KAPLAN

TEST PREP AND ADMISSIONS

ACT®*

Course Book

Copyright ©2015 Kaplan, Inc.

Let's Get Started.

Thanks for choosing Kaplan for your ACT* Preparation. Get ready to experience Kaplan ACT and score higher—guaranteed or your money back.†

STEP 1

Check the contents of your ACT Kit.

You should have the following:

✔ ACT Course Book

STEP 2

Take your Diagnostic Test.

When you go to your first session, you'll take a full-length ACT. This Diagnostic Test establishes a baseline of your performance and feeds your custom study plan into your online resources. When your Diagnostic Test results are available, you'll get an email to log in and check out your Smart Reports™!

STEP 3

Log into your online resources.

You should have received an email with your log-in information. Go to kaptest.com/myhome and log into your online resources. Once you've logged in, you can:

- View your Diagnostic Test results.

- On your syallabus, click on each Classroom Session to find your assignments for before and after each class.

- Click on your My Performance tab to get overviews of your progress and areas to study.

Ready to score higher? Log in to get started.

Didn't receive your log-in information? Visit kaptest.com/myhome, and we'll resend it.
Need help? Call 1-800-KAP-TEST or email us at customer.care@kaplan.com.

TEST PREP

*ACT is a registered trademark of ACT, Inc. †Conditions and restrictions apply. For complete guarantee eligibility requirements, visit kaptest.com/hsg.

AC4098F

How to Use Kaplan's Digital Flashcards

To Access Kaplan's Digital Flashcards

1. Go to www.kaptest.com and log in using your username and password.
2. You will see a link to the flashcards; click the "Launch" button to access.
3. For more information, including technical specifications and instructions for bookmarking them on your mobile device, go to "Help" on the upper right-hand corner of the flashcard homepage.

How to Use the Flashcards

Like print flashcards, the first side of the card asks the question. In the example below, the question is "How do you solve an *inequality*"? Once you have answered the question, click "View Answer."

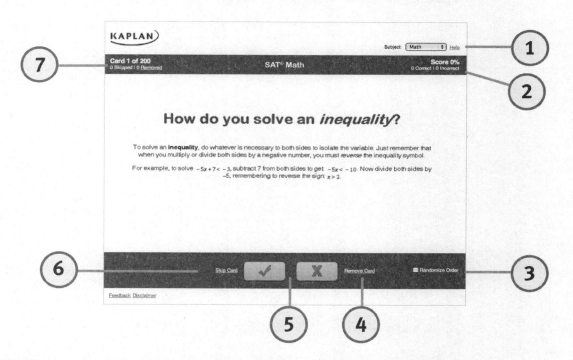

1. **Choose Subject:** Use this drop down and only flashcards for that subject will be displayed.
2. **Score:** Your score is displayed here.
3. **Randomize Cards:** The original setting has the cards in a set order. Check the "Randomize Order" box to randomize the cards. If you unselect, you go back to the set order.
4. **Remove Card:** Takes the card out of the deck. Go to "Removed" to add back in.
5. **Scoring:** Select the green check if you answered correctly or the red X if you got it wrong.
6. **Skip Card:** Goes on to the next card but keeps it in the deck so you can review later.
7. **Track Cards:** This tells you the card number and how many cards you have skipped or removed during the current session.

CONTENTS

Session 1

Session 2

Session 3

Session 4

Session 5

Session 6

Answers and Explanations

Appendix 1: Practice Test E

Appendix 2

TABLE OF CONTENTS

	Welcome to Your Kaplan ACT Course
	Introduction to the ACT
	Introduction to ACT English and Writing

Welcome to Your Kaplan ACT Course!

Congratulations on taking this important step in your college admissions process! By studying with Kaplan, you'll maximize your score on the ACT—a major factor in your overall application.

Our experience shows that the best ACT score increases result from active engagement in the preparation process. Kaplan will give you direction, focus your prep, and teach you the specific skills and effective test-taking strategies you need to know for the ACT. We will help you achieve your top performance on Test Day, but the effort you put into test preparation is crucial. The more you invest in preparing for the ACT, the greater your chances of achieving your target score and getting into your top-choice college!

This Course Guide serves as an overview of Kaplan's ACT program. Read it carefully. You'll get answers to the following important questions:

- How is the course structured?

- What do I do if I miss a class?

- What homework will I need to do?

- What materials does Kaplan provide, and how do I use them effectively?

- What are my online resources, and how do I access them?

- How can I achieve my best score on Test Day?

Are you registered for the ACT? Kaplan cannot register you for the official ACT. If you have not already registered for an upcoming ACT test date, visit the ACT's official website at www.act.org for online registration and for information on registration deadlines, test sites, and fees. The ACT is administered each year in September, October, December, February,* April, and June. Regular registration deadlines are usually four weeks prior to the test date. Your high school guidance office may have more information on registering for the ACT.

*No test centers in New York are scheduled for February test administration.

KAPLAN

ACT Course Structure

Your Kaplan ACT course will consist of ten sessions: four full-length, 4-hour ACT practice tests and six dynamic lessons with your instructor. In addition to your tests and lessons, your Kaplan program includes the *Lesson Book*, online and *Lesson Book* homework assignments, additional practice tests and materials, and online digital flashcards.

There are three things you need to do to master the ACT:

1. Know the content.

2. Know the test.

3. Know the strategies.

The Kaplan ACT course will help you do these three things—and raise your score—in a fun, interactive way. The ACT is not an intelligence test, and it's not an indicator of how successful you will be in life. Once you realize that and put the ACT into perspective, you can relax and get to the business of preparing. You *can* prepare for the ACT, just as you get ready for other tests.

Practice Tests

Kaplan's ACT practice tests are just like the real thing, only your scores don't count toward the college admissions process. By taking four full-length, 4-hour proctored ACT practice tests, you will prepare yourself for the actual Test Day experience. After each test, you will log in to your online resources to access a score report that breaks down your performance in each section and compares your practice test scores as you progress through the course. Based on your performance on these tests and your online assignments, your online syllabus will customize your study plan to help you improve more efficiently and effectively. The Answers and Explanations for each practice test can be found on your personal syllabus. Always consult your instructor with any questions or concerns.

Do you want even more practice tests? For additional practice tests, log on to www.kaptest.com.

Lessons

In your class sessions, your expert Kaplan instructor will review the key concepts tested on the ACT and teach you Kaplan's proven methods and strategies for each question type. Each lesson will cover all five sections of the ACT and will be interactive, so be ready to participate! You will need your ACT Lesson Book for all instructional sessions.

Homework

You need to reinforce what you learn in class by practicing the Kaplan methods and strategies on your own. Written homework will be assigned after every class session. In addition, you should complete the engaging online videos, interactive guided practice, and test-like quizzes. The quizzes should be taken after each teaching session. The videos and guided practice should be done in preparation for the next lesson. Your online homework can be found on your online syllabus. Your instructor will provide you with the written assignment.

Did you miss a session? If you miss a session or practice test, you can make it up by either attending the same session with another class or by viewing the Lesson On Demand and doing all the online work associated with that lesson. To find a makeup session with another class, log on to your Courses and Services page at www.kaptest.com and use the Makeup Session Finder.

ACT Course Materials

Your Kaplan ACT Student Kit contains the following items that you will use in preparation for Test Day:

Course Book

This book contains the lessons and activities you'll be working on in each session and most of the homework assignments you'll complete between sessions. It also contains the answers and explanations for each session's classwork and homework assignments.

Remember Bring this book, a calculator, and a couple of pencils to every class.

In addition to the ACT Course Book, you'll use:

Online resources, including quizzes, digital flashcards, and make-up classes

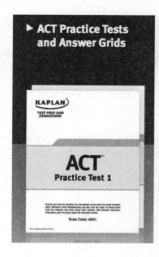

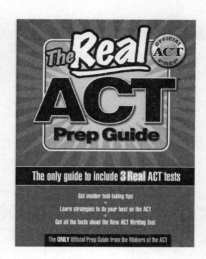

These items are only found in ACT Premier Tutoring kits

Your Online Resources

A variety of resources are available to you on your personalized online syllabus at www.kaptest.com/myhome.

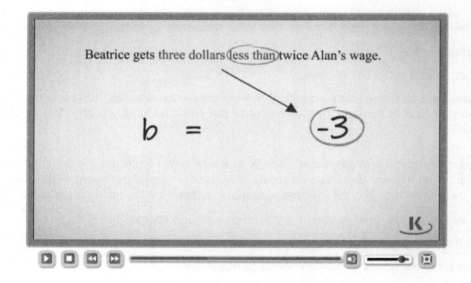

Quizzes

Each quiz is focused on a particular aspect of the ACT and will take approximately 10–15 minutes to complete. After each class session, you will have a set of quizzes to complete as homework.

Instructional Videos

If you struggled with a quiz, you can view an instructional video, led by a Kaplan-trained instructor, that focuses on a specific aspect of the ACT. Each video will take between four and eight minutes to complete.

Additional Online Practice Tests

You also have access to six additional full-length online timed practice tests. After you submit your answers online, you'll receive a comprehensive Smart Report. Use this report to guide your subsequent practice.

Smart Reports

Smart Reports analyzes your practice test results and generates personalized feedback to help you raise your score.

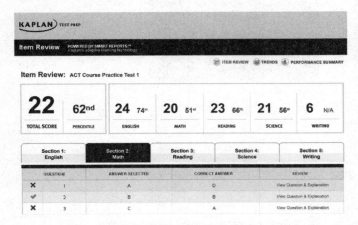

Access your online full-length practice tests and other resources by following these steps:

1. Go to kaptest.com.

2. Click on Log In at the top of the page.

3. Log in using the username and password that were emailed to you and/or your parents when you enrolled in your Kaplan course. They were sent to the email address you provided with your class registration.

Don't have your username and password? Check your junk email folder for the original username and password email from Kaplan. If you cannot locate your username and password, visit www.kaptest.com and click on the link next to "Forgot your username and password?" to have it sent again.

4. Once you are logged in, read and accept the terms and conditions.

5. Complete the Background and Goal Setting survey.

6. Begin work with your online videos and practice questions.

Take your online resources with you by logging in to Smart Reports from your web-enabled cell phone or other smart device.

| **KAPLAN**

ACT SmartPoints

The ACT tests certain skills more often than others. Students who want to maximize their scores need to master the skills that are tested the most, and they need an easy way to organize their study around these concepts. By analyzing previously released tests, Kaplan is able to apply a point value to each tested skill on the ACT and show students "where the points are." These point values are called SmartPoints.

Each section of the ACT is scored on a scale that ranges from 1 to 36 points. This means there are 36 points available to earn on each section of the test: English, Math, Reading, and Science.

Point Value	English
7	Connections
6	Verb Tenses
5	Punctuation
5	Word Choice
5	Wordiness
4	Writing Strategy
3	Sentence Sense
1	Organization
36	Total

Point Value	Reading
12	Detail
8	Inference
8	Generalization
6	Function
1	Vocab-in-Context
1	Writer's View
36	Total

Point Value	Science
13	Scientific Reasoning
12	Figure Interpretation
11	Patterns
36	Total

Point Value	Math
7	Plane Geometry
7	Variable Manipulation
6	Proportions and Probability
6	Coordinate Geometry
3	Operations
3	Patterns, Logic, and Data
2	Number Properties
2	Trigonometry
36	Total

Are you uncertain about how to start studying? Match the SmartPoints chart above to your Smart Report from your first ACT practice test. Focus your practice on the SmartPoints categories that have large point values and that are your weakest areas. You need to master the large categories before you think about working on the smaller ones.

Analyzing Your Tests Online

Your Kaplan practice test results are essential for your preparation for Test Day. Take some time to analyze which SmartPoint categories are your strengths and which ones still provide an opportunity for score improvement.

Practice: Analyze a Hypothetical Student's Practice Test

First, let's analyze this hypothetical student's score as an example of what you'll do with your online score report as homework.

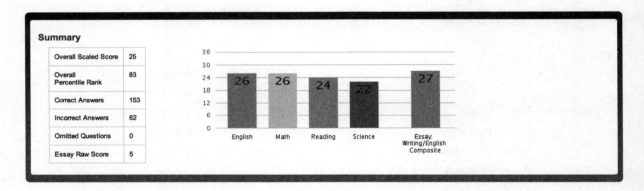

Write down the student's score by section:

English _____ Math _____ Reading _____ Science _____

Essay Writing/English Composite _____

Answer Detail

Using this student's Math and Reading Answer Detail pages, answer the questions that follow.

Answer Detail

| Download Test | Download Answers & Explanations |

View Math Set ▼

Section 2:

Question Number	Answer Selected	Correct Answer
01	D	D
02	F	J
03	D	E
04	K	K
05	B	C
06	K	K
07	B	B
08	H	K
09	E	E
10	G	K
11	D	D
12	H	H
13	C	C
14	J	H
15	D	C
16	G	G
17	B	D
18		H
19	D	D
20	H	H
21	E	E
22	G	H
23	E	D
24	F	F
25	C	D
26	H	G
27	C	C
28	G	H
29	B	B
30	K	K

Question Number	Answer Selected	Correct Answer
31	C	C
32	H	H
33	A	E
34	K	K
35	A	A
36	H	J
37	A	A
38	J	G
39	C	C
40	G	G
41	B	B
42	H	H
43	C	C
44	F	K
45	A	A
46	F	G
47	E	E
48	G	G
49	E	E
50	J	K
51	B	E
52	K	K
53	D	B
54	G	G
55	C	D
56	J	K
57	B	C
58	J	H
59	B	D
60	H	J

Section 3:

Question Number	Answer Selected	Correct Answer
01	C	C
02	G	G
03	B	B
04	F	F
05	D	D
06	H	H
07	B	C
08	H	G
09	B	B
10	H	H
11	A	B
12	G	H
13	A	B
14	F	F
15	C	C
16	J	J
17	A	B
18	G	H
19	B	B
20	G	H

1. Did the student answer a series of questions incorrectly at the end of the Math Test? **Yes/No**

2. Did the student answer a series of questions incorrectly at the beginning of the Math Test? **Yes/No**

3. Did the student leave a group of questions blank at the end of either test? **Yes/No**

4. Did the student answer a group of Reading questions incorrectly? **Yes/No**

If You Circled Yes

1. If the student answered a series of questions incorrectly at the end of the Math Test, he or she is likely answering questions without taking enough time to solve them accurately. If you don't have enough time to solve a question or eliminate any answer choices, you should pick a Letter of the Day.

2. If the student answered some early Math questions incorrectly, he or she is probably working too quickly. Remember, early questions—which are likely to be low in difficulty—are worth as many points as the high-difficulty questions at the end of the section.

3. If there are questions left blank at the end of a section, the student probably ran out of time. The student can work on budgeting time more carefully while not rushing to answer every question. It's best for students to spend time on questions they are likely to answer correctly.

4. If the student answered a group of questions incorrectly on the Reading Test, he or she may have misunderstood the passage. You should spend enough time (about three minutes) on a passage to get a basic understanding of it and look up details as needed.

Individual Test Analysis

For each test (English, Math, Reading, and Science), it's important to review how you did in each SmartPoint category, recognize where you performed well, and find one area for more in-depth review and practice. Let's take a look again at how this would work for this hypothetical student for the Reading Test.

Here is a screenshot of this student's Reading Test Smart Report score breakdown:

Reading

Scaled Score	Correct Answers	Incorrect Answers	Omitted Questions
20	25	15	0

For question-by-question detail, please see answer details

	SmartPoint	Number of Questions	Percentage Answered Correctly
Very Important	Detail	19	58%
	Generalization	7	57%
	Inference	7	57%
Important	Function	1	100%
Not as Important	Writers View	3	100%
	Vocab-in-Context	3	67%

Why are certain SmartPoint categories called "Very Important"?

_____

_____

Which SmartPoint category is worth the most points? _____

In which SmartPoint category does this student have the most correct answers? _____

_____

In which category does this student have the most incorrect answers? _____

In-Depth Review of One SmartPoint Category:

Next, the student would read through the Answers & Explanations for the one Reading Test SmartPoint category on which the most questions were either missed or omitted. You should select one SmartPoint category for in-depth review for English, Math, Reading, and Science. Below is an example of an Answer & Explanation for an Inference question from the Reading Test.

1. **C**

Category: Inference

Difficulty: Medium

Strategic Advice: Remember that the answer to an Inference question will not stray far from something said in the passage.

Getting to the Answer: The passage indicates that the search required all possible assistance because of its importance. The process also sounds very laborious. Look for a choice that incorporates these ideas.

(A) Opposite; the difficulty of the search required the participation of many people.

(B) Opposite; the passage makes clear that the search was far from "simple."

(C) This matches your prediction.

(D) Distortion; the passage does not say that the search resulted in lowered production but states that garlic consumption by a cow can affect a day's dairy production.

Reviewing Your Practice Test

Just as you analyzed the score of the hypothetical student, so, too, is it essential that you review your score report in the same way. First, log in at www.kaptest.com/myhome with your email address and password. Once you're logged in, click on My Smart Reports.

Then, review your overall score and write it down in your Course Book for easy reference.

English _____ Math _____ Reading _____ Science _____

Combined Essay Writing/English _____ Overall _____

Next, scroll down to the Answer Detail and answer the questions below while reviewing the Smart Report for your practice test results.

1. Did you answer a series of questions incorrectly at the end of the Math Test? **Yes/No**

2. Did you answer a series of questions incorrectly at the beginning of the Math Test? **Yes/No**

3. Did you leave a group of questions blank or randomly guess at the end of any test section? **Yes/No**

4. Did you answer a group of Reading Test questions incorrectly? **Yes/No**

If You Circled Yes

1. If you answered a series of questions incorrectly at the end of the Math Test, you are likely answering questions that you don't have enough time to solve accurately. If you don't have enough time to solve a question or eliminate any answer choices, choose a Letter of the Day.

2. If you answered some early Math Test questions incorrectly, you are probably working too quickly. Remember, early questions—which are likely to be low in difficulty—are worth as many points as the high-difficulty questions at the end of the Math Test.

3. If you left questions blank or randomly guessed the answers at the end of a section, you probably ran out of time. Work on budgeting your time more carefully but don't rush to answer every question. Spend your valuable time on questions you're likely to answer correctly.

4. If you answered a group of Reading Test questions incorrectly, you may have misunderstood the passage. Spend enough time (about three minutes) on a passage to get a basic understanding of it and then look up details as needed.

Test-by-Test Analysis

For English, Math, Reading, and Science, make a check mark beside the SmartPoint category in which you answered the most questions correctly. Then, circle the SmartPoint category in which you answered the most questions incorrectly. You should have a total of four check marks and four circled categories. For each circled SmartPoint category, read through the Answers and Explanations for the questions in that category on your Diagnostic Test.

Your Study Schedule

Take the time now to plan out your anticipated study schedule leading up to Test Day.

MONTH

Sunday	Monday	Tuesday	Wednesday	Thursday	Friday	Saturday

MONTH

Sunday	Monday	Tuesday	Wednesday	Thursday	Friday	Saturday

MONTH

Sunday	Monday	Tuesday	Wednesday	Thursday	Friday	Saturday

How to Achieve Your Best Score

Set up a weekly schedule—and stick to it. Students who set up and then follow a disciplined schedule for their preparation are more confident and ready for Test Day. Schedule your class sessions, practice tests, and time to do homework between them on the calendar on page 17.

Make use of all the materials in your Kaplan course. You have a wealth of materials in your Student Kit and online; both should play a role in your preparation. Don't let the box collect dust under your bed! Use the online flashcards for a few minutes each day, complete additional practice in your Course Book, and log on to your online resources a few times a week to complete quizzes and watch videos in your areas of opportunity.

Complete the homework. After every lesson, your instructor will assign written homework from the Lesson Book. The homework is designed to reinforce what you did in class. You will also need to watch the instructional videos and complete the online guided practice and quizzes. Just attending class will not raise your score; you must practice on your own!

Always use the Kaplan Methods when you practice. Every time you do homework questions or take a practice test, you need to use the Kaplan Methods. The Methods may slow you down or trip you up initially, but with practice, they will become second nature and help you improve your score on Test Day.

Be patient. Your test-taking skill will improve with sustained, patient effort. Don't get frustrated if you don't see immediate results. Mistakes and wrong answers are a natural and necessary part of improvement. Also, some students see improvement in their practice test scores right away, but many students don't see results until their third or fourth practice test. If you are dedicated to making the most out of your class sessions, and if you are committed to your study schedule, your score will increase!

Concentrate on process, not performance. Getting questions right or wrong in class or at home is meaningless. You won't see the same questions on Test Day! Instead, you will see problems like those you have practiced, so *how* you get to the right answers and avoid the wrong answers is much more important. Always review your homework and practice tests by reading the full explanations for every question, even those you answered correctly. You need to make sure that you answered correctly because you solved correctly, not because you guessed correctly.

What can you do about pacing and time management on Test Day? At the beginning of your study, timing should be a secondary concern. First, concentrate on developing the mental approach needed to answer questions effectively. Focus on knowing how to solve them correctly and quickly. When you are comfortable with the Kaplan Methods, start working on timed practice both in test sections and on full-length tests.

Introduction to the ACT

The ACT: What Will You See?

Section	Timing	On the Test	Seconds per question
1	45 minutes	English Test 75 questions	36
2	60 minutes	Math Test 60 questions	60
3	35 minutes	Reading Test 40 questions	52
4	35 minutes	Science Test 40 questions	52
5	30 minutes	Writing Test (Optional) 1 essay	

ACT Scoring

Connect the terms on the left to their definitions on the right.

1. Raw Score   a. The number that describes how many students received a lower score than you did

2. Scaled Score   b. The number that compares your results to other students' results

3. Percentile   c. The number that results from a calculation of your correct answers

Four of the five tests on the ACT are multiple-choice. The scaled scoring for each of these four tests ranges from 1 to 36. The average of all four scaled scores results in your Composite Score:

$$\frac{English + Math + Reading + Science}{4}$$

How many points do you earn for a correct answer? _____

How many points do you lose for an incorrect answer? _____

Raw score = _____

What does this mean?

- NEVER skip an ACT problem.

- If you run out of time and don't know the answer, pick a Letter of the Day.

How can eliminating answer choices help? _____

_____

_____

Which scores do colleges and universities primarily look at? _____

Pacing on the ACT

The **Math Test** contains questions that vary in content and complexity. It is arranged in order of difficulty.

_____ minutes long

_____ total questions on the Math Test

_____ minutes per question

Pre-Algebra/Elementary Algebra

40%

30% Intermediate Algebra/ Coordinate Geometry

30%

Plane Geometry/ Trigonometry

The **English, Reading,** and **Science Test** questions are grouped according to the passage they pertain to.

English	Reading	Science
_____ passages	_____ passages	_____ passages
_____ questions per passage	_____ questions per passage	_____ questions per passage
_____ minutes per passage	_____ minutes per passage	_____ minutes per passage

A low-difficulty question is worth_____ a high-difficulty question.

Answer 60 Math questions. Omit zero Math questions.	Answer 30 Math questions. Pick a Letter of the Day for the remaining 30 Math questions.
On average, this student spent _____ minutes per question.	On average, this student spent _____ minutes per question.
Answer 24 of the questions correctly. Answer 36 of the questions incorrectly.	Answer 35 of the questions correctly. Answer 25 of the questions incorrectly.
This student's raw score is 24.	This student's raw score is 35.
This student's scaled score is _____.	This student's scaled score is _____.

The **Writing Test** is optional.

- There is one essay prompt.
- An essay that does not address the topic receives a score of zero.
- The Combined English/Writing score includes your performance on the essay.
- 30 minutes are allowed for the Writing Test.
- Your essay is scored by two graders, each of whom scores the essay on a scale of 1–6 for a combined score of 2–12.

The Writing score does not affect your scores from the multiple-choice tests or the Composite score, but it does combine with your English Test results for a **Combined English/Writing score.**

The Kaplan Method for ACT English and Writing

A. The Combined English/Writing score is made up of the English Test and the Writing Test or essay.

B. The English Test is always the _____ test on the ACT. It will be _____ minutes long and have _____ questions.

C. It has _____ passages, each of which has exactly _____ questions. This means you have approximately _____ minutes to spend on each passage.

D. What's on the English Test?

1. _____

2. _____

3. _____

4. _____

5. _____

6. _____

E. What's NOT on the English Test?

1. _____

2. _____

3. _____

F. **The Kaplan Method for ACT English**

1. _____

_____

2. _____

_____

3. _____

_____

[1] People often complain <u>that are</u> generation is politically apathetic. [2] Just twenty-five years ago, it
₁ (appears under "that are")
was common for students to join strikes and antiwar protests. [3] These days, though, most young
people are more likely to be found watching MTV or texting their friends than rallying to support a
treasured belief.

1. (A) NO CHANGE
   (B) which are
   (C) that our
   (D) about our

G. Some questions will ask you to select the most concise and relevant answer. To answer these
questions correctly, watch out for answer choices that are:

1. _____

2. _____

H. More than one answer choice may be grammatically correct. If that is the case, look for
_____.

I. When "OMIT the underlined portion" is an answer, it is often correct.

J. If more than one remaining answer choice seems possible, ask yourself:

1. _____

2. _____

3. _____

[1] People often complain <u>that are</u> generation is politically apathetic. [2] Just twenty-five years ago, it
₁
was common for students to join strikes and antiwar protests. [3] These days, though, most young
people are more likely to be found watching MTV or texting their friends than rallying to support a
treasured belief.

[4] <u>As for myself</u>, I certainly was no different. [5] Appallingly ignorant of current events, I never read a
₂
paper or watched the news, but I knew all about the personal lives of popular TV and movie stars. ▢3

2. (F) NO CHANGE
   (G) In regards to my own experience,
   (H) In comparison to other teenagers today,
   (J) OMIT the underlined portion.

3. Suppose that the author wants to add the following sentence to the passage:

   "Then something happened that changed my outlook forever."

   This sentence would be best placed at the end of sentence:
   (A) 1
   (B) 2
   (C) 4
   (D) 5

Quiz

Basketry may be the world's earliest
<u>handicraft, the oldest</u> examples of basketry are 10,000
1
years old. These ancient <u>fragments, which have been</u>
2
preserved well in the dry environment of Danger Cave,
Utah, show that early Native Americans knew the art of
weaving semi-rigid materials into useful objects. The
remains of baskets are also found on every continent.
Materials, rather than technique or decoration, <u>is</u> usually
3
most useful in identifying a <u>baskets' origin</u>. Willow, just
4
pliant enough to be either woven or plaited, is the favored
basket-making material of northern Europe. In other areas,
basket makers use relatively rigid materials, such as bamboo
and rattan. Africa has yielded the widest variety of basket-
making <u>materials including palm</u> leaves, tree roots,
and grasses.   5

1. (A) NO CHANGE
    (B) handicraft and the oldest
    (C) handicraft. The oldest
    (D) handicraft but the oldest

2. (F) NO CHANGE
    (G) fragments, which are
    (H) fragments which have been
    (J) fragments, which will have been

3. (A) NO CHANGE
    (B) are
    (C) was
    (D) were

4. (F) NO CHANGE
    (G) baskets origin
    (H) baskets' origins
    (J) basket's origin

5. (A) NO CHANGE
    (B) materials. They included palm
    (C) materials included palm
    (D) materials, including palm

Watching a craftsperson weave a basket can be a
marvelous experience. The craftsperson, <u>who works quick</u>
6
and gracefully, passes the weft over and under the
foundation element, or warp. <u>Because each culture</u> has its
7
own unique basket-making patterns, the most common
and most beautiful patterns worldwide are twillings and
twinings.

Unfortunately, the traditional art of basket making
<u>having been eroded</u> by the pressures of commercialism.
8
Many modern craftspeople must choose <u>among traditioned</u>
9
<u>artistry</u> and financial security. Sadly, few factory-made
baskets today show the delicate, geometric designs of the
solitary artisan. Indeed, the handmade basket has become
an "artwork." Now, collectors who prize the work of the
traditional basket maker may fly thousands of miles in order
to purchase genuine designs. Under such financial pressure,
how long will the basket maker be able to <u>preserve their</u>
standards?   10

6. (F) NO CHANGE
    (G) who worked quick
    (H) who worked quickly
    (J) who works quickly

7. (A) NO CHANGE
    (B) Although each culture
    (C) But each culture
    (D) Despite each culture

8. (F) NO CHANGE
    (G) will have been eroded
    (H) has been eroded
    (J) have been eroded

9. (A) NO CHANGE
    (B) among traditional artistry
    (C) between traditional artistry
    (D) between traditioned artistry

10. (F) NO CHANGE
    (G) preserve there
    (H) preserve they're
    (J) preserve his or her

Point Builder	The Kaplan Method for ACT Math
Point Builder	Picking Numbers
Point Builder	Backsolving
7 Points	Variable Manipulation
	Quiz

The Kaplan Method for ACT Math

A. The Mathematics Test is always the _____ test on the ACT. It will be _____ minutes long and have _____ questions.

B. **The Kaplan Method for ACT Math**

1. _____

2. _____

3. _____

    a. _____

    b. _____

    c. _____

    d. _____

4. _____

Picking Numbers

A. With Kaplan's math strategies, you can avoid algebra on about $\frac{1}{3}$ of the ACT Math questions you'll see on Test Day.

B. Some questions present abstract situations. Picking Numbers means replacing fuzzy unknowns with concrete numbers.

"X" $\Rightarrow$ 3

"an even integer" $\Rightarrow$ _____

"a prime number less than 20" $\Rightarrow$ _____

1. For all $f > 1$, what does the expression $\frac{5f^6}{5f^9}$ equal?
   (A) $\frac{1}{2}$
   (B) $-f^3$
   (C) f^3
   (D) $-\frac{1}{f^3}$
   (E) $\frac{1}{f^3}$

C. Make sure the numbers you pick follow the rules of the questions and are easy to work with.

D. You can Pick Numbers when:

1. _____

_____

_____

2. _____

_____

_____

)) REMEMBER
In percent questions, everything should cost $100, all objects should travel at 100 miles per hour, and you should have 100 of any item.

2. A certain television set is discounted 20% on Monday and then discounted another 25% on Tuesday. What is the total percent discount applied to the price of the television on Monday and Tuesday?

(F) 35%

(G) 40%

(H) 45%

(J) 50%

(K) 55%

)) REMEMBER
When a question asks about odd or even numbers, you'll need to pick one of each.

3. Which of the following expressions will produce an odd number for any integer a?

(A) a^2

(B) $a^2 + 1$

(C) $2a^2 + 1$

(D) $3a^2 + 2$

(E) $4a^2 + 4$

Backsolving

A.   Since the ACT is a multiple-choice test, you know the correct answer must be one of the five given options! When you Backsolve, you let the ACT pick numbers for you.

B.   For most questions, you'll start with choice (C) or (H).

C.   If a question asks for the smallest possible value, _____

_____

If a question asks for the largest possible value, _____

_____

D.   You can Backsolve when:

_____

_____

_____

_____

)) REMEMBER
You can avoid complicated algebra by Backsolving.

4. Set *A* contains 7 consecutive even integers. If the average of Set *A*'s integers is 46, which of the following is the smallest integer of Set *A*?

(F) 36

(G) 38

(H) 40

(J) 42

(K) 44

5. What is the value of *x* if $\frac{x+1}{x-3} - \frac{x+2}{x-4} = 0$?

(A) −2

(B) −1

(C) 0

(D) 1

(E) 2

)) REMEMBER
Use the space provided in your booklet to clearly show your work.

6. Michelle is pulling gummy worms out of a bag that only has green and orange gummy worms in it. In her first handful, she pulled out 10 orange worms and 6 green worms. Setting these worms aside, she pulled out a second handful, and 40% of these were orange. After both handfuls, 50% of all the worms pulled were orange. How many worms did Michelle pull out in her second handful if she only pulled whole worms?

(F) 20

(G) 26

(H) 30

(J) 36

(K) 40

Variable Manipulation: 7 SmartPoints

Terms to Know

- Equations
- Inequalities
- In terms of
- Polynomials

A. The order of operations and other rules for manipulating numbers also apply to variables.

If $D = RT$, what is R in terms of D and T?_____

B. Cardinal rule of equations: _____

_____

C. Be particularly careful when working with fractions.

D. Inequalities are just like equations, with the exception that multiplying or dividing by a negative number flips the inequality sign.

7. Which of the following inequalities is equivalent to $-2 - 4x \le -6x$?

    (A) $x \ge -2$
    (B) $x \ge 1$
    (C) $x \ge 2$
    (D) $x \le -1$
    (E) $x \le 1$

)) REMEMBER
With variables in the answer choices, Picking Numbers is a great strategy if the algebra seems complicated.

8. If $a = 4$, what is the value of $\dfrac{4a^4 + 64b}{16}$?

    (F) $\dfrac{1}{4} + 4b$
    (G) $4 + 16b$
    (H) $64 + 4b$
    (J) $32 + 16b$
    (K) $16 + 64b$

)) REMEMBER
If a problem asks for a specific value and there are concrete numbers in the answer choices, you can Backsolve.

9. If $5x + 3 = -17$, then $x = ?$

    (A) -25
    (B) -7
    (C) -4
    (D) $\dfrac{1}{3}$
    (E) 4

Variable Manipulation: 7 SmartPoints

A. Many questions will ask you to translate English into math.

Translation Table	
Equals, is, was, will be, has, costs, adds up to, is the same as	$=$
Times, of, multiplied by, product of, twice, double, half, triple	$\times$
Divided by, per, out of, each, ratio of _____ to _____	$\div$
Plus, added to, sum, combined, together, and, more than, total, also	$+$
Minus, subtracted from, less than, decreased by, difference between	$-$
What, how much, how many, the cost of, Joe's wage	x

B. When you choose variables, pick letters that are easy to remember.

Bob's age and Carol's age $\Rightarrow$ *B, C*

number of cats and number of dogs $\Rightarrow$ _____

price of cucumbers and price of carrots $\Rightarrow$ _____

C. Picking Numbers and Backsolving can make many word problems a snap.

)) REMEMBER
For other word problems, you'll
need to solve an equation.

10. Brandy has a collection of comic books. If she adds 15 to the number
of comic books in her collection and multiplies the sum by 3, the
result will be 65 fewer than 4 times the number of comic books in her
collection. How many comic books are in her collection?

(F) 50
(G) 85
(H) 110
(J) 145
(K) 175

)) REMEMBER
Backsolving often works well on
word problems.

11. The toll for driving a segment of a certain freeway is $1.50 plus
25 cents for each mile traveled. Joy paid a $25.00 toll for driving a
segment of the freeway. How many miles did she travel?

(A) 75
(B) 94
(C) 96
(D) 100
(E) 106

Variable Manipulation: 7 SmartPoints

Formulas to Know

Distributive Property	$a(b + c) = ab + ac$
FOIL	$(a + b)(c + d) = ac + ad + bc + bd$
Classic Quadratic Equations	$(x + y)^2 = x^2 + 2xy + y^2$
	$(x - y)^2 = x^2 - 2xy + y^2$
	$(x + y)(x - y) = x^2 - y^2$

Terms to Know

- Combination
- Factor
- Substitution
- Variable

A. FOIL means_____

B. Many questions will require you to factor a complicated expression.

$a^2 + (b + c) \, a + bc = (a + b)(a + c)$

$x^2 + 5x + 6 = $ _____

C. Remember the classic quadratic equations to factor quickly on Test Day.

D. You can solve for any number of variables as long as you have an equal number of equations. Expect to see questions about two equations with two unknowns.

E. Substitution is solving either equation for one variable in terms of the other, then substituting that into the other equation.

F. Combination is adding the equations.

》REMEMBER
Picking Numbers is a good strategy if an expression is difficult to simplify algebraically.

12. What is the value of $2x + y$ if $4x^2 + 6xy + 2y^2 = 32$ and $x + y = 4$?

   (F) 3
   (G) 4
   (H) 5
   (J) 6
   (K) 7

》REMEMBER
Be very careful with negative signs. They're easy to forget.

13. For all $x \neq 8$, $\dfrac{x^2 - 11x + 24}{8 - x} = ?$

   (A) $8 - x$
   (B) $3 - x$
   (C) $x - 3$
   (D) $x - 8$
   (E) $x - 11$

》REMEMBER
Substitution and combination will both work on almost any question with multiple equations, but one is usually easier for any given question.

14. What is the solution for x in the system of equations below?
   $3x + 4y = 31$
   $3x - 4y = -1$

   (F)   4
   (G)   5
   (H)   6
   (J)   9
   (K) 10

Quiz

1. An aquarium contains dolphins, sharks, and whales. There are twice as many dolphins as whales and eight fewer sharks than dolphins and whales combined. If there are x whales, which of the following represents the number of sharks?

   (A) $5x$
   (B) $3x - 8$
   (C) $10 + x$
   (D) $\sqrt{24x}$
   (E) $3\sqrt{x - 8}$

2. At a recent tryout for a soccer team, 1 out of 3 players who tried out was asked to come to a second tryout. After the second tryout, 75% of those asked to the second tryout were offered places on the team. If 18 players were offered places, how many players went to the first tryout?

   (F) 18
   (G) 24
   (H) 48
   (J) 56
   (K) 72

3. Of the participants at a certain conference, $\frac{1}{3}$ are anthropologists, $\frac{1}{2}$ are biologists, and the remaining 12 participants are chemists. Each participant specializes in only one field. What is the total number of participants at the conference?

   (A) 36
   (B) 48
   (C) 60
   (D) 72
   (E) 76

4. If $x \neq 4$ and $x \neq -4$, then the expression $\dfrac{4x}{x^2 - 16} - \dfrac{3x}{x - 4}$ is equivalent to which of the following?

   (F) $\dfrac{x}{x^2 - x - 20}$
   (G) $\dfrac{x}{x^2 - 20}$
   (H) $\dfrac{-5x}{x^2 - 16}$
   (J) $\dfrac{-3x^2 - 8x}{x^2 - 16}$
   (K) $\dfrac{-3x^2 + 16}{x^2 - 16}$

5. The formula for converting a Fahrenheit temperature reading to Celsius is $C = \dfrac{5}{9}(F - 32)$ where C is the reading in degrees Celsius and F is the reading in degrees Fahrenheit. Which of the following is the Fahrenheit equivalent to a reading of 95° Celsius?

   (A) 35° F
   (B) 53° F
   (C) 63° F
   (D) 203° F
   (E) 207° F

6. If $-3x + 7 \leq 4$ and x is an integer, which of the following statements must be true?

   (F) $x > 0$
   (G) $x \leq 1$
   (H) $x \leq -1$
   (J) $x \leq 0$
   (K) $x \leq 3$

Point Builder	The Kaplan Method for ACT Reading
Point Builder	Active Reading and Passage Mapping
Point Builder	Natural Science and Prose Fiction
	Quiz

The Kaplan Method for ACT Reading

A. The Reading Test is always the _____ test on the ACT. It will be _____ minutes long and have _____ questions.

B. It has _____ passages, each of which has exactly _____ questions. This means you have approximately _____ minutes to spend on each passage.

C. What makes ACT Reading challenging?

_____

_____

_____

_____

D. **The Kaplan Method for ACT Reading**

1. _____

   • _____

   • _____

2. _____

3. _____

   • _____

Active Reading and Passage Mapping

A. *Active reading* means:

_____

_____

While you read, you should ask questions like:

_____

_____

_____

B. A *passage map* is:

_____

_____

Passage I

I have a soft spot in my heart (and maybe my head) for tearjerker movies. In fact, until I saw the made-for-cable film *Why Me?* I had always thought,
Line "Nothing beats a good cry." But this film has
(5) made me reconsider. Sometimes, a movie is so bad that producing a tear is more of a response than the film deserves. From the threadbare plot that consists mainly of one improbable setback after another to the total lack of chemistry between the usually satisfying
(10) Sandie Findlay and her on-screen daughter Tiffany Jackson, *Why Me?* is entirely lacking in character development. Even the family dog seems more like a stuffed animal than a real pet.

The plot, such as it is, revolves around Henrietta
(15) (Findlay), a single mother with a fairly normal life. Naturally, this changes shortly after you see her sitting in her doctor's waiting room, fending off frantic phone calls from her domineering boss. Suffice it to say, Henrietta loses her job and is diagnosed with
(20) a disease (one unheard of even on the corniest soap opera) before the first commercial break. That's all I'll say about the plot—not because I don't want to give it away, but because I already have.

Of course, even this might have become moving
(25) with some kind of convincing acting by Findlay or Jackson. Though some have charged that Findlay coasts on her reputation from her glory days, I usually find that she does much with whatever she is given. Unfortunately, it appears here as if she and
(30) Jackson have never even met before, making the concept of them as mother and daughter implausible at best. Director Sarah Connelly certainly doesn't help matters, showily cuing the viewer with music that is either melodramatic or dirge-like. I guess she figures
(35) we won't know when to grab the tissue otherwise.

So if you like tearjerker movies, look elsewhere. You'll only feel like a fool for watching this one.

1. _____

2. _____

3. _____

4. _____

》 **REMEMBER**
Why is more important than *what*.

1. The phrase, "I already have" (line 23) serves primarily to:

    (A) recommend that viewers avoid the movie.

    (B) stress the poor performance of the movie's stars.

    (C) emphasize the weakness of the movie's storyline.

    (D) convey the author's reluctance to reveal key points in the movie's plot.

》 **REMEMBER**
Keep straight who said what.

2. According to the author, the performance of the actress Sandie Findlay in the film *Why Me?* is:

    (F) surprisingly compelling.

    (G) typically poor.

    (H) uncharacteristically disappointing.

    (J) overly annoying.

Natural Science and Prose Fiction

NATURAL SCIENCE PASSAGES	
What makes them different?	**Focus on...**
	1. summarizing each paragraph.
	2. keeping good passage notes.
	3. keeping an eye out for keywords.
	4. not getting caught up in details.

PROSE FICTION	
What makes them different?	**Focus on...**
	1. the characters.
	2. feelings and relationships.
	3. the author's tone and diction.

Passage II

NATURAL SCIENCE: The following passage is excerpted from "The Transformer," by John W. Coltman. Reprinted with permission. (© 1988 by Scientific American, Inc.)

The transformer is an essential component of modern electric power systems. Simply put, it can convert electricity with a low current and a high
Line voltage into electricity with a high current and a low
(5) voltage (and vice versa) with almost no loss of energy. The conversion is important because electric power is transmitted most efficiently at high voltages but is best generated and used at low voltages. Were it not for transformers, the distance separating generators
(10) from consumers would have to be minimized; many households and industries would require their own power stations, and electricity would be a much less practical form of energy.

In addition to its role in electric power systems,
(15) the transformer is an integral component of many things that run on electricity. Desk lamps, battery chargers, toy trains, and television sets all rely on transformers to cut or boost voltage. In its multiplicity of applications, the transformer can range from tiny
(20) assemblies the size of a pea to behemoths weighing 500 tons or more. This article will focus on the transformers in power systems, but the principles that govern the function of electrical transformers are the same regardless of size or application.
(25) The English physicist Michael Faraday discovered the basic action of the transformer during his pioneering investigations of electricity in 1831. Some 50 years later, the advent of a practical transformer,

containing all the essential elements of the modern
(30) instrument, revolutionized the infant electric lighting industry. By the turn of the century, alternating-current power systems had been universally adopted and the transformer had assumed a key role in electrical transmission and distribution.
(35) Yet the transformer's tale does not end in 1900. Today's transformers can handle 500 times the power and 15 times the voltage of their turn-of-the-century ancestors; the weight per unit of power has dropped by a factor of 10, and efficiency typically
(40) exceeds 99 percent. These advances reflect the marriage of theoretical inquiry and engineering that first elucidated and then exploited the phenomena governing transformer action.

Faraday's investigations were inspired by the
(45) Danish physicist Hans Christian Oersted, who had shown in 1820 that an electric current flowing through a conducting material creates a magnetic field around the conductor. At the time, Oersted's discovery was considered remarkable, since electricity
(50) and magnetism were thought to be separate and unrelated forces. If an electric current could generate a magnetic field, it seemed likely that a magnetic field could give rise to an electric current.

In 1831, Faraday demonstrated that in order for a
(55) magnetic field to induce a current in a conductor, the field must be changing. Faraday caused the strength of the field to fluctuate by making and breaking the electric circuit generating the field; the same effect can be achieved with a current whose direction
(60) alternates in time. This fascinating interaction of electricity and magnetism came to be known as electromagnetic induction.

)) REMEMBER
When prediction is impractical, work through the choices; good notes will still help you to qualify or discard answer choices quickly.

3. Which of the following statements is best supported by the passage?

(A) Faraday was the first to show how an electric current can produce a magnetic field.

(B) Oersted was the first to utilize transformers in a practical application, by using them to power electric lights.

(C) Oersted coined the term "electromagnetic induction."

(D) Faraday showed that, when a magnetic field is changing, it can produce an electric current in a conducting material.

)) REMEMBER
Good notes will help you to avoid selecting Misused Detail answer choices as you look for the correct choice.

4. The passage suggests that advances in the efficiency of the transformer are:

(F) based solely on Faraday's discovery of electromagnetic induction.

(G) attributable to a combination of engineering and theoretical study.

(H) most likely at a peak that cannot be surpassed.

(J) found in transformers that weigh 500 tons or more.

Quiz

Passage III

PROSE FICTION: This passage is an adapted excerpt from Jane Austen's novel *Emma*. In this passage, Emma confronts a change in her previously happy life.

Emma Woodhouse—handsome, clever, and rich, with a comfortable home and happy disposition—seemed to unite some of the best
Line blessings of existence. She had lived nearly
(5) twenty-one years in the world with very little to distress or vex her. She was the youngest of the two daughters of a most affectionate, indulgent father, and had—in consequence of her sister's marriage—been mistress of his house from a very early period.
(10) Her mother had died too long ago for her to have more than an indistinct remembrance of her caresses, and her place had been taken by an excellent governess who had fallen little short of a mother in affection.
(15) Sixteen years had Miss Taylor been in Mr. Woodhouse's family, less as a governess than a friend, very fond of both daughters, but particularly of Emma. Between them it was more the intimacy of sisters. Even before Miss Taylor
(20) had ceased to hold the nominal office of governess, the mildness of her temper had hardly allowed her to impose any restraint. The shadow of authority being now long passed away, they had been living together as friend and friend very mutually
(25) attached, and Emma doing just what she liked—highly esteeming Miss Taylor's judgment, but directed chiefly by her own. The real evils, indeed, of Emma's situation were the power of having rather too much her own way and a disposition to
(30) think a little too well of herself; these were the disadvantages which threatened alloy to her many enjoyments. The danger, however, was at present so unperceived that they did not by any means rank as misfortunes with her.
(35) Sorrow came—a gentle sorrow—but not at all in the shape of any disagreeable consciousness. Miss Taylor married. It was Miss Taylor's loss which first brought grief. It was on the wedding day of this beloved friend that Emma first sat in
(40) mournful thought of any continuance. The wedding over, and the bride-people gone, she and her father were left to dine together, with no prospect of a third to cheer a long evening. Her father composed himself to sleep after dinner, as
(45) usual, and she had then only to sit and think of what she had lost.

The marriage had every promise of happiness for her friend. Mr. Weston was a man of unexceptionable character, easy fortune, suitable
(50) age, and pleasant manners. There was some satisfaction in considering with what self-denying, generous friendship she had always wished and promoted the match, but it was a black morning's work for her. The want of Miss Taylor would be
(55) felt every hour of every day. She recalled her past kindness—the kindness, the affection of sixteen years—how she had taught her and how she had played with her from five years old, how she had devoted all her powers to attach and amuse her in
(60) health, and how she had nursed her through the various illnesses of childhood. A large debt of gratitude was owing here, but the intercourse of the last seven years—the equal footing and perfect unreserve which had soon followed Isabella's
(65) marriage, on their being left to each other—was yet a dearer, tenderer recollection. She had been a friend and companion such as few possessed: intelligent, well informed, useful, gentle, knowing all the ways of the family, interested in all its
(70) concerns, and peculiarly interested in her, in every pleasure, every scheme of hers—one to whom she could speak every thought as it arose, and who had such an affection for her as could never find fault.

How was she to bear the change? It was true
(75) that her friend was going only half a mile from them, but Emma was aware that great must be the difference between a Mrs. Weston, only half a mile from them, and a Miss Taylor in the house. With all her advantages, natural and domestic,
(80) she was now in great danger of suffering from intellectual solitude.

1. As described in the passage, Emma's relationship with Miss Taylor can best be characterized as:

   (A) similar to a mother-daughter relationship.
   (B) similar to the relationship between sisters or best friends.
   (C) weaker than Emma's relationship with her sister.
   (D) stronger than Miss Taylor's relationship with her new husband.

2. It is most reasonable to infer from Emma's realization in lines 76–78 ("great...house") that:

   (F) Miss Taylor will no longer be a part of Emma's life.
   (G) Emma is happy about the marriage because now she will have more freedom.
   (H) Emma regrets that her relationship with Miss Taylor will change.
   (J) Emma believes that her relationship with Miss Taylor will become stronger.

3. Based on the passage, Emma could best be described as:

   (A) sweet and naïve.
   (B) self-centered and naïve.
   (C) self-centered and headstrong.
   (D) unappreciative and bitter.

QUARTER 4

SESSION 1

Point Builder	What Is ACT Science?
Point Builder	The Kaplan Method for ACT Science

What Is ACT Science?

A. The Science Test is always the _____ test on the ACT. It will be _____ minutes long and have _____ questions.

B. It has _____ passages. This means you have approximately _____ minutes to spend on each passage.

C. ACT Science tests how well you can do the following:
- Identify the Purpose, Method, and Results of an experiment.
- Scan and interpret figures to identify variables and patterns.
- Apply Scientific Reasoning.

D. You already have a working knowledge of the sciences from high school. The Science Test contains passages about the following subjects:

_____

_____

_____

_____

_____

E. You will see three kinds of passages:

_____ Data Representation passages, each with _____ questions

_____ Research Summary passages, each with _____ questions

_____ Conflicting Viewpoints passage with _____ questions

F. Don't worry! Almost all of the information you need to answer the questions will be in the passage!

The Kaplan Method for ACT Science

A. The Purpose of an experiment is the main idea. Ask yourself:

_____

_____

B. The Method is how the researchers set up the experiment.

_____

_____

C. The Results are what the researchers have found out. They can be presented in the form of a graph or chart.

D. By practicing passage mapping, you will train yourself to identify the Purpose, Method, and Results automatically by Test Day!

E. **The Kaplan Method for ACT Science**

1. _____

_____

2. _____

_____

3. _____

_____

Passage I

Animal behaviorists researched how bats respond to abnormalities in their environments. Because bats are nocturnal animals, the researchers used light to represent abnormality. The researchers devised two experiments to examine the effect of light on bat behavior in groups and in isolation.

Experiment 1

Twenty-five groups, each consisting of 6 bats, were placed in 25 separate simulated caves. The environment of the caves replicated the natural habitat of the bats. Twice during nocturnal hours, a beam of light was sent into the simulated caves for 3 minutes at a time. This procedure was repeated 21 times in the course of 3 weeks, at varying times during the nocturnal hours. Throughout the trials, not one bat was observed to respond to the light.

Experiment 2

Twenty-five bats were placed in 25 separate simulated caves. The environment of the caves replicated the natural habitat of the bats. Twice during nocturnal hours, a beam of light was sent into the simulated caves for 3 minutes at a time. This procedure was repeated 21 times in the course of 3 weeks, at varying times during the nocturnal hours. Eighteen of the isolated bats responded to the light with extremely agitated and nervous behavior. Seven of those bats attempted to escape from the research environment.

What is the Purpose of both experiments?
_____
_____
_____

What is the Method of Experiment 1?
_____
_____
_____

What are the Results of Experiment 1?
_____
_____
_____

What is the Method of Experiment 2?
_____
_____
_____

What are the Results of Experiment 2?
_____
_____
_____

The Kaplan Method for ACT Science

A.   Identify the independent and dependent variables.

     • An independent variable is changed to determine its relationship to the dependent variable.

     • Independent variables answer the question, "What do I change?"

     • Dependent variables answer the question, "What do I observe?"

B.   Identify the information needed.

C.   Identify the pattern in that information.

D.   **The Kaplan Method for ACT Science**

     1. Map the passage, identifying and marking the Purpose, Method, and Results of the experiment.

     2. _____

     _____

     3. _____

     _____

E.   ACT Science overwhelmingly tests reasoning ability. In fact, it used to be called the Science Reasoning Test. Almost every question can be answered using only the information on the page.

F.   Know the general scope of the experiment or passage and where to find information if a question asks for it.

G.   **The Kaplan Method for ACT Science**

     1. Map the passage, identifying and marking the Purpose, Method, and Results of the experiment.

     2. Scan figures, identifying variables and patterns.

     3. _____

     _____

Passage I

Animal behaviorists researched how bats respond to abnormalities in their environments. Because bats are nocturnal animals, the researchers used light to represent abnormality. The researchers devised two experiments to examine the effect of light on bat behavior in groups and in isolation.

Experiment 1

Twenty-five groups, each consisting of 6 bats, were placed in 25 separate simulated caves. The environment of the caves replicated the natural habitat of the bats. Twice during nocturnal hours, a beam of light was sent into the simulated caves for 3 minutes at a time. This procedure was repeated 21 times in the course of 3 weeks, at varying times during the nocturnal hours. Throughout the trials, not one bat was observed to respond to the light.

Experiment 2

Twenty-five bats were placed in 25 separate simulated caves. The environment of the caves replicated the natural habitat of the bats. Twice during nocturnal hours, a beam of light was sent into the simulated caves for 3 minutes at a time. This procedure was repeated 21 times in the course of 3 weeks, at varying times during the nocturnal hours. Eighteen of the isolated bats responded to the light with extremely agitated and nervous behavior. Seven of those bats attempted to escape from the research environment.

1. According to the passage, the bats responded to a beam of light when:

   (A) it was sent into the simulated caves 21 times during the week.
   (B) seven of the bats attempted to escape from the research environment.
   (C) they were isolated in 25 separate caves.
   (D) they were placed in groups of 6.

2. Which of the following factors was intentionally varied in Experiment 1 and Experiment 2?

   (F) Duration of the beam of light
   (G) The time of day during which the light was sent into the caves
   (H) The bats' behavior when exposed to light
   (J) The number of bats exposed to the light

Quiz

Passage II

Humans can experience toxic symptoms when concentrations of mercury (Hg) in the blood exceed 200 parts per billion (ppb). Frequent consumption of foods high in Hg content contributes to high Hg levels in the blood. On average, higher Hg concentrations are observed in people whose diets consist of more extreme amounts of certain types of seafood. A research group proposed that sea creatures that live in colder waters acquire greater amounts of Hg than those that reside in warmer waters. The researchers performed the following experiments to examine this hypothesis.

Experiment 1

Samples of several species of consumable sea life caught in the cold waters of the northern Atlantic Ocean were chemically prepared and analyzed using a cold vapor atomic fluorescence spectrometer (CVAFS), a device that indicates the relative concentrations of various elements and compounds found within a biological sample. Comparisons of the spectra taken from the seafood samples with those taken from samples of known Hg levels were made to determine the exact concentrations in ppb. Identical volumes of tissue from eight different specimens for each of four different species were tested, and the results are shown in Table 1, including the average concentrations found for each species.

Table 1				
Specimen	Hg concentration in cold-water species (ppb):			
	Cod	Crab	Swordfish	Shark
1	160	138	871	859
2	123	143	905	820
3	139	152	902	839
4	116	177	881	851
5	130	133	875	818
6	134	148	880	836
7	151	147	910	847
8	109	168	894	825
Average	133	151	890	837

Experiment 2

Four species caught in the warmer waters of the Gulf of Mexico were examined using the procedure from experiment 1. The results are shown in Table 2.

Table 2				
Specimen	Hg concentration in warm-water species (ppb):			
	Catfish	Crab	Swordfish	Shark
1	98	113	851	812
2	110	122	856	795
3	102	143	845	821
4	105	128	861	803
5	94	115	849	798
6	112	136	852	809
7	100	129	863	815
8	117	166	837	776
Average	105	125	852	804

1. A researcher, when using the CVAFS, was concerned that lead (Pb) in the tissue samples might be interfering with the detection of Hg. Which of the following procedures would best help the researcher explore this problem?

   (A) Flooding the sample with a large concentration of Pb before using the CVAFS
   (B) Using the CVAFS to examine a nonbiological sample
   (C) Collecting tissue from additional species
   (D) Testing a sample with known concentrations of Hg and Pb

2. The governments of many nations require frequent testing of seafood to determine Hg concentration levels. According to the experiments, in order to determine the maximum concentration of Hg found in a collection of seafood specimens, from which of the following specimens would it be best to take sample tissue?

   (F) A crab caught in cold water
   (G) A swordfish caught in cold water
   (H) A catfish caught in warm water
   (J) A swordfish caught in warm water

3. Which of the following factors was intentionally varied in Experiment 2?

   (A) The volume of tissue tested
   (B) The method by which the marine organisms were caught
   (C) The species of marine organism tested
   (D) The method of sample analysis

4. Given that sharks and swordfish are both large, predatory animals and that catfish and crabs are smaller, nonpredatory animals, do the results of Experiment 2 support the hypothesis that the tissue of larger predatory fish exhibits higher levels of Hg than does the tissue of smaller species?

   (F) Yes; the lowest concentration of Hg was found in swordfish.
   (G) Yes; both swordfish and shark had Hg concentrations that were higher than those found in either catfish or crab.
   (H) No; the lowest concentration of Hg was in catfish.
   (J) No; both catfish and crab had concentrations of Hg that were higher than those found in either swordfish or shark.

5. How might the results of the experiments be affected if the chemical preparation described in Experiment 1 introduced Hg-free contaminants into the sample, resulting in a larger volume of tested material? The measured concentrations of Hg would be:

   (A) the same as the actual concentrations for both cold-water and warm-water specimens.
   (B) higher than the actual concentrations for both cold-water and warm-water specimens.
   (C) lower than the actual concentrations for cold-water specimens but higher than the actual concentrations for warm-water specimens.
   (D) lower than the actual concentrations for both cold-water and warm-water specimens.

Session 1 Homework

	Required	Recommended	Appendix
Quarter 1			
The Kaplan Method for ACT English	1–10		
Quarter 2			
Variable Manipulation	1–10	11–20	
Quarter 3			
Natural Science Passages	1–5	6–10	
Prose Fiction Passages	11–15	16–20	
Quarter 4			
The Kaplan Method for ACT Science	1–11		

HOMEWORK

Quarter 1

Urban Legends

Since primitive times, societies have created,
<u>1</u>
<u>and told</u> legends. Even before the development of
<u>1</u>
written language, cultures would orally pass down
these popular stories. These stories served the dual
purpose of entertaining audiences and
<u>also transmitting</u> values and beliefs from
<u>2</u>
generation to generation. <u>Indeed</u> today we have
<u>3</u>
many more permanent ways of handing down our
beliefs to future generations, we continue to create
and tell legends. In our technological society, a new
form of folktale has <u>emerged: the</u> urban legend.
<u>4</u>

Urban legends are stories we all have heard; they
are supposed to have really happened, but are never
<u>verifiable however</u>. It seems that the people
<u>5</u>
involved can never be found. Researchers of the
urban legend call the elusive participant in such
supposed "real-life" events a FOAF—a Friend of a
Friend.

1. (A) NO CHANGE
   (B) created and told
   (C) created, and telling
   (D) created and telling

2. (F) NO CHANGE
   (G) also transmit
   (H) of transmitting
   (J) of transmit

3. (A) NO CHANGE
   (B) But
   (C) And
   (D) Although

4. (F) NO CHANGE
   (G) emerged; the
   (H) emerged the
   (J) emerged, the

5. (A) NO CHANGE
   (B) verified however
   (C) verified, however
   (D) verified

Urban legends have some characteristic features.
They are often humorous in nature, with a surprise
<u>ending and a conclusion</u>. One such legend is the
<u>6</u>
tale of the hunter who was returning home from
an unsuccessful hunting trip. On his way home,
he accidentally hit and killed a deer on a deserted
highway. Even though he knew it was illegal, he
decided to keep the deer, and he <u>loads it in</u>
<u>7</u>
the back of his station wagon. As the hunter
continued, driving, the deer—<u>he was</u> only
<u>8</u>
temporarily knocked unconscious by the car—
woke up and began thrashing around. The hunter
panicked, stopped the car, ran to the ditch, and
watched the enraged deer destroy his car. Another
legend involves alligators in the sewer systems of
major metropolitan areas. According to the story,
before alligators were a protected <u>species, people</u>
<u>9</u>
vacationing in Florida purchased baby alligators to
take home as souvenirs.
<u>Between 1930 and 1940, nearly a million</u>
<u>10</u>
<u>alligators in Florida were killed for the value of their</u>
<u>10</u>
<u>skin, used to make expensive leather products such as</u>
<u>10</u>
<u>boots and wallets</u>. After the novelty of having a pet
<u>10</u>
alligator wore off, many people flushed their baby
souvenirs down toilets. Legend has it that the baby
alligators found a perfect growing and breeding
environment in city sewer systems, where they thrive
to this day on the ample supply of rats.

6. (F) NO CHANGE
   (G) ending; and a conclusion
   (H) ending
   (J) ending, and a conclusion

7. (A) NO CHANGE
   (B) loads it into
   (C) loaded it in
   (D) loading it in

8. (F) NO CHANGE
   (G) which was
   (H) they were
   (J) which is

9. (A) NO CHANGE
   (B) species people
   (C) species; people
   (D) species because

10. (F) NO CHANGE
    (G) Between 1930 and 1940, nearly a million alligators were killed and used to make expensive leather products such as boots and wallets.
    (H) Between 1930 and 1940, they killed nearly a million alligators in Florida for the value of their skin, used to make expensive leather products such as boots and wallets.
    (J) OMIT the underlined portion.

Quarter 2

1. At a local theater, adult tickets cost $8 and student tickets cost $5. At a recent show, 500 tickets were sold for a total of $3,475. How many adult tickets were sold?

   (A) 125
   (B) 200
   (C) 325
   (D) 400
   (E) 450

2. If $x \neq 0$, and $x^2 - 3x = 6x$, then $x = ?$

   (F) −9
   (G) −3
   (H) $\sqrt{9}$
   (J) 3
   (K) 9

3. If $\frac{3}{zy} = \frac{2y}{x}$, then x is equal to which of the following?

   (A) $\frac{2zy^2}{3}$
   (B) $\frac{3zy^2}{2}$
   (C) $\frac{2z}{3}$
   (D) $\frac{3}{2zy^2}$
   (E) $6zy^2$

4. If $\frac{\left(x^2\right)^3}{2} = 32$ which of the following is a possible value of x ?

   (F) −3
   (G) 2
   (H) 3
   (J) 4
   (K) 5

5. Dr. Hasenpfeffer's physics midterm has 60 questions. He scores the test as follows: for each correct answer, he gives 2 points; for each incorrect answer, he subtracts $\frac{2}{3}$ of a point; for unanswered questions, he neither gives nor subtracts points. If Denise scored a 68 and did not answer 2 of the questions, how many questions did she answer correctly?

   (A) 34
   (B) 36
   (C) 38
   (D) 40
   (E) 42

6. For what value of k can the expression $x^2 + kx + 15$ be factored as $(x - 3)(x - 5)$?

   (F) −15
   (G) −8
   (H) 0
   (J) 8
   (K) 15

7. If $k - 3 = -\frac{5}{3}$, then $3 - k = ?$

   (A) $-\frac{5}{3}$
   (B) $-\frac{3}{5}$
   (C) $\frac{3}{5}$
   (D) $\frac{5}{3}$
   (E) $\frac{7}{3}$

8. Which of the following is the solution statement for the inequality $-3 < 4x - 5$?

   (F) $x > -2$
   (G) $x > \frac{1}{2}$
   (H) $x < -2$
   (J) $x < \frac{1}{2}$
   (K) $x < 2$

9. If $x > 0$ and $y > 0$, $\frac{\sqrt{x}}{x} + \frac{\sqrt{y}}{y}$ is equivalent to which of the following?

   (A) $\frac{2}{\sqrt{xy}}$

   (B) $\frac{\sqrt{x} + \sqrt{y}}{\sqrt{xy}}$

   (C) $\frac{x + y}{xy}$

   (D) $\frac{\sqrt{x + \sqrt{y}}}{\sqrt{x + y}}$

   (E) $\frac{x + y}{\sqrt{xy}}$

10. If $9^{2x-1} = 3^{3x+3}$ then $x = $?

   (F) -4

   (G) $-\frac{4}{7}$

   (H) $-\frac{7}{4}$

   (J) 2

   (K) 5

11. For all $x \neq 0$, $\frac{x^2 + x^2 + x^2}{x^2} = $?

   (A) 3

   (B) $3x$

   (C) x^2

   (D) x^3

   (E) x^4

12. The expression $7n - 8$ will equal 6 if n equals:

   (F) 1

   (G) 2

   (H) 3

   (J) 4

   (K) 5

13. Joan has q quarters, d dimes, n nickels, and no other coins in her pocket. Which of the following represents the total number of coins in Joan's pocket?

   (A) $q + d + n$

   (B) $5q + 2d + n$

   (C) $0.25q + 0.10d + 0.05n$

   (D) $(25 + 10 + 5)(q + d + n)$

   (E) $25q + 10d + 5n$

14. At a school trivia competition, contestants can answer 2 kinds of questions: easy questions and hard questions. Easy questions are worth 3 points, and hard questions are worth 5 points. Nicole knows that she correctly answered 21 questions and that she had a total of 79 points. How many hard questions did she answer correctly?

   (F) 7

   (G) 8

   (H) 12

   (J) 13

   (K) 15

15. What is the sum of the values of x for which $2x^2 = 2x + 12$?

   (A) -2

   (B) -1

   (C) 0

   (D) 1

   (E) 2

16. Miguel is at a bookstore buying books, each of which usually costs $12.60. He learns that the books are on sale and that he can buy 5 books for a total of $55.00. If he buys the books on sale, by what amount is the price of *each* book reduced?

   (F) $ 0.32

   (G) $ 1.60

   (H) $ 1.93

   (J) $ 2.52

   (K) $11.00

17. Which of the following is the solution statement for the inequality $3 < -4x - 5$?

   (A) $x > -2$

   (B) $x > \frac{1}{2}$

   (C) $x < -2$

   (D) $x < \frac{1}{2}$

   (E) $x < 2$

18. For all $x > 0$, $\dfrac{1}{1 + \frac{1}{x}} = $?

   (F) $x + 1$

   (G) $\frac{x}{x + 1}$

   (H) $x + 2$

   (J) $\frac{x}{x + 2}$

   (K) $\frac{x}{2}$

19. If $ax + y = 23$, $3x - y = 9$, and $x = 8$, what is the value of a?

    (A) 1
    (B) 3
    (C) 5
    (D) 8
    (E) 15

20. $\sqrt{(x^2 + 4)^2} - (x + 2)(x - 2) = ?$

    (F) $2x^2$
    (G) $x^2 - 8$
    (H) $2(x - 2)$
    (J) 0
    (K) 8

Quarter 3

Passage I

NATURAL SCIENCE: The following passage is excerpted from "Earth's Ozone Shield Under Threat," by France Bequette (© *Unesco Courier,* June 1992, Vol. 45, Issue 6, p. 26).

The ozone layer, the tenuous layer of gas that surrounds our planet between 12 and 45 kilometers above our surface, is being rapidly depleted.
Line Seasonally occurring holes have appeared in it over
(5) the poles, and, more recently, over the temperate regions of the Northern Hemisphere. The threat is a serious one since the ozone layer traps almost all incoming ultraviolet radiation, which is harmful to all living organisms—humans, animals, and plants.
(10) Even though the ozone layer is 25 kilometers thick, the atmosphere in it is very tenuous, and the total amount of ozone, compared with other atmospheric gases, is quite small. If all of the ozone in a vertical column reaching up through the atmosphere
(15) were to be compressed to sea-level pressure, it would form a layer only a few millimeters thick.

Detailed study of the ozone layer began comparatively recently, the earliest observations being made in 1930 by the English scientist Sydney
(20) Chapman. These initial observations were taken up by the World Meteorological Organization (WMO), which established the Dobson network of one hundred observation stations. Since 1983, on the initiative of WMO and the United Nations Environment
(25) Programme (UNEP), seven of these stations have been entrusted with the task of making long-term forecasts of the likely evolution of our precious shield.

In 1958, the researchers who permanently monitor the ozone content of the layer above the South Pole
(30) began to observe several seasonal variations. From June, there was a slight reduction in ozone content that reached a minimum in October. In November, there was a sudden increase in the ozone content. The fluctuations appeared to result from the
(35) natural phenomena of wind effects and temperature change.

However, although the October minimum remained constant until 1979, the total ozone content over the pole was steadily diminishing until, in 1985,
(40) public opinion was finally roused by reports of a "hole" in the ozone layer and observations were intensified. The culprits responsible for the hole had already been identified as being supersonic aircraft, such as the Concorde (although these have now been
(45) exonerated), and the notorious compounds known as chlorofluorocarbons, or CFCs. Synthesized in 1928 by chemists working at General Motors in the United States, CFCs are compounds of atoms of carbon, chlorine, and fluorine. Having the advantage of being
(50) nonflammable, nontoxic, and noncorrosive, they came into widespread use in the 1950s. They are widely used in refrigerators, air conditioners, the "bubbles" in the foam plastic used, for example, in car seats, and as insulation in buildings.
(55) In 1989, they represented a market valued at over $1 billion and a labor force of 1.6 million. Of the twenty-five countries producing CFCs, the United States, France, the United Kingdom, Japan, and Germany accounted for three-quarters of the total
(60) world production of some 1.2 million tons.

These figures give some idea of the importance of the economic interests that are at stake in any decision to ban the industrial use of CFCs. But, with CFCs incriminated by scientists, the question arose as to
(65) whether we were prepared to take the risk of seeing an increase in the number of cases of skin cancer, eye ailments such as cataracts, or even a lowering of the human immune-defense system, all effects that would follow further depletion of the ozone layer.
(70) The Montreal Protocol was the first world agreement aimed at halting the production of CFCs. As more evidence emerged concerning the seriousness of the threat, it became apparent that the protocol was not stringent enough and, year by year,
(75) its severity was increased until, in 1990 in London, seventy countries agreed to stop all production of CFCs by the year 2000.

Unfortunately, even if the entire world were to agree today to halt all production and use of CFCs,
(80) this would not provide an immediate solution to the problem. A single molecule of chlorine can destroy

from 10,000 to 100,000 molecules of ozone. Furthermore, CFCs have a lifespan of between 75 and
Line 400 years, and they take ten years to reach the ozone
(85) layer. In other words, what we are experiencing now results from CFCs emitted 10 years ago.

Industrialists are now urgently searching for substitute products. Some, such as propane, are too dangerous because they are flammable; others, the
(90) HCFCs, might prove to be toxic and to contribute to the greenhouse effect, i.e., to the process of global warming. Nevertheless, nobody can say that the situation will not right itself, whether in the short term or long term, if we ourselves lend a hand.

1. As it is used in the passage, the term *right* (line 93) most likely means:

    (A) affirm
    (B) fix
    (C) stand up
    (D) topple

2. According to the passage, the public first became aware of the depletion of the ozone layer in:

    (F) 1930
    (G) 1958
    (H) 1979
    (J) 1985

3. According to the passage, all of the following contribute to changes in the ozone layer EXCEPT:

    (A) supersonic aircraft
    (B) chlorofluorocarbons
    (C) temperature changes
    (D) wind effects

4. The main point of the seventh paragraph (lines 61–69) is to:

    (F) highlight the number of CFCs produced every year.
    (G) criticize the countries responsible for producing CFCs.
    (H) indicate the economic interests at stake in the CFC debate.
    (J) list the most important members of the Montreal Protocol.

5. Based on information in the passage, which of the following would most likely result if all production of CFCs were to end today?

    (A) Scientists would have to replace the quantities of ozone already lost.
    (B) The ozone layer would only return to normal levels after 75 years.
    (C) Scientists would also have to destroy all chlorine molecules in the atmosphere.
    (D) The benefits would not be experienced for another 10 years.

6. According to the passage, forecasts about the future of the ozone layer are made by:

    (F) the WMO
    (G) the Dobson network
    (H) the Montreal Protocol
    (J) UNEP

7. According to the passage, which of the following does NOT represent a reason that substitutes for CFCs may be problematic?

    (A) They are flammable.
    (B) They may be toxic.
    (C) They may contribute to global warming.
    (D) They are prohibitively expensive.

8. According to the passage, the ozone layer is:

    (F) a few millimeters thick
    (G) 12 kilometers thick
    (H) 25 kilometers thick
    (J) more than 25 kilometers thick

9. Which of the following statements is best supported by the fourth paragraph (lines 28–35)?

    (A) Researchers studying the ozone layer above the South Pole were not alarmed by the results of their study.
    (B) Seasonal variations in the ozone layer did not occur before 1958.
    (C) The ozone layer is more at risk over the South Pole than it is over other areas.
    (D) The first studies of ozone layer depletion overestimated its severity.

10. The main conclusion reached in the passage about the threat to the ozone layer is that:

    (F) the cost of banning CFCs altogether may make it an impractical answer.

    (G) finding alternative products to CFCs may provide a long-term remedy to the situation.

    (H) halting production of CFCs is unlikely to produce a solution to the problem.

    (J) agreements between CFC-producing countries need to be more strictly enforced.

Passage II

PROSE FICTION: The passage below is an adapted excerpt from *Bleak House*, by Charles Dickens. In this passage, Esther recounts some of her childhood experiences.

I can remember, when I was a very little girl indeed, I used to say to my doll when we were alone together, "Now, Dolly, I am not clever, you know very
Line well, and you must be patient with me, like a dear!"
(5) My dear old doll! I was such a shy little thing that I seldom dared to open my lips, and never dared to open my heart, to anybody else. It almost makes me cry to think what a relief it used to be to me when I came home from school of a day to run upstairs to my
(10) room and say, "Oh, you dear faithful Dolly, I knew you would be expecting me!" and then to sit down on the floor, leaning on the elbow of her great chair, and tell her all I had noticed since we parted.

I was brought up, from my earliest childhood
(15) remembrance—like some of the princesses in the fairy stories, only I was not charming—by my godmother. At least, I only knew her as such. She was a good, good woman! She went to church three times every Sunday, and to morning prayers on Wednesdays and
(20) Fridays, and to lectures whenever there were lectures; and never missed. She was handsome; and if she had ever smiled, would have been (I used to think) like an angel—but she never smiled. She was always grave and strict. She was so very good herself, I thought,
(25) that the badness of other people made her frown all her life. It made me very sorry to consider how good she was and how unworthy of her I was, and I used ardently to hope that I might have a better heart; and I talked it over very often with the dear old doll, but I never loved
(30) my godmother as I ought to have loved her and as I felt I must have loved her if I had been a better girl.

I had never heard my mama spoken of. I had never been shown my mama's grave. I had never been told where it was.

(35) Although there were seven girls at the neighboring school where I was a day boarder, and although they called me little Esther Summerson,

I knew none of them at home. All of them were older than I, to be sure (I was the youngest there
(40) by a good deal), but there seemed to be some other separation between us besides that, and besides their being far more clever than I was and knowing much more than I did. One of them in the first week of my going to the school (I remember it very well) invited
(45) me home to a little party, to my great joy. But my godmother wrote a stiff letter declining for me, and I never went. I never went out at all.

It was my birthday. There were holidays at school on other birthdays—none on mine. There were
(50) rejoicings at home on other birthdays, as I knew from what I heard the girls relate to one another—there were none on mine. My birthday was the most melancholy day at home in the whole year.

Dinner was over, and my godmother and I were
(55) sitting at the table before the fire. The clock ticked, the fire clicked; not another sound had been heard in the room or in the house for I don't know how long. I happened to look timidly up from my stitching, across the table at my godmother, and I saw in her
(60) face, looking gloomily at me, "It would have been far better, little Esther, that you had had no birthday, that you had never been born!"

I broke out crying and sobbing, and I said, "Oh, dear godmother, tell me, pray do tell me, did Mama
(65) die on my birthday?"

"No," she returned. "Ask me no more, child!"

I put up my trembling little hand to clasp hers or to beg her pardon with what earnestness I might, but withdrew it as she looked at me, and laid it on my
(70) fluttering heart. She said slowly in a cold, low voice—I see her knitted brow and pointed finger—"The time will come—and soon enough—when you will understand this better and will feel it too. I have forgiven her"—but her face did not relent—"the
(75) wrong she did to me, and I say no more of it, though it was greater than you will ever know. Forget your mother and leave all other people to forget her. Now, go!"

I went up to my room, and crept to bed, and laid
(80) my doll's cheek against mine wet with tears, and holding that solitary friend upon my bosom, cried myself to sleep. Imperfect as my understanding of my sorrow was, I knew that I had brought no joy at any time to anybody's heart and that I was to no one
(85) upon earth what Dolly was to me.

Dear, dear, to think how much time we passed alone together afterwards, and how often I repeated to the doll the story of my birthday and confided to her that I would try as hard as ever I could to repair
(90) the fault I had been born with. I hope it is not self-indulgent to shed these tears as I think of it.

11. According to the passage, Esther only remembers:

    (A) being brought up by her parents for a short time.
    (B) being brought up by her mother for a short time.
    (C) being brought up by her godmother for a short time.
    (D) being brought up by her godmother.

12. It is most likely that Esther thinks of her doll as:

    (F) her only friend and confidante.
    (G) only an amusing plaything.
    (H) like a sister to her.
    (J) a beautiful toy that is too fragile to touch.

13. As it is used in the passage, "stiff"(line 45) most closely means:

    (A) difficult to bend.
    (B) overly formal.
    (C) unchanging.
    (D) lifeless.

14. Which of the following most likely contributes to Esther's belief that she has been born with a fault (line 90)?

    (F) Her birthday is never celebrated.
    (G) She has never heard anyone talk about her father.
    (H) Her godmother told her that she should never have been born.
    (J) Her godmother does not let her attend birthday parties.

15. Esther's godmother's words, actions, and facial expression as described in paragraph 10 (lines 67–76) suggest that she:

    (A) wishes to scold Esther for pestering her about her birthday.
    (B) does not know what happened to Esther's mother.
    (C) continues to resent Esther's mother.
    (D) has forgotten Esther's mother.

16. According to the passage, Esther's childhood can be most accurately characterized as:

    (F) an adventure.
    (G) a time of loneliness and confusion.
    (H) a period of dedication to education and self-improvement.
    (J) a period of attempting to become more like her godmother.

17. From Esther's statement, "I was to no one upon earth what Dolly was to me" (lines 84–85), it is reasonable to infer that Esther:

    (A) believes that no one loves her.
    (B) believes that she will never become friends with the girls at school.
    (C) believes that her godmother doesn't love her.
    (D) transferred her love for her mother to Dolly.

18. In the passage, it is implied that all of the following contribute to separating Esther from the other girls at her school EXCEPT:

    (F) the other girls are older than Esther.
    (G) Esther's godmother does not allow Esther to socialize with the other girls outside of school.
    (H) Esther believes that the other girls are much smarter.
    (J) Esther's self-indulgence makes the other girls not want to be around her.

19. According to the passage, one reason that Esther thinks of her godmother as a "good, good woman" (lines 17–18) is:

    (A) that her smile is like that of an angel.
    (B) that she forgave Esther's mother.
    (C) that she frequently attends church services.
    (D) that she gave Esther a doll.

20. In the passage, Esther describes herself as a child as:

    (F) self-indulgent and not very clever.
    (G) shy and not very clever.
    (H) shy and faithful.
    (J) self-indulgent and faithful.

Quarter 4

Passage 1

The extent to which a solute will dissolve in a given solvent is dependent on several factors, including conditions of temperature and pressure and the electrochemical natures of the solute and solvent.

A high school chemistry teacher assigned 24 students the project of measuring the solubilities in distilled water of several pairs of common sodium (Na) and potassium (K) salts at various temperatures. The pairs were $NaCl$ and KCl, $NaNO_3$ and KNO_3, and $NaClO_3$ and $KClO_3$. All measurements were conducted under normal atmospheric pressure. After pooling and averaging all the data, the students plotted solubility curves to produce the graph below.

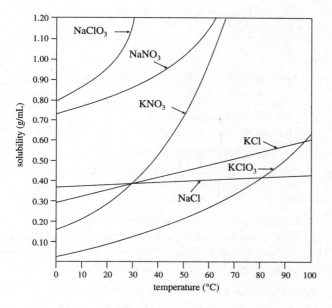

1. For the salts given, which of the following conclusions can be drawn concerning the relationship between solubility and temperature?

    (A) As the temperature increases, the solubility increases.

    (B) As the temperature increases, the solubility decreases.

    (C) As the temperature increases, the solubility remains the same.

    (D) Solubility and temperature are unrelated.

2. How does the solubility data for $NaCl$ and KCl differ from the data for the two other pairs of salts?

    (F) For the other two pairs, the K salt is always more soluble than the Na salt.

    (G) For the other two pairs, the Na salt is always more soluble than the K salt.

    (H) The Na salts are usually not soluble in water.

    (J) The K salts are usually not soluble in water.

3. A student wishes to make a 1-liter solution containing equal amounts of KNO_3 and $KClO_3$ in distilled water at 50°C and under normal atmospheric pressure. The limiting factor is:

    (A) the decomposition temperatures of the two salts.

    (B) the solubility of KNO_3.

    (C) the solubility of $NaClO_3$.

    (D) the solubility of $KClO_3$.

4. For which of the following salts would it be possible to dissolve more than 0.65 g/mL at 65°C?

    (F) Any of the Na salts

    (G) Any of the K salts

    (H) Either of the NO_3 salts

    (J) Either of the ClO_3 salts

5. Based on the data in the passage, which solute exhibits the greatest variation of solubility with temperatures between 0°C and 60°C?

    (A) $NaCl$

    (B) KCl

    (C) KNO_3

    (D) $KClO_3$

Passage 2

As part of an ecological impact study, factors affecting the rate of algae growth were investigated by measuring the relative amounts of algal blooms produced under various conditions.

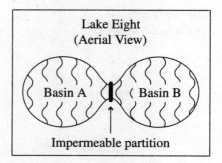

Experiment 1

The two basins of Lake Eight were separated by an impermeable partition. The experimenters varied the temperatures in different regions of each basin. Basin A was fertilized with phosphorus, carbon, and nitrogen, whereas basin B received only carbon and nitrogen. Two months after fertilization, the number of algal blooms per square meter of surface area of water was measured, yielding the data in Table 1.

Table 1

	Additives	Temperature (°C)	Algal blooms per square meter
Basin A	phosphorus, carbon, and nitrogen	10 25 35	0.18 0.48 0.56
Basin B	carbon and nitrogen	10 25 35	0.04 0.07 0.08

Experiment 2

In Experiment 2, sodium bicarbonate ($NaHCO_3$), which reacts with water to produce carbon dioxide (CO_2), replaced phosphorus, yielding the data in Table 2.

Table 2

	Additives	Temperature (°C)	Algal blooms per square meter
Basin A	$NaHCO_3$, Carbon, and nitrogen	10 25 35	0.26 0.56 0.78
Basin B	carbon and nitrogen	10 25 35	0.04 0.07 0.08

6. According to the experimental results, for any given temperature, which of the following combinations would most likely result in the greatest production of blooms?

    (F) Carbon, nitrogen, and sodium bicarbonate

    (G) Carbon, nitrogen, and phosphorus

    (H) Carbon and nitrogen

    (J) Carbon and hydrogen

7. According to the data, what effect does raising the temperature of the water have on the rate of algae production?

    (A) It always decreases the rate of production.

    (B) It always increases the rate of production.

    (C) It increases the rate of production for some additives and decreases the rate of production for other additives.

    (D) It has no effect on the rate of production.

8. If carbon, nitrogen, and sodium bicarbonate were added to a basin at 40°C, after 2 months the number of algal blooms in 1 square meter of surface area would most likely be approximately:

    (F) 0.25

    (G) 0.51

    (H) 0.91

    (J) 2.5

9. From the results of Experiment 2, it can be inferred that the carbon dioxide:

    (A) promotes algae growth.

    (B) inhibits algae growth.

    (C) does not affect algae growth.

    (D) promotes algae growth only at certain temperatures.

10. Extensive algal blooms cause pollution problems. Detergents are one of the major sources of phosphorus in fresh water. To reduce the pollution associated with algal blooms, it would be most useful to:

    (F) increase the amount of detergent present.

    (G) decrease the amount of detergent present.

    (H) replace the phosphorus in detergents with sodium bicarbonate.

    (J) balance the phosphorus added to detergents with equal amounts of sodium bicarbonate.

11. Which of the following was a controlled variable in Experiment 1?

    (A) The number of algal blooms produced per square meter

    (B) The rate of algae growth

    (C) The surface area of the basin

    (D) The temperature of the water

TABLE OF CONTENTS

Quarter 1	Session 1 Homework Review · Preview Quiz · Session Objectives
Quarter 2	Sentence Sense · Run-ons · Fragments · Parallelism · Modifiers · Punctuation · Commas · Semicolons & Colons · Dashes & Apostrophes · Quiz
Quarter 3	The Kaplan Method for Reading Comprehension · Detail Questions · Vocab-in-Context Questions · Generalization Questions · Quiz
Quarter 4	The ACT Writing Test: What to Expect · The Kaplan Method for Essay Writing · Quiz
	Homework

Quarter 1	Session 1 Homework Review
Quarter 1	Preview Quiz
Quarter 1	Session Objectives

Session 1 Homework Review

Math

18. For all $x > 0$, $\dfrac{1}{1 + \frac{1}{x}} = ?$

(F) $x + 1$

(G) $\dfrac{x}{x + 1}$

(H) $x + 2$

(J) $\dfrac{x}{x + 2}$

(K) $\dfrac{x}{2}$

5. Dr. Hasenpfeffer's physics midterm has 60 questions. He scores the test as follows: for each correct answer, he gives 2 points; for each incorrect answer, he subtracts $\frac{2}{3}$ of a point; for unanswered questions, he neither gives nor subtracts points. If Denise scored a 68 and did not answer two of the questions, how many questions did she answer correctly?

(A) 34

(B) 36

(C) 38

(D) 40

(E) 42

10. If $9^{2x-1} = 3^{3x+3}$, then $x = ?$

(F) -4

(G) $-\dfrac{7}{4}$

(H) $-\dfrac{10}{7}$

(J) 2

(K) 5

READING

Passage I

NATURAL SCIENCE: The following passage is excerpted from "Earth's Ozone Shield Under Threat," by France Bequette (© *Unesco Courier,* June 1992, Vol. 45, Issue 6, p. 26).

The ozone layer, the tenuous layer of gas that surrounds our planet between 12 and 45 kilometers above our surface, is being rapidly depleted.
Line Seasonally occurring holes have appeared in it over
(5) the poles, and, more recently, over the temperate

regions of the Northern Hemisphere. The threat is a serious one since the ozone layer traps almost all incoming ultraviolet radiation, which is harmful to all living organisms—humans, animals, and plants.
(10) Even though the ozone layer is 25 kilometers thick, the atmosphere in it is very tenuous, and the total amount of ozone, compared with other atmospheric gases, is quite small. If all of the ozone in a vertical column reaching up through the atmosphere
(15) were to be compressed to sea-level pressure, it would form a layer only a few millimeters thick.

Detailed study of the ozone layer began comparatively recently, the earliest observations being made in 1930 by the English scientist Sydney
(20) Chapman. These initial observations were taken up by the World Meteorological Organization (WMO), which established the Dobson network of one hundred observation stations. Since 1983, on the initiative of WMO and the United Nations Environment
(25) Programme (UNEP), seven of these stations have been entrusted with the task of making long-term forecasts of the likely evolution of our precious shield.

In 1958, the researchers who permanently monitor the ozone content of the layer above the South
(30) Pole began to observe several seasonal variations. From June, there was a slight reduction in ozone content that reached a minimum in October. In November, there was a sudden increase in the ozone content. The fluctuations appeared to result from the
(35) natural phenomena of wind effects and temperature change.

However, although the October minimum remained constant until 1979, the total ozone content over the pole was steadily diminishing until, in 1985,
(40) public opinion was finally roused by reports of a "hole" in the ozone layer and observations were intensified. The culprits responsible for the hole had already been identified as being supersonic aircraft, such as the Concorde (although these have now been
(45) exonerated), and the notorious compounds known as chlorofluorocarbons, or CFCs. Synthesized in 1928 by chemists working at General Motors in the United States, CFCs are compounds of atoms of carbon, chlorine, and fluorine. Having the advantage of being
(50) nonflammable, nontoxic, and noncorrosive, they came into widespread use in the 1950s. They are widely used in refrigerators, air conditioners, the "bubbles" in the foam plastic used, for example, in car seats, and as insulation in buildings.
(55) In 1989, they represented a market valued at over $1 billion and a labor force of 1.6 million. Of the twenty-five countries producing CFCs, the United States, France, the United Kingdom, Japan, and Germany accounted for three-quarters of the total
(60) world production of some 1.2 million tons.

These figures give some idea of the importance of the economic interests that are at stake in any decision to ban the industrial use of CFCs. But, with CFCs incriminated by scientists, the question arose as to
(65) whether we were prepared to take the risk of seeing an increase in the number of cases of skin cancer, eye ailments such as cataracts, or even a lowering of the human immune-defense system, all effects that would follow further depletion of the ozone layer.
(70)   The Montreal Protocol was the first world agreement aimed at halting the production of CFCs. As more evidence emerged concerning the seriousness of the threat, it became apparent that the protocol was not stringent enough and, year by year,
(75) its severity was increased until, in 1990 in London, seventy countries agreed to stop all production of CFCs by the year 2000.
        Unfortunately, even if the entire world were to agree today to halt all production and use of CFCs,
(80) this would not provide an immediate solution to the problem. A single molecule of chlorine can destroy from 10,000 to 100,000 molecules of ozone. Furthermore, CFCs have a lifespan of between 75 and
Line 400 years, and they take ten years to reach the ozone
(85) layer. In other words, what we are experiencing now results from CFCs emitted 10 years ago.
        Industrialists are now urgently searching for substitute products. Some, such as propane, are too dangerous because they are flammable; others, the
(90) HCFCs, might prove to be toxic and to contribute to the greenhouse effect, i.e., to the process of global warming. Nevertheless, nobody can say that the situation will not right itself, whether in the short term or long term, if we ourselves lend a hand.

1. As it is used in the passage, the term *right* (line 93) most likely means:

    (A) affirm
    (B) fix
    (C) stand up
    (D) topple

3. According to the passage, all of the following contribute to changes in the ozone layer EXCEPT:

    (A) supersonic aircraft
    (B) chlorofluorocarbons
    (C) temperature changes
    (D) wind effects

5. Based on information in the passage, which of the following would most likely result if all production of CFCs were to end today?

    (A) Scientists would have to replace the quantities of ozone already lost.
    (B) The ozone layer would only return to normal levels after 75 years.
    (C) Scientists would also have to destroy all chlorine molecules in the atmosphere.
    (D) The benefits would not be experienced for another 10 years.

10. The main conclusion reached in the passage about the threat to the ozone layer is that:

    (F) the cost of banning CFCs altogether may make it an impractical answer.
    (G) finding alternative products to CFCs may provide a long-term remedy to the situation.
    (H) halting production of CFCs is unlikely to produce a solution to the problem.
    (J) agreements between CFC-producing countries need to be more strictly enforced.

SCIENCE

Passage II

The extent to which a solute will dissolve in a given solvent is dependent on several factors, including conditions of temperature and pressure and the electrochemical natures of the solute and solvent. A high school chemistry teacher assigned 24 students the project of measuring the solubilities in distilled water of several pairs of common sodium (Na) and potassium (K) salts at various temperatures. The pairs were NaCl and KCl, $NaNO_3$ and KNO_3, and $NaClO_3$ and $KClO_3$. All measurements were conducted under normal atmospheric pressure. After pooling and averaging all the data, the students plotted solubility curves to produce the graph below.

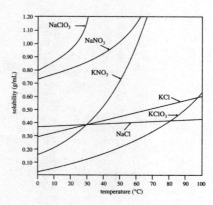

1. For the salts given, which of the following conclusions can be drawn concerning the relationship between solubility and temperature?

   (A) As the temperature increases, the solubility increases.

   (B) As the temperature increases, the solubility decreases.

   (C) As the temperature increases, the solubility remains the same.

   (D) Solubility and temperature are unrelated.

3. A student wishes to make a 1-liter solution containing equal amounts of KNO_3 and $KClO_3$ in distilled water at 50°C and under normal atmospheric pressure. The limiting factor is:

   (A) the decomposition temperatures of the two salts.

   (B) the solubility of KNO_3.

   (C) the solubility of $NaClO_3$.

   (D) the solubility of $KClO_3$.

4. For which of the following salts would it be possible to dissolve more than 0.65 g/mL at 65°C?

   (F) Any of the Na salts

   (G) Any of the K salts

   (H) Either of the NO_3 salts

   (J) Either of the ClO_3 salts

Preview Quiz

Passage I

WHY LIONS ROAR

Research by biologists and environmental scientists has found several reasons that lions roar. Lions, which live in groups called prides, are very social creatures that communicate with one another in many ways. <u>Roaring</u>, the
1
sound most often associated with lions, <u>perform</u> several key
2
functions within the pride.

<u>One of these defense</u> involves protecting the pride's
3
land. When prides take large pieces of land and claim them as their own, they will roar to keep away intruders, <u>those are usually</u> other lions. This "No Trespassing"
4
warning serves to keep the peace because it helps prevent competing prides from fighting over food or for mates.

<u>Frequently, everyday</u> activities like hunting call upon
5
animals' sharp instincts; in order to reunite, the pride members roar to find one another.

1. (A) NO CHANGE
   (B) Roaring
   (C) Roaring:
   (D) Roaring is

2. (F) NO CHANGE
   (G) perform,
   (H) performs,
   (J) performs

3. (A) NO CHANGE
   (B) One of these, defense,
   (C) One of these being defense,
   (D) One of these is defense and it

4. (F) NO CHANGE
   (G) most often these are
   (H) and are typically
   (J) usually

5. (A) NO CHANGE
   (B) Quite regularly, everyday
   (C) Many times, everyday
   (D) Everyday

Passage II

Astronomers noted more than 150 years ago that sunspots wax and wane in number in an 11-year cycle. Ever since, people have speculated that the solar cycle
Line might exert some influence on Earth's weather. In this
(5) century, for example, scientists have linked the solar cycle to droughts in the American Midwest. Until recently, however, none of these correlations has held up under close scrutiny.

One problem is that sunspots themselves are
(10) so poorly understood. Observations have revealed that the swirly smudges represent areas of intense magnetic activity where the sun's radiant energy has been blocked. They are also considerably cooler than bright regions of the sun. Scientists have not been
(15) able, however, to determine just how sunspots are created or what effect they have on the solar constant (a misnomer that refers to the sun's total radiance at any instant).

The latter question, at least for now, seems to
(20) have been resolved by data from the *Solar Maximum Mission* satellite, which has monitored the solar constant since 1980, the peak of the last solar cycle. As the number of sunspots decreased through 1986, the satellite recorded a gradual dimming of the sun.
(25) Over the past year, as sunspots have proliferated, the sun has brightened. The data suggest that the sun is 0.1 percent more luminous at the peak of the solar cycle, when the number of sunspots is greatest, than at its nadir, according to Richard C. Willson of the
(30) Jet Propulsion Laboratory and Hugh S. Hudson of the University of California at San Diego.

The data show that sunspots do not themselves make the sun shine brighter. Instead, when a sunspot appears, it initially causes the sun to dim slightly,
(35) but then after a period of weeks or months, islands of brilliance called faculas usually emerge near the sunspot and more than compensate for its dimming effect. Willson says faculas may represent regions where energy that initially was blocked beneath a
(40) sunspot has finally breached the surface.

Does the subtle fluctuation in the solar constant manifest itself in Earth's weather? Some recent reports offer statistical evidence that it does, albeit indirectly. The link seems to be mediated by a phenomenon
(45) known as the quasi-biennial oscillation (QBO), a 180-degree shift in the direction of stratospheric winds above the Tropics that occurs about every two years.

Karin Labitzke of the Free University of Berlin and Harry van Loon of the National Center for
(50) Atmospheric Research in Boulder, Colorado, were the first to uncover the QBO link. They gathered temperature and air-pressure readings from various latitudes and altitudes over the past three solar cycles. They found no correlation between the solar cycle
(55) and their data until they sorted the data into two categories: those gathered during the QBO's west phase (when the stratospheric winds blow west) and those gathered during its east phase. A remarkable correlation appeared: Temperatures and pressures
(60) coinciding with the QBO's west phase rose and fell in accordance with the solar cycle.

Building on this finding, Brian A. Tinsley of the National Science Foundation discovered a statistical correlation between the solar cycle and the position
(65) of storms in the North Atlantic. The latitude of storms during the west phase of the QBO, Tinsley found, varied with the solar cycle: Storms occurring toward the peak of a solar cycle traveled at latitudes about six degrees nearer the Equator than storms
(70) during the cycle's nadir.

Labitzke, van Loon, and Tinsley acknowledge that their findings are still rather mysterious. Why does the solar cycle seem to exert more of an influence during the west phase of the QBO than
(75) it does during the east phase? How does the 0.1 percent variance in solar radiation trigger the much larger changes—up to six degrees Celsius in polar regions—observed by Labitzke and van Loon? Van Loon says simply, "We can't explain it."
(80) Nonetheless, John A. Eddy of the National Center for Atmospheric Research thinks these QBO findings as well as the Solar Maximum Mission data "look like breakthroughs" in the search for a link between the solar cycle and weather. With further research
(85) into how the oceans dampen the effects of solar flux, these findings may lead to models that have some predictive value. The next few years may be particularly rich in solar flux.

6. According to the passage, the main source of information about the effect of sunspots on the solar constant is provided by:

(F) studies of droughts in the Midwest.

(G) data from the Solar Maximum Mission satellite.

(H) temperature and air pressure readings taken in Colorado.

(J) discussions among various eminent astronomers.

7. The main purpose of this passage is to:

(A) explain why scientists have failed to find any direct correlation between sunspots and the solar constant.

(B) describe a possible correlation between the solar cycle and Earth's weather.

(C) describe the solar cycle and its relation to the solar constant.

(D) prove conclusively that sunspots dramatically influence Earth's weather.

Passage III: Writing

Read the following and pick a side: yes or no. Ask yourself, "Why do I think that?" Note your reasons below.

A growing number of high schools have stopped publishing an honor roll at the end of each marking period. They are concerned that the existence of an honor roll increases pressure on students. Some schools have even ceased awarding such honors as valedictorian and salutatorian, claiming that these distinctions foster too much competition. Your school is considering doing away with both the honor roll and the valedictorian and salutatorian honors. Some students support this idea, saying that rewarding academic excellence damages the self-esteem of those students who do not make honors. Others feel it's unfair because they work hard for their grades. These students believe that the public recognition is good preparation for competition in the real world.

Reason 1

_____

_____

Reason 2

_____

_____

Reason 3

_____

_____

Session Objectives

QUARTER 2—8 SMARTPOINTS

- Learn the Kaplan Method for ACT English—Point Builder.

SENTENCE SENSE—3 SMARTPOINTS

- Identify and correct run-on sentences.
- Identify and correct sentence fragments.
- Identify and correct parallelism errors.
- Identify and correct modifier errors.

PUNCTUATION—5 SMARTPOINTS

- Commas
- Semicolons & colons
- Dashes & apostrophes

QUARTER 3—21 SMARTPOINTS

- The Kaplan Method for Reading Comprehension—Point Builder
- Answer Detail questions—12 points.
- Answer Vocab-in-Context questions—1 point.
- Answer Generalization questions by predicting an answer that aligns with the purpose of the passage—8 points.

QUARTER 4—POINT BUILDER

- The ACT Writing Test: What to Expect—Point Builder
- The Kaplan Method for Essay Writing—Point Builder

3 SmartPoints	Sentence Sense: Run-ons · Fragments · Parallelism · and Modifiers
5 SmartPoints	Punctuation: Commas · Semicolons · Colons · Dashes · and Apostrophes

The Kaplan Method for English

1. Read until you have enough information to identify the issue.

2. Eliminate answer choices that don't address the issue.

3. Plug in the remaining answer choices and choose the one that is the most correct, concise, and relevant.

Sentence Sense: 3 SmartPoints

Run-ons

A. A complete sentence = _____

_____

B. An **independent clause** expresses a complete thought and can stand alone as a sentence.

Emily purchased her shoes online.

Dependent clauses cannot stand alone as sentences.

While Emily purchased her shoes online.

C. If a sentence has more than one independent clause, the clauses must be properly combined. Otherwise, the sentence is a run-on.

There are three ways to correct a run-on like this:

I know English now, I didn't know it before I came to America.

1. Use a semicolon *without* a FANBOYS word.

I know English now; I didn't know it before I came to America.

2. Use a relationship word to make one clause dependent.

Although I know English now, I didn't know it before I came to America.

3. Use a comma and a FANBOYS conjunction.

I know English now, but I didn't know it before I came to America.

D. The FANBOYS conjunctions are:

F _____

A _____

N _____

B _____

O _____

Y _____

S _____

Fragments

A.   A **fragment** is a group of words that is missing one of the elements needed for a sentence.

A group of words that does contain a subject and predicate verb but still does not express a complete thought is a special type of fragment called a _____.

Parallelism

A.   Items in a series, list, or compound must be parallel in form.

Over the summer, I plan to *work, read*, and *swim*.

Series and lists may consist of *nouns, adjectives, adverbs,* or *verb forms*.

Check for parallelism if the sentence contains...	Examples of parallel forms	Parallel elements in example
a list	Before you leave, you should **charge** your phone, **clean** your room, and **find** your keys.	3 verb phrases
a compound (words joined by *and* or *or*)	I don't like **swimming** or **hiking**.	2 *–ing* gerunds
an idiomatic phrase like *both ... and* and *not only ... but also*	It's necessary not only **to prepare thoroughly** but also **to listen carefully**.	2 verb phrases that start with to
a comparison	Your **homework** is just as important as your **participation** in class.	2 nouns
related nouns	**Students** who complete all of their homework **assignments** will be rewarded with higher **grades**.	3 plural nouns that are related in the sentence

Modifiers

A. A **modifier** is a word or group of words that describes, clarifies, or provides more information about another part of the sentence.

B. **Adjectives** are single-word modifiers that describe nouns and pronouns.

Amanda bought the fuchsia love seat from a garage sale.

C. **Adverbs** are single-word modifiers that describe verbs, adjectives, or other adverbs.

Ian conducted his lab experiment efficiently.

D. A **modifying phrase** must be properly placed for what it is intended to modify. In many cases, an introductory phrase or clause will modify the first noun that follows.

Rushing to the scene, emergency responders quickly sealed off the crime scene and stabilized victims.

E. Tips for spotting modifying phrases on the ACT:

1. When modifying phrases are tested, the modifying phrase often appears at the beginning of a sentence.

2. Modifying phrases often start with or include words that end in *–ing* or *–ed*, such as *attempting* or *emboldened*.

3. A comma appears between an introductory modifying phrase and the rest of the sentence.

Espresso 89

For years, friends in my neighborhood complained in the area about the lack of a good coffee shop. The discussions at times became passionate, and it seemed that my neighbors believed that a coffee shop would cure just about any problem our suburban neighborhood faced. Not a coffee drinker, my friends who thought that a place to buy coffee would make such a difference were hard for me to understand. Then, a coffee shop called Espresso 89 finally opened in the neighborhood. Six months after opening, I understand what all of the fuss was about.

1. Which of the following is the best placement for the underlined phrase?

   (A) Where it is now
   (B) After the word "friends"
   (C) After the word "neighborhood"
   (D) After the word "shop" (ending the sentence with a period)

2. Which of the following replacements for the underlined segment of the sentence would NOT be acceptable?

   (F) passionate it
   (G) passionate; it
   (H) passionate. It
   (J) passionate—it

3. (A) NO CHANGE
   (B) my friends thinking a place to buy coffee would make such a difference was hard for me to understand.
   (C) having a hard time understanding why my friends thought a place to buy coffee would make such a difference
   (D) I had a hard time understanding why my friends thought a place to buy coffee would make such a difference

4. (F) NO CHANGE
   (G) It opened six months ago,
   (H) Six months after it opened,
   (J) Opening six months ago,

It's not as though I've suddenly converted to a daily diet of lattes and cappuccinos. (However, I have gotten in the habit of buying chai, a delicious spiced tea.) Instead, I have discovered that a coffee shop can be about more than coffee. Ingrid and Gus, the owners of Espresso 89 running their shop as something of a community center for the area.

They began by inviting a local artist to display her paintings on the walls of the shop and holding a "gallery" opening for the occasion. They encouraged other local artists to sign up for future opportunities to share their work with the coffee-drinking public. Two or three nights a week, Espresso 89 hosts music or literary events that provide entertainment and the opportunity for local artists to share their craft. Another public performance is the weekly children's story hour, it is when one corner of the shop is filled with parents and their toddlers listening to storybook after storybook read by a retired elementary school teacher.

The owners of the shop have also made Espresso 89 available to different groups for small meetings. Local book clubs, knitting clubs, and even American Sign Language clubs meet there on a regular basis. Every so often, local politicians at the shop hold events, sharing information with or explaining government services to constituents.

5. (A) NO CHANGE
    (B) Espresso 89. Run
    (C) Espresso 89, run
    (D) Espresso 89, running

6. (F) NO CHANGE
    (G) To create evenings that provide entertainment and the opportunity to host music or literary events, local artists share their craft with Espresso 89 two or three nights a week.
    (H) To provide entertainment and the opportunity to share their craft, two or three nights a week local artists at Espresso 89 host created evenings.
    (J) Sharing their craft, evenings hosted by Espresso 89 provide entertainment and an opportunity for local artists two or three nights a week.

7. (A) NO CHANGE
    (B) this is when one
    (C) when one
    (D) one

8. Which of the following would be the best placement for the underlined segment of the sentence?

    (F) Where it is now.
    (G) after the word "events."
    (H) after the word "information."
    (J) after the word "government."

Punctuation: 5 SmartPoints

Punctuation questions will deal with:

1. _____

2. _____

3. _____

4. _____

5. _____

Commas

A. Use commas to set off three or more items in a series or list.

Duke Ellington made a name for himself as a leader, an arranger, and a pianist.

B. Use a comma to separate independent clauses connected by a FANBOYS conjunction.

Chocolate ants have yet to catch on in this country, but Americans do enjoy their chocolate.

C. Use a comma to separate an introductory phrase from the rest of the sentence.

In the late 1960s, NASA began to study the feasibility of developing a reusable space transportation system.

D. Use commas to separate nonessential information from the rest of the sentence.

On January 24th, 1848, while inspecting the mill's runoff into the river, Marshall saw two shiny objects below the surface of the water.

Semicolons & Colons

A.   Use semicolons to _____

Word of the discovery got out; workers began quitting their jobs and heading into the hills to look for the source of the gold that had washed down the river.

B.   Use semicolons to _____

Mary bought apples, eggs, and oranges; Donna bought cereal, juice, and milk; and Alex bought cinnamon rolls, muffins, and bacon.

C.   Use colons to _____

_____

Ellington recorded several of his best-known hits during this period: "Black and Tan Fantasy," "Hot and Bothered," and "Rockin' in Rhythm."

When a colon is underlined, examine its usage carefully; this is the only colon usage rule that is tested on the ACT.

Fly Fishing

One thing that keeps many beginners from joining in the fun of fly rod fishing isn't a lack of <u>interest; it</u> is the
9
confusion of trying to assemble that first outfit, or collection of gear. It seems that there are countless choices out there, and it is only when one begins to acquire the basic <u>information;</u> that the confusion dissipates.
10
First of all, any new rod will almost certainly be made of graphite. If one did want a rod made of split <u>bamboo: the</u>
11
favorite of most advanced fly fishers, one certainly could find it; a little shopping around can unearth bamboo rods that are not much more expensive than some of the better graphite ones. On the other hand, basic outfits in graphite start retailing for around a hundred dollars, and these will have almost everything the beginner needs, lacking only leaders and flies.

Any newcomer to the sport should try to get some basic casting instruction before buying a rod. Basic fly casting can be self-taught in a couple of hours, but working with an instructor might reduce this to less than an hour. Beginners will have more success with a rod that is at least eight feet long. Shorter rods might cost a few dollars less, but the rationale behind this choice concerns <u>ease of use and longer</u>
12
rods handle line better, deal with wind better, and, in a boat, help keep one's line above a partner's head. All else being equal, longer rods are generally easier to use.

9. Which of the following alternatives to the underlined portion would NOT be acceptable?
   - (A) interest; rather, it
   - (B) interest—it
   - (C) interest it
   - (D) interest. It

10. (F) NO CHANGE
    (G) information,
    (H) information—
    (J) information

11. (A) NO CHANGE
    (B) bamboo;
    (C) bamboo—
    (D) bamboo,

12. (F) NO CHANGE
    (G) ease of use, which longer
    (H) ease of use: longer
    (J) ease of use, longer

Dashes & Apostrophes

A. Use a dash to _____

He left for Baltimore with—No wait. He left for Washington.

B. Use a dash or dashes to _____

_____.

Rockwell's Space Transportations Division handled all facets—design, development, and testing—of the reusable orbiter.

C. Use an apostrophe to _____.

Paris is the world's most romantic city.

D. Use an apostrophe to _____

_____.

They've built the largest sandcastle on record.

E. To check whether *it's* is appropriate, replace it in the sentence with *it is* or *it has*. If the sentence doesn't make sense with *it is* or *it has*, *it's* is incorrect.

The tree frog, for example, blends perfectly into its surroundings. When it holds still, it's nearly invisible.

Music in the Park

Some people think of classical music as too boring, too academic, or simply too long to enjoy. They feel like music without lyrics is lacking in emotion or is just too difficult to focus on. For many years, I was among those who thought that classical music wasn't for them. But when a friend took me to see the New York Philharmonic in Central Park—a free performance usually scheduled twice each <u>summer</u>, my
13
whole perception of orchestras and classical music changed.

I knew that there would be a large audience for the performance, but I didn't think the atmosphere would be festive. In contrast to my expectations, the audience wasn't made up of retirees and studious <u>types; there</u> were young
14
people on dates, families with small children, and groups of friends enjoying a summer picnic. Thousands of people had spread out blankets to enjoy the music. As the sky turned pink and purple with the setting sun, the <u>musicians'</u> tuned
15
their instruments in preparation for the show.

By the end of the first piece, *Mendelssohn's Symphony No. 4 in A Major*, I was hooked. The <u>sounds' of the orchestra's</u> many instruments captured
16
the attention of everyone in the park, including me. The second piece was Tchaikovsky's *1812 Overture*, and the members of the audience hushed their already whispered conversations to hear the song's dynamics among the brass, strings, woodwinds, and percussion. <u>Its'</u> emotional
17
ending, punctuated with booming cannons and church bells, made me realize that classical music didn't have to be boring at all.

13. (A) NO CHANGE
    (B) summer
    (C) summer—
    (D) summer;

14. Of the following options to replace the underlined portion, which would NOT be acceptable?
    (F) types—there
    (G) types there
    (H) types. There
    (J) types; instead, there

15. (A) NO CHANGE
    (B) musicians
    (C) musician's
    (D) musicians,

16. (F) NO CHANGE
    (G) sounds of the orchestras
    (H) sound's of the orchestra's
    (J) sounds of the orchestra's

17. (A) NO CHANGE
    (B) It's
    (C) Its
    (D) Their

Quiz

Passage I

The History of Telecommunications

The history of telecommunications over the past two
<u>   </u>
1
centuries is known by few of the people who use cellular
<u>   </u>

phones today. Until the early nineteenth century, the fastest

way to send a message was by horseback rider. That

changed dramatically <u>in 1844, Samuel Morse presented</u>

<u>his electric telegraph system at that time.</u> He successfully
2
sent a message from Washington, D.C. to Baltimore.

<u>Another invention of Samuel Morse was the Morse Code.</u>
3
Soon, America was linked coast-to-coast by telegraph wires.

Three decades later, Alexander Graham Bell invented the

telephone. The modern era of telecommunications

<u>having begun.</u>
4
While the cellular phone may be new, wireless

communication <u>almost dates back a hundred years.</u> By
5
the late 1800s, inventor Guglielmo Marconi was already

experimenting with radio <u>waves, he</u> developed a tower that
6
could transmit a radio signal over several miles.

1. (A) NO CHANGE
   (B) The history of telecommunications over the past two centuries, known by few of the people who use cellular phones today.
   (C) Few of the people who use cellular phones today know the history of telecommunications over the past two centuries.
   (D) The past two centuries of the history of telecommunications are known by few of the people who use cellular phones today.

2. (F) NO CHANGE
   (G) in 1844, when Samuel Morse presented his electric telegraph system.
   (H) in 1844. When Samuel Morse presented his electric telegraph system.
   (J) in 1844; when Samuel Morse presented his electric telegraph system.

3. (A) NO CHANGE
   (B) Samuel Morse also invented the Morse Code.
   (C) The Morse Code was another invention by Samuel Morse.
   (D) OMIT the underlined portion.

4. (F) NO CHANGE
   (G) beginning.
   (H) had begun.
   (J) will begin.

5. (A) NO CHANGE
   (B) dates back a hundred (almost) years.
   (C) dates back a hundred years almost.
   (D) dates back almost a hundred years.

6. (F) NO CHANGE
   (G) waves, but he
   (H) waves he
   (J) waves. He

Passage II

The Fires at Yellowstone

<u>During the summer of 1988 I</u> watched Yellowstone
7
National Park go up in flames. In June, fires ignited by

lightning had been allowed to burn unsuppressed because

park officials expected that the usual summer rains

would douse the flames. However, the rains never came.

A plentiful fuel supply of fallen logs and pine needles

was <u>available, and winds</u> of up to 100 mph whipped
8

the spreading fires along and carried red-hot embers to other areas, creating new fires. By the time park officials succumbed to the pressure of public opinion and decided to try to extinguish the flames; it was too late. The situation
9
remained out of control in spite of the efforts of 9,000 fire fighters who were using state-of-the-art equipment. By September, a large segment of Yellowstone—more than
10
720,000 acres—had been affected by fire. Nature was only
10
able to curb the destruction; the smoke did not begin to clear until the first snow arrived on September 11.

As an ecologist whose studied forests for 20 years,
11
I knew that this was not nearly the tragedy it seemed to be. Large fires are, after all, necessary in order that the
12
continued health of the forest ecosystem be maintained. Fires thin out overcrowded areas and allow the sun to reach species of plants stunted by shade. Ash fertilizes the soil, and fire smoke kills forest bacteria. In the case of the lodgepole pine, fire is essential to reproduction, the
13
pines' cones only open when exposed to temperatures
14
greater than 112 degrees.

The fires in Yellowstone did result in some loss of
15
wildlife, but overall, the region's animals proved to be
15
fire-tolerant and fire-adaptive. Large animals such as bison were often seen grazing and bedding down in meadows near burning forests. Also, the fire posed little threat to the members of any endangered animal species in the park.

My confidence in the natural resilience of the forest has been borne out in the years since the fires ravaged Yellowstone. Judging from recent pictures of the park, the forest was not destroyed; it was rejuvenated.
16

7. (A) NO CHANGE
   (B) During the summer of 1988, I
   (C) During the summer of 1988; I
   (D) During the summer of 1988: I

8. (F) NO CHANGE
   (G) available and winds
   (H) available. And winds
   (J) available—and winds

9. (A) NO CHANGE
   (B) extinguish the flames. It was too late.
   (C) extinguish the flames, it was too late.
   (D) extinguish the flames it was too late.

10. (F) NO CHANGE
    (G) Yellowstone: more than 720,000 acres had been affected
    (H) Yellowstone, more than 720,000 acres had been affected
    (J) Yellowstone. More than 720,000 acres had been affected

11. (A) NO CHANGE
    (B) who's studied
    (C) whos' studied
    (D) whose's studied

12. (F) NO CHANGE
    (G) Large fires are, after all necessary
    (H) Large fires are after all, necessary
    (J) Large fires are after all necessary

13. (A) NO CHANGE
    (B) reproduction the
    (C) reproduction—the
    (D) reproduction; the

14. (F) NO CHANGE
    (G) pine's cones
    (H) pines's cones
    (J) pines cone's

15. (A) NO CHANGE
    (B) some loss of wildlife but
    (C) some loss of wildlife; but
    (D) some loss of wildlife. But

16. (F) NO CHANGE
    (G) was not destroyed, it was
    (H) was not destroyed it was
    (J) was not destroyed: it was

Point Builder	The Kaplan Method for Reading Comprehension
12 SmartPoints	Detail Questions
1 SmartPoint	Vocab-in-Context Questions
8 SmartPoints	Generalization Questions
	Quiz

The Kaplan Method for Reading Comprehension

1. _____
   - _____
   - _____

2. _____
   - _____

3. _____
   - _____

Detail Questions: 12 SmartPoints

A. Detail questions ask about _____
_____
_____

B. You can spot them because they _____
_____
_____

C. To answer them effectively, you must _____
_____
_____

Passage I

Natural Science: This passage is adapted from "The Quasar 3C 273," by Thierry Courvoisier and E. Ian Robinson. It originally appeared in *Scientific American*, June 1991, Volume 264. Reprinted with permission. (© 1991 by Scientific American, Inc.)

The quasar 3C 273 lies about one-fifth of the way from Earth to the edge of the known universe. Of all the objects in the cosmos, only a few other quasars
Line surpass the energy and activity of 3C 273. On an
(5) average day, it is more luminous than 1,000 galaxies, each containing 100 billion stars. During one remarkable day in February 1988, the quasar erupted with a burst of radiation equivalent to lighting up stars the size of our sun at the rate of 10 million per second.

(10) By monitoring 3C 273 in all domains of the electromagnetic spectrum and by observing variations in its luminosity, astronomers have begun to understand quasars and the physical processes that power them.

(15) Since quasars were first identified some 28 years ago, astronomers have come to realize that quasars are the cores of extremely active galaxies. Quasars are unmatched in luminosity and hence are the most distant objects that can be detected in the universe.

(20) One of the most important discoveries about quasars is that their luminosity can vary greatly over periods of less than a year. This variability led investigators to the conclusion that the tremendous energy of quasars is radiated from a region many times smaller than the
(25) cores of ordinary galaxies.

Quasars are powered by the gravitational energy that is released as gas and dust fall toward the quasars' massive, dense centers. Some of this energy channels particles into beams, blasting material out into the
(30) host galaxy at speeds close to that of light. Most of the energy is converted into radiation by a wide range of physical processes, probably occurring at different distances from the core. Yet quasars exhibit many phenomena that cannot be explained, and they remain
(35) among the most enigmatic objects in the universe.

On the whole, we know more about 3C 273 than any other quasar. It possesses a very wide range of properties, not all of which are shared by all quasars. The wealth of activity displayed by 3C 273, however,
(40) is a key to helping astronomers understand the phenomena at work in quasars.

The task of observing 3C 273 is as challenging as it is rewarding. After traveling through space for more than a billion years, only a tiny fraction of
(45) the radiation from 3C 273 reaches Earth. Capturing this radiation requires frequent observations using a battery of ground-based telescopes and satellite-borne instruments.

The effort began more than a century ago. The
(50) object known today as 3C 273 was first recorded on photographic plates as astronomers surveyed the stars in the constellation Virgo. It looked like nothing more than an ordinary, moderately bright star. Then in 1962, Cyril Hazard and his colleagues at Sydney
(55) University discovered that the starlike object occupied the same position in the sky as a strong source of radio waves. The radio emitter had been previously identified as 3C 273, which stood for number 273 in the Third Cambridge Catalogue of Radio Sources.
(60) Objects such as 3C 273 were subsequently described as quasi-stellar radio sources, or quasars.

In 1963, Maarten Schmidt of the Mount Wilson and Palomar Observatories deduced that the quasar 3C 273 was about three billion light-years away from
(65) Earth. The implications of this discovery were extraordinary. The quasar was by far the most luminous and distant object ever observed. Soon a few other quasars were identified that seemed to be even farther away and brighter than 3C 273. At the
(70) time, many of Schmidt's colleagues had good reason to question these results. Yet as modern astronomers review the evidence collected during the past 28 years, we find little room to doubt that Schmidt was right.

Where in the passage does the author mention what 3C 273 stands for?

_____

What part of the passage discusses Maarten Schmidt's discovery?

_____

)) REMEMBER
With Detail questions, you will
be able to put your finger on
specific parts of the passage that
lead to the correct choice.

1. According to the passage, what characteristic of quasars makes them the most distant objects that can be detected in the universe?

   (A) Their density
   (B) Their size
   (C) Their luminosity
   (D) Their puzzling behavior

)) REMEMBER
Detail questions usually contain
tempting wrong answer choices
that distort or misuse details
from the passage.

2. According to the passage, astronomers study quasars and the physical processes that power them by:

   (F) observing 3C 273 through ground-based telescopes.
   (G) monitoring the electromagnetic spectrum of 3C 273.
   (H) enlarging satellite photographs of distant galaxies.
   (J) investigating phenomena that cannot be easily explained.

)) REMEMBER
Pay close attention to words
that are all in caps in the
question stem.

3. In the passage, which of the following is NOT a fact provided about the quasar 3C 273?

   (A) All quasars have the same properties as 3C 273.
   (B) Its luminosity can vary, with some extreme peaks of radiation production.
   (C) It is typically more luminous than a thousand galaxies.
   (D) It is located more than a billion light-years away from Earth.

Vocab-in-Context Questions: 1 SmartPoint

A. Vocab-in-Context questions ask you to _____

_____

_____

B. You can spot them because they _____

_____

_____

C. The words they ask about are _____

_____

_____

_____

D. To answer them effectively, you must _____

_____

_____

As it is used in line 39, the word "wealth" most nearly means: _____

---

4. As it is used in line 10, the word "domains" most nearly means:

   (F) homes.
   (G) specialties.
   (H) territories.
   (J) areas.

>> **REMEMBER**
The most common meaning of a word will often be listed and will usually be wrong.

---

5. When the author writes, "we find little room to doubt that Schmidt was right" (lines 72–73), he most likely means that:

   (A) one should not believe Schmidt's findings.
   (B) everyone in the field agrees with Schmidt's findings.
   (C) the bulk of available scientific evidence supports Schmidt's findings.
   (D) efforts to confirm Schmidt's findings should be expanded.

>> **REMEMBER**
Sometimes a question will ask you to give the meaning of a phrase or to identify a clearer restatement of it.

Generalization Questions: 8 SmartPoints

A.   Generalization questions ask about _____

_____

_____

B.   You can spot them because they _____

_____

_____

_____

C.   To answer them effectively, you must _____

_____

_____

What is the main idea of the passage? _____

_____

)) REMEMBER
Primary-purpose questions accompany almost every ACT passage.

6.   The primary purpose of the passage is to:

(F)   compare and contrast the luminosity of several celestial bodies.

(G)   offer technical analysis of all quasars.

(H)   discuss the characteristics and discovery of a phenomenon.

(J)   chronicle the history of quasars and their effect on the Earth.

Quiz

Passage II

Social Science: The following passage is excerpted from *The Heart of Man* by Erich Fromm (© 1964 by Erich Fromm. Reprinted with permission of HarperCollins Publishers). The passage describes two types of violence and possible causes of those types of violence.

The distinction between various types of violence is based on the distinction between their respective unconscious motivations. Only the understanding of
Line the unconscious dynamics of behavior permits us to
(5) understand the behavior itself, its roots, its course, and the energy with which it is charged.

The most normal and non-pathological form of violence is playful violence. We find it in those forms in which violence is exercised in the pursuit of
(10) displaying skill, not in the pursuit of destruction, not motivated by hate or destructiveness. Examples of this playful violence can be found in many instances, from the war games of primitive tribes to the Zen Buddhist art of sword fighting. In all such games of fighting,
(15) it is not the aim to kill; even if the outcome is the death of the opponent it is, as it were, the opponent's fault for having "stood in the wrong spot." Naturally, if we speak of the wish to destroy in playful violence, this refers to only the ideal type of such games. In
(20) reality, one would often find unconscious aggression and destructiveness hidden behind the explicit logic of the game. But even this being so, the main motivation in this type of violence is the display of skill, not destructiveness.

(25) Of much greater practical significance than playful violence is reactive violence. By reactive violence, I understand that violence that is employed in the defense of life, freedom, dignity, property— one's own or that of others. It is rooted in fear, and
(30) for this very reason it is probably the most frequent form of violence: The fear can be real or imagined, conscious or unconscious. This type of violence is in the service of life, not of death; its aim is preservation, not destruction. It is not entirely the
(35) outcome of irrational passions, but, to some extent, of rational calculation; hence it also implies a certain proportionality between end and means. It has been argued that from a higher spiritual plane, killing— even in defense—is never morally right. But most of
(40) those who hold this conviction admit that violence in the defense of life is of a different nature than violence which aims at destructiveness for its own sake.

Very often, the feeling of being threatened and the resulting reactive violence are not based on reality,
(45) but on the manipulation of man's mind; political and religious leaders persuade their adherents that they are threatened by an enemy, and thus arouse the subjective response of reactive hostility. Hence, the distinction between just and unjust wars is a most questionable
(50) one, since usually each side succeeds in presenting its position as a defense against an attack. There is hardly a case of an aggressive war that could not be couched in terms of defense. The question of who claimed defense rightly is usually decided by the victors,
(55) and sometimes only much later by more objective historians. The tendency of pretending that any war is a defensive one shows two things. First of all is that the majority of people, at least in most civilized countries, cannot be made to kill and to die unless they
(60) are first convinced that they are doing so in order to defend their lives and freedom; second, it shows that it is not difficult to persuade millions of people that they are in danger of being attacked, and hence, that they are called upon to defend themselves. Such persuasion
(65) depends most of all on a lack of independent thinking and feeling, and on the emotional dependence of the vast majority of people on their political leaders. Provided there is this dependence, almost anything presented with force and persuasion will be accepted
(70) as real. The psychological results of the acceptance of a belief in an alleged threat are, of course, the same as those of a real threat. People feel threatened and, in order to defend themselves, are willing to kill and to destroy. In the case of paranoid delusions of
(75) persecution, we find the same mechanism, only not on a group basis, but on an individual one. In both instances, subjectively, the person feels in danger and reacts aggressively.

Another aspect of reactive violence is the kind
(80) of violence that is produced by frustration. We find aggressive behavior in animals, children, and adults when a wish or a need is frustrated. Such aggressive behavior constitutes an attempt, although often a futile one, to attain the frustrated aim through the use
(85) of violence. It is clearly an aggression in the service of life, and not one for the sake of destruction. Since frustration of needs and desires has been an almost universal occurrence in most societies even to the present day, there is no reason to be surprised that
(90) violence and aggression are constantly produced and exhibited.

1. As it is used in the passage, the word "couched" (line 52) means:

   (A) described.
   (B) fought.
   (C) planned.
   (D) reclined.

2. According to the passage, people who react violently when frustrated:

   (F) have replaced constructive motives with destructive ones.
   (G) are reliving the frustrating experiences of their childhood.
   (H) want to take revenge on the source of their frustration.
   (J) do so in order to achieve their desired goal.

3. According to the passage, which of the following are aspects of reactive violence?

   (I)   Irrational passions
   (II) Rational calculation
   (III) Imaginary fears

   (A) I only
   (B) I and II only
   (C) II and III only
   (D) I, II, and III

4. As it is used in the passage, the term "reactive violence" primarily refers to:

   (F) violence exercised in order to display skill.
   (G) violence undertaken in the defense of life and freedom.
   (H) violence committed for the sake of destruction.
   (J) violence only used in an attempt to attain frustrated goals.

5. It is most reasonable to infer that the author of the passage believes that:

   (A) the frustration of needs and desires is no longer a common aspect of human life.
   (B) animals, children, and adults all have similar needs and desires that they attempt to fulfill through violent means.
   (C) the examination of the unconscious causes of violence leads to a better understanding of the violence itself.
   (D) reactive violence is usually sparked by the desire for destruction.

6. The main idea of the passage is that:

   (F) a better understanding of violence could prevent wars from occurring.
   (G) people commit violent acts for a variety of different reasons.
   (H) reactive violence is the most significant form of human violence.
   (J) all forms of violence are rooted in subconscious fears.

Point Builder	The ACT Writing Test: What to Expect
Point Builder	The Kaplan Method for Essay Writing

The ACT Writing Test: What to Expect

A. The ACT Writing Test is always the _____ test of the ACT. It is optional.

B. The ACT Writing Test requires you to be _____.

C. You will have _____ minutes to complete the ACT Writing Test.

D. Each essay will be scored by graders, on a scale of _____ to _____,

for a total score ranging between _____ and _____.

E. An essay will receive a score of 0 if:

1. _____

2. _____

3. _____

4. _____

F. Essays are scored _____, meaning that they will be graded

based on _____. There is no _____ for errors.

G. The essay measures your ability to _____

and to _____.

Essay graders are looking for very specific things, including:

1. Understanding of the prompt
2. Understanding of the complexity of the issue
3. Development of ideas
4. Focus
5. Organization
6. Transitions
7. Introductory and concluding sentences
8. Language skills
9. Correct grammar and sentence structure

Your essay score will not be affected by:

1. _____

2. _____

3. _____

| KAPLAN

The Kaplan Method for Essay Writing

A.   The Kaplan Method for Essay Writing

1. _Prompt_
2. _Plan_
3. _Produce_
4. _Proofread_

B.   "Prompt" means _____.

Students receive a score of _____ for an essay that fails to address the prompt.

Prompt

As many employers stress an increased awareness of the global economy, high school and college students look to expand their understanding of foreign cultures. Successfully interacting with other nations requires diplomacy and general knowledge about customs and communication. In order to have meaningful interaction with a foreign culture, is it necessary to both learn the language and live within that culture for an extended period of time? Considering the importance of positive interactions with foreign states, it is important to identify effective ways of engaging with other cultures.

Read and carefully consider these perspectives. Each suggests a particular way of thinking about ways of meaningfully interacting with other cultures.

Perspective One	Perspective Two	Perspective Three
It is not necessary to live in another country or even learn the language to have a significant positive interaction with a foreign culture. It is possible to have a meaningful cultural experience simply by engaging in basic cultural experiences like eating ethnic cuisine, learning about traditional clothing, or familiarizing yourself with indigenous music and cultural celebrations.	It is unrealistic to expect people to live within other cultures in order to learn about them. Not only would that require considerable time and resources, but also there are too many cultures throughout the world from which to choose. Rather than encouraging people to travel, it is better to provide objective information about other cultures in high school and college courses.	Living in a foreign nation is the ideal way to learn about another culture, and schools should provide opportunities for students to do so during their high school and college careers. Students will learn the most by far about both a new culture as well as their own culture by immersing themselves in the surroundings of a foreign nation. In addition to fostering comprehensive learning experiences, spending time in a different country provides students with valuable opportunities to forge positive cultural interactions that are much harder to experience without visiting the foreign nation.

Essay Task

Write a unified, coherent essay in which you evaluate multiple perspectives on meaningful interactions with other cultures. In your essay, be sure to:

- analyze and evaluate the perspectives given
- state and develop your own perspective on the issue
- explain the relationship between your perspective and those given

Your perspective may be in full agreement with any of the others, in partial agreement, or wholly different. Whatever the case, support your ideas with logical reasoning and detailed, persuasive examples.

Planning Your Essay

You may wish to consider the following as you think critically about the task:

- Strengths and weaknesses of the three given perspectives
  - What insights do they offer, and what do they fail to consider?
  - Why might they be persuasive to others, or why might they fail to persuade?
- Your own knowledge, experience, and values
  - What is your perspective on this issue, and what are its strengths and weaknesses?
  - How will you support your perspective in your essay?

According to the directions, you must _____

_____

_____

Plan—Thesis Sentence

As many employers stress an increased awareness of the global economy, high school and college students look to expand their understanding of foreign cultures. Successfully interacting with other nations requires diplomacy and general knowledge about customs and communication. In order to have meaningful interaction with a foreign culture, is it necessary not simply to learn the language, but to live within that culture for an extended period of time? Considering the importance of positive interactions with foreign states, it is important to identify effective ways of engaging with other cultures.

A. "Plan" means _____

_____

B. What keywords from this prompt might be used in this essay? _____

_____

C. Your thesis sentence needs to _____

_____

_____

D. Your discussion of the three perspectives should _____

_____

_____

Write your thesis sentence for this prompt on the lines below:

_____

_____

_____

_____

_____

How does your perspective compare and contrast to the three perspectives given?

_____

_____

_____

_____

_____

Plan—Supporting Data

A. To write a strong essay, you must have _____

_____

_____

B. The examples that you provide in support of your thesis must be both _____ and _____.

To make your examples specific, think of a concrete situation. Be prepared to write about particular aspects of the situation. Doing so will help you avoid making mere generalizations, a common weakness of lower-scoring essays.

For an example to be relevant, it must relate to your thesis and/or one of the perspectives.

Consider this introductory paragraph:

Understanding another person's culture and language is key to effectively interacting with people of different countries. But how does one go about doing this? Is it necessary to actually live in another country to understand its culture? Can a person learn as much as necessary without traveling, but through experiencing basic aspects of the culture, such as its food and music? Or can schools provide enough information to understand another culture by teaching it objectively, such as through textbooks? Each point of view has positive and negative aspects, and I support the point of view which advocates engaging in basic cultural experiences, though I would take that further to include the necessity of learning the language and going beyond basic experiences.

Which examples constitute *specific* examples that could be used to support the thesis stated in that paragraph?

	Specific	Not Specific
1. People who attend traditional weddings learn about other cultures.		
2. Attending a quinceañera provides an opportunity to enjoy Latin American food like enchiladas, tamales, and pan de polvo, and traditional songs, such as *De Niña a Mujer* and *La Ultima Muñeca*.		
3. After I returned from the Chinese New Year parade held in my neighborhood, I immediately bought two new e-books on Chinese culture.		
4. I had no interest in learning about Costa Rica until I took Spanish 101; simply knowing a handful of phrases really sparked my interest in that country at large and Costa Ricans in particular.		

Which examples constitute *relevant* examples that could be used to support the thesis stated in that paragraph?

	Relevant	Not Relevant
1. Everyone should try sushi at least once in his or her lifetime.		
2. Learning how to speak French is easier than learning how to speak Spanish in the beginning, but it gets harder by the second year.		
3. After reading an article about Thorrablot, Iceland's month-long homage to the nation's Viking heritage, I wanted to learn more about the sparsely populated country.		
4. Translating several of Pablo Neruda's poems was enough to spark my interest in Chilean culture in general.		
5. I wasn't interested in Hawaiian culture until I went to live with my aunt in Honolulu during the summer between my sophomore and junior year.		

Plan—Organize, Using Kaplan's Essay Template

¶1: Introductory paragraph
- Introductory statement
- Thesis

¶2: 1st body paragraph
- Describe Perspective One
  - Strengths/weaknesses
  - Insights it offers/Insights it fails to consider
  - Persuasive/Fails to persuade
- Specifically state whether you agree, disagree, or partially agree/disagree with this perspective

¶3: 2nd body paragraph
- Describe Perspective Two
  - Strengths/weaknesses
  - Insights it offers/Insights it fails to consider
  - Persuasive/Fails to persuade
- Specifically state whether you agree, disagree, or partially agree/disagree with this perspective

¶4: 3rd body paragraph
- Describe Perspective Three
  - Strengths/weaknesses
  - Insights it offers/Insights it fails to consider
  - Persuasive/Fails to persuade
- Specifically state whether you agree, disagree, or partially agree/disagree with this perspective

¶5: 4th body paragraph
- Describe your thesis
  - Provide specific, relevant support
  - Discuss the strengths/weaknesses of your thesis
  - Explain how your thesis fits in among Perspectives One, Two, and Three
- Include a single, conclusion sentence at the end of your 4th body paragraph to wrap up your essay.

Quiz

Now that you've completed the prompt and plan phase, practice producing. Using your thesis from the previous pages, write a body paragraph for your essay. Support your argument and make sure to use evidence that is specific and relevant. Finally, remember to tie your evidence back to your main point before completing the paragraph.

_____
_____
_____
_____
_____
_____
_____
_____
_____
_____
_____
_____
_____
_____
_____
_____
_____
_____
_____
_____
_____
_____
_____
_____

Session 2 Homework

English	Basic Assignment	Additional Practice	In the Appendix
Sentence Sense/Punctuation	Questions 1–20	Questions 21–40	Page 585
Reading			
3 Question Types	Questions 1–10	Questions 11–20	
Essay Writing	Complete the Essay		
Online			
Quizzes and Workshops	English Quiz Reading Quiz Writing Quiz	English Workshop Reading Workshop Writing Workshop	

HOMEWORK

Quarter 2

Passage I

The Library System

In the past ten years, library systems have become <u>increasingly computerized, this has led</u>
1
<u>to speculation</u> about the future of libraries. Some
1
people believe that not only the card catalogue, but also the library stacks themselves, will eventually be rendered obsolete. It is quite likely, they say, that in the next decade or so, <u>books as we know them will</u>
2
<u>be replaced by electronic data.</u>
2

This thought presents an interesting picture of the future. <u>Instead of spending a cozy evening with a</u>
3
<u>good book, curling up with a laptop computer.</u> With
3
all the intriguing possibilities the future holds, we are inclined to ignore the past. <u>While the future state</u>
4
<u>may be interesting to predict of the library system,</u> it
4
has a rich history as well.

Libraries may have originated as early as the third millennium BCE in Babylonia. There, clay tablets were <u>used and utilized</u> for record-keeping purposes
5
and stored in a temple. In the seventh century BCE, <u>approximately 20,000 tablets organized by the King</u>
6
<u>of Assyria have been recovered for an enormous</u>
6
<u>collection of fragments.</u> The first libraries to store
6
books were fourth-century BCE Greek temples established in conjunction with the various schools of philosophy. In the second century CE, libraries were founded in monasteries. Not until the thirteenth century <u>was university libraries created.</u>
7

During the Renaissance, a series of societal changes began to transform the library system into the form we have today: the emergence of a middle class, a growth in literacy, and the invention of the printing press. <u>Although</u> wars and revolutions served to hinder
8
the development of the library system in England. For example, Henry VIII ordered the destruction of countless manuscripts and disbanded some monastic libraries. <u>Henry VIII was married six times.</u>
9

In the days of King Henry, many English citizens were pondering the fate of the nascent library system. Today's societal changes are likewise causing some of us <u>to consider the same thing,</u>
10
<u>although in ways that medieval readers could never</u>
10
<u>have imagined.</u> Have we progressed from clay
10
tablets to paperbacks only to trade our paperbacks in for microchips?

1. (A) NO CHANGE
   (B) increasingly computerized: this has led to speculation
   (C) increasingly computerized, which has led to speculation
   (D) increasingly computerized. Leading to speculation

2. (F) NO CHANGE
   (G) electronic data will replace books as we know them.
   (H) books as we know them being replaced by electronic data.
   (J) books as we know them are replaced by electronic data.

3. (A) NO CHANGE
   (B) Instead of spending a cozy evening with a good book, curling up with a laptop computer instead.
   (C) Curling up with a laptop computer instead of spending a cozy evening with a good book.
   (D) Instead of spending a cozy evening with a good book, we may be curling up with a laptop computer.

4. (F) NO CHANGE
   (G) While predicting the future state may be interesting of the library system,
   (H) While predicting the future state of the library system may be interesting,
   (J) While the future of the library system may be an interesting state to predict,

5. (A) NO CHANGE
   (B) used—and utilized—
   (C) used
   (D) used, and therefore utilized,

6. (F) NO CHANGE
   (G) having organized an enormous collection, approximately 20,000 tablets and fragments have been recovered by the King of Assyria.
   (H) an enormous collection of records organized by the King of Assyria: approximately 20,000 tablets and fragments recovered.
   (J) the King of Assyria organized an enormous collection of records; approximately 20,000 tablets and fragments have been recovered.

7. (A) NO CHANGE
   (B) were university libraries created.
   (C) was the creation of university libraries.
   (D) were libraries created at any universities.

8. (F) NO CHANGE
   (G) Despite
   (H) However,
   (J) Even though

9. (A) NO CHANGE
   (B) Henry VIII, having been married six times.
   (C) Six times, Henry VIII was married.
   (D) OMIT the underlined portion.

10. (F) NO CHANGE
    (G) to consider the same thing, it is in ways that medieval readers could never have imagined.
    (H) to have consideration of the same thing, although it is in ways that medieval readers could never have imagined.
    (J) to consider the same thing, although in ways that medieval readers will never be able to imagine.

Passage II

Liberal Arts Education

Although the concept of liberal arts has existed since the time of ancient Greece, the parameters over the centuries have remained relatively
11
unchanged of liberal arts study. In essence, liberal
11
arts are defined as "any study given to reflection

and free inquiry." This not always being the case,
12
however.
12

In medieval times, the seven liberal arts were divided into two parts: the Trivium ("the three roads") and the Quadrivium ("the four roads"). The Trivium consisted of grammar, rhetoric, and logic, the Quadrivium consisted of arithmetic,
13
geometry, astronomy, and harmonics. However, the
13
description of a liberal arts college is somewhat more limiting. A liberal arts college generally awards a Bachelor of Arts degree after four years of study, primarily enrolls full-time students between the ages of 18 and 24, typically has between 800 and 1,800 students, and does not provide professional or vocational preparation.

The liberal arts have been the primary focus of
14
undergraduate education in the United States since it was a British colony. The late 1800s saw an expansion of liberal arts colleges as the right to education began to include minorities and women. The number of liberal arts colleges in the United States steady increased throughout the twentieth
15
century as private universities, state universities, and community colleges all sought to give their
16
undergraduates a broad education.

The content of liberal arts study still focuses on the arts, humanities, and sciences, and the
17
basic notion of forming well-rounded students in
17
these areas is still the concept behind liberal arts education today. There is some concern, however, that the philosophy behind liberal arts education is out of step with the times in which today's students are living. Responding to this concern, courses in
18
computer science and information technology have
18
been added to the curriculum of many colleges and
18
universities. Does this mean the end of liberal arts
18
education as it has been practiced since the days of Martianus Capella? I don't believe so. Most liberal
19
arts colleges award Master's and doctoral degrees
19
as well. The study of liberal arts may have to
19

evolve with the times, but its basic premise— that well-rounded students are well-educated students— remain as valid today as it was in medieval times.
20

11. (A) NO CHANGE
    (B) over the centuries of liberal arts study have remained relatively unchanged.
    (C) of liberal arts study have remained relatively unchanged over the centuries.
    (D) of liberal arts study remaining relatively unchanged over the centuries.

12. (F) NO CHANGE
    (G) This has not always been the case, however.
    (H) Although this has not always been the case.
    (J) OMIT the underlined selection.

13. (A) NO CHANGE
    (B) logic; while the Quadrivium consisted of arithmetic, geometry, astronomy, and harmonics.
    (C) logic, so the Quadrivium consisted of arithmetic, geometry, astronomy, and harmonics.
    (D) logic; the Quadrivium consisted of arithmetic, geometry, astronomy, and harmonics.

14. (F) NO CHANGE
    (G) The liberal arts has been
    (H) The liberal arts having been
    (J) The liberal arts being

15. (A) NO CHANGE
    (B) steadily increased
    (C) increased in a steady fashion
    (D) increased in a steadily fashion

16. (F) NO CHANGE
    (G) give its
    (H) giving their
    (J) gave its

17. (A) NO CHANGE
    (B) sciences; and the basic notion of forming well-rounded students
    (C) sciences. And the basic notion of forming well-rounded students
    (D) sciences: and the basic notion of forming well-rounded students

18. (F) NO CHANGE
    (G) Responding to this concern, computer science and information technology courses have been added to the curriculum of many colleges and universities.
    (H) Responding to this concern, computer science and information technology are the subject of courses that have been added to the curriculum of many colleges and universities.
    (J) Responding to this concern, many colleges and universities have added courses in computer science and information technology to the curriculum.

19. (A) NO CHANGE
    (B) Master's and doctoral degrees are awarded by most liberal arts colleges as well.
    (C) Most degrees awarded by liberal arts colleges are Master's and doctoral ones.
    (D) OMIT the underlined portion.

20. (F) NO CHANGE
    (G) remaining as valid today
    (H) remains as valid today
    (J) remained as valid today

Passage III

The Mystery of Stonehenge

On Salisbury plain in England west of the town
21
of Amesbury, stands a strange and mysterious
21
artifact of the distant past: Stonehenge. These stone
22
monoliths stand as a silent testimony to an ancient people. Who those people were and how they constructed these imposing circles of stones is a mystery that has puzzled scientists for ages.

From a distance—Stonehenge doesn't seem
23
very large, but when you get closer, it takes
24
your breath away. The tallest upright stone is
22 feet; with another eight feet to hold it in place.
25
The stones weigh up to four tons each, and they may have come from as far away as the Prescelly
26
Mountains—nearly 240 miles away.
26

For many years, it was thought that Stonehenge had been built by <u>the Druids; who were an ancient</u>
27
<u>Celtic people.</u> Modern scholars <u>have determined</u>
27   28
<u>however</u> that Stonehenge had already been standing
28
for 2,000 years before the Druids. There are many other <u>legends, stories, and theories</u> that people
29
have come up with about the origin of Stonehenge, including a story about giants from Africa and a story involving <u>King Arthurs magician,</u> Merlin. The
30
truth remains elusive. We know roughly when the structure was built, but we have no clear idea who built it or why.

21. (A) NO CHANGE
    (B) England, west of the town of Amesbury stands
    (C) England, west of the town of Amesbury, stands
    (D) England west of the town of Amesbury stands

22. (F) NO CHANGE
    (G) artifact of the distant past Stonehenge
    (H) artifact, of the distant past, Stonehenge
    (J) artifact of the distant past; Stonehenge

23. (A) NO CHANGE
    (B) From a distance Stonehenge
    (C) From a distance, Stonehenge,
    (D) From a distance, Stonehenge

24. (F) NO CHANGE
    (G) large but when,
    (H) large; but when
    (J) large but when

25. (A) NO CHANGE
    (B) 22 feet, with another eight feet
    (C) 22 feet—with another eight feet
    (D) 22 feet with another eight feet

26. (F) NO CHANGE
    (G) the Prescelly Mountains: nearly 240 miles away.
    (H) the Prescelly Mountains nearly 240 miles away.
    (J) the Prescelly Mountains nearly, 240 miles away.

27. (A) NO CHANGE
    (B) the Druids who, were an ancient Celtic people.
    (C) the Druids, who were an ancient Celtic people.
    (D) the Druids—who were an ancient Celtic people.

28. (F) NO CHANGE
    (G) have determined, however
    (H) have determined however,
    (J) have determined, however,

29. (A) NO CHANGE
    (B) legends, stories and theories
    (C) legends stories, and theories
    (D) legends, stories, and theories,

30. (F) NO CHANGE
    (G) King Arthur's magician
    (H) King Arthurs' magician
    (J) King Arthurs's magician

Passage IV

Frankenstein

The character of Frankenstein did not originate in Hollywood. Rather, the legendary mad scientist who sought to reanimate lifeless bodies was <u>the creation</u>
31
<u>of, Mary Wollstonecraft Shelley,</u> who was married to
31
famed poet Percy Bysshe Shelley. Her *Frankenstein,*

or the Modern Prometheus, <u>published in 1818</u> is
32
considered one of the greatest horror tales of all time.

Mary Shelley created her nightmarish subject in response to a bet. <u>She, her husband Lord Byron, and</u>
33
<u>Byron's physician;</u> had a contest to see who could
33
write the best ghost story. Although it was begun <u>whimsically her tale</u> became a serious examination
34
of the fate of an individual who decides to overstep moral and social bounds.

<u>Shelley's novel tells</u> the story of a scientist,
35
Dr. Victor Frankenstein, who discovers the secret of bringing corpses back to life and creates a monster with material from graveyards, dissecting rooms, and slaughterhouses. Despite the monster's <u>gruesome appearance; he</u> is basically good.
36

The monster, who is nameless, only becomes evil when his creator refuses to accept and care for him. After being rejected by Dr. Frankenstein and all other people with whom he comes into contact, the monster becomes violent. One by one, the monster murders the people Dr. Frankenstein cares for the most, his younger brother, his best friend, and
37
his wife. The tale ends as Dr. Frankenstein chases the monster to the North Pole, where both of them eventually die.

Although it is a horror story, Mary Shelley's
38
Frankenstein is respected by many as a literary
38
classic. The continued popularity of the story is also evidenced by the numerous films that have been based on it. Some versions like *Young Frankenstein*
39
provide a humorous retelling of the story: other
40
versions, like the most recent *Mary Shelley's*
40
Frankenstein, attempt to be faithful to the original.

31. (A) NO CHANGE
    (B) the creation of: Mary Wollstonecraft Shelley.
    (C) the creation of Mary Wollstonecraft Shelley.
    (D) the creation of—Mary Wollstonecraft Shelley.

32. (F) NO CHANGE
    (G) published in 1818,
    (H) published in 1818;
    (J) published, in 1818,

33. (A) NO CHANGE
    (B) She, her husband Lord Byron, and Byron's physician,
    (C) She, her husband Lord Byron and Byron's physician,
    (D) She, her husband, Lord Byron, and Byron's physician

34. (F) NO CHANGE
    (G) whimsically; her tale
    (H) whimsically, her tale
    (J) whimsically. Her tale

35. (A) NO CHANGE
    (B) Shelleys novel tells
    (C) Shelley's novel tells,
    (D) Shelleys' novel tells

36. (F) NO CHANGE
    (G) gruesome appearance, he
    (H) gruesome appearance. He
    (J) gruesome appearance he

37. (A) NO CHANGE
    (B) the most his
    (C) the most: his
    (D) the most; his

38. (F) NO CHANGE
    (G) horror story. Mary Shelley's *Frankenstein*
    (H) horror story; Mary Shelley's *Frankenstein*
    (J) horror story Mary Shelley's *Frankenstein*

39. (A) NO CHANGE
    (B) Some versions, like *Young Frankenstein*
    (C) Some versions, like, *Young Frankenstein,*
    (D) Some versions, like *Young Frankenstein,*

40. (F) NO CHANGE
    (G) of the story, other versions,
    (H) of the story; other versions,
    (J) of the story—other versions,

Quarter 3

Passage I

Humanities: This passage is excerpted from *A History of Women Artists,* by Hugo Munsterberg. (© 1975 by Hugo Munsterberg.) Reprinted with permission of Clarkson N. Potter, Inc., a division of Crown Publishers, Inc.

There can be little doubt that women artists have been most prominent in photography and that they have made their greatest contribution in this field.
Line One reason for this is not difficult to ascertain.
(5) As several historians of photography have pointed out, photography, being a new medium outside the traditional academic framework, was wide open to women and offered them opportunities that the older fields did not.

(10) All these observations apply to the first woman to have achieved eminence in photography—Julia Margaret Cameron. Born in 1815 in Calcutta into an upper-middle-class family and married to Charles Hay Cameron, a distinguished jurist and member of
(15) the Supreme Court of India, Julia Cameron was well known as a brilliant conversationalist and a woman of personality and intellect who was unconventional to the point of eccentricity. Although the mother of six children, she adopted several more and still found
(20) time to be active in social causes and literary activities. After the Camerons settled in England in 1848 at Freshwater Bay on the Isle of Wight, she became the center of an artistic and literary circle that included such notable figures as the poet Alfred, Lord Tennyson,
(25) and the painter George Frederick Watts. Pursuing numerous activities and taking care of her large family, Mrs. Cameron might have been remembered as still another rather remarkable and colorful Victorian lady had it not been for the fact that, in 1863, her daughter
(30) presented her with photographic equipment, thinking her mother might enjoy taking pictures of her family and friends. Although 48 years old, Mrs. Cameron took up this new hobby with enormous enthusiasm and dedication. She was a complete beginner, but within a
(35) very few years she developed into one of the greatest photographers of her period and a giant in the history of photography. She worked ceaselessly and mastered the technical processes of photography, at that time far more cumbersome than they are today, turning her
(40) coal house into a darkroom and her chicken house into a studio. To her, photography was a "divine art," and in it she found her vocation. In 1864, she wrote triumphantly under one of her photographs, "My First Success," and from then until her death in Ceylon in
(45) 1874, she devoted herself wholly to this art.

Working in a large format (her portrait studies are usually about 11 inches by 14 inches) and requiring a long exposure (on the average five minutes), she produced a large body of work that stands up
(50) as one of the notable artistic achievements of the Victorian period. The English art critic Roger Fry believed that her portraits were likely to outlive the works of artists who were her contemporaries. Her friend Watts, then a very celebrated portrait painter,
(55) inscribed on one of her photographs, "I wish I could paint such a picture as this." Her work was widely exhibited, and she received gold, silver, and bronze medals in England, the United States, Germany, and Austria. No other female artist of the nineteenth
(60) century achieved such acclaim, and no other woman photographer has ever enjoyed such success.

Her work falls into two main categories on which her contemporaries and people today differ sharply. Victorian critics were particularly impressed by
(65) her allegorical pictures, many of them based on the poems of her friend and neighbor Tennyson. Contemporary taste much prefers her portraits and finds her narrative scenes sentimental and sometimes in bad taste. Yet, not only Julia Cameron, but also
(70) the painters of that time loved to depict subjects such as *Pray God, Bring Father Safely Home*. Still, today her fame rests upon her portraits for, as she herself said, she was intent upon representing not only the outer likeness but also the inner greatness
(75) of the people she portrayed. Working with the utmost dedication, she produced photographs of such eminent Victorians as Tennyson, Browning, Carlyle, Trollope, Longfellow, Watts, Darwin, Ellen Terry, Sir John Herschel, who was a close friend of hers, and
(80) Mrs. Duckworth, the mother of Virginia Woolf.

1. Which of the following conclusions can be most reasonably drawn from the passage's discussion of Julia Margaret Cameron?

    (A) She was a traditional homemaker until she discovered photography.

    (B) Her work holds a significant place in the history of photography.

    (C) She was unable to achieve in her lifetime the artistic recognition she deserved.

    (D) Her eccentricity has kept her from being taken seriously by modern critics of photography.

2. According to the passage, Cameron is most respected by modern critics for her:

(F) portraits.

(G) allegorical pictures.

(H) use of a large format.

(J) service in recording the likenesses of so many nineteenth-century figures.

3. The author uses which of the following methods to develop the second paragraph (lines 10–45)?

(A) A series of anecdotes depicting Cameron's energy and unconventionality.

(B) A presentation of factual data demonstrating Cameron's importance in the history of photography.

(C) A critique of Cameron's early work.

(D) A chronological account of Cameron's background and artistic growth.

4. The author uses the details in lines 37–41 ("She worked...a studio.") to indicate:

(F) the economic constraints that Cameron had to overcome.

(G) the reason that modern critics don't value Cameron's work.

(H) the depth of Cameron's commitment to her art.

(J) the extent of the challenges facing nineteenth-century photographers.

5. When the author says that Cameron had found "her vocation" (line 42), his main point is that photography:

(A) offered Cameron an escape from the confines of conventional social life.

(B) became the main interest of her life.

(C) became her primary source of income.

(D) provided her with a way to express her religious beliefs.

6. The main point of the third paragraph (lines 46–61) is that Cameron:

(F) achieved great artistic success during her lifetime.

(G) is the greatest photographer that ever lived.

(H) was considered a more important artist during her lifetime than she is now.

(J) revolutionized photographic methods in the Victorian era.

7. The author cites the opinions of an art critic and a "celebrated portrait painter" (lines 51–56) in order to:

(A) illustrate the significance of Cameron's artistic accomplishments.

(B) emphasize Victorian critics' preference for Cameron's allegorical work.

(C) detail the envy Cameron's peers felt toward her.

(D) counter the negative assessments of Cameron's work by more recent critics.

8. The author offers *Pray God, Bring Father Safely Home* as an example of:

(F) a portrait of a celebrated Victorian.

(G) an allegorical subject of the sort that was popular during the Victorian era.

(H) a photograph in which Cameron sought to show a subject's outer likeness and inner greatness.

(J) a photograph by Cameron that was scoffed at by her contemporaries.

9. According to the passage, which of the following opinions of Cameron's work was held by Victorian critics but is NOT held by modern critics?

(A) Photographs should be based on poems.

(B) Her portraits are too sentimental.

(C) Narrative scenes are often in bad taste.

(D) Her allegorical pictures are her best work.

10. The author's treatment of Cameron's development as a photographer can best be described as:

(F) respectful.

(G) condescending.

(H) neutral.

(J) defensive.

Passage II

Natural Science: This passage is excerpted from a textbook about the solar system and discusses research that examines the possibility of life on Mars.

When the first of the two Viking landers touched down on Martian soil on July 20, 1976 and began to send camera images back to Earth, the scientists at
Line the Jet Propulsion Laboratory could not suppress a
(5) certain nervous anticipation. Like people who hold a ticket to a lottery, they had a one-in-a-million chance of winning. The first photographs that arrived, however, did not contain any evidence of life. What was revealed was merely a barren landscape littered with rocks and
(10) boulders. The view resembled nothing so much as a flat section of desert. In fact, the winning entry in a contest at J.P.L. for the photograph most accurately predicting what Mars would look like was a snapshot taken from a particularly arid section of the Mojave Desert.

(15) The scientists were soon ready to turn their attention from visible life to microorganisms. The twin Viking landers carried experiments designed to detect organic compounds. Researchers thought it possible that life had developed on early Mars just as it is thought to
(20) have developed on Earth, through the gradual chemical evolution of complex organic molecules. To detect biological activity, Martian soil samples were treated with various nutrients that would produce characteristic by-products if life forms were active in the soil. The
(25) results from all three experiments were inconclusive. The fourth experiment heated a soil sample to look for signs of organic material but found none—an unexpected result because organic compounds were thought to have been present due to the steady
(30) bombardment of the Martian surface by meteorites.

The absence of organic materials, some scientists speculated, was the result of intense ultraviolet radiation penetrating the atmosphere of Mars and destroying organic compounds in the soil.
(35) Although Mars' atmosphere was at one time rich in carbon dioxide and thus thick enough to protect its surface from the harmful rays of the sun, the carbon dioxide had gradually left the atmosphere and been converted into rocks. This means that
(40) even if life had gotten a start on early Mars, it could not have survived the exposure to ultraviolet radiation that occurred when the atmosphere thinned. Mars never developed a protective layer of ozone as Earth did.

(45) Despite the disappointing Viking results, there are those who still keep open the possibility of life on Mars. They point out that the Viking data cannot be considered the final word on Martian life because the two landers only sampled limited—and
(50) uninteresting—sites. The Viking landing sites were not chosen for what they might tell of the planet's biology. They were chosen primarily because they appeared to be safe for landing a spacecraft. The landing sites were on parts of the Martian plains that appeared
(55) relatively featureless according to orbital photographs.

The type of terrain that these researchers suggest may be a possible hiding place for active life has an Earthly parallel: the ice-free region of southern Victoria Land, Antarctica, where the temperatures
(60) in some dry valleys average below zero. Organisms known as endoliths, a form of blue-green algae that has adapted to this harsh environment, were found living inside certain translucent, porous rocks in these Antarctic valleys. The argument based on this
(65) discovery is that if life did exist on early Mars, it is possible that it escaped worsening conditions by similarly seeking refuge in rocks. Skeptics object, however, that Mars in its present state is simply too dry, even compared with Antarctic valleys, to sustain
(70) any life whatsoever.

Should Mars eventually prove to be barren of life, as some suspect, then this would have a significant impact on the current view of the chemical origins of life. It could be much more difficult to get life started on a
(75) planet than scientists thought before the Viking landings.

11. The word "active," as used in line 25, most nearly means:

(A) moving.
(B) energetic.
(C) dormant.
(D) present.

12. The main function of the fourth paragraph (lines 45–55) in relation to the passage as a whole is to indicate that:

(F) the Viking program was unsuccessful due to poor selection of landing sites.
(G) the results of the Viking program do not necessarily prove that Mars is devoid of life.
(H) the detection of life on Mars was not a primary objective of the Viking program.
(J) scientists were not expecting to discover life on the Martian plains.

13. According to the passage, scientists expected the presence of organic compounds on Mars to be a result of:

    (A) alien civilizations.
    (B) ultraviolet radiation.
    (C) meteor bombardment.
    (D) atmospheric activity.

14. The passage suggests that an important difference between Mars and Earth is that, unlike Earth, Mars:

    (F) accumulated organic compounds in its soil.
    (G) lies in the path of harmful rays of ultraviolet radiation.
    (H) once possessed an atmosphere rich in carbon dioxide.
    (J) could not sustain any life that developed.

15. According to the passage, the surface of Mars most resembles:

    (A) the ice valleys of Antarctica.
    (B) a very dry section of a desert.
    (C) that of Earth's moon.
    (D) that of Earth, if it lacked its ozone layer.

16. The main point of the second paragraph (lines 15–31) is that:

    (F) scientists were disappointed by the inconclusive results of their experiments.
    (G) theories about how life developed on Earth were shown to be flawed.
    (H) there was no experimental confirmation that life exists on Mars.
    (J) meteorite bombardment of the Martian surface is less constant than scientists predicted.

17. The researchers' argument that life may exist in Martian rocks rests on the idea that:

    (A) life evolved in the same way on two different planets.
    (B) organisms may adopt identical survival strategies in similar environments.
    (C) life developed in the form of a blue-green algae on Mars.
    (D) organisms that survived in Antarctica could survive on Mars.

18. According to the passage, the results of the Viking program could eventually have a "significant impact" (line 72) because:

    (F) future expeditions to Mars may take samples from many different sites.
    (G) current theories about how life began on Earth may have to be changed.
    (H) scientists may be forced to acknowledge that life does not exist on other planets.
    (J) the focus of research into the evolution of life may shift to Antarctica.

19. According to the passage, any organic materials that existed on Mars were probably destroyed by:

    (A) carbon dioxide in the atmosphere.
    (B) the planet's arid conditions.
    (C) ultraviolet radiation.
    (D) bombardment by meteorites.

20. According to the passage, scientists treated Martian soil samples with nutrients in order to:

    (F) test for the presence of life forms.
    (G) verify the results of their experiments.
    (H) investigate ways of starting life on other planets.
    (J) find evidence of meteorite bombardment.

Quarter 4

American History Curriculum

Educators and curriculum designers continuously debate the best way to teach American history to high school students. Whether students are reading historical interpretations or primary source documents, teachers often put the most emphasis on memorizing important names and dates. Although history is generally regarded as a compilation of facts, should high school students be expected to learn more about history than general information regarding famous people and events? Given the richness of American history, it is worthwhile to explore best practices in presenting the story of the United States to students.

Read and carefully consider these perspectives. Each suggests a particular way of teaching American history.

Perspective One	**Perspective Two**	**Perspective Three**
It is important to focus on a nation's prominent historical leaders when studying history. Leaders are representative of the nation as a whole, so studying historical figures provides a full perspective.	The clearest lens through which to view a nation's history is the welfare of its entire population. It is only through an examination of the ways in which society has been affected by historical events that students will truly understand a nation's foundation.	In order to learn the story of America, students need to know what happened when and who influenced those events. Familiarity with and testing of important dates and events is the most effective way to study history. Students need to know what happened in years past in order to plan for the future.

Essay Task

Write a unified, coherent essay in which you evaluate multiple perspectives on the most effective way to teach American history to high school students. In your essay, be sure to:

- analyze and evaluate the perspectives given
- state and develop your own perspective on the issue
- explain the relationship between your perspective and those given

Your perspective may be in full agreement with any of the others, in partial agreement, or wholly different. Whatever the case, support your ideas with logical reasoning and detailed, persuasive examples.

Planning Your Essay

Use the space below and on the next page to generate ideas and plan your essay. You may wish to consider the following as you think critically about the task:

- Strengths and weaknesses of the three given perspectives
  - What insights do they offer, and what do they fail to consider?
  - Why might they be persuasive to others, or why might they fail to persuade?
- Your own knowledge, experience, and values
  - What is your perspective on this issue, and what are its strengths and weaknesses?
  - How will you support your perspective in your essay?

Use this page to *plan* your essay.
Your work on this page will *not* be scored.

Begin WRITING TEST here.

	Test Review
	Homework Review
	Preview Quiz
	Session Objectives

Test Review

Your Kaplan Practice Test results not only tell you how well you did, but also tell you what to do before your next test. Review your results carefully to determine a study plan.

English _____ **Math** _____ **Reading** _____ **Science** _____ **Writing** _____

English

1. In which three SmartPoint categories did you perform the best?

_____

_____

_____

2. Which three categories need the most improvement?

_____

_____

_____

3. How can you improve? (*Circle those that apply.*)

- Learn and practice Kaplan Methods and Strategies.
- Improve grammar knowledge.
- Budget time.
- Practice more questions.
- Eliminate choices before guessing.

Mathematics

4. In which three SmartPoint categories did you perform the best?

_____

_____

_____

5. Which three categories need the most improvement?

_____

_____

_____

6. How can you improve? (*Circle those that apply.*)

- Learn and practice Kaplan Methods and Strategies.
- Improve math knowledge.
- Budget time.
- Practice more questions.
- Eliminate choices before guessing.

Reading

7. In which three SmartPoint categories did you perform the best?

_____

_____

_____

8. Which three categories need the most improvement?

_____

_____

_____

9. How can you improve? (*Circle those that apply.*)

- Learn and practice Kaplan Methods and Strategies.
- Budget time.
- Practice more questions.
- Eliminate choices before guessing.
- Read actively.

Science

10. In which three SmartPoint categories did you perform the best?

_____

_____

_____

11. Which three categories need the most improvement?

_____

_____

_____

12. How can you improve? (*Circle those that apply.*)

- Learn and practice Kaplan Methods and Strategies.
- Budget time.
- Practice more questions.
- Eliminate choices before guessing.
- Focus on the purpose, method, and results.

Writing

Review the Essay-scoring information on page 330 to help you evaluate what improvements you can make to boost your Essay score.

Session 2 Homework Review

The Library System

In the days of King Henry, many English citizens were pondering the fate of the nascent library system.

Today's societal changes are likewise causing some of us <u>to consider the same thing, although in ways</u> <u>that medieval readers could never have imagined.</u> Have we progressed from clay tablets to paperbacks

10

only to trade our paperbacks in for microchips?

10. (F) NO CHANGE
   (G) to consider the same thing, it is in ways that medieval readers could never have imagined.
   (H) to have consideration of the same thing, although it is in ways that medieval readers could never have imagined.
   (J) to consider the same thing, although in ways that medieval readers will never be able to imagine.

Liberal Arts Education

The number of liberal arts colleges in the United States <u>steady increased</u> throughout the twentieth

15

century as private universities, state universities, and community colleges all sought to give their

undergraduates a broad education.

15. (A) NO CHANGE
   (B) steadily increased
   (C) increased in a steady fashion
   (D) increased in a steadily fashion

The Mystery of Stonehenge

On Salisbury Plain in England, west of the town of Amesbury, stands a strange and mysterious

<u>artifact of the distant past: Stonehenge.</u> These stone monoliths stand as a silent testimony to an

22

ancient people.

22. (F) NO CHANGE
   (G) artifact of the distant past Stonehenge
   (H) artifact, of the distant past, Stonehenge
   (J) artifact of the distant past; Stonehenge

Frankenstein

The continued popularity of the story is also evidenced by the numerous films that have been based

on it. <u>Some versions like *Young Frankenstein*</u> provide a humorous retelling of the story: other versions,
                              39
like the most recent *Mary Shelley's Frankenstein*, attempt to be faithful to the original.

39. (A) NO CHANGE
    (B) Some versions, like *Young Frankenstein*
    (C) Some versions, like, *Young Frankenstein,*
    (D) Some versions, like *Young Frankenstein,*

Reading

Humanities

3. The author uses which of the following methods to develop the second paragraph (lines 10–45)?

    (A) A series of anecdotes depicting Cameron's energy and unconventionality
    (B) A presentation of factual data demonstrating Cameron's importance in the history of photography
    (C) A critique of Cameron's early work
    (D) A chronological account of Cameron's background and artistic growth

7. The author cites the opinions of an art critic and a "celebrated portrait painter" (lines 51–56) in order to:

    (A) illustrate the significance of Cameron's artistic accomplishments.
    (B) emphasize Victorian critics' preference for Cameron's allegorical work.
    (C) detail the envy Cameron's peers felt toward her.
    (D) counter the negative assessments of Cameron's work by more recent critics.

Natural Science

12. The main function of the fourth paragraph (lines 45–55) in relation to the passage as a whole is to indicate that:

    (F) the Viking program was unsuccessful due to poor selection of landing sites.
    (G) the results of the Viking program do not necessarily prove that Mars is devoid of life.
    (H) the detection of life on Mars was not a primary objective of the Viking program.
    (J) scientists were not expecting to discover life on the Martian plains.

17. The researchers' argument that life may exist in Martian rocks rests on the idea that:

    (A) life evolved in the same way on two different planets.
    (B) organisms may adopt identical survival strategies in similar environments.
    (C) life developed in the form of a blue-green algae on Mars.
    (D) organisms that survived in Antarctica could survive on Mars.

Preview Quiz

1. If $\left(\frac{1}{2} + \frac{1}{6}\right) - \left(\frac{1}{12} + \frac{1}{3}\right)$ is calculated and the result is reduced to simplest terms, what is the numerator of this fraction?

   (A) 1
   (B) 2
   (C) 3
   (D) 4
   (E) 5

2. From 1970 to 1980, the population of City Q increased by 20 percent. From 1980 to 1990, the population increased by 30 percent. What was the combined percent increase for the period 1970–1990?

   (F) 25%
   (G) 26%
   (H) 36%
   (J) 50%
   (K) 56%

3. Which of the following is the solution statement for the inequality $3 < 4x - 5$?

   (A) $x > -2$
   (B) $x > \frac{1}{2}$
   (C) $2 < x$
   (D) $x < \frac{1}{2}$
   (E) $x < 2$

4. If $a(x) = \sqrt{x^2 + 7}$ and $b(x) = x^3 - 7$, then what is the value of $\frac{a(3)}{b(2)}$?

   (F) $\frac{\sqrt{11}}{20}$
   (G) $\frac{1}{4}$
   (H) $\sqrt{11}$
   (J) 4
   (K) $4\sqrt{11}$

5. A well-known fiction magazine pays writers for articles at a rate of $0.35 per word for the first 500 words and $0.25 per word for each word over 500 words. If the magazine paid $1,050 for a set of three articles, each of which had exactly the same number of words, how many words long was any one of the articles?

   (A) 1,000
   (B) 1,200
   (C) 2,400
   (D) 3,600
   (E) 4,000

Session Objectives

Quarter 2—13 SmartPoints

Ratios—2 SmartPoints

- Set up ratios.
- Use ratio charts to solve problems about proportions.

Averages—2 SmartPoints

- Apply the average formula and find the mean, median, and mode of a set of numbers.

Percents—2 SmartPoints

- Apply the percent formula or Pick Numbers to solve a percent problem.

Variable Manipulation—7 SmartPoints

- Solve an inequality for an unknown variable and know when to change the inequality sign.
- Solve an absolute value equation for an unknown.
- Manipulate number lines.

Quarter 3—14 SmartPoints

Operations—3 SmartPoints

- Multiply and divide exponents without a calculator.
- Rationalize a radical.
- Solve a logarithm.

Probability, Proportions, and Rates—6 SmartPoints

- Find the probability of compound events.
- Solve problems that involve the relationships among distance, rate, and time.

Patterns, Logic, and Data—3 SmartPoints

- Distinguish between arithmetic and geometric sequences and solve for the nth term of each.
- Apply logic to answer math questions.
- Differentiate between permutations and combinations and use the appropriate calculator functions or equations.
- Combine matrices.

Trigonometry—2 SmartPoints

- Use basic trig functions, such as sine, cosine, and tangent.

Quarter 4—23 SmartPoints

Figure Interpretation—12 SmartPoints

- Scan and interpret figures to interpret variables and patterns.

Patterns—11 SmartPoints

- Apply the Kaplan Method for ACT Science to Patterns questions.

2 SmartPoints	Ratios
2 SmartPoints	Averages
2 SmartPoints	Percents
7 SmartPoints	Variable Manipulation

Ratios: 2 SmartPoints

A.   Ratios can be written $x{:}y$ or $\frac{x}{y}$.

B.   Always determine if you have been given a part-to-part or a part-to-whole ratio before you perform ratio calculations.

If there are 3 boys and 5 girls in a class, what is the ratio of

boys to girls? _____

girls to boys? _____

boys to students? _____

C.   With only a ratio, you cannot find the actual total, but you can find its multiples. With a ratio and one number, you can find the total. If the ratio of dogs to cats in a pet store is 2:5 and there are 10 dogs, how many pets are there? _____

D.   To combine ratios, give them a common term. The ratio of a to b is 3 to 4 and the ratio of b to c is 3 to 5. What is the ratio of a to c?

a	:	b	:	c
3	:	4	:	
		3	:	5
___	:	___		
	:	___	:	___
___	:		:	___

E.   A proportion is a set of two equal ratios.

)) REMEMBER
If you aren't sure how to set up a ratio problem, try a Kaplan Strategy, like Backsolving.

1. In a certain string ensemble, the ratio of men to women is 5:3. If there is a total of 24 people in the ensemble, how many women are there?

    (A) 12
    (B) 11
    (C) 10
    (D) 9
    (E) 8

2. What value of x solves the following proportion?

$$\frac{2}{9} = \frac{x}{15}$$

(F) $2\frac{2}{5}$

(G) 3

(H) $3\frac{1}{3}$

(J) $4\frac{1}{3}$

(K) $5\frac{1}{2}$

» REMEMBER
When you see fractions set equal to each other, think "cross multiply."

Averages: 2 SmartPoints

A. The average (or arithmetic mean) formula of a set of terms is:

_____

What is the average of 3, 6, and 18?

_____

How else can you write the average formula?

_____

_____

B. The median of a set of numbers is: _____

What is the median of {4, 17, $\frac{1}{2}$, 8, 12.5}? _____

C. The mode is the number that appears most often. Not all sets of numbers have a mode.

What is the mode of {2, 2, 2, 3, 3, 4}? _____

» REMEMBER
Backsolving works well on many averages problems.

3. Randy scored 150, 195, and 160 in 3 bowling games. What should she score on her next bowling game if she wants to have an average score of exactly 175 for the 4 games?

   (A) 205
   (B) 195
   (C) 185
   (D) 175
   (E) 165

Percents: 2 SmartPoints

A. You should know two important percent formulas for Test Day:

Percent = _____

Percent change = _____

B. Many ACT questions involve percents and percent change.

What percent of 75 is 25? _____

A store increased the price of a $20 sweater to $25. What was the percent increase in the price of the sweater?

_____

---

4. Ernesto is shopping at a store that is having a clearance sale. Everything in the store is 25 percent off. If Ernesto buys a shirt originally priced at $22.00 and a 6 percent sales tax is added, what will be the total price of the shirt?

(F) $29.15
(G) $23.10
(H) $18.66
(J) $17.49
(K) $16.50

» REMEMBER
Don't just combine the percents—that is a sure way to make a careless mistake!

---

5. A certain television set is discounted 20 percent on Monday and then discounted another 25 percent on Tuesday. What is the total percent discount applied to the price of the television on Monday and Tuesday?

(A) 35%
(B) 40%
(C) 45%
(D) 50%
(E) 55%

» REMEMBER
When you Pick Numbers for percent questions, everything should cost $100, all objects should travel at 100 miles per hour, and you should have 100 of any item.

Variable Manipulation: 7 SmartPoints
Inequalities

A. Follow the Cardinal Rule of Inequalities: Perform operations with inequalities just as you would equalities (equations), except when:

_____

_____

---

6. If $8 - 2x > 6$, which of the following describes all of the possible values of x?

   (F) $x < -7$

   (G) $x > -7$

   (H) $x > -2$

   (J) $x < 1$

   (K) $x > 1$

B. The test maker has two consistent ways to make inequalities harder:

_____

_____

_____

_____

Absolute Value

C.   The absolute value of a number is its distance from zero on the
number line. Because distance cannot be negative, absolute value
is always positive or zero.

Number	Absolute Value
7	7
–7	7
−8, 8	8
−N, N	N

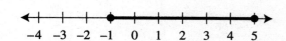

7. If the number line above shows the range of possible values for some
number b, which of the following shows the same possible values
for b?

   (A) $|b - 1| \leq 5$
   (B) $|b - 2| \leq 3$
   (C) $|b - 2| \leq 5$
   (D) $|b - 5| \leq 1$
   (E) $|b - 5| \leq 2$

Quiz

1. The table below displays Jamie's income for each of the years 1989–1994. Which of the years 1990–1994 shows the greatest percent increase over the previous year?

Year	Income
1989	$20,000
1990	$25,000
1991	$30,000
1992	$33,000
1993	$36,000
1994	$44,000

   (A) 1990

   (B) 1991

   (C) 1992

   (D) 1993

   (E) 1994

2. The ratio of girls to boys in a class is 3:5. If the total number of students is 32, how many more boys are there than girls?

   (F) 3

   (G) 5

   (H) 8

   (J) 12

   (K) 20

3. At the end of the season, a team's ratio of wins to losses was 3:5. If there were no ties, what percentage of its games did the team win?

   (A) $33\frac{1}{3}\%$

   (B) $37\frac{1}{2}\%$

   (C) 40%

   (D) 60%

   (E) 75%

4. Which of the following is the solution statement for the inequality $-3 < 4x - 5$?

   (F) $x > -2$

   (G) $x > \frac{1}{2}$

   (H) $x < -2$

   (J) $x < -\frac{1}{2}$

   (K) $x < 2$

5. What is the average of the expressions $2x + 5$, $5x - 6$, and $-4x + 2$?

   (A) $x - \frac{1}{3}$

   (B) $x + \frac{1}{4}$

   (C) $x + \frac{1}{3}$

   (D) $3x + 3$

   (E) $3x - 3$

3 SmartPoints	Operations
6 SmartPoints	Probability, Proportions, and Rates
3 SmartPoints	Patterns, Logic, and Data
2 SmartPoints	Trigonometry

Operations: 3 SmartPoints

A. Before doing calculations, simplify any parts of the expression that involve exponents, radicals, or imaginary numbers.

Exponents

$a^b \cdot a^c = a^{b+c} \Rightarrow 4^3 \cdot 4^2 = $ _____

$\dfrac{a^b}{a^c} = a^{b-c} \Rightarrow \dfrac{4^3}{4^2} = $ _____

$(a^b)^c = a^{bc} \Rightarrow (4^3)^2 = $ _____

$a^0 = 1$

$a^{-b} = \dfrac{1}{a^b} \Rightarrow 4^{-3} = $ _____

$a^{\frac{b}{c}} \Rightarrow \sqrt[c]{a^b} = (\sqrt[c]{a})^b \Rightarrow 4^{\frac{3}{2}} = $ _____

Radicals

$\sqrt{ab} = \sqrt{a} \cdot \sqrt{b} \Rightarrow \sqrt{50} = $ _____

$\sqrt{\dfrac{a}{b}} \cdot \dfrac{\sqrt{a}}{\sqrt{b}} \Rightarrow \sqrt{\dfrac{4}{9}} = $ _____

1. What is the greatest integer smaller than $\sqrt{250}$?

 (A) 15
 (B) 16
 (C) 17
 (D) 19
 (E) 20

B. Perform operations with imaginary numbers just like you would with any other variable, then substitute –1 anywhere you see i^2. All imaginary numbers follow the same pattern of values: _____

C. Logarithms are simply another form of exponent properties.
$\log_3 9 = 2$ means _____

2. If $\log_x 100 = 2$, then $x = ?$

(F) 1
(G) 10
(H) 50
(J) 100
(K) 200

Probability, Proportions, and Rates: 6 SmartPoints

Probability

A. The probability that something will happen is _____

B. The probability that two independent events will both happen is the probability of the first times the probability of the second.

)) REMEMBER
First, find the probability of each event.

---

3. Nancy and Meghan are playing a game that involves flipping a 2-sided coin designated heads and tails and rolling a 6-sided die numbered 1 through 6. What is the probability of getting heads on the coin and an even number on the die?

   (A) $\frac{1}{2}$

   (B) $\frac{1}{4}$

   (C) $\frac{1}{6}$

   (D) $\frac{1}{8}$

   (E) $\frac{1}{12}$

Proportions and Rates

C. A rate can be any something per something.

_____

_____

_____

rate = $\frac{distance}{time}$ can also be written:

_____ or _____

A train travels at a speed of 75 miles per hour. How many minutes does it take to travel 40 miles?

_____

Rate problems are also easily solved by setting up proportions.

)) REMEMBER
Include the units of measurements when setting up proportions to ensure accuracy.

---

4. A car travels 288 miles in 6 hours. At that rate, how many miles will it travel in 8 hours?

   (F)   60

   (G) 216

   (H) 368

   (J)   376

   (K) 384

Patterns, Logic, & Data: 3 SmartPoints

Sequences and Patterns

A. Arithmetic sequences are formed by adding some constant to the previous term.

9, 6, 3, _____

$a_n = a_1 + (n-1)r$

B. Geometric sequences are formed by multiplying each term by some constant.

2, 6, 18, _____

$a_n = a_1(r^{n-1})$

C. Some ACT questions will deal with repeating sequences. On those problems, consider number properties and divisibility rules to solve.

---

5. The first and second terms of a geometric sequence are $2n$ and $4n$, in that order. What is the 500th term of the sequence?

   (A) $2n^{500}$
   (B) $2n^{499}$
   (C) $2^{499}n$
   (D) $2^{500}n$
   (E) n^{500}

» REMEMBER
Picking Numbers can be a great strategy for problems with variables in the question stem and the answer choices.

Geometric Visualization

D. Some questions may not even look like math at first. Read them carefully and be sure you understand the situation before making any calculations.

E. Sketching the situation is often helpful, but keepin in mind the difference between two dimensions and three dimensions.

» REMEMBER
Think about what a three-dimensional figure looks like from other angles.

6. Eighteen identical cubes are put together to form the rectangular solid shown in the diagram below.

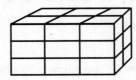

How many cubes have exactly one side that is visible from the outside of the solid?

(F) 0
(G) 1
(H) 2
(J) 3
(K) 4

Permutations and Combinations

F. Permutations are sequences; order matters. Combinations are groups; order doesn't matter.

How many different ways can four people stand in line? ___24___

How many different groups of two people can you make from a group of four people?
___6___

Matrices

G. To combine matrices, multiply the row of the first matrix by the column of the second.

$$\begin{bmatrix} a & b \\ c & d \end{bmatrix} \cdot \begin{bmatrix} e & f \\ g & h \end{bmatrix} = \begin{bmatrix} ae + bg & af + bh \\ ce + dg & cf + dh \end{bmatrix}$$

Trigonometry: 2 SmartPoints

Formulas to Know

$$\text{sine} = \frac{\text{opposite}}{\text{hypotenuse}}$$

$$\text{cosine} = \frac{\text{adjacent}}{\text{hypotenuse}}$$

$$\text{tangent} = \frac{\text{opposite}}{\text{adjacent}}$$

Trignometric Functions

$$\text{cosecant} = \frac{1}{\text{sine}} = \frac{\text{hypotenuse}}{\text{opposite}}$$

$$\text{secant} = \frac{1}{\text{cosine}} = \frac{\text{hypotenuse}}{\text{adjacent}}$$

$$\text{cotangent} = \frac{1}{\text{tangent}} = \frac{\text{adjacent}}{\text{opposite}}$$

Inverse Trigonometric Functions

$$\text{arcsin} = \sin^{-1}\theta$$

$$\text{arcos} = \cos^{-1}\theta$$

$$\text{arctan} = \tan^{-1}\theta$$

Classic Trigonometric Equations

$$\sin^2\theta + \cos^2\theta = 1$$

$$\frac{\sin A}{a} = \frac{\sin B}{b} = \frac{\sin C}{c}$$

A.   Trigonometry is one of the most predictable topics on the ACT Math Test. You're almost guaranteed to see _____four_____ Trigonometry questions on Test Day.

Basic Trig Identities

B. ACT Trig tests three basic concepts: sine, cosine, and tangent. You can remember which Trigonometry function to use on Test Day by using the acronym SOHCAHTOA.

7. To determine the height h of a tree, Roger stands b feet from the base of the tree and measures the angle of elevation from the base of the tree to be θ, as shown in the figure below. Which of the following illustrates the relationship between h and b?

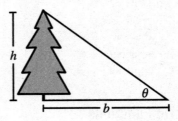

(A) $\sin \theta = \dfrac{h}{b}$

(B) $\sin \theta = \dfrac{b}{h}$

(C) $\sin \theta = \dfrac{b}{b + h}$

(D) $\sin \theta = \dfrac{h}{\sqrt{b^2 + h^2}}$

(E) $\sin \theta = \dfrac{\sqrt{b^2 + h^2}}{b}$

Other Trig Identities

C. You may also see reciprocal and inverse trig functions. Use your calculator to solve these.

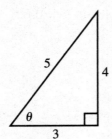

$\theta = $ _____

D. The ACT may measure angles in degrees or radians, which are proportional to each other.

$$\frac{\text{degree measure}}{360} = \frac{\text{radian measure}}{2\pi}$$

E. Some questions will also ask you to understand how degree/radian measures impact a trig ratio's sign. Draw a right triangle in the appropriate quadrant of a coordinate grid to determine whether the ratio is positive or negative.

8. If $0° < \theta < 90°$ and $\cos \theta = \frac{5\sqrt{2}}{8}$ then $\tan \theta = ?$

(F) $\frac{8}{5\sqrt{2}}$

(G) $\frac{\sqrt{7}}{5}$

(H) $\frac{\sqrt{14}}{8}$

(J) $\frac{5}{\sqrt{7}}$

(K) $\frac{8}{\sqrt{14}}$

Quiz

1. What is the value of $(-2)^{-3} + (-3)^{-2}$?

   (A) $-\dfrac{17}{72}$

   (B) $-\dfrac{1}{72}$

   (C) 0

   (D) $\dfrac{1}{72}$

   (E) $\dfrac{17}{72}$

2. When $\dfrac{4}{11}$ is written as a decimal, what is the 100th digit after the decimal point?

   (F) 3

   (G) 4

   (H) 5

   (J) 6

   (K) 7

3. A company is packing boxes of decorative tiles. If each tile weighs 0.23 pounds, approximately how many tiles would it take to fill a box with 100 pounds of tiles?

   (A) 10

   (B) 23

   (C) 230

   (D) 435

   (E) 500

4. Alicia is playing a game in which she draws marbles from a box. There are 50 marbles, numbered 01 through 50. Alicia draws one marble from the box and sets it aside, then draws a second marble. If both marbles have the same units digit, then Alicia wins. If the first marble she draws is numbered 25, what is the probability that Alicia will win on her next draw?

   (F) $\dfrac{1}{50}$

   (G) $\dfrac{1}{25}$

   (H) $\dfrac{2}{25}$

   (J) $\dfrac{4}{49}$

   (K) $\dfrac{1}{10}$

5. The following two logical statements are both true. If the length of side $\overline{QR}$ of regular hexagon A is 6, then the shortest distance from the center to an edge is $3\sqrt{3}$.

   The shortest distance from the center to an edge of regular hexagon A is NOT $3\sqrt{3}$.

   Which of the following must also be true?

   (A) The length of side $\overline{QR}$ is 6.

   (B) The length of side $\overline{QR}$ is NOT 6.

   (C) The length of side $\overline{QR}$ is $3\sqrt{3}$.

   (D) The shortest distance from the center to an edge is 6.

   (E) The shortest distance from the center to an edge is NOT 6.

6. The figure below is one of the triangular glass fragments that Bob collects. Which of the following expressions is the value of Z? (Note: The law of sines states that for a triangle with sides of lengths a, b, and c and opposite angles of measure A, B, and C, respectively, $\frac{\sin A}{a} = \frac{\sin B}{b} = \frac{\sin C}{c}$).

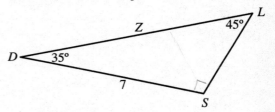

   (F) $\dfrac{7 \sin 35°}{\sin 45°}$

   (G) $\dfrac{7 \sin 35°}{\sin 100°}$

   (H) $\dfrac{7 \sin 45°}{\sin 100°}$

   (J) $\dfrac{7 \sin 100°}{\sin 35°}$

   (K) $\dfrac{7 \sin 100°}{\sin 45°}$

12 SmartPoints	Figure Interpretation
11 SmartPoints	Patterns

Figure Interpretation—12 SmartPoints

A. As in the ACT Reading Test, all the information necessary to answer the questions will be in the passage.

B. The Kaplan Method for ACT Science is closely linked to reading comprehension and active reading.

C. The Kaplan Method for ACT Science

1. Map the passage, identifying and marking the Purpose, Method, and Results of the experiment.

2. Scan figures, identifying variables and patterns.

3. Find support for the answer in the passage.

D. Step 2 of the Kaplan Method for ACT Science will provide the information you need to answer figure interpretation questions.

E. During Step 2 of the Kaplan Method for ACT Science, ask yourself:

_____

_____

_____

F. Don't be intimidated by technical terminology. Usually, you simply need to find the information in the passage.

Passage I

The acceleration of an object at the surface of Earth due to gravity is called *g* and is measured in m/sec². While its standard definition is 9.78 m/sec², *g* actually varies with latitude and altitude.

A physicist wished to study, in detail, variations in *g* due to these factors and so measured the gravitational acceleration of a 5 kg block in a vacuum at various latitudes. She plotted her results in Figure 1 below.

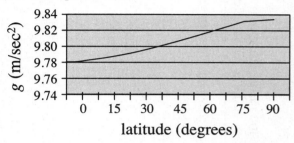

The physicist also wanted to study gravitational acceleration as a function of elevation above sea level at a latitude of 15 degrees. She again measured the gravitational acceleration of a 5 kg block in a vacuum, this time at various altitudes. Her results are shown in Table 1 below.

Table 1	
Elevation above sea level (m)	**Gravitational acceleration (m/sec²)**
0	9.78
250	9.77
500	9.76
750	9.74
1,000	9.72
1,500	9.65
2,000	9.60

What does Figure 1 show?

_____

What are the units of measurement?

_____

What is the dependent variable in Figure 1?

_____

What is the independent variable in Figure 1?

_____

What does Table 1 show?

_____

What is the independent variable in Table 1?

_____

What is the mass of the block?

_____

What is the gravitational acceleration when the block is 500 meters above sea level?

_____

Passage II

Astronomers want to know the effects of atmospheric conditions on the impact of an asteroid-to-Earth collision. The most common hypothesis is that the presence of moisture in Earth's atmosphere significantly reduces the hazardous effects of such a collision. One researcher has decided to create a laboratory model of Earth. The researcher has the ability to control the amount of moisture surrounding the model. The researcher has also created models of asteroids at various sizes. The researcher will use a collision indicator (see Table 1 below) based on the Torino scale to measure the results of two experiments.

Table 1	
Collision rating (Torinos)	**Collision indicator**
0 to 0.9	A collision capable of little destruction
1 to 3.9	A collision capable of localized destruction
4 to 6.9	A collision capable of regional destruction
7 to 10	A collision capable of global catastrophe

Experiment 1

The researcher simulated collisions on the Earth model with asteroid models equivalent to mass ranging from 100,000 kg to 1,000,000 kg. The controlled moisture level of the model Earth's atmosphere was 86%. The effects of the collisions were recorded and rated according to the collision indicator.

Experiment 2

The researcher simulated collisions on the Earth model with asteroid models equivalent to the same mass as in Experiment 1. The controlled moisture level of the model Earth's atmosphere in this experiment was 12%. The effects of the collisions were recorded and rated according to the collision indicator. The results of both experiments are shown in Figure 1.

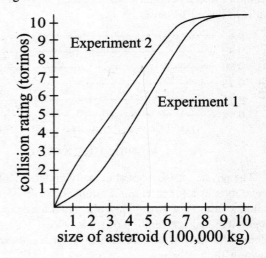

1. If the asteroid that killed the dinosaurs rated 9 Torinos on the collision indicator, and if Earth's atmospheric moisture level at that time was approximately 86 percent, then how large was the asteroid that impacted Earth, according to this research?

   (A) 200,000 kg
   (B) 500,000 kg
   (C) 700,000 kg
   (D) 1,000,000 kg

)) **REMEMBER**
Find support for the answer in the passage. Where is the information you need?

2. In a simulated asteroid-to-Earth collision, a 400,000 kg asteroid received a collision rating of 4. The amount of moisture in the atmosphere was most likely closest to:

(F) 0%

(G) 12%

(H) 86%

(J) 100%

)) **REMEMBER**
Draw lines on the graph with your pencil and use a second pencil to keep them straight. Sometimes, the figures will be small, and eyeballing the answer won't cut it.

3. What would be the result, according to the Torino scale, of a 500,000 kg asteroid colliding with Earth at an atmospheric moisture level of 12 percent?

(A) A collision capable of little destruction

(B) A collision capable of localized destruction

(C) A collision capable of regional destruction

(D) A collision capable of global catastrophe

›› REMEMBER
More difficult questions will often require you to combine information from two different figures.

Passage III

Physicists and medical technicians can detect the amount of radiation emitted by unstable isotopes as they spontaneously decay into other elements. The half-life of these radioactive isotopes is the amount of time necessary for one-half of the initial number of their nuclei to decay. The decay curves of two radioactive thorium isotopes ($^{231}_{90}$Th and $^{234}_{90}$Th) are graphed below as functions of the ratio of N, the number of nuclei remaining after a given time period, to N_0, the initial number of nuclei. The results are recorded in Figure 1 and Figure 2 below.

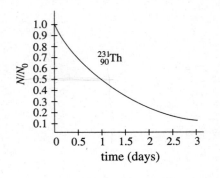 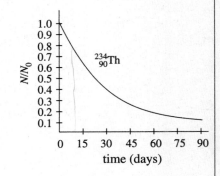

In order to study the correlation between isotope decay and radiation, the technicians also measured and recorded the amount of radiation emitted (measured in mega electron volts) as 1 g samples of the two isotopes decayed. The results are recorded in Figure 3.

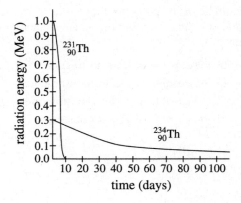

4. According to Figure 1, the half-life of $^{231}_{90}$Th is approximately:

    (F) 1 day.

    (G) 2.5 days.

    (H) 25 days.

    (J) 58 days.

5. On the basis of the data presented in Figure 3, how many MeV of radiation per day would one predict should be released from a 1-g sample of $^{234}_{90}$Th after 60 days?

    (A) 1.0 MeV
    (B) 0.7 MeV
    (C) 0.4 MeV
    (D) 0.1 MeV

6. If a decaying sample of $^{234}_{90}$Th that initially weighed 1 g is emitting 0.2 MeV of radiation per day, what is the ratio of its remaining nuclei to its initial number of nuclei?

    (F) 0.4
    (G) 0.55
    (H) 0.8
    (J) 1.0

» REMEMBER
If you don't recall reading anything about math terms or formulas, remember that the answer is in the figures and the passage.

Passage IV

Blue-green algae are actually not algae at all but photosynthesizing bacteria. They are often blue or green in color but are common in other colors as well, especially pink and red. In large numbers, they appear as a thick, slimy coating on aquatic rocks and plants. They are capable of smothering plants and may release toxins that are harmful to fish. Some varieties of red tide are caused by blue-green algae.

Like other bacteria, blue-green algae reproduce through a process wherein one cell divides completely to form two distinct cells. The average time for a colony of blue-green algae to divide and for its population to double is called the generation time. Table 1 shows the *generation time* for different varieties of blue-green algae in the presence of different nutrients and at differing temperatures.

Table 1			
Algae	**Growth medium**	**Temp. (°C)**	**Generation time (mins)**
Aphanothece gelatinosa	Na_3PO_4	30	42
Arthrospira fusiformis	K_4SiO_4	30	103
Chroococcus submarinus	NH_4NO_4	30	231
Dactylococcopsis salina	Na_3PO_4	38	259
Geitlerinema carotinosum	NH_4NO_4	38	39
Gloeothece rupestris	K_4SiO_4	38	61
Kalagnymene spiralis	Na_3PO_4	38	131
Merismopedia glauca	NH_4NO_4	38	751
Rhabdoderma rubrum	NH_4NO_4	38	225
Synechococcus unigames	K_4SiO_4	30	321
Synechococcus leopoliensis	NA_3PO_4	30	458
Thermosynechthoccus valcanitis	K_4SiO_4	38	56

Because blue-green algae cannot travel in search of necessary nutrients, the population density of a colony also affects its generation time. Figure 1 shows the generation time of a colony of *Dactylococcopsis salina* as a function of its population per square centimeter at 38°C.

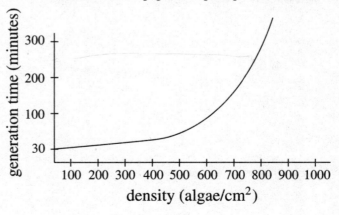

7. On the basis of the data presented in Table 1, if *Arthrospira fusiformis* was placed in a petri dish containing potassium silicate (K_4SiO_4) at 30°C, its generation time would most likely be:

   (A) less than 50 min.
   (B) between 51 and 70 min.
   (C) between 71 and 90 min.
   (D) between 91 and 110 min.

8. If a colony of *Dactylococcopsis salina* covered a pond floor with a density of 400 algae per square centimeter, what would you expect its generation time to be?

   (F) About 20 min
   (G) About 50 min
   (H) About 100 min
   (J) About 200 min

9. Based on the data recorded in Table 1, which of the following blue-green algae growing in the presence of ammonium nitrate (NH_4NO_4) took the longest amount of time to double its population?

   (A) *Merismopedia glauca*
   (B) *Geitlerinema carotinosum*
   (C) *Croococcus submarinus*
   (D) *Rabdoderma rubrum*

10. Twelve tanks of water were enriched with sodium phosphate (Na_3PO_4). One of the varieties of blue-green algae from Table 1 was introduced into each tank, and the water was heated to 38°C. Which of the following algae would be predicted to take closest to 2 hours to double its population?

    (F) *Geitlerinema carotinosum*
    (G) *Kalagnymene spiralis*
    (H) *Rhabdoderma rubrum*
    (J) *Dactylococcopsis salina*

11. According to the information in Figure 1, what was the approximate population density, in algae/cm^2, of the colony of *Dactylococcopsis salina* that was studied in Table 1?

    (A) 100
    (B) 300
    (C) 800
    (D) 1,000

Patterns—11 SmartPoints

A.   Patterns questions test your knowledge of the passage in predictable ways.

Some will ask you to identify general trends in the data. Examples include:

_____

_____

_____

Some will ask you to predict what will happen for data points beyond a graph or a table.

Other questions will introduce a new variable and ask you to determine how it will behave based on the patterns in the passage.

You may also be asked to find an equation that describes the relationship between the variables in a table.

B.   When Patterns questions ask you to find values for points that aren't shown, expect that trends will continue as indicated by the tables and figures.

C.   Regardless of the question type, the Kaplan Method for ACT Science will be the same:

1. **Map** the passage, identifying and marking the Purpose, Method, and Results of the experiment.

2. **Scan** figures, identifying variables and patterns.

3. **Find support** for the answer in the passage.

D.   When scanning figures, ask yourself:

_____

_____

E.   Patterns questions are similar to the Reading section's Inference questions. Though the information is not explicitly stated, the correct answer will be directly supported by facts from the passage.

Passage V

Most natural substances can occur in any of three *phases* (states of matter): solid, liquid, or gas. The molecular, ionic, and atomic structures of a substance determine the conditions under which it will experience a phase change. A phase diagram indicates the phases of a substance under different conditions of temperature and pressure. The conditions of a transition occur between adjacent phases, with two or more phases coexisting, and are represented by solid lines. Figure 1 below shows the phase diagram for water, and Figure 2 shows the phase diagram for carbon dioxide.

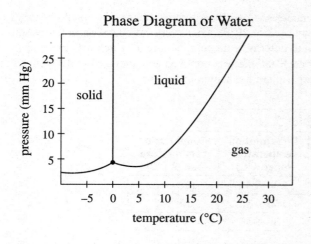

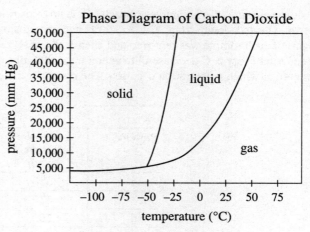

Based on Figure 1, how does water transition from solid to liquid at a pressure greater than 5 mm Hg?

Greater than zero

According to Figure 1, liquid transitions to gas when (circle one):
Pressure: increases/decreases
Temperature: increases/decreases

Based on Figure 2, carbon dioxide exists in liquid phase between what two temperatures?

_−50 to 50_

Passage VI

Many proteins undergo denaturation upon heating. A denatured protein is unfolded and can no longer perform its normal biological functions. Denaturation usually occurs over a temperature range. Some proteins can fold back (renature) into their original conformation when the temperature is decreased. A series of experiments was performed to determine the denaturation and renaturation behavior of three different proteins.

Experiment 1

Fifteen separate 15-mL samples of each of the proteins ribonuclease (Rase), carboxypeptidase (Case), and hexokinase (Hase) were heated slowly from 20°C to 160°C and cooled slowly back to 20°C. After every 5°C increase in temperature, 0.002 mL of each sample was removed and chemically analyzed to determine the temperature at which denaturation occurred. After every 5°C decrease in temperature, 0.002 mL of each sample was removed and analyzed to determine the temperature at which renaturation occurred. The results of the experiment are shown in Table 1.

Table 1			
Protein	Molecular weight (amu)	Denaturation temperature range (°C)	Renaturation temperature range (°C)
Rase	856	135–145	110–135
Case	672	150–155	60–140
Hase	759	85–95	—

Experiment 2

Solubility is also a measure of protein denaturation. A protein can be considered fully denatured when its solubility drops to zero. Each 0.002 mL sample of ribonuclease, carboxypeptidase, and hexokinase was dissolved in 10 mL of ethyl alcohol, and its solubility was measured. The solubility measurements were taken in 5°C increments as the samples were heated from 20°C to 160°C and again as they were cooled from 160°C to 20°C. The results are shown in Figure 1 and Figure 2.

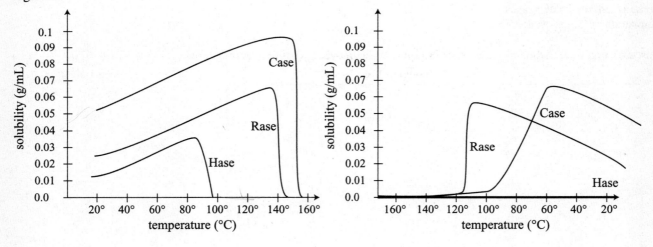

12. If the protein Rase were heated to 150°C and then cooled to 40°C, which of the following plots would its solubility curve most likely resemble?

F.

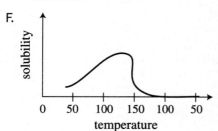

G.

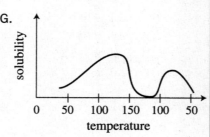

H.

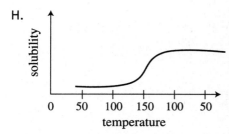

J.

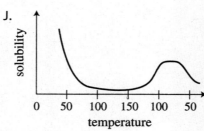

13. According to Figures 1 and 2, what would most likely be the solubility of Case in 10 mL of ethyl alcohol at 0°C?

(A) 0.055 g/mL

(B) 0.045 g/mL

(C) 0.015 g/mL

(D) 0.0 g/mL

⟩⟩ REMEMBER
Make sure you understand the patterns in the data before you make a prediction.

)) REMEMBER
When you're extending a line on a graph, be careful to continue its shape and direction.

14. A fourth protein, ovalbumin, denaturates between 115°C and 130°C and renaturates between 70°C and 100°C. According to Figure 1, its solubility curve would:

(F) peak at 85°C.

(G) peak at 95°C.

(H) peak at 105°C.

(J) peak at 115°C.

Passage VII

A high school physics class wished to determine the best way of calculating D, a snowmobile's *total braking distance*. They defined D as the total distance a snowmobile requires to stop from the moment the driver first sees a "stop" signal until the snowmobile comes to a complete stop.

The class used two methods. In Method 1, S is the distance traveled before the driver could begin the braking process when a driver reaction time of 0.8 sec was assumed, and T is the average distance traveled after the brakes are applied. Method 2 assumes that D is simply the initial speed in ft/sec times 2 sec. Table 1 shows the results of both methods with various initial speeds.

Table 1

Initial speed (mi/hr)	Initial speed (ft/sec)	Method 1			Method 2
		S (ft)	T (ft)	D (ft)	D (ft)
25	37	30	28	58	74
35	51	41	75	116	102
45	66	53	144	197	132
55	81	65	245	310	162

The class then plotted the D they calculated through Method 1 and the D they calculated through Method 2. The results are shown in Figure 1.

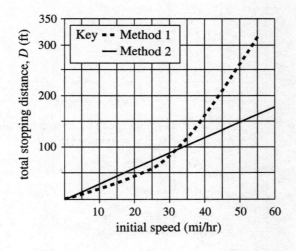

15. In Method 1, D can be calculated using the formula:

    (A) $S + T$

    (B) $S - T$

    (C) $\dfrac{S}{T}$

    (D) ST

)) **REMEMBER**
Some Patterns questions will introduce new variables that behave similarly to the patterns in the passage.

16. According to either Table 1 or Figure 1, if a snowmobile is traveling at an initial speed of 75 mi/hr, what will its D be according to Method 2?

   (F)   Less than 100 ft
   (G)   Between 105 and 200 ft
   (H)   Between 205 and 300 ft
   (J)   Greater than 300 ft

17. S for an initial speed of 25 mi/hr, compared to S for an initial speed of 55 mi/hr, is approximately:

   (A) $\frac{1}{4}$ as large.
   (B) $\frac{1}{2}$ as large.
   (C)   2 times as large.
   (D)   4 times as large.

Quiz

Passage I

A conductor's resistance (R) is defined as the extent to which it opposes *conductivity* (the flow of electricity). Resistance depends not only on the conductor's resistivity (ρ) but also on the conductor's length (L) and cross-sectional area (A). The resistivity of a conductor is a physical property of the material and varies with temperature.

A research team designing a new appliance was researching the best type of wire to use in a particular circuit. The most important consideration was the wire's resistance. The team studied the resistance of wires made from four metals: gold (Au), aluminum (Al), tungsten (W), and iron (Fe). Two lengths and two *gauges* (diameters) of each type of wire were tested at 20°C. The results are recorded in Table 1.

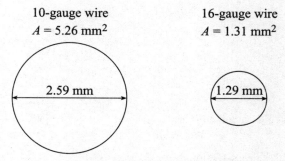

10-gauge wire
$A = 5.26$ mm^2

2.59 mm

16-gauge wire
$A = 1.31$ mm^2

1.29 mm

Note: area of circle = πr^2

Table 1				
Material	**Resistivity (ρ)**	**Length (cm)**	**Cross-sectional area (mm^2)**	**Resistance (R)**
Au	2.44	1.0	5.26	46.4
Au	2.44	1.0	1.31	186.0
Au	2.44	2.0	5.26	92.8
Au	2.44	2.0	1.31	372.0
Al	2.83	1.0	5.26	53.8
Al	2.83	1.0	1.31	216.0
Al	2.83	2.0	5.26	107.6
Al	2.83	2.0	1.31	432.0
W	5.51	1.0	5.26	105.0
W	5.51	1.0	1.31	421.0
W	5.51	2.0	5.26	210.0
W	5.51	2.0	1.31	842.0
Fe	10.00	1.0	5.26	190.0
Fe	10.00	1.0	1.31	764.0
Fe	10.00	2.0	5.26	380.0
Fe	10.00	2.0	1.31	1,528.0

1. Of the wires tested, resistance increases for any given material as which parameter is decreased?

   (A) Length
   (B) Cross-sectional area
   (C) Resistivity
   (D) Gauge

2. Given the data in Table 1, which of the following best expresses resistance in terms of resistivity (ρ), cross-sectional area (A), and length (L)?

   (F) $\dfrac{\rho A}{L}$

   (G) $\dfrac{\rho L}{A}$

   (H) ρAL

   (J) $\dfrac{AL}{\rho}$

3. Which of the following wires would have the highest resistance?

   (A) A 1 cm aluminum wire with a cross-sectional area of 3.31 mm^2
   (B) A 2 cm aluminum wire with a cross-sectional area of 3.31 mm^2
   (C) A 1 cm tungsten wire with a cross-sectional area of 0.66 mm^2
   (D) A 2 cm tungsten wire with a cross-sectional area of 0.66 mm^2

4. According to the information given, which of the following statements is (are) correct?

   (I) 10-gauge wire has a larger diameter than 16-gauge wire.
   (II) Gold has a higher resistivity than tungsten.
   (III) Aluminum conducts electricity better than iron.

   (F) I only
   (G) II only
   (H) III only
   (J) I and III only

5. Which of the following graphs best represents the relationship between the resistivity of a tungsten wire and its length?

   (A)
   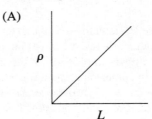

   (B)
   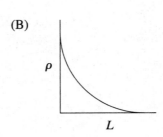

   (C)
   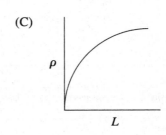

   (D)
   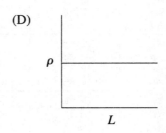

Session 3 Homework

Math	Basic Assignment	Additional Practice	In the Appendix
Ratios, Averages, Percents	Questions 1–10	Questions 11–12	Pages 515–518
Exponents, Rates, Sequences, & Trig	Questions 1–10	Questions 11–15	Pages 517, 531–533, 537–539
Science	**Basic Assignment**	**Additional Practice**	
Patterns & Figure Interpretation	Passages I–III Questions 1–16	Passages IV–V Questions 17–27	

HOMEWORK

Quarter 2

Required

1. Jay drove 300 miles in 5 hours of actual driving time. By driving an average of 10 miles per hour slower, Jay would have added how many hours of actual driving time?

   (A) 1
   (B) 3
   (C) 14
   (D) 23
   (E) 114

2. On Monday, a shirt was priced at $80.00. On Wednesday, the shirt was put on sale for 25 percent off its original price. On Saturday, the price was further reduced by 20 percent and marked FINAL. What was the FINAL price of the shirt?

   (F) $32.00
   (G) $36.00
   (H) $40.00
   (J) $44.00
   (K) $48.00

3. In a company of 50 people, the 30 males have an average age of 42 and the 20 females have an average age of 37. To the nearest year, what is the average age of the company's workforce?

   (A) 39
   (B) 40
   (C) 41
   (D) 42
   (E) 43

4. The points A, B, C, D, and E are located on a number line in that order. The length of AB is twice the length of BC, the length of BC is twice the length of CD, and the length of CD is twice the length of DE. If the length of AE is 45, what is the length of BD?

   (F) 3
   (G) 6
   (H) 12
   (J) 18
   (K) 21

5. A survey asked students in a school if they were in favor of having a dress code. Of the students who responded, 40 percent were in favor, 35 percent were not in favor, and 40 students were undecided. How many students were in favor of having a dress code?

   (A) 30
   (B) 40
   (C) 64
   (D) 80
   (E) 160

6. Franklin leaves school and rides his bike east at a constant rate. At the same time, Mariah leaves the same school and bikes west at a rate that is 3 miles per hour faster than Franklin is riding. At the end of 2 hours, the two bikes are 54 miles apart. How many miles did Mariah ride?

   (F) 24
   (G) 26
   (H) 28
   (J) 30
   (K) 32

7. A number line contains points W, X, Y, and Z. Point X is between points W and Y. Point Z is between Y and X. Which of the following inequalities must be true?

   (A) $XY < WX$
   (B) $XZ < WX$
   (C) $XZ < YZ$
   (D) $YZ < WX$
   (E) $YZ < XY$

8. Which of the following is a solution to $|x^2 - 8| - 4 = 0$

   (F) 2
   (G) $\sqrt{3}$
   (H) 2, $-\sqrt{3}$
   (J) 4, $-\sqrt{3}$
   (K) $3\sqrt{2}$

9. Tom uses 10 ounces of chocolate chips to make a batch of 24 cookies. How many ounces of chocolate chips will Tom need for 96 cookies?

   (A) 10
   (B) 20
   (C) 30
   (D) 40
   (E) 50

10. If 125 percent of a number is 470, what is 50 percent of the number?

    (F) 168
    (G) 188
    (H) 208
    (J) 228
    (K) 248

Recommended

11. The temperature, t, in degrees Fahrenheit, in Summerville on an August day satisfies the inequality, $|t - 94| \leq 10$. Which of the following temperatures, in degrees Fahrenheit, is NOT in this range?

    (A) 82
    (B) 90
    (C) 96
    (D) 98
    (E) 104

12. Mary's goal is to collect 200 cans of food during a food drive. During her first four days, she averaged 10 cans per day. With 10 days remaining, Mary must average how many cans per day to meet her goal?

    (F) 12
    (G) 14
    (H) 16
    (J) 18
    (K) 20

Quarter 3

Required

1. Which of the following is equal to $\dfrac{(3.0 \times 10^4)(8.0 \times 10^9)}{1.2 \times 10^6}$?

   (A) 2.0×10^6
   (B) 2.0×10^7
   (C) 2.0×10^8
   (D) 2.0×10^{30}
   (E) 2.0×10^{31}

2. What is the value of $9^{-\frac{3}{2}}$?

   (F) -27
   (G) $-13\frac{1}{2}$
   (H) $\frac{-1}{27}$
   (J) $\frac{1}{27}$
   (K) $13\frac{1}{2}$

3. $(\sqrt{8} + \sqrt{6})(\sqrt{8} - \sqrt{6}) = ?$

   (A) 1
   (B) 2
   (C) $\sqrt{7}$
   (D) $\sqrt{14}$
   (E) 7

4. Which of the following is equivalent to $\sqrt{0.0016}$?

   (F) 0.04
   (G) 0.08
   (H) 0.004
   (J) 0.0004
   (K) 0.0008

5. Jan types at an average rate of 12 pages per hour. At that rate, how long will it take Jan to type 100 pages?

    (A) 8 hours and 3 minutes
    (B) 8 hours and 15 minutes
    (C) 8 hours and 20 minutes
    (D) 8 hours and 30 minutes
    (E) 8 hours and 33 minutes

6. Jamal has a suitcase that contains 10 white socks. He wants to add enough black socks so that the probability of randomly selecting a white sock is $\frac{1}{5}$. How many black socks should Jamal add to the suitcase?

    (F) 30
    (G) 35
    (H) 40
    (J) 45
    (K) 50

7. In the geometric sequence 3, 12, r, 192, . . . what is the value of r, the third term?

    (A) 24
    (B) 36
    (C) 48
    (D) 60
    (E) 96

8. In the figure below, point C is the center of the circle and D is 37°. Which of the following expresses the length of the radius?

    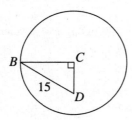

    (F) 15 sin 53°
    (G) 15 sin 37°
    (H) 15 cos 37°
    (J) 15 tan 53°
    (K) 15 tan 37°

9. If $0° < \theta < 90°$ and $\sin \theta = \dfrac{\sqrt{11}}{2\sqrt{3}}$, then what is the value of $\cos \theta$?

    (A) $\dfrac{1}{2\sqrt{3}}$

    (B) $\dfrac{1}{\sqrt{11}}$

    (C) $\dfrac{2\sqrt{3}}{\sqrt{11}}$

    (D) $2\sqrt{3}$

    (E) $\sqrt{11}$

10. Elizabeth wants to determine the height of a flagpole. She stands 100 feet from the base of the flagpole and measures the angle of elevation to be 40°, as shown in the figure below. Which of the following is the best approximation of the height of the flagpole, in feet?

    (Note: sin 40° ≈ 0.643
                cos 40° ≈ 0.766
                tan 40° ≈ 0.839)

    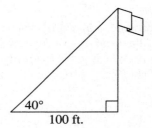

    (F) 40
    (G) 50
    (H) 64
    (J) 77
    (K) 84

Recommended

11. What is the value of $(5\sqrt{3})^2$?

    (A) 15
    (B) $10\sqrt{3}$
    (C) $25\sqrt{3}$
    (D) 30
    (E) 75

12. What 3 numbers should be placed in the blanks below so that the difference between consecutive numbers is the same?

12, ___ , ___ , ___ , 32

(F) 16, 22, 28
(G) 17, 22, 27
(H) 20, 22, 30
(J) 22, 24, 30
(K) 23, 29, 31

13. Assume these three statements are true:

All cats in Cooperville are gray.
Cat A is gray.
Cat B is in Cooperville.

Which of the following statements must also be true, based on the statements above?

(A) Cat A is in Cooperville.
(B) Cat A is not in Cooperville.
(C) Cat B is gray.
(D) Cat B is not gray.
(E) Cat B is black.

14. The triangles in the figure below share one side. Given that $\sin (a + b) = \sin a \cos b + \sin b \cos a$ for all a and b, what is the value of $\sin (x + y)$?

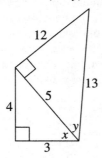

(F) $\dfrac{46}{65}$
(G) $\dfrac{48}{65}$
(H) $\dfrac{51}{65}$
(J) $\dfrac{56}{65}$
(K) $\dfrac{65}{56}$

15. In the figure below, ΔPQR is a right triangle, and p, q, and r represent the lengths, in units, of the sides of the triangle. What is the cosecant of $\angle Q$?

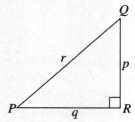

(A) $\dfrac{p}{q}$
(B) $\dfrac{p}{r}$
(C) $\dfrac{q}{p}$
(D) $\dfrac{q}{r}$
(E) $\dfrac{r}{q}$

Quarter 4

Required

Passage I

The utilization and replenishment of Earth's carbon supply is a cyclical process involving all living matter. This cycle is shown in Figure 1 below.

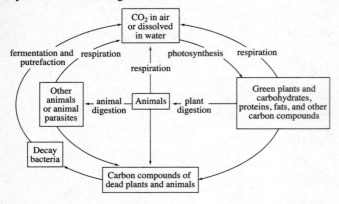

1. Which of the following statements is (are) consistent with the carbon cycle as presented in the diagram?

   I. A non-plant-eating animal does not participate in the carbon cycle.

   II. Both plant and animal respiration contribute CO_2 to Earth's atmosphere.

   III. All CO_2 is released into the air by respiration.

   (A) I only
   (B) II only
   (C) I and II only
   (D) II and III only

2. A direct source of CO_2 in the atmosphere is:

   (F) the fermentation of green-plant carbohydrates.
   (G) the photosynthesis of tropical plants.
   (H) the digestion of plant matter by animals.
   (J) the respiration of animal parasites.

3. Which of the following best describes the relationship between animal respiration and photosynthesis?

   (A) Respiration and photosynthesis serve the same function in the carbon cycle.
   (B) Animal respiration provides vital gases for green plants.
   (C) Animal respiration prohibits photosynthesis.
   (D) There is no relationship between respiration and photosynthesis.

4. The elimination of which of the following would likely cause Earth's carbon cycle to come to a complete halt?

   (F) Green plants
   (G) Animals
   (H) Animal digestion
   (J) Decay bacteria

5. What effect would a sudden drop in the amount of Earth's decay bacteria have on the amount of carbon dioxide in the atmosphere?

   (A) The CO_2 level would drop to a life-threatening level since the bacteria are the sole source of CO_2.
   (B) The CO_2 level would rise because the bacteria usually consume CO_2.
   (C) The CO_2 level might decrease slightly, but there are other sources of CO_2.
   (D) The CO_2 level would increase slightly due to an imbalance in the carbon cycle.

Passage II

A solution is defined as a mixture of two or more substances. The *solvent* is the liquid into which the *solute*, usually a solid or gas, is dissolved.

Solutions that can conduct an electrical current are called *electrolytes*. The current is conducted through an electrolyte by the solute. Solutions that cannot conduct an electric current are called *nonelectrolytes*. The voltage of a current traveling through a solution can be measured by a device called a voltameter. A simple circuit—consisting of a battery, solution, light emitting diode (LED), and voltameter—is diagrammed below in Figure 1.

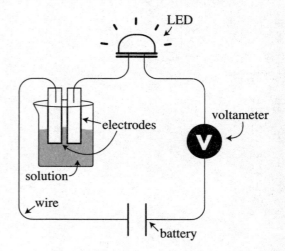

Researchers conducted the following experiments to determine whether increasing the solute in a solution or increasing the temperature of the solution would increase the solution's conductivity.

Experiment 1

Researchers mixed six solutions, each containing 10.0 grams (g) of solute dissolved in 100 milliliters (mL) of water at 35°C. The water was also tested for conductivity without the addition of solute. The results of Experiment 1 are shown in Table 1.

Table 1	
Solute	Voltameter reading (volts)
Water (H_2O)	0.0
Sodium chloride (NaCl)	5.4
Glucose ($C_{12}H_{22}O_{11}$)	0.0
Potassium fluoride (KF)	5.1
Magnesium chloride ($MgCl_2$)	1.6
Acetic acid ($HC_2H_3O_2$)	1.9

Experiment 2

The researchers repeated Experiment 1, this time tripling the amount of solute in each solution to 30.0 g. The solute was again dissolved in 100 mL of water at 35°C. The results of Experiment 2 are shown in Table 2.

Table 2	
Solute	Voltameter reading (volts)
Water (H_2O)	0.0
Sodium chloride (NaCl)	10.6
Glucose ($C_{12}H_{22}O_{11}$)	0.0
Potassium fluoride (KF)	9.7
Magnesium chloride ($MgCl_2$)	2.6
Acetic acid ($HC_2H_3O_2$)	3.0

Experiment 3

Experiment 2 was repeated with 30.0 g of solute dissolved in 100 mL of water. This time, however, researchers heated the water to 70°C. The results of Experiment 3 are shown in Table 3.

Table 3	
Solute	Voltameter reading (volts)
Water (H_2O)	0.0
Sodium chloride (NaCl)	1.3
Glucose ($C_{12}H_{22}O_{11}$)	0.0
Potassium fluoride (KF)	13.1
Magnesium chloride ($MgCl_2$)	4.0
Acetic acid ($HC_2H_3O_2$)	4.9

6. Increasing the amount of solute in a solution increases the conductivity of the solution in each of the following solutes EXCEPT for:

   (F) NaCl
   (G) $C_{12}H_{22}O_{11}$
   (H) $HC_2H_3O_2$
   (J) $MgCl_2$

7. On the basis of the results of each of the three experiments, which of the following solutions of $MgCl_2$ should conduct the most electricity?

   (A) 10 g in 100 mL of H_2O at 35°C
   (B) 20 g in 100 mL of H_2O at 35°C
   (C) 20 g in 200 mL of H_2O at 35°C
   (D) 30 g in 100 mL of H_2O at 70°C

8. If the researchers had dissolved 30 g of $C_{12}H_{22}O_{11}$ and 30 g of $HC_2H_3O_2$ in 100 mL of H_2O at 70°C, the voltameter could be expected to read approximately:

   (F) 0.0 volts
   (G) 2.5 volts
   (H) 4.9 volts
   (J) 7.5 volts

9. If Experiment 2 were repeated, only this time the water was heated to 50°C, the conductivity of the electrolyte solutions would most likely:

(A) decrease for all except NaCl.
(B) all stay the same.
(C) all increase.
(D) increase for all except NaCl.

10. Which of the following objectives best explains why H_2O alone was tested in all three experiments?

(F) To test whether H_2O was the solute or the solvent
(G) To determine the amount of conductivity that could be attributed to H_2O
(H) To test whether H_2O would dissolve all of the salts equally
(J) To prove that H_2O conducts electricity well

11. According to the results of all three experiments, which effects would be most appropriate to test next to learn more about conductivity in a solution?

(A) How temperature influences conductivity
(B) How solute color influences conductivity
(C) How water influences conductivity
(D) How different solvents influence conductivity

Passage III

Scientists at a national park recently conducted three studies to analyze the relationship between monarch caterpillars and the milkweed plants they populate.

Study 1

Scientists compared two different species of milkweed plants—one that is populated by the monarch caterpillars (monarch plants) and one that is not populated by monarch caterpillars (non-monarch plants). The results are shown in Table 1 below.

Table 1		
	Monarch plants	**Non-monarch plants**
Leaves	Thick Low pH High concentration of plant proteins	Thin High pH Low concentration of plant proteins
Stems	Surrounded by bare ground	Surrounded by weeds and other plants
Blossoms	Present purple and fragrant produce nectar	Not present
Sunlight	Partial sun	Direct, all-day sun
Caterpillars	20–30 per plant	< 3 per plant

Study 2

The scientists also did a comparison study of monarch caterpillars and a closely related species of caterpillar that does not feed on milkweed plants. The results are shown in Table 2 below.

Table 2		
	Monarch caterpillars	**Non-monarch caterpillars**
Coloring	Yellow, white, and black	Orange and black
Activity	Active in daytime	Active at night and day
Nutrition	Plant-based proteins and nectar	Animal-based proteins
Breeding sites	Milkweed leaves	Tall trees

Study 3

A patch of wild milkweed was divided into three groups. All of the monarch caterpillars were removed from the plants in Group 1. The monarch caterpillars on the plants in Group 2 remained untouched. The plants in Group 3 consisted entirely of a species of non-monarch milkweed. All of the plants in the three groups received equal amounts of rainfall and sunlight and were initially very healthy. The number of living plants in each group was tallied on the 1st and 60th days of the study. The results are shown in Table 3 below.

Table 3					
Day	Group 1		Group 2		Group 3	
	Alive	Dead	Alive	Dead	Alive	Dead
1	65	0	70	0	68	0
60	30	35	65	5	45	23

The dead plants in Group 1 had been eaten by insects, birds, and grazing mammals. The dead plants in Groups 2 and 3 did not show evidence of having been killed by grazing mammals.

12. How does the design of Study 3 differ from that of Study 1?

    (F) In Study 1, physical characteristics of monarch caterpillars were examined, and in Study 3, characteristics of milkweed plants were examined.

    (G) In Study 1, milkweed plants were examined, and in Study 3, the relationship between milkweed plants and caterpillars was examined.

    (H) In Study 1, monarch caterpillars were removed from milkweed plants, and in Study 3, monarch caterpillars were studied in their native environments.

    (J) In Study 1, monarch caterpillars were examined, and in Study 3, non-monarch caterpillars were examined.

13. Based on the information in Table 1, which of the following characteristics likely protects non-monarch milkweed plants from being eaten by birds, insects, or grazing animals?

    (A) High pH
    (B) High concentration of plant proteins
    (C) Purple blossoms
    (D) Sharp thorns

14. According to the passage, how many monarch caterpillars were likely living on each monarch milkweed plant in Group 2 in Study 3?

    (F) Fewer than 3
    (G) Between 5 and 10
    (H) Between 10 and 20
    (J) Between 20 and 30

15. Scientists identified a new species of milkweed during their research and were able to classify it as a non-monarch milkweed. What could have been some characteristics of the new milkweed?

    (A) Thin leaves; no blossoms; grows in direct sunlight

    (B) Low pH; surrounded by weeds; low concentration of plant proteins

    (C) Fragrant blossoms; grows in partial sun; low pH

    (D) High pH; fewer than 3 caterpillars per plant; thick leaves

16. According to the information in all 3 tables, plant proteins and nectar play what role for monarch caterpillars and monarch milkweeds?

    (F) Plant proteins repel grazing animals, whereas nectar is a food source for monarch caterpillars.

    (G) Nectar repels grazing animals, whereas plant proteins are a food source for monarch caterpillars.

    (H) Both plants proteins and nectar repel grazing animals.

    (J) Monarch caterpillars use both plant proteins and nectar as food sources.

Recommended

Passage IV

A spring of length L and coefficient k was hung from a ceiling. A block of mass m was attached to the bottom of the spring, as shown in Figure 1.

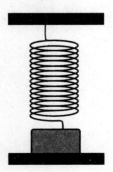

When the weight was released, the spring stretched and then bounced back, as shown in Figure 2.

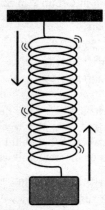

The *oscillation time* was the time it took for the spring to stretch and then bounce back up to a maximum height. The oscillation times of a spring of fixed length L and various masses m on the surface of Earth, Saturn's largest moon Titan, and Jupiter are shown in Figure 3. Figure 4 shows the oscillation time for the same spring with $m = 300$ g and various L on the same 3 surfaces. The gravitational acceleration at each surface is shown in Table 1.

Table 1	
Planet or moon	**Gravitational acceleration at surface of planet or moon (m/sec^2)**
Jupiter	24.9
Earth	9.8
Titan	1.1

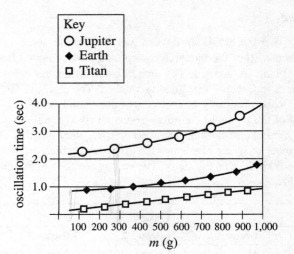

Figure 3

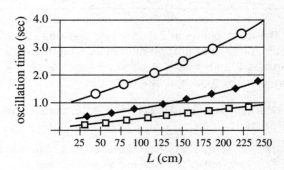

Figure 4

17. Based on the data in Figure 3, what would be the expected oscillation time on the surface of Earth of the spring with a 50 g mass attached?

   (A) 2.0 sec
   (B) 1.3 sec
   (C) 1.0 sec
   (D) 0.8 sec

18. According to Figure 4, the spring with $m = 300$g attached will have an oscillation time of 3.0 sec on Earth if L is approximately:

   (F) 1000 cm.
   (G) 350 cm.
   (H) 200 cm.
   (J) 100 cm.

19. According to the information in the passage, which statement best describes the relationship between gravitational acceleration and oscillation time?

    (A) As gravitational acceleration increases, oscillation time decreases.

    (B) As gravitational acceleration increases, oscillation time increases.

    (C) As gravitational acceleration increases, oscillation time stays the same.

    (D) There is no constant relationship between gravitational acceleration and oscillation time.

20. The spring in Figure 3 has an oscillation time of 2.25 sec on Jupiter's surface. In order to give the same oscillation time for the same spring on Earth's surface, m would have to be approximately:

    (F) 50 times greater than that at Jupiter's surface.

    (G) 50 times less than that at Jupiter's surface.

    (H) 15 times greater than that at Jupiter's surface.

    (J) 15 times less than that at Jupiter's surface.

21. The gravitational acceleration on the surface of the planet Mercury is approximately 3.7 m/sec^2. Based on the relationships shown in Figure 4, the spring's oscillation time for a given m on Mercury would be:

    (A) greater than its oscillation time on Earth.

    (B) greater than its oscillation time on Jupiter.

    (C) greater than its oscillation time on Earth, but less than its oscillation time on Jupiter.

    (D) greater than its oscillation time on Titan, but less than its oscillation time on Earth.

Passage V

Scientists at a university noticed unusual plant and algae growth in a pond on their campus. They sampled the water and also discovered very high concentrations of bacteria. Significant increases in the growth of plants, algae, and bacteria in ponds are often caused by an excess of growth nutrients, especially phosphates and nitrates. Phosphates typically enter ponds by attaching to soil or stream sediment particles and washing in with rainwater. Nitrates typically are flushed in by *groundwater* (water moving through the soil) or streams. To determine how the nutrients were entering the pond, the scientists conducted two experiments.

Experiment 1

The scientists speculated that phosphates might be entering the pond by seeping from wastewater systems buried behind dormitories that border the pond. Sampling wells were placed to intercept groundwater flowing from the dormitories to the pond. The samples were collected daily, and the results are shown in Table 1.

Table 1		
Date	Nitrate concentration (mg/L)	Phosphate concentration (mg/L)
Dormitory 1		
June 1	19.1	8.3
June 2	17.7	6.6
June 3	18.5	9.2
June 4	19.1	9.0
June 5	22.5	7.9
Dormitory 2		
June 1	23.9	7.9
June 2	26.4	10.1
June 3	23.1	10.8
June 4	22.7	9.5
June 5	19.5	8.6

Experiment 2

The pond was also situated close to neighboring farmland, and the scientists suspected that runoff water carrying fertilizers was another source of the nutrients. They collected water and suspended sediment samples from two streams that carried water from the fields to the pond. The streams collected water from the farmland through rainstorms and snowmelt. The results are shown in Table 2.

Table 2

Date	Suspended sediment concentration (mg/L)	Nitrate concentration (mg/L)	Phosphate concentration (mg/L)
Stream 1			
June 1	33.5	35.5	7.1
June 2	42.0	33.4	9.3
June 3	512.9	36.8	52.6
June 4	1668.2	62.4	102.9
June 5	687.5	57.0	55.7
Stream 2			
June 1	12.3	11.3	6.7
June 2	18.4	26.5	12.9
June 3	24.1	29.7	26.8
June 4	19.2	21.3	16.4
June 5	12.3	12.5	9.2

22. Which of the following is a difference between the sampling procedures in Experiment 1 and Experiment 2?

   (F) In Experiment 1, samples were taken weekly, while in Experiment 2, samples were taken daily.
   (G) In Experiment 1, only nitrates were measured, while in Experiment 2, both nitrates and phosphates were measured.
   (H) In Experiment 1, groundwater was sampled, while in Experiment 2, stream water was sampled.
   (J) In Experiment 1, algae concentrations were measured, while in Experiment 2, bacteria concentrations were measured.

23. Based on the data in Table 2, as phosphate concentration increases, the concentration of suspended sediment in Stream 1:

   (A) increases.
   (B) decreases.
   (C) doesn't change.
   (D) decreases, then increases.

24. According to the data in Table 1, on which date were nitrate concentrations from Dormitory 2 the highest?

   (F) June 1
   (G) June 2
   (H) June 3
   (J) June 4

25. What was the scientists' hypothesis concerning pond algae growth in Experiment 2?

   (A) Wastewater contamination from dormitories decreases pond algae growth.
   (B) Runoff from fertilized farmland increases pond algae growth.
   (C) Bacteria inhibit pond algae growth.
   (D) High rainfall increases pond algae growth.

26. Given the results of Experiments 1 and 2, which of the following measures would most likely reduce phosphorous and nitrogen input into the pond?

   (F) Increasing the number of dormitories near the pond
   (G) Increasing the amount of fertilizer used on the farmland
   (H) Installing pipes to carry wastewater from the dormitories to a central treatment facility
   (J) Removing plants from the pond

27. As phosphates move farther from their source, they are more likely to be absorbed by the soil (removed from the water). Which of the following would most likely be the approximate phosphate concentration for Dormitory 1 on June 2 if the sampling well were farther away from the dormitory?

   (A) 6.0 mg/L
   (B) 7.0 mg/L
   (C) 8.0 mg/L
   (D) 9.0 mg/L

TABLE OF CONTENTS

Quarter 1	**Homework Review · Preview Quiz · Session Objectives**
Quarter 2	**Inference Questions · Writer's View Questions · Function Questions**
Quarter 3	**Connections · Verb Tense · Wordiness · Word Choice**
Quarter 4	**Writing Strategy · Organization**
	Homework

	Homework Review
	Preview Quiz
	Session Objectives

Homework Review

2. What is the value of $9^{-\frac{3}{2}}$?

   (F) -27

   (G) $-13\frac{1}{2}$

   (H) $\frac{-1}{27}$

   (J) $\frac{1}{27}$

   (K) $13\frac{1}{2}$

3. In a company of 50 people, the 30 males have an average age of 42 and the 20 females have an average age of 37. To the nearest year, what is the average age of the company's workforce?

   (A) 39

   (B) 40

   (C) 41

   (D) 42

   (E) 43

6. Franklin leaves school and rides his bike east at a constant rate. At the same time, Mariah leaves the same school and bikes west at a rate that is 3 miles per hour faster than Franklin is riding. At the end of 2 hours, the two bikes are 54 miles apart. How many miles did Mariah ride?

   (F) 24

   (G) 26

   (H) 28

   (J) 30

   (K) 32

6. Jamal has a suitcase that contains 10 white socks. He wants to add enough black socks so that the probability of randomly selecting a white sock is $\frac{1}{5}$. How many black socks should Jamal add to the suitcase?

   (F) 30

   (G) 35

   (H) 40

   (J) 45

   (K) 50

9. If $0° < \theta < 90°$ and $\sin\theta = \frac{\sqrt{11}}{2\sqrt{3}}$, then what is the value of $\cos\theta$?

   (A) $\frac{1}{2\sqrt{3}}$

   (B) $\frac{1}{\sqrt{11}}$

   (C) $\frac{2\sqrt{3}}{\sqrt{11}}$

   (D) $2\sqrt{3}$

   (E) $\sqrt{11}$

Passage III

Scientists at a national park recently conducted three studies to analyze the relationship between monarch caterpillars and the milkweed plants they populate.

Study 1

Scientists compared two different species of milkweed plants—one that is populated by the monarch caterpillars (monarch plants) and one that is not populated by monarch caterpillars (non-monarch plants). The results are shown in Table 1 below.

Table 1		
	Monarch plants	**Non-monarch plants**
Leaves	Thick Low pH High concentration of plant proteins	Thin High pH Low concentration of plant proteins
Stems	Surrounded by bare ground	Surrounded by weeds and other plants
Blossoms	Present; purple and fragrant, produce nectar	Not present
Sunlight	Partial sun	Direct, all-day sun
Caterpillars	20–30 per plant	< 3 per plant

Study 2

The scientists also did a comparison study of monarch caterpillars and a closely related species of caterpillar that does not feed on milkweed plants. The results are shown in Table 2 below.

Table 2

	Monarch caterpillars	Non-monarch caterpillars
Coloring	Yellow, white, and black	Orange and black
Activity	Active in daytime	Active at night and day
Nutrition	Plant-based proteins and nectar	Animal-based proteins
Breeding sites	Milkweed leaves	Tall trees

Study 3

A patch of wild milkweed was divided into three groups. All of the monarch caterpillars were removed from the plants in Group 1. The monarch caterpillars on the plants in Group 2 remained untouched. The plants in Group 3 consisted entirely of a species of non-monarch milkweed. All of the plants in the three groups received equal amounts of rainfall and sunlight and were initially very healthy. The number of living plants in each group was tallied on the 1st and 60th days of the study. The results are shown in Table 3 below.

Table 3

Day	Group 1		Group 2		Group 3	
	Alive	Dead	Alive	Dead	Alive	Dead
1	65	0	70	0	68	0
60	30	35	65	5	45	23

The dead plants in Group 1 had been eaten by insects, birds, and grazing mammals. The dead plants in Groups 2 and 3 did not show evidence of having been killed by grazing mammals.

13. Based on the information in Table 1, which of the following characteristics likely protects non-monarch milkweed plants from being eaten by birds, insects, or grazing animals?

    (A) High pH
    (B) High concentration of plant proteins
    (C) Purple blossoms
    (D) Sharp thorns

16. According to the information in all 3 tables, plant proteins and nectar play what role for monarch caterpillars and monarch milkweeds?

    (F) Plant proteins repel grazing animals, whereas nectar is a food source for monarch caterpillars.
    (G) Nectar repels grazing animals, whereas plant proteins are a food source for monarch caterpillars.
    (H) Both plants proteins and nectar repel grazing animals.
    (J) Monarch caterpillars use both plant proteins and nectar as food sources.

Preview Quiz

For four months in the fall of 1940, citizens of the Puget Sound area of Washington <u>are using</u> one of the most
1
illustrious, and most dangerous, suspension bridges ever built. The Tacoma Narrows Bridge, or "Galloping Gertie," enjoyed a relatively short life compared to similar structures in the United States. <u>Also</u> in its short career, "Gertie" taught
2
important lessons on what to do—and what not to do—when building a suspension bridge.

[1] The closest point was the Tacoma Narrows, a windy 2,800-foot gap that, at the time, appeared to be the ideal place for a suspension bridge. [2] Spanning the length of the Narrows, the Tacoma Narrow Bridge was the third-largest span in the world at the time and was hailed by the public as a triumph of engineering. [3] State officials <u>in</u> Washington
3
saw a need for a bridge across Puget Sound to connect the city of Tacoma, on the mainland, with the Olympic Peninsula <u>on the other side of the Sound</u>. [4] Construction
4
began in November of 1938, and the bridge was officially opened on July 1, 1940.

1. (A) NO CHANGE
   (B) used
   (C) will use
   (D) might have used

2. (F) NO CHANGE
   (G) For example
   (H) But
   (J) Finally

3. (A) NO CHANGE
   (B) from
   (C) between
   (D) among

4. (F) NO CHANGE
   (G) on the other side
   (H) on the Sound
   (J) on the other side of Puget Sound

5. What would be the most logical order of sentences in paragraph 2?
   (A) NO CHANGE
   (B) 2, 1, 4, 3
   (C) 2, 4, 3, 1
   (D) 3, 1, 4, 2

Session Objectives

Quarter 2—15 SmartPoints

Inference Questions—8 SmartPoints
- Answer Inference questions by predicting an answer and looking for support in the passage.

Writer's View Questions—1 SmartPoint
- Answer Writer's View questions by predicting an answer and looking for support in the passage.

Function Questions—6 SmartPoints
- Answer Function questions by predicting an answer and looking for support in the passage.

Quarter 3—23 SmartPoints

Connections—7 SmartPoints
- Use transitions to clearly reflect the flow of a paragraph or passage.

Verb Tense—6 SmartPoints
- Identify the six tested verb tenses: present, past, future, present perfect, past perfect, and future perfect.

Wordiness—5 SmartPoints
- Recognize redundancy in a sentence.

Word Choice—5 SmartPoints
- Match a plural subject with a plural verb and a singular subject with a singular verb.
- Replace nouns with appropriate pronouns.
- Recognize appropriate pronouns and replace inappropriate pronouns.
- Differentiate between *who* and *whom*, *which* and *that*, *their* and *there*, *when* and *where*, as well as identify when *being* is used incorrectly.
- Recognize common idiomatic expressions.

Quarter 4—5 SmartPoints

Writing Strategy—4 SmartPoints
- Decide whether information in a passage makes sense, is relevant, or is in the correct place.

Organization—1 SmartPoint
- Learn how to correctly organize individual paragraphs and a passage as a whole.

8 SmartPoints	Inference Questions
1 SmartPoint	Writer's View Questions
6 SmartPoints	Function Questions
Quiz	

Inference Questions—8 SmartPoints

A. Inference questions ask you to

_____

_____

_____

B. You must remember that

_____

_____

_____

C. Tempting wrong answer choices

_____

_____

_____

Passage I

Prose Fiction: This passage is an adapted excerpt from Willa Cather's *O Pioneers!* This novel, set in the Nebraska prairie, was originally published in 1913.

Carl had changed, Alexandra felt, much less than one might have expected. He had not become a self-satisfied city man. There was still something homely
Line and wayward and personal about him. Even his clothes
(5) were unconventional. He seemed to shrink into himself as he used to do, as if he were afraid of being hurt.

That evening, Carl and Alexandra were sitting in the flower garden. The gravel paths glittered in the moonlight, and below them the fields lay white and still.
(10) "You know, Alexandra, I've been thinking how strangely things work out. I've been away engraving other people's pictures, and you've stayed at home and made your own." Carl pointed toward the sleeping landscape. "How in the world have you done it? How
(15) have your neighbors done it?"

"We hadn't much to do with it, Carl. The land pretended to be poor because nobody knew how to work it right; then, suddenly, it worked itself. It woke up out of its sleep and stretched itself, and it was so
(20) big, so rich, that we found we were rich, just from sitting still. You remember when I began to buy land. For years I was always squeezing and borrowing until I was ashamed to show my face in the banks. And then, all at once, men began to come to me offering
(25) to lend me money! Then I built this house—for Emil, really. I want you to see Emil, Carl. He is so different from the rest of us!"

"How different?"

"Oh, you'll see! I'm sure it was to have children like
(30) Emil, to give them a chance, that Father left Sweden."

"Is he going to farm here with you?"

"He shall do whatever he wants to," Alexandra declared. "He is going to have a real chance; that's what I've worked for!"

(35) "How about Lou and Oscar? They've done well, haven't they?"

"Yes, very well; but they are different, and now that they have farms of their own I don't see so much of them. We divided the land equally when Lou
(40) married. They have their own way of doing things, and they don't altogether like my way. Perhaps they think me too independent. But I've had to think for myself for many years and am not likely to change. On the whole, though, we take as much comfort in each other
(45) as most brothers and sisters do."

Alexandra looked at Carl with her calm, deliberate eyes. "Why are you dissatisfied with yourself?" she asked earnestly.

Her visitor winced and paused. "You see," he
(50) said, "measured by your standards here, I'm a failure. I couldn't buy even one of your cornfields. I've enjoyed many things in New York, but I've got nothing to show for it."

"But you show for it yourself, Carl. I'd rather
(55) have had your freedom than my land."

Carl shook his head mournfully. "Freedom so often means that one isn't needed anywhere. Here you have a background of your own; you would be missed. But in the cities there are thousands of rolling stones
(60) like me. We're all alike, paying exorbitant rent for a few square feet of space near the heart of things; we have no ties, we know nobody, we own nothing. When people die, they scarcely know where to bury them."

Alexandra was silent. He knew that she understood
(65) what he meant. At last she said slowly, "And yet I would rather have Emil grow up like that than like his brothers. We pay a high rent, too, though we pay differently. We grow hard and heavy. We don't move lightly and easily as you do, and our minds get stiff. If
(70) the world were no wider than my cornfields, I wouldn't feel that it was worthwhile to work. No, I would rather have Emil like you. I felt that as soon as you came."

How has city life changed Carl? _____

How does Alexandra feel about her success? _____

》 REMEMBER
Locate a part of the passage that can help you make a prediction.

1. The passage suggests that Alexandra wants Emil to:

   (A) take over the management of her farm someday.
   (B) choose a profession other than farming.
   (C) grow up to be like Lou and Oscar.
   (D) move to New York with Carl.

》 REMEMBER
The correct answer will be only a small logical step from what is stated in the passage.

2. Alexandra's assessment of Carl in the first paragraph implies that she is:

   (F) charmed by his eccentric appearance.
   (G) perplexed about why he has come home.
   (H) relieved that he seems unchanged.
   (J) surprised by her own lack of sympathy for him.

3. Carl's comments in lines 49–53 ("You see ... show for it.") suggest that he feels:

   (A) lucky to have escaped the hardships of farm life.
   (B) fortunate to have met many interesting people in New York.
   (C) dissatisfied with the quality of life in Nebraska.
   (D) unable to account satisfactorily for the life he has led.

)) REMEMBER
Inference questions sometimes refer to specific portions of the passage, much as Detail questions do.

Writer's View Questions—1 SmartPoint

A. Writer's View questions ask about _____

_____

_____

B. You can spot them because they _____

_____

_____

C. To answer them effectively, you must _____

_____

_____

KAPLAN

This Page Intentionally Left Blank

)) REMEMBER

Writer's View questions may pull from different parts of the passage or from the passage as a whole.

4. The depiction of the conversation between Carl and Alexandra suggests that the author sympathizes with:

(F) Carl's longing for the simple life.

(G) Alexandra's idea of "freedom."

(H) Lou's opinion of Alexandra.

(J) Alexandra's disdain for the "city man."

)) REMEMBER

Active Reading will help you successfully answer Writer's View questions.

5. Which of the following statements made by Alexandra in the passage best captures the author's characterization of her?

(A) "He is going to have a real chance; that's what I've worked for!" (lines 33–34)

(B) "Why are you dissatisfied with yourself?" (lines 47–48)

(C) "But I've had to think for myself for many years and am not likely to change." (lines 42–43)

(D) "We pay a high rent, too, though we pay differently." (lines 67–68)

Function Questions—6 SmartPoints

A. Function questions ask about

_____

_____

_____

B. They may ask about the function of a

1. _____

2. _____

3. _____

4. _____

5. _____

6. _____

C. You can spot them because they

_____

_____

_____

D. To answer them effectively, you should

_____

_____

_____

Passage II

Humanities: The passage below is an excerpt from *American Houses* by Philip Langdon (© 1987 by Philip Langdon).

People carry in their minds a picture of what constitutes an "American house." For most of us, it is and has long been a freestanding dwelling that rises
Line from its own piece of land. Whether that piece of land is
(5) a 40-foot-wide lot on a city street or an expanse of farmland stretching off toward the horizon is almost irrelevant; what matters is that the house stands as an individual object, separate from the walls of its neighbors. This may not be the sort of dwelling in
(10) which every American actually lives—millions inhabit apartment buildings and blocks of row houses—yet the detached house holds such an allure for the imagination that it remains a national ideal, in good times and bad, in periods both of dense urban development and of
(15) outward suburban dispersal. So deeply embedded in the country's consciousness is the ideal of a freestanding dwelling that even young children, when asked to draw a house, will unhesitatingly make a sketch of a family-sized dwelling with a pitched roof on top, a few
(20) windows in its facade, and a prominent front door.

Some of the details that embellish this notion of the American house have, of course, changed greatly with the passage of time. In the 1850s, when the landscape of architect Andrew Jackson Downing exerted a major
(25) influence on residential design, the image of an American house would have included verandas and vestibules, parlors, and pantries. In the 1920s, a decade enchanted by "Old English" architecture but also gripped by a concern for cleanliness, it often summoned
(30) up a picturesque, even quaint, exterior with arched doorways and a steeply pitched roof, yet with a shiny white-surfaced kitchen and bathroom within. In the 1960s, the prevailing vision was of a house that had substituted a back patio or deck for the front porch and
(35) had added a "family room" as a casual, unceremonious alternative to the formality of the living room.

Despite such modifications, the governing ideal remained constant in its essentials—an individual residence enclosing a comfortable amount of space
(40) beneath the slopes of its roof and enjoying dominion over a certain amount of land beyond its walls. Gradually, too, the American house was accompanied by a standard arrangement of its grounds. In the front grew a neatly kept lawn, setting a scene that possessed
(45) a measure of dignity and repose. To the rear, a more informal yard provided a space for relaxation and outdoor recreation. Side yards acted as buffers against the noise and nosiness of neighbors, while at the same time making each household feel more autonomous.

(50) This was by no means a perfect or universal way to provide shelter, but it did satisfy many of the needs of millions of people. From East Coast to West, vast numbers of houses were built in accordance with the common image of the American house—dwellings set
(55) apart from one another in a pattern that suited, above all, the interests of families.

Today much of this arrangement has lost its important reason for being: the traditional family—a working husband, a wife who stays home, and their not-
(60) yet-grown children—until recently the predominant form of American household, now makes up a minority of America's population. As the population and the workforce have dramatically changed, the house has been pressed to adapt. Detached dwellings accounted
(65) for 80 percent of the newly constructed private housing in the United States as late as 1975; a decade later, the proportion had steadily diminished to 62 percent. Instead of an "American house," it has become more accurate to speak in the plural: "American houses." The
(70) nation has entered a period in which many houses are distinguished less by their lingering similarities than by how they diverge both from one another and from homes of the past.

Why does the author mention "Old English" architecture?

_____

Why does the author discuss the traditional family?

_____

Passage II

Humanities: The passage below is an excerpt from *American Houses* by Philip Langdon (© 1987 by Philip Langdon).

People carry in their minds a picture of what constitutes an "American house." For most of us, it is and has long been a freestanding dwelling that rises
Line from its own piece of land. Whether that piece of land is
(5) a 40-foot-wide lot on a city street or an expanse of farmland stretching off toward the horizon is almost irrelevant; what matters is that the house stands as an individual object, separate from the walls of its neighbors. This may not be the sort of dwelling in
(10) which every American actually lives—millions inhabit apartment buildings and blocks of row houses—yet the detached house holds such an allure for the imagination that it remains a national ideal, in good times and bad, in periods both of dense urban development and of
(15) outward suburban dispersal. So deeply embedded in the country's consciousness is the ideal of a freestanding dwelling that even young children, when asked to draw a house, will unhesitatingly make a sketch of a family-sized dwelling with a pitched roof on top, a few
(20) windows in its facade, and a prominent front door.

Some of the details that embellish this notion of the American house have, of course, changed greatly with the passage of time. In the 1850s, when the landscape of architect Andrew Jackson Downing exerted a major
(25) influence on residential design, the image of an American house would have included verandas and vestibules, parlors, and pantries. In the 1920s, a decade enchanted by "Old English" architecture but also gripped by a concern for cleanliness, it often summoned
(30) up a picturesque, even quaint, exterior with arched doorways and a steeply pitched roof, yet with a shiny white-surfaced kitchen and bathroom within. In the 1960s, the prevailing vision was of a house that had substituted a back patio or deck for the front porch and

(35) had added a "family room" as a casual, unceremonious alternative to the formality of the living room.

Despite such modifications, the governing ideal remained constant in its essentials—an individual residence enclosing a comfortable amount of space
(40) beneath the slopes of its roof and enjoying dominion over a certain amount of land beyond its walls. Gradually, too, the American house was accompanied by a standard arrangement of its grounds. In the front grew a neatly kept lawn, setting a scene that possessed
(45) a measure of dignity and repose. To the rear, a more informal yard provided a space for relaxation and outdoor recreation. Side yards acted as buffers against the noise and nosiness of neighbors, while at the same time making each household feel more autonomous.

(50) This was by no means a perfect or universal way to provide shelter, but it did satisfy many of the needs of millions of people. From East Coast to West, vast numbers of houses were built in accordance with the common image of the American house—dwellings set
(55) apart from one another in a pattern that suited, above all, the interests of families.

Today much of this arrangement has lost its important reason for being: the traditional family—a working husband, a wife who stays home, and their not-
(60) yet-grown children—until recently the predominant form of American household, now makes up a minority of America's population. As the population and the workforce have dramatically changed, the house has been pressed to adapt. Detached dwellings accounted
(65) for 80 percent of the newly constructed private housing in the United States as late as 1975; a decade later, the proportion had steadily diminished to 62 percent. Instead of an "American house," it has become more accurate to speak in the plural: "American houses." The
(70) nation has entered a period in which many houses are distinguished less by their lingering similarities than by how they diverge both from one another and from homes of the past.

6. The author uses the example of the child's sketch, at the end of paragraph 1, in order to:

(F) emphasize the simplicity of design in the typical American house.

(G) show the connection between the traditional family and the traditional American house.

(H) support the idea that the ideal of the American house pervades American society.

(J) indicate that the desire for the American house begins at a very early age.

7. The primary function of the fourth paragraph (lines 50–56) in relation to the passage as a whole is most likely to:

(A) provide an example of the point made in the preceding paragraph.

(B) highlight a shortcoming of the model discussed in the first part of the passage.

(C) sum up the author's main idea to that point before taking the subject in a new direction.

(D) put forth the principal counterargument to the author's thesis.

8. The author refers to "a shiny white-surfaced kitchen and bathroom" (lines 31–32) in order to:

    (F) show a detail common to all versions of the "American house."

    (G) explain which rooms had to be moved to make way for the "family room" of the 1960s.

    (H) point out how unsanitary the homes of the 1850s were.

    (J) exemplify the 1920s focus on cleanliness in the home.

》 REMEMBER
The best approach to Function questions is to actively read the passage.

Quiz

Prose Fiction: The following passage is an excerpt from "Graduation" by Jon Krupp.

Rosemary sat at her kitchen table, working at a crossword puzzle. Crosswords were nice; they filled the time and kept the mind active. She
Line needed just one word to complete this morning's
(5) puzzle. The clue was "A Swiss river," and the first of its three letters was "A." Unfortunately, Rosemary had no idea what the name of the river was and could not look it up. Her atlas was on the desk, and the desk was in the guestroom,
(10) currently being occupied by her grandson Victor. Looking up over the tops of her bifocals, Rosemary glanced at the kitchen clock—it was almost 10 a.m. Land sakes! Did the boy intend to sleep all day? She noticed that the arthritis in her
(15) wrist was throbbing, and she put down her pen. At 87 years of age, she was glad she could still write at all. She had decided long ago that growing old was like slowly turning to stone; you could not take anything for granted. She stood up
(20) slowly, painfully, and started walking to the guestroom.

The trip, although only a distance of about 25 feet, seemed to take a long while. Late in her ninth decade now, Rosemary often experienced
(25) an expanded sense of time, with present and past tense intermingling in her mind. One minute she was padding in her slippers across the living room carpet, the next she was back on the farm where she'd grown up, a sturdy little girl
(30) treading the path behind the barn just before dawn. In her mind's eye, she could still pick her way among the stones in the darkness, more than 70 years later.

Rosemary arrived at the door to the
(35) guestroom. It stood slightly ajar, and she peered through the opening. Victor lay sleeping on his side, his arms bent, his expression slightly pained. "Get up, lazy bones," she wanted to say. Even in childhood, Rosemary had never slept
(40) past 4 a.m.; there were too many chores to do. How different things were for Victor's generation! Her youngest grandson behaved as if he had never done a chore in his life. Twenty-one years old, he had driven down to Florida to visit
(45) Rosemary in his shiny new car, a gift from his doting parents. Victor would finish college soon, and his future appeared bright—if he ever got out of bed, that is.

Something Victor had said last night over
(50) dinner had disturbed her. Now what was it? Oh yes, he had been talking about one of his college courses—a "gut," he had called it. When she had asked him to explain the term, Victor said it was a course that you took simply because it was easy
(55) to pass. Rosemary, who had not even had a high school education, found the term repellent. If she had been allowed to continue her studies, she would never have taken a "gut."

The memory flooded back then, still as
(60) painful as an open wound all these years later. It was the first day of high school. She had graduated from grammar school the previous year, but her father had forbidden her to go on to high school that fall, saying that she was needed on the farm.
(65) After much tearful pleading, she had gotten him to promise that next year, she could start high school. She had endured a whole year of chores instead of books, with animals and rough farmhands for company instead of people her own age. Now, at
(70) last, the glorious day was at hand. She had put on her best dress (she owned two), her heart racing in anticipation. But her father was waiting for her as she came downstairs.

"Where do you think you're going?" he asked.
(75) "To high school, Papa."
"No, you're not. Take that thing off and get back to work." "But Papa, you promised!"
"Do as I say!" he thundered.
There was no arguing with Papa when he
(80) spoke that way. Tearfully, she had trudged upstairs to change clothes. Rosemary still wondered what life would have been like if her father had not been waiting at the bottom of the stairs that day, or if somehow she had found the
(85) strength to defy him.

9. The passage suggests that Rosemary's attitude toward the physical afflictions of old age is generally one of:

   (A) sadness.
   (B) acceptance.
   (C) resentment.
   (D) optimism.

10. It can be inferred from the passage that Rosemary is disturbed by Victor's:

   (F) intention to drop out of college.
   (G) disregard for her harsh upbringing.
   (H) overlong stay at her home.
   (J) willingness to take courses that are easy to pass.

11. Which of the following best describes the method by which the author reveals elements of Rosemary's character?

   (A) Depicting a series of hardships and how she overcame them
   (B) Tracing her life from her early inability to go to school to her later bitterness over that fact
   (C) Exploring her regret over the greatest disappointment in her life
   (D) Using an occurrence in the present to trigger her recollection of a past event

12. Information given in the passage suggests that Rosemary's father:

   (F) did not love Rosemary.
   (G) valued pursuing an education over working on the farm.
   (H) frequently changed his mind once he had made a decision.
   (J) intimidated Rosemary.

13. The author includes Rosemary's memory of her father in lines 59–81 to:

   (A) describe how she was raised.
   (B) explain why Rosemary judges Victor so harshly.
   (C) show what life was like when Rosemary was Victor's age.
   (D) demonstrate that Rosemary was prone to crying.

14. The use of quotation marks around the word "gut" (line 51) serves to:

   (F) demonstrate what kind of college course Victor is taking.
   (G) highlight that Rosemary does not understand Victor's slang.
   (H) underscore Rosemary's disdain for the word and what it represents.
   (J) show that Rosemary is unfamiliar with the term.

7 SmartPoints	Connections
6 SmartPoints	Verb Tense
5 SmartPoints	Wordiness
5 SmartPoints	Word Choice
Quiz	

Connections—7 SmartPoints

A. Connections questions will deal with:

1. _____

_____

2. _____

_____

3. _____

_____

B. To determine the right answer, ask yourself how the ideas presented relate to each other. Some possible relationships include:

_____

_____

_____

_____

Medusa

For more than two thousand years, Medusa has been a prominent image in the world of art and the world of myth. As far back as 200 B.C., images of Medusa, the defeated Gorgon, abounded. The shield of Alexander the Great, on the other hand, was graced with an image of the mythical
                        1
Medusa with her locks of live serpents and a gaze that could turn men into stone.

Medusa was surely one of the most threatening figures of ancient Greek mythology. One of the three Gorgon sisters, she had purportedly been known for her beauty. However, she aroused the anger of the goddess
          2
Athena, who turned Medusa's once lovely hair to snakes. With the power to turn anyone who looked upon her into stone, Medusa was feared and thought impossible to defeat. Indeed, Medusa finally did meet her end at the hands of
3
Perseus. Perseus was helped by Athena and Hermes, another major Greek god. Perseus was given a powerful sword, a helmet that made him invisible, winged sandals that enabled

him to fly, and a highly polished shield. Using these gifts, Perseus was able to invisibly sneak up on the sleeping Gorgon, use the shield as a mirror to protect himself from Medusa's direct gaze, and cut off the monster's head.

1. (A) NO CHANGE
   (B) as a result,
   (C) for example,
   (D) finally,

2. (F) NO CHANGE
   (G) beauty. Also,
   (H) beauty, also
   (J) beauty, however

3. (A) NO CHANGE
   (B) Nevertheless,
   (C) In addition,
   (D) Because of this,

Verb Tense—6 SmartPoints

A. Verb Tense questions will deal with:

1. _____

_____

2. _____

B. The six verb tenses are:

Present: I *come* to class **every week.**
Past: I *came* to class **last week.**
Future: I *will come* to class **next week.**
Present Perfect: I *have come* to every class **so far.**
Past Perfect: **Before I enrolled in my Kaplan course,** I *had not taken* an ACT class.
Future Perfect: **By the end of the course,** I *will have come* to every class.

Mary's Attic

I thought the tour of my friend's new house was finished as we came to a stop outside her bedroom on the third floor. But Mary had something else in mind. "Do you want to go up to the attic?" she asked me, her eyes sparkling with mischief. "My dad says no one <u>goes</u> up there for forty years!"
4

I wasn't thrilled about the idea of exploring the dark, musty space overhead. In the past, I <u>would of hesitated</u>
5
whenever Mary suggested risky or dangerous activities, but this time I just nodded, trying to appear nonchalant. Mary yanked on the cord dangling from the wooden door; as if by magic, a staircase unfolded, the bottom step landing directly in front of my feet. I looked up into the looming darkness, imagining cobwebs crawling with eight-legged monsters, and shuddered.

I took a deep breath, hoping Mary wouldn't notice, and gripped the ladder. As I placed my foot on the bottom rung, I wondered how my best friend had failed to remember I had a terrible fear of spiders. "The sooner you <u>got</u> this over with, the better," I whispered to myself.
6

4. (F) NO CHANGE
   (G) will have gone
   (H) still goes
   (J) has gone

5. (A) NO CHANGE
   (B) hesitated
   (C) will hesitate
   (D) must hesitate

6. (F) NO CHANGE.
   (G) had got
   (H) get
   (J) are getting

Wordiness—5 SmartPoints

A. Wordiness questions will deal with:

1. _____

2. _____

3. _____

B. When you see "OMIT the underlined portion" as an answer choice, ask yourself whether:

_____

_____

_____

Gregory Hines, a Beloved Icon

During the last five decades of the 20th century, Gregory Hines has enriched musical theater with his performances <u>for more than fifty years</u> as a dancer, singer
7
and star of the Broadway stage. A multitalented artist, he was also employed as an actor, a director, and a producer in television and film.

Hines began performing as a dancer <u>when he was the</u>
8
<u>age of five years old.</u> He toured professionally in nightclubs
8
across the country with his older brother, Maurice, as the duo The Hines Kids. At eight, he made his Broadway debut and remained a star of the stage in <u>a variety of</u> musicals,
9
including *Eubie!, Sophisticated Ladies,* and *Comin' Uptown.* He received a Tony award for Best Actor for his work in *Jelly's Last Jam* in 1993, as well as three Tony nominations from 1979 to 1981.

7. (A) NO CHANGE
   (B) for fifty more years
   (C) for fifty years
   (D) OMIT the underlined portion.

8. (F) NO CHANGE
   (G) when he was five
   (H) at the age of five years
   (J) at an age, starting at five,

9. Which of the following alternatives to the underline portion would be LEAST acceptable?
   (A) various
   (B) an assortment of
   (C) different
   (D) various and different

Word Choice—5 SmartPoints

A. Word Choice questions will deal with:

1. _____

2. _____

3. _____

4. _____

B. A verb must agree with its subject noun in person and number.
A stamp *sticks* to an envelope.
Stamps *stick* to envelopes.

C. Only the conjunction _____ forms a compound subject requiring a plural verb form.

Danny and Jared _____ members of the fencing club.

Either Danny or Jared _____ a member of the fencing club.

D. A pronoun must agree with its antecedent in person and number.
Keron won the competition because *he* had prepared the most.
The fans wanted tickets so badly that *they* stood in line for hours before the box office opened.

E. Use _____ and _____ when referring to people; use _____

or _____ to refer to any other nouns.

Internet Advertising

Twenty years ago, large companies hoped to reach their target markets through advertisements in national magazines and network television. Smaller companies utilized local newspapers, phone books, and radio stations to reach their local customers. Of course, companies large and small still buy advertisements in mass media outlets <u>that reaches</u> large
$$\underline{\hspace{2cm}}_{10}$$
numbers of consumers. Now, though, businesses also use Internet advertising, including company websites, banner advertisements, and ads generated by search engines to reach more specifically targeted audiences. Small, local businesses have benefited <u>with greatness from</u> the marketing
$$\underline{\hspace{2cm}}_{11}$$
opportunities presented by the Internet. Small specialty shops once were relatively limited to local populations of customers, but today those same shops can have customers from around the world. With a website and a few well-placed Internet advertisements, a small company can make itself known to potential customers <u>which</u>, regardless of
$$\underline{\hspace{2cm}}_{12}$$
where they live, are excited about the company's products.

10. (F) NO CHANGE
    (G) which reached
    (H) that reach
    (J) who reach

11. (A) NO CHANGE
    (B) greatly from
    (C) most greatly with
    (D) a great amount by

12. (F) NO CHANGE
    (G) whom,
    (H) who,
    (J) who

Quiz

My Great-Grandmother

Even in the early part of the twentieth century, people were used to consider it unusual, even shocking, for a
<u>13</u>
woman to work outside the home; however, my great-grandmother Ella was not only a nurse-midwife but also a professional photographer. Ella was born in 1882. Although by the time I was born she <u>will have died</u>, I grew up hearing
<u>14</u>
stories of her amazing accomplishments. Ella decided to pursue medicine because her father, an eminent doctor, was <u>known for</u> his forward-thinking ideas about women's
<u>15</u>
abilities in the workforce. His work—coupled <u>for</u>
<u>16</u>
that of her adored older brother, also a doctor—<u>which strongly influenced</u> Ella's interests. At the age of
<u>17</u>
twenty-two, Ella married my great- grandfather Frederick, a young chemist who worked in her brother's hospital laboratory. Soon, Ella started to learn about the newly created discipline of photography. Many chemists were the first to take up the hobby of <u>the newly created</u> art
<u>18</u>
form, because chemicals were necessary to process the film. Ella's husband was able to teach her how to use the chemicals, and she began to take photographs of children whose mothers she knew from her nursing career. While her contemporaries believed that art should be staid and serious, Ella found that capturing children at play <u>produced</u> joyful,
<u>19</u>
beautiful art.

Ella mounted her first photography show in 1910, the same year that she and her husband, <u>whom</u> published a
<u>20</u>
scientific paper that year, welcomed the birth of their first child. By 1920, three more children had been born, and the family was complete. In 1925, Ella was recognized for her photography by her hometown, when the city asked her to take official school portraits in the public schools. She <u>would spend</u> two months there, capturing candid pictures of
<u>21</u>
the school day as well as the official pictures. The candids

are still proudly displayed in the front hall of the town elementary school, where parents and children can walk past and gaze at the smiling faces from long ago.

My great-grandmother was truly one of those rare persons <u>whom combined</u> artistic talent with a love of
<u>22</u>
children and an interest in documenting daily life. I look back on her works now to inspire my own artistic pursuits.

13. (A) NO CHANGE
    (B) were use to
    (C) used to
    (D) use to

14. (F) NO CHANGE
    (G) will die
    (H) had died
    (J) dies

15. Which of the following alternatives to the underlined portion would be LEAST acceptable?
    (A) renowned for
    (B) admired for
    (C) infamous for
    (D) celebrated for

16. (F) NO CHANGE
    (G) together by
    (H) with
    (J) DELETE the underlined portion.

17. (A) NO CHANGE
    (B) strongly influences
    (C) strongly influencing
    (D) strongly influenced

18. (F) NO CHANGE
    (G) this
    (H) which
    (J) a newly created

19. Which of the following alternatives to the underlined portion would NOT be acceptable?
    (A) created
    (B) resulted in
    (C) prepared
    (D) yielded

20. (F) NO CHANGE
    (G) by whom
    (H) whose
    (J) who

21. (A) NO CHANGE
    (B) would of spent
    (C) would
    (D) spent

22. (F) NO CHANGE
    (G) whom had combined
    (H) who combined
    (J) that combined

QUARTER 4

4 SmartPoints	Writing Strategy
1 SmartPoint	Organization
	Quiz

Writing Strategy—4 SmartPoints

A. Writing Strategy questions will deal with:

1. _____

2. _____

3. _____

_____

_____

4. _____

_____

_____

Community-Supported Agriculture

This spring, my family joined our local community-supported agriculture, or CSA, association. We wanted to eat more organic, locally grown foods, and this seemed like a natural place to start. The CSA works like this: before the growing season begins on the farm, people have the opportunity to buy a "share" of the year's crop. Then the farm delivers a box of vegetables and fruit each week. The box is filled with the farmer's harvest. ⬚1 The farmer is guaranteed payment for the year, no matter what variables the growing season presents, and share members are guaranteed regular access to a variety of local, organic fruits and vegetables.

Right away, we discovered that fresh, in-season food is delicious. ⬚2

1. The writer is considering rewriting the phrase "the farmer's harvest" in the preceding sentence to read: "whatever was harvested that week on the farm." Should the writer keep the phrase as it is or make the revision?
   - (A) Keep the phrase as it is, because it is more concise than the proposed revision.
   - (B) Keep the phrase as it is, because it does not use the ambiguous language of the proposed revision.
   - (C) Make the revision, because it adds detail that is relevant to the point being made in the paragraph.
   - (D) Make the revision, because it emphasizes the benefits of the CSA.

2. The writer is considering deleting the phrase "no matter what variables the growing season presents" from the preceding sentence. If the writer deletes this phrase, the paragraph would primarily lose:
   - (F) information that explains why the narrator's family joined the CSA.
   - (G) an additional explanation of why farmers sell to CSAs.
   - (H) a contrast between farmers who sell to CSAs and those who do not.
   - (J) nothing, because the essay focuses on the members' experience in the CSA, not the farmer's.

Writing Strategy—4 SmartPoints

A. If asked to add or delete information, ask yourself:

_____

_____

I had never liked broccoli before, but one bunch that came in our second June box changed my mind. ⬚3 My younger brother is usually reluctant to try new foods, but so far he has tried and liked both kale and turnips from the CSA. Of the four people in my family, my mother

is definitely the most accomplished cook. ⬚4

We have, however, run into a minor problem with the CSA vegetable boxes. That problem is zucchini, and lots of it. Each week in July, we received at least six zucchini in our box. First we just grilled the zucchini. ⬚5 By the third week, when we received ten zucchini, it was time to get creative. We found and tried out recipes for zucchini soup, zucchini casserole, zucchini bread, zucchini pizza, and even zucchini brownies. Though everything was actually rather tasty, except for the brownies, we'll all be a bit relieved when zucchini season is over. By then, though, tomato season will have begun, and we'll have to figure out how to prepare countless tomatoes each week. I hope we don't have to resort to tomato

3. The writer is considering removing the phrase "that came in our second June box" from the preceding sentence. Should the phrase be kept or deleted?
   (A) Kept, because it emphasizes that fresh, in-season vegetables were delivered to the family in a box.
   (B) Kept, because it clarifies the word "bunch" as well as the main idea of the paragraph.
   (C) Deleted, because the preceding paragraph introduced the idea of vegetable boxes.
   (D) Deleted, because it draws the reader's focus from the vegetables to the season.

4. Given that all of the choices are true statements, which one provides a conclusion to this paragraph that is most consistent with other information in the paragraph?
   (F) NO CHANGE
   (G) Before we joined the CSA, the most unusual vegetable my brother was willing to eat was a carrot.
   (H) The cardboard boxes are recycled each week, and the CSA even provides composting services on-site.
   (J) We pick up our vegetables from the farmer's delivery every Thursday afternoon.

5. At this point in the essay, the writer would like to insert the following true statement: "Then we made pasta with sautéed zucchini." Should the writer insert this sentence here?
   (A) Yes, because it helps to establish the range of the family's cooking skills.
   (B) Yes, because it helps to emphasize the main idea of this paragraph.
   (C) No, because it is unnecessarily repetitive.
   (D) No, because it does not specify what type of pasta the family made.

brownies! [6]

> Question 6 asks about the preceding passage as a whole.

6. If the writer's goal were to write a brief essay about the purpose and organization of community-supported agriculture, would this essay successfully accomplish that goal?

   (F) Yes, because it explains how community-supported agriculture works.

   (G) Yes, because it fully describes both the benefits and drawbacks of community-supported agriculture.

   (H) No, because it focuses instead on one family's personal experience with community-supported agriculture.

   (J) No, because it fails to provide an overview of how membership in a community-supported agriculture association works.

Organization—1 SmartPoint

A. Organization questions will deal with:

1. _____
_____
_____

2. _____
_____
_____

B. To renumber sentences or paragraphs, begin by determining which sentence or paragraph makes the most logical introduction to the paragraph or to the passage.

> The paragraphs in this passage may not be in the most logical order. Each paragraph is numbered in brackets, and question 8 will ask you to choose the appropriate order.

Nature's Disguises

Some animals change their coloring with the seasons. The stoat, a member of the weasel family, is known as the ermine in winter, because its brown fur changes to white. Chameleons are perhaps the most versatile of all animals that change their protective coloration. The chameleon changes its color in just a few minutes to that of the surface upon which it happens to be sitting.

While animals like the chameleon use their coloring as a way of hiding from predators, the skunk uses its distinctive white stripe as a way of standing out from its surroundings. Far from placing it in danger, the skunk's visibility actually protects it by distinguishing it from other animals. The skunk warns its predators to avoid its infamous stink. Think about it: Would your appetite be whetted by the skunk's odor?

Researchers have been investigating how animal species have come to use coloring as a means of protecting themselves. One study has shown that certain animals have glands that release special hormones, resulting in the change of skin or fur color. Therefore, not all the animals that camouflage themselves have these glands. The topic endures as one of the many mysteries of the natural world.

(1) The tree frog, for example, blends perfectly into its surroundings. (2) This camouflage enables the tree frog to hide from other animals that would be interested in eating it. (3) Animals have a variety of ways of protecting themselves from enemies. (4) Some animals alter their shape or color to blend in with their environment. (5) When it sits motionless, a background of leaves completely hides the tree frog.

7. What would be the most logical order of sentences in paragraph 4?

   (A) NO CHANGE
   (B) 3, 1, 4, 2, 5
   (C) 4, 1, 5, 2, 3
   (D) 3, 4, 1, 5, 2

8. What would be the most logical order of paragraphs for this essay?

   (F) 3, 1, 4, 2
   (G) 1, 2, 4, 3
   (H) 4, 1, 2, 3
   (J) 2, 1, 3, 4

Quiz

The Other Side of Chocolate

[9] The first people known to have made chocolate were the Aztecs, a people who used cacao seeds to make [10] a bitter but tasty drink. However, it was not until Hernan Cortez's exploration of Mexico in 1519. That Europeans [11] first learned of chocolate.

Cortez came to the New World in search of gold, but his interest was also fired by the Aztecs' strange drink. When Cortez returned to Spain, his ship's cargo held three chests of cacao beans. It was from these beans that Europe experienced its first taste of what seemed to be a very unusual beverage. The drink soon became popular among those people wealthy enough to afford it. [12] Over the next century, cafés specializing in chocolate drinks began to appear throughout Europe. [13]

[1] People all over the world enjoy chocolate bars, chocolate sprinkles, and even chocolate soda. [2] The chocolate ant phenomenon has yet to take over America, but Americans do enjoy their chocolate nonetheless. [3] In fact, Asia has cultivated the delicacy of chocolate-covered ants! [4] Of course, chocolate is very popular today. [14]

[1] Many chocolate lovers around the world were ecstatic to hear that chocolate may actually be good for you. [2] Researchers say chocolate contains a chemical that could prevent cancer and heart disease. [3] New research measures the amount of catechins, the chemical thought to be behind the benefits, in different types of chocolate. [4] The studies show that chocolate is very high in catechins. [5] The research is likely to be welcomed by those with a sweet tooth, although dentists may be less pleased. [15]

9. The author wants to add a sentence at the beginning of this paragraph to introduce the essay. Which of the following sentences would best serve this purpose?

   (A) Europeans and Aztecs were among the first people to make chocolate.
   (B) Chocolate is one of the most popular snack foods in the world today.
   (C) Cacao beans were first brought to Europe from Mexico in the sixteenth century.
   (D) The word *chocolate* is used to describe a variety of foods made from the beans of the cacao tree.

10. (F) NO CHANGE
    (G) Aztecs, and they used
    (H) Aztecs a people that use
    (J) Aztecs, who used

11. (A) NO CHANGE
    (B) 1519 that
    (C) 1519, that
    (D) 1519:

12. The purpose of this sentence is to:
    (F) describe the limited appeal chocolate initially had in Europe.
    (G) indicate that chocolate was once very expensive.
    (H) explain why Cortez brought chocolate back to Spain.
    (J) explain why the author refers to the beverage made from chocolate as "unusual."

13. The author is considering the addition of another sentence here that briefly describes one of the first European cafés to serve a chocolate drink. This addition would:
    (A) weaken the author's argument.
    (B) provide some interesting detail.
    (C) not fit with the topic of the paragraph.
    (D) highlight the author's opinion of chocolate.

14. What would be the most logical order of sentences in this paragraph?
    (F) NO CHANGE
    (G) 4, 1, 3, 2
    (H) 2, 3, 4, 1
    (J) 4, 3, 1, 2

15. The author is considering adding the following sentence to this paragraph: "This substance is also found in tea." Is this appropriate?
    (A) Yes, after sentence 2.
    (B) Yes, after sentence 3.
    (C) Yes, after sentence 4.
    (D) No, tea is outside the scope of this passage.

Question 16 asks about the preceding passage as a whole.

16. Suppose the author were given the assignment of writing about culinary trends in history. Would this essay satisfy the requirement?

(F) Yes, because the essay discusses many culinary trends in history.

(G) Yes, because the essay shows how chocolate has been used over time.

(H) No, because the essay focuses too much on chocolate in present times.

(J) No, because the essay only covers chocolate.

Homework

	Required	Recommended	In the Appendix
Quarter 2			
Inference Questions	#1, 5, 7, 9		
Writer's View Questions	#4, 20		
Function Questions	#14, 17		
Other		#2–3, 6, 8, 10–13, 15–16, 18–19	
Quarter 3			
Connections	#2, 5		
Verb Tense	#10–11, 14, 18, 20, 24–25		Pages 544–547
Wordiness	#1, 3–4, 7–8, 16, 19, 21–23, 30		Pages 594–595
Word Choice	#12–13, 15, 17, 26–29		
Other		#6, 9	
Quarter 4			
Writing Strategy	#2–5, 7–11, 13		
Organization	#1, 6, 12		

HOMEWORK

Quarter 2

Passage I

Prose Fiction: This passage is adapted from Katherine Mansfield's short story "Miss Brill," which was originally published in *The Garden Party and Other Stories*. In the passage, Miss Brill wears an old fur for her weekly visit to the park.

Miss Brill was glad that she had decided on her fur. Dear little thing! It was nice to feel it again. She had taken it out of its box that afternoon, shaken out
Line the moth powder, given it a good brush, and rubbed
(5) the life back into the dim little eyes. "What has been happening to me?" said the sad little eyes. Oh, how sweet it was to see them snap at her again.

There were a number of people out this afternoon, far more than last Sunday. And the band
(10) sounded louder.

Only two people shared her "special" seat: a fine old man in a velvet coat, his hands clasped over a huge carved walking stick, and a big old woman, sitting upright, with a roll of knitting on her
(15) embroidered apron. They did not speak. This was disappointing, for Miss Brill always looked forward to the conversation. She had become really quite expert, she thought, at listening as though she didn't listen, at sitting in on other people's lives just for a
(20) minute while they talked round her.

To and fro, in front of the flowerbeds and the band rotunda, the couples and groups paraded, stopped to talk, to greet, to buy a handful of flowers from the old beggar who had his tray fixed to the railings. Other
(25) people sat on the benches and green chairs, but they were nearly always the same, Sunday after Sunday, and—Miss Brill had often noticed—there was something funny about nearly all of them. They were odd, silent, nearly all old, and from the way they stared
(30) they looked as though they'd just come from dark little rooms or even—even cupboards!

Two young girls in red came by and two young soldiers in blue met them, and they laughed and paired and went off arm-in-arm. A beautiful woman came
(35) along and dropped her bunch of violets, and a little boy ran after to hand them to her, and she took them and threw them away as if they'd been poisoned. Dear me! Miss Brill didn't know whether to admire that or not.

Oh, how fascinating it was! How she enjoyed it!
(40) How she loved sitting here, watching it all! It was like a play. It was exactly like a play. Who could believe

the sky at the back wasn't painted? But it wasn't till a little brown dog trotted on solemnly and then slowly trotted off, like a little "theatre" dog, a little dog that
(45) had been drugged, that Miss Brill discovered what it was that made it so exciting. They were all on the stage. They weren't only the audience, not only looking on; they were acting. Even she had a part and came every Sunday. No doubt somebody would have
(50) noticed if she hadn't been there; she was part of the performance after all.

The band had been having a rest. Now they started again. And what they played was warm, sunny, yet there was just a faint chill—not sadness—no, not
(55) sadness—a something that made you want to sing. The tune lifted, lifted, the light shone; and it seemed to Miss Brill that in another moment all of them, all the whole company, would begin singing. The young ones, the laughing ones who were moving together, they would
(60) begin, and the men's voices, very resolute and brave, would join them. And then she too, she too, and the others on the benches—they would come in with a kind of accompaniment—something low, that scarcely rose or fell, something so beautiful, so moving...
(65) Just at that moment a boy and girl came and sat down where the old couple had been. They were beautifully dressed; they were in love. The hero and heroine, of course, just arrived from his father's yacht. And still soundlessly singing, still with that trembling
(70) smile, Miss Brill prepared to listen.

"No, not now," said the girl. "Not here, I can't."

"But why? Because of that stupid old thing at the end there?" asked the boy. "Why does she come here at all—who wants her? Why doesn't she keep her silly
(75) old mug at home?"

"It's her fur which is so funny," giggled the girl.

On her way home, Miss Brill usually bought a slice of honey-cake at the baker's. It was her Sunday treat. Sometimes there was an almond in her slice,
(80) sometimes not. It made a great difference. If there was an almond it was like carrying home a tiny present—a surprise—something that might very well not have been there.

But today she passed the baker's by, climbed the
(85) stairs, went into the little dark room—her room like a cupboard—and sat down. She sat there for a long time. The box that the fur came out of was on the bed. She unclasped the necklet quickly; quickly, without looking, laid it inside. But when she put the lid on she
(90) thought she heard something crying.

1. The passage suggests that Miss Brill goes to the park because:

   (A) she wants to show off her fox fur.

   (B) it is where she meets new friends.

   (C) she enjoys listening to other people's conversations.

   (D) she loves to hear the band play.

2. According to the passage, Miss Brill observes which of the following?

   (F) A woman throwing away poisoned violets

   (G) Two young girls meeting two young soldiers

   (H) An old man planting flowers

   (J) The young lovers boarding a yacht

3. According to the passage, Miss Brill changes her normal Sunday routine by:

   (A) talking with the young boy and girl.

   (B) becoming an actress on stage.

   (C) watching the actions of others in the park.

   (D) going home without stopping at the baker's for a slice of honey-cake.

4. Based on her depiction of Miss Brill, the author seems to perceive this character as:

   (F) a lonely woman who finds entertainment in watching and listening to others.

   (G) an outgoing woman who is an expert at listening to others' problems.

   (H) an unattractive woman who is frequently ridiculed.

   (J) an elderly woman who dreams of pursuing an acting career.

5. It is most reasonable to infer from the description of the boy and girl as "The hero and heroine, of course, just arrived from his father's yacht" (lines 67–68) that Miss Brill:

   (A) is well acquainted with them.

   (B) has heard from others in the park that they are in love.

   (C) thinks of them as actors on the stage of the park.

   (D) is overly concerned about their relationship.

6. As it is used in the passage, *company* (line 58) most closely means:

   (F) a group of guests.

   (G) a group of friends and acquaintances.

   (H) a group of actors or performers.

   (J) a business organization.

7. From the passage, it is most reasonable to infer that after Miss Brill listens to the boy and girl's conversation (lines 71–76), she realizes that:

   (A) her dream of acting on stage is unrealistic.

   (B) she can no longer enjoy her Sundays in the park.

   (C) many people in the park think of her as an interesting character in the "play" that takes place in the park.

   (D) some people in the park think that she is odd.

8. According to the passage, Miss Brill gets the idea that Sundays in the park are like an exciting play in which she participates when she:

   (F) sees the old woman knitting.

   (G) watches a dog slowly trot by.

   (H) sings with the other people in the park.

   (J) takes her fur out of storage.

9. From Miss Brill's memory of taking her fur out of storage (lines 1–7), it is most reasonable to infer that she thought of the fur:

   (A) as something like a pet.

   (B) only as a fashion accessory.

   (C) as part of her costume for the stage.

   (D) as an accessory that others might think of as humorous.

10. From the last paragraph of the passage, it is most reasonable to infer that:

    (F) Miss Brill will never return to the park.

    (G) Miss Brill no longer cares about her fur.

    (H) Miss Brill feels like crying about that day's experience in the park.

    (J) Miss Brill will no longer eavesdrop on other people's conversations.

Passage II

Humanities: This passage is excerpted from *A History of Women Artists* by Hugo Munsterberg (© 1975 by Hugo Munsterberg). Reprinted with permission of Clarkson N. Potter, Inc., a division of Crown Publishers, Inc.

There can be little doubt that women artists have been most prominent in photography and that they have made their greatest contribution in this field. One
Line reason for this is not difficult to ascertain. As
(5) several historians of photography have pointed out, photography, being a new medium outside the traditional academic framework, was wide open to women and offered them opportunities that the older fields did not.
(10)   All these observations apply to the first woman to have achieved eminence in photography—Julia Margaret Cameron. Born in 1815 in Calcutta into an upper-middle-class family and married to Charles Hay Cameron, a distinguished jurist and member of the
(15) Supreme Court of India, Julia Cameron was well known as a brilliant conversationalist and a woman of personality and intellect who was unconventional to the point of eccentricity. Although the mother of six children, she adopted several more and still found time
(20) to be active in social causes and literary activities. After the Camerons settled in England in 1848 at Freshwater Bay on the Isle of Wight, she became the center of an artistic and literary circle that included such notable figures as the poet Alfred, Lord Tennyson
(25) and the painter George Frederick Watts. Pursuing numerous activities and taking care of her large family, Mrs. Cameron might have been remembered as still another rather remarkable and colorful Victorian lady had it not been for the fact that, in 1863, her daughter
(30) presented her with photographic equipment, thinking her mother might enjoy taking pictures of her family and friends. Although 48 years old, Mrs. Cameron took up this new hobby with enormous enthusiasm and dedication. She was a complete beginner, but within a
(35) very few years she developed into one of the greatest photographers of her period and a giant in the history of photography. She worked ceaselessly and mastered the technical processes of photography, at that time far more cumbersome than they are today, turning her
(40) coal house into a darkroom and her chicken house into a studio. To her, photography was a "divine art," and in it she found her vocation. In 1864, she wrote triumphantly under one of her photographs, "My First Success," and from then until her death in Ceylon in
(45) 1874, she devoted herself wholly to this art.

Working in a large format (her portrait studies are usually about 11 inches by 14 inches) and requiring a long exposure (on the average 5 minutes), she produced a large body of work that stands up as one
(50) of the notable artistic achievements of the Victorian period. The English art critic Roger Fry believed that her portraits were likely to outlive the works of artists who were her contemporaries. Her friend Watts, then a very celebrated portrait painter, inscribed on one of
(55) her photographs, "I wish I could paint such a picture as this." Her work was widely exhibited, and she received gold, silver, and bronze medals in England, the United States, Germany, and Austria. No other female artist of the nineteenth century achieved such
(60) acclaim, and no other woman photographer has enjoyed such success.

Her work falls into two main categories on which her contemporaries and people today differ sharply. Victorian critics were particularly impressed by her
(65) allegorical pictures, many of them based on the poems of her friend and neighbor Tennyson. Contemporary taste much prefers her portraits and finds her narrative scenes sentimental and sometimes in bad taste. Yet, not only Julia Cameron, but also the painters of that time
(70) loved to depict subjects such as *Pray God, Bring Father Safely Home*. Still, today her fame rests upon her portraits for, as she herself said, she was intent upon representing not only the outer likeness but also the inner greatness of the people she portrayed.
(75) Working with the utmost dedication, she produced photographs of such eminent Victorians as Tennyson; Browning; Carlyle; Trollope; Longfellow; Watts; Darwin; Ellen Terry; Sir John Herschel, who was a close friend of hers; and Mrs. Duckworth, the mother
(80) of Virginia Woolf.

11. Which of the following conclusions can be most reasonably drawn from the passage's discussion of Julia Margaret Cameron?

   (A) She was a traditional homemaker until she discovered photography.

   (B) Her work holds a significant place in the history of photography.

   (C) She was unable to achieve in her lifetime the artistic recognition she deserved.

   (D) Her eccentricity has kept her from being taken seriously by modern critics of photography.

12. According to the passage, Cameron is most respected by modern critics for her:

    (F) portraits.
    (G) allegorical pictures.
    (H) use of a large format.
    (J) service in recording the likenesses of so many nineteenth-century figures.

13. The author uses which of the following methods to develop the second paragraph (lines 10–45)?

    (A) A series of anecdotes depicting Cameron's energy and unconventionality
    (B) A presentation of factual data demonstrating Cameron's importance in the history of photography
    (C) A critique of Cameron's early work
    (D) A chronological account of Cameron's background and artistic growth

14. The author uses the details in lines 37–41 ("She worked...a studio.") to indicate:

    (F) the economic constraints that Cameron had to overcome.
    (G) the reason that modern critics don't value Cameron's work.
    (H) the depth of Cameron's commitment to her art.
    (J) the extent of the challenges facing nineteenth-century photographers.

15. When the author says that Cameron had found "her vocation" (line 42), his main point is that photography:

    (A) offered Cameron an escape from the confines of conventional social life.
    (B) became the main interest of her life.
    (C) became her primary source of income.
    (D) provided her with a way to express her religious beliefs.

16. The main point of the third paragraph (lines 46–61) is that Cameron:

    (F) achieved great artistic success during her lifetime.
    (G) is the greatest photographer that ever lived.
    (H) was considered a more important artist during her lifetime than she is now.
    (J) revolutionized photographic methods in the Victorian era.

17. The author cites the opinions of an art critic and a "celebrated portrait painter" (lines 51–56) in order to:

    (A) illustrate the significance of Cameron's artistic accomplishments.
    (B) emphasize Victorian critics' preference for Cameron's allegorical work.
    (C) detail the envy Cameron's peers felt toward her.
    (D) counter the negative assessments of Cameron's work by more recent critics.

18. The author offers *Pray God, Bring Father Safely Home* as an example of:

    (F) a portrait of a celebrated Victorian.
    (G) an allegorical subject of the sort that was popular during the Victorian era.
    (H) a photograph in which Cameron sought to show a subject's outer likeness and inner greatness.
    (J) a photograph by Cameron that was scoffed at by her contemporaries.

19. According to the passage, which of the following opinions of Cameron's work was held by Victorian critics but is NOT held by modern critics?

    (A) Photographs should be based on poems.
    (B) Her portraits are too sentimental.
    (C) Narrative scenes are often in bad taste.
    (D) Her allegorical pictures are her best work.

20. The author's treatment of Cameron's development as a photographer can best be described as:

    (F) respectful.
    (G) condescending.
    (H) neutral.
    (J) defensive.

Quarter 3

Sherlock Holmes

Sherlock Holmes, the <u>ingenious and extremely clever</u>
1
detective with the deer-stalker hat, pipe, and magnifying glass, is a universally recognizable character. Everyone knows of Holmes's ability to solve even the most bizarre mysteries through the application of cold logic. <u>Therefore,</u>
2
<u>everyone</u> is also familiar with the phrase "Elementary, my
2
dear Watson," Holmes's perennial response to the requests

of his baffled sidekick, Dr. Watson, for an explanation of his amazing deductions. <u>Strictly speaking, of course, Holmes's "deductions" were not deductions at all, but inductive inferences.</u>
    3

Not as many people know about the creator of Sherlock Holmes, Sir Arthur Conan Doyle. Fans of Holmes might be surprised to discover that Conan Doyle did not want <u>to be engraved forever in the memory of the people</u> as
    4
the author of the Sherlock Holmes stories. <u>In fact,</u> Conan
    5
Doyle sent Holmes to his death at the end of the second book of short stories and subsequently felt a great sense of relief. Having had enough of his famous character by that time, <u>Sherlock Holmes would never divert him again from more serious writing, he promised himself.</u> It took
    6
eight years and the offer of a princely sum of money before Conan Doyle could be persuaded to revive the detective. <u>Conan Doyle was also knighted by the Queen of England,
    7
although not for his literary work.</u>
    7

Admirers of Holmes's coldly scientific approach to his detective work may also be taken aback when they learn that Conan Doyle was deeply immersed in spiritualism. For example, he and his family attempted to communicate with the dead by automatic writing, <u>thought to be a method of
    8
talking with those no longer among the living,</u> and through
    8
a spiritual medium, an individual who supposedly could contact those in the world beyond. Conan Doyle claimed to have grasped materialized hands and watched heavy objects swimming through the air during sessions led by the medium. Convinced by these experiences of the validity of paranormal <u>phenomena, that he lectured</u> on spiritualism
    9
in towns and villages throughout Britain. Conan Doyle seems never to have asked himself why those in the other world would manifest themselves in such curious ways or to have reflected on the fact that many of these effects are the standard trappings of cheating mediums. One has to wonder, <u>what will Sherlock Holmes have to say?</u>
    10

1. (A) NO CHANGE
   (B) ingenious
   (C) ingenious, extremely clever
   (D) cleverly ingenious

2. (F) NO CHANGE
   (G) Although everyone
   (H) For this reason, everyone
   (J) Everyone

3. (A) NO CHANGE
   (B) Strictly speaking Holmes's "deductions" were not deductions at all but inductive inferences.
   (C) Holmes's "deductions" were, strictly speaking, not deductions at all but inductive inferences.
   (D) OMIT the underlined portion.

4. (F) NO CHANGE
   (G) to go down in the annals of history
   (H) to be permanently thought of forever
   (J) to be remembered

5. (A) NO CHANGE
   (B) Despite this,
   (C) Regardless,
   (D) Yet

6. (F) NO CHANGE
   (G) the diversion of Sherlock Holmes, he promised himself, would never again keep him from more serious writing.
   (H) more serious writing consumed all his time from then on.
   (J) he promised himself that Sherlock Holmes would never again divert him from more serious writing.

7. (A) NO CHANGE
   (B) Although not for his literary work, Conan Doyle was also knighted by the Queen of England.
   (C) Knighted by the Queen of England, although not for his literary work, Conan Doyle was also.
   (D) OMIT the underlined portion.

8. (F) NO CHANGE
   (G) a means of getting in touch with those beyond the grave,
   (H) thought to be a method of talking with the dead,
   (J) OMIT the underlined portion.

9. (A) NO CHANGE
   (B) phenomena, he lectured
   (C) phenomena was he that he lectured
   (D) phenomena. He lectured

10. (F) NO CHANGE
    (G) what would Sherlock Holmes have said?
    (H) what is Sherlock Holmes going to say?
    (J) what had Sherlock Holmes said?

My Rafting Adventure

White-water rafting being a favorite pastime of mine
                           11
for several years. I have drifted down many challenging
North American rivers, including the Snake, the Green,
and the Salmon. I have spent some of my best moments
in dangerous rapids, yet nothing have ever matched the
                                    12
thrill I experienced facing my first rapids, on the Deschutes
River. My father and me spent the morning floating down
        13
a calm and peaceful stretch of the Deschutes in his wooden
MacKenzie river boat. This trip was the wooden boat's first
time down rapids, as well as mine. I could hear the water
roar as we approached Whitehorse Rapids. I felt much like
                                            14
a novice skier peering down her first steep slope; I was
scared but excited. The water churned, covering me with a
refreshing spray. My father, toward the stern, controlled the
oars. The carefree expression he usually wore on the river
had been replaced from a look of intense concentration as
                      15
he maneuvered around the boulders that dotted our path.
To release tension, we began to holler like kids on a roller
coaster, our voices echoing across the water as we lurched
violently about. Suddenly we came to a jarring halt
and stop; the left side of the bow was wedged on a large
16
rock. A whirlpool whirled around us; if we capsized, we
would be sucked into the undertow. Instinctively, I threw
all of my weight toward the right side of the tilting boat.
                                       17
Luckily, it was just enough force to dislodge us, and we
continued on down for about ten minutes of spectacular
rapids. Later that day, we will go through Buckskin Mary
                        18
Rapids and Boxcar Rapids. When we pulled up on the

bank that evening, we saw that the boat had received its
first scar: that scar was a small hole on the upper bow from
               19
the boulder we had wrestled with. In the years to come,
we went down many rapids and the boat receiving many
                                        20
bruises, but that trip through Whitehorse was the most
memorable one of all.

11. (A) NO CHANGE
    (B) have been
    (C) has been
    (D) was

12. (F) NO CHANGE
    (G) has ever matched
    (H) having ever matched
    (J) ever matched

13. (A) NO CHANGE
    (B) Both my father and me
    (C) My father as well as I
    (D) My father and I

14. (F) NO CHANGE
    (G) feel
    (H) had felt
    (J) discovered that I was feeling

15. (A) NO CHANGE
    (B) of a look
    (C) by a look
    (D) for a look

16. (F) NO CHANGE
    (G) or stop
    (H) and stopped
    (J) OMIT the underlined portion.

17. (A) NO CHANGE
    (B) on the tilting boat.
    (C) that tilted the boat.
    (D) that the boat tilted.

18. (F) NO CHANGE
    (G) would have gone through
    (H) go through
    (J) went through

19. (A) NO CHANGE
    (B) this scar was
    (C) a scar which was
    (D) OMIT the underlined portion.

20. (F) NO CHANGE
    (G) was receiving
    (H) received
    (J) receive

The History of Marbles

Taws, alleys, and flints are the names of particular kinds of marbles. The names of marbles may originate <u>from its</u> appearance, as in "cloudies," their use, as in
21
"shooters," or their original material. "Alleys," for example, were once made of alabaster. Marbles may be made from many different materials. In the eighteenth century, marbles were actually made from marble chips. Nowadays, marbles may consist of glass, baked clay, steel, onyx, plastic, or agate. Perhaps the key word regarding <u>marbles are "variety."</u>
22
Marbles can be <u>manipulated by</u> a variety of ways.
23
"Knuckling" is a technique in which the bottom of the hand is balanced against the ground while a marble placed against the forefinger is shot outward with the thumb. Marbles <u>can also be thrown, rolling, dropped, and even kicked.</u>
24
<u>There were also many varieties</u> of marble games. The most
25
common American version involves winning opponents' marbles by knocking them out of a designated area with one's own marbles. Another popular game is taw, also known as ringtaw or ringer, the object of which is to shoot marbles arranged like a cross out of a large ring. Players in a pot game such as moshie try to knock one another's marbles into a hole. In nineholes or bridgeboard, players shoot <u>his or her marbles</u> through numbered arches on a
26
board.

The popularity of marbles <u>spans centuries</u> and crosses
27
cultural boundaries as well. The first marble games took place in antiquity. <u>It was played with</u> nuts, fruit pits, or
28
pebbles. Even the great Augustus Caesar, <u>in addition with</u>
29
his Roman playmates, was known to have played marble games as a child. During Passover, Jewish children have customarily used filberts as marbles. Several traditional Chinese games are also played with marbles.

So, although most people consider the game of marbles to be just for children, <u>it actually has a complex history</u>. And
30
if anyone accuses you of having marbles in your head, you might ask them what kind.

21. (A) NO CHANGE
    (B) by its
    (C) from there
    (D) from their

22. (F) NO CHANGE
    (G) marbles is "variety."
    (H) marbles being "variety."
    (J) marbles were "variety."

23. (A) NO CHANGE
    (B) manipulated with
    (C) manipulated within
    (D) manipulated in

24. (F) NO CHANGE
    (G) are used for throwing, rolling, dropping, and even kicking.
    (H) can also be thrown, rolled, dropped, and even kicked.
    (J) can also throw, roll, drop, and kick.

25. (A) NO CHANGE
    (B) Many varieties also being
    (C) There are also many varieties
    (D) There was also many varieties

26. (F) NO CHANGE
    (G) your marbles
    (H) their marbles
    (J) our marbles

27. (A) NO CHANGE
    (B) span centuries
    (C) spanning centuries
    (D) spans hundreds of years

28. (F) NO CHANGE
    (G) They were played with
    (H) They were playing with
    (J) It plays with

29. (A) NO CHANGE
    (B) additionally with
    (C) along with
    (D) having the addition of

30. (F) NO CHANGE
    (G) it actual has a complex history.
    (H) the history that they have is actually complex.
    (J) it has a history that is actually complex.

Quarter 4

The paragraphs in this passage may not be in the most logical order. Each paragraph is numbered in brackets, and question 6 will ask you to choose the appropriate order.

Urban Legends

[1] Even though he knew it was illegal, he decided to keep the deer, and he loaded it in the back of his station wagon. They are often humorous in nature with a surprise ending. Urban legends have some characteristic features. As the hunter continued driving, the deer, which was temporarily knocked unconscious by the car, woke up and began thrashing around. On his way home, he accidentally hit and killed a deer on a deserted highway. The hunter panicked, stopped the car, ran to the ditch, and watched the enraged deer destroy his car. One such legend is the tale of the hunter who was returning home from an unsuccessful hunting trip.

Although today's technology enhances our ability to tell and retell urban legends, the Internet can also serve as a monitor of urban legends. Many websites are dedicated to researching the validity of commonly told urban legends. According to those websites, most legends, including the ones told here, have no basis in reality.

In addition to urban legends that are told from friend to friend, a growing number of urban legends are passed along through the Internet and email. One of the more popular stories is about a woman who was unwittingly charged $100 for a cookie recipe she requested at an upscale restaurant.

[2] To get her money's worth, this woman supposedly copied the recipe for the delicious cookies and forwarded it via email to everyone she knew.

Urban legends are stories we all have heard; they are supposed to have really happened, but they are never verifiable. It seems that the people involved can never be found. Researchers of the urban legend call the elusive participant in such supposed "real-life" events an FOAF—Friend of a Friend.

One legend involves alligators in the sewer systems of major metropolitan areas. According to the story, before alligators were a protected species, people vacationing in

Florida purchased baby alligators to take home as souvenirs. After the novelty of having a pet alligator wore off, many people flushed their baby souvenirs down toilets. Legend has it that the baby alligators found a perfect growing and breeding environment in city sewer systems, where they thrive to this day on the ample supply of rats.

Since primitive times, societies have told legends. Even before the development of written language, cultures would orally pass down these popular stories. [3] These stories served the dual purpose of entertaining audiences and transmitting values and beliefs from generation to generation. Although today we have many more permanent ways of handing down our beliefs to future generations, we continue to create and tell legends. In our technological society, a new form of folk tales has emerged: the urban legend.

1. What would be the most logical order of sentences in paragraph 1?

    (A) NO CHANGE
    (B) 3, 2, 7, 5, 1, 4, 6
    (C) 2, 6, 4, 1, 5, 7, 3
    (D) 3, 7, 5, 4, 1, 6, 2

2. The writer includes the example of the cookie recipe in order to:

    (F) rebut the assumption that all urban legends are untrue.
    (G) show that some urban legends could not be spread if it weren't for the Internet.
    (H) provide an example to support the premise of the paragraph.
    (J) provide an example to disprove the premise of the paragraph.

3. Suppose that the author wants to insert a sentence here to describe the different kinds of oral stories told by these societies. Which of the following sentences would best serve that purpose?

    (A) These myths and tales varied in substance from the humorous to the heroic.
    (B) These myths and tales were often recited by paid storytellers.
    (C) Unfortunately, no recording of the original myths and tales exists.
    (D) Sometimes it took several evenings.

Questions 4–6 ask about the preceding passage as a whole.

4. The author wants to insert the following sentence: "Other urban legends seem to be designed to instill fear." What would be the most logical placement for this sentence?

    (F) After the last sentence of paragraph 6
    (G) After the first sentence of paragraph 3
    (H) Before the first sentence of paragraph 5
    (J) After the last sentence of paragraph 5

5. Suppose that the author were assigned to write an essay comparing the purposes and topics of myths and legends in primitive societies and in our modern society. Would this essay fulfill that assignment?

    (A) Yes, because the essay describes myths and legends from primitive societies and from modern society.
    (B) Yes, because the essay provides explanations of possible purposes and topics for myths and legends from primitive societies and from modern society.
    (C) No, because the essay does not provide enough information about the topics of the myths and legends in primitive societies to make a valid comparison.
    (D) No, because the essay doesn't provide any information on the myths and legends of primitive societies.

6. What would be the most logical order of paragraphs for this essay?

    (F) NO CHANGE
    (G) 4, 3, 5, 2, 1, 6
    (H) 6, 4, 1, 5, 3, 2
    (J) 2, 6, 4, 3, 1, 5

The Space Shuttle

The Space Transportation System Space Shuttle Program, administered by the National Aeronautics and Space Administration (NASA), started before today's high school students were born. In the late 1960s and early 1970s, NASA and the United States Air Force conducted years of study to assess the feasibility of developing a reusable space transportation system. Previous spacecraft were disposable, single-use vehicles. In 1972, NASA selected Rockwell's Space Transportation Systems Division to design, develop, and test an orbiter.

The first prototype—the *Enterprise*—was rolled out on September 17, 1976. After nearly an additional year of testing, the *Enterprise* took off from the back of a 747 jet airliner on August 12, 1977, demonstrating that it could indeed fly and land like an airplane. However, the *Enterprise* was not equipped for real space flight. This claim went to *Columbia*, the second orbiter and the first to fly into space.

So began a complex tale of advances and difficulties for the U.S. space shuttle program. Pushing the boundaries of scientific, technological, and human invention, the intricacy of the program leaves a wide window for potential errors. It has made historic achievements while encountering serious obstacles.

[7] The shuttle program has accomplished significant firsts. Mission specialist Sally K. Ride was the first U.S. female in space in 1983. The following year, the *Challenger* carried Ride and mission specialist Kathryn D. Sullivan for the first flight with two women. Sullivan became the first female in the United States to walk in space. John Glenn was the first astronaut to fly 36 years after his original 1962 flight, in which he was the first American to orbit Earth. [8]

Not all shuttle experiments are successful though. Furthermore, financing for the program is substantial. An average mission costs about $400 million solely for launching and operating the shuttle—without the expenses of the payload (or satellite) that is carried into orbit. The average cost of the original missions in 1981 would have been about $200 million, based on the inflation rate between then and now. [9]

7. Which of the following most effectively and appropriately introduces this paragraph?

    (A) NO CHANGE
    (B) As with any difficult task, you experience many advances and difficulties.
    (C) The U.S. space shuttle program was a complete success from then on.
    (D) Although there were many obstacles, as you will see, the space shuttle program turned out to be a great investment.

8. What is the purpose of this paragraph, as it relates to the rest of the essay?

    (F) To highlight some of the successes of the shuttle program
    (G) To outline the history of the shuttle program
    (H) To predict the future of the shuttle program
    (J) To provide an alternative reason for the cost of the shuttle program

9. Which of the following sentences could best be added to the end of this essay as a conclusion?

   (A) Therefore, the shuttle program is too expensive for NASA to keep.

   (B) As you can see, the shuttle program abounds with success.

   (C) Yet despite these high costs, the shuttle program is an important aspect of NASA.

   (D) NASA will improve upon the shuttle program in years to come.

Question 10 asks about the preceding passage as a whole.

---

10. This essay's opening with a statement about the age of high school students provides a:

    (F) contradiction to the main idea that the shuttle program has had successes and failures.

    (G) concrete framework for the essay's readers to understand the history of the shuttle program.

    (H) general history of NASA's greatest accomplishments.

    (J) brief summary of the topic of the essay.

Maria Merian

At a time when it was considered daring, even shocking by many, to be a female painter, Maria Sibylla Merian was not only a painter but also a zoologist and botanist. Merian was born in Frankfurt in 1647. Although her father died when she was three years old, he had a lasting influence on her. A publisher and engraver, Merian's father was known for his production of a volume of scientific flower engravings. Her stepfather, a flower painter, also shared similar interests.

At the age of eighteen, Merian married Johann Andreas Graff, yet another painter who specialized in flower still-lifes. In 1679, Merian published the first of a three-volume study of 186 insects of Europe. Some of her observations were revolutionary. While her contemporaries believed that insects somehow sprang from the mud, Merian found that they have a distinct life cycle. She also discovered that each kind of insect has a predilection for a particular plant.

[11] Her second volume of engravings followed in 1684, the same year she separated from her husband. Sometime in the 1690s, they divorced.

[12] (1) Merian was one of the first people to travel to the New World for biological research. (2) In 1699, the city of Amsterdam funded a trip to the Dutch colony of Surinam on the South American coast. (3) She spent two years there

pursuing her studies, assisted by her two daughters. (4) In 1705, she published 60 large copper plates of her watercolor and oil studies and sketches.

Merian's final work was an illustrated history of the insects of Europe. This adventurous woman was one of those rare persons who combine artistic talent and skill with scientific insight. Her work contributed to many different fields.

11. The writer could most strengthen the essay at this point by adding a paragraph consisting of which of the following?

    (A) More examples of Merian's innovations

    (B) A discussion of the contributions of Merian's contemporaries

    (C) The sentence "Yes, a predilection for particular plants," to add rhetorical emphasis

    (D) A bibliography of contemporary articles on Merian's work

12. For unity and coherence in this paragraph, it would be best to place the numbered sentences in what order?

    (F) As they are now

    (G) Place sentence 4 before sentence 1

    (H) Place sentence 3 before sentence 2

    (J) Place Sentence 3 after Sentence 4

Question 13 asks about the preceding passage as a whole.

---

13. The intended audience for this passage is probably readers who:

    (A) wish to know more about Medieval Europe.

    (B) are professional art historians.

    (C) are interested in art history.

    (D) intend to travel to Amsterdam.

TABLE OF CONTENTS

	Test Review
	Homework Review
	Preview Quiz
	Session Objectives

Test Review

Your Kaplan practice test results not only tell you how well you did but also tell you what to do before your next test. Review your results carefully to determine a study plan.

English _____ **Math** _____ **Reading** _____ **Science** _____ **Writing** _____

English

1. In which three SmartPoint categories did you perform the best?

_____

_____

2. Which three need the most improvement?

_____

_____

Review these SmartPoint categories to see how you can improve your score in these categories.

3. How can you improve? (*circle those that apply*)
- Learn and practice Kaplan Methods and strategies.
- Improve grammar knowledge.
- Budget time more effectively.
- Practice more questions.
- Eliminate choices before guessing.

Mathematics

4. In which three SmartPoint categories did you perform the best?

_____

_____

5. Which three need the most improvement?

_____

_____

Review these SmartPoint categories to see how you can improve your score in these categories.

6. How can you improve? (*circle those that apply*)

- Learn and practice Kaplan Methods and strategies.
- Improve math knowledge.
- Budget time more effectively.
- Practice more questions.
- Eliminate choices before guessing.

Reading

7. In which three SmartPoint categories did you perform the best?

_____

_____

8. Which three need the most improvement?

_____

_____

Review these SmartPoint categories to see how you can improve your score in these categories.

9. How can you improve? (*circle those that apply*)

- Learn and practice Kaplan Methods and strategies.
- Budget time more effectively.
- Practice more questions.
- Eliminate choices before guessing.
- Read actively.

Science

10. In which three SmartPoint categories did you perform the best?

_____

_____

11. Which three need the most improvement?

_____

_____

Review these SmartPoint categories to see how you can improve your score in these categories.

12. How can you improve? (*circle those that apply*)

- Learn and practice Kaplan Methods and strategies.
- Budget time more effectively.
- Practice more questions.
- Eliminate choices before guessing.
- Focus on the purpose, method, and results.

Essay

Review the essay-scoring rubric and evaluate what improvements you can make to boost your essay score.

Session 4 Homework Review

1. The passage suggests that Miss Brill goes to the park because:

    (A) she wants to show off her fox fur.
    (B) it is where she meets new friends.
    (C) she enjoys listening to other people's conversations.
    (D) she loves to hear the band play.

2. Based on her depiction of Miss Brill, the author seems to perceive this character as:

    (F) a lonely woman who finds entertainment in watching and listening to others.
    (G) an outgoing woman who is an expert at listening to others' problems.
    (H) an unattractive woman who is frequently ridiculed.
    (J) an elderly woman who dreams of pursuing an acting career.

17. The author cites the opinions of an art critic and a "celebrated portrait painter" (lines 51–56) in order to:

    (A) illustrate the significance of Cameron's artistic accomplishments.
    (B) emphasize Victorian critics' preference for Cameron's allegorical work.
    (C) detail the envy Cameron's peers felt toward her.
    (D) counter the negative assessments of Cameron's work by more recent critics.

Not as many people know about the creator of Sherlock Holmes, Sir Arthur Conan Doyle. Fans of Holmes might be surprised to discover that Conan Doyle did not want to be engraved forever in the memory of the people as the author of the Sherlock Holmes stories. In fact, Conan Doyle sent
                                                                                                   5
Holmes to his death at the end of the second book of short stories and subsequently felt a great sense of relief.

5. (A) NO CHANGE
    (B) Despite this,
    (C) Regardless,
    (D) Yet

Conan Doyle seems never to have asked himself why those in the other world would manifest themselves in such curious ways or to have reflected on the fact that many of these effects are the standard trappings of cheating mediums. One has to wonder, what will Sherlock Holmes have to say?
                                                                                                   10

10. (F) NO CHANGE
    (G) what would Sherlock Holmes have said?
    (H) what is Sherlock Holmes going to say?
    (J) what had Sherlock Holmes said?

Suddenly we came to a jarring halt <u>and stop</u>; the left side of the bow was wedged on a large rock.
16
A whirlpool whirled around us; if we capsized, we would be sucked into the undertow. Instinctively,

I threw all of my weight toward the right side <u>of the tilting boat.</u>
17

16. (F) NO CHANGE
    (G) or stop
    (H) and stopped
    (J) OMIT the underlined portion.

17. (A) NO CHANGE
    (B) on the tilting boat.
    (C) that tilted the boat.
    (D) that the boat tilted.

[3]

In addition to urban legends that are told from friend to friend, a growing number of urban legends are passed along through the Internet and email. One of the more popular stories is about a woman who was unwittingly charged $100 for a cookie recipe she requested at an upscale restaurant. To get her money's worth, this woman supposedly copied the recipe for the delicious cookies and forwarded it via email to everyone she knew. 8

2. The writer includes the example of the cookie recipe in order to:

    (F) rebut the assumption that all urban legends are untrue.
    (G) show that some urban legends could not be spread if it weren't for the Internet.
    (H) provide an example to support the premise of the paragraph.
    (J) provide an example to disprove the premise of the paragraph.

[1]

(1) Even though he knew it was illegal, he decided to keep the deer, and he loaded it in the back of his station wagon. (2) They are often humorous in nature with a surprise ending. (3) Urban legends have some characteristic features. (4) As the hunter continued driving, the deer, which was temporarily knocked unconscious by the car, woke up and began thrashing around. (5) On his way home, he accidentally hit and killed a deer on a deserted highway. (6) The hunter panicked, stopped the car, ran to the ditch, and watched the enraged deer destroy his car. (7) One such legend is the tale of the hunter who was returning home from an unsuccessful hunting trip. 9

1. What would be the most logical order of sentences in paragraph 1?

    (A) NO CHANGE
    (B) 3, 2, 7, 5, 1, 4, 6
    (C) 2, 6, 4, 1, 5, 7, 3
    (D) 3, 7, 5, 4, 1, 6, 2

Preview Quiz

Passage I
Two scientists discuss their views of the quark model.

Scientist 1

According to the quark model, each proton consists of three quarks: two up quarks, which carry a charge of +2/3 each, and one down quark, which carries a charge of −1/3. All mesons, one of which is the π+ particle, are composed of one quark and one antiquark, and all baryons, one of which is the proton, are composed of three quarks. The quark model explains the numerous types of mesons that have been observed. It also successfully predicted the essential properties of the γ meson. Individual quarks, the only particles with a fractional charge, have not been observed because they are absolutely confined within baryons and mesons. However, the results of deep inelastic scattering experiments indicate that the proton has a substructure. In these experiments, high-energy electron beams were fired into protons. While most of the electrons that collided with the proton passed right through, a few bounced back. The number of electrons scattered through large angles indicated that there are three distinct lumps within the proton.

Scientist 2

The quark model is seriously flawed. Conventional scattering experiments should be able to split the proton into its constituent quarks, if they existed. Once the quarks were free, it would be easy to distinguish quarks from other particles using something as simple as the Millikan oil-drop experiment, because they would be the only particles that carried fractional charge. Furthermore, the lightest quark would be stable because there is no lighter particle for it to decay into. Quarks would be so easy to produce, identify, and store that they would have been detected if they truly existed. In addition, the quark model violates the Pauli exclusion principle, which originally was believed to hold for electrons but has been found to hold for all particles of half-integer spin. The Pauli exclusion principle states that no two particles of half-integer spin can occupy the same state. The Δ^{++} baryon, which supposedly consists solely of three up quarks, violates the Pauli exclusion principle because two of those quarks would be in the same state. Therefore, the quark model must be replaced.

1. Which of the following would most clearly strengthen Scientist 1's hypothesis?

   (A) Detection of the Δ^{++} baryon
   (B) Detection of a particle with fractional charge
   (C) Detection of mesons
   (D) Detection of baryons

2. Which of the following are reasons why Scientist 2 claims quarks should have been detected, if they existed?

   I.   They have a unique charge.
   II. They are confined within mesons and baryons.
   III. They are supposedly fundamental particles and, therefore, could not decay into any other particle.

   (F) I only
   (G) II only
   (H) I and III only
   (J) I, II, and III

3. A straight line in the coordinate plane passes through the points with (x,y) coordinates (5,2) and (−3,0). What are the (x,y) coordinates of the point at which the line passes through the y-axis?

   (A) $\left(0, \frac{5}{4}\right)$
   (B) $\left(0, \frac{3}{4}\right)$
   (C) $(0, 0)$
   (D) $\left(0, -\frac{5}{4}\right)$
   (E) $(0, -3)$

4. Line t in the standard (x,y) coordinate plane has a y intercept of −3 and is parallel to the line having the equation $3x - 5y = 4$. Which of the following is an equation for line t?

   (F) $y = -\frac{3}{5}x + 3$
   (G) $y = -\frac{3}{5}x - 3$
   (H) $y = \frac{3}{5}x + 3$
   (J) $y = \frac{5}{3}x + 3$
   (K) $y = \frac{3}{5}x - 3$

5. In the figure below, points *A, B,* and *C* lie on the circumference of the circle centered at *O*. If ∠*OAB* measures 50° and ∠*BCO* measures 60°, what is the measure of ∠*AOC*?

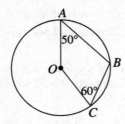

(A) 110°

(B) 120°

(C) 130°

(D) 140°

(E) 150°

6. When water is poured into rectangular box *A*, which has a base that measures 4 inches by 9 inches, the water comes to a height of 10 inches. If the same amount of water is poured into box *B*, which has a base that measures 5 inches by 6 inches, the water will come to a height of how many inches? (Assume that both boxes are tall enough to contain the water without overflow.)

(F) 8

(G) 9

(H) 10

(J) 11

(K) 12

Session Objectives

Quarter 2—13 SmartPoints

Scientific Reasoning Questions—13 SmartPoints

- Explain why experiments are set up the way they are and what they are set up to test.
- Learn how to think like a scientist

Conflicting Viewpoints Passages—Point Builder

- Identify and underline scientists' opinions to answer Conflicting Viewpoints questions.

Quarter 3—6 SmartPoints

Coordinate Geometry—6 SmartPoints

- Manipulate number lines.
- Define and graph $y = mx + b$ and find the slope and y-intercept of a line.
- Find the equations of lines that are parallel and perpendicular to $y = mx + b$.
- Graph a parabola.

Quarter 4—7 SmartPoints

Plane Geometry—7 SmartPoints

- Recognize properties of parallel lines cut by a transversal.
- Define the terms *parallel*, *tangent*, and *perpendicular*.
- Explain the basic properties of a triangle.
- Use the Pythagorean theorem to solve for an unknown side.
- Memorize common Pythagorean triplets and recognize their multiples.
- Apply the properties of special right triangles (45–45–90 and 30–60–90).
- Name different polygons and state the total angle measure of each.
- Recognize the properties of regular polygons.

13 SmartPoints	Scientific Reasoning Questions
Point Builder	Conflicting Viewpoints Passages
	Quiz

Scientific Reasoning Questions—13 SmartPoints

A. Scientific Reasoning questions essentially require you to use your logic skills and are very similar to Reading questions. Some of the questions you should ask yourself are explicitly related to Active Reading:

_____

_____

_____

_____

B. The key to successfully answering Scientific Reasoning questions is

_____

_____

C. It's very important that you effectively map the passage and identify the Purpose and Method of the experiments.

D. Many Scientific Reasoning passages include multiple experiments and will ask questions about the differences between experiments or differences in experimental procedure.

Passage I

The Brazilian tree frog (*Hyla faber*) exchanges gases through both its skin and lungs. The exchange rate depends on the temperature of the frog's environment. A pair of experiments was performed to investigate this dependence.

Experiment 1

Fifty frogs were placed in a controlled atmosphere that, with the exception of temperature, was designed to simulate their native habitat. The temperature was varied from 5°C to 25°C, and equilibrium was attained before each successive temperature change. The amount of oxygen absorbed by the frogs' lungs and skin per hour was measured, and the results for all the frogs were averaged. The results are shown below in Table 1.

Table 1		
Temperature (°C)	Moles O_2 absorbed/hr	
	Skin	Lungs
5	15.4	8.3
10	22.7	35.1
15	43.6	64.9
20	42.1	73.5
25	40.4	78.7

Experiment 2

The same frogs were placed under the same conditions as in Experiment 1. For this experiment, the amount of carbon dioxide eliminated through the skin and lungs was measured. The results are averaged and shown below in Table 2.

Table 2		
Temperature (°C)	Moles CO_2 eliminated/hr	
	Skin	Lungs
5	18.9	2.1
10	43.8	12.7
15	79.2	21.3
20	91.6	21.9
25	96.5	21.4

What is the purpose of these experiments?

To investigate the exchange rate based on temperature

Method of Experiment 1: _Oxygen absorbed_

Method of Experiment 2: _CO$_2$ absorbed_

>> **REMEMBER**

The factor that researchers intentionally vary is the independent variable.

>> **REMEMBER**

Remember to look for patterns between the independent and dependent variables.

What was the independent variable in the experiments above?

Temperature

What were the dependent variables?

In these experiments, as temperature increased, what happened to the gases?

1. Which of the following factors did researchers intentionally vary?

   (A) The number of frogs studied
   (B) The humidity of the frogs' simulated habitats
   (C) The temperature of the frogs' simulated habitats
   (D) The amount of oxygen in the frogs' simulated habitats

)) **REMEMBER**
When reading about multiple experiments, keep straight who did what.

2. Experiment 1 and Experiment 2 differed in that Experiment 2:

   (F) used a different species of tree frog.
   (G) studied a broader range of temperatures.
   (H) measured oxygen absorption through the skin only.
   (J) measured carbon dioxide elimination.

)) **REMEMBER**
Why an experiment was designed a certain way is more important than what was done.

3. Which of the following best explains why the researchers allowed the temperature in the simulated habitats to achieve equilibrium before each temperature change? The researchers wanted to allow:

   (A) time for additional oxygen to be removed from the habitats.
   (B) time for the frogs to adjust their oxygen absorption to the new temperature.
   (C) time for the researchers to increase or decrease carbon dioxide levels in the habitats.
   (D) time for the habitats' humidity level to adjust with the new temperature.

)) **REMEMBER**
Most experiments boil down to varying one factor while controlling the rest.

4. Which of the following best explains why the frogs were placed in a controlled atmosphere designed to simulate their native habitats?

   (F) The researchers wanted to manipulate some variables but leave other elements as they are naturally.
   (G) The researchers wanted to exclude natural predators from the frogs' environment.
   (H) The researchers wanted to be able to control the frogs' food supply.
   (J) The researchers wanted to be able to control the frogs' oxygen intake.

Passage II

When potassium nitrate (KNO_3) reacts with a particular rhodium complex, two different substances can potentially be formed. Substance 1 is a pale green solid with a melting point of approximately 85.0°C. Substance 2 is a dark blue solid with a melting point of approximately 62.5°C. To learn more about which reaction conditions encourage the formation of each product, chemists performed a series of experiments.

Experiment 1

Two 200-mL solutions (Solution A and Solution B) of the rhodium complex were prepared. The chemists used an acid to lower the pH of Solution A to pH 5.0 and a base to raise the pH of Solution B to pH 8.2. The two solutions were identical in all other ways.

When the chemists added 50 mL of KNO_3 to Solution A, a dark blue solid with a melting point of 62°C formed. When they added 50 mL of KNO_3 to Solution B, a yellow solid with a melting point of 76°C was formed. These results are shown in Table 1.

Table 1				
Solution	**pH**	**Melting point (°C)**	**Color**	**State**
A	5.0	62	Dark blue	Solid
B	8.2	76	Yellow	Solid

Experiment 2

Two more 200-mL solutions of the rhodium complex were prepared as in Experiment 1. Again, 50 mL of KNO_3 were added to each solution. Then the solutions were heated to 125°C for 30 minutes. A dark blue solid with a melting point of 62°C formed from Solution A, and a pale green solid with a melting point of 85°C formed from Solution B. These results are shown in Table 2.

Table 2			
Solution	**Melting point (°C)**	**Color**	**State**
A	62	Dark blue	Solid
B	85	Pale green	Solid

Experiment 3

Chemists again prepared two 200-mL rhodium complexes as in Experiments 1 and 2. Fifty mL of KNO_3 were added to each complex, as was a small amount of sodium acetate. The solutions were then heated to 125°C for 30 minutes. Solution A remained unchanged as a green liquid. Solution B formed a pale green solid with a melting point of 84.5°C. These results are shown in Table 3 below.

Table 3			
Solution	**Melting point (°C)**	**Color**	**State**
A	–	Green	Liquid
B	84.5	Pale green	Solid

5. Which factor did the chemists leave unchanged in all three experiments?

    (A) The temperature of the solutions
    (B) The initial amount of rhodium complex present
    (C) The amount of sodium acetate present
    (D) The amount of rhodium complex and the amount of sodium acetate present

)) REMEMBER
Conditions, factors, and *variables* all mean the same thing and usually signify a Scientific Reasoning question.

6. In order to learn more about the formation of Substance 1 and Substance 2, what experiment should the chemists perform next?

    (F) Varying the concentration of the solutions
    (G) Testing with a pH level of 7
    (H) Heating the solutions to 175°C
    (J) Freezing the solutions

)) REMEMBER
The correct answer will build on factors that have already been shown to have some effect on the experiment.

7. Other chemists have suggested that Substance 2 may react to form other, more easily dissolved products in the presence of certain acetates. This hypothesis is best supported by the fact that:

    (A) Substance 1 forms at a different pH than Substance 2.
    (B) Solution A yields a different color solid when heated.
    (C) Substance 2 is unstable in the presence of Substance 1.
    (D) no solid forms in Solution A when sodium acetate is added prior to heating.

Point Builder: Conflicting Viewpoints Passages

A. Conflicting Viewpoints passages require you to understand, evaluate, and compare theories. They may ask you to

_____

_____

_____

_____

_____

B. These questions can go beyond the scope of information in the passage. The correct answers, however, will always

_____

C. Remember _Keep straight who said what?_____

_____

_____

D. Scientific Reasoning questions occur primarily on Conflicting Viewpoints passages. The method for approaching these passages is different from the method for the other passages:

1. Read the introductory text and the first author's viewpoint and then answer the questions that ask only about the first author's viewpoint.

2. Read the text for the second author's viewpoint and then answer the questions that ask only about the second author's viewpoint.

3. Answer the questions that refer to both authors' viewpoints.

Passage III

The distinction between *eukaryotic* (nucleated) and *prokaryotic* (nonnucleated) cells is basic to modern biology. The first prokaryotes appeared two billion years before the first eukaryotes. Most single-celled organisms, such as bacteria, are prokaryotes, and most complex organisms consist of eukaryotic cells. Eukaryotes contain *mitochondria*, which are enclosed by inner and outer membranes. It has been suggested that mitochondria-containing eukaryotes evolved from a symbiotic relationship between two types of prokaryotes. Two scientists debate the issue.

Scientist 1

Eukaryotes developed from a symbiotic relationship between two types of prokaryotes. Early prokaryotes did not require O_2; there was no free O_2 in Earth's atmosphere until prokaryotes began releasing O_2 as a metabolic by-product. Eventually, some prokaryotes became *aerobic*, capable of utilizing free O_2. They were engulfed by *anaerobes*, prokaryotes that could not metabolize O_2. The aerobes gained a secure environment and a continuous food supply, while the anaerobes gained the ability to survive in an oxygen-rich environment. Over time, the symbiotic partners lost their independence, and the aerobic prokaryotes evolved into mitochondria. Mitochondrial DNA differs both genetically and structurally from the DNA in the eukaryotic cell's nucleus.

What is Scientist 1's viewpoint?

_____

_____

Scientist 2

Mitochondria could not have originated outside the eukaryotic cell. Although mitochondria synthesize several of the enzymes necessary for their own function, most mitochondrial proteins are controlled by genes in the nucleus of the eukaryotic cell and are synthesized outside of the mitochondria. Mitochondrial DNA and ribosomal proteins differ from those of bacteria. Therefore, mitochondria could not have evolved from aerobic prokaryotes. It is far more likely that eukaryotes developed directly from a single type of prokaryote and that mitochondria developed from the membrane of that prokaryote.

What is Scientist 2's viewpoint?

_____

_____

8. Scientist 2 emphasizes the differences between mitochondria and bacteria in order to:

   (F) prove that mitochondria could not have evolved from aerobic prokaryotes.
   (G) illustrate the superior aerobic capacity of mitochondria.
   (H) argue that bacteria are genetically less complex than mitochondria.
   (J) demonstrate the prokaryotic nature of mitochondria.

9. Mitochondrial DNA molecules are circular, having the same structure as prokaryotic DNA. This information weakens the viewpoint of:

   (A) Scientist 1 only.
   (B) Scientist 2 only.
   (C) both Scientist 1 and Scientist 2.
   (D) neither Scientist 1 nor Scientist 2.

Passage IV

Schizophrenia is a mental disorder that severely impacts the way 2.5 million Americans think, feel, and act. It is a disorder that makes it difficult for a person to tell the difference between real and imagined experiences or to behave normally in social situations. Two researchers discuss possible causes of schizophrenia.

Researcher 1

Schizophrenia is an organic disorder. Mounting pharmacological evidence suggests that schizophrenia is somehow related to hyperactivity of the dopaminergic system. The cause of the hyperactivity has yet to be determined. Some leading possibilities are a simple overrelease of dopamine (a neurotransmitter), overreaction to a dopaminergic stimulus by nerve receptors, overactivity in a related system, underactivity in an antagonist system, or a defect in a feedback mechanism. Antipsychotic drugs used in the treatment of schizophrenia are known to block dopamine receptors. Patients using these drugs sometimes develop side effects identical to Parkinson's disease, which is primarily a state of dopamine deficiency. Radioisotope studies clearly show that such antipsychotics bind to dopamine receptors in the brain and that the degree of binding correlates quite strongly with the anti-schizophrenic efficacy of the drug.

What is Researcher 1's viewpoint?

_____

_____

_____

Researcher 2

There is as yet no clear-cut evidence that all schizophrenics produce increased levels of dopamine, let alone that such levels are the causative agent of schizophrenia. If schizophrenia were caused by hyperactivity of the dopaminergic system, one would expect schizophrenics to display increased levels of homovanillic acid and decreased levels of serum prolactin. Such is not the case, however. Moreover, dopamine blockers effectively relieve most states of agitation and psychosis, whether or not the patient shows signs of schizophrenia. Schizophrenia is not an organic aliment but an emotional disorder. It is caused by childhood exposure to chronically dysfunctional communications within the family. One or both parents habitually emit double-blind messages (communications with multiple, conflicting levels of meaning that the child can neither accept nor reject). The child is mystified both by the constant injection of hidden meaning into seemingly routine messages and by the denial that such hidden meanings exist. The cognitive problems of many schizophrenics strongly resemble their families' transactional patterns of illogic and denial.

What is Researcher 2's viewpoint?

_____

_____

_____

10. Both researchers would agree that:

    (F) some of the symptoms of schizophrenia can be treated with drugs.

    (G) some of the symptoms of schizophrenia are similar to those of Parkinson's disease.

    (H) schizophrenia is caused by chemical imbalances.

    (J) schizophrenia is caused by early childhood exposure to dysfunctional communications.

>> **REMEMBER**
When a question stem asks for agreement, answer choices that refer to the opinion of just one researcher are incorrect.

11. Which of the following actions would Researcher 2 suggest to prevent schizophrenia in an individual?

    (A) Blocking the dopaminergic receptors

    (B) Suppressing the release of dopamine

    (C) Facilitating effective family communication

    (D) Giving the individual regular blood transfusions

>> **REMEMBER**
The correct answer will hinge on Researcher 2's hypothesis. Identify that first.

12. Some scientists have proposed that schizophrenia is caused by a virus, contracted before birth, that targets neurotransmitters. If true, this would support:

    (F) both researchers' hypotheses.

    (G) neither researcher's hypothesis.

    (H) Researcher 1's hypothesis.

    (J) Researcher 2's hypothesis.

>> **REMEMBER**
In which passage is the topic of neurotransmitters discussed?

Quiz

Passage V

A series of experiments was performed to study the environmental factors that affect the size and number of leaves on the *Cycas* plant.

Experiment 1

Five groups of 25 *Cycas* seedlings, all 2–3 cm tall, were allowed to grow for 3 months, each group at a different humidity level. All of the groups were kept at 75°F and received 9 hours of sunlight a day. The average leaf lengths, widths, and densities are shown in Table 1.

Table 1			
% Humidity	Average length (cm)	Average width (cm)	Average density* (leaves/cm)
15	5.6	1.6	0.13
35	7.1	1.8	0.25
55	9.8	2.0	0.56
75	14.6	2.6	0.61
95	7.5	1.7	0.52
* Number of leaves per 1 cm of plant stalk			

Experiment 2

Five new groups of 25 seedlings, all 2–3 cm tall, were allowed to grow for 3 months, each group receiving different amounts of sunlight at a constant humidity of 55%. All other conditions were the same as in Experiment 1. The results are shown in Table 2.

Table 2			
Sunlight (hrs/day)	Average length (cm)	Average width (cm)	Average density* (leaves/cm)
0	5.3	1.5	0.2
3	12.4	2.4	0.59
6	11.2	2.0	0.56
9	8.4	1.8	0.26
12	7.7	1.7	0.19
* Number of leaves per 1 cm of plant stalk			

Experiment 3

Five new groups of 25 seedlings, all 2–3 cm tall, were allowed to grow at a constant humidity of 55% for 3 months at different daytime and nighttime temperatures. All other conditions were the same as in Experiment 1. The results are shown in Table 3.

Table 3			
Day/night temperature (°F)	Average length (cm)	Average width (cm)	Average density* (leaves/cm)
85/85	6.8	1.5	0.28
85/65	12.3	2.1	0.53
65/85	8.1	1.7	0.33
75/75	7.1	1.9	0.45
65/65	8.3	1.7	0.39
* Number of leaves per 1 cm of plant stalk			

1. Which of the following conclusions can be made based on the results of Experiment 2 alone?

(A) The seedlings do not require long daily periods of sunlight to grow.

(B) The average leaf density is independent of the humidity the seedlings grew in.

(C) The seedlings need more water at night than during the day.

(D) The average length of the leaves increases as the amount of sunlight increases.

2. Seedlings grown at a 40% humidity level under the same conditions as in Experiment 1 would have average leaf widths closest to:

(F) 1.6 cm.

(G) 1.9 cm.

(H) 2.2 cm.

(J) 2.5 cm.

3. According to the experimental results, under which set of conditions would a *Cycas* seedling be most likely to produce the largest leaves?

(A) 5% humidity and 3 hours of sunlight

(B) 75% humidity and 3 hours of sunlight

(C) 95% humidity and 6 hours of sunlight

(D) 75% humidity and 6 hours of sunlight

4. Which variable remained constant throughout all of the experiments?

(F) The number of seedling groups

(G) The percent of humidity

(H) The daytime temperature

(J) The nighttime temperature

5. It was assumed in the design of the three experiments that all of the *Cycas* seedlings were:

(A) more than 5 cm tall.

(B) equally capable of germinating.

(C) equally capable of producing flowers.

(D) equally capable of further growth.

6. As a continuation of the three experiments listed, it would be most appropriate to next investigate:

(F) how many leaves more than 6.0 cm long there are on each plant.

(G) which animals consume *Cycas* seedlings.

(H) how the mineral content of the soil affects the leaf size and density.

(J) what time of year the seedlings have the darkest coloring.

Passage VI

At the deepest part of the breath, when the lungs have the greatest force, the lungs fill up the rib cage and then lift the ribs. The ribs lift the spine, and the force is transferred from the top of the spine to a bone of the skull called the occipital bone. The result is a yawn. Yawning has been associated with drowsiness or weariness, as well as acute myocardial infarction and aortic dissection (vasovagal reactions). However, the reasons why humans yawn remain unconfirmed. Two different viewpoints are presented below.

Scientist 1

Yawning is the human body's way of crying out for more oxygen in the bloodstream. Most yawns occur when a person is tired or bored. At such times, the body is not functioning at its optimal level and requires an increase in oxygen to return to normal activities. The respiratory system responds to this need by inducing a yawn. The deep breath of a yawn provides a sudden increase in the amount of oxygen in the blood and simultaneously rids the body of the excess carbon dioxide that has accumulated because of oxygen deficiency.

Scientist 2

Recent studies have shown that the number of times a person yawns is not affected by the amount of oxygen in the air he or she breathes. Oxygen-rich, oxygen-depleted, and normal air all lead to the same average number of yawns in a given time period. Respiration, therefore, is not the primary function of yawning. It is far more likely that yawning is actually a stretching mechanism. Both stretching and yawning most commonly occur during periods of tiredness. Particularly striking support for this theory is found in the behavior of people who are paralyzed on one side of their bodies from a stroke. It has been observed that such people can stretch limbs on the otherwise paralyzed sides of their bodies when they yawn.

7. There is no correlation between the amount of oxygen in the air and the number of times a person yawns in a day. This statement, if true, would best support the view of:

   (A) Scientist 1, because respiration is not a function of yawning.

   (B) Scientist 1, because stretching is not a function of yawning.

   (C) Scientist 2, because respiration is not a function of yawning.

   (D) Scientist 2, because stretching is not a function of yawning.

8. According to Scientist 2, the best evidence that respiration is not the primary function of yawning is that:

   (F) frequency of yawning is not affected by oxygen levels.

   (G) individuals who are paralyzed on one side can stretch their mobile sides by yawning.

   (H) most yawns occur when a person is bored or tired.

   (J) most people yawn regardless of whether or not they're tired.

9. Scientist 1 states that yawning is a body's way of bringing more oxygen into the bloodstream. Which of the following statements, if true, counters this?

   (A) A person's blood oxygen levels neither increase nor decrease after a yawn.

   (B) A person's blood oxygen levels always increase after a yawn.

   (C) A person's blood carbon dioxide levels always decrease after a yawn.

   (D) A person's muscles are insufficiently stretched by a yawn.

10. Scientist 1 and Scientist 2 would agree that:

    (F) yawns are caused by tiredness or boredom.

    (G) the primary cause of yawns is biological, not social.

    (H) yawns are caused by acute myocardial infarction and aortic dissection.

    (J) yawns are caused by a need to stretch.

11. According to Scientist 1, which of the following would keep a person from yawning?

    (A) Increase the amount of carbon dioxide in the bloodstream.

    (B) Stretch throughout the day.

    (C) Reduce pressure on the lungs.

    (D) Increase the amount of oxygen in the bloodstream.

12. According to the passage, yawning is associated with:

    (F) pain in the top of the spine and the occipital bone.

    (G) insufficient lung capacity.

    (H) cancer and autoimmune diseases.

    (J) acute myocardial infarction and aortic dissection.

13. A sleep center study found that individuals who had been awake for more than 24 hours yawned 1.5 times more frequently than those who had been awake for fewer than 12 hours. What conclusion would each scientist draw from this information?

    (A) Scientist 1 would conclude that a lack of sleep caused an increased need to stretch; Scientist 2 would conclude that a lack of sleep caused an increased need for oxygen.

    (B) Scientist 1 would conclude that a lack of sleep caused an increased need for oxygen; Scientist 2 would conclude that a lack of sleep caused an increased need to stretch.

    (C) Both scientists would agree that a lack of sleep caused an increased need for oxygen.

    (D) Both scientists would agree that a lack of sleep caused an increased need to stretch.

6 SmartPoints	Coordinate Geometry
	Quiz

Coordinate Geometry—6 SmartPoints

A. Questions that involve number lines can be solved quickly on Test Day.

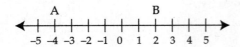

What do the following represent?

$\overline{AB}$ $\overleftrightarrow{AB}$

$\overrightarrow{AB}$ AB

B. Points, lines, and curves can all be plotted on the coordinate plane. Points in the coordinate plane are always written (x,y).

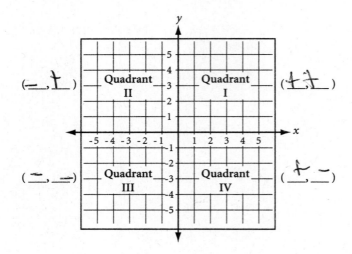

C. The midpoint of two endpoints—say (x_1,y_1) and (x_2,y_2)—is simply the average of the x-coordinates and the average of the y-coordinates.

The midpoint formula is _____

The Pythagorean theorem can be used to find the distance between any two points in the coordinate plane.

The distance between the same two endpoints can be expressed as _____

_____

1. What is the length of *AB* in the diagram below?

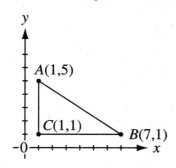

(A) 52
(B) 12
(C) $2\sqrt{13}$
(D) 4
(E) $\sqrt{13}$

D. Most ACT Math questions about Coordinate Geometry focus on linear equations.

For any equation in the form $y = mx + b$,

$m =$

$b =$

2. What is the *y*-intercept of the line that passes through the points (1, 21) and (4, 42)?

$$y - 21 = 7(x - 1)$$

(F) 0
(G) 7
(H) 9
(J) 14
(K) 19

» REMEMBER
Convert equations in standard form to slope-intercept form to easily identify the slope.

E. Parallel lines have _____.

Perpendicular lines have _____.

)) **REMEMBER**
Apply information from the
question stem to a given figure.

3. Which of the following is parallel to $4x + 3y = 15$?

  (A) $y = -\frac{4}{3}x - 5$

  (B) $y = \frac{3}{4}x + 5$

  (C) $y = \frac{3}{4}x - 5$

  (D) $y = \frac{4}{3}x + 5$

  (E) $y = 3x + 5$

4. In the figure below, point G is the midpoint of FH, and $HJ = JK$. If $HK = 18$, what is the value of GJ?

  (F) 13

  (G) 18

  (H) 22

  (J) 24

  (K) 26

F. High-difficulty questions that are found near the end of the ACT test include graphs of parabolas and circles.

G. The equation of a circle is _____.

$$x^2 + y^2 = 36$$

5. In the standard (x,y) coordinate plane, the graph of $x^2 + y^2 - 36 = 0$ depicts which of the following?

   (A) A square with a side of 6
   (B) A cube with a side of 36
   (C) An ellipse centered at the origin
   (D) A circle with a diameter of 6
   (E) A circle with a diameter of 12

» REMEMBER
Draw equations in the answer choices on the coordinate plane to visually determine the answer.

Solve It

- When two lines or curves intersect, they have the same values of x and y at the point of intersection.
- By applying your operations skills to the coordinates of a point, you can relocate the point on the coordinate plane.
- Ask yourself, "Can I pick numbers?" or "Can I backsolve?"

6. The parabola in the figure below will NEVER intersect with which of the following?

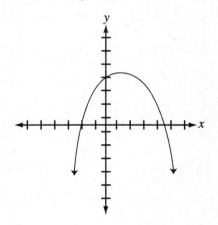

   (F) $y = 2$
   (G) $3x - y = 0$
   (H) $4x - 2y + 16 = 0$
   (J) $4x + 2y - 16 = 0$
   (K) $y = x^2$

$$-2y = -4x - 16$$
$$y = 2x + 8$$

$$2y = -4x + 16$$
$$y = -2x + 8$$

$$(x+2)(x-4.5) = 0$$
$$x^2 +$$

H. With quadratic equations, FOIL and factor to simplify:

FOIL stands for _____.

Factor the following: $x^2 + 21x - 72$

_____.

7. If $x^2 - 4x - 6 = 6$, what are the possible values for x?

(A) 4, 12
(B) −6, 2
(C) −6, −2
(D) 6, 2
(E) 6, −2

8. Which of the following is an equation for the graph in the standard (x, y) coordinate plane below?

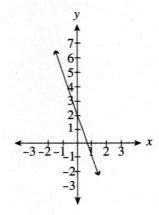

(F) $y = 3x - 2$
(G) $y = -3x + 2$
(H) $y = 2x + \frac{1}{2}$
(J) $y = \frac{1}{3}x + 2$
(K) $y = -\frac{1}{3}x + 2$

Quiz

1. What is the length of a line segment that has end points with (x, y) coordinates $(-2, 6)$ and $(3, -6)$?

   (A) 1
   (B) 5
   (C) 10
   (D) 13
   (E) 17

2. What are the coordinates of the point of intersection of AB and its perpendicular bisector?

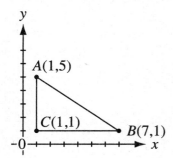

   (F) (1, 1)
   (G) (4, 3)
   (H) (3, 4)
   (J) (3, 1)
   (K) (1, 4)

3. Points $V(-2, -7)$ and $W(4, 5)$ determine the line segment $\overline{VW}$ in the standard (x, y) coordinate plane. If the midpoint of $\overline{VW}$ is $(1, p)$, what is the value of p?

   (A) −2
   (B) −1
   (C) 1
   (D) 2
   (E) 6

4. Line m passes through the point (4, 3) in the standard (x, y) coordinate plane and is perpendicular to the line described by the equation $y = -\frac{4}{5}x + 6$. Which of the following equations describes line m?

   (F) $y = \frac{5}{4}x + 2$
   (G) $y = -\frac{5}{4}x + 6$
   (H) $y = \frac{4}{5}x - 2$
   (J) $y = -\frac{4}{5}x + 2$
   (K) $y = \frac{5}{4}x - 2$

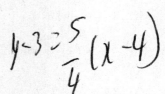

5. In the standard (x, y) coordinate plane shown in the figure below, points A and B lie on line m, and point C lies below it. The coordinates of points A, B, and C are (0, 5), (5, 5), and (3, 3), respectively. What is the shortest distance from point C to line m?

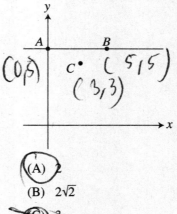

   (A) 2
   (B) $2\sqrt{2}$
   (C) 3
   (D) $\sqrt{13}$
   (E) 5

6. In the standard (x,y) coordinate plane, line l is perpendicular to the line containing the points $(5,6)$ and $(6,10)$. What is the slope of line l?

(F) -4

(G) $-\frac{1}{4}$

(H) $\frac{1}{4}$

(J) 4

(K) 8

7. If $x^2 - 6x + 1 = -4$, what are the possible values for x?

(A) $-6, 1$

(B) $-5, 1$

(C) $-5, -1$

(D) $5, 1$

(E) $5, -1$

8. $\sqrt{(x^2 + 4)^2} - (x + 2)(x - 2) = ?$

(F) $2x^2$

(G) $x^2 - 8$

(H) $2(x - 2)$

(J) 0

(K) 8

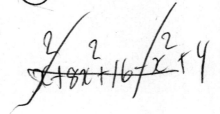

7 SmartPoints	Plane Geometry
	Quiz

Plane Geometry—7 SmartPoints
Lines and Angles
Formulas to Know

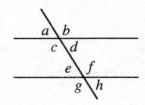

$\angle a = \angle d = \angle e = \angle h$

$\angle b = \angle c = \angle f = \angle g$

$\angle a + \angle b = 180°$

Terms to Know

Acute angle

Bisector

Complementary angles

Degree

Measure

Midpoint

Obtuse angle

Parallel (||)

Perpendicular (⊥)

Right angle

Supplementary angles

Vertical angles

A. The most basic figures of plane geometry are the following:

_____ *lines and angles* _____

1. $\overline{PQ}$ is perpendicular to $\overline{RS}$. Q is a point on $\overline{RS}$ If L is in the interior of $\angle PQS$ which of the following can be the measure of $\angle LQR$?

(A) 110°
(B) 90°
(C) 70°
(D) 50°
(E) 30°

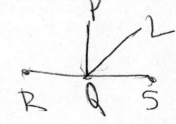

B. A line that divides an angle or another line into two equal pieces ___ *bisects* ___ it.

C. Lines can intersect in many ways.

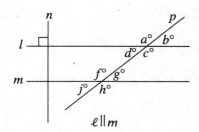

D. Angles that make up a line are supplementary and add up to 180°. Which angles in the figure above are supplementary?

_____

E. Angles that are across from each other are vertical and are equal. Which angles in the figure above are vertical?

_____

2. In the figure below, $\overline{CD}$ is parallel to $\overline{AB}$ and $\overline{PQ}$ intersects $\overline{CD}$ at R and $\overline{AB}$ at T. If the measure of $\angle CRP$ is 110°, what is the measure of $\angle ATQ$?

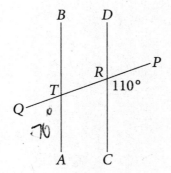

(F) 30°
(G) 50°
(H) 70°
(J) 90°
(K) 110°

)) REMEMBER
When a transversal crosses two parallel lines, all the acute angles are equal, and all the obtuse angles are equal.

Triangles
Formulas to Know

$A = \frac{1}{2}bh$

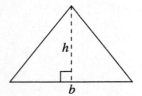

Ratios of Sides

45:45:90
$x:x:x\sqrt{2}$

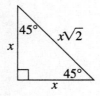

30:60:90
$x:x\sqrt{3}:2x$

Pythagorean Theorem

$a^2 + b^2 = c^2$

Pythagorean Triplets

3:4:5

5:12:13

A. About a third of ACT geometry questions focus on triangles.

B. All triangles have three things in common:

1. The sum of the interior angles of a triangle equals 180°.

2. Triangle Inequality Theorem: Any side of the triangle is less than the sum of, and greater than the difference between, the other two sides.

3. The area of a triangle is one-half of its base times its height.

---

3. In the figure below, $\overline{BD}$ bisects $\angle ABC$. The measure of $\angle ABC$ is 100°, and the measure of $\angle BAD$ is 60°. What is the measure of $\angle BDC$?

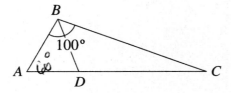

(A) 80°
(B) 90°
(C) 100°
(D) 110°
(E) 120°

C. Right triangles appear most often. Always look for hidden right triangles within complex figures.

D. Similar triangles have _____ *equal* _____ angles and _____ *proportional* _____ sides.

4. In the figure below, $AC = 10$, $BC = 6$, $CD = 9$, and $\angle ABC$ is a right angle. If $\overline{AC}$ is parallel to $\overline{ED}$ what is the length of $\overline{AE}$?

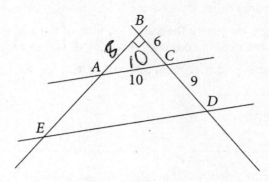

(F)   8
(G)   10
(H)   12
(J)   15
(K)   30

5. A ladder 20 feet long is placed against a wall such that the foot of the ladder is 12 feet from the wall. How many feet above the ground is the top of the ladder?

(A)   8
(B)   12
(C)   15
(D)   16
(E)   18

Circles

Formulas to Know

Area = πr^2

Circumference = $2\pi r$

Diameter = $2r$

Circles

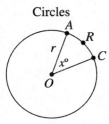

$$\frac{x}{360°} = \frac{\text{length}_{ARC}}{\text{circumference}} = \frac{\text{area}_{AOC}}{\text{area of a circle}}$$

A. Nearly everything you'll need to know about a circle is based on its radius.

---

6. What is the area, in square inches, of a circle with a circumference of 2π inches?

   (A) $\frac{\pi}{2}$

   (B) π

   (C) 2π

   (D) 4π

   (E) 8π

B. A line tangent to a circle is perpendicular to the radius at the point of contact.

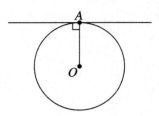

)) REMEMBER

Be careful not to mix up radius and diameter. This easy mistake to make will lead you right into a trap answer choice.

7. The circle below has a diameter of 6 inches. What is the length, in inches, of the arc that has a central angle of 60°?

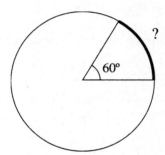

(A) π
(B) $\dfrac{3\pi}{2}$
(C) 2π
(D) 3π
(E) 6π

$$\frac{1}{6} = \frac{x}{6\pi}$$

Polygons
Formulas to Know

Squares

Area = s^2

Perimeter = $4s$

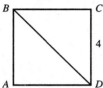

Squares

Rectangles

Area = bh

Perimeter = $2\ell + 2w$

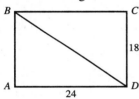

Rectangles

Parallelograms

Area = bh

Perimeter = $2\ell + 2w$

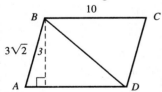

Parallelograms

Trapezoids

Area = $\dfrac{(b_1 + b_2)h}{2}$

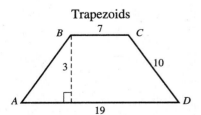

Trapezoids

A. Know the properties of polygons on Test Day.

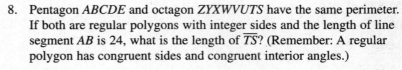

8. Pentagon *ABCDE* and octagon *ZYXWVUTS* have the same perimeter. If both are regular polygons with integer sides and the length of line segment *AB* is 24, what is the length of $\overline{TS}$? (Remember: A regular polygon has congruent sides and congruent interior angles.)

    (F) 11
    (G) 15
    (H) 19
    (J) 23
    (K) 27

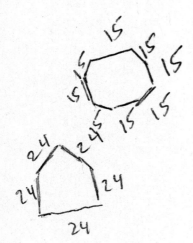

B. There are four major types of quadrilaterals: squares, rectangles, parallelograms, and trapezoids.

C. Every time you add a side to a figure, you add 180° to the sum of the interior angles.

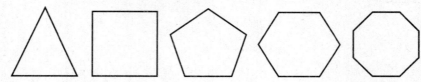

Rectangular Solids
Formulas to Know

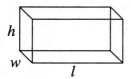

Volume = *lwh*
Surface area = 2*lw* + 2*lh* + 2*wh*

Cylinders

Volume = $\pi r^2 h$
Surface area = $2\pi r^2 + 2\pi rh$

Cubes

Volume = s^3
Surface area = $6s^2$

A. Complex and composite figures should be broken down into simple parts. Move information from one part of the figure to the next.

9. The figure below shows square *OABC* and a circle centered at *O*. If points *A* and *C* are on the circumference of the circle and the area of the square is 16, what is the area of the circle?

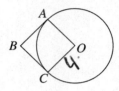

(A) 4
(B) 4π
(C) 8π
(D) 32
(E) 16π

B. Occasionally, a problem may require you to find the area of a shaded section of a figure. For these problems, it is sometimes easier to find the area of the unshaded section and subtract it from the area of the entire figure.

)) REMEMBER
Break composite and complex figures into simple shapes that you know.

10. The circle in the figure below is inscribed in a square with a perimeter of 16 inches. What is the area of the shaded region in square inches?

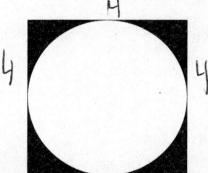

(F) 4π
(G) $16 - 2\pi$
(H) $16 - 4\pi$
(J) $8 - 2\pi$
(K) $8 - 4\pi$

C. The ACT will ask not only about the volume (*v*) but also the surface (*SA*) area of a rectangular prism, right cylinder, or cube. The surface area of a solid is _____.

11. In the figure below, a wooden plank is shown with its dimensions in inches. If Marcus wants to spray-paint every surface of the plank, how much paint, in square inches, will Marcus need?

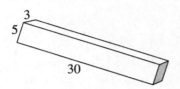

    (A) 38
    (B) 76
    (C) 240
    (D) 450
    (E) 510

12. As part of a Navy training exercise, paratroopers are trained to target circular landing zones, represented in the figure below. Paratroopers must land within a shaded area inscribed in the circle to pass the exercise. This area is shaped like an isosceles triangle. If the base of the triangle passes through the center of the circle and the circumference of the circle is 36π, what is the area of the landing triangle?

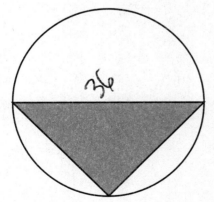

    (F) 36
    (G) 72
    (H) 108
    (J) 144
    (K) 324

Quiz

1. In the figure below, line *m* is parallel to line *n*, point *A* lies on line *m*, and points *B* and *C* lie on line *n*. If ∠*BAC* is a right angle, what is the measure of *y*?

    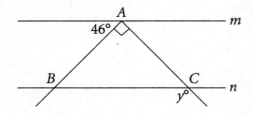

    (A) 54°
    (B) 90°
    (C) 124°
    (D) 136°
    (E) 154°

2. Lines *E*, *F*, and *G* are parallel lines cut by transversal *H* as shown below. What is the value of *a* + *b* + *c* + *d*?

    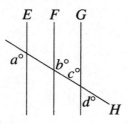

    (F) 180
    (G) 270
    (H) 360
    (J) 540
    (K) Cannot be determined from the given information.

3. What is the area in square units of the figure below?

    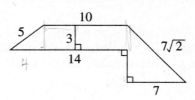

    (A) 147
    (B) 108.5
    (C) 91
    (D) 60.5
    (E) 39 + 7√2

4. If triangle *ABC* below is equilateral with side lengths 4√2, and $\overline{BD}$ is perpendicular to $\overline{AC}$, what is the length of $\overline{BD}$?

    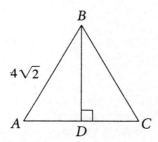

    (F) 2√2
    (G) 2√6
    (H) 3√3
    (J) 3√6
    (K) 4

5. In the figure below, x is closest to which of the following?

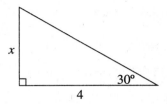

    (A) 2.3
    (B) 3.0
    (C) 4.2
    (D) 5.0
    (E) 6.9

6. In the parallelogram $WXYZ$ shown below, $\overline{WX}$ is 8 centimeters long. If the parallelogram's perimeter is 30 centimeters, how many centimeters long is $\overline{XY}$?

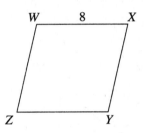

    (F) $3\frac{3}{4}$
    (G) 7
    (H) 8
    (J) 11
    (K) 14

7. What is the volume, in cubic inches, of the cylinder shown in the figure below?

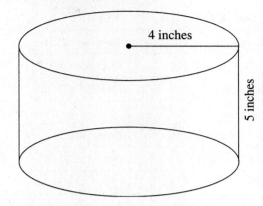

    (A) 20π
    (B) 40π
    (C) 60π
    (D) 80π
    (E) 100π

Homework

Science	Basic Assignment	Additional Practice	Appendix
Scientific Reasoning	Questions 1–6	Questions 14–25	
Conflicting Viewpoints	Questions 7–13	Questions 26–32	
Math			
Coordinate Geometry	Questions 1–10	Questions 11–15	
Plane Geometry	Questions 1–10	Questions 11–19	Pages 534–540
Online			
Quizzes and Workshops	Scientific Reasoning Quiz Conflicting Viewpoints Quiz Coordinate Geometry Quiz Plane Geometry Quiz	Scientific Reasoning Workshop Conflicting Viewpoints Workshop Coordinate Geometry Workshop Plane Geometry Workshop	

HOMEWORK

Quarter 2

Passage I

Ground-level ozone gas is a major component of urban smog. It is not emitted directly as a pollutant but is formed through a complex set of chemical reactions involving hydrocarbons, nitrogen oxides, and sunlight. The rate of ozone production increases with sunlight intensity and temperature and therefore peaks during hot summer afternoons.

The hydrocarbons and nitrogen oxides from which ozone is formed come primarily from fossil fuel–burning engines. Students at an urban high school hypothesized that their school buses emit more hydrocarbons when the engines idle for three minutes than they do when the drivers turn off the engines and then restart them. The students performed a series of experiments to test their hypothesis.

Experiment I

Students connected a collection bag to the exhaust pipe of one of their school buses. The bus's engine was started, and the exhaust was captured by the collection bag. A syringe was then used to extract a 5-mL sample of the exhaust. The exhaust was injected into a *gas chromatograph*, which separates mixtures of gases into their individual components. Students compared the exhaust to mixtures of known hydrocarbon concentration samples to determine what percent, by volume, of the sample was composed of hydrocarbons. The bus was started, and samples of the exhaust were collected and extracted at 30-second intervals. Exhaust samples from two other buses were also collected. The results are reproduced below in Table 1.

Table 1			
Time after starting (sec)	Percent of hydrocarbons in the exhaust		
	Bus 1 1984 Model X	Bus 2 1982 Model X	Bus 3 1996 Model X
30	10.3	9.0	5.4
60	11.2	9.8	4.9
90	12.0	13.2	6.0
120	10.5	22.9	4.9
150	9.6	21.0	4.5
180	9.5	20.1	4.2
210	9.4	19.2	4.2
240	9.3	19.2	3.8

Experiment 2

The exhaust of the buses was collected and tested again after the buses had been allowed to idle for 15 minutes, using the same procedure as Experiment 1. The results are reproduced below in Table 2.

Table 2			
Time after starting (min)	Percent of hydrocarbons in the exhaust		
	Bus 1 1984 Model X	Bus 2 1982 Model X	Bus 3 1996 Model X
15.0	5.5	6.1	1.8
15.5	5.5	6.1	1.8
16.0	5.4	6.2	1.8
16.5	5.4	6.2	1.8
17.0	5.4	6.1	1.8
17.5	5.4	6.1	1.8
18.0	5.3	6.1	1.8
18.5	5.3	6.1	1.8

1. Several students in the class also hypothesized that, at any given time, the exhaust of newer buses contains a lower percent of hydrocarbons on average than the exhaust of older buses. Do the results of Experiment 1 support this hypothesis?

   (A) Yes; the highest percent of hydrocarbons was found in the exhaust of the 1996 bus.
   (B) Yes; the lowest percent of hydrocarbons was found in the exhaust of the 1996 bus.
   (C) No; the highest percent of hydrocarbons was found in the exhaust of the 1982 bus.
   (D) No; the lowest percent of hydrocarbons was found in the exhaust of the 1982 bus.

2. One student was concerned that the school's gas chromatograph was unable to distinguish between the hydrocarbons and the carbon monoxide in the bus's exhaust. Which of the following procedures could the student follow to investigate this possibility?

   (F) Adding hydrocarbons to the bag before collecting exhaust
   (G) Getting a sample of exhaust from a teacher's car
   (H) Testing oxygen in the gas chromatograph
   (J) Testing a sample with known volumes of hydrocarbons and carbon monoxide in the gas chromatograph

3. Which of the following best explains why the students collected exhaust samples in a collection bag?

   (A) To keep air and other gases from contaminating the exhaust samples

   (B) To allow outside air and gases to mix with the exhaust samples equally

   (C) To capture only the hydrocarbons in the exhaust

   (D) To filter out sediments from the exhaust

4. Which factor of Experiment 1 did the students vary?

   (F) The time of day at which the samples were taken

   (G) The instruments used to collect the exhaust samples

   (H) The age of the buses tested

   (J) The amount of exhaust collected from the buses

5. Many states require that buses undergo emissions testing to pass an annual inspection. If the goal of the test is to determine peak emissions, then when, based on the results of the students' experiments, should the exhaust be sampled?

   (A) After 30–60 seconds

   (B) After 90–120 seconds

   (C) After 210–240 seconds

   (D) After 15 minutes

6. The main purpose of Experiment 2 was to:

   (F) determine the percentage of hydrocarbons in the exhaust of a warm, idling bus.

   (G) calibrate the gas chromatograph.

   (H) determine the percentage of nitrogen oxides in a bus's exhaust.

   (J) test the effectiveness of the exhaust collection bag.

Passage II

While the *focus* (point of origin) of most earthquakes lies less than 20 km below Earth's surface, certain unusual seismographic readings indicate that some activity originates at considerably greater depths. Below, two scientists discuss the possible causes of deep-focus earthquakes.

Scientist 1

Surface earthquakes occur when rock in Earth's crust fractures to relieve stress. However, below 50 km, rock is under too much pressure to fracture normally. Deep-focus earthquakes are caused by the pressure of fluids trapped in Earth's tectonic plates. As a plate is forced down into the mantle by convection, increases in temperature and pressure cause changes in the crystalline structure of minerals such as serpentine. In adopting a denser configuration, the crystals dehydrate, releasing water. Other sources of fluid include water trapped in pockets of deep-sea trenches and carried down with the plates. Laboratory work has shown that fluids trapped in rock pores can cause rock to fail at lower shear stresses. In fact, at the Rocky Mountain Arsenal, the injection of fluid wastes into the ground accidentally induced a series of shallow-focus earthquakes.

Scientist 2

Deep-focus earthquakes cannot result from normal fractures because rock becomes ductile at the temperatures and pressures that exist at depths greater than 50 km. Furthermore, mantle rock below 300 km is probably totally dehydrated because of the extreme pressure. Therefore, trapped fluids could not cause quakes below that depth. A better explanation is that deep-focus quakes result from the slippage that occurs when rock in a descending tectonic plate undergoes a phase change in its crystalline structure along a thin plane parallel to a stress. Just such a phase change and resultant slippage can be produced in the laboratory by compressing a slab of calcium magnesium silicate. The pattern of deep-quake activity supports this theory. In most seismic zones, the recorded incidence of deep-focus earthquakes corresponds to the depths at which phase changes are predicted to occur in mantle rock. For example, little or no phase change is thought to occur at 400 km, and indeed, earthquake activity at this level is negligible. Between 400 and 680 km, activity once again increases. Although seismologists initially believed that earthquakes could be generated at depths as low as 1,080 or 1,200 km, no foci have been confirmed below 700 km. No phase changes are predicted for mantle rock below 680 km.

7. Scientists 1 and 2 agree on which point?

   (A) Deep-focus earthquake activity does not occur below 400 km.

   (B) Fluid allows tectonic plates to slip past one another.

   (C) Water can penetrate mantle rock.

   (D) Rock below 50 km will not fracture normally.

8. Which of the following is evidence that would support the hypothesis of Scientist 1?

   (F) The discovery that water can be extracted from mantle-like rock at temperatures and pressures similar to those found below 300 km.

   (G) Seismographic indications that earthquakes occur 300 km below the surface of Earth.

   (H) The discovery that phase changes occur in the mantle rock at depths of 1,080 km.

   (J) An earthquake underneath Los Angeles that was shown to have been caused by water trapped in sewer lines

9. Both scientists assume that:

   (A) deep-focus earthquakes are more common than surface earthquakes.

   (B) trapped fluids cause surface earthquakes.

   (C) Earth's crust is composed of mobile tectonic plates.

   (D) deep-focus earthquakes cannot be felt on Earth's surface crust without special recording devices.

10. To best refute Scientist 2's hypothesis, Scientist 1 might:

   (F) find evidence of other sources of underground water.

   (G) record a deep-focus earthquake below 680 km.

   (H) find a substance that doesn't undergo phase changes even at depths equivalent to 680 km.

   (J) show that rock becomes ductile at depths of less than 50 km.

11. According to Scientist 1, the earthquake at Rocky Mountain Arsenal occurred because:

   (A) serpentine or other minerals dehydrated and released water.

   (B) fluid wastes injected into the ground compressed a thin slab of calcium magnesium silicate.

   (C) fluid wastes injected into the ground flooded pockets of a deep-sea trench.

   (D) fluid wastes injected into the ground lowered the shear stress failure point of the rock.

12. Scientist 2's hypothesis would be strengthened by evidence showing that:

   (F) water evaporates at high temperatures and pressures.

   (G) deep-focus earthquakes can occur at 680 km.

   (H) stress has the same effect on mantle rock that it has on calcium magnesium silicate.

   (J) water pockets exist at depths below 300 km.

13. The information in the passage indicates that:

   (A) most earthquakes originate near Earth's surface.

   (B) most earthquakes originate hundreds of kilometers below Earth's surface.

   (C) deep-sea earthquakes often are caused by volcanic activity.

   (D) earthquakes are Earth's most destructive natural phenomenon.

Passage III

Osmosis is the diffusion of a solvent (often water) across a semipermeable membrane from the side of the membrane with a lower concentration of dissolved material to the side with a higher concentration of dissolved material. The result of osmosis is an equilibrium—an even distribution—on both sides of the membrane. To prevent osmosis, external pressure must be applied to the side with the higher concentration of dissolved material. *Osmotic pressure* is the external pressure required to prevent osmosis. The apparatus shown below was used to measure osmotic pressure in the following experiments.

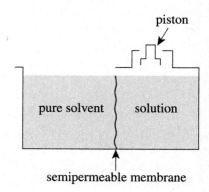

Experiment 1

Aqueous (water-based) solutions containing different concentrations of sucrose were placed in the closed side of the apparatus. The open side was filled with water. The plain water also contained a blue dye. The osmotic pressure created by the piston was measured for each solution at various temperatures. The results are shown in Table 1.

Table 1

Concentration of sucrose solution (mol/L)	Temperature (K)	Osmotic pressure (atm)
1.00	298.0	24.47
0.50	298.0	12.23
0.10	298.0	2.45
0.05	298.0	1.22
1.00	348.0	28.57
0.50	348.0	14.29
0.10	348.0	2.86
0.05	348.0	1.43

Experiment 2

Sucrose solutions of four different organic solvents were investigated in the same manner as in Experiment 1, with all trials at 298 K. The results are shown in Table 2.

Table 2

Solvent	Concentration of sucrose solution (mol/L)	Osmotic pressure (atm)
Ethanol	0.50	12.23
Ethanol	0.10	2.45
Acetone	0.50	12.23
Acetone	0.10	2.45
Diethyl ether	0.50	12.23
Diethyl ether	0.10	2.45
Methanol	0.50	12.23
Methanol	0.10	2.45

14. In Experiment 1, the scientists investigated the effect of:

(F) solvent and concentration on osmotic pressure.
(G) volume and temperature on osmotic pressure.
(H) concentration and temperature on osmotic pressure.
(J) temperature on atmospheric pressure.

15. What was the most likely purpose of the dye placed in the sucrose solutions in Experiments 1 and 2?

(A) The dye showed when osmosis was completed.
(B) The dye showed the presence of ions in the solutions.
(C) The dye was used to make the experiment more colorful.
(D) The dye was used to make the onset of osmosis visible.

16. According to the experimental results, osmotic pressure is dependent upon the:

(F) solvent and temperature only.
(G) solvent and concentration only.
(H) temperature and concentration only.
(J) solvent, temperature, and concentration.

17. A 0.10 mol/L aqueous sucrose solution is separated from an equal volume of pure water by a semipermeable membrane. If the solution is at a pressure of 1 atm and a temperature of 298 K, the pure water:

(A) will diffuse across the semipermeable membrane from the sucrose solution side to the pure water side.
(B) will diffuse across the semipermeable membrane from the pure water side to the sucrose solution side.
(C) will not diffuse across the semipermeable membrane.
(D) will diffuse across the semipermeable membrane, but the direction of diffusion cannot be determined.

18. Which of the following conclusions can be drawn from the experimental results?

I. Osmotic pressure is independent of the solvent used.
II. Osmotic pressure is only dependent upon the temperature of the system.
III. Osmosis occurs only when the osmotic pressure is exceeded.

(F) I only
(G) III only
(H) I and II only
(J) I and III only

19. According to Experiment 2, if methanol is used as a solvent, what pressure must be applied to a 0.50 mol/L solution of sucrose at 298 K to prevent osmosis?

(A) 24.46 atm
(B) 12.23 atm
(C) 2.45 atm
(D) 1.23 atm

Passage IV

Indigo buntings (*Passerina cyanea*), night-flying songbirds, are known to migrate each fall to Central America from their breeding grounds in the eastern United States. They then reverse the journey each spring. Researchers conducted the following experiments to determine how *Passerina cyanea* orient themselves during migration.

Experiment 1

Passerina cyanea, in indoor cages that permitted full view of the sky while blocking ground objects, were observed in April and September. The results are recorded in Figure 1 below.

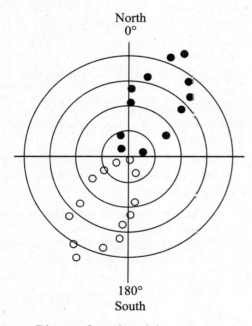

Distance from the origin represents
the number of birds observed in the
direction indicated, where 0° = true north;

● = April and ○ = September.

Figure 1

Experiment 2

Passerina cyanea were observed in a planetarium during April and September under both normal and "reversed" projections (i.e., fall constellations in April and spring constellations in September). The results are recorded in Figures 2a and 2b below.

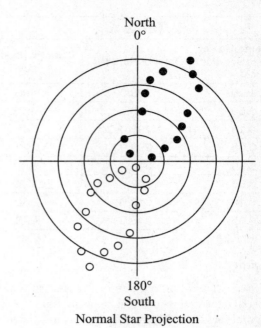

Normal Star Projection

Figure 2a

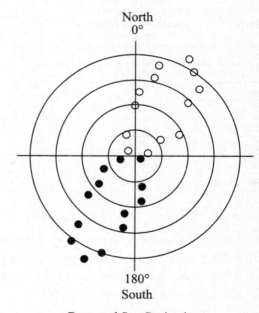

Reversed Star Projection

Figure 2b

Experiment 3

Two groups of newborn indigo buntings (*Passerina cyanea*) were raised by researchers in isolation from adult birds, one group in a planetarium with normal night skies projected and the other group in a windowless room with diffuse illumination. Both groups were observed during September in a planetarium with fall constellations projected. The observations are recorded in Figure 3 below.

North
0°

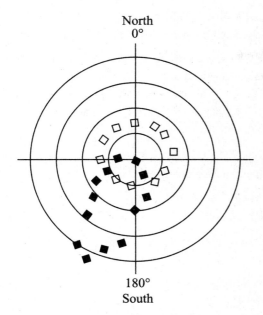

180°
South

■ = planetarium-raised birds
□ = birds raised in windowless room

Figure 3

20. The results of which experiment(s) suggest that indigo buntings that are not exposed to the stars cannot orient themselves during migration?

(F) Experiment 1 only
(G) Experiment 2 only
(H) Experiment 3 only
(J) Experiments 2 and 3 only

21. Which experiment should researchers perform next to determine more about the ability of *Passerina cyanea* to orient themselves for migration?

(A) Place adult *Passerina cyanea* in cages with a full view of the sky and ground objects.
(B) Feed adult *Passerina cyanea* a diet consisting primarily of insects.
(C) Raise newborn *Passerina cyanea* in cages with a full view of the sky and ground objects.
(D) Raise newborn *Passerina cyanea* in a windowless room until the age of 3 months and then allow them to view the stars.

22. The purpose of Experiment 3 was to test whether the indigo bunting's ability to choose a migration direction is influenced by:

(F) being raised from birth without adults and in windowless rooms.
(G) seasonal temperature variations.
(H) whether the bird is raised indoors or outdoors.
(J) the presence of other species of migratory birds.

23. Which of the following observations, if true, would weaken the hypothesis that indigo buntings use star positions as a directional guide during migration?

I. Newborn indigo buntings, raised with adult birds in a windowless room, orient themselves correctly when placed in outdoor cages on clear nights in September.
II. Indigo buntings in outdoor cages orient themselves correctly during April and September on completely overcast nights.
III. Other species of migratory birds fly by day when stars are invisible.

(A) I only
(B) II only
(C) III only
(D) I and III only

24. If a group of newborn *Passerina cyanea* raised in a windowless room as in Experiment 3 was observed during April in a planetarium with spring constellations, the birds would probably display:

(F) no particular orientation.
(G) an orientation similar to that of planetarium-raised birds.
(H) a predominantly eastward orientation.
(J) a predominantly westward orientation.

25. If a group of newborn buntings was isolated from adult birds and raised in outdoor cages, the birds most likely would:

(A) orient themselves correctly only in April.
(B) orient themselves correctly only in September.
(C) orient themselves correctly in both April and September.
(D) orient themselves correctly in neither April nor September.

CONFLICTING VIEWPOINTS

Passage V

Two scientists discuss their views on the quark model.

Scientist 1

According to the quark model, each proton consists of three quarks: two up quarks, which carry a charge of +2/3 each, and one down quark, which carries a charge of −1/3. All mesons, one of which is the π+ particle, are composed of one quark and one antiquark, and all baryons, one of which is the proton, are composed of three quarks. The quark model explains the numerous types of mesons that have been observed. It also successfully predicted the essential properties of the γ meson. Individual quarks, the only particles with a fractional charge, have not been observed because they are absolutely confined within baryons and mesons. However, the results of deep inelastic scattering experiments indicate that the proton has a substructure. In these experiments, high-energy electron beams were fired into protons. While most of the electrons that collided with the proton passed right through, a few bounced back. The number of electrons scattered through large angles indicated that there are three distinct lumps within the proton.

Scientist 2

The quark model is seriously flawed. Conventional scattering experiments should be able to split the proton into its constituent quarks, if they existed. Once the quarks were free, it would be easy to distinguish quarks from other particles using something as simple as the Millikan oil-drop experiment, because they would be the only particles that carried fractional charge. Furthermore, the lightest quark would be stable because there is no lighter particle for it to decay into. Quarks would be so easy to produce, identify, and store that they would have been detected if they truly existed. In addition, the quark model violates the Pauli exclusion principle, which originally was believed to hold for electrons but has been found to hold for all particles of half-integer spin. The Pauli exclusion principle states that no two particles of half-integer spin can occupy the same state. The Δ++ baryon, which supposedly consists solely of three up quarks, violates the Pauli exclusion principle because two of those quarks would be in the same state. Therefore, the quark model must be replaced.

26. Which of the following could Scientist 1 use to counter Scientist 2's point about the Pauli exclusion principle?

    (F) Evidence that quarks do not have half-integer spin

    (G) Evidence that the Δ++ baryon exists

    (H) Evidence that quarks have fractional charge

    (J) Evidence that quarks have the same spin as electrons

27. If Scientist 1's hypothesis is correct, the Δ++ baryon should have a charge of:

    (A) −1

    (B) 0

    (C) +1

    (D) +2

28. According to Scientist 2, the quark model is flawed because:

    (F) the existence of individual baryons cannot be experimentally verified.

    (G) the existence of individual quarks cannot be experimentally verified.

    (H) particles cannot have fractional charge.

    (J) it doesn't include electrons as elementary particles.

29. Scientist 1 believes that some of the high-energy electrons that were aimed into the proton in the deep inelastic scattering experiments bounced back because:

    (A) they hit quarks.

    (B) they hit other electrons.

    (C) they were repelled by the positive charge on the proton.

    (D) they hit baryons.

30. The fact that deep inelastic scattering experiments revealed a proton substructure of three lumps supports the quark model because:

    (F) protons are mesons, and mesons supposedly consist of three quarks.

    (G) protons are mesons, and mesons supposedly consist of one quark and one antiquark.

    (H) protons are baryons, and baryons supposedly consist of three quarks.

    (J) protons are baryons, and baryons supposedly consist of one quark and one antiquark.

Quarter 3

1. What is the sum of the values of x for which
    $2x^2 = 2x + 12$?

    (A) –2
    (B) –1
    (C) 0
    (D) 1
    (E) 2

2. How much greater is the y-intercept of the line
    $5x + 7y = 49$ than that of the line $7y - 6x = 21$?

    (F) –1
    (G) 2
    (H) 4
    (J) 13
    (K) 28

3. Which of the following represents the midpoint of
    $(x + 4, x + 5)$ and $(x + 2, x - 1)$?

    (A) $(x - 3, x - 3)$
    (B) $(x - 3, x + 3)$
    (C) $(x + 3, x - 2)$
    (D) $(x + 3, x)$
    (E) $(x + 3, x + 2)$

4. The line that passes through the points $(1, 1)$ and
    $(2, 16)$ in the standard (x, y) coordinate plane is
    parallel to the line that passes through the points
    $(-10, -5)$ and $(a, 25)$. What is the value of a?

    (F) –15
    (G) –10
    (H) –8
    (J) –4
    (K) 10

5. In the standard (x, y) coordinate plane, at which
    x-value does the line described by $3x + y = 9$ intersect
    the x-axis?

    (A) –9
    (B) –3
    (C) $-\frac{1}{3}$
    (D) 3
    (E) 9

6. In the standard (x, y) coordinate plane, three corners
    of a rectangle are $(2, -2)$, $(-5, -2)$, and $(2, -5)$.
    Where is the rectangle's fourth corner?

    (F) $(2, 5)$
    (G) $(-2, 5)$
    (H) $(-2, 2)$
    (J) $(-2, -5)$
    (K) $(-5, -5)$

7. What is the slope of any line parallel to the line
    $4x + 3y = 9$?

    (A) –4
    (B) $-\frac{4}{3}$
    (C) $\frac{4}{9}$
    (D) 4
    (E) 9

8. Which of the following best describes the graph on the
    number line below?

    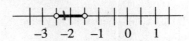

    (F) $-|x| = -2$
    (G) $-|x| < 0.5$
    (H) $-3 < x < -1$
    (J) $-1.5 < x < -2.5$
    (K) $-1.5 > x > -2.5$

9. In the (x, y) coordinate plane, what is the y-intercept of
    the line $12x - 3y = 12$?

    (A) –4
    (B) –3
    (C) 0
    (D) 4
    (E) 12

10. Among the points graphed on the number line below,
    which is closest to e? (Note: $e \approx 2.718281828$.)

    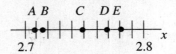

    (F) A
    (G) B
    (H) C
    (J) D
    (K) E

11. In the standard (x, y) coordinate plane, if the x-coordinate of each point on a line is 9 more than 3 times the y-coordinate, the slope of the line is:

    (A) -9

    (B) -3

    (C) $\frac{1}{3}$

    (D) 3

    (E) 9

12. In the standard (x, y) coordinate plane, what is the slope of the line through the origin and $\left(\frac{1}{3}, \frac{3}{4}\right)$?

    (F) $\frac{1}{4}$

    (G) $\frac{1}{3}$

    (H) $\frac{5}{12}$

    (J) $\frac{3}{4}$

    (K) $\frac{9}{4}$

13. In the standard (x, y) coordinate plane, if the distance between the points $(r, 6)$ and $(10, r)$ is 4 coordinate units, which of the following could be the value of r?

    (A) 3

    (B) 4

    (C) 7

    (D) 8

    (E) 10

14. From 1970 to 1980, the population of City Q increased by 20%. From 1980 through 1990, the population increased by 30%. What was the combined percent increase for the period 1970–1990?

    (F) 25%

    (G) 26%

    (H) 36%

    (J) 50%

    (K) 56%

Quarter 4

1. A rectangle is two times as wide as it is long, and x represents the area of the rectangle in square centimeters. If both the length and width are doubled, what will be the area in square centimeters of the new rectangle in terms of x?

   (A) $2x$
   (B) $3x$
   (C) $4x$
   (D) $6x$
   (E) $8x$

2. A certain triangle has a height three times as long as its base. If it has an area of 216 square inches, what is the length in inches of its base?

   (F) 6
   (G) 12
   (H) 18
   (J) 54
   (K) 108

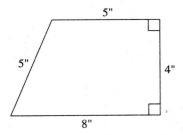

3. The figure shown below belongs in which of the following classifications?

   (I) Polygon
   (II) Quadrilateral
   (III) Rectangle
   (IV) Trapezoid

   (A) I only
   (B) II only
   (C) IV only
   (D) I, II, and III only
   (E) I, II, and IV only

4. If the lengths, in inches, of all three sides of a triangle are integers, and one side is 7 inches long, what is the smallest possible perimeter of the triangle, in inches?

   (F) 9
   (G) 10
   (H) 15
   (J) 21
   (K) 24

5. The two rectangles in the figure below have the same area. What is a expressed in terms of b?

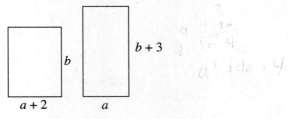

   (A) $\dfrac{2b}{3}$
   (B) $\dfrac{3b}{2}$
   (C) $\dfrac{2}{3b}$
   (D) $\dfrac{3}{2b}$
   (E) $b - 1$

6. In the figure below, the area of parallelogram $PQRS$ is 24 square units. The length of $\overline{QR}$ is 6 units, $\overline{QT}$ is perpendicular to $\overline{PS}$ and T is the midpoint of $\overline{PS}$. What is the perimeter, in units, of $PQRS$?

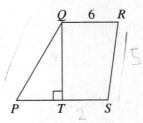

   (F) 20
   (G) 22
   (H) 24
   (J) 26
   (K) 28

7. In the figure below, the circle centered at R is tangent to the circle centered at S. Point S is on the circumference of circle R. If the area of circle R is 6 square inches, what is the area, in square inches, of circle S?

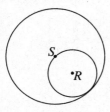

(A) 12
(B) 24
(C) 36
(D) 12π
(E) 36π

8. In the figure below, O is the center of the circle and P, O, and Q are collinear. If $\angle ROQ$ measures 50°, what is the measure of $\angle RPQ$?

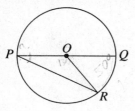

(F) 20°
(G) 25°
(H) 30°
(J) 35°
(K) 40°

9. What is the measure of $\angle ABC$ in the figure below?

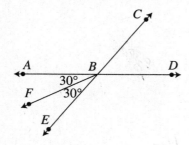

(A) 30°
(B) 60°
(C) 90°
(D) 120°
(E) Cannot be determined from the information given.

10. A triangle has sides with lengths 6, 8, and 10 units, and a square has a perimeter of 28 units. What is the positive difference, in square units, between the area of the triangle and the area of the square?

(F) 1
(G) 4
(H) 25
(J) 100
(K) 148

11. In the figure below, $\overline{AB} = 20$, and $\overline{BC} = 15$, $\angle ADB$ and $\angle ABC$ are right angles. What is the length of $\overline{AD}$?

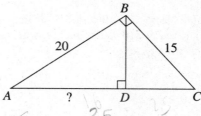

(A) 9
(B) 12
(C) 15
(D) 16
(E) 25

12. Jolene is wrapping a present. She wants to wrap it with two pieces of ribbon, as shown below. Both pieces of ribbon must go completely around the present. How much ribbon, in inches, does she need to wrap this present?

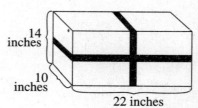

(F) 92
(G) 102
(H) 112
(J) 120
(K) 136

13. How many feet long is the diameter of a circle that has a circumference of 36π feet?

(A) 12
(B) 18
(C) 6π
(D) 36
(E) 18π

14. What is the area, in square inches, of the trapezoid below?

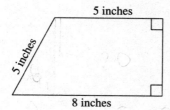

5 inches

5 inches

8 inches

(F) 22
(G) 24
(H) 26
(J) 28
(K) 32.5

15. In the figure below, O is the center of the circle, and C, D, and E are points on the circumference of the circle. If $\angle OCD$ measures 70° and $\angle OED$ measures 45°, what is the measure of $\angle CDE$?

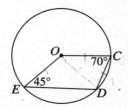

(A) 25°
(B) 45°
(C) 70°
(D) 90°
(E) 115°

16. In isosceles triangle ABC, $\overline{AB}$ and $\overline{BC}$ are congruent. If $\angle CAB = 27°$, what is the measure of $\angle ABC$?

(F) 27°
(G) 54°
(H) 90°
(J) 126°
(K) 153°

17. The diagonal of a square has a length of 8 inches. What is the area of the square, in square inches?

(A) $4\sqrt{2}$
(B) $8\sqrt{2}$
(C) 16
(D) 32
(E) 64

18. The inside diagonal of the square picture frame shown below is $4\sqrt{2}$ inches long. Its outside dimensions are 6 inches by 6 inches. What is the width (w), in inches, of this picture frame?

(F) $\dfrac{1}{\sqrt{2}}$
(G) 1
(H) $\sqrt{2}$
(J) 2
(K) $2\sqrt{2}$

19. In triangle XYZ below, $\overline{XS}$ and $\overline{SZ}$ are 3 and 12 units, respectively. If the area of XYZ is 45 square units, how many units long is altitude $\overline{YS}$?

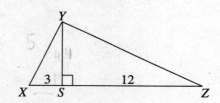

(A) 3
(B) 6
(C) 9
(D) 12
(E) 15

TABLE OF CONTENTS

	Analyzing Your Test
	Session 5 Homework Review
	Preview Quiz
	Session Objectives

Analyzing Your Test

Your Kaplan Practice Test results not only tell you how well you did, but also tell you what to do before your next test. Review your results carefully to determine a study plan.

Math

1. In which three SmartPoint categories did you perform the best?

   _____

2. Which three need the most improvement?

   _____

3. How can you improve? (*circle those that apply*)
   - Learn and practice Kaplan strategies.
   - Improve math knowledge.
   - Budget time more effectively.
   - Practice more questions.
   - Avoid questions that you're unlikely to answer correctly.
   - Eliminate choices before guessing.

Reading

4. In which three SmartPoint categories did you perform the best?

   _____

5. Which three need the most improvement?

   _____

6. How can you improve? (*circle those that apply*)
   - Learn and practice Kaplan strategies.
   - Read actively.
   - Budget time more effectively.
   - Practice more questions.
   - Eliminate choices before guessing.

English

7. In which three SmartPoint categories did you perform the best?

    _____

8. Which three need the most improvement?

    _____

9. How can you improve? (*circle those that apply*)
    - Learn and practice Kaplan strategies.
    - Practice more questions.
    - Budget time more effectively.
    - Eliminate choices before guessing.
    - Avoid questions that you're unlikely to answer correctly.
    - Improve grammar knowledge.

Science

10. In which SmartPoint category did you perform the best?

    _____

11. Which needs the most improvement?

    _____

12. How can you improve? (*circle those that apply*)
    - Learn and practice Kaplan strategies.
    - Read actively.
    - Practice more questions.
    - Budget time more effectively.
    - Eliminate choices before guessing.

Essay

13. How can you improve? (*circle those that apply*)
    - Plan essay before beginning to write.
    - Use stronger examples in essay.

RESPONSE SUMMARY

Ask yourself these questions when looking at the Response Summary on your Practice Test results. Revisit them after each test to identify trends in your test-taking methods.

1. Did you leave a group of questions blank at the end of a section? **Yes/No**

2. Did you answer a group of English questions incorrectly? **Yes/No**

3. Did you answer a group of Reading questions incorrectly? **Yes/No**

4. Did you answer a series of questions incorrectly at the end of a Math section? **Yes/No**

5. Did you answer a series of questions incorrectly at the beginning of a Math section? **Yes/No**

6. Did you answer a series of questions incorrectly on the Science section? **Yes/No**

7. Did you answer more questions incorrectly in the Reading/Science sections than the Math/English ones? **Yes/No**

If You Circled Yes

1. If you left questions blank at the end of a section, you probably ran out of time. Work on budgeting your time more carefully, but don't rush to answer every question. Spend your valuable time on questions you're likely to answer correctly.

2. If you answered a group of English questions incorrectly, you may be reading too quickly or not reading the parts of the passage where there are no underlined words. Read the passages for comprehension and grammar.

3. If you answered a group of Reading questions incorrectly, you may have misunderstood the passage. Spend enough time (about 3 minutes) on a passage to get a basic understanding of it and look up details as needed. Map the passage!

4. If you answered a series of questions incorrectly at the end of a Math section, you are likely answering questions that you don't have enough time to solve accurately. If you don't have enough time to solve a question or eliminate any answer choices, you should still guess, since you do not lose any points for an incorrect answer.

5. If you answered some early Math questions incorrectly, you are probably working too quickly. Remember, early questions, which are likely to be lower-difficulty questions, are worth as many points as the higher-difficulty questions at the end of the section.

6. If you answered a group of Science questions incorrectly, you may have misunderstood the experiments or read the results too quickly. Research the answer and predict and match your prediction to the answer choices.

7. If you are answering more questions incorrectly later in the test, you are probably fatigued. Take more timed, full-length practice tests, which Kaplan offers online, to build your test-taking stamina.

Session 5 Homework Review

Session 5, Quarter 2: Science

Passage V

While the *focus* (point of origin) of most earthquakes lies less than 20 km below Earth's surface, certain unusual seismographic readings indicate that some activity originates at considerably greater depths. Below, two scientists discuss the possible causes of deep-focus earthquakes.

Scientist 1

Surface earthquakes occur when rock in Earth's crust fractures to relieve stress. However, below 50 km, rock is under too much pressure to fracture normally. Deep-focus earthquakes are caused by the pressure of fluids trapped in Earth's tectonic plates. As a plate is forced down into the mantle by convection, increases in temperature and pressure cause changes in the crystalline structure of minerals such as serpentine. In adopting a denser configuration, the crystals dehydrate, releasing water. Other sources of fluid include water trapped in pockets of deep-sea trenches and carried down with the plates. Laboratory work has shown that fluids trapped in rock pores can cause rock to fail at lower shear stresses. In fact, at the Rocky Mountain Arsenal, the injection of fluid wastes into the ground accidentally induced a series of shallow-focus earthquakes.

Scientist 2

Deep-focus earthquakes cannot result from normal fractures because rock becomes ductile at the temperatures and pressures that exist at depths greater than 50 km. Furthermore, mantle rock below 300 km is probably totally dehydrated because of the extreme pressure. Therefore, trapped fluids could not cause quakes below that depth. A better explanation is that deep-focus quakes result from the slippage that occurs when rock in a descending tectonic plate undergoes a phase change in its crystalline structure along a thin plane parallel to a stress. Just such a phase change and resultant slippage can be produced in the laboratory by compressing a slab of calcium magnesium silicate. The pattern of deep-quake activity supports this theory. In most seismic zones, the recorded incidence of deep-focus earthquakes corresponds to the depths at which phase changes are predicted to occur in mantle rock. For example, little or no phase change is thought to occur at 400 km, and indeed, earthquake activity at this level is negligible. Between 400 and 680 km, activity once again

increases. Although seismologists initially believed that earthquakes could be generated at depths as low as 1,080 or 1,200 km, no foci have been confirmed below 700 km. No phase changes are predicted for mantle rock below 680 km.

7. Scientists 1 and 2 agree on which point?

(A) Deep-earthquake activity does not occur below 400 km.

(B) Fluid allows tectonic plates to slip past one another.

(C) Water can penetrate mantle rock.

(D) Rock below 50 km will not fracture normally.

8. Which of the following is evidence that would support the hypothesis of Scientist 1?

(F) The discovery that water can be extracted from mantle-like rock at temperatures and pressures similar to those found below 300 km.

(G) Seismographic indications that earthquakes occur 300 km below the surface of Earth.

(H) The discovery that phase changes occur in the mantle rock at depths of 1,080 km.

(J) An earthquake underneath Los Angeles that was shown to have been caused by water trapped in sewer lines.

9. Both scientists assume that:

(A) deep-focus earthquakes are more common than surface earthquakes.

(B) trapped fluids cause surface earthquakes.

(C) Earth's crust is composed of mobile tectonic plates.

(D) deep-focus earthquakes cannot be felt on Earth's crust without special recording devices.

10. To best refute Scientist 2's hypothesis, Scientist 1 might:

(F) find evidence of other sources of underground water.

(G) record a deep-focus earthquake below 680 km.

(H) find a substance that doesn't undergo phase changes even at depths equivalent to 680 km.

(J) show that rock becomes ductile at depths of less than 50 km.

11. According to Scientist 1, the earthquake at Rocky Mountain Arsenal occurred because:

    (A) serpentine or other minerals dehydrated and released water.
    (B) fluid wastes injected into the ground compressed a thin slab of calcium magnesium silicate.
    (C) fluid wastes injected into the ground flooded pockets of deep-sea trench.
    (D) fluid wastes injected into the ground lowered the shear stress failure point of the rock.

12. Scientist 2's hypothesis would be strengthened by evidence showing that:

    (F) water evaporates at high temperatures and pressures.
    (G) deep-focus earthquakes can occur at 680 km.
    (H) stress has the same effect on mantle rock that it has on calcium magnesium silicate.
    (J) water pockets exist at depths below 300 km.

13. The information in the passage indicates that:

    (A) most earthquakes originate near Earth's surface.
    (B) most earthquakes originate hundreds of kilometers below Earth's surface.
    (C) deep-sea earthquakes often are caused by volcanic activity.
    (D) earthquakes are Earth's most destructive natural phenomenon.

Session 5, Quarter 3: Math

2. How much greater is the y-intercept of the line $5x + 7y = 49$ than that of the line $7y - 6x = 21$?

    (F) −1
    (G) 2
    (H) 4
    (J) 13
    (K) 28

4. The line that passes through the points $(1, 1)$ and $(2, 16)$ in the standard (x, y) coordinate plane is parallel to the line that passes through the points $(-10, -5)$ and $(a, 25)$. What is the value of a?

    (A) −15
    (B) −10
    (C) −8
    (D) −4
    (E) 10

8. Which of the following best describes the graph on the number line below?

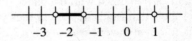

    (A) $-|x| = -2$
    (B) $-|x| < 0.5$
    (C) $-3 < x < -1$
    (D) $-1.5 < x < -2.5$
    (E) $-1.5 > x > -2.5$

$7y = -5x + 49$

$y = -\dfrac{5}{7}x + 7$

$7y = 6x + 21$

$y = \dfrac{6}{7}x + 3$

$\dfrac{25 + 5}{-10-}$

$$\sqrt{r^2 - 12r + 36 + r^2 - 20r + 160}$$

13. In the standard (x,y) coordinate plane, if the distance between the points $(r, 6)$ and $(10, r)$ is 4 coordinate units, which of the following could be the value of r?

(F) 3
(G) 4
(H) 7
(J) 8
(K) 10

$$\sqrt{(r-6)^2 + (10-r)^2} = 4$$

Session 5, Quarter 4: Math

5. The two rectangles in the figure below have the same area. What is a expressed in terms of b?

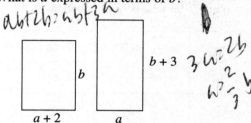

$ab + 2b = ab + 3n$

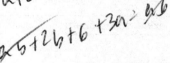

$b + 3$ $3n = 2b$

$n = \frac{2}{3}b$

(A) $\dfrac{2b}{3}$

(B) $\dfrac{3b}{2}$

(C) $\dfrac{2}{3b}$

(D) $\dfrac{3}{2b}$

(E) $b - 1$

$\dfrac{b}{a+2} = \dfrac{b+3}{n}$

$ab + 2b + 6 + 3a = ab$

6. In the figure below, the area of parallelogram $PQRS$ is 24 square units. The length of $\overline{QR}$ is 6 units, $\overline{QT}$ is perpendicular to $\overline{PS}$, and T is the midpoint of $\overline{PS}$. What is the perimeter, in units, of $PQRS$?

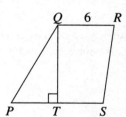

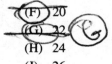

(F) 20
(G) 22
(H) 24
(J) 26
(K) 28

11. In the figure below, $\overline{AB} = 20$, $\overline{BC} = 15$, and $\angle ADB$ and $\angle ABC$ are right angles. What is the length of $\overline{AD}$?

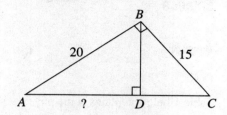

(A) 9
(B) 12
(C) 15
(D) 16
(E) 25

15. In the figure below, O is the center of the circle, and C, D, and E are points on the circumference of the circle. If $\angle OCD$ measures $70°$ and $\angle OED$ measures $45°$, what is the measure of $\angle CDE$?

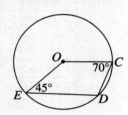

(F) 25°
(G) 45°
(H) 70°
(J) 90°
(K) 115°

Preview Quiz

Science

Passage I

READ

Table 1 below contains some physical properties of common optical materials. The refractive index of a material is a measure of the amount by which light is bent upon entering the material. The transmittance range is the range of wavelengths over which the material is transparent.

Table 1				
Material	Refractive index for light of 0.589 μm	Transmittance range (μm)	Useful range for prisms (μm)	Chemical resistance
Lithium fluoride	1.39	0.12–6	2.7–5.5	Poor
Calcium fluoride	1.43	0.12–12	5–9.4	Good
Sodium chloride	1.54	0.3–17	8–16	Poor
Quartz	1.54	0.20–3.3	0.20–2.7	Excellent
Potassium bromide	1.56	0.3–29	15–28	Poor
Flint glass*	1.66	0.35–2.2	0.35–2	Excellent
Cesium iodide	1.79	0.3–70	15–55	Poor
*Flint glass is lead oxide–doped quartz.				

1. According to Table 1, which material(s) will transmit light at 25 μm?

    (A) Potassium bromide only
    (B) Potassium bromide and cesium iodide
    (C) Lithium fluoride and cesium iodide
    (D) Lithium fluoride and flint glass

2. A scientist hypothesizes that any material with poor chemical resistance would have a transmittance range wider than 10 μm. The properties of which of the following materials contradict this hypothesis?

    (F) Lithium fluoride
    (G) Flint glass
    (H) Cesium iodide
    (J) Quartz

Session Objectives

Quarter 2—9 SmartPoints

Kaplan Method for Reading Comprehension: Active Reading Review—Point Builder
- Review and practice the Kaplan Method for Reading Comprehension and understand how it helps earn points on Test Day.
- Review Active Reading strategies.

Prose Fiction—9 SmartPoints
- Understand how prose fiction passages are different from the other passage types and practice implementing appropriate passage-mapping tactics.

Quarter 3

Essay ReKap—Point Builder
- Understand and practice how to implement the Kaplan Method for Essay Writing to produce a high-scoring essay.

Know What to Expect: Scoring Review—Point Builder
- Learn what ACT essay graders are looking for in a high-scoring essay.

The Kaplan Method for ACT English: Style and Usage—Point Builder
- Review the Kaplan Method for ACT English and how to implement it effectively.

Quarter 4—36 SmartPoints

The Kaplan Method for Math—Point Builder
- Review the Kaplan Method for Math and practice implementing it under timed conditions.

The Kaplan Method for Science: Figure Interpretation, Patterns, Scientific Reasoning, and Conflicting Viewpoints—36 points
- Review the Kaplan Method for Science and how it applies to different passage and question types.
- Practice applying the Kaplan Method to Science passages with Test Day timing.

Test Day Checklist—Point Builder
- Feel confident about what to do between now and Test Day and how to get your best score on the actual exam.

	Reading Comprehension ReKap
	The Kaplan Method for Paired Passages
	Quiz

Reading Comprehension ReKap

A. The Kaplan Method for ACT Reading

1. _Actively read the passage._
2. _Read the question stems._
3. _Predict, Select answer:_

B. The ACT Reading Test consists of __4__ passages, each with __10__ questions, which you must complete in __35__ minutes. This gives you __8-7__ minutes per passage, so moving through the passages and their respective questions quickly and confidently is essential.

C. Active Reading means:

_____

_____

D. Active Reading Rules

1. Why is more important than what.

2. Support for the answer is ALWAYS in the passage.

3. Predict before you peek.

4. Keep straight who said what.

E. The ACT Reading section has four passage types:

Prose Fiction   Humanities
Social Science   Natural Sciences

F. The ACT Reading section has six question types:

Writer's View
Inference
Detail
Function
Generalization
Vocab In context

G. Prose Fiction passages differ from the other three passage types because they have a _less predictable_ structure and the questions focus on _character development / adjectives_

H. Your Passage Maps for Prose Fiction passages should include _notes about characters_

While actively reading, pay special attention to _adjectives_

The Kaplan Method for Paired Passages

1. Read Passage A and answer the questions about it.

2. Read Passage B and answer the questions about it.

3. Answer questions asking about both passages.

Paired Passages

Paired Passages provide two passages that deal with the same topic or related topics.

Some questions ask about only one of the passages, while others ask you to consider both. The passage or passages each question addresses is clearly labeled.

Paired Passages will not appear on all administrations of the ACT. When they do, they will replace one of the single passages, and will make up about 25% of your Reading score.

LITERARY NARRATIVE: Passage A is adapted from the essay "The Language Barrier or Silence" by Joseph Fellows. Passage B is adapted from the essay "The First and Last Time" by Randy Benson.

Passage A by Joseph Fellows

I hadn't slept the night before I left, nor could I even doze on the plane; I was so horribly jetlagged when I landed that I had to wait another day and a
Line half before I could realign my sleep cycle. Piqued
(5) and red-eyed is not how I had envisioned my first day abroad. I had also hoped to have a little bit of the German language under my belt before mingling with locals. Unfortunately, the absurdly unpredictable nature of the *der/die/das* articles
(10) frustrated me so much that I never really got past the general salutations and simple, commonly-used phrases. I was therefore stubbornly determined to get as much mileage out of *Danke* and *Bitte* as I could. Every German person in Tegel Airport must have
(15) thought me incredibly gracious but dimwitted.

I tried saying *Freut mich, Sie kennenzulernen* (nice to meet you) to the cab driver that I hailed, and after three tries, each receiving a quizzical stare in return, I gave up and simply told him my destination in
(20) English. I then squeezed myself into the tiny Peugeot; evidently, SUVs are not fashionable in Europe.

The bed and breakfast I had booked was nice—very quaint, but obviously a tourist spot.

The owner was a scowling old woman who said
(25) little and waddled around, pointing and grunting, rightfully assuming I was linguistically stunted. Otherwise, I found the room and common areas charming and quiet. Thoroughly intimidated by the locals and their language, I decided to take a walk
(30) through historic Berlin in hopes of bonding with the nature and architecture, rather than the people. I was immediately glad that I did.

Despite being exhausted and surly, I found myself awestruck and humbled by the ubiquitous
(35) artistry of the city. Despite knowing little about World War II and having been born forty years after, I was profoundly affected by my first view of the Kaiser Wilhelm *Gedächtniskirche* (Memorial Church), with its crushed steeple and bomb-ravaged
(40) stone walls, existing in jarring juxtaposition to the surrounding modern architecture.

Further east near the Berlin Zoo, I found a lovely park along the murky water of the *Landwehrkanal* and was beckoned by the wafting aroma of a nearby
(45) Currywurst cart. It was a struggle to count out the unfamiliar Euro coins, but I finally managed to pay for my meal, which I took with me on a walk north through a huge forest area. Eventually, I came to a massive traffic circle. In the midst of this automotive
(50) maelstrom of Berlin rush hour stood the magnificent *Siegessäule* (Victory Column). The immaculate craftsmanship against the verdant horizon and cerulean sky—there are no words in any language to describe it. So I sat on a stone bench, smiled
(55) contentedly, and said nothing.

Questions 1–3 ask about Passage A.

1. The author includes the interaction with the cab driver (lines 16–20) in order to:

   A. explain how the narrator got from the airport to the bed and breakfast.

   B. provide an example of the narrator's aggravation with the German language.

   C. show the affinity that the narrator has for the German language.

   D. explain how to greet someone unfamiliar in German.

)) **REMEMBER**
Two-thirds of the questions in a Paired Passage set deal with only one passage, so most of these questions will not be any more challenging than the questions from any other single reading passage.

2. In the third paragraph, the narrator's decision to go for a walk is prompted by:

   F. his insecurity that developed as a result of his difficulty with the German language.

   G. his anger towards the owner of the bed and breakfast.

   H. his eagerness to sightsee and experience the culture of the city.

   J. his stubborn determination to succeed at speaking the German language.

)) **REMEMBER**
Expect to see questions for Passage A that feature answer choices with information from Passage B. Following Step 1 of the Kaplan Method for Paired Passages helps you eliminate these answer choices quickly and save time!

3. The narrator states that "there are no words" to describe the view at the *Siegessäule* because the narrator:

   A. can't speak German well enough to translate the description thoroughly.

   B. is too frustrated with the German language to take the time to depict its beauty.

   C. feels that any explanation of the beauty of the scene could not do it justice.

   D. chose to sit quietly on the stone bench rather than say anything.

Passage B by Randy Benson

My room was gray and windowless, with a
cement floor painted blood-red. The mattress had no
sheets, but I was too disoriented to care. Bad way to
start the semester. Why had I picked up with Greg,
(60) anyway?

After we stored our bags in a locker at Termini,
Greg marched me to a trattorìa where we feasted on
pasta, fish, veal, salad, cheese, and fruit. After the
meal, Greg took me on a bistro-and-basilica tour.
(65) "C'mon, Paisan'. I'm gonna show you how to do
Rome right."

After two churches and two restaurants, I said to
Greg, "I understand loving the food here. But what's
your thing with churches?"
(70) Greg looked at me like I had a trinity of heads.
"I know you're not really that clueless, Paisan'. Quit
being such a middle-class American sophomore and
ask me a real question, like 'Gee, Greg, that bone
church we just went through makes me wonder
(75) whatever would possess a herd of Capuchin monks
to make artistic masterpieces out of their own
skeletal remains.'"

Actually, the thought of the bone church made
the hunk of Fontinella cheese I'd just wolfed down
(80) twist in my stomach. "No. I don't wanna talk about
the bones. I wanna know why you're dragging me
through churches. Is it just a scenic way to pace
ourselves between bistros?"

"You mean to tell me, Paisan', that you really got
(85) nothing out of St. Peter's?"

I wasn't going to admit it to Greg, but St. Peter's
really was kind of awesome. Made my jaw drop,
actually.

"Eh. It's a big church. Who cares?"
(90) "*You* should, Paisan'. This is *Rome*, man. The
Republic. The Empire. The Church. In a place like
this, I shouldn't have to agitate you into an outburst
of culture. Up 'til now, everything about life has
numbed you. This place is gonna wake up your
(95) soul." At this, he pushed another hunk of Fontinella
at me, and I had no confidence that it would sit any
better than the last after one more church full of
bones.

After seven more churches and three more bistros,
(100) we finally ground to a halt at the Cafe Montespiné.
The locals gawked at the Americani, and engaged
Greg in conversations that mixed French, Greek,
Italian, and Martian. We dragged ourselves out of
Montespiné at four-thirty in the morning, with half
(105) of our new-found friends still acting like the night
was just starting.

Which is why I woke up this morning, bleary-
eyed, in the previous night's clothes, my head heavy
as a crushed Italian moon-rock breakfast roll. Maybe
(110) not the best way to start the semester. But I have to
admit—it *was* quite a start.

Questions 4–6 ask about Passage B.

4. The last paragraph of Passage B (lines 107–111) summarizes:

   F. the narrator's transition from sleep to regret for staying out the previous night.

   G. the narrator's transition from sleep to a celebratory embrace of new life-circumstances.

   H. the narrator's recognition of the previous night as a unique way to begin the stay in Rome.

   J. the narrator's return to a reality happily without Greg.

5. In Passage B, the narrator's descriptions of Greg suggest that the narrator sees Greg as:

   A. too daring and bold to be a traveling companion in the future.

   B. intriguing enough to follow and see what happens next.

   C. too numb to experience any pleasure in Rome.

   D. a religious fanatic.

6. In Passage B, the author uses line 86 ("I wasn't going to admit it to Greg") in order to:

   F. illustrate the narrator's unwillingness to follow Greg's scheme.

   G. argue that admiration of Roman churches is more privately held matter.

   H. call attention to the jaw-dropping nature of St. Peter's.

   J. suggest the favorable influence that Greg's tour is having on the narrator.

Questions 7–9 ask about both passages.

7. Compared to Passage B's narrator, Passage A's narrator spends more time discussing:

    A. the history of the city he is visiting.

    B. his interactions with the local people.

    C. the various religious landmarks he encounters.

    D. his inability to speak the foreign language fluently.

8. Which of the following statements best summarizes the similarity or difference of the tone of the two passages?

    F. Passage A is impersonal and historical, while Passage B is thoughtfully nostalgic.

    G. Passage A is animated and comical, while Passage B is serious and introspective.

    H. Both passages begin with a sense of trepidation but end with an air of equability and serenity.

    J. Both passages begin humorously and end on a note of introspection.

9. While Passage A straightforwardly recounts the narrator's experiences abroad, Passage B is more:

    A. colloquial.

    B. informative.

    C. didactic.

    D. impersonal.

	Essay ReKap
	Know What to Expect: Scoring Review
	Proofread: The Final Step
	English ReKap
	English Practice

Essay ReKap

A. Although the ACT Writing Test is optional, some colleges require it, and others may use it as an additional indicator of your abilities. We strongly suggest that you take the Writing Test along with your ACT.

B. The Kaplan Method for Essay Writing will help you make the best use of the 30 minutes you have to complete your essay.

1. Prompt: *1-2 minutes*

2. Plan: *4-6 minutes*

3. *Produce* : 20–22 minutes

4. *Proofread* : 2–3 minutes

C. Using Kaplan's Essay Template will help to ensure that you satisfy all of the parts of the assignment outlined in the Essay Task.

Kaplan's Essay Template

¶1: Introductory paragraph
- Introductory statement
- Thesis

¶2: 1st body paragraph
- Describe Perspective One
  - Strengths/weaknesses
  - Insights it offers/Insights it fails to consider
  - Persuasive/Fails to persuade
- Specifically state whether you agree, disagree, or partially agree/disagree with this perspective

¶3: 2nd body paragraph
- Describe Perspective Two
  - Strengths/weaknesses
  - Insights it offers/Insights it fails to consider
  - Persuasive/Fails to persuade
- Specifically state whether you agree, disagree, or partially agree/disagree with this perspective

¶4: 3rd body paragraph
- Describe Perspective Three
  - Strengths/weaknesses
  - Insights it offers/Insights it fails to consider
  - Persuasive/Fails to persuade
- Specifically state whether you agree, disagree, or partially agree/disagree with this perspective

¶5: 4th body paragraph
- Describe your thesis
  - Provide specific, relevant support
  - Discuss the strengths/weaknesses of your thesis
  - Explain how your thesis fits in among Perspectives One, Two, and Three
- Include a single, conclusion sentence at the end of your 4th body paragraph to wrap up your essay.

Know What to Expect: Scoring Review

A. Essay Scoring

- The essay is scored by holistically two readers, who each assigns a score between _____0_____ and __6__.

- The scores are added together to generate a final essay score that is between _____0_____ and __12__.

- You will receive a separate score that combines your score on the essay with your scores on the English and Reading tests. This is called an ELA Score and will be between __1__ and __36__.

B. To earn a high score on your essay, you must:

- evaluate and analyze multiple perspectives.
- clearly state and substantiate your own perspective.
- structure your argument logically and organize your writing clearly.
- write persuasively, using correct grammar, syntax, word usage and mechanics.

C. Your essay score will not be affected by:

- your point of view.
- factual errors.
- a few spelling or grammatical errors.

D. Don't waste time trying to figure out what the graders want you to say. Your essay score is based on how well you support your position, NOT which position you support.

E. Keep these two important facts in mind as you prepare for your Writing Test:

1. __Address the prompt,__
2. __Evaluate each Perspective,__

F. What should you do between now and Test Day to prepare for the essay?

_____

_____

_____

_____

Proofread: The Final Step

A.   Your essay does not have to be error-free to receive a strong score.

B.   During the "Proofread" step of the Kaplan Method, you should do the following:

_____

_____

C.   Use proofreading symbols to make neat, legible changes to your essay. If you want to cross something out, draw a single line through it:

~~my error~~

If you want to add something, use a caret:

I left out a word here.
⌃
right

Or an asterisk:

I *something.   *forgot

If you want to indicate the beginning of a new paragraph, use this symbol:

This ends one idea. ¶ This begins a new
idea and a new paragraph.

D.   Proofread the following sample essay. Make neat, legible changes to the essay when necessary.

Memorizing facts isn't a good way to learn history. They are hard to remember and don't

tell us ~~nothing~~ about what really happened. In my opinion, ~~I think~~ the better way to learn   *Anything*

history is by studying about a countries leader. This way we can see if they made good or   *Country's*

bad decisions. I think that the only reason to study history is to see if we can learn some thing

that will help us do better in the future. By seeing if most of the people did better or worse,   *Something*

we can know what to do better next time.

English ReKap

A.   The ACT English Test consists of _____75_____ questions, which you must complete in _____45_____ minutes. This gives you approximately 35 seconds per question, so moving through the questions quickly and confidently is essential.

B.   The Kaplan Method for ACT English will help you do just that.

1. _Read enough to identify the issue_
2. _Eliminate answer choices_
3. _Select an answer_

C.   Keep these two important facts in mind as you prepare for Test Day:

1. _____

Unlike some standardized tests, the ACT has no wrong-answer penalty. Consequently, you should answer every question, even if you have to guess. Use your Kaplan strategies to eliminate all the answer choices you can and then make your best guess from the remaining choices.

2. _____

Don't get bogged down on a single difficult question. Make your best guess or circle the question in your test booklet and come back to it later. If you do skip a question, make sure you also skip the corresponding number on your answer grid.

D.   What should you do between now and Test Day to maximize your English score?
- Complete all homework.
- Use time that would otherwise be "wasted" — waiting in line, at doctors' offices, at the school bus stop — to access the flashcards on your cell phone.
- Email your Kaplan instructor with any questions.

Quiz

Medusa

For more than two thousand years, Medusa has been a prominent image in the world of art and the world of myth. As far back as 200 B.C., images of Medusa, the defeated Gorgon, abounded. The shield of Alexander the Great, <u>on the other hand</u>, was graced with an image of the
<u>   1</u>
mythical Medusa with her locks of live serpents and a gaze that could turn men into stone.

Medusa was surely one of the most threatening figures of ancient Greek mythology. One of the three Gorgon sisters, she had purportedly been known for her <u>beauty. However,</u> she aroused the anger of the goddess
<u>   2</u>
Athena, who turned Medusa's once lovely hair to snakes. With the power to turn anyone who looked upon her into stone, Medusa was feared and thought impossible to defeat.

<u>Indeed</u>, Medusa finally did meet her end at the hands of
<u> 3</u>
Perseus. Perseus was helped by Athena and Hermes, another major Greek god. Perseus was given a powerful sword, a helmet that made him invisible, winged sandals that enabled him to fly, and a highly polished shield. Using these gifts, Perseus was able to invisibly sneak up on the sleeping Gorgon, use the shield as a mirror to protect himself from Medusa's direct gaze, and cut off the monster's head.

1. (A) NO CHANGE

    (B) as a result,

    (C) for example,

    (D) finally,

2. (F) NO CHANGE

    (G) beauty. Also,

    (H) beauty, also

    (J) beauty, however

3. (A) NO CHANGE

    (B) Nevertheless,

    (C) In addition,

    (D) Because of this,

The Legend of Robin Hood

The story of Robin Hood and his band of merry men has become one of the most popular traditional tales in English literature, <u>since</u> there is no conclusive evidence that
<u>   4</u>
a man named Robin Hood ever actually existed.

Robin is the hero in a series of ballads dating from at least the fourteenth century. These ballads tell of <u>discontent and unhappiness</u> among the lower classes
<u>   5</u>
in the north of England during a turbulent time that led to the Peasant's Revolt of 1381. A good deal of the rebellion against authority stemmed from the restriction of hunting rights. These early ballads reveal the cruelty that was a part of medieval life.

4. (F) NO CHANGE

    (G) because

    (H) although

    (J) furthermore

5. (A) NO CHANGE

    (B) discontentedness and unhappiness

    (C) discontent and displeasure

    (D) discontent

According to the ballads, Robin Hood was a rebel. He was a hero for common people, which was <u>furthermore</u>
<u>   6</u>
something rarely seen in the literature of the time.

6. (F) NO CHANGE

    (G) in fact

    (H) consequently

    (J) OMIT the underlined portion

Many of the most striking episodes depict him and his companions robbing and killing representatives of authority on behalf of the oppressed—<u>nonetheless</u>, giving the gains
<u>   7</u>
<u>to the poor people who did not have a lot of money</u>. Their
<u>   8</u>
most frequent enemy was the Sheriff of Nottingham, a local

agent of the central government. While Robin could be ruthless with <u>those persons who were known to have</u> abused
9
their power, he was kind to the oppressed.

7. (A) NO CHANGE

   (B) however,

   (C) that is,

   (D) since,

8. (F) NO CHANGE

   (G) the poor

   (H) the poor without money

   (J) the poor people without money

9. (A) NO CHANGE

   (B) persons who were known to have

   (C) those who

   (D) those persons who

<u>On the other hand, King Arthur was a hero for the</u>
10
noble. <u>Anyways,</u> the nature of the legend was distorted by
11
the suggestion that Robin was a fallen nobleman.

10. (F) NO CHANGE

   (G) A hero for the noble, on the other hand, was King Arthur.

   (H) King Arthur was a heroic noble, on the other hand.

   (J) OMIT the underlined portion.

11. (A) NO CHANGE

   (B) In the eighteenth century,

   (C) After years,

   (D) Subsequently,

Writers adopted this new element <u>as eagerly as new</u>
12
<u>kittens.</u> Robin was also given a love interest, Maid Marian.

<u>After</u> such major changes had been incorporated,
13
audiences still continued to relish Robin's story. The legend of Robin Hood inspired several movies, a television series, and a Broadway musical during the twentieth century. Whether or not an actual Robin Hood lived in ancient Britain, the legendary Robin has lived in the popular imagination for more than six hundred years.

12. (F) NO CHANGE

   (G) as eager as new kittens.

   (H) eagerly.

   (J) as eagerly.

13. Which of the following would NOT be an acceptable alternative for the underlined portion?

   (A) Unless

   (B) When

   (C) Once

   (D) Even after

	Math ReKap
Point Builder	**Dealing with Difficult Math Questions**
	Math Quiz
	Science ReKap
	Science Practice
	Science Knowledge
	Scientific Method
	Science Quiz
	ACT Test Day To-Do List

Math ReKap

A.   The Kaplan Method for ACT Math

1. _____?

2. _____?

3. _____?

   a. _____

   b. _____

   c. _____

   d. _____

4. _____?

B.   You have _____ minutes to answer _____ questions. That's _____ minute(s) per question.

C.   You should answer _____ questions first. Why?

_____

_____

---

1. What is the largest integer less than $\sqrt{42}$?

   (A) 5

   (B) 6

   (C) 7

   (D) 9

   (E) 20

Dealing with Difficult Math Questions

A. What makes some questions difficult?

_____

_____

_____

_____

2. Which of the following expressions represents the length of $\overline{VX}$ shown in the figure below?

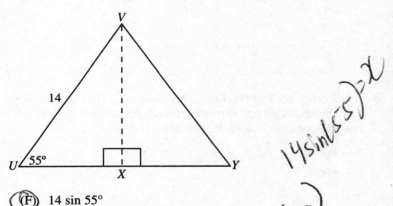

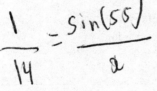

(F) 14 sin 55°

(G) 14 cos 55°

(H) 14 tan 55°

(F) $\dfrac{14}{\sin 55°}$

(K) $\dfrac{14}{\cos 55°}$

B. How do you deal with difficult questions?

• Relax! Every question is worth the same number of points, so focus on easier questions first.

• Use your Kaplan strategies, like Picking Numbers and Backsolving.

• If you're not sure how to get started, ask yourself:

_____

3. Bob and his wife Linda both leave their house at 7:30 A.M. to commute to work. Bob drives 60 mph and goes north for half an hour, then east for one hour. Linda drives 50 mph and goes east for 1 hour, then north for half an hour. Which of the following is an expression for the number of miles apart Bob and Linda are at 9:00 A.M., when they each arrive at work?

(A) $3(60 - 50)$

(B) $\sqrt{(60 - 50)^2 + (25 - 30)^2}$

(C) $\sqrt{(60 - 50)^2 + (25 + 30)^2}$

(D) $\sqrt{(60 + 50)^2 + (25 - 30)^2}$

(E) $\sqrt{(3 - 60)^2 + (3 - 30)^2}$

4. Listed below are five functions, each denoted $g(x)$, with each formula involving the same real number constant $a \geq 3$. If $f(x) = 3^x$, which of these five functions yields the greatest value for $f(g(x))$, for all $x > 2$?

(F) $g(x) = ax$

(G) $g(x) = \dfrac{a}{x}$

(H) $g(x) = \dfrac{x}{a}$

(J) $g(x) = a + x$

(K) $g(x) = \log_a x$

5. In 2000, the population of Town A was 9,400, and the population of Town B was 7,600. Since then, each year, the population of Town A has decreased by 100, and the population of Town B has increased by 100. Assuming that in each case the rate is constant, in what year will the two populations be equal?

(A) 2008

(B) 2009

(C) 2010

(D) 2018

(E) 2019

6. If $^n\sqrt{45} = 3^n\sqrt{5}$ then $n = ?$

(F) 1

(G) 2

(H) 3

(J) 4

(K) 5

)) REMEMBER
Use the extra space provided in your test booklet to work through a problem in an organized way.

7. Mark's rectangular flowerbed is twice as long as it is wide. He wants to build a rectangular vegetable garden that is twice as long and twice as wide as the flowerbed. The area of the vegetable garden will be how many times as large as the area of the flowerbed?

(A) 2

(B) 3

(C) 4

(D) 6

(E) 8

$2w \quad w$

$4w \quad 2w^2$

)) REMEMBER
When a problem asks for a concrete value and there are numbers in the answer choices, Backsolve.

Math Quiz

1. In a class, 10 students are receiving honors credit. This number is exactly 20% of the total number of students in the class. How many students are in the class?

   (A) 12
   (B) 15
   (C) 18
   (D) 20
   (E) 50

2. In the figure below, points A, B, and C are on a straight line. What is the measure of angle DBE?

   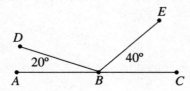

   (F) 60°
   (G) 80°
   (H) 100°
   (J) 120°
   (K) 140°

3. What is the fifth term of the arithmetic sequence 7, 4, 1, ...?

   (A) −5
   (B) −2
   (C) 1
   (D) 4
   (E) 7

   $7-3(n-1)$

   $-3n+10$

4. What value of C solves the following proportion: $\frac{20}{8} = \frac{C}{10}$?

   (F) 4
   (G) 16
   (H) 18
   (J) 22
   (K) 25

   $8C = 200$

   $C = 25$

5. If G, H, and K are distinct points on the same line, and $\overline{GK} \cong \overline{HK}$, then which of the following must be true?

   (A) G is the midpoint of $\overline{HK}$.
   (B) H is the midpoint of $\overline{GK}$.
   (C) K is the midpoint of $\overline{GH}$.
   (D) G is the midpoint of $\overline{KH}$.
   (E) K is the midpoint of $\overline{KG}$.

6. Four pieces of yarn, each 1.2 meters long, are cut from the end of a ball of yarn that is 50 meters long. How many meters of yarn are left?

   (F) 45.2
   (G) 45.8
   (H) 46.8
   (J) 47.2
   (K) 47.8

7. If $x = -2$, then $14 - 3(x + 3)$?

   (A) −1
   (B) 11
   (C) 14
   (D) 17
   (E) 29

8. A car dealership expects an increase of 15% of its current annual sales of 3,200 cars. What are its new annual sales expected to be?

   (F) 3,215
   (G) 3,248
   (H) 3,680
   (J) 4,700
   (K) 4,800

9. If $x^4 = 90$ (and x is a real number), then x lies between which two consecutive integers?

   (A) 2 and 3
   (B) 3 and 4
   (C) 4 and 5
   (D) 5 and 6
   (E) 6 and 7

Science ReKap

A. The ACT Science Test consists of ___ passages with ___ questions, which you must complete in _____ minutes. This gives you _____ seconds per question, so moving through the passages and their respective questions quickly and confidently is essential.

B. You can attack passages in any order! Before you begin work, quickly preview the section to decide which passages to do first and which to do later.

C. The Kaplan Method for ACT Science:

1. _____

2. _____

3. _____

D. For Conflicting Viewpoints passages, alter your approach slightly:

1. _____

   _____

2. _____

   _____

3. _____

   _____

E. Answer every question, even if you have to guess. Use your Kaplan strategies to eliminate all the answer choices you can. Then make your best guess from the remaining choices.

F. On many Science Test questions, the fastest way to the correct answer is to eliminate answer choices that are obviously wrong.

G. Like the Reading Test, wrong answer types come in several common forms:

- Misused Detail:

   _____

   _____

- Opposite:

   _____

   _____

- Out of Scope:

  _____

  _____

- Half Right/Half Wrong:

  _____

  _____

H.   Recognizing and eliminating wrong answer choices will increase your odds of guessing the correct answer.

Science Knowledge

A. Occasionally, the ACT Science Test will contain questions about science knowledge. The answers to these questions will not be stated explicitly in the passage.

B. Your familiarity with basic high school science topics is enough to successfully answer these questions on Test Day.

Passage II

Aerobic cellular respiration is the process by which organisms oxidize organic molecules, like sugars, and derive energy (ATP) from the molecular bonds that are broken. Respiration is the opposite of photosynthesis and can be summarized by the following chemical equation: $C_6H_{12}O_6 + 6O_2 \rightarrow 6CO_2 + 6H_2O + 36$ ATP. Simply stated, this equation means that oxygen combines with sugars to break molecular bonds, releasing the energy (in the form of ATP) contained in those bonds. In eukaryotic cellular respiration, energy is released from sugars, and water is formed as a by-product. The mitochondria use the energy released in this oxidation to synthesize ATP through a series of metabolic pathways. The theoretical maximum yield of cellular respiration is 36 ATP per molecule of glucose metabolized.

1. Which of the following represents carbon dioxide in the chemical equation shown in the passage?

   (A) $C_6H_{12}O_6$
   (B) H_2O
   (C) CO_2
   (D) ATP

Scientific Method

A. ACT Science questions often require you to understand the function of different elements in an experimental setup.

B. As you read passages that have multiple experiments, use the Kaplan Method for ACT Science to locate the three elements of the Scientific Method—the Purpose, Method, and Results of the experiment.

Purpose: _____

_____

Method: _____

_____

Results: _____

_____

C. When you locate them, you should _____ the Purpose, _____ the Method, and _____ the Results.

Science Quiz

Passage I

A panel of engineers designed and built a pressurized structure to be used for shelter by geologists during extended research missions near the South Pole. The design consisted of 4 rooms, each with its own heating and air pressure control systems. During testing, the engineers found the daily average air temperature, in degrees Celsius (°C), and daily average air pressure, in millimeters of mercury (mm Hg), in each room. The data for the first 5 days of their study are given in Table 1 and Table 2.

Table 1

Day	Daily average air temperature (°C)			
	Room 1	Room 2	Room 3	Room 4
1	19.64	19.08	18.67	18.03
2	20.15	19.20	18.46	18.11
3	20.81	19.19	18.62	18.32
4	21.06	19.51	19.08	18.91
5	21.14	19.48	18.60	18.58

Table 2

Day	Daily average air pressure (mm Hg)			
	Room 1	Room 2	Room 3	Room 4
1	748.2	759.6	760.0	745.2
2	752.6	762.0	758.7	750.3
3	753.3	760.2	756.5	760.4
4	760.1	750.8	755.4	756.8
5	758.7	757.9	754.0	759.5

1. The lowest daily average air pressure recorded during the first 5 days of the study was:

    (A) 762.0 mm Hg.
    (B) 745.2 mm Hg.
    (C) 21.14 mm Hg.
    (D) 18.03 mm Hg.

2. According to Table 2, daily average air pressures were recorded to the nearest:

    (F) 0.01 mm Hg.
    (G) 0.1 mm Hg.
    (H) 1.0 mm Hg.
    (J) 10 mm Hg.

3. Which of the following graphs best represents a plot of the daily average air temperature versus the daily average air pressure for Room 4?

    (A)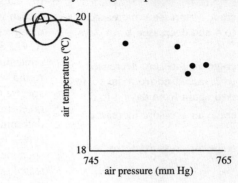

    (B)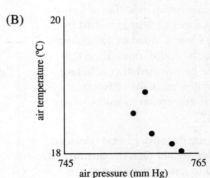

    (C)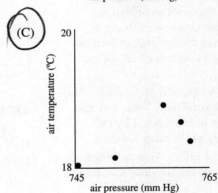

    (D)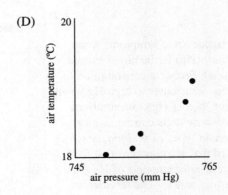

4. Which of the following most accurately describes the changes in the daily average air pressure in Room 3 during days 1–5?

(F) The daily average air pressure increased from days 1 to 4 and decreased from days 4 to 5.

(G) The daily average air pressure decreased from days 1 to 2, increased from days 2 to 4, and decreased again from days 4 to 5.

(H) The daily average air pressure increased only.

(J) The daily average air pressure decreased only.

5. Suppose the *heat absorption modulus* of a room is defined as the quantity of heat absorbed by the contents of the room divided by the quantity of heat provided to the entire room. Based on the data, would one be justified in concluding that the heat absorption modulus of Room 1 was higher than the heat absorption modulus of any of the other rooms?

(A) Yes, because the quantity of heat provided to Room 1 was greater than the quantity of heat provided to any of the other rooms.

(B) Yes, because the quantity of heat not absorbed by the contents of Room 1 was greater than the quantity of heat not absorbed by the contents of any of the other rooms.

(C) No, because the quantity of heat absorbed by the contents of Room 1 was less than the quantity of heat absorbed by the contents of any of the other rooms.

(D) No, because the information provided is insufficient to determine heat absorption modulus.

Passage II

Humans can experience toxic symptoms when concentrations of mercury (Hg) in the blood exceed 200 parts per billion (ppb). Frequent consumption of foods high in Hg content contributes to high Hg levels in the blood. On average, higher Hg concentrations are observed in people whose diets consist of more extreme amounts of certain types of seafood. A research group proposed that sea creatures that live in colder waters acquire greater amounts of Hg than those that reside in warmer waters. The researchers performed the following experiments to examine this hypothesis.

Experiment 1

Samples of several species of consumable sea life caught in the cold waters of the northern Atlantic Ocean were chemically prepared and analyzed using a cold vapor atomic fluorescence spectrometer (CVAFS), a device that indicates the relative concentrations of various elements and compounds found within a biological sample. Comparisons of the spectra taken from the seafood samples with those taken from samples of known Hg levels were made to determine the exact concentrations in parts per billion (ppb). Identical volumes of tissue from eight different specimens for each of four different species were tested, and the results are shown in Table 1, including the average concentrations found for each species.

Table 1

Specimen	Hg concentration in cold-water species (ppb):			
	Cod	Crab	Swordfish	Shark
1	160	138	871	859
2	123	143	905	820
3	139	152	902	839
4	116	177	881	851
5	130	133	875	818
6	134	148	880	836
7	151	147	910	847
8	109	168	894	825
Average	133	151	890	837

Experiment 2

Four species caught in the warmer waters of the Gulf of Mexico were examined using the procedure from Experiment 1. The results are shown in Table 2.

Table 2

Specimen	Hg concentration in warm-water species (ppb):			
	Catfish	Crab	Swordfish	Shark
1	98	113	851	812
2	110	122	856	795
3	102	143	845	821
4	105	128	861	803
5	94	115	849	798
6	112	136	852	809
7	100	129	863	815
8	117	116	837	776
Average	105	125	852	804

6. Given that shark and swordfish are both large, predatory animals, and catfish and crab are smaller, nonpredatory animals, do the results of Experiment 2 support the hypothesis that the tissue of larger predatory fish exhibits higher levels of Hg than does the tissue of smaller species?

   (F) Yes; the lowest concentration of Hg was found in swordfish.

   (G) Yes; both swordfish and shark had Hg concentrations that were higher than those found in either catfish or crab.

   (H) No; the lowest concentration of Hg was in catfish.

   (J) No; both catfish and crab had concentrations of Hg that were higher than those found in either swordfish or shark.

7. A researcher, when using the CVAFS, was concerned that lead (Pb) in the tissue samples might be interfering with the detection of Hg. Which of the following procedures would best help the researcher explore this trouble?

   (A) Flooding the sample with a large concentration of Pb before using the CVAFS

   (B) Using the CVAFS to examine a nonbiological sample

   (C) Collecting tissue from additional species

   (D) Testing a sample with known concentrations of Hg and Pb

8. Based on the results of the experiments and the data in the table below, sharks caught in which of the following locations would most likely possess the largest concentrations of Hg in February?

Location	Average water temperature (°F) for February
Northern Atlantic Ocean	33
Gulf of Mexico	70
Northern Pacific Ocean	46
Tampa Bay	72

   (F) Northern Atlantic Ocean

   (G) Northern Pacific Ocean

   (H) Gulf of Mexico

   (J) Tampa Bay

9. Which of the following factors was intentionally varied in Experiment 2?

   (A) The volume of tissue tested

   (B) The method by which the marine organisms were caught

   (C) The species of marine organism tested

   (D) The method of sample analysis

10. The governments of many nations require frequent testing of seafood to determine Hg concentration levels. According to the experiments, in order to determine the maximum concentration of Hg found in a collection of seafood specimens, from which of the following specimens would it be best to take sample tissue?

    (F) A crab caught in cold water

    (G) A swordfish caught in cold water

    (H) A catfish caught in warm water

    (J) A swordfish caught in warm water

11. How might the results of the experiments be affected if the chemical preparation described in Experiment 1 introduced Hg-free contaminants into the sample, resulting in a larger volume of tested material? The measured concentrations of Hg would be:

    (A) the same as the actual concentrations for both cold-water and warm-water specimens.

    (B) higher than the actual concentrations for both cold-water and warm-water specimens.

    (C) lower than the actual concentrations for cold-water specimens but higher than the actual concentrations for warm-water specimens.

    (D) lower than the actual concentrations for both cold-water and warm-water specimens.

ACT Test Day To-Do List

Week Before the Test

- Finish up any required homework assignments, including online quizzes.

- Focus your additional practice on the question types or subject areas in which you usually score highest. Now is the time to sharpen up your best skills, not to cram new information.

- Make sure you are registered for the test. Remember, Kaplan did not register you. If you missed the registration deadlines, you can find out more about standby testing locations on the testmaker's website.

- Confirm the location of your test site. Never been there before? Make a practice run to make sure you know exactly how long it will take to get from your house to your test site.

- Get a great night's sleep two days before the test.

Day Before the Test

- Review the Kaplan Methods and strategies that you've learned in class.

- Review sample passages and questions, your formula page, and your English flashcards.

- Put new batteries in your calculator.

- Pack your backpack or bag for Test Day with the following items:
    - ✓ Photo ID
    - ✓ Registration slip or printout
    - ✓ Directions to your test site location
    - ✓ Five or more sharpened No. 2 pencils (no mechanical pencils)
    - ✓ Pencil sharpener
    - ✓ Eraser
    - ✓ Calculator (make sure it's an acceptable one!)
    - ✓ Extra batteries
    - ✓ Nonprohibited timepiece
    - ✓ Tissues
    - ✓ Prepackaged snacks, like granola bars
    - ✓ Bottled water, juice, or sports drink
    - ✓ Sweatshirt, sweater, or jacket

Night Before the Test

- No studying!

- Do something relaxing that will take your mind off the test, like watching a movie or having a quiet dinner out with friends.

- Set your alarm to wake up early enough that you won't feel rushed.

- Go to bed early, but not too much earlier than you usually do. You want to fall asleep quickly, not spend hours tossing and turning.

Morning of the Test

- Dress comfortably and in layers. You need to be prepared for any temperature.

- Eat a filling breakfast but don't stray too far from your usual routine. If you normally aren't a breakfast eater, don't eat a huge meal but make sure you have something substantial.

- As you eat breakfast, read something! You need to warm up your brain so you don't go into the test cold. Read a few pages of a newspaper, a magazine, or a novel.

- Get to your test site early. There is likely to be some confusion about where to go and how to sign in, so allow yourself plenty of time even if you are taking the test at your school.

- Leave your cell phone at home or in your car. Many test sites do not allow them in the building.

- While you're waiting to sign in or be seated, read a book, review flash cards, or do other things to warm up for the test.

During the Test

- Be calm and confident. You're ready for this!

- Remember that while the ACT is a four-hour marathon, it is also a series of short sections. Focus on the section you're working on at that moment; don't think about previous or upcoming sections.

- Use the Kaplan Methods as often as you can.

- Pacing is extremely important on Test Day! Don't linger too long on any one question. Mark it and come back to it later.

- Can't figure out an answer? Try to eliminate some choices and guess strategically. There will be plenty of questions you CAN answer, so spend your time on those!

- NEVER omit an ACT question. If you don't know the answer or if the question is too time-consuming, pick a Letter of the Day and move on.

- If you find yourself losing concentration, getting frustrated, or stressing about the time, stop for 30 seconds. Close your eyes, put your pencil down, take a few deep breaths, and relax your shoulders. You'll be much more productive after taking a few moments to relax.

- Use your breaks effectively. Your first break is after the Mathematics Test. During this time, go to the restroom, eat your snacks, and get your energy up for the next section. There is another break before the writing test. ...During this time, use the restroom, then eat your snacks and get your energy up...

After the Test

- Congratulate yourself! Also, reward yourself by doing something fun. You've earned it.

- If you got sick during the test or if something else happened that may have negatively affected your score, you can cancel your scores by the Thursday after your Saturday test date. Request a score cancellation form by contacting ACT Registration or by visiting the testmaker's website for more information. If you have questions about whether or not you should cancel your scores, or about how to report your scores to colleges or your high school, call us at 1-800-KAPTEST.

- Your scores will be available online 2–8 weeks after your test and will be mailed to you in approximately 8 weeks.

- Email your instructor with your ACT scores. We want to hear how you did!

Good Luck on Test Day!

Homework

Reading	Basic Assignment	Additional Practice
Humanities Passage	questions 1–10	
Essay		
Planning Your Essay Exercise	Prompt 1	Prompt 2
English	"The Sloth"	"The History of Marbles"
Math	Questions 1–9	Questions 10–14
Science	Passage I	Passage II

HOMEWORK

Reading

Passage I

Humanities: The following passage is excerpted from *A Short History of Western Civilization* by John Harrison, Richard Sullivan, and Dennis Sherman. (©1990 by McGraw-Hill, Inc. Reprinted with permission of McGraw-Hill.)

Enlightenment ideas were put forth by a variety of intellectuals who in France came to be known as the *philosophes*. *Philosophes* is French for philosophers,
Line and in a sense these thinkers were rightly considered
(5) philosophers, for the questions they dealt with were philosophical: How do we discover truth? How should life be lived? What is the nature of God? But on the whole the term has a meaning different from the usual meaning of "philosopher." The *philosophes* were
(10) intellectuals, often not formally trained or associated with a university. They were usually more literary than scientific. They generally extended, applied, popularized, or propagandized ideas of others rather than originating those ideas themselves. The *philosophes* were more
(15) likely to write plays, satires, pamphlets, or simply participate in verbal exchanges at select gatherings than to write formal philosophical books.

It was the *philosophes* who developed the philosophy of the Enlightenment and spread it to much of
(20) the educated elite in Western Europe (and the American colonies). Although the sources for their philosophy can be traced to the Scientific Revolution in general, the philosophes were most influenced by their understanding of Newton, Locke, and English institutions.

(25) The *philosophes* saw Newton as the great synthesizer of the Scientific Revolution, who rightly described the universe as ordered, mechanical, material, and only originally set in motion by God, who since then has remained relatively inactive.
(30) Newton's synthesis showed to the *philosophes* that reason and nature were compatible: Nature functioned logically and discernibly, and what was natural was also reasonable. Newton exemplified the value of reasoning based on concrete experience. The
(35) *philosophes* felt that his empirical methodology was the correct path to discovering truth.

John Locke (1632–1704) agreed with Newton but went further. This English thinker would not exempt even the mind from the mechanical laws of the
(40) material universe. In his *Essay Concerning Human Understanding* (1691), Locke pictured the human brain at birth as a blank sheet of paper on which nothing would ever be written except sense

perception and reason. What human beings become
(45) depends on their experiences—on the information received through the senses. Schools and social institutions could therefore play a great role in molding the individual from childhood to adulthood. Human beings were thus by nature far more malleable
(50) than had been assumed. This empirical psychology of Locke rejected the notion that human beings were born with innate ideas or that revelation was a reliable source of truth. Locke also enunciated liberal and reformist political ideas in his *Second Treatise of Civil*
(55) *Government* (1690), which influenced the *philosophes*. On the whole, Locke's empiricism, psychology, and politics were appealing to the *philosophes*.

England, not coincidentally the country of Newton and Locke, became the admired model for
(60) many of the philosophes. They tended to idealize it, but England did seem to allow greater individual freedom, tolerate religious differences, and evidence greater political reform than other countries, especially France. England seemed to have gone furthest in
(65) freeing itself from traditional institutions and accepting the new science of the seventeenth century. Moreover, England's approach seemed to work, for England was experiencing relative political stability and prosperity. The *philosophes* wanted to see in their own countries
(70) much of what England already seemed to have.

Many *philosophes* reflected the influence of Newton, Locke, and English institutions, but perhaps the most representative in his views was Voltaire (1694–1778). Of all leading figures of the
(75) Enlightenment, he was the most influential. Voltaire, the son of a Paris lawyer, became the idol of the French intelligentsia while still in his early twenties. His versatile mind was sparkling; his wit was mordant. An outspoken critic, he soon ran afoul of both church
(80) and state authorities. First he was imprisoned in the Bastille; later he was exiled to England. There he encountered the ideas of Newton and Locke and came to admire English parliamentary government and tolerance. In *Letters on the English* (1732), *Elements*
(85) *of the Philosophy of Newton* (1738), and other writings, he popularized the ideas of Newton and Locke, extolled the virtues of English society, and indirectly criticized French society. Slipping back into France, he was hidden for a time and protected by a
(90) wealthy woman who became his mistress. Voltaire's facile mind and pen were never idle. He wrote poetry, drama, history, essays, letters, and scientific treatises— ninety volumes in all. Few people in history have dominated their age intellectually as did Voltaire.

1. According to the passage, the *philosophes* can best be described as:

   (A) writers swept up by their mutual admiration of John Locke.
   (B) professors who lectured in philosophy at French universities.
   (C) intellectuals responsible for popularizing Enlightenment ideas.
   (D) scientists who furthered the work of the Scientific Revolution.

2. Based on information provided in the passage, which of the following would most likely have been written by Voltaire?

   (F) A treatise criticizing basic concepts of the Scientific Revolution
   (G) A play satirizing society in France
   (H) A collection of letters mocking the English Parliament
   (J) A sentimental poem expounding the virtues of courtly love

3. According to the passage, Locke felt that schools and social institutions could "play a great role in molding the individual" (lines 46–48) because:

   (A) human beings were born with certain innate ideas.
   (B) of human nature.
   (C) society owes each individual the right to an education.
   (D) the human mind is chiefly influenced by experience.

4. Based on the information in the passage, which of the following describes Newton's view of the universe?

   I. The universe was initially set in motion by God.
   II. Human reason is insufficient to understand the laws of nature.
   III. The universe operates in a mechanical and orderly fashion.

   (F) I only
   (G) I and II only
   (H) I and III only
   (J) II and III only

5. According to the passage, which of the following works questioned the idea that revelation was a reliable source of truth?

   (A) *Letters of the English*
   (B) *Second Treatise of Civil Government*
   (C) *Elements of the Philosophy of Newton*
   (D) *Essay Concerning Human Understanding*

6. The passage supports which of the following statements concerning the relationship between Newton and Locke?

   (F) Locke's psychology contradicted Newton's belief in an orderly universe.
   (G) Locke maintained that Newton's laws of the material universe also applied to the human mind.
   (H) Newton eventually came to accept Locke's revolutionary ideas about the human mind.
   (J) Newton's political ideas were the basis of Locke's liberal and reformist politics.

7. It can be inferred from the passage that the *philosophes* believed that society should do each of the following EXCEPT:

   (A) allow greater personal freedom.
   (B) break loose from traditional institutions.
   (C) tolerate religious differences.
   (D) question the new science of the time.

8. Based on the passage, the authors apparently regard England's political stability and economic prosperity as:

   (F) evidence that political reforms could bring about a better way of life.
   (G) the reason that the *philosophes* did not idealize England's achievement.
   (H) the result of Voltaire's activities after he was exiled to England.
   (J) an indication that the Scientific Revolution had not yet started.

9. The passage suggests that the French political and religious authorities during the time of Voltaire:

   (A) allowed little in the way of free speech.
   (B) overreacted to Voltaire's mild satires.
   (C) regarded the *philosophes* with indifference.
   (D) accepted the model of English parliamentary government.

10. As it is used in the passage, *treatises* (line 92) most nearly means:

    (F) formal trade agreements between two or more countries.
    (G) extensive written discussions or examinations of specific topics.
    (H) documents evidencing the end of conflict between warring countries.
    (J) narratives designed to teach moral lessons.

For each of the following prompts, write a compelling thesis sentence. Then plan your essay using Kaplan's Essay Template. For extra practice, complete each essay to ready yourself for Test Day.

Prompt 1

Education Technology

Education technology (ed tech) companies gather data about the elementary through high school students who use their products. Some for-profit and not-for-profit ed tech providers have pledged to protect student data so that it is not sold to outside companies that may target students with advertisements, or compile profiles that could be harmful for students later in life. However, student data is extremely valuable in helping both for-profit and not-for-profit companies develop effective educational software that records student progress and adapts lessons to meet individual needs. While schools have a responsibility to protect students, some argue that all ed tech companies should be allowed to buy student data to develop better educational products, even if the data is used for commercial purposes. As ed tech continues to evolve, it is important to develop policies that both protect and benefit students.

Read and carefully consider these perspectives. Each suggests a particular way of thinking about sharing student data.

Perspective One	Perspective Two	Perspective Three
Information gathered about anyone under the age of 18 should be wholly protected. Even though student data may aid in ed tech advancements, the activities of minors should not be accessed by any entity other than the provider, and the data should not be sold to third parties. It is better to save students from possible harm than to take a risk, even if the goal is to foster innovation.	There is a clear distinction between educational initiatives and for-profit strategies. Student data should exclusively be available to not-for-profit ed tech developers who provide software at little or no cost to students and educators.	Using software that tracks student progress in real time relies on continuous access of student data. Therefore, there is no reason to expect that the very data that provides immediate adaptation for students will be inaccessible to ed tech companies—whether for-profit or not.

Essay Task

Write a unified, coherent essay in which you evaluate multiple perspectives on sharing student data. In your essay, be sure to:

- analyze and evaluate the perspectives given
- state and develop your own perspective on the issue
- explain the relationship between your perspective and those given

Your perspective may be in full agreement with any of the others, in partial agreement, or wholly different. Whatever the case, support your ideas with logical reasoning and detailed, persuasive examples.

Planning Your Essay

Use the space below and on the back cover to generate ideas and plan your essay. You may wish to consider the following as you think critically about the task:

- Strengths and weaknesses of the three given perspectives
  - What insights do they offer, and what do they fail to consider?
  - Why might they be persuasive to others, or why might they fail to persuade?
- Your own knowledge, experience, and values
  - What is your perspective on this issue, and what are its strengths and weaknesses?
  - How will you support your perspective in your essay?

Prompt 2

College Tuition

As the cost of college continues to rise, some states are creating programs that provide free or reduced tuition for students who are accepted into community colleges and state universities. While these programs require considerable amounts of taxpayer money, proponents argue that a more educated population benefits the entire nation. Should states continue to fund these programs despite the exorbitant cost? Considering that affording college costs is a major factor in students' decision to pursue higher education, it is prudent for politicians and educators to explore this issue.

Read and carefully consider these perspectives. Each suggests a particular approach to alleviating the burden of college tuition for students.

Perspective One	Perspective Two	Perspective Three
While attending college is expensive, studies show that it is worth the investment by students. As long as students have access to low-interest loans they can pay off later, when they are gainfully employed, states have no obligation to help students pay for college.	Money that is currently funding reduced or free tuition should instead be spent on programs that aid college graduates in securing employment that will allow them to make loan payments. Students will have more incentive to graduate if they know they will be able to get a job, and repaying their student loans teaches both responsibility and proper fiscal planning.	Despite the cost to taxpayers, in-state college tuition should be free or greatly reduced for all students who receive acceptance letters. Providing affordable education will help more students attend and complete college, which betters society as a whole.

Essay Task

Write a unified, coherent essay in which you evaluate multiple perspectives on alleviating the burden of college tuition for students. In your essay, be sure to:

- analyze and evaluate the perspectives given
- state and develop your own perspective on the issue
- explain the relationship between your perspective and those given

Your perspective may be in full agreement with any of the others, in partial agreement, or wholly different. Whatever the case, support your ideas with logical reasoning and detailed, persuasive examples.

Planning Your Essay

Use the space below and on the back cover to generate ideas and plan your essay. You may wish to consider the following as you think critically about the task:

- Strengths and weaknesses of the three given perspectives
  - What insights do they offer, and what do they fail to consider?
  - Why might they be persuasive to others, or why might they fail to persuade?
- Your own knowledge, experience, and values
  - What is your perspective on this issue, and what are its strengths and weaknesses?
  - How will you support your perspective in your essay?

Quarter 3: English

The Sloth

More than half the world's <u>current living plant</u> and
₁
animals species live in tropical rain forests. Four square
miles of a Central American rain forest can be home to up
to 1,500 species of flowering plants, 700 species of trees,
400 species of birds, and 125 species of mammals. Of these
mammals, the sloth is the most unsual.

Unlike most mammals, the sloth is usually upside
down. A sloth does just about everything upside down,
including sleeping, eating, mating, and giving birth.

<u>Its' unique</u> anatomy allows the sloth to spend most of the
₂
time hanging from one tree branch or another, high in the
canopy of rain forest trees.

1. (A) NO CHANGE
   (B) currently existing plant
   (C) living plant
   (D) plant

2. (F) NO CHANGE
   (G) It's unique
   (H) Its unique
   (J) Its uniquely

About the size of a large domestic <u>cat, the</u> sloth hangs
₃
from its unusally long limbs and long, hook-like claws. The
muscles in the sloth's limbs seemed to be specially designed
for clinging to things.

In fact, a sloth's limbs are <u>so specific</u> adapted to upside-
₄
down life that a sloth is essentially incapable of walking
on the ground. <u>Instead, they</u> must crawl or drag itself with
₅
its massive claws. This makes it easy to see why the sloth
rarely leaves its home in the trees. <u>Because</u> it cannot move
₆
swiftly on the ground, the sloth is an excellent swimmer.

3. (A) NO CHANGE
   (B) cat; the
   (C) cat. The
   (D) cat, but the

4. (F) NO CHANGE
   (G) so specific and
   (H) so specified
   (J) so specifically

5. (A) NO CHANGE
   (B) Instead, it
   (C) However, they
   (D) In addition, it

6. (F) NO CHANGE
   (G) Despite
   (H) Similarly,
   (J) Though

A sloth can hang upside down and, without moving the
rest of its body, turn 180 degres so that it <u>was looking</u>
₇
at the ground. A sloth can rotate its forelimbs in all
directions, so it can easily reach the leaves that make up
its diet. The sloth can also roll itself up into a ball in order
<u>to protect and defend itself</u> from predators.
₈
<u>The howler monkey, another inhabitant of the rain</u>
₉
<u>forest, is not as flexible as the sloth.</u> The best defense a
₉
sloth has from predator such as jaguars and large snakes,
though, is its camoflauge. During the rainy season, the
sloth's thick brown or gray fur is usually covered with a
coat of blue-gree <u>algae. Which</u> helps it blend in with its
₁₀
forest surroundings. Another type of camouflage is the
sloth's incredibly slow movement; it often moves less than
100 feet during a 24-hour period.

7. (A) NO CHANGE
   (B) had been looking
   (C) will have the ability to be looking
   (D) can look

8. (F) NO CHANGE
    (G) protects and defends itself
    (H) protects itself.
    (J) protect itself.

9. (A) NO CHANGE
    (B) Another inhabitant of the rain forest, the howler monkey, is not as flexible as the sloth.
    (C) Not as flexible as the sloth is the howler monkey, another inhabitant of the rainforest.
    (D) OMIT the underlined portion.

10. (F) NO CHANGE
    (G) algae, which
    (H) algae, being that it
    (J) algae

The History of Marbles

Taws, alleys, and flints are the names of particular kinds of marbles. The names of marbles may originate

from its appearance, as in "cloudies"; their use, as in
—————
11

"shooters"; or their original material.

"Alleys," for example, were once made of alabaster. Marbles may be made from many different materials. In the eighteenth century, marbles were actually made from marble chips. Nowadays, marbles may consist of glass, baked clay, steel, onyx, plastic, or agate. Perhaps, the key word regarding marbles are "variety."
—————————————
12

11. (A) NO CHANGE
    (B) by its
    (C) from there
    (D) from their

12. (F) NO CHANGE
    (G) marbles is "variety."
    (H) marbles being "variety."
    (J) marbles were "variety."

Marbles can be manipulated by a variety of ways.
                    —————————————
                          13

"Knuckling" is a technique in which the bottom of the hand is balanced against the ground while a marble placed against the forefinger is shot outward toward the thumb. Marbles can also be thrown, rolling, dropped, and even kicked.
—————————————————————————————————
                          14

13. (A) NO CHANGE
    (B) manipulated with
    (C) manipulated within
    (D) manipulated in

14. (F) NO CHANGE
    (G) are used for throwing, rolling, dropping, and even kicking.
    (H) can also be thrown, rolled, dropped, and even kicked.
    (J) can also throw, roll, drop and kick.

There were also many varieties of marble games.
—————————————————————————————————
                     15

The most common American version involves winning opponents' marbles by knocking them out of a designated area with one's own marbles. Another popular game is taw, also known as ringtaw or ringer, the object of which is to shoot marbles arranged like a cross out of a large ring. Players in a pot game such as moshie try to knock one another's marbles into a hole. In nineholes, or bridgeboard, players shoot his or her marbles through numbered arches on
          —————————————
                 16

the board.

15. (A) NO CHANGE
    (B) Many varieties are being
    (C) There are also many varieties
    (D) There was also many varieties

16. (F) NO CHANGE
    (G) your marbles
    (H) their marbles
    (J) our marbles

The popularity of marbles <u>spans centuries</u> and crosses
                              17
cultural boundaries. The first marble games took place in
antiquity. <u>It was played with</u> nuts, fruit pits, or pebbles.
                18
Even the great Augustus Caesar, <u>in addition with</u> his Roman
                                      19
playmates, was known to have played marble games as a
child. During Passover, Jewish children have customarily
used filberts as marbles. Several traditional Chinese games
are also played with marbles.

17. (A) NO CHANGE
    (B) span centuries
    (C) spanning centuries
    (D) spans hundreds of years

18. (F) NO CHANGE
    (G) They were played with
    (H) They were playing with
    (J) It plays with

19. (A) NO CHANGE
    (B) additionally with
    (C) along with
    (D) having the addition of

So, although most people consider the game of marbles
to be just for children, <u>it actually has a complex history.</u> If
                                                    20
anyone accuses you of having marbles in your head, you
might ask what kind.

20. (F) NO CHANGE
    (G) it actual has a complex history.
    (H) the history that they have is actually complex.
    (J) it has a history that is actually complex.

Quarter 4: Math

1. $\triangle PQR$ has side lengths a, b, and c, as shown in the figure below. A dotted line segment (d) originates at point P and is perpendicular to $\overline{QR}$. What is the ratio of the length of d to the length of $\overline{PQ}$?

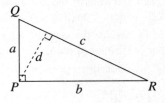

   (A) $\dfrac{a}{c}$

   (B) $\dfrac{b}{c}$

   (C) 1

   (D) $\dfrac{a}{b}$

   (E) $\dfrac{b}{a}$

2. How many different integer values of n satisfy the inequality $\frac{1}{11} < \frac{3}{n} < \frac{1}{9}$?

   (F) 1
   (G) 2
   (H) 3
   (J) 4
   (K) 5

3. A spider drops straight down from its web to the ground, a distance of 4.3 inches. If a bird, also on the ground, has an angle of inclination to the web of 37°, as shown below, what is the distance between the spider and the bird?

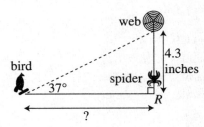

   (A) $\dfrac{4.3}{\tan 37°}$

   (B) $4.3 \tan 37°$

   (C) $\dfrac{4.3}{\sin 37°}$

   (D) $4.3 \sin 37°$

   (E) $\dfrac{4.3}{\cos 37°}$

4. How many points do the graphs of all three of the following equations have in common?

$$-2y = x + 4$$
$$-2y = -x + 4$$
$$5y = -6x + 8$$

(F) 0

(G) 1

(H) 2

(J) 3

(K) infinitely many

5. The figure below shows a vertical crosssection of a shovel used for moving large volumes of sand. The shovel is 40 inches (in.) wide and 35 in. long. The bottom is horizontal for 25 in. and then slopes up, and the sides are vertical. What is the volume of sand, in cubic inches, that is required to fill the shovel to a depth, as shown, of 15 inches on the deep side and 10 inches on the shallow side?

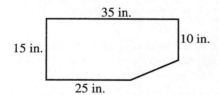

(A) 500

(B) 18,600

(C) 20,000

(D) 21,000

(E) 24,000

6. Line segments $\overline{WX}$, $\overline{XY}$, and $\overline{YZ}$ in the rectangular box shown below, have lengths of 12 centimeters, 5 centimeters, and 13 centimeters, respectively. What is the sine of angle ZWY?

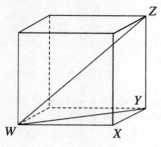

(F) 1

(G) $\frac{12}{13}$

(H) $\frac{\sqrt{2}}{2}$

(J) $\frac{5}{13}$

(K) $\frac{2\sqrt{2}}{3}$

7. Felicia knows that $(a - b)^2 \neq a^2 - b^2$, but she wonders if it's ever true in special cases. She works on this and finds that $(a - b)^2 = a^2 - b^2$ if and only if:

(A) $a = 0$

(B) $b = 0$

(C) $a = 0$ and $b = 0$

(D) $a = 0$ or $b = 0$

(E) $b = 0$ or $a = b$

8. A certain rectangle is $(x + 3)$ units long and $(x + 7)$ units wide. If a square with sides of length x is removed from the interior of the rectangle, which of the following is an expression for the remaining area?

(F) 10

(G) 21

(H) $2x + 10$

(J) $10x + 21$

(K) $x^2 + 10x + 21$

9. In 3 fair coin tosses, what is the probability of obtaining at least 2 heads? (Note: In a fair coin toss, the 2 outcomes, heads and tails, are equally likely.)

(A) $\frac{1}{8}$

(B) $\frac{3}{8}$

(C) $\frac{1}{2}$

(D) $\frac{2}{3}$

(E) $\frac{7}{8}$

10. In the standard (x,y) coordinate plane, if the distance between $(a,2)$ and $(16,a)$ is 10 units, which of the following could be the value of a?

   (F) 10
   (G) 6
   (H) −6
   (J) −8
   (K) −10

11. If $x = \frac{1}{3}t + 2$ and $y = 4 - t$, which of the following expresses y in terms of x?

   (A) $y = 2 - \frac{1}{3}x$
   (B) $y = 4 - x$
   (C) $y = 10 - 3x$
   (D) $y = -2 - 3x$
   (E) $y = 6 - 3x$

12. The complex number i is defined such that $i^2 = -1 (i - 1)^2 (i + 1) =$?

   (F) $i - 1$
   (G) $i - 2$
   (H) $i - 3$
   (J) $2i - 2$
   (K) $-2i + 2$

13. Which of the following is the equation of the largest circle that can be inscribed in the ellipse with equation $\frac{(x - 3)^2}{16} = \frac{(y + 2)^2}{25} = 1$?

   (A) $(x - 3)^2 + (y + 2)^2 = 400$
   (B) $(x - 3)^2 + (y + 2)^2 = 25$
   (C) $(x - 3)^2 + (y + 2)^2 = 16$
   (D) $x^2 + y^2 = 25$
   (E) $x^2 + y^2 = 16$

14. For the area of a square to triple, the new side lengths must be the old side lengths multiplied by:

   (F) $\sqrt{3}$.
   (G) 3.
   (H) 9.
   (J) $\sqrt{27}$.
   (K) 27.

Quarter 4: Science

Passage I

Table 1 below contains some physical properties of common optical materials. The refractive index of a material is a measure of the amount by which light is bent upon entering the material. The transmittance range is the range of wavelengths over which the material is transparent.

Table 1				
Material	Refractive index for light of 0.589 μm	Transmittance range (μm)	Useful range for prisms (μm)	Chemical resistance
Lithium fluoride	1.39	0.12–6	2.7–5.5	Poor
Calcium fluoride	1.43	0.12–12	5–9.4	Good
Sodium chloride	1.54	0.3–17	8–16	Poor
Quartz	1.54	0.20–3.3	0.20–2.7	Excellent
Potassium bromide	1.56	0.3–29	15–28	Poor
Flint glass*	1.66	0.35–2.2	0.35–2	Excellent
Cesium iodide	1.79	0.3–70	15–55	Poor
*Flint glass is lead oxide–doped quartz.				

1. When light travels from one medium to another, total internal reflection can occur if the first medium has a higher refractive index than the second. Total internal reflection could occur if light were traveling from:

   (A) lithium fluoride to flint glass.
   (B) potassium bromide to cesium iodide.
   (C) quartz to potassium bromide.
   (D) flint glass to calcium fluoride.

2. Based on the information in Table 1, how is the transmittance range related to the useful prism range?

   (F) The transmittance range is always narrower than the useful prism range.
   (G) The transmittance range is narrower than or equal to the useful prism range.
   (H) The transmittance range increases as the useful prism range decreases.
   (J) The transmittance range is wider than and includes within it the useful prism range.

3. The addition of lead oxide to pure quartz has the effect of:

   (A) decreasing the transmittance range and the refractive index.

   (B) decreasing the transmittance range and increasing the refractive index.

   (C) increasing the transmittance range and the useful prism range.

   (D) increasing the transmittance range and decreasing the useful prism range.

Passage II

When the *Voyager 2* spacecraft passed near Triton, the largest moon of Neptune, the pictures it transmitted of the surface became a source of controversy. Two views are presented below.

Scientist 1

The images of Triton seem to indicate recent volcanic activity, probably measured in millions or tens of millions of years. We can see no large-scale blemishes from around 4 billion years ago, when, shortly after the formation of our solar system, swarms of planetoids struck elsewhere. Many features are clearly visible that appear to be recentlyformed lava lakes, similar to the ice-lava lakes found on Jupiter's moon Ganymede. Other features resemble the icy slush found flowing from fractures on Uranus's Ariel. There even seems to be ongoing volcanic activity; this would explain the dark streaks seen in several places on the surface. We know that Triton's surface is covered with a thick layer of methane and nitrogen ice. It would take only a relatively small amount of internal heat to boil nitrogen to drive a nitrogen volcano. It can't be ruled out that Triton has a source of internal heat, like the radioactive decay within Earth, that supplies sufficient energy for volcanic reactions.

Scientist 2

The surface features we have observed on Triton can all be explained without assuming any volcanism within the last 4 billion years. Undoubtedly, Triton was molten for some time past the earliest days of the solar system. Its unusual orbit—it revolves in the direction opposite to the planet's rotation—indicates that it was captured by Neptune. The original orbit must have been highly elliptical and the gravitational stresses enormous, leading to frictional heating. But Triton has been settled into its current orbit for billions of years. Closer examination of the *Voyager* 2

images, particularly the higher-resolution pictures, shows many small craters on Triton due to the impact of small meteorites over a long period of time. What appear as lava lakes and volcanic-flows form fractures are most likely the result of the glacier-like movement of the methane-nitrogen polar ice caps. The dark streaks are probably the result of methane-nitrogen "snowfall." Finally, Triton's size—much smaller than that of Earth—rules out the possibility of internal heating.

4. Scientists 1 and 2 would be most likely to agree that:

   (F) volcanic activity has occurred on Triton within the last million years.

   (G) Triton may be internally heated by natural radioactive decay.

   (H) Triton is covered by a thick layer of methane and nitrogen ice.

   (J) nitrogen and methane "snow" falls on Triton.

5. Scientist 2 points out that many small craters have been seen on Triton, particularly in the higher-resolution images, in order to:

   (A) contradict Scientist 1's claim that there are no signs of planetoids having struck Triton.

   (B) provide evidence of recent volcanic activity on Triton.

   (C) demonstrate that some of Triton's surface features have evolved over a long period of time.

   (D) emphasize that Scientist 1's view is based on lower-resolution images of Triton.

6. Which of the following instruments, if included in a future mission to Triton, would supply additional information likely to resolve the controversy between Scientists 1 and 2?

   I. A mass spectrometer capable of chemically analyzing Triton's surface
   II. An infrared sensor able to determine surface and subsurface temperatures
   III. A subatomic particle detector thatcould determine core radioactivity

   (F) I and II only

   (G) II and III only

   (H) I and III only

   (J) I, II, and III

7. Scientists 1 and 2 disagree about:

   (A) the presence of dark streaks visible in images of Triton.
   (B) the physical process responsible for the features seen in images of Triton.
   (C) the chemical composition of the surface of Triton.
   (D) the origin of Triton.

8. Which of the following discoveries, if true, would most conclusively support the viewpoint of Scientist 1?

   (F) The surface of Triton has the same composition as the surfaces of Ganymede and Ariel.
   (G) The apparent small craters seen in the high-resolution pictures of Triton were introduced by faulty image processing.
   (H) Further inspection of images from Triton reveals an erupting volcano.
   (J) Triton is shown not to have been captured by Neptune but to have originated together with Neptune.

9. New research suggests that slow radioactive decay may persist in a body much smaller than Earth for up to 10 billion years. This information, if true, best supports the viewpoint of:

   (A) Scientist 1.
   (B) Scientist 2.
   (C) both Scientist 1 and Scientist 2.
   (D) neither Scientist 1 nor Scientist 2.

10. Based on Scientist 2's description of Triton's orbit, what must be true about a typical moon?

   (F) Most moons travel in elliptical orbits.
   (G) Most moons revolve in the direction of their planet's rotation.
   (H) Most moons are much smaller than the planets they orbit.
   (J) Most moons are less than 10,000 km from the planets they orbit.

ANSWERS AND EXPLANATIONS

Lesson Answers & Explanations

Quarter 1

Lesson Answer Key

1. **C**
2. **J**
3. **D**

1. C

Category: Word Choice
Difficulty: Low
Strategic Advice: Be aware of words that sound alike but have different meanings.
Getting to the Answer: This sentence uses the verb "are" in place of the possessive pronoun "our." Both (C) and (D) correct the pronoun, but the preposition "about" in (D) doesn't make sense in context.

2. J

Category: Wordiness
Difficulty: Medium
Strategic Advice: When "OMIT the underlined portion" is one of the answer choices, it's frequently the correct choice. Determine whether the underlined portion is necessary and relevant in context.
Getting to the Answer: The author makes it clear that she is talking about herself through her use of the pronoun "I." All of the other answer choices are unnecessary to the sense of the passage.

3. D

Category: Writing Strategy
Difficulty: Medium
Strategic Advice: Some Writing Strategy questions will require you to read the entire passage; others will relate to specific parts of the passage only. Remember the first step of the Kaplan Method: read until you have enough information to identify the issue.
Getting to the Answer: The new sentence talks about a change in the writer's outlook, so look for a logical place to introduce a contrast. Placing the new sentence anywhere but at the end of Paragraph 2 interrupts the flow of the narrative.

Quiz Answer Key

1. **C**
2. **F**
3. **B**
4. **J**
5. **D**
6. **J**
7. **B**
8. **H**
9. **C**
10. **J**

1. C

Category: Sentence Sense
Difficulty: Low
Strategic Advice: As written, the sentence is a run-on, which is formed when two independent clauses are not properly combined.
Getting to the Answer: (**C**) is the only answer choice that properly combines the two independent clauses; it does so by making each its own sentence.

2. F

Category: Word Choice
Difficulty: Low
Strategic Advice: Sometimes, ACT sentences will be correct as written.
Getting to the Answer: The sentence refers to "ancient fragments," so we need to use past or past-perfect tense, as in (F) and (H). The word "which" will always have a comma before it, so (**F**) is the correct answer. No change is necessary. (G), (H), and (J) all introduce new errors.

3. B

Category: Word Choice
Difficulty: Medium
Strategic Advice: The ACT will often separate a subject and a verb with nonessential information. Ignore it and place the subject and verb together to let your ear lead you to the correct answer.
Getting to the Answer: The subject of the underlined verb is the plural "Materials," which requires a plural verb: "are," so (**B**) is correct. While (D) is also in the plural verb form, it is in the past tense and changes the original meaning of the sentence.

4. J

Category: Punctuation
Difficulty: Medium
Strategic Advice: When punctuation is underlined, make sure it is being used correctly. An apostrophe is used before an "s" to show possession of a single object; it is used after an "s" to denote possession of plural objects.

Getting to the Answer: The sentence refers to the origin of the singular "basket," so the apostrophe should be between the "t" and the "s," as in (**J**).

5. D

Category: Punctuation
Difficulty: High
Strategic Advice: Commas should set off supplementary or explanatory phrases or words.

Getting to the Answer: While (B) seems to correct the error, "They" is ambiguous. Therefore, (**B**) is incorrect. (D) appropriately offsets the type of materials with a comma, rendering the list explanatory or supplementary.

6. J

Category: Word Choice
Difficulty: Low
Strategic Advice: When a modifier (an adjective, adverb, or modifying phrase) is underlined, match what it is modifying and make sure the correct modifier is being used.

Getting to the Answer: Because "works" is used here as a verb, the word that describes it must be an adverb. (H) and (J) both correct the error, but (**H**) makes the sentence past tense, which is incorrect given the context of the passage.

7. B

Category: Connections
Difficulty: Medium
Strategic Advice: Determine the relationship between two parts of a sentence to figure out what kind of connection is required.

Getting to the Answer: This sentence needs to start with a word or phrase that shows a contrast, not a word or phrase that shows a cause-and-effect relationship. (**B**) uses "Although," which is an appropriate contrast connection. (C) and (D) also introduce contrast words, but they make the sentence ungrammatical.

8. H

Category: Verb Tense
Strategic Advice: Look out for *–ing* verbs used alone, as they often create sentence fragments.
Getting to the Answer: As written, this is a sentence fragment. (The gerund [*–ing*] verb form cannot be the main verb in a sentence.) The other verbs in the sentence are in present tense, so we need to choose a present-tense verb, (**H**).

9. C

Category: Word Choice
Difficulty: Medium
Strategic Advice: When choosing from two things, use "between." When choosing from three or more things, use "among."

Getting to the Answer: The craftspeople must choose "between" artistry and security—that's two things, so use "between." While (C) and (D) both correct this error, "traditioned" in the original sentence and (D) is not a word; the correct word is "traditional."

10. J

Category: Word Choice
Difficulty: Medium
Strategic Advice: Match pronouns to their antecedent (the word the pronoun is replacing) in gender, number, and case.

Getting to the Answer: Because "basket maker" is singular, the pronoun that refers to it must also be singular. (G) and (H) are homonyms of "their," which is a plural pronoun and therefore incorrect. Only (**J**) makes the pronoun match the antecedent.

Quarter 2

Lesson Answer Key

1. **E**
2. **G**
3. **C**
4. **H**
5. **D**
6. **F**
7. **E**
8. **H**
9. **C**
10. **H**
11. **B**
12. **G**
13. **B**
14. **G**

1. E

Category: Number Properties
Difficulty: Low
Strategic Advice: When you divide variables with exponents, the answer is their difference.
Getting to the Answer: We know that $\frac{5}{5}$ becomes 1 and $\frac{f6}{f9}$ becomes f^{-3} or $\frac{1}{f^3}$.

2. G

Category: Proportions and Probability
Difficulty: Medium
Strategic Advice: When Picking Numbers for percent problems, you should start with 100 to make your calculations easier.
Getting to the Answer: Say original cost = $100. Then Monday's cost = $100 − $100(0.2) = $80 and Tuesday's cost = $80 − $80(0.25) = $60.
Percent change = $\frac{\$100 - \$60}{\$100}$ 100% = 40%

3. C

Category: Number Properties
Difficulty: Medium
Strategic Advice: Variables in the answer choices let you know you can Pick Numbers.
Getting to the Answer: Pick a value of a that follows the rules in the question stem (is an integer) and is

easy to work with: say, $a = 1$. Then evaluate each answer choice:

(A) $1^2 = 1$
(B) $1^2 + 1 = 1 + 1 = 2$
(C) $2(1)^2 + 1 = 2 + 1 = 3$
(D) $3(1)^2 + 2 = 3 + 2 = 5$
(E) $4(1)^2 + 4 = 4 + 4 = 8$

(A), (C), and (D) are all odd when $a = 1$. Since this question asks for the expression that is odd for *any* value of a, try another number for these choices. If $a = 2$, then:

(A) $2^2 = 4$
(C) $2(2)^2 + 1 = 2(4) + 1 = 8 + 1 = 9$
(D) $3(2)^2 + 2 = 3(4) + 2 = 12 + 2 = 14$

Only (**C**) is odd for both $a = 1$ and $a = 2$, so it must be correct.

4. H

Category: Patterns, Logic & Data
Difficulty: Medium
Strategic Advice: When a problem contains sets, drawing it out can help you visualize the answer.
Getting to the Answer: Since the integers in Set A are consecutive, their average must equal their middle term. In a set of 7 integers, the middle one is the fourth term. To find the smallest term, count backward from 46: 46, 44, 42, 40. That's (H). You can also answer this question by using Kaplan's Backsolving strategy. Start with (H). If 40 is the smallest integer of Set A, then the next six consecutive integers must be 42, 44, 46, 48, 50, and 52. Take the average of these 7 integers:

$$\frac{40 + 42 + 44 + 46 + 48 + 50 + 52}{7} = \frac{322}{7} = 46$$

This matches the condition in the question stem: The average of these consecutive integers equals 46. (**H**) must be the correct answer.

5. D

Category: Variable Manipulation
Difficulty: High
Strategic Advice: If an equation looks complicated enough that you'd get confused trying to solve it algebraically, you can Backsolve.
Getting to the Answer: As always, start with the middle number, (C):

$$\frac{0 + 1}{0 - 3} - \frac{0 + 2}{0 - 4} = \frac{1}{-3} - \frac{2}{-4} = -\frac{1}{3} + \frac{1}{2} \neq 0$$

Zero doesn't work, but it's hard to see whether a bigger or smaller number is necessary. If you're not sure which direction to go, just pick the one that looks easier to work with. In this case, that's (**D**):

$$\frac{1+2}{1-3} - \frac{1+2}{1-4} = \frac{2}{-2} - \frac{3}{-3} = -1 - (-1) = 0.$$

6. F

Category: Proportions and Probability

Difficulty: Medium

Strategic Advice: If a problem with numerical choices seems difficult to set up, use Backsolving instead.

Getting to the Answer: Read the word problem carefully to isolate the key details that will lead you to the correct answer. In the problem, Michelle pulls gummy worms from the bag twice. For the answer to be correct, 50% of all worms pulled must be orange after Michelle's second handful. Therefore, the total number of orange worms pulled must equal the total number of gummy worms that have a different color.

The correct choice represents the number of worms pulled in her second handful, 40% of which are orange. Since Michelle only pulled whole worms, you can eliminate (G) and (J) right away, as 40% of 26 or 36 does not result in a whole number. Backsolve the remaining choices, starting with (H):

If Michelle pulled 30 worms the second time, 30 × 40% = 12 of them would be orange. Therefore, she would have 12 + 10 = 22 orange worms and (30 − 12) + 6 = 24 worms of other colors. Because 22 ≠ 24, eliminate (H).

You could try either (F) or (K). Let's start with (K): 40 × 40% = 16 orange worms. Therefore, Michele has 16 + 10 = 26 orange worms and (40 − 16) + 6 = 30 worms of other colors. Because 26 ≠ 30, eliminate (K). Now for (F): 20 × 40% = 8 orange worms. Michelle has 8 + 10 = 18 orange worms and (20 − 8) + 6 = 18 worms of other colors. Then 18 = 18, so (**F**) is the correct answer.

7. E

Category: Variable Manipulation

Difficulty: Medium

Strategic Advice: If you multiply or divide by a negative number, you must reverse the direction of the inequality sign.

Getting to the Answer:

$$-2 - 4x \leq -6x$$
$$-2 \leq -2x$$
$$1 \geq x$$
$$x \leq 1$$

8. H

Category: Variable Manipulation

Difficulty: Medium

Strategic Advice: On problems with complex fractions, simplifying before multiplying will save you valuable time on Test Day.

Getting to the Answer: Since $a = 4$, the fraction becomes $\frac{4(4)^4 + 64b}{16} = \frac{4^5 + 64b}{16}$. You could evaluate 4^5, but you'll save yourself some work if you notice that the denominator and the coefficient for b can both be represented in base 4 as well. Rewriting the problem with base 4, you have the following:

$$\frac{4^5 + 4^3 b}{4^2} = 4^3 + 4b = 64 + 4b$$

9. C

Category: Variable Manipulation

Difficulty: Low

Strategic Advice: Whenever you're working with an equation, you must do the same thing to both sides.

Getting to the Answer:

$$5x + 3 = -17$$
$$5x = -20$$
$$x = -4$$

10. H

Category: Variable Manipulation

Difficulty: Medium

Strategic Advice: Always read word problems carefully, particularly if you need to translate them into algebra problems.

Getting to the Answer: Call the number of comic books in Brandy's collection C. Then translate the question stem into an equation. First, "she adds 15 to the number," which means $C + 15$. Then she "multiplies the sum by 3," so you have $3(C + 15)$. "The result will be" indicates an equal sign, and "65 less than 4 times the number" is $4C - 65$. So this sentence can be written $3(C + 15) = 4C - 65$. Now solve for C:

$$3c + 45 = 4c - 65$$
$$110 = c$$

You could also Backsolve, plugging each answer choice into the question stem until you find one that works with the information there.

11. B

Category: Variable Manipulation

Difficulty: Medium

Strategic Advice: Backsolving works well on many word problems.

Getting to the Answer: Start with the middle choice, (H). If Joy drove 96 miles, she would have paid $1.50 + $0.25(96) = $25.50. This is too much, so go to (B). If she drove 94 miles, she would have paid $1.50 + $0.25(94) = $25.00. (B) is correct.

You could also set up an equation. If m is the number of miles traveled, the toll is $1.50 + 0.25m$. Joy paid $25.00, so we set up this equation:

$1.50 + 0.25m$ = $25.00

0.25m$ = $23.50

$$\frac{\$23.50}{\$.25} = 94$$

12. G

Category: Variable Manipulation

Difficulty: Medium

Strategic Advice: If you don't know what to do with a quadratic equation, try factoring it.

Getting to the Answer: You are given the value of $x + y$. To make use of it, reverse FOIL the equation $4x^2 + 6xy + 2y^2 = 32$ and try to factor out an $x + y$:

$4x^2 + 6xy + 2y^2 = 32$

$(2x + 2y)(2x + y) = 32$

$2(x + y)(2x + y) = 32$

Now substitute 4 for $x + y$ and solve for $2x + y$:

$2(4)(2x + y) = 32$

$8(2x + y) = 32$

$2x + y = 4$

Therefore, **(G)** is correct. Alternatively, you could simplify the quadratic equation first by dividing both sides by 2, to get the lowest-possible numbers to work with.

13. B

Category: Variable Manipulation

Difficulty: Medium

Strategic Advice: To factor a quadratic equation, find factors of the last term that, when added together, equal the middle term.

Getting to the Answer:

$$\frac{x^2 - 11x + 24}{8 - x} = \frac{(x-8)(x-3)}{8-x}$$

$$= \frac{-(8-x)(x-3)}{8-x}$$

$$= -(x-3)$$

$$= 3 - x$$

14. G

Category: Variable Manipulation

Difficulty: Medium

Strategic Advice: Either combination or substitution will work for a given set of equations, but one will usually be easier. Because this question already has +4y and −4y, combination is the best choice here.

Getting to the Answer:

$$\begin{array}{r} 3x + 4y = 31 \\ +3x - 4y = -1 \\ \hline 6x = 30 \\ x = 5 \end{array}$$

Notice that $y = 4$, so (F) is a trap.

Quiz

Answer Key

1. **B**
2. **K**
3. **D**
4. **J**
5. **D**
6. **F**

1. B

Category: Variable Manipulation

Difficulty: Low

Strategic Advice: Stay organized by working with each piece of information separately.

Getting to the Answer: If x represents the number of whales, "twice as many dolphins as whales" indicates that there are 2x dolphins. Therefore, "dolphins and whales combined" is 2x + x, or 3x. Since there are eight fewer sharks, the correct answer is (B). However, you can also find this answer by using the Picking Numbers strategy. Pick a small, positive number for the number of whales, like 5. If there are 5 whales and "twice as many dolphins as whales," there must be 10 dolphins. Combine the number of whales and dolphins and subtract 8 from that sum to find the number of sharks: $(5 + 10) - 8 = 15 - 8 = 7$. Plug in 5 for x to determine the answer choice that will give you a final value of 7:

(A) $5(5) = 25$. Eliminate.

(B) $3x - 8 = 15 - 7 = 8$. Keep this answer choice.

(C) $10 + 5 = 15$. Eliminate.

(D) $\sqrt{24 \times 5} = \sqrt{120} \neq 7$. Eliminate.

(E) $3\sqrt{5} - 8 \neq 7$. Eliminate.

(**B**) is the only answer choice that works.

2. K

Category: Proportions and Probability

Difficulty: Medium

Strategic Advice: When there are numbers in the question stem and in the answer choices, think Backsolving.

Getting to the Answer: Start with the middle choice: H. If 48 players tried out for the team and $\frac{1}{3}$ of students were asked to come to a second tryout, then $48 \times \frac{1}{3} = 16$ players were invited to the second tryout. The question states that 18 players were offered parts, so you already know that (H) is far too small. (F) and (G) are likewise going to be too small, so eliminate all three answer choices and move on to J: $\frac{56}{3} = 18\frac{2}{3}$ players invited to a second tryout. You can't have $\frac{2}{3}$ of a soccer player, so (J) can't be the correct answer. That leaves (**K**).

3. D

Category: Variable Manipulation

Difficulty: Medium

Strategic Advice: Complicated word problems are great situations for Backsolving.

Getting to the Answer: The numbers in the answer choices represent the number of people at the conference. Start with (C) and see whether each number fits the information in the question stem:

(C). If there are 60 participants, then there are $\frac{60}{3} = 20$ anthropologists and $\frac{60}{2} = 30$ biologists. That leaves $60 - 20 - 30 = 10$ chemists, which is not enough. Move to the next higher number: (D). If there are 72 participants, then there are $\frac{72}{3} = 24$ anthropologists and $\frac{72}{2} = 36$ biologists, leaving $72 - 24 - 36 = 12$ chemists. Perfect!

4. J

Category: Variable Manipulation

Difficulty: High

Strategic Advice: When a question has all variables in the answer choices, it is a good time to Pick Numbers. Most numbers that fit the rules of the question will get you the right answer, but some will be easier to work with than others. In this case, glancing at the denominators in the question tells us we want something larger than 4, to avoid working with negatives unnecessarily. 6 would work, but since there are multiples and factors of 8 in the question, that may be even easier.

Getting to the Answer: Let $x = 8$:

$$\frac{4x}{x^2 - 16} - \frac{3x}{x - 4} = \frac{4(8)}{(8)^2 - 16} - \frac{3(8)}{(8) - 4} = \frac{32}{64 - 16} - \frac{24}{4}$$
$$= \frac{32}{48} - \frac{6}{1} = -5\frac{1}{3}$$

Choice (J) is the only answer that will yield this same result:

$$\frac{-3x^2 - 8x}{x^2 - 16} = \frac{-3(8)^2 - 8(8)}{(8)^2 - 16} = \frac{-192 - 64}{48} = \frac{-256}{48} = -5\frac{1}{3}$$

You could also solve algebraically by finding a common denominator:

$$\frac{4x}{x^2 - 16} - \frac{3x}{x - 4} \times \frac{(x + 4)}{(x + 4)} = \frac{4x - 3x^2 - 12x}{(x - 4)(x + 4)} = \frac{-3x^2 - 8x}{x^2 - 16},$$

which is choice (**J**).

When finding a common denominator, if you spotted the classic quadratic $x^2 - 16$ (the difference of squares), you'd know that $(x+4)$ would be a good choice!

5. D

Category: Variable Manipulation

Difficulty: Medium

Strategic Advice: Both Backsolving and algebra work well here. If you Backsolve, you can save time by noticing that C will be less than F (unless F is -40 or less). This lets you eliminate (A), (B), and (C) right away.

Getting to the Answer: Plug in 95 for C and solve for F:

$$95 = \frac{5}{9}(F - 32)$$
$$\frac{9}{5} \times 95 = \frac{9}{5} \times \frac{5}{9}(F - 32)$$
$$171 = (F - 32)$$
$$203 = F$$

6. F

Category: Variable Manipulation

Difficulty: Medium

Strategic Advice: If the answer you come up with isn't one of the answer choices, carefully consider which of the choices means the same thing. Don't just pick one that looks similar.

Getting to the Answer:

$$-3x + 7 \leq 4$$
$$-3x \leq -3$$
$$x \geq 1$$

(Since you divided by a negative number, you must change the direction of the inequality sign.) This is not one of the answer choices, but think about what it means: if x is greater than or equal to 1, then it must be greater than 0. (**F**) is correct.

Quarter 3

Answer Key

1. **C**
2. **H**
3. **D**
4. **G**

PASSAGE I

1. C

Category: Function

Difficulty: Low

Strategic Advice: With Function questions, be sure to concentrate on the specific word or phrase in question. Then read around it to determine context.

Getting to the Answer: The second paragraph relates the plot of the movie and concludes, "That's all I'll say about the plot—not because I don't want to give it away, but because I already have." The author is implying that this short description is all there is to say about the plot because it is so simple. From the rest of the paragraph, you know that the author doesn't think very highly of the plot, so look for an answer in keeping with this negative tone.

(A) Misused Detail; although the author does feel that the film is not worthwhile, the sentence in question is more limited in scope and only addresses the film's plot.

(B) Misused Detail; this discussion occurs in the third paragraph, not the second.

(**C**) This matches the tone and content of the prediction.

(D) Opposite; the author says that he's not worried about giving away the plot.

2. H

Category: Detail

Difficulty: Medium

Strategic Advice: Clues to the answer may appear in more than one place in the passage.

Getting to the Answer: In the first paragraph, the author says that the actress is "usually satisfying." In the third paragraph, the author says that the acting is poor but that Findlay usually "does much with whatever she is given." In other words, she is usually good but is lousy in this movie.

(F) Opposite; in this movie, she's boring, not "compelling."

(G) Opposite; she's usually good.

(**H**) This matches the thrust of your prediction.

(J) Extreme; although the author criticizes the actress's performance, he never says that it's "annoying." Instead, it seems to be simply uninspired.

PASSAGE II

3. D

Category: Inference

Difficulty: High

Strategic Advice: When prediction is not feasible, work through the choices, using your notes to help you eliminate your way to the correct one.

Getting to the Answer: As you compare the choices to your notes, you should see that two choices start with "Faraday" and two start with "Oersted." With that in mind, your notes should draw you to paragraphs 5 and 6. Do a quick re-skim of those two paragraphs and then quickly work through the choices.

(A) Distortion; paragraph 5 indicates that it was Oersted who did this.

(B) Out of Scope; the author does not suggest that either physicist was involved in this.

(C) Distortion; this term comes in the "Faraday" paragraph. The author doesn't indicate who "coined the term." Note that underlining that term in the passage helps in finding it quickly. You can get the correct answer without necessarily knowing what "electromagnetic induction" is.

(**D**) Correct; this is supported by the first part of paragraph 6.

4. G

Category: Inference
Difficulty: Medium
Strategic Advice: The organization that good notes provide should keep you safe from falling for Misused Details.

Getting to the Answer: Your notes should indicate that the author discusses "advances in the efficiency of the transformer" in paragraph 4. After you review the paragraph, you can predict *reflective of "the marriage of theoretical inquiry and engineering"* (line 40).

(F) Misused Detail; the author doesn't use this detail from the last paragraph in relation to such advances, and the word "solely" is extreme.

(**G**) Correct; this captures what is in the text.

(H) Out of Scope; the author never suggests this, and the word "cannot" is extreme.

(J) Misused Detail; the author doesn't use this detail from the second paragraph in relation to such advances.

Quiz

Answer Key

PASSAGE III

1. **B**
2. **H**
3. **C**

1. B

Category: Detail
Difficulty: Low
Strategic Advice: Remember that support for the answer will be in the passage.

Getting to the Answer: Your notes should have led you to paragraph 2. Based on that, you can predict that *they're like sisters* (see lines 18–19).

(A) Distortion; the end of paragraph 1 implies something close to this, but it speaks about "affection," not their relationship.

(**B**) Correct; this matches the prediction and the text.

(C) Out of Scope; Austen doesn't state or imply this.

(D) Out of Scope; Austen makes no such comparison.

2. H

Category: Inference
Difficulty: Medium
Strategic Advice: You should usually be able to handle questions with line references quickly, saving time for more difficult questions.

Getting to the Answer: Read around the reference. You should be able to come up with a prediction along these lines: *Even though they won't be far from each other, their friendship won't be as close.*

(F) Extreme; the passage doesn't support so strong a statement as "no longer."

(G) Opposite; she had nearly unlimited freedom when Miss Taylor was around.

(**H**) Correct; the wording is slightly different, but it still matches the main idea of the prediction.

(J) Opposite; the passage indicates that she fears the relationship will become weaker.

3. C

Category: Generalization
Difficulty: Medium
Strategic Advice: Even on questions drawing from the entire passage, you will still be able to find specific points in support of the correct choice.

Getting to the Answer: Since the answer is "based on the passage," you should review all of your notes regarding Emma. This should lead to predictions like *sad* and *used to getting her way.*

(A) Out of Scope; while Austen does depict some positive characteristics of Emma, these are not referenced.

(B) Distortion; the passage supports the first one, but not the second. Emma seems very realistic in assessing the future of her relationship with Mrs. Weston.

(**C**) Correct; this matches the characterization in the passage, especially lines 25–30.

(D) Extreme; the passage never shows Emma's sadness turning into bitterness or ingratitude.

Quarter 4

Answer Key

1. **C**
2. **J**

PASSAGE I

1. C

Category: Scientific Reasoning

Difficulty: Low

Strategic Advice: Mapping the passage and marking the Purpose, Method, and Results of the experiments will help you locate the answer.

Getting to the Answer: Based on your notes, you can determine that experiment 1 does not produce a response to the beam of light. Therefore, experiment 2 must have produced the desired response. In experiment 2, the bats were isolated in 25 separate simulated caves, (**C**).

(A) is incorrect because the beam of light was sent into the caves 21 times over the course of 3 weeks. Moreover, the number of exposures did not vary and was not a factor in the experiments. (B) is incorrect because the escape attempts were extensions of the bats' response to the light, not the reason for their reaction. (D) is incorrect because placing the bats in groups of 6 was the method of experiment 1, which did not produce a response to light.

2. J

Category: Scientific Reasoning

Difficulty: Low

Strategic Advice: Understanding and marking the Method of the experiment will help you predict what the answer will look like before you look at the answer choices.

Getting to the Answer: Experiments 1 and 2 differ in the number of bats placed in simulated caves. The Method of experiment 1 has groups of 6 bats in simulated caves, whereas the Method of experiment 2 isolates the bats. Therefore, the intentionally varied factor in experiment 1 is the number of bats exposed to the beam of light, (**J**).

(F) is incorrect because the duration of the beam of light never changes.

(G) is incorrect because the behaviorists do not change the time of exposure.

(H) is incorrect because the bats' behavior is the result of the experiments, not the variable.

Quiz

Answer Key

1. **D**
2. **G**
3. **C**
4. **G**
5. **D**

PASSAGE II

1. D

Category: Scientific Reasoning

Difficulty: High

Passage type: Research Summary

Strategic Advice: Refer to the passage to understand the process in question on Scientific Method questions. In this case, refer to the description of CVAFS.

Getting to the Answer: The passage mentions that CVAFS "indicates the relative concentrations of various elements and compounds." A properly working CVAFS, then, should be able to correctly measure the relative concentrations of Hg and Pb. Using a sample of known concentrations of Hg and Pb, as in (**D**), would support or reject the accuracy of the CVAFS in detecting the presence of Pb. Nothing in the passage supports either (A) or (C). (B) is similarly unrelated to the passage.

2. G

Category: Patterns

Difficulty: Medium

Passage type: Research Summary

Strategic Advice: Questions like this use a lot of words to hide a very simple concept. In this case, all you're really asked to do is identify which fish would be most likely to have the greatest Hg concentration.

Getting to the Answer: Tables 1 and 2 tell you that swordfish have the highest Hg concentrations and that cold-water fish have higher Hg concentrations than the same species in warm water. Therefore, a swordfish caught in cold water would likely have the greatest Hg concentration of all the listed specimens, making (**G**) correct.

3. C

Category: Scientific Reasoning

Difficulty: Low

Passage type: Research Summary

Strategic Advice: The factors intentionally varied are the ones researchers purposefully changed in the course of the experiment.

Getting to the Answer: Look back at Table 2. It shows that researchers intentionally tested four different kinds of fish, which matches (**C**).

(A) is incorrect since the volume of tissue was never discussed.

(B) is incorrect because all four species in experiment 2 were extracted from water of the same temperature.

(D) is incorrect since CVAFS is the only method of analysis mentioned.

4. G

Category: Scientific Reasoning
Difficulty: Low
Passage type: Research Summary
Strategic Advice: Before looking at the choices, determine for yourself what factors would support the given hypothesis or cause it to be rejected. In this case, the hypothesis would be supported only if the results showed higher Hg concentrations in swordfish and shark than in catfish and crab.

Getting to the Answer: The results do indeed show higher Hg concentrations for swordfish and shark, so the hypothesis is confirmed as in (**G**).

The "Yes" part of (F) is correct, but the reason given contradicts the data in Table 2, so it is incorrect.

(H) is also incorrect; the lowest Hg concentration was indeed in catfish, but this does not cause the hypothesis to be rejected.

(J) contradicts the data in Table 2.

5. D

Category: Scientific Reasoning
Difficulty: Medium
Passage type: Research Summary
Strategic Advice: Think about the experimental Method used and try to predict an answer before looking at the choices.

Getting to the Answer: Increasing the volume of tested material while maintaining the same volume of Hg in the sample would lead to a smaller fraction of Hg content, regardless of water temperature. (**D**) is perfect.

(C) is incorrect because nothing in the passage indicates that the contamination would affect warm- and cold-water fish differently.

Homework Answers and Explanations
Quarter 1

Answer Key

1. **B**
2. **H**
3. **D**
4. **F**
5. **D**
6. **H**
7. **C**
8. **G**
9. **A**
10. **J**

1. B

Category: Punctuation
Difficulty: Low
Strategic Advice: When punctuation (like a comma) is underlined, make sure it's necessary and being used correctly.

Getting to the Answer: The comma is not necessary here, so choose an answer that omits it. (B) and (D) both do this, but (D) changes "told" to "telling," which is incorrect.

2. H

Category: Word Choice
Difficulty: Medium
Strategic Advice: Items in a compound construction must be in parallel form.

Getting to the Answer: The "dual purpose" implies a compound construction. "Also transmitting" must match "of entertaining." Replace the "also" with "of," like in (**H**).

3. D

Category: Sentence Sense
Difficulty: High
Strategic Advice: Two independent clauses must be combined properly. You can do this by making one clause subordinate or dependent.

Getting to the Answer: While (B), (C), and (D) all make the first clause subordinate, only (**D**) makes sense within the context of the sentence and passage.

4. F

Category: Punctuation

Difficulty: Medium

Strategic Advice: Colons can be used to introduce or name a concept that's just been described.

Getting to the Answer: This use of the colon is correct; no change is necessary.

5. D

Category: Wordiness

Difficulty: Medium

Strategic Advice: When, inside the same sentence, you have two words that mean the same thing, one of the words should be omitted.

Getting to the Answer: The sentence uses "but" a couple of words before "verifiable." Therefore, "however" is redundant and should be eliminated.

6. H

Category: Wordiness

Difficulty: Low

Strategic Advice: When you see two words joined by "and," make sure they don't have the same meaning.

Getting to the Answer: The word "conclusion" is unnecessary because it expresses the same thing as the word "ending," which has already been used. Omit "and a conclusion."

7. C

Category: Verb Tenses

Difficulty: Low

Strategic Advice: When multiple verbs are used in a sentence, make sure they are the same tense unless a change of time period is specifically mentioned.

Getting to the Answer: "Knew" and "decided" establish the verb tense as past, so "load it in" must be "loaded it in" to be consistent with the other two verbs.

8. G

Category: Word Choice

Difficulty: Medium

Strategic Advice: Use "who" and "whom" to refer to people. Use "that" and "which" to refer to animals or things.

Getting to the Answer: The pronoun "he" is incorrect because the sentence already has a subject. (G) and (J) correct the error by replacing "he" with "which," but (J) changes the verb tense.

9. A

Category: Punctuation

Difficulty: Medium

Strategic Advice: Use commas to offset nonessential information in a sentence both before and after the nonessential phrase.

Getting to the Answer: A comma appears before "before alligators were a protected species," a phrase the sentence could do without. A comma must come after it as well, so it is correct as written.

10. J

Category: Writing Strategy

Difficulty: Medium

Strategic Advice: If a sentence has nothing to do with the topic of the passage and there's an option to omit it, take that option.

Getting to the Answer: The fact that alligator skin was used to make boots and wallets is irrelevant to the passage's topic of urban legends.

Quarter 2

Answer Key

1. **C**
2. **K**
3. **A**
4. **G**
5. **D**
6. **G**
7. **D**
8. **G**
9. **B**
10. **K**
11. **A**
12. **G**
13. **A**
14. **G**
15. **D**
16. **G**
17. **C**
18. **G**
19. **A**
20. **K**

1. C

Category: Variable Manipulation
Difficulty: Medium
Strategic Advice: Algebra and Backsolving both work well on word problems like this one. Use whichever you find more comfortable.

Getting to the Answer: To solve this problem algebraically, first translate it into math. At $8 per adult ticket and $5 per student ticket, the total amount of money collected can be written as $8a + 5s = 3,475$. Since there were 500 tickets total, $s + a = 500$, or $s = 500 - a$. This lets you get the first equation in terms of one variable so you can solve it. Plug this equation for s into the first equation and solve for a:

$8a + 5(500 - a) = 3,475$

$8a + 2,500 - 5a = 3,475$

$3a = 975$

$a = 325$

To Backsolve, start with (C). If there are 325 adult tickets, then there are $500 - 325 = 175$ student

tickets. The total amount of money collected would be $325(8) + 175(5) = 2,600 + 875 = 3,475$ dollars. Since this is the total in the question stem, (**C**) is correct.

2. K

Category: Variable Manipulation
Difficulty: Medium
Strategic Advice: Factoring an equation is easier when one side is equal to zero.

Getting to the Answer:

$x^2 - 3x = 6x$

$x^2 - 9x = 0$

$x(x - 9) = 0$

$x = 0$ or $x = 9$

Since the question stem states that $x \neq 0$, (**K**) must be correct. Backsolving would also work well here; you would want to start by checking the easiest-to-solve choices: (J) and (K).

3. A

Category: Variable Manipulation
Difficulty: Medium
Strategic Advice: The first step to solving most questions about fractions set equal to each other is to crossmultiply.

Getting to the Answer:

$\dfrac{3}{zy} = \dfrac{2y}{x}$

$3x = 2zy^2$

$x = \dfrac{2zy^2}{3}$

4. G

Category: Variable Manipulation
Difficulty: Medium
Strategic Advice: Backsolving and algebra will both work on problems like this.

Getting to the Answer:

$\dfrac{(x^2)^3}{2} = 32$

$x^6 = 64$

Note that, while square roots must be positive, either 8 or -8 can be squared to get 64. Therefore, $x = 2$ or $x = -2$.

5. **D**

Category: Variable Manipulation

Difficulty: Medium

Strategic Advice: Backsolving works well on complicated word problems like this one.

Getting to the Answer: Start with (C). If Denise answered 38 of the questions correctly and skipped 2, then she answered $60 - 38 - 2 = 20$ questions incorrectly. She gets 2 points for every correct question and loses $\frac{2}{3}$ of a point for every incorrect question, so she would earn $38(2) - 20\left(\frac{2}{3}\right) = 76 - \frac{40}{3} = \frac{228}{3} - \frac{40}{3} = \frac{188}{3} = 62\frac{2}{3}$ points. This is too low, so try (D). If Denise answered 40 questions correctly, she made $40(2) - 18\left(\frac{2}{3}\right) = 80 - 12 = 68$ points. Perfect!

6. **G**

Category: Variable Manipulation

Difficulty: Low

Strategic Advice: The most obvious way to answer a question isn't necessarily the fastest.

Getting to the Answer: Here, it's much faster to simply multiply out the given factorization than to try plugging in values of k to factor the quadratic expression: $(x - 3)(x - 5) = x^2 - 5x - 3x + 15 = x^2 - 8x + 15$. Thus, $k = -8$.

Notice that (J) is a trap. Always be aware of negative signs.

7. **D**

Category: Variable Manipulation

Difficulty: Low

Strategic Advice: Even a very straightforward question can trip you up if you're careless. Watch those negative signs and be careful with your arithmetic.

Getting to the Answer:

$$k - 3 = -\frac{5}{3}$$
$$k = \frac{5}{3} + 3 = \frac{-5}{3} + \frac{9}{4} = \frac{4}{3}$$
$$3 - k = \frac{9}{3} - \frac{4}{3} = \frac{5}{3}$$

8. **G**

Category: Variable Manipulation

Difficulty: Low

Strategic Advice: The direction of an inequality sign changes if you multiply or divide by a negative number.

Other than that, they act exactly like equations—you must always do the same thing to both sides.

Getting to the Answer:

$$-3 < 4x - 5$$
$$2 < 4x$$
$$\frac{1}{2} < x$$

9. **B**

Category: Variable Manipulation

Difficulty: High

Strategic Advice: Picking Numbers is a great alternative to algebra when you're trying to work with complicated expressions like this.

Getting to the Answer: Say $x = 4$ and $y = 9$. Then $\frac{\sqrt{x}}{x} + \frac{\sqrt{y}}{y} = \frac{\sqrt{4}}{4} + \frac{\sqrt{9}}{9} = \frac{2}{4} + \frac{3}{9} = \frac{18}{36} + \frac{12}{36} = \frac{30}{36} = \frac{5}{6}$. Which of the answer choices also equal $\frac{5}{6}$?

(A) $\frac{2}{\sqrt{4 \cdot 9}} = \frac{2}{\sqrt{36}} = \frac{2}{6} = \frac{1}{3}$ No.

(B) $\frac{\sqrt{4} + \sqrt{9}}{\sqrt{4 \cdot 9}} = \frac{2 + 3}{\sqrt{36}} = \frac{5}{6}$ Yes.

(C) $\frac{4 + 9}{4 \cdot 9} = \frac{13}{36}$ No.

(D) $\frac{\sqrt{4} + \sqrt{9}}{\sqrt{4 + 9}} = \frac{2 + 3}{\sqrt{13}} = \frac{5}{\sqrt{13}}$ No.

(E) $\frac{4 + 9}{\sqrt{4 \cdot 9}} = \frac{13}{\sqrt{36}} = \frac{13}{6}$ No.

Only (B) equals $\frac{5}{6}$ when $x = 4$ and $y = 9$, so (B) is correct. To solve algebraically, you need to reexpress and give the fractions a common denominator:

$$\frac{\sqrt{x}}{x} + \frac{\sqrt{y}}{y} = \frac{1}{\sqrt{x}} + \frac{1}{\sqrt{y}} = \frac{\sqrt{y}}{(\sqrt{x} \times \sqrt{y})} + \frac{\sqrt{x}}{(\sqrt{y} \times \sqrt{x})} = \frac{(\sqrt{y} + \sqrt{x})}{(\sqrt{xy})}$$

10. **K**

Category: Variable Manipulation

Difficulty: Medium

Strategic Advice: To solve for variables in exponents, you first need to get the two sides of the equation in terms of the same base. Backsolving is also a good alternative here.

Getting to the Answer:

$$9^{2x - 1} = 3^{3x + 3}$$
$$(3^2)^{2x - 1} = 3^{3x + 3}$$
$$3^{4x - 2} = 3^{3x + 3}$$
$$4x - 2 = 3x + 3$$
$$x = 5$$

11. **A**

Category: Variable Manipulation

Difficulty: Low

Strategic Advice: Expressions can be treated just like variables. In this case, you can work with x^2 as a variable.

Getting to the Answer:

$$\frac{x^2 + x^2 + x^2}{x^2} = \frac{3x^2}{x^2} = 3$$

12. **G**

Category: Variable Manipulation

Difficulty: Low

Strategic Advice: Simple Variable Manipulation questions like this one are usually easier to solve algebraically than by Backsolving. Since you might have to plug in several numbers, Backsolving can be slow.

Getting to the Answer:

$$7n - 8 = 6$$
$$7n = 14$$
$$n = 2$$

13. **A**

Category: Variable Manipulation

Difficulty: Low

Strategic Advice: Read questions carefully! This one doesn't want to know how many dollars or cents worth of money Joan has, only how many coins she has.

Getting to the Answer: Joan has q quarters, d dimes, and n nickels, so she has a total of $q + d + n$ coins.

14. **G**

Category: Variable Manipulation

Difficulty: Medium

Strategic Advice: Both Backsolving and algebra work well here. If you choose to Backsolve this problem, be sure you plug in the answer choices for the number of hard questions, not the number of easy questions.

Getting to the Answer: To solve algebraically, set up an equation relating the number of questions of each type (e for easy and h for hard) to the number of points Nicole got: $3e + 5h = 79$. Since she correctly answered 21 questions, $e + h = 21$ and $e = 21 - h$. Plug this into the above equation and solve for h:

$$3(21 - h) + 5h = 79$$
$$63 - 3h + 5h = 79$$
$$2h = 16$$
$$h = 8$$

To Backsolve, start with (H). If Nicole got 12 hard questions right, she got $21 - 12 = 9$ easy questions right for a total of $9(3) + 12(5) = 27 + 60 = 87$ points. This is too many, so she must have gotten fewer hard questions right. Try (G). If she got 8 hard questions, then she got $21 - 8 = 13$ easy questions right. This would give her a total of $13(3) + 8(5) = 39 + 40 = 79$ points—just right.

15. **D**

Category: Variable Manipulation

Difficulty: Medium

Strategic Advice: Since this question asks about the sum of the solutions of the equation, it cannot be Backsolved. You must factor the equation and solve for x.

Getting to the Answer:

$$2x^2 = 2x + 12$$
$$2x^2 - 2x - 12 = 0$$
$$2(x^2 - x - 6) = 0$$
$$x^2 - x - 6 = 0$$
$$(x - 3)(x + 2) = 0$$
$$x = 3 \text{ or } x = -2$$
$$3 + (-2) = 1$$

Be sure not to pick (A), which is one of the possible values of x. That's not what this question asks for.

16. **G**

Category: Variable Manipulation

Difficulty: Low

Strategic Advice: Since the question asks about the price of each book, get both prices in terms of one book.

Getting to the Answer: Each book usually costs $12.60. On sale for $55 for 5 books, each book costs $11. So, $12.60 - $11 = $1.60.

17. **C**

Category: Variable Manipulation

Difficulty: Medium

Strategic Advice: Remember to change the direction of the inequality sign when you multiply or divide by a negative number.

Getting to the Answer:

$$3 < -4x - 5$$
$$8 < -4x$$
$$-2 > x$$

(Since you divide by -4, you must flip the inequality sign.)

18. **G**

Category: Variable Manipulation

Difficulty: High

Strategic Advice: Picking Numbers is a great substitute for complicated algebra.

Getting to the Answer: To solve this one algebraically, you need to give the fractions in the denominator a common denominator:

$$\frac{1}{1 + \frac{1}{x}} = \frac{1}{\frac{x}{x} + \frac{1}{x}} = \frac{1}{\frac{x+1}{x}} = \frac{x}{x+1}$$

19. **A**

Category: Variable Manipulation

Difficulty: High

Strategic Advice: Some questions take several steps to solve.

Getting to the Answer: First, plug in 3 for x. Then, solve the second equation for y. Go back to the first equation and plug in the value of y so that you can solve for a.

$3(8) - y = 9$

$24 - y = 9$

$15 = y$

$a(8) + 15 = 23$

$8a = 8$

$a = 1$

20. **K**

Category: Variable Manipulation

Difficulty: High

Strategic Advice: Even terrible-looking expressions can be simplified. Look for classic quadratics and parts of the expression that cancel out.

Getting to the Answer:

$\sqrt{(x^2 + 4)^2} - (x + 2)(x - 2) = (x^2 + 4) - (x^2 - 4)$
$= x^2 + 4 - x^2 + 4 = 8$

Quarter 3

Answer Key

1. **B**
2. **J**
3. **A**
4. **H**

5. **D**
6. **G**
7. **D**
8. **H**
9. **A**
10. **G**
11. **D**
12. **F**
13. **B**
14. **F**
15. **C**
16. **G**
17. **A**
18. **J**
19. **C**
20. **G**

PASSAGE I

In this passage, the author details the dangers resulting from the deterioration of Earth's ozone layer, as well as attempts to address this problem. After introducing the subject in paragraph 1, the author explains in paragraph 2 how little ozone is in the layer. The next paragraph recounts the history of the study of the layer. Paragraph 4 discusses seasonal fluctuations in ozone content in the middle of the last century. The fifth paragraph moves on to the more dire problem of actual holes in the layer, brought on by the proliferation of CFCs. Paragraphs 6 and 7 describe the size of the CFC industry and the competition between health and economic interests. Paragraph 8 details efforts to limit CFCs, but the next paragraph suggests that the spread of these compounds may be too extensive to overcome. The author closes by detailing options for the future, concluding that nations must still make an effort to fix the problem.

1. **B**

Category: Vocab-in-Context

Difficulty: Medium

Strategic Advice: Be sure to read for context before jumping at any familiar meanings.

Getting to the Answer: In the first part of the paragraph, the author paints a pessimistic picture. "Nevertheless" indicates a change of direction, however, so you can forecast something positive like *correct*.

(A) Out of Scope; this alludes to a more common definition of this word as an adjective.

(B) Correct; this makes sense in context.

(C) Out of Scope; this related meaning doesn't make sense here.

(D) Distortion; this twists the word's meaning.

2. J

Category: Detail

Difficulty: Medium

Strategic Advice: Skim if you're unsure; dates are easy to spot in the passage.

Getting to the Answer: Read the question carefully; you need the date when "the public" became aware of the problem. Paragraph 5 indicates that "public opinion was finally roused" in 1985.

(F) Misused Detail; this was the year when scientists first began to observe the ozone layer.

(G) Misused Detail; this was the year when scientists first began to notice seasonal variations in the content of the ozone layer.

(H) Misused Detail; this year relates to "the October minimum" (paragraph 5).

(J) Correct; the text supports this.

3. A

Category: Detail

Difficulty: Medium

Strategic Advice: These questions will seem much easier if you have taken good notes that lead you quickly to details.

Getting to the Answer: Your notes should indicate that paragraphs 4 and 5 address seasonal fluctuations and outright "holes" in the layer. Compare the choices to the paragraphs and remember that three of them will be confirmed by the passage.

(A) Correct; paragraph 5 indicates that such aircraft have been "exonerated," meaning they do not cause these changes.

(B) Opposite; paragraph 5 identifies CFCs as a cause of changes to the ozone layer.

(C) Opposite; the last sentence of the fourth paragraph identifies temperature changes as impacting the content of the ozone layer.

(D) Opposite; the last sentence of the fourth paragraph identifies wind effects as impacting the content of the ozone layer.

4. H

Category: Generalization

Difficulty: Medium

Strategic Advice: For main-point questions, looking at the passage again shouldn't be necessary. Your notes should be sufficient.

Getting to the Answer: Your notes should tell you that the seventh paragraph discusses the conflict between economic and health interests resulting from CFCs. Use this as your prediction.

(F) Misused Detail; this comes from the previous paragraph.

(G) Distortion; the author offers no such criticism.

(H) Correct; the wording is a little different, but this matches the prediction well enough.

(J) Out of Scope; the author doesn't give such a list.

5. D

Category: Inference

Difficulty: Medium

Strategic Advice: Remember that Inference questions ask for a conclusion drawn from a detail stated in the passage; finding that detail is the first step.

Getting to the Answer: Consult your notes to see where the author discusses such a scenario— paragraph 9. At the end of the paragraph, you see that it takes ten years for the effects of CFCs to be felt. You can infer from this information that *the world would start to see benefits ten years from now if CFC production were banned today*.

(A) Out of Scope; there is no information in the passage to suggest that scientists would have to—or even could—replace lost ozone.

(B) Distortion; the paragraph does reference this figure, but you cannot draw this inference from it.

(C) Out of Scope; the author does not suggest this.

(D) Correct; this matches the prediction and is supported by the text.

6. G

Category: Detail

Difficulty: Medium

Strategic Advice: If your notes don't help you, remember that proper names and acronyms are easy to spot when skimming.

Getting to the Answer: This may not have registered in your notes. If you skim for these names, you see that three of them appear in the third paragraph. There you will also see that stations from the Dobson network "have been entrusted" with this task.

(F) Misused Detail; the WMO established the Dobson network but doesn't fulfill the role in question.

(G) Correct; this matches what you find in the text.

(H) Misused Detail; this comes from paragraph 8.

(J) Misused Detail; like the WMO, UNEP is involved but doesn't actually make the forecasts.

7. D

Category: Detail
Difficulty: Low

Strategic Advice: With NOT questions, be careful that you answer the question being asked.

Getting to the Answer: Your notes should tell you that "substitutes for CFCs" are discussed in the last paragraph. Reread the paragraph, eliminating choices as you see them in the paragraph.

(A) Opposite; this appears in line 89.

(B) Opposite; this appears in line 90.

(C) Opposite; this appears in lines 90–92.

(D) Correct; the passage does not state this.

8. H

Category: Detail
Difficulty: Low

Strategic Advice: With Detail questions, the answer is in the passage; be careful, though, not to mistake a Misused Detail for the answer.

Getting to the Answer: The stem itself is broadly worded, but a quick look at the choices and your notes should send you to paragraph 2, which clearly states that the layer "is 25 kilometers thick."

(F) Misused Detail; the author says it "would form" such a thin layer if it were compressed.

(G) Misused Detail; this comes from the previous paragraph and refers to the distance from the ozone layer to the surface of the earth.

(H) Correct; paragraph 2 confirms this.

(J) Out of Scope; nothing in the passage supports this.

9. A

Category: Inference
Difficulty: High

Strategic Advice: You may be unable to predict an answer for broadly phrased questions, but you should still get a sense of what you need from your notes before tackling the choices.

Getting to the Answer: First, consult your notes for this paragraph; it discusses seasonal fluctuations in the ozone layer above the South Pole. Then work through the choices to see which statement most logically flows from the ideas laid out in the paragraph.

(A) Correct; the author states in the last sentence that the variations "appeared to result from... natural phenomena," a result that doesn't sound very alarming. Greater concern over the ozone layer is discussed in the next paragraph.

(B) Distortion; the author only states that researchers "began to observe" these variations above the South Pole in that year. That doesn't mean that such variations couldn't have occurred before then, over the South Pole or elsewhere.

(C) Out of Scope; the paragraph doesn't support this distinction.

(D) Out of Scope; in this paragraph, the author only states that these researchers monitored the layer. No estimate, either "more" or "less," is suggested.

10. G

Category: Generalization
Difficulty: Medium

Strategic Advice: When asked for main conclusions, look to your notes and the last paragraph.

Getting to the Answer: Your notes should lead you to the last paragraph. The author ends it on an optimistic note, saying that a solution to the ozone problem might be found if nations "lend a hand." He says this after acknowledging that today's substitute products present problems of their own. Predict something like *substitutes for CFCs hold some hope.*

(F) Misused Detail; this draws from paragraph 7, but it is not the main conclusion.

(G) Correct; this matches the prediction.

(H) Distortion; this twists a statement made in paragraph 9.

(J) Distortion; such agreements have been becoming stricter.

PASSAGE II

In the first two paragraphs, Esther recalls her devotion to her doll, Dolly. In paragraph 3, she describes her godmother as a stern, church going woman. Esther notes in the next paragraph that she knows nothing about her mother. Paragraph 5 details her lack of friends, and paragraph 6 discusses how this birthday, like all others, was not celebrated. In paragraphs 7–10, Esther's godmother makes Esther feel that she would have been better off if she had not been born; Esther's godmother also refers to a wrong that was done to her by Esther's mother. In paragraphs 11 and 12, Esther cries herself to sleep, feeling despondent but thankful for her only friend, Dolly.

11. D

Category: Detail

Difficulty: Low

Strategic Advice: If the question stem doesn't offer many clues, take a quick scan of the choices to help your research.

Getting to the Answer: Your overall recollection of the passage can help, but check early in the passage. Paragraph 3 begins, "I was brought up, from my earliest remembrance…by my godmother."

(A) Out of Scope; the passage doesn't support this.

(B) Out of Scope; the passage doesn't support this.

(C) Distortion; the passage indicates that Esther has always been with her godmother.

(**D**) Correct; this matches the text.

12. F

Category: Generalization

Difficulty: Low

Strategic Advice: The benefit of Generalization questions is that you can find support for the correct answer in more than one place.

Getting to the Answer: Your notes should help you see that, in the first two paragraphs, Esther views her doll as *her only friend*. This idea is repeated in lines 79–81: "I went up to my room, and crept to bed, and laid my doll's cheek against mine…holding that solitary friend upon my bosom."

(**F**) Correct; this matches the text.

(G) Opposite; Dolly is much more than that to Esther.

(H) Out of Scope; the passage doesn't support this characterization.

(J) Opposite; the passage indicates that she holds her.

13. B

Category: Vocab-in-Context

Difficulty: Medium

Strategic Advice: Remember to avoid the more common meanings of the word.

Getting to the Answer: Read the entire sentence. Dickens uses "stiff" to describe the tone of the letter that Esther's godmother wrote to decline the invitation to another student's birthday party. He earlier describes the godmother as stern and humorless. Predict *rigidly formal*.

(A) Out of Scope; this is a common meaning that doesn't fit the context.

(**B**) Correct; this matches the prediction.

(C) Distortion; this is close, but it doesn't fully capture the godmother's attitude.

(D) Out of Scope; this draws from an alternate meaning of the word that doesn't fit the context.

14. F

Category: Inference

Difficulty: High

Strategic Advice: When you receive a line reference, you normally won't have to stray far from it to find the answer.

Getting to the Answer: Read the reference closely. While many aspects of Esther's life combine to make it dispiriting, she dwells on the "fault" here in connection with her uncelebrated birthday.

(**F**) Correct; this is consistent with the paragraph.

(G) Distortion; Esther thinks this about her mother.

(H) Distortion; Esther only imagines that her godmother tells her this.

(J) Distortion; the birthday in question is Esther's own and not related to someone else's party.

15. C

Category: Inference

Difficulty: Medium

Strategic Advice: Don't make a big logical leap; the correct answer will be close to what is stated in the passage.

Getting to the Answer: Reread the paragraph if necessary to find support for your prediction. The question is rather open-ended, but you could predict something like *still bitter* and look for the choice consistent with at least that tone.

(A) Out of Scope; the passage doesn't support this.

(B) Out of Scope; the passage doesn't support this.

(**C**) Correct; despite the godmother's statement that she has forgiven Esther's mother, her demeanor suggests resentment.

(D) Opposite; the paragraph suggests she has not forgotten her at all.

16. G

Category: Generalization
Difficulty: Medium

Strategic Advice: Your notes should be sufficient to help describe the main character.

Getting to the Answer: Your notes should help you predict that Esther's childhood is *sad and lonely,* as evidenced by her description of Dolly as her only friend and her unpleasant home life.

(F) Distortion; this has too positive a tone.

(**G**) Correct; this is consistent with the passage.

(H) Distortion; Esther feels that she could be a better person, but this is a manifestation of her confusion and loneliness.

(J) Distortion; Again, Esther feels that she could be a better person, but this is a manifestation of her confusion and loneliness.

17. A

Category: Inference
Difficulty: Medium

Strategic Advice: Remember to predict an answer if at all possible. It will keep you from falling for trap answers.

Getting to the Answer: Read closely around the cited reference. Before it, Esther says, "I knew that I had brought no joy at any time to anybody's heart." Predict *she was unloved.*

(**A**) Correct; this matches the prediction.

(B) Extreme; the passage doesn't support the belief that she will "never" become friends with these girls.

(C) Distortion; Esther might believe this, but it is too narrow a conclusion to draw from this statement.

(D) Out of Scope; the passage doesn't support this specific statement.

18. J

Category: Generalization
Difficulty: Medium

Strategic Advice: Reading passages are quite long; your notes will help you when you don't see a line reference in the question.

Getting to the Answer: Your notes should tell you that Esther considers this point in paragraph 5. Check the choices against the paragraph to see which choice is NOT mentioned or implied.

(F) Opposite; this is mentioned in the paragraph.

(G) Opposite; this is implied in the paragraph.

(H) Opposite; this is mentioned in the paragraph.

(**J**) Correct; Esther describes herself as "self-indulgent" elsewhere in the passage, but nothing indicates that the other girls feel this way.

19. C

Category: Detail
Difficulty: Medium

Strategic Advice: Detail questions with line references should take very little time on Test Day.

Getting to the Answer: Read around the citation. Esther lists many qualities, including the frequency with which her godmother attends church. Use the paragraph to confirm your choice.

(A) Distortion; Esther speaks hypothetically: "if she had ever smiled...but she never" did.

(B) Misused Detail; this comes from a later paragraph.

(**C**) Correct; this matches the text.

(D) Out of Scope; you don't see in this excerpt who gave Esther the doll.

20. G

Category: Detail
Difficulty: Medium

Strategic Advice: On some Detail questions, you will have to research more than just a limited part of the passage.

Getting to the Answer: Esther does most of the "speaking" in the passage, so it may seem unclear where to look. If necessary, rely on your impression of her from your notes to help eliminate answers.

(F) Distortion; Esther worries in the last paragraph that she may be self-indulgent. She doesn't actually describe herself that way.

(**G**) Correct; in the first paragraph, Esther says, "Now, Dolly, I am not clever" (line 3). In the second paragraph, Esther describes herself as "such a shy little thing" (line 5).

(H) Misused Detail; Esther describes Dolly, not herself, as "faithful" in the second paragraph.

(J) Distortion; Esther worries in the last paragraph that she may be self-indulgent. She doesn't actually describe herself that way.

Quarter 4

Answer Key

1. **A**
2. **G**
3. **D**
4. **H**
5. **C**
6. **F**
7. **B**
8. **H**
9. **A**
10. **G**
11. **D**

PASSAGE I

1. A

Category: Patterns

Difficulty: Low

Strategic Advice: When you're looking for the relationship between two variables on a line graph, check to see if they go up or down together, stay the same, or if one goes down as the other goes up.

Getting to the Answer: All six lines rise from left to right across the graph, indicating that solubility goes up as temperature goes up. (B), (C), and (D) contradict this information.

2. G

Category: Patterns

Difficulty: Medium

Strategic Advice: When you're asked to look for trends between pairs on a line graph, mark up the graph so that you can easily distinguish one pair from the next. You might choose to draw squiggly or jagged lines over the solubility lines for NaCl and KCl.

Getting to the Answer: Start by looking at the solubility curves of $NaClO_3$ and $KClO_3$. They have the same shape, but the Na salt's solubility line is much higher than the K salt's solubility line. The same is true for $NaNO_3$ and KNO_3, with the Na salt solubility line again higher than the K salt solubility line. NaCl and KCl are the only pair of salts whose solubility lines cross, at a little below 30°C. Below that temperature, NaCl is more soluble; above it, KCl is more soluble. That makes NaCl and KCl different from the other two

salts, whose Na salt solubilities are always above their corresponding K salt solubilities.Therefore, (**G**) is correct.

(F) contradicts the information in the graph—the Na salts are more soluble than the K salts, not the other way around.

(H) and (J) are incorrect because all of the salts are soluble in water.

3. D

Category: Figure Interpretation

Difficulty: Medium

Strategic Advice: The question stem will tell you where in the figure you'll find your answer.

Getting to the Answer: This question asks about a solution at 50°C, so start there. Considerably less $KClO_3$ than KNO_3 will dissolve in water at this temperature (about 0.20 g/mL versus about 0.70 g/mL). As equal amounts of $KClO_3$ and KNO_3 are added to the solution, the $KClO_3$ salt will stop dissolving sooner. Therefore, the solubility of $KClO_3$ is the limiting factor, (**D**).

You could easily eliminate (A) and (C) using the Scientific Method—decomposition temperature is never mentioned in the passage, and $NaClO_3$ isn't mentioned in the question stem.

4. H

Category: Figure Interpretation

Difficulty: Medium

Strategic Advice: When a question gives you a specific range of values for the *x*- or *y*-axis, make sure you focus your attention within that range.

Getting to the Answer: To find the solubility of the different salts at 65°C, draw a vertical line up from the *x*-axis, starting halfway between 60°C and 70°C. To find solubilities greater than 0.65 g/mL, draw a horizontal line across the graph, starting halfway between 0.60 g/mL and 0.70 g/mL on the *y*-axis. Only three of the solubility curves ever rise above 0.65 g/mL: those for $NaClO_3$, $NaNO_3$, and KNO_3, all of which do so below 65°C. None of the answer choices includes all three of those salts, but (**H**) lists two of the three. The other three answer choices contain salts with solubilities below 0.65 g/mL at 65°C.

5. C

Category: Figure Interpretation

Difficulty: Low

Strategic Advice: Unless the question stem specifically tells you to make guesses about what might happen beyond the range of a figure, consider only the given data when answering questions.

Getting to the Answer: The phrase "exhibits the greatest variation of solubility" means "has the biggest change in solubility." The question stem limits you to the range between 0°C and 60°C. Because you only know what the graph shows you, don't assume anything about what the salts might do if you extended the solubility lines beyond 1.20 g/mL. KNO_3 starts very low (about 0.16 g/mL) and comes close to the top of the graph (about 1.00 g/mL) at 60°C, so it shows the greatest increase in solubility over the specified range. The solutes in (A), (B), and (D) have much smaller changes in solubility over the given temperature range.

PASSAGE II

6. **F**

Category: Figure Interpretation
Difficulty: Low

Strategic Advice: When you're asked to find which set of conditions yielded a certain result, go back to the figures to find the result first and then trace back to find the cause.

Getting to the Answer: Carbon and nitrogen were used in both basins in both experiments, but phosphorus and sodium bicarbonate ($NaHCO_3$) were used only in basin A in experiment 1 and experiment 2, respectively. Regardless of whether phosphorus or sodium bicarbonate was used in basin A, basin A always produced a higher density of algal blooms than basin B for any given temperature, so (H) is incorrect. A higher density of algal blooms was recorded for basin A with sodium bicarbonate than for basin A with phosphorus, so (**F**) is correct and (G) is incorrect. You could have immediately eliminated (J), as hydrogen was not added to either basin in either experiment.

7. **B**

Category: Patterns
Difficulty: Low

Strategic Advice: When a question asks you to find a broad trend, make sure you check every relevant experiment before you draw conclusions.

Getting to the Answer: For either experiment, and within either basin, algal bloom density increases as temperature increases, (**B**).

8. **H**

Category: Patterns
Difficulty: Medium

Strategic Advice: Sometimes, a question will ask you to predict what might happen if a variable was extended beyond the range shown in the data.

Getting to the Answer: Sodium bicarbonate was used only in basin A during experiment 2, so that's where to look to find the answer. Since algal-bloom density increased with temperature during the experiment, and since 40°C is a little higher than the highest temperature recorded, the number of algal blooms in one square meter of surface area could reasonably be expected to be a little bit greater than the maximum experimental density of 0.78 blooms per square meter, which was recorded at 35°C. Therefore, (**H**) is the best answer.

9. **A**

Category: Scientific Reasoning
Difficulty: Low

Strategic Advice: If a question stem asks about a term or substance you didn't see in the data, check the supporting paragraphs.

Getting to the Answer: Carbon dioxide (CO_2) is not listed in either table, but it is mentioned in the paragraph for experiment 2 as a product of $NaHCO_3$ and water. In that experiment, the addition of $NaHCO_3$ was the only difference between basins A and B. The higher algal bloom density at each temperature in basin A can therefore be attributed to the addition of the $NaHCO_3$ and the consequent production of CO_2. Hence, you can infer that carbon dioxide encourages the growth of algae.

10. **G**

Category: Scientific Reasoning
Difficulty: Low

Strategic Advice: Sometimes a question will use a lot of words to disguise a very simple concept.

Getting to the Answer: Look for a choice that would decrease algal-bloom density. Decreasing the amount of detergent would decrease the amount of phosphorus in the water, which would in turn reduce algal blooms and the associated pollution. (**G**), then, is correct.

(F) and (H) would probably increase the growth of algal blooms.

(J) can be ruled out because nothing in the passage addresses the presence of both phosphorus and sodium bicarbonate.

11. D

Category: Scientific Reasoning

Difficulty: Medium

Strategic Advice: Understanding the scientific method will help you score points on method questions.

Getting to the Answer: A "controlled variable" is one that is altered directly by the researchers. The paragraph under experiment 1 states that the researchers "varied the temperatures," so (**D**) is correct.

(A) is incorrect because the number of algal blooms was measured, not controlled, by the researchers.

(B) is incorrect because the rate of algal growth was not controlled by the researchers.

(C) is incorrect because the surface area of each basin is constant.

ANSWERS AND EXPLANATIONS

Preview Quiz Answers and Explanations

Answer Key

1. **A**
2. **J**
3. **B**
4. **J**
5. **D**
6. **G**
7. **B**

PASSAGE I: WHY LIONS ROAR

1. A

Category: Punctuation

Difficulty: Medium

Strategic Advice: Keep tested punctuation rules in mind; other uses will be incorrect on the ACT.

Getting to the Answer: This sentence is punctuated correctly; the phrase set off by the commas is not essential to the meaning of the sentence. By eliminating the first comma, (B) incorrectly leaves the subject and verb of the sentence separated by a comma. (C) misuses the colon, which—on the ACT—will only be correct when used to introduce or emphasize a brief explanation, description, or list. (D) creates a sentence that is grammatically incorrect.

2. J

Category: Word Choice

Difficulty: Medium

Strategic Advice: The test maker frequently places a plural object near a verb with a singular subject. Always determine the predicate verb of an underlined noun; it will not generally be the verb closest to the underlined noun in the sentence.

Getting to the Answer: The singular "Roaring," not the plural "lions," is the subject of the verb "perform." (J) puts the verb in the proper singular form without introducing any additional errors.

(G) does not address the error and also incorrectly places a comma between the verb and its object.

(H) corrects the agreement error but also inserts the incorrect comma.

3. B

Category: Punctuation

Difficulty: High

Strategic Advice: Always read for logic as well as usage and style.

Getting to the Answer: As written, this sentence uses the plural "these" to modify the singular "defense." By putting commas around "defense," (B) makes "One of these" refer to "functions" and identifies "defense" as a function of roaring. (C) creates a sentence that is grammatically incorrect. (D) is unnecessarily wordy.

4. J

Category: Sentence Sense

Difficulty: Medium

Strategic Advice: There are several ways to correct a run-on sentence, but only one answer choice will do so without introducing any new errors.

Getting to the Answer: This sentence is a run-on; the underlined selection begins a new independent clause. (J) corrects the error by making the final clause dependent. (G) does not address the error. Not just unnecessarily wordy, (H) actually changes the meaning of the sentence.

5. D

Category: Wordiness

Difficulty: Medium

Strategic Advice: Use context clues to determine when words are used redundantly.

Getting to the Answer: Something that is described as "everyday" can be assumed to be done "frequently"; (D) eliminates the redundancy and (B) and (C) use words or phrases that are redundant with "everyday."

PASSAGE II

6. G

Category: Detail

Difficulty: Medium

Strategic Advice: More often than not, you will not be given line references. Taking good notes is the key to finding answers in the passage.

Getting to the Answer: Your notes should lead you to paragraphs 2 and 3. The author states that "the *Solar*

Maximum Mission satellite, which has monitored the solar constant," seems to have resolved "the latter question" of the relationship between sunspots and the solar constant. Look for a choice referencing the satellite.

(F) Out of Scope; while the author mentions such droughts, he doesn't mention any studies of them.

(**G**) Correct; this matches what you're looking for.

(H) Distortion; this twists a detail from later in the passage.

(J) Out of Scope; the author doesn't bring up any such "discussions."

7. **B**

Category: Generalization

Difficulty: Medium

Strategic Advice: You should be predicting this for every passage you read. If you do, you'll move quickly through such questions.

Getting to the Answer: If you're unsure of purpose, the opening and closing paragraphs will usually help you. Here the second sentence of the passage says, "people have speculated that the solar cycle might exert some influence on Earth's weather" (lines 3–4). The concluding paragraph suggests that the findings discussed in the passage point to "a link between the solar cycle and weather" (lines 84–85). Predict something like *discuss the connection between the solar cycle and weather.*

(A) Opposite; scientists have not "failed." They seem to be making progress.

(**B**) Correct; this matches the thrust of the prediction.

(C) Distortion; this leaves out the impact on Earth's weather.

(D) Extreme; the passage makes clear that nothing has been "conclusively" proven.

PASSAGE III

Strategy: Make sure you've chosen a distinct side. Don't use any middle ground. Pick a side that can help you create an argument. You want an opposing side to push against. For your thesis, make sure that side is stated clearly in a complete sentence without using language such as "I think," "In my opinion," or "I believe." That is implied; this is your essay. Once you've picked your side, support it ("Because...") with either specific references from the text or specific and relevant experiences from your own life or knowledge. Your "Because" cannot be "Because I think so," but must always be "Because of this compelling evidence...

Lesson Answers & Explanations

Quarter 2

Answer Key

1. **D**
2. **F**
3. **D**
4. **H**
5. **C**
6. **F**
7. **C**
8. **G**
9. **C**
10. **J**
11. **D**
12. **H**
13. **C**
14. **G**
15. **B**
16. **J**
17. **C**

1. **D**

Category: Sentence Sense

Difficulty: Medium

Strategic Advice: Incorrect placement of a prepositional phrase can create an illogical sentence.

Getting to the Answer: To figure out the correct placement of the underlined prepositional phrase, determine what it describes and then move it to that part of the sentence. In this sentence, the underlined portion logically describes the shop, so (**D**) is correct. (A) is illogical, while (B) and (C) are repetitious.

2. **F**

Category: Punctuation

Difficulty: Low

Strategic Advice: If a sentence has more than one complete thought, make sure the correct punctuation and/or connecting word is used.

Getting to the Answer: This sentence has two complete thoughts, which can be separated by a coordinating conjunction and a comma (as in the original), separated by a semicolon (as in (G)), separated into two sentences (as in (H)), or separated by a dash that emphasizes the second part of the sentence (as in (J)). By omitting punctuation, (F) creates a run-on.

3. D

Category: Sentence Sense
Difficulty: Medium
Strategic Advice: The person or thing described by an introductory phrase should be placed as close in the sentence as possible to its description.
Getting to the Answer: In this sentence, the introductory phrase describes the writer, so the first-person pronoun should follow the description. Only (**D**) correctly orders the sentence. (A) and (B) illogically make it sound as though the friends are "not a coffee drinker," and both introduce an agreement error. (C) creates a sentence fragment.

4. H

Category: Sentence Sense
Difficulty: Medium
Strategic Advice: Make sure that your choice doesn't correct one error only to introduce another.
Getting to the Answer: As it is, the beginning phrase illogically describes the subject of the sentence, "I." (H) corrects the error by inserting the pronoun "it," turning the descriptive phrase into a dependent clause and clarifying that the coffee shop, not the writer of the passage, opened six months ago. (G) corrects the modification error but creates a comma splice. (J) does not correct the original error.

5. C

Category: Word Choice
Difficulty: Medium
Strategic Advice: An –*ing* word without a helping verb isn't a complete verb.
Getting to the Answer: As it is written, this is a sentence fragment—without a helping verb such as *were* or *are*, the verb is incomplete. (**C**) corrects the verb error and inserts the comma necessary to set the descriptive information off from the rest of the sentence. (B) creates two sentence fragments. (D) uses the comma correctly but does not address the verb error.

6. F

Category: Sentence Sense
Difficulty: High
Strategic Advice: A complicated sentence is not necessarily incorrect. Make sure that your choice does not introduce an error that does not appear in the original.
Getting to the Answer: This sentence is correct as written. (G), (H), and (J) all use word orders that confuse meaning and create illogical relationships.

7. C

Category: Sentence Sense
Difficulty: Medium
Strategic Advice: When a comma separates two complete thoughts, a coordinating conjunction (*for, and, nor, but, or, yet, so*) must also be used.
Getting to the Answer: The sentence is a comma splice—two complete thoughts incorrectly separated by only a comma. (**C**) corrects this by making the second half of the sentence a dependent clause describing the story hour. (B) and (D) change the wording but repeat the comma splice error.

8. G

Category: Sentence Sense
Difficulty: Medium
Strategic Advice: For the meaning of a sentence to be clear, descriptive information needs to be placed next to the thing, person, or action it describes.
Getting to the Answer: The underlined prepositional phrase describes where the events happen, so the phrase should immediately follow events, as in (**G**). The other choices confuse the meaning of the sentence.

9. C

Category: Punctuation
Difficulty: High
Strategic Advice: A semicolon or dash can join two independent clauses, or a period can break them into separate sentences. Any of these would be correct answers.
Getting to the Answer: An answer that incorrectly eliminates the semicolon without replacing it will create a grammatical error. (**C**) runs the two independent clauses together without punctuation. (A) correctly uses a semicolon. (B) correctly uses an em dash. (D) turns the two independent clauses into individual sentences, which is grammatically correct.

10. J

Category: Punctuation
Difficulty: Medium

Strategic Advice: A semicolon should join two independent clauses.

Getting to the Answer: The second clause here is dependent, so the semicolon is incorrect. No punctuation is needed before the relative pronoun, so (**J**) fixes the error. (G) incorrectly uses a comma. (H) incorrectly uses a dash, which is used to set off explanatory elements or indicate a break in thought.

11. D

Category: Punctuation
Difficulty: Medium

Strategic Advice: A colon does not introduce a modifying phrase in the middle of a sentence.

Getting to the Answer: The modifying phrase describes a bamboo rod, so it should not be introduced by a colon. The modifying phrase should be set off by commas, as in (**D**). (B) uses a semicolon, which should be used to separate independent clauses. (C) uses a dash incorrectly; it would only be correct if the modifying clause were followed by a dash as well.

12. H

Category: Punctuation
Difficulty: High

Strategic Advice: A colon is used to introduce an item or items that illustrate the preceding statement.

Getting to the Answer: The ideas following the coordinating conjunction work to illustrate the point made earlier in the sentence, so "and" is used incorrectly. (**H**) correctly introduces the examples with a colon. (G) uses a relative pronoun without a verb, which is incorrect. (J) uses a comma, which creates a run-on sentence.

13. C

Category: Punctuation
Difficulty: Low

Strategic Advice: When used to set off descriptive information from the main part of a sentence, punctuation marks come in pairs.

Getting to the Answer: The beginning of the descriptive phrase in this sentence is set off by a dash, so the end of the phrase should also be set off by a dash. (**C**) is correct. (A) uses a comma instead of the necessary dash. (B) incorrectly omits the necessary punctuation. (D) uses a semicolon instead of the necessary dash. A semicolon should be used to connect two complete but related thoughts, which is not the case in this sentence.

14. G

Category: Punctuation
Difficulty: Medium

Strategic Advice: Read the question carefully—sometimes you are asked to choose the one option that would create an incorrect sentence.

Getting to the Answer: This sentence has two complete but related thoughts. The only choice that does not create a grammatically correct sentence is (**G**)—by omitting any punctuation, it creates a run-on. (F) correctly uses a dash to emphasize the second half of the sentence.
(H) correctly uses a period, creating two complete sentences. (J) correctly uses a semicolon to separate two independent clauses and a contrasting transition.

15. B

Category: Punctuation
Difficulty: Low

Strategic Advice: Use an apostrophe to indicate a contraction or to show possession.

Getting to the Answer: The apostrophe here is incorrect; the possessive is not needed until later in the sentence. (**B**) corrects the error by deleting the apostrophe. (C) uses an incorrect apostrophe and incorrectly makes the noun singular. (D) inserts a comma that creates a sentence structure error.

16. J

Category: Punctuation
Difficulty: Medium

Strategic Advice: When a word with an apostrophe is underlined, check the context of the sentence to see if the word needs to show possession.

Getting to the Answer: In this sentence, the "many instruments" belong to the singular noun "orchestra," so only "orchestra" needs to show possession; "sounds" is plural but not possessive in the sentence. (F) and (H) both incorrectly make "sounds" possessive, while (G) omits the necessary apostrophe in "orchestra's."

17. **C**

Category: Punctuation

Difficulty: Medium

Strategic Advice: Know the difference between *its* and *it's*: *it's* is the contraction for *it is,* and *its* is the possessive form of *it.*

Getting to the Answer: *Its'* is never correct. The sentence calls for the possessive *its,* as the pronoun refers to the "song" mentioned in the previous sentence. (B) uses the contraction, which would be grammatically incorrect. (D) uses the wrong pronoun; the "emotional ending" belongs to the singular "song," not to the plural "members of the audience" or "dynamics." Therefore, (**C**) is correct.

Quiz

Answer Key

1. **C**
2. **G**
3. **D**
4. **H**
5. **D**
6. **J**
7. **B**
8. **F**
9. **C**
10. **F**
11. **B**
12. **F**
13. **D**
14. **G**
15. **A**
16. **F**

1. **C**

Category: Sentence Sense

Difficulty: Medium

Strategic Advice: When an underlined sentence uses the passive voice, expect to find an active version of the sentence among the answer choices.

Getting to the Answer: "History...is known" is passive; "Few...know the history" is active. (**C**) is the best choice here. (B) creates a sentence fragment. (D) does not address the incorrect use of passive voice.

2. **G**

Category: Sentence Sense

Difficulty: Medium

Strategic Advice: One way to correct a run-on sentence is to make one of the clauses subordinate.

Getting to the Answer: (**G**) corrects this run-on by making the second clause subordinate. The second sentence in (H) is a fragment. (J) misuses a semicolon, which is only used in this type of sentence to join independent clauses.

3. **D**

Category: Wordiness

Difficulty: Medium

Strategic Advice: Always consider relevance when OMIT is offered as an answer choice.

Getting to the Answer: The Morse Code is outside the scope of this passage. OMIT is the correct choice here.

4. **H**

Category: Verb Tenses

Difficulty: Medium

Strategic Advice: The *–ing* verb form cannot be the main verb in an independent clause.

Getting to the Answer: As written, this is a sentence fragment. (H) replaces the gerund (*–ing*) verb form with the correct tense, "had begun." (G) does not address the error. The verb phrase in (J) is inappropriate in context; verbs using "will" indicate actions that will take place in the future.

5. **D**

Category: Sentence Sense

Difficulty: Medium

Strategic Advice: Determining the logical use of modifying words will help you answer word order questions.

Getting to the Answer: Here, "almost" is intended to modify the phrase, "a hundred years"; (**D**) makes this clear. (B) and (C) are awkwardly worded.

6. **J**

Category: Punctuation

Difficulty: High

Strategic Advice: There are several ways to correct a run-on sentence, but only one answer choice will do so without introducing additional errors.

Getting to the Answer: Here, (**J**) makes the run-on into two separate sentences. (G) adds a FANBOYS conjunction, but "but" does not appropriately relate the ideas in the two clauses. (H) does not address the error.

7. B

Category: Punctuation
Difficulty: Medium
Strategic Advice: Use a comma to separate an introductory clause from the rest of the sentence.

Getting to the Answer: (**B**) correctly inserts the necessary comma. (A) uses no punctuation; (C) and (D) misuse the semicolon and colon, respectively.

8. F

Category: Punctuation
Difficulty: Medium
Strategic Advice: Use a comma between an independent clause and one beginning with a FANBOYS conjunction.

Getting to the Answer: This sentence needs NO CHANGE. (G) omits the necessary comma. The second sentence in (H) begins with a coordinating conjunction. This usage is common in everyday speech but is not good ACT style. (J) misuses the dash.

9. C

Category: Punctuation
Difficulty: Medium
Strategic Advice: When used to combine clauses, the semicolon is only correct if both clauses are independent.

Getting to the Answer: The first clause here is not independent; the semicolon is incorrect. (**C**) correctly replaces it with a comma. The first sentence in (B) is a fragment. (D) creates a run-on.

10. F

Category: Punctuation
Difficulty: High
Strategic Advice: Make sure underlined dashes are used to set off brief explanatory material.

Getting to the Answer: The dashes here are used correctly. The colon is misused in (G). This phrase could be correctly set off with two commas as well,

but a single comma, as in (H), is incorrect. The first sentence in (J) is a fragment.

11. B

Category: Punctuation
Difficulty: High
Strategic Advice: Apostrophes are used only in pronoun contractions, not in pronoun possessives.

Getting to the Answer: The possessive "whose" is incorrect here; the contraction for *who has*, in (**B**), is correct. The spellings in (C) and (D) are never correct.

12. F

Category: Punctuation
Difficulty: Medium
Strategic Advice: Words and phrases like "after all," "however," and "in fact" should be set off with commas.

Getting to the Answer: This sentence needs NO CHANGE. (G), (H), and (J) fail to set off the phrase.

13. D

Category: Punctuation
Difficulty: Medium
Strategic Advice: Use a semicolon to join two independent clauses.

Getting to the Answer: Only a semicolon (**D**) can correctly join two independent clauses, not a colon (A) or a dash (C). (B) creates a run-on.

14. G

Category: Punctuation
Difficulty: High
Strategic Advice: Use context to determine correct noun forms.

Getting to the Answer: Since the singular "pine" is used in the first clause, "pine's" is the correct possessive. (H) is incorrect in form. (J) makes the wrong word possessive.

15. A

Category: Punctuation
Difficulty: Medium
Strategic Advice: Use a comma with clauses joined by a FANBOYS conjunction.

Getting to the Answer: NO CHANGE is needed here. (B) omits a needed comma. (C) misuses the semicolon. (D) creates a sentence fragment.

16. F

Category: Punctuation

Difficulty: Medium

Strategic Advice: A semicolon can be used to combine two independent clauses.

Getting to the Answer: This sentence needs NO CHANGE. (G) and (H) create run-on sentences. (J) misuses the colon.

Quarter 3

Answer Key

1. **C**
2. **G**
3. **A**
4. **J**
5. **C**
6. **H**

PASSAGE I

1. C

Category: Detail

Difficulty: Low

Strategic Advice: Taking notes on the big issue behind each paragraph helps in locating the answers to questions.

Getting to the Answer: Your notes should lead you back to paragraph 3, specifically the statement, "Quasars are unmatched in luminosity and hence are the most distant objects that can be detected" (lines 17–19). The Keyword "hence" establishes luminosity as the reason quasars can be seen. Predict an answer of *luminosity.*

(A) Misused Detail; density is not a reason quasars can be detected.

(B) Out of Scope; the author doesn't mention "size" in this paragraph.

(C) Correct; it matches perfectly.

(D) Misused Detail; puzzling behavior is not a reason that quasars can be detected.

2. G

Category: Detail

Difficulty: Medium

Strategic Advice: Many trap answers do come from the passage, but they have been distorted in some way.

Getting to the Answer: Your notes should lead you back to paragraph 2, where the author states that "astronomers have begun to understand quasars" "by monitoring 3C 273 in all domains of the electromagnetic spectrum" (lines 10–13). This quote makes a great prediction.

(F) Misused Detail; this appears in paragraph 6.

(G) Correct; this matches the quote nicely.

(H) Distortion; this misrepresents a detail from paragraph 7.

(J) Misused Detail; this appears in paragraph 4.

3. A

Category: Detail

Difficulty: Medium

Strategic Advice: Don't let your guard down. Three choices will be in the passage; the correct one will not be there.

Getting to the Answer: Nothing in the question stem helps to limit your search of the passage. Compare the choices to your notes and confirm the presence of the three incorrect answer choices in the text.

(A) This contradicts a statement made in line 38. "All," the first word, also should have given you pause. Extreme language like this often appears in incorrect choices

(B) Opposite; this is supported by paragraphs 1 and 3.

(C) Opposite; this fact appears in paragraph 1.

(D) Opposite; this fact appears in paragraph 8.

4. J

Category: Vocab-in-Context

Difficulty: Medium

Strategic Advice: Beware of primary meanings of words among the choices. Predicting first will protect you.

Getting to the Answer: Read the sentence containing the word and rephrase it in your own words with a simpler synonym for *domains* as it is used in the sentence. *Areas* makes a good prediction.

(F) Out of Scope; this relates to a common meaning of *domain,* but it doesn't make sense in context.

(G) Out of Scope; this relates to a common meaning of the word, but it doesn't make sense in context.

(H) Out of Scope; this is the primary meaning of the word, but it doesn't work in the context of the sentence.

(J) Correct; this matches your prediction well.

5. C

Category: Vocab-in-Context

Difficulty: Medium

Strategic Advice: Treat phrases in context as you would treat a single word in context. Read the sentence and restate it in simpler terms.

Getting to the Answer: The sentence before the one given in the stem indicates a period of doubt over Schmidt's thesis. The next sentence, though, begins with the Keyword "Yet," indicating a change in direction: There no longer must have been "good reason to question" his results. So you can predict that "little room to doubt" means *no good reason to doubt,* or that *the theory is well accepted.*

(A) Opposite; be careful to interpret "little...doubt" properly. This means that the findings are most likely correct.

(B) Extreme; there might be a very small minority who disagree.

(C) Correct; this matches the tone and thrust of your prediction.

(D) Out of Scope; this distorts "little room" into a concern with expanding, or providing more room.

6. H

Category: Generalization

Difficulty: Low

Strategic Advice: Always know the main idea of a passage before moving on to the questions.

Getting to the Answer: The author's primary purpose is to describe quasar 3C 273's discovery and how the discovery has taught scientists about the properties of quasars. Also, for these questions, use the *vertical scan* technique: Scan the verbs that start each answer choice, eliminating any that do not match the author's purpose (e.g., "chronicle" in (J)).

(F) Distortion; the author compares 3C's luminosity to that of other celestial bodies, but it's not the primary purpose.

(G) Extreme; it is too strong to say the author offers technical analysis of *all* quasars; the author merely focuses on 3C.

(H) Correct; this matches your prediction.

(J) Distortion; while the author chronicles the history of 3C 273's discovery, the passage never discusses histories of other quasars or their effect on Earth.

Quiz

Answer Key

1. **A**
2. **J**
3. **D**
4. **G**
5. **C**
6. **G**

1. A

Category: Vocab-in-Context

Difficulty: High

Strategic Advice: You can deduce the meaning of virtually any term, familiar or unfamiliar, in a passage by interpreting the surrounding context.

Getting to the Answer: Go back to the referenced line and reread the surrounding sentences. The author maintains that each side in a war can present "its position as a defense against an attack" (lines 50–51). He follows this with the statement that an aggressive war can almost always "be couched in terms of defense." *Presented,* from the prior sentence, makes a great prediction.

(A) Correct; this matches your prediction very well.

(B) Misused Detail; this does not fit the context of the word.

(C) Out of Scope; this doesn't fit the context.

(D) Out of Scope; this draws from an alternate meaning of "couch."

2. J

Category: Detail

Difficulty: Medium

Strategic Advice: Make sure you study the question stem for all clues to the detail's location in the text.

Getting to the Answer: Your notes should lead you to the point where the author discusses frustration—the final paragraph. He states that violence caused by frustration can be "an attempt...to attain the frustrated aim" (lines 83–84). Look for a match with this idea.

(F) Opposite; the author states that such aggression is "not...for the sake of destruction."

(G) Out of Scope; the author doesn't mention this.

(H) Out of Scope; the author doesn't mention revenge.

(**J**) Correct; this matches the idea you predicted.

3. D

Category: Detail

Difficulty: Medium

Strategic Advice: Remember that taking good notes will help you to find answers most quickly in the passage.

Getting to the Answer: Your notes should show you that the author explains the concept of reactive violence in the third paragraph. Reread the description to see which of these items are listed, confirming any of the Roman numeral statements as you come across them. You first see that reactive violence is "rooted in fear" that "can be real or imagined" (lines 29–31). So Statement III is included; eliminate (A) and (B). The author goes on to state that reactive violence is "not entirely the outcome of irrational passions, but, to some extent, of rational calculation" (lines 34–36). So Statements I and II are also included, meaning that (D) is correct.

(A) Distortion; all three statements reflect aspects of this type of violence.

(B) Distortion; all three statements reflect aspects of this type of violence.

(C) Distortion; all three statements reflect aspects of this type of violence.

(**D**) Correct; all three statements reflect aspects of this type of violence.

4. G

Category: Vocab-in-Context

Difficulty: Medium

Strategic Advice: For terms that seem peculiar to the passage, return to the author's first reference to them. You'll usually find defining language there.

Getting to the Answer: Early in the passage, the author defines reactive violence as "violence that is employed in the defense of life, freedom, dignity, property" (lines 27–28). Use that as your prediction.

(F) Misused Detail; this is the definition of playful violence.

(**G**) Correct; this matches your prediction.

(H) Opposite; the author states that the goal of reactive violence "is preservation, not destruction" (lines 33–34).

(J) Distortion; this is not the "only" situation when reactive violence is used.

5. C

Category: Generalization

Difficulty: High

Strategic Advice: With broadly-worded questions, keep the author's main idea and tone in mind as you work through the choices.

Getting to the Answer: Prediction is difficult here. Work through the choices, using your notes to confirm or discard answer choices.

(A) Opposite; you can find this discussed in the last paragraph. The author refers to this frustration as an "almost universal" occurrence. Nothing indicates that this commonality has ceased.

(B) Distortion; the author does not indicate that all of these entities have "similar" needs and desires.

(**C**) Correct; the first paragraph states, "Only the understanding of the unconscious dynamics of behavior permits us to understand the behavior itself" (lines 3–5). The rest of the passage then examines the "unconscious dynamics" behind different kinds of violence.

(D) Opposite; this contradicts the author's statement in lines 33–34.

6. G

Category: Generalization

Difficulty: High

Strategic Advice: Your notes should always contain a summation of the main idea. Be alert, though, for choices that sound good at first but contain slight distortions.

Getting to the Answer: Rely on your notes as well as the introduction given to the passage. The author discusses two types of violence and then goes into detail about the different aspects and causes of these types. Use this as your prediction.

(F) Extreme; the author never talks about preventing wars.

(**G**) Correct; this captures the thrust of your prediction.

(H) Distortion; the author never maintains that reactive violence is the "most" significant form of human violence. He only states that it is of "greater practical significance than playful violence" (lines 25–26).

(J) Distortion; the author only states that reactive violence is "rooted in subconscious fears" (paragraph 3).

Quarter 4

Example Essay

SCORE OF 6

¶1: Understanding another person's culture and language is key to effectively interacting with people of different countries. But how does one go about doing this? Is it necessary to actually live in another country to understand its culture? Can a person learn as much as necessary without traveling, but through experiencing basic aspects of the culture, such as its food and music? Or can schools provide enough information to understand another culture by teaching it objectively, such as through textbooks? Each point of view has positive and negative aspects, and I support the point of view which advocates engaging in basic cultural experiences, though I would take that further to include the necessity of learning the language and going beyond basic experiences.

¶2: The perspective of encouraging students to actually travel to and live in another country is, perhaps, the most theoretically attractive but also the most extreme and unworkable. While it is true that immersion in another culture is a fast way to understand its people and maybe your own country, and provides opportunities to create positive cultural interactions, living in another country is not only expensive, but may be prohibitive for other reasons, perhaps because some students may not be able to leave their families for one reason or another, or some may need specialized services not available in a host country. In terms of schools providing this opportunity, which one assumes means the schools pay for it, it is obvious that not all schools have the money to do this and even those with a large endowment cannot send all students abroad. Finally, the thinking itself is flawed, relying on the assumption that one must become a part of another culture to understand it is like saying that to understand evolution, you have to go through it yourself, or to understand flight you need to build an airplane. Though living in another country is an enticing idea, it cannot be implemented fairly for all students, and would require far more money than most schools can afford, and, in the long run, is not necessary for learning and understanding others.

¶3: Those who advocate for learning by objective means echo several of the concerns above, but go further by saying that students can learn everything they need about other countries through objective teaching. This means that students would learn primarily through textbooks, a cold and dry way to learn about another country. It is possible to provide a lot more exciting experiences, even objective ones, such as hearing the language spoken or watching travel videos. Those who support this argument also say that there are too many countries from which to choose. This is a fallacious argument, since no one is suggesting that students could choose to go to any country. Schools would have to research those countries which would provide the safest, best and most important experience for students, limit the options to those countries, and limit the number of students going to each one. In any case, learning without having an opportunity to actually be hands-on, at least to a minimal extent, is not an effective way to learn.

¶4: Finally, the perspective that it is possible to learn a lot about another country by experiencing components of its culture without traveling is a useful idea. Certainly if one were to eat the native foods, listen to the music and take part in its celebrations, one would get a close look at the important basic ideas of the country. This is the benefit of population diversity and one which many people these days take advantage of. My family loves to go to ethnic fairs and eat foreign foods; in fact, sushi is one of my favorite foods and through eating it I've learned several Japanese words, how to use chopsticks, and how to order it politely. When I do these things, in a limited way I become a part of the Japanese culture and can understand how and why Japanese do the same things. My brother loves reggae music and listens to Bob Marley all the time. The rhythms and instruments have given me insights into the people who sing these songs. Engaging in another country's cultural events is an important way to understand the culture.

¶5: For the most part, then, I agree that it is not necessary to actually live in another country for an extended period of time, but engaging in cultural experiences can teach you a lot about other cultures, as my experiences with sushi support. But I would add that it is vital, not optional, to learn the language of the culture and to go beyond basic cultural components. To be able to think and speak in a foreign language is to be able to get into the mind of the country's people. Just sharing sushi doesn't promote real interaction. You have to be able to talk with each other and share ideas as well as food, to create positive interactions. Finally, it is important to go beyond basic components, which may provide only a surface look at the culture. Inviting school speakers from other countries, joining a different culture's social club, going on field trips to culturally-specific areas of the city, perhaps even having a school program which pretends that, in a certain week, students live in another country and have to represent that country, will help them immerse themselves in the culture without actually living in it. It would be lovely if we could all travel to a different country, but since this is often financially impossible to do, the best substitute is to immerse oneself in as much of the country's culture as possible without actually living there; when we are comfortable with the cultures of other countries, we are open and accepting, and create positive interactions.

Homework Answers & Explanations

Quarter 2

Answer Key

1. **C**
2. **G**
3. **D**
4. **H**
5. **C**
6. **J**
7. **B**
8. **H**
9. **D**
10. **F**
11. **C**
12. **G**
13. **D**
14. **F**
15. **B**
16. **F**
17. **A**
18. **J**
19. **D**
20. **H**
21. **C**
22. **F**
23. **D**
24. **F**
25. **B**
26. **F**
27. **C**
28. **J**
29. **A**
30. **G**
31. **C**
32. **G**
33. **D**
34. **H**
35. **A**
36. **G**
37. **C**
38. **F**
39. **D**
40. **H**

THE LIBRARY SYSTEM

1. C

Category: Punctuation

Difficulty: Medium

Strategic Advice: One way of correcting a run-on error is to make one of the independent clauses subordinate.

Getting to the Answer: As written, this sentence is a run-on. (**C**) corrects this by making the second clause dependent. (B) misuses the colon. The second sentence created by (D) is a fragment.

2. G

Category: Word Choice

Difficulty: Medium

Strategic Advice: The passive voice will not always be wrong on the ACT, but always look for a more active way to express the underlined selection.

Getting to the Answer: (**G**) eliminates the passive voice; none of the other choices does. Additionally, (H) creates a sentence fragment and (J) introduces a verb tense that is inappropriate for an action that will happen in the future.

3. D

Category: Punctuation

Difficulty: Medium

Strategic Advice: A sentence can have multiple nouns and verbs and still be a fragment.

Getting to the Answer: This sentence is a fragment since it has no independent clause. (**D**) corrects this without introducing any additional errors. Neither (B) nor (C) addresses the error; additionally, (B) uses "instead" redundantly.

4. H

Category: Sentence Sense

Difficulty: Low

Strategic Advice: Use logic to determine the best word order in context.

Getting to the Answer: Here, "future state" refers to "library system"; the word order in (**H**) is the most logical. Neither (G) nor (J) makes the sentence logical.

5. C

Category: Wordiness

Difficulty: Low

Strategic Advice: When the underlined selection consists of two words joined by "and," check to see if they mean essentially the same thing.

Getting to the Answer: "Used" and "utilized" mean the same thing; only (**C**) omits the redundancy.

6. J

Category: Sentence Sense

Difficulty: High

Strategic Advice: Expect to see two or three word order questions on your ACT.

Getting to the Answer: Here, (**J**) is the only choice that is both logical and grammatically correct. (F) does not make sense, and (G) and (H) create sentence fragments.

7. B

Category: Word Choice

Difficulty: Medium

Strategic Advice: A verb must agree in number with its subject noun, which may appear after the verb in a sentence.

Getting to the Answer: Here, the subject of the singular verb form "was" is actually the plural "libraries." Both (B) and (D) change the verb, but (D) is unnecessarily wordy. (C) does not address the error.

8. H

Category: Word Choice

Difficulty: Medium

Strategic Advice: Sometimes, changing one word is all that's needed to correct a sentence fragment.

Getting to the Answer: Here, changing "Although" (which makes a clause dependent) to "However" (which does not) turns this fragment into a complete sentence. None of the other choices corrects the error.

9. D

Category: Wordiness

Difficulty: Low

Strategic Advice: Always check for relevance when OMIT is one of the answer choices.

Getting to the Answer: The number of times Henry VIII was married is irrelevant in context; (**D**) is the correct choice here.

10. F

Category: Punctuation

Difficulty: High

Strategic Advice: About 25% of the sentences on your ACT English Test will require NO CHANGE.

Getting to the Answer: This sentence is correct as written. (G) creates a run-on sentence. (H) is awkward and unnecessarily wordy. The future verb phrase "will...be able to" in (J) is inappropriate in context.

LIBERAL ARTS EDUCATION

11. C

Category: Sentence Sense

Difficulty: High

Strategic Advice: Use logic to determine the best word order in context.

Getting to the Answer: It is the "parameters of liberal arts study" that "have remained...unchanged over the centuries." (**C**) provides the most logical word order here.

12. G

Category: Word Choice

Difficulty: Low

Strategic Advice: The –*ing* verb form cannot serve as the main verb in an independent clause.

Getting to the Answer: As written, this sentence is a fragment. (G) corrects this. (H) does not address the error. Omitting this sentence, as (J) suggests, would eliminate a necessary transition to the next paragraph.

13. D

Category: Word Choice

Difficulty: High

Strategic Advice: Although there are a number of ways to correct a run-on sentence, only one answer choice will do so without introducing additional errors.

Getting to the Answer: (B), (C), and (D) all address the run-on error. However, (B) uses a semicolon while also making the second clause dependent, and the conjunction "so" in (C) creates a cause-and-effect relationship between the clauses that is inappropriate in context.

14. F

Category: Sentence Sense

Difficulty: Medium

Strategic Advice: About one out of every four English Test questions will require NO CHANGE.

Getting to the Answer: This sentence is correct as written. (G) uses a singular verb form with a plural subject. (H) and (J) create sentence fragments.

15. B

Category: Word Choice

Difficulty: Medium

Strategic Advice: Adjectives can only modify nouns and pronouns; all other parts of speech are modified by adverbs.

Getting to the Answer: This sentence uses an adjective ("steady") to modify a verb ("increased"). Both (B) and (C) correct the error, but (C) is unnecessarily wordy. (D) incorrectly uses the adverb "steadily" to modify the noun "fashion."

16. F

Category: Word Choice

Difficulty: Medium

Strategic Advice: Check underlined verbs and pronouns for agreement errors.

Getting to the Answer: Here, both the verb and pronoun are used correctly. The infinitive "to give" is idiomatically correct with "sought," and "their" agrees with its plural antecedent "colleges." (G) and (J) use a singular pronoun with a plural antecedent; (H) and (J) do not properly construct the infinitive.

17. A

Category: Punctuation

Difficulty: Medium

Strategic Advice: Carefully examine the differences in answer choices involving punctuation.

Getting to the Answer: The comma is used correctly here; the sentence needs NO CHANGE. (B) and (D) misuse the semicolon and the colon, respectively; the second sentence formed by (C) is a fragment.

18. J

Category: Sentence Sense

Difficulty: High

Strategic Advice: An introductory clause generally modifies the first noun that follows it.

Getting to the Answer: As written, this sentence tells us that "courses in computer science and information technology" are "Responding to this concern." (J) puts the logical noun phrase, "many colleges and universities," after the modifying clause. (G) does not address the error. (H) uses incorrect grammatical structure.

19. D

Category: Wordiness

Difficulty: Medium

Strategic Advice: When OMIT is among the answer choices, carefully examine the underlined material for relevance.

Getting to the Answer: Information about additional degrees offered by liberal arts colleges is irrelevant to this passage and should be omitted.

20. H

Category: Word Choice
Difficulty: Medium
Strategic Advice: A verb must agree with its subject noun, which may not be the noun closest to it in the sentence.

Getting to the Answer: Although the plural "students" is the closest noun to the verb "remain," the verb's subject is actually the singular "premise." (H) corrects the agreement error. (G) creates a run-on sentence. (J) uses a verb tense that is inappropriate in context.

THE MYSTERY OF STONEHENGE

21. C

Category: Punctuation
Difficulty: Medium
Strategic Advice: Set off supplemental information between two commas.

Getting to the Answer: As written, this sentence only has one of the required commas. (C) corrects the error. (B) also has only one of the necessary commas; (D) omits both needed commas.

22. F

Category: Punctuation
Difficulty: High
Strategic Advice: Use a colon to introduce and/or emphasize a brief explanation, quotation, or list.

Getting to the Answer: This sentence needs NO CHANGE. (G) makes the sentence difficult to follow. (H) inappropriately sets off a prepositional phrase in commas. (J) misuses the semicolon.

23. D

Category: Punctuation
Difficulty: Medium
Strategic Advice: Using a comma to set off an introductory phrase makes a sentence easier to understand.

Getting to the Answer: The introductory phrase, "From a distance," should be set off with a comma. The dash in (A) is used incorrectly. (B) uses no punctuation at all. (C) incorrectly adds a comma after "Stonehenge."

24. F

Category: Punctuation
Difficulty: Medium
Strategic Advice: Use a comma when joining an independent clause to a clause beginning with a FANBOYS conjunction.

Getting to the Answer: This sentence needs NO CHANGE. (G) places the comma incorrectly. (H) uses a semicolon to join an independent and a subordinate clause. (J) omits the necessary comma.

25. B

Category: Punctuation
Difficulty: Medium
Strategic Advice: A semicolon can only combine independent clauses.

Getting to the Answer: Here, a semicolon is used to join an independent clause to a dependent one; (B) correctly replaces the semicolon with a comma. (C) misuses the dash. (D) omits the necessary comma.

26. F

Category: Punctuation
Difficulty: High
Strategic Advice: A dash can be used to emphasize a brief explanatory element.

Getting to the Answer: The dash is correctly used here to emphasize the distance the stones are thought to have been carried. (G) misuses the colon. (H) uses no punctuation, making the sentence confusing. Although a comma could also be correct here, (J) places it incorrectly.

27. C

Category: Punctuation
Difficulty: Medium
Strategic Advice: A semicolon can only combine independent clauses.

Getting to the Answer: Here, a semicolon is used to combine an independent clause with a dependent one. (C) correctly replaces the semicolon with a comma. (B) places the comma incorrectly. (D) misuses the dash.

28. J

Category: Punctuation
Difficulty: Medium
Strategic Advice: Words and phrases like "after all," "however," and "in fact" should be set off with commas.
Getting to the Answer: Only (J) properly sets off "however" between two commas. (G) and (H) only add one of the necessary commas.

29. A

Category: Punctuation
Difficulty: Medium
Strategic Advice: In a series of three or more, separate items with commas.
Getting to the Answer: This sentence is correct as written. (B) and (C) each leave out a necessary comma. The comma after "theories" in (D) is incorrect.

30. G

Category: Punctuation
Difficulty: Medium
Strategic Advice: Use 's to create the possessive form of a noun.
Getting to the Answer: Here, since the magician "belonged" to King Arthur, the possessive form in (G) is correct. (F) is the plural, rather than the possessive, form. (H) and (J) form the possessive incorrectly.

FRANKENSTEIN

31. C

Category: Punctuation
Difficulty: Low
Strategic Advice: A comma will not be correct if used to separate a preposition from its object.
Getting to the Answer: Here, the comma after "of" is incorrect; (C) eliminates it. Neither the colon in (B) nor the dash in (D) is correct.

32. G

Category: Punctuation
Difficulty: Medium
Strategic Advice: Make sure supplemental information within a sentence is set off by two commas.

Getting to the Answer: This sentence has the first comma correctly placed, but the second one is omitted. (G) and (J) correctly add the second comma, but (J) also adds an incorrect comma after "published." (H) uses a semicolon instead of the required comma.

33. D

Category: Punctuation
Difficulty: High
Strategic Advice: A semicolon should not be placed between a sentence's subject and that subject's verb.
Getting to the Answer: The semicolon after "physician" is incorrect; (D) eliminates it. (B) replaces the semicolon with a comma, which is also incorrect between a subject and its verb. (C) eliminates the necessary comma after "Byron."

34. H

Category: Punctuation
Difficulty: Medium
Strategic Advice: An introductory phrase should be set off with a comma.
Getting to the Answer: The introductory phrase, "Although it was begun whimsically," should be set off from the rest of the sentence by a comma; (H) does so. (G) incorrectly joins an independent and a subordinate clause with a semicolon. The first sentence in (J) is a fragment.

35. A

Category: Punctuation
Difficulty: Low
Strategic Advice: Use 's to create the possessive form of a noun.
Getting to the Answer: This sentence uses the possessive form correctly. (B) eliminates the necessary apostrophe. (C) uses the possessive correctly, but the comma after "tells" is incorrect. (D) forms the possessive incorrectly.

36. G

Category: Punctuation
Difficulty: Medium
Strategic Advice: When two clauses are joined by a semicolon, check to see if they are both independent.
Getting to the Answer: Here, the first clause is

subordinate, so the semicolon is incorrect. (**G**) properly replaces the semicolon with a comma. The first sentence in (H) is a fragment. (J) omits the necessary comma.

37. C

Category: Punctuation

Difficulty: High

Strategic Advice: A colon can be used to introduce a brief list.

Getting to the Answer: The comma here makes the sentence hard to understand; replacing it with a colon, as (**C**) does, makes the meaning clear. (B) eliminates the comma, but the sentence is still hard to understand. (D) misuses the semicolon.

38. F

Category: Punctuation

Difficulty: Medium

Strategic Advice: Use a comma to set off an introductory clause.

Getting to the Answer: This sentence needs NO CHANGE; the comma is correct here. The first sentence in (G) is a fragment. (H) misuses the semicolon. (J) incorrectly eliminates the comma.

39. D

Category: Punctuation

Difficulty: High

Strategic Advice: Set off explanatory clauses within a sentence between two commas.

Getting to the Answer: As written, this sentence does not set off the phrase "like *Young Frankenstein*," making the sentence confusing. (**D**) correctly adds and places the necessary commas. (B) correctly places a comma before the phrase, but not after it. (C) incorrectly adds a third comma after "like."

40. H

Category: Punctuation

Difficulty: Medium

Strategic Advice: Use a semicolon to combine independent clauses.

Getting to the Answer: The colon between these two independent clauses is incorrect; (**H**) correctly replaces it with a semicolon. (G) creates a run-on sentence. (J) misuses the dash.

Quarter 3

Answer Key

1. **B**
2. **F**
3. **D**
4. **H**
5. **B**
6. **F**
7. **A**
8. **G**
9. **D**
10. **F**
11. **D**
12. **G**
13. **C**
14. **J**
15. **B**
16. **H**
17. **A**
18. **H**
19. **C**
20. **F**

PASSAGE I

1. B

Category: Generalization

Difficulty: Medium

Strategic Advice: With generally worded questions, look for the choice that best matches the author's purpose and tone.

Getting to the Answer: The author's purpose is to discuss the impressive photographic work of Julia Margaret Cameron. In the second paragraph, the author describes her as "the first woman to have achieved eminence in photography." Look for a choice that matches this focus.

(A) Distortion; she was far from "a traditional homemaker," and this part of her life was hardly the focus of the passage.

(**B**) Correct; the author says as much, and the last paragraph indicates that he is not alone.

(C) Opposite; paragraph 3 contradicts this.

(D) Distortion; any "eccentricity" was not so significant as to prevent her from being appreciated.

2. F

Category: Detail
Difficulty: Low
Strategic Advice: When you don't receive a line reference, count on your notes to help you find support for the answer in the passage.
Getting to the Answer: Look to your notes to find where the author discusses "modern critics": the last paragraph. In lines 66–67, the author writes, "Contemporary taste much prefers her portraits."
(F) Correct; this matches what you find in the text.
(G) Opposite; modern critics don't like these works.
(H) Misused Detail; this comes from paragraph 3.
(J) Out of Scope; the author never suggests this.

3. D

Category: Generalization
Difficulty: High
Strategic Advice: When faced with a question on a paragraph, first consult your notes on the paragraph.
Getting to the Answer: Your notes should indicate that the author uses this paragraph to give background on Cameron's life and on her interest in photography. The dates used in the passage tell you that he does this chronologically. Use this as your prediction.
(A) Out of Scope; the author lists a series of chronological facts, not "anecdotes" (short stories).
(B) Distortion; the paragraph also discusses her personal life, and her importance to the field comes after this.
(C) Out of Scope; the author never mentions this.
(D) Correct; this matches the prediction well.

4. H

Category: Function
Difficulty: Medium
Strategic Advice: On Function questions, remember to read around the reference (sometimes as much as the entire paragraph) to understand what the author is doing.
Getting to the Answer: Near the end of the paragraph, the author indicates that Cameron

"worked ceaselessly" and overcame the technological limitations of the time. All of this shows how she "devoted herself wholly to this art" (line 45). Use this as the basis for your prediction.
(F) Distortion; the first part of the second paragraph indicates that she was relatively well off.
(G) Distortion; modern critics do value her portraits.
(H) Correct; this matches the prediction.
(J) Out of Scope; the passage focuses on only one such photographer.

5. B

Category: Vocab-in-Context
Difficulty: Medium
Strategic Advice: Some Vocab-in-Context questions will ask you to "translate" a phrase.
Getting to the Answer: Read around the reference for context. Cameron considered photography a "divine art," to which she was wholly devoted. You can predict something like *was her purpose in life*.
(A) Distortion; the second paragraph suggests that Cameron's social life was anything but conventional.
(B) Correct; this matches the prediction nicely.
(C) Out of Scope; this draws from a different meaning of "vocation."
(D) Out of Scope; don't be misled by "divine" and "devoted." The author is not speaking about Cameron's religious beliefs.

6. F

Category: Generalization
Difficulty: Medium
Strategic Advice: A question on the main point of a passage or paragraph can be easily answered if you're taking good notes.
Getting to the Answer: Return to your notes on the third paragraph; they should reflect that it details Cameron's record of success. Look for a match to that.
(F) Correct; this matches the gist of the prediction.
(G) Extreme; to say that she is "the greatest photographer that ever lived" goes beyond anything stated or implied in the passage.
(H) Misused Detail; the third paragraph does not mention modern appraisals of Cameron.
(J) Out of Scope; the author does not make such a statement.

7. A

Category: Function
Difficulty: High
Strategic Advice: The function of a part of the passage will be closely tied to the text immediately surrounding it. You shouldn't have to look far.
Getting to the Answer: The author introduces these two assessments directly after lauding Cameron's achievements as "notable." He follows their comments by saying that no other woman photographer can match her level of success. The two opinions emphasize how impressive her accomplishments were.
(**A**) Correct; this matches the purpose of the reference.
(B) Misused Detail; this comes from the next paragraph.
(C) Out of Scope; don't misconstrue Watts' inscription (lines 55–56). Nothing in the paragraph suggests any "envy."
(D) Misused Detail; this pulls from the next paragraph.

8. G

Category: Detail
Difficulty: Low
Strategic Advice: You should be able to find distinctive details (such as proper names or italicized words) easily, even without line references.
Getting to the Answer: You shouldn't have taken any detailed names down in your notes, but a quick skim of the passage should help you find this title quickly. Read a few lines before, and you should see that this is an example of the "allegorical...native scenes" that Victorian critics loved and modern critics devalue.
(F) Distortion; this work is contrasted with the portraits.
(**G**) Correct; this matches what the author writes in the paragraph.
(H) Distortion; this refers to an aspect of Cameron's photographic portraits, not her allegorical work.
(J) Opposite; Cameron's contemporaries liked works such as this.

9. D

Category: Detail
Difficulty: Medium
Strategic Advice: Don't get confused on NOT questions; make sure you're answering the question that was asked.

Getting to the Answer: Check your notes to determine where the two sets of critics are discussed: the last paragraph. Based on your notes, you could predict that modern critics would not agree with the high esteem that Victorians felt for Cameron's allegorical pictures.
(A) Distortion; while Cameron did base some of her photographs on poems, neither set of critics takes a stand on the practice.
(B) Distortion; the author never states that Victorian critics felt this way about any of her work.
(**C**) Opposite; based on the paragraph, modern critics would agree with this.
(D) Correct; the author makes clear that the two camps disagree on this matter.

10. F

Category: Writer's View
Difficulty: Medium
Strategic Advice: Many Writer's View questions can be answered with a quick review of the author's purpose and tone.
Getting to the Answer: The author says that Cameron "achieved eminence" (line 11) in her field, that she "devoted herself wholly to this art" (line 45), and that "No other female artist of the nineteenth century achieved such acclaim" (lines 58–60). You can predict *appreciative*, or even something as simple as *positive*.
(**F**) Correct; this matches the author's tone.
(G) Opposite; this is too negative.
(H) Distortion; the author uses too many words of praise for this to work.
(J) Out of Scope; the passage doesn't support this characterization.

PASSAGE II

11. D

Category: Vocab-in-Context
Difficulty: Medium
Strategic Advice: Remember to avoid the most common meaning of a word on Vocab-in-Context questions.
Getting to the Answer: Return to the line referenced and read as much of the surrounding text as you need to. At the beginning of the sentence, the author states that the experiments were performed "to detect biological activity." Keep in mind that the thrust of the

passage is about finding any form of life on Mars. You can predict something like *present* or *in existence.*

(A) Out of Scope; this is a common meaning of the word, but it doesn't fit the context.

(B) Out of Scope; this is a common meaning of the word, but it doesn't fit the context.

(C) Out of Scope; nothing in the paragraph supports this.

(D) Correct; this matches the prediction.

12. G

Category: Function

Difficulty: High

Strategic Advice: When looking for a "big picture" answer, don't fall for misused or distorted details.

Getting to the Answer: Check your notes for the fourth paragraph and skim it again if you need help. The author describes some flaws in the Viking program to show why some still hold out hope for finding life on Mars. Use this as your prediction.

(F) Distortion; while this may be true, this is too narrow to match the scope of the passage overall.

(G) Correct; this is consistent with the overall purpose of the passage.

(H) Opposite; the passage contradicts this.

(J) Distortion; the passage indicates that, even though the odds were long, scientists were still hopeful.

13. C

Category: Detail

Difficulty: Medium

Strategic Advice: When you aren't given a line reference, your notes become even more critical for saving time.

Getting to the Answer: Consult your notes to see where experiments with "organic compounds" are discussed: paragraph 2. There you read that scientists' failure to find organic material was unexpected "because at least organic compounds from the steady bombardment of the Martian surface by meteorites were thought to have been present" (lines 28–31). Predict *bombardment by meteorites.*

(A) Out of Scope; the paragraph doesn't mention this.

(B) Misused Detail; the author discusses this in the next paragraph.

(C) Correct; the paragraph supports this.

(D) Misused Detail; the author discusses this in the next paragraph.

14. J

Category: Inference

Difficulty: Medium

Strategic Advice: When you receive limited help from the question stem, count on your notes to help you confirm or rule out choices based on the passage.

Getting to the Answer: The question stem does not point to any one paragraph definitively; the author discusses many such differences. You can certainly predict that Mars seems unable to sustain life the way that Earth does. Look for a choice in line with that.

(F) Opposite; this is more specific than the prediction, but a check of your notes will rule this out. According to the second paragraph, no organic compounds were found in Martian soil.

(G) Distortion; the third paragraph addresses this but never says that Earth is not in the path of such radiation. The difference is that Earth has a "protective layer of ozone."

(H) Distortion; Earth still does possess such an atmosphere.

(J) Correct; this matches the thrust of the author.

15. B

Category: Detail

Difficulty: Low

Strategic Advice: With Detail questions, the answer is in the passage. Don't slip into making an inference.

Getting to the Answer: Let your notes help you find the reference to what Mars resembles. The last sentence of the first paragraph indicates that "the photograph most accurately predicting what Mars would look like was a snapshot taken from a particularly arid section of the Mojave Desert." This works as a prediction.

(A) Misused Detail; the author refers to this in a later paragraph.

(B) Correct; the first paragraph supports this.

(C) Out of Scope; the author never states this.

(D) Distortion; the third paragraph may seem to suggest this, but you are looking for something that the author actually states.

16. H

Category: Generalization

Difficulty: Medium

Strategic Advice: If you're taking good notes, questions on the main idea of a passage or paragraph will present few problems.

Getting to the Answer: Your notes should indicate that this paragraph discusses four experiments carried out by the Viking landers. These experiments were designed to detect signs of life but were unsuccessful. Look for a match to this general idea.

(F) Distortion; the paragraph never states this. Also, the paragraph centers more on the results than on the scientists' reaction to them.

(G) Out of Scope; no such conclusions are suggested about Earth.

(**H**) Correct; this matches your research.

(J) Distortion; the results do not suggest this.

17. A

Category: Inference
Difficulty: High

Strategic Advice: With generally worded questions, skim your notes and look for the choice that matches the general thrust of the passage.

Getting to the Answer: Check your notes to see where "Martian rocks" are discussed: paragraph 5. The author states that some scientists hypothesize that life on Mars may have "escaped worsening conditions by... seeking refuge in rocks" (lines 64–67), as happened on Earth. Predict that the idea assumes that *Earth and Mars are similar in some basic way.*

(**A**) Correct; this matches the prediction and the thrust of the argument.

(B) Distortion; this is too specific to be an idea on which the argument can rest.

(C) Extreme; the paragraph doesn't support this.

(D) Distortion; the idea in the paragraph emphasizes similarity in the environments, not in these specific organisms.

18. H

Category: Detail
Difficulty: Low

Strategic Advice: Detail questions with line references shouldn't take long at all; they're like an open-book test.

Getting to the Answer: The last paragraph states, "Should Mars eventually prove to be barren of life... it could be much more difficult to get life started on a planet than scientists thought before." Predict that

scientists will have to reevaluate the chances for life on other planets.

(F) Out of Scope; while the fourth paragraph might seem to suggest this, it has nothing to do with the given reference.

(G) Out of Scope; the passage does not state this.

(**H**) Correct; this matches what the author writes in paragraph 5.

(J) Distortion; this twists a detail from the previous paragraph.

19. C

Category: Detail
Difficulty: Medium

Strategic Advice: If the question stem doesn't seem to give any clues, skim your notes to help you find the match.

Getting to the Answer: Your notes should indicate that paragraph 3 suggests why there seems to be no life on Mars: the effect of UV rays. Look for a match to this idea.

(A) Opposite; carbon dioxide had provided protection from such radiation.

(B) Misused Detail; this comes from the first paragraph.

(**C**) Correct; the paragraph supports this.

(D) Opposite; paragraph 2 indicates that this should have enabled the existence of some organic material.

20. F

Category: Detail
Difficulty: Medium

Strategic Advice: Consult your notes, research the passage, and beware of Misused Details.

Getting to the Answer: Your notes should lead you to the second paragraph. The author states, "To detect biological activity, Martian soil samples were treated with various nutrients" (lines 22–23). Predict *to detect biological activity.*

(**F**) Correct; this matches up with the text

(G) Out of Scope; these were standalone experiments, not follow-ups.

(H) Out of Scope; the experiments were focused on Mars.

(J) Misused Detail; this is mentioned later in the paragraph, but was not the aim of the experiments.

Quarter 4

Example Essays

Score of 6

A good understanding of American history is an important part of a well-rounded education. History enables us to understand how and why our culture and political systems came about. Just as scientific discoveries build one upon the other, our knowledge of social systems improves when we understand their foundations through the study of history. Because of this importance, teachers look for the best way to teach history. Three of these include focusing on the lives of important leaders, concentrating on the welfare of the society as a whole, and focusing on the important events and dates. Since simple memorization of dates and events does not lead to a deeper understanding of the development of our culture or social systems, history should be taught by examining the development of the entire population, as shaped by the lives and decisions of important leaders.

Some would argue that the single focus of history should be the lives of prominent figures. Especially in American history, where most of the important leaders were democratically elected by a majority of the population, major historical characters could be considered as representative of the nation as a whole, because voters are unlikely to choose candidates with values and backgrounds much different from their own. However, this view overlooks the very exceptionality built into the electoral process. In order to persuade the majority of people to vote for him, a candidate must possess attributes or talents that distinguish him, and make him preferable to his opponent. The example of Abraham Lincoln is illustrative. While Lincoln came from a humble background, similar to that of many rural Americans of his time, his penetrating thinking and persuasive oratory set him apart and were not characteristic of the population as a whole. Lincoln's personal history is an important backdrop to the decisions he made that shaped US history, however, what is most necessary for Americans to understand and appreciate are the changes he brought to the entire nation through his leadership of the North during the Civil War, and through his Emancipation Proclamation. This is why it is necessary to supplement the study of the lives of national leaders with the understanding of how their decisions affected the population as a whole.

The best understanding of history comes through examining the development, or lack of it, of the entire population. While great changes are inspired or instigated by great leaders, these changes must be perpetuated by the population as a whole if they are to be effective. My grandparents and teachers have told me that, when they were growing up, there were "White Only" restrooms and water fountains. Even as recently as 50 years ago, some Americans were subjected to open discrimination, despite the Emancipation Proclamation and the efforts of Abraham Lincoln. What is most important for Americans to understand through the study of history is how our society and culture have developed since Lincoln's bold decision. We have moved from enslaving persons of African descent, through enshrining discrimination in law, to electing Barack Obama, a president of African descent, twice by the votes of a majority of the population. Understanding the dynamics and developments that led to this remarkable turnaround are the most important aspects of history, and support the idea that the optimal teaching of history is done through analysis of the welfare of the entire population of a nation, as shaped by the decisions of its leaders.

The least valuable understanding of history comes through memorization of dates and events. Although some argue that knowledge of dates and events is necessary for us to learn from the past, if a person could recite the precise date of the signing of the Emancipation Proclamation, or the dates of Barack Obama's inaugurations, that knowledge is insufficient to describe or explain the effects of those events. A general knowledge of the approximate time of major events is enough to analyze their impact, and again, their impact is best measured by evaluating the development, or lack of it, of the population of the nation as a whole.

The study of history enables us to understand how societies progress, and to use the knowledge of the past to make better decisions in the present. In order to do this, we must have some metric to evaluate the success of the choices made in the past, and the welfare of the society as a whole is an excellent measure, and should be the focus of teaching history. Some may argue that determining the development of a nation is a subjective measure because different sectors of the population may be improving, while others seem to be deteriorating. Surely the slave owners in Lincoln's time thought that the destruction of their system of labor was not a "development" but an unfair theft of a crucial asset of their livelihood by the government. However, this argument overlooks the fact that, through the lens of history, we are able to easily evaluate the effectiveness of most decisions. For example, no reasonable person could argue that the Emancipation Proclamation was not beneficial for the US nation as a whole, and that Hitler's decisions proved to be disastrous for the people of Germany. The welfare of the population as a whole can be used to measure the effectiveness of historical decisions, so it should be the central theme in history courses. Because the study of history should help us make better decisions in the present, the best way to learn from history is to study how decisions of the past have improved society as a whole.

SCORE OF 3

History should be studied by examining the welfare of the entire population, because these are the people who make up the country. The leaders are just individuals who are part of the whole country. Memorizing dates is hard and doesn't teach us anything but the dates.

I don't think studying the lives of the country's leaders helps us understand history, because they are just one person. Abraham Lincoln was a great man. He came from a poor background to be president, but there haven't been a lot of other people like him. Even if we know everything about Lincoln and his life, we don't know very much about history.

If we study the entire population, it can help us know if things got better or worse under a president. For example, under Lincoln the slaves were freed, so their lives got a lot better. Because Lincoln made things better for so many people, he is considered a great president. So when we study history, we should think about whether or not the lives of most of the people got better.

Memorizing dates and events isn't a good way to learn history. They are hard to remember and don't tell us anything about what really happened. My friend can memorize stuff quickly, and always gets good grades on history tests, but I can't.

In my opinion, the only reason to study history is to see if we can learn something that will help us do better in the future. By seeing if most of the people did better or worse, we can know what to do better next time. Because leaders are just one person, and because knowing dates doesn't help us to know what to do better in the future, history should be taught by studying the welfare of the entire population.

SCORE OF 1

There are 3 ways to study history. You can focus on a nation's prominent historical leaders, on the welfare of the entire population or on what happened when and who influenced those events. I think you should focus on the welfare of the entire population b/c everyone is important and this way you'll know the most about the most people. Leaders are just one person and history is about everyone together. Dates are just numbers and they are hard to learn.

ANSWERS AND EXPLANATIONS

Preview Quiz Answers & Explanations

Answer Key

1. **A**
2. **K**
3. **C**
4. **J**
5. **B**

1. A

Category: Operations
Difficulty: Low
Strategic advice: Always follow the order of operations and be sure to give fractions a common denominator before adding or subtracting them.
Getting to the answer: Do what's in parentheses first:

$$\left(\frac{1}{2} + \frac{1}{6}\right) - \left(\frac{1}{12} + \frac{1}{3}\right)$$
$$= \left(\frac{6}{12} + \frac{2}{12}\right) - \left(\frac{1}{12} + \frac{4}{12}\right)$$
$$= \left(\frac{8}{12}\right) - \left(\frac{5}{12}\right)$$
$$= \frac{3}{12}$$
$$= \frac{1}{4}$$

Don't forget to simplify the fraction before you select your answer.

2. K

Category: Proportions and Probability
Difficulty: Medium
Strategic advice: Again, you can't just add the percents since the first increase is a percentage of the 1970 population and the second increase is a percentage of the 1980 population.
Getting to the answer: Pick a number for the original population of City Q and see what happens to the population. 100 is an easy number with which to work. If the city had 100 people in 1970, the 20% increase would result in 100(1.20) = 120 people in 1980. The 30% increase would produce 120(1.30) = 156 people in 1990. This is an increase of 156 − 100 = 56 people, for a percent increase of $\frac{56}{100}$. 100% = 56%, or (**K**). Note that (J) is a trap. If you just added the given percents together, you'd get 50%, but since the second percent is a percent of a larger number than the first, the actual answer is larger.

3. C

Category: Variable Manipulation
Difficulty: Low
Strategic advice: Solve inequalities just the same as you would equations, but look out for multiplying or dividing by negative numbers.
Getting to the answer:

$3 < 4x - 5$

$8 < 4x$

$2 < x$

(Since you divide by −4, you must flip the inequality sign.)

4. J

Category: Patterns, Logic & Data
Difficulty: Medium
Strategic advice: Most functions questions, like this one, rely on substitution. Make sure your Operations skills are up to snuff and always read the question carefully.
Getting to the answer:

$$\frac{a(3)}{b(2)}$$
$$= \frac{\sqrt{3^2 + 7}}{(2)^3 - 7}$$
$$= \frac{\sqrt{9 + 7}}{8 - 7}$$
$$= \frac{\sqrt{16}}{1}$$
$$= 4$$

5. B

Category: Proportions and Probability
Difficulty: High
Strategic advice: Complicated word problems like this can be solved algebraically or Backsolved. Use whichever method you find more comfortable.
Getting to the answer: To Backsolve, calculate the amount of money the magazine would pay for three articles of the length in each answer choice. Start with the middle choice, (C). If each article were 2,400 words long, then the magazine would pay $0.35 per word for the first 500 words and $0.25 per word for the remaining 1,900 words, for a total of $0.35(500) + $0.25(1,900) = $175 + $475 = $650 per article. Since there are three articles, the magazine would

pay $650(3) = $1,950 all together. This is too much, so go to the next-smaller answer choice, (B). If each article were 1,200 words long, the magazine would pay $0.35(500) + $0.25(700) = $175 + $175 = $350 for each article, for a total of $350(3) = $1,050. This is exactly what they paid, so (**B**) is correct. You could also solve this problem algebraically. If the number of words in an article is x, the magazine pays $0.35(500) + $0.25(x − 500) for each article. Since the magazine paid $1,050 for all three articles, each article was worth $\frac{\$1,050}{3}$ = $350. Set these equal and solve for x:

$0.35(500) + $0.25(x − 500) = $350

$175 + $0.25x − $125 = $350

$0.25x = $300

$x = 1,200

Quarter 2

Answer Key

1. **D**
2. **H**
3. **B**
4. **J**
5. **B**
6. **J**
7. **B**

1. D

Category: Proportions and Probability

Difficulty: Medium

Strategic advice: Always be alert to exactly what a ratio is telling you. Is it men to women or women to men?

Getting to the answer: Since the ratio of men to women is 5:3, the ratio of women to ensemble members is 3:8. There's a total of 24 people, so $\frac{3}{8} = \frac{x}{24}$, where x is the number of women in the ensemble.

$\frac{3}{8} = \frac{x}{24}$

$8x = 24 \cdot 3$

$x = \frac{72}{8} = 9$

You don't need to work through the proportion if you notice that the number of people is 3 times the total of the proportion, so the number of women must be three times the number of women in the proportion. If

working through the proportion doesn't go well, notice that all the answer choices are also whole numbers, meaning this question can be solved with Backsolving.

2. H

Category: Proportions and Probability

Difficulty: Low

Strategic Advice: Be careful when converting improper fractions into mixed fractions.

Getting to the Answer:

$\frac{2}{9} = \frac{x}{15}$

$9x = 15 \cdot 2$

$x = \frac{30}{9} = \frac{10}{3} = 3\frac{1}{3}$

3. B

Category: Operations

Difficulty: Medium

Strategic advice: Backsolving is often a great way to solve averaging problems.

Getting to the answer: The average of a set of numbers is the sum of the numbers divided by the number of numbers. You can either set up an equation involving the missing score or try plugging each of the possible scores into the question stem to see which one works. If you Backsolve, remember to start with the middle number:

(C) $\frac{150 + 195 + 160 + 185}{4} = \frac{690}{4} = 172.5$

Too low? Try the next-largest number.

(B) $\frac{150 + 195 + 160 + 195}{4} = \frac{700}{4} = 175$

Perfect! To solve the problem algebraically, call the missing score x and set up the average equation:

$\frac{150 + 195 + 160 + x}{4} = 175$

$505 + x = 700$

$x = 195$

4. J

Category: Operations

Difficulty: Medium

Strategic advice: Converting percent increases and decreases into decimal multipliers will help save time on questions like this one.

Getting to the answer: If everything in the store is 25% off, then it costs 75% of its original price. The

6% sales tax means that the price must be multiplied by 1.06. Put this all together to find that a shirt originally priced at $22.00 costs ($22.00)(0.75)(1.06) = $17.49.

5. **B**

Category: Operations
Difficulty: Medium

Strategic advice: When Picking Numbers for percents problems, you should start with 100 to make your calculations easier.

Getting to the answer: Say original cost = $100. Then Monday's cost = $100 – $100(0.2) = $80, and Tuesday's cost = $80 – $80(0.25) = $60.

Discount = $100 – $60 = $40.

Percent change = $\frac{\$40}{\$100}$. 100% = 40%.

6. **J**

Category: Variable Manipulation
Difficulty: Medium

Strategic advice: If you multiply or divide by a negative number, you must reverse the direction of the inequality sign.

Getting to the answer:

$8 - 2x > 6$

$-2x > -2$

$x < 1$

7. **B**

Category: Number Properties
Difficulty: Medium

Strategic advice: One approach to this question is to solve each of the answer choices to get a range of values for b and then see which one gives you the same range as that shown in the figure. A faster approach is to think of absolute value as a distance. You can see that the values in the figure are centered at 2 and include everything up to and including 3 units away from the center. Therefore, the distance between b and 2 must be less than or equal to 3, so $|b - 2| \leq 3$.

Getting to the answer:

$|b - 2| \leq 3$

$-3 \leq b - 2 \leq 3$

$-1 \leq b \leq 5$

Notice that at the extreme values, the inequalities will be equal. Plug the extreme values from the graph into each inequality to see which one works. When $b = -1$, $|b - 2| = |(-1) - 2| = |-3| = 3$, and when b = 5, $|b - 2| = |(5) - 2| = |3| = 3$, so (**B**) is correct.

Quiz

1. **A**
2. **H**
3. **B**
4. **G**
5. **C**

1. **A**

Category: Proportions and Probability
Difficulty: High

Strategic advice: The largest *actual* increase is not necessarily the largest *percent* increase.

Getting to the answer: Percent increase is the actual increase over the original amount, so you are looking for the largest increase, in dollar amounts, from the smallest original amount. Although the $8,000 increase from 1993 to 1994 is the largest dollar amount, it starts from a larger original amount than the other years and therefore may not be the largest *percent* increase. The increases from 1989 to 1990 and 1990 to 1991 are both $5,000, so you can already eliminate (B), since its original amount is larger. Similarly, the increases from 1991 to 1992 and 1992 to 1993 are $3,000, and they both start from a larger original amount than (A). Evaluate the remaining answer choices:

(A) $\frac{\$5,000}{\$20,000}$. 100% = 25%

(E) $\frac{\$8,000}{\$36,000}$. 100% = 22.2%

The percent increase from 1989 to 1990 is larger.

2. **H**

Category: Proportions and Probability
Difficulty: Medium

Strategic advice: Before you bubble in an answer, double-check to be sure it's what the question was asking for.

Getting to the answer: First, find the number of girls and boys in the class. If g is the number of girls, then $\frac{3}{8} = \frac{g}{32}$ and $g = \frac{32 \cdot 3}{8} = 12$. Since there are

32 total students, there are 32 − 12 = 20 boys. The difference between the number of boys and the number of girls is 20 − 12 = 8, or (**H**). Notice that (J) and (K) are traps—one is the number of girls and the other is the number of boys.

3. **B**

Category: Proportions and Probability
Difficulty: Medium
Strategic advice: Whenever you're working with ratios, pay attention to whether they're part:part or part:whole ratios.
Getting to the answer: Since the ratio of wins to losses was 3:5, the ratio of wins to games was 3:8. Convert this into a percent: $\frac{3}{8} \cdot 100\% = 37\frac{1}{2}\%$.

4. **G**

Category: Variable Manipulation
Difficulty: Low
Strategic advice: The direction of an inequality sign changes if you multiply or divide by a negative number. Other than that, they act exactly like equations—you must always do the same thing to both sides.
Getting to the answer:
$-3 < 4x - 5$
$2 < 4x$
$\frac{1}{2} < x$

5. **C**

Category: Proportions and Probability
Difficulty: Medium
Strategic advice: The average is the sum of the terms divided by the number of terms.
Getting to the answer:
$\frac{(2x+5)+(5x-6)+(-4x+2)}{3} = \frac{3x+1}{3} = x + \frac{1}{3}$

Quarter 3

Answer Key

1. **A**
2. **G**
3. **B**
4. **K**
5. **D**

6. **H**
7. **D**
8. **G**

1. **A**

Category: Operations
Difficulty: Low
Strategic advice: This question is a great opportunity to use your calculator, but it can be solved mathematically as well. The square root of a number is the factor of the number that when multiplied by itself gives you the original number.
Getting to the answer: If you plug the square root of 250 into your calculator, it will come out to approximately 15.81, so the greatest integer smaller than that is 15. To solve this mathematically, you can find the two perfect squares that ($\sqrt{250}$) is between: ($\sqrt{225}$) and ($\sqrt{256}$), or 15 and 16. So, 15 is the largest integer less than ($\sqrt{250}$).

2. **G**

Category: Operations
Difficulty: High
Strategic advice: Remember how to re-order logarithms with the mnemonic device "Apes Chew Bananas." That is the order the numbers appear in a logarithm, and you must simply put them back in alphabetical order to create a proper exponent. Log$_a$c = b becomes $a^b = c$, and vice versa.
Getting to the answer: Using the Apes Chew Bananas device, we know that Log$_x$100 = 2 is equivalent to $x^2 = 100$. Simplify by taking the square root of both sides. $\sqrt{x^2} = \sqrt{100}$ gives us $x = 10$.

3. **B**

Category: Proportions and Probability
Difficulty: Medium
Strategic advice: The probability that two independent events will both occur is the probability of the first times the probability of the second.
Getting to the answer: The probability that the coin will land heads-up is $\frac{1}{2}$ (1 desired outcome, heads, over 2 possible outcomes, heads or tails). The probability that the die will land on an even number is also $\frac{1}{2}$ (3 even numbers over 6 possible numbers). Therefore, the probability that the coin will land on

heads and the die will land on an even number is $\frac{1}{2} \cdot \frac{1}{2} = \frac{1}{4}$.

4. K

Category: Proportions and Probability

Difficulty: Medium

Strategic advice: Using proportions is a great way to solve simple rate problems.

Getting to the answer: Just set up a proportion:

$$\frac{288 \text{ miles}}{6 \text{ hours}} = \frac{x \text{ miles}}{8 \text{ hours}}$$

$$x = \frac{(288)8}{6} = 384$$

5. D

Category: Patterns, Logic & Data

Difficulty: High

Strategic advice: You'll want to have the equation of a geometric sequence memorized by Test Day—it may come in handy.

Getting to the answer: The nth term of a geometric sequence is represented by the equation $a_n = a_1(r^{n-1})$, where n is the term you're looking for, a_1 is the first term of the sequence, and r is the ratio between terms. The first term of this sequence is $a_1 = 2n$. The ratio between the terms is $r = \frac{4n}{2n} = 2$. Therefore, the 500th term is $a_{500} = 2n(2^{500-1}) = 2n(2^{499})$. This isn't one of the listed answer choices, though, so there must be a way to simplify further. $2n$ is really $2^1 n$, so it can be combined with 2^{499}, leaving $2^{500}n$, which is (**D**).

6. H

Category: Patterns, Logic, & Data

Difficulty: Medium

Strategic advice: Remember to account for parts of three-dimensional figures that aren't shown in diagrams.

Getting to the answer: As you can see in the diagram, there are two layers of 9 cubes each (one in front and one in back). The cubes on the corners each have 3 faces on the outside, the cubes in the middle of each side each have 2 faces on the outside, and the cube in the middle has 1 face on the outside. Since there are two layers, there are two cubes with exactly one face that is visible from the outside of the solid: one in front and one in back.

7. D

Category: Trigonometry

Difficulty: High

Strategic advice: Glancing at the answer choices can help you figure out just what the question is asking for. Here, it's looking for the relationship between b and h that could be given by $\sin \theta$.

Getting to the answer: $\sin \theta = \frac{\text{opposite}}{\text{hypotenuse}} =$ The side opposite θ is the height, h. You can find the hypotenuse, $\sqrt{b^2 + h^2}$ by using the Pythagorean theorem. Just plug these into the equation you know for $\sin \theta$ to find $\sin \theta = \frac{h}{\sqrt{b^2 + h^2}}$.

8. G

Category: Trigonometry

Difficulty: Medium

Strategic advice: The mnemonic SOHCAHTOA can help you remember the basic trig functions.

Getting to the answer: Sketch a triangle that includes the information from the question.

$Cosine = \frac{\text{adjacent}}{\text{hypotenuse}}$, so the triangle described by $\cos \theta = \frac{5\sqrt{2}}{8}$ is

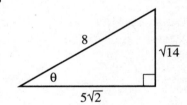

The opposite side can be found by the Pythagorean theorem:

$$(5\sqrt{2})^2 + b^2 = 8^2$$
$$50 + b^2 = 64$$
$$b^2 = 14$$
$$b = \sqrt{14}$$

$$\tan \theta = \frac{\text{opposite}}{\text{adjacent}}$$

$$= \frac{\sqrt{14}}{5\sqrt{2}}$$

$$= \frac{\sqrt{7} \cdot \sqrt{2}}{5 \cdot \sqrt{2}}$$

$$= \frac{\sqrt{7}}{5}$$

Quiz

Answer Key

1. **B**
2. **J**
3. **D**
4. **J**
5. **B**
6. **K**

1. B

Category: Operations

Difficulty: Low

Strategic advice: Most people find it easier to work with negative exponents when they are written as fractions.

Getting to the answer:

$(-2)^{-3} + (-3)^{-2} = \dfrac{1}{(-2)^3} + \dfrac{1}{(-3)^2}$

$= \dfrac{1}{-8} + \dfrac{1}{9} = \dfrac{-9}{72} + \dfrac{8}{72} + \dfrac{-1}{72}$

2. J

Category: Patterns, Logic & Data

Difficulty: Medium

Strategic advice: When a question asks for something that seems to require hours of calculation, such as the 100th digit after the decimal, look for a pattern instead of using brute calculation.

Getting to the answer: Divide 4 by 11 and see what the first few terms after the decimal are: $\dfrac{11}{4}$ = 0.363636….Every odd term (the first, third, and so on) is 3. Every even term is 6. Since 100 is an even number, the 100th digit after the decimal will be 6.

3. D

Category: Proportions and Probability

Difficulty: Medium

Strategic advice: Backsolve or set up a proportion.

Getting to the answer: To Backsolve, start with the middle choice and see how much that many tiles would weigh:

(C) 0.23 pounds per tile × 230 tiles = 52.9 pounds. Not enough.

(D) 0.23 pounds per tile × 435 tiles = 100.05 pounds. Since this question asks for an approximate number

of tiles, this is correct. To solve algebraically, set up a proportion:

$\dfrac{0.23 \text{ pounds}}{1 \text{ tile}} = \dfrac{100 \text{ pounds}}{x \text{ tile}}$

$0.23x = 100$

$x = 434.7861$, which rounds to 435. Only round off if the question includes language such as "approximately how many" or "about how much."

4. J

Category: Proportions and Probability

Difficulty: Medium

Strategic advice: The probability that something will happen is the number of desired outcomes over the number of possible outcomes.

Getting to the answer: Once Alicia has drawn the marble numbered 25, there are 49 marbles left in the box, or 49 possible outcomes. How many of these are desired outcomes? Alicia wins if she draws a marble with the same units digit as the one she already drew, so there are 4 winning marbles (05, 15, 35, and 45). Therefore, the probability that she will win on her next draw is $\dfrac{4}{49}$.

5. B

Category: Patterns, Logic & Data

Difficulty: Medium

Strategic advice: Be sure to read logic problems very carefully.

Getting to the answer: When you see a statement of the form "If (A), then (B)," you know that if the length of QR is 6, so the shortest distance from the edge to the center is $3\sqrt{3}$. Since the shortest distance is NOT $3\sqrt{3}$, the length of QR cannot be 6. (**B**) is correct.

6. K

Category: Trigonometry

Difficulty: Medium

Strategic advice: On Test Day, be on the lookout for problems that simply ask you to plug values into a given formula. They may look tough, but they won't require you to do much math.

Getting to the answer: The problem is asking for the expression that represents the value of Z. With the values of two of the three angles known, we can determine that the unmarked angle is 180° − 35° − 45° = 100°. We are given the length of $\overline{DS}$ along with its opposite angle, so plug that information into the law of sines to solve for Z:

$$\frac{\sin 45°}{7} = \frac{\sin 100°}{Z}$$

$$Z \sin 45° = \sin 7100°$$

$$Z = \frac{7 \sin 100°}{\sin 45°}$$

So (**K**) is correct.

Quarter 4

Answer Key

1. **C**
2. **H**
3. **D**
4. **F**
5. **D**
6. **G**
7. **D**
8. **G**
9. **A**
10. **G**
11. **C**
12. **G**
13. **B**
14. **J**
15. **A**
16. **H**
17. **B**

PASSAGE II

1. C

Category: Figure Interpretation
Difficulty: Low
Strategic advice: Be sure you're looking at the appropriate line on a graph when there is more than one!

Getting to the answer: You'll have to get out your pencil and draw a horizontal line on the graph to find the exact place where a collision rating of 9 Torinos intersects the line corresponding to Experiment 1. Then, draw a vertical line from that point down and you'll see that it corresponds to roughly 700,000 kg on the x-axis. That's (**C**).

(A) is incorrect because an asteroid weighing 200,000 kg would only have caused an impact with a collision rating of 1 Torino.

(B) is incorrect because a 500,000 kg asteroid would have caused an impact with a collision rating of 6 Torinos.

(D) is incorrect because a 1,000,000 kg asteroid would have caused an impact with a collision rating of 10 Torinos, which is too high.

2. H

Category: Figure Interpretation
Difficulty: Low
Strategic advice: Sometimes, you'll need to combine information from a figure with information in the text of a passage.

Getting to the answer: Draw a vertical line from the 4 on the x-axis and a horizontal line from the 4 on the y-axis. The two lines intersect on the line for Experiment 1. The passage tells you that the moisture level for Experiment 1 was 86%, so (**H**) is correct.

(F) An atmospheric moisture level of 0% wasn't studied by the researchers, but if the trends are correct, it would have caused far more damage than a 4 on the Torino scale.

(G) A moisture level of 12% would mean a Torino rating of 6 or 7 for a 400,000 kg asteroid.

(J) A moisture level of 100% was not studied, but it would probably result in less damage.

3. D

Category: Figure Interpretation
Difficulty: Low
Strategic advice: Common mistakes students make on questions often show up as wrong answer choices, so be careful!

Getting to the answer: First, check to see which experiment simulated an atmospheric moisture level of 12%: Experiment 2. Then draw a line from 500,000 kg on the x-axis straight up until you intersect the line for Experiment 2. Draw a line from that intersection across to the y-axis. It falls somewhere between 7 and 8. Now, go to the first table and find out what kind of destruction a 7 or 8 on the Torino scale represents. The answer is (**D**), a collision capable of global catastrophe. (A), (B), and (C) are too low to be correct.

PASSAGE III

4. F

Category: Figure Interpretation

Difficulty: Low

Strategic advice: Don't forget to check the passage for terms and definitions.

Getting to the answer: In the introduction to the passage, the "half-life" of an isotope is defined as the amount of time needed for one-half of the initial number of nuclei to decay. To figure out the half-life of $^{231}_{90}$Th, look at the first graph. When half of the nuclei have decayed, the $\frac{N}{N_0}$ ratio will be $\frac{N}{N_0}$ or 0.5. (Think about it this way: If you started with 100 nuclei and half decayed, you'd have 50 left. That's an $\frac{N}{N_0}$ ratio of $\frac{50}{100}$ or 0.5.) Draw a horizontal line across the graph from 0.5 on the y-axis. Where that line intersects the curve, draw a vertical line down to the x-axis. This line intersects the x-axis right around 1.0, which means the amount of time it takes for half of the nuclei to decay is about 1 day. (**F**) matches perfectly.

5. D

Category: Figure Interpretation

Difficulty: Medium

Strategic advice: Ask yourself, where is the information you need?

Getting to the answer: MeV data are shown in Figure 3. Find the point where a line drawn up from 60 days on the x-axis intersects the graph that corresponds to $^{234}_{90}$Th. Then draw a line across from this point of intersection to the y-axis. It lands at approximately 0.1 MeV, (**D**).

6. G

Category: Figure Interpretation

Difficulty: Medium

Strategic advice: There are lots of chances to make mistakes on questions that ask you to jump back and forth between diagrams, so pay extra attention.

Getting to the answer: You'll have to work backwards to answer this question. First, find out how many days old the sample of $\frac{N}{N_0}$ Th is. Then use the other graph to find $\frac{N}{N_0}$. Draw a line From 0.2 MeV on Figure 3 across to where it intersects the line corresponding

to $^{234}_{90}$Th. Be sure you don't confuse it with the line corresponding to $^{231}_{90}$Th. Your line should intersect the plot at about 20 days. Your sample is 20 days old. Now, go to Figure 2. Draw a vertical line up from 20 days to where it intersects the graph. Draw a horizontal line from this point to the y-axis. It falls between 0.5 and 0.6. (**G**) is a perfect match.

(F) is too low to be correct.

(H) and (J) are far too high.

PASSAGE IV

7. D

Category: Figure Interpretation

Difficulty: Low

Strategic advice: Take advantage of a table's neat organization and grab easy points like these.

Getting to the answer: Locate *Arthrospira fusiformis* on Table 1 and read across. In the presence of potassium silicate and at 30°C, its generation time is 103 minutes. The range presented in (**D**) encompasses this time. (A), (B), and (C) are too low to be correct

8. G

Category: Figure Interpretation

Difficulty: Medium

Strategic advice: You already scanned the figures in Step 2 of the Kaplan Method for ACT Science, so you should know where to go to find the answer.

Getting to the answer: Figure 1 plots algae density against generation time for *Dactylococcopsis salina,* so start there. Draw a line from 400 on the x-axis to the curve, and then draw a horizontal line to the y-axis. It intersects the axis at about 50 minutes, which matches (**G**).

(F) can't be correct because the generation time can't be less than 30 minutes.

(H) would be the generation time for a density of about 600 algae/cm².

(J) would be the generation time for a density of about 750 algae/cm².

9. A

Category: Figure Interpretation

Difficulty: Medium

Strategic advice: Time is of the essence on the ACT, so work quickly but accurately.

Getting to the answer: As you locate each algae on Table 1, jot its generation time down next to the answer choice. Then you won't have to remember which was the highest. *Merismopedia glauca*, (A), has the longest generation time at 751 minutes.

10. G

Category: Figure Interpretation

Difficulty: Medium

Strategic advice: Be careful when converting units on ACT Science questions.

Getting to the answer: Jot the generation times down next to each answer choice to eliminate any chance for error. *Katagnymene spiralis*, (**G**), is closest to 2 hours, at 131 minutes.

You can eliminate (F) and (H) because they were grown in NH_4NO_3, not Na_3PO_4.

11. C

Category: Figure Interpretation

Difficulty: High

Strategic advice: There are plenty of chances to make mistakes on questions that involve multiple figures, so work carefully.

Getting to the answer: Start with Table 1 and find the generation time of the algae—259 minutes. Now, move to Figure 1 and draw a line from 259 on the *y*-axis across until you intersect the graph. Draw a line down from that point to the *x*-axis. It lands at about 800 algae/cm². That is closest to (**C**).

PASSAGE VI

12. G

Category: Patterns

Difficulty: Medium

Strategic advice: Identify some key data that will have to be on the correct plot.

Getting to the answer: According to Figure 1, the solubility of Rase peaks at 135°C. Therefore, solubility on the correct graph should also peak at 135°C. Eliminate (H) and (J) because they show solubility peaking at 155°C and at less than 50°C, respectively. Figure 2 shows the solubility of Rase as it is cooled returning between 120°C and 100°C. Eliminate (F) because the solubility doesn't return as Rase cools in this graph. That leaves (**G**), which is the correct answer.

13. B

Category: Patterns

Difficulty: Medium

Strategic advice: When you extend a line on a graph beyond what is shown, make sure you follow the shape of the curve.

Getting to the answer: The question stem directs you to both figures, but you can find the answer on either one, so pick whichever you like best. (If they were to give different answers, the question would be impossible to answer!) Draw a line up from where 0°C would be and extend the line representing Case until it intersects that line. It looks like the intersection would happen at about 0.045 g/mL, or (**B**).

(A) can't be right because it is higher than the solubility at 20°C, and solubility clearly drops with decreasing temperature.

(C) is the solubility of Rase at 0°C.

(D) is the solubility of Hase at 0°C.

14. J

Category: Patterns

Difficulty: High

Strategic advice: This question is tricky because it requires you to combine information from Table 1 with information from Figure 1 but only directs your attention to Figure 1.

Getting to the answer: To find the answer, you must first ask yourself, "Where in respect to the denaturation range does solubility peak?" You're given three proteins and the ranges of their denaturation, and you can read their peak solubility in Figure 1. It appears that each protein solubility peaks just before the denaturation process begins, so you should expect that the solubility of ovalbumin peaks just before its denaturation begins, at 115°C, or (**J**).

(F) is incorrect because it is where the solubility of Hase peaks.

(G) and (H) are incorrect because they are too low.

PASSAGE VII

15. A

Category: Patterns

Difficulty: Medium

Strategic advice: When you're asked to find a formula, identify general trends and then Backsolve.

Getting to the answer: A quick glance at the answer choices tells you that you're either adding, subtracting, multiplying, or dividing S by T to get D. Look at the first row of Table 1. Since D is bigger than S or T, you're not dividing or subtracting, so cross off (G) and (H). It's easy to see that 30 + 28 = 58, so you're adding, (F).

16. H

Category: Patterns
Difficulty: Low

Strategic advice: The question stem tells you either Table 1 or Figure 1 can be used to answer this question, so pick whichever one appeals to you more.

Getting to the answer: Either continue the straight line that represents Method 2 to 75 mi/hr or use Table 1 to estimate D. The straight line from Figure 1, if extended, gives a D of about 225 ft, (H). Looking at Table 1, you can see that each 10 mi/hr increase in initial speed increases D by about 30 ft. So an initial speed of 75 mi/hr would have a D that's about 60 ft greater than the D at 55 mi/hr, or 222 ft.

(J) might be tempting if you were looking at Method 1 instead of Method 2.

17. B

Category: Patterns
Difficulty: Low

Strategic advice: Don't overthink simple questions! Grab the points and then move on.

Getting to the answer: According to Table 1, S for an initial speed of 25 mi/hr is 30 ft. S for an initial speed of 55 mi/hr is 65 ft. 30 is about half of 65, so (B) is correct. You know that 30 is less than 65, so you could always eliminate (C) and (D) (which would make 30 larger than 65) and then guess.

Quiz

Answer Key

1. B
2. G
3. D
4. J
5. D

1. B

Category: Patterns
Difficulty: Medium

Strategic advice: Make sure you don't get confused when a question asks you about an inverse relationship—that is, one variable increases while another decreases.

Getting to the answer: According to Table 1, decreasing the cross-sectional area of a given wire always increases resistance, so (B) is correct.

(A) is incorrect because Table 1 shows that resistance goes up with length, which is the opposite of the relationship you're looking for.

(C) is incorrect because resistivity is constant for each material and can't be increased or decreased. (D) is tricky, because gauge varies *inversely* with cross-sectional area, so it varies *directly* with resistance.

2. G

Category: Patterns
Difficulty: High

Strategic advice: When you're finding an equation to describe a relationship, figure out the placement of one variable at a time and eliminate as you go.

Getting to the answer: Since you just determined in the previous question that resistance goes up as area (A) goes down, cross off any answer choices that don't have A in the denominator. That's everything but (G), which is the correct answer.

3. D

Category: Patterns
Difficulty: High

Strategic advice: Questions that require many steps, like this one, are time-consuming and best saved for last.

Getting to the answer: Compare the choices two at a time. The wires in choices (A) and (B) are both made of aluminum and have the same cross-sectional area; only their lengths are different. Doubling the length doubles the resistance, so (B) will have a higher resistance than (A). Cross off (A). By similar reasoning, (D) will have a higher resistance than (C), so cross off (C). (B) and (D) differ in both cross-sectional area and material. You can approximate from Table 1 that (B) will have a resistance of about 230 (about halfway between the resistance for a 2-cm aluminum wire with a cross-sectional area of 5.26 and the same wire with a cross-sectional area of 1.31). (D) will have a resistance of about double that of the 2-cm tungsten wire with a cross-sectional area of 1.31, or about 1,700. That's higher than 230, the resistance of (B), so (D) is the correct answer.

4. J

Category: Figure Interpretation

Difficulty: Medium

Strategic advice: Since Statement I is so easy to read off Table 1 and it appears frequently in the answer choices, start there.

Getting to the answer: Check the diagram next to Table 1 to see whether a 10-gauge wire has a larger diameter than a 16-gauge wire. It does, so eliminate (G) and (H) because they don't contain Statement I. You don't have to check Statement II because it's not in any of the remaining answer choices.

To figure out whether Statement III is true, you'll have to check Table 1. It shows that the resistance of an iron (Fe) wire is much higher than that of an aluminum (Al) wire with the same length and cross-sectional area. How does that relate to conductivity? The first sentence of the passage defines the resistance of a conductor as "the extent to which it opposes *conductivity* (the flow of electricity)." Since iron has a higher resistance than aluminum, iron must not conduct electricity as well. Therefore, Statement III is true, and (J) is correct

5. D

Category: Patterns

Difficulty: Medium

Strategic advice: Use the third and fourth Figure questions before you predict an answer.

Getting to the answer: Table 1 shows that the resistivity of a material doesn't change when wire length changes. Therefore, the graph of resistivity versus length for a tungsten wire (or any other wire) is a horizontal line, (D).

Homework Answers and Explanations
Quarter 2

Answer Key

1. **A**
2. **K**
3. **B**
4. **J**
5. **C**
6. **J**
7. **E**
8. **F**
9. **D**
10. **G**
11. **A**
12. **H**

1. A

Category: Averages

Difficulty: Medium

Strategic advice: Write the Average rate formula, and then plug in the information from the question.

Getting to the answer: Average rate = total distance ÷ total time. Since you need to find Jay's average rate: 300 miles (total distance) ÷ 5 hours (total time) = 60 miles per hour. If Jay drove 10 miles per hour slower, he would be driving 50 miles per hour. Now apply the formula with Jay's new rate: 50 mph = 300 miles ÷ x hours. Solve for x. At the new rate, Jay's trip takes 6 hours, or 1 hour longer. Select answer choice (A).

2. K

Category: Percents

Difficulty: Low

Strategic advice: Remember: You can't simply add the percent changes. Go step-by-step.

Getting to the answer: 80 – (25%)80 = 60. 60 – (20%)60 = 48. Select answer choice (K).

3. B

Category: Averages

Difficulty: High

Strategic advice: Start by writing the relevant formulas and then fill in the pieces of information you have from the question stem. ACT questions will often ask you to work with the sum of the terms.

Getting to the answer: Write the Average formula: *average = sum of terms/number of terms*. The average age will be the sum of the male ages plus the sum of the female ages divided by the total number of employees. *Average age = sum of male ages + sum of female ages/number of employees*. To find this, you must find the sum of male ages and sum of female ages independently.

Because 42 = *sum of male ages/30*, *sum of male ages* is 1,260. Because 37 = *sum of female ages/20*, *sum of female ages* is 740. Thus, the average age of all employees = (1,260 + 740)/50 = 40. Select answer choice (**B**).

4. J

Category: Number Lines
Difficulty: Medium

Strategic advice: If the test maker doesn't give you a diagram, make a sketch! Don't forget Step 4: Am I finished?

Getting to the answer: If your variable is changing geometrically, start with the smallest;

$DE = x$; $CD = 2x$; $BC = 4x$; $AB = 8x$; $15x = 45$; $x = 3$. What is the question? $BD = 6x = 18$. Answer choice (**J**).

5. C

Category: Percents
Difficulty: Medium

Strategic advice: Because all of the answer choices are whole numbers, this is a good candidate for Backsolving. Remember to start with (**C**).

Getting to the answer: You know what percent of students were in favor of uniforms (40%), but not what that number actually is. To find it, note that the 40 undecided students must be 25%, since 75% already voted. 40 is 25% of 160. 40% (in favor) of 160 is 64.

6. J

Category: Ratios
Difficulty: Medium

Strategic advice: Backsolving works well when you see integers in your answer choices.

Getting to the answer: Start with answer choice (**H**). If Mariah rode 28 miles in 2 hours, her rate was 14 miles per hour. If they were 54 miles apart after

two hours, that means Franklin rode 54 − 28 miles, or 26 miles in two hours, for a rate of 13 miles per hour. 13 mph is not 3 mph less than 14, so Mariah must have ridden further than 28 miles. Eliminate (F), (G), and (H). Try (J) next. If Mariah went 30 miles in 2 hours, her rate was 15 mph. Franklin, then, must have ridden 24 miles in 2 hours at a rate of 12 mph. Mariah's rate is 3 mph more than Franklin's, so (**J**) is our answer.

7. E

Category: Number Lines
Difficulty: Medium

Strategic advice: If the test maker doesn't give you a diagram, make a sketch!

Getting to the answer: The sketch of the number line places Z between X and Y, thus the distance between Y and Z must be less than the distance between X and Y. Choose (**E**).

8. F

Category: Absolute Value
Difficulty: Medium

Strategic advice: In an Absolute Value problem, remember to solve the positive and negative result.

Getting to the answer:

$x^2 - 8 =$ either 4 or −4. If it's the positive, $x^2 = 12$, or $x = 2\sqrt{3}$. That doesn't appear as an answer, so solve for $x^2 - 8 = -4$. $x^2 = 4$, or $x = 2$. Answer choice (**F**) is correct.

9. D

Category: Ratios
Difficulty: Low

Strategic advice: Always ask yourself whether this is a part-to-part ratio or a part-to-whole ratio?

Getting to the answer: This question provides us with a part-to-whole ratio: 10 oz chocolate chips for 24 cookies. Set up a proportion: $\frac{10}{24} = \frac{x}{96}$.
Cross multiply: $24x = 960$. $x = 40$, or (**D**).

10. G

Category: Percents
Difficulty: Low

Strategic advice: The English word "of" translates to the Math word "times."

Getting to the answer: $n(125\%) = 470$; $n = 376$. $376(50\%) = 188$. Answer (**G**) is correct.

11. A

Category: Absolute Value

Difficulty: High

Strategic advice: When solving an absolute value inequality, put the positive and negative values of the inequality on both sides of the absolute value expression and solve.

Getting to the answer: When we clear the brackets, $-10 \le t - 94 \le 10$; $84 \le t \le 104$. Only 82 falls outside of the range. Be careful of answer choice (E). Because the range is inclusive, 104 is part of the solution set. Choose (**A**).

12. H

Category: Averages

Difficulty: Medium

Strategic advice: More difficult questions require that you work step-by-step. Make sure you know what the question is asking.

Getting to the answer: Avg. cans per day $= \dfrac{\text{sum of cans}}{\text{number of days}}$; $10 = \dfrac{\text{sum of cans so far}}{4 \text{ days}}$. So, Mary has collected 40 cans so far, and she needs 160 more cans. She has 10 days left to collect them: Avg. cans per day $= \dfrac{160 \text{ cans}}{10 \text{ days}} = 16$ cans per day. Select answer choice (**H**).

Quarter 3

Answer Key

1. **C**
2. **J**
3. **B**
4. **F**
5. **C**
6. **H**
7. **C**
8. **G**
9. **A**
10. **K**
11. **E**
12. **G**

13. **C**
14. **J**
15. **E**

1. C

Category: Operations

Difficulty: Medium

Strategic advice: Work carefully on problems that contain many steps.

Getting to the answer:
$$\frac{(3.0 \times 10^4)(8.0 \times 10^9)}{1.2 \times 10^6} = \frac{3 \times 8}{1.2} \times \frac{10^4 \times 10^9}{10^6}$$
$$= \frac{24}{1.2} \times 10^{4+9-6} = 20 \times 10^7 = 2.0 \times 10^8$$

2. J

Category: Operations

Difficulty: Medium

Strategic advice: Sometimes it's easier to rewrite fractional and negative exponents.

Getting to the answer: Remember that a negative exponent means "1 over," and the denominator of a fractional exponent is the root. $9^{-\frac{3}{2}} = \dfrac{1}{(\sqrt[2]{9})^3} = \dfrac{1}{3^3} = \dfrac{1}{27}$.

3. B

Category: Operations

Difficulty: Medium

Strategic advice: Sometimes you need to work through part of a problem before you can simplify it.

Getting to the answer:
$(\sqrt{8} + \sqrt{6})(\sqrt{8} - \sqrt{6})$
$= 8 - \sqrt{8 \cdot 6} + \sqrt{8 \cdot 6} - 6$
$= 8 - 6 = 2$

4. F

Category: Operations

Difficulty: Low

Strategic advice: While raising a fraction to a power gives you a smaller fraction, taking the root of a fraction gives you a bigger fraction.

Getting to the answer:
$$\sqrt{0.0016} = \sqrt{\frac{16}{10,000}} = \frac{4}{100} = 0.04$$

Just by knowing that the answer must be bigger than 0.0016, you could have eliminated choices (J) and (K).

5. C

Category: Proportions and Probability

Difficulty: Medium

Strategic advice: Keep an eye on the units. Many questions will require you to convert minutes into hours, or vice versa.

Getting to the answer: Set up a proportion: $\frac{12 \text{ pages}}{60 \text{ mins}} = \frac{100 \text{ pages}}{x \text{ mins}}$. $12x = 6000$, so $x = 500$ mins, which is 8 hours and 20 minutes.

6. H

Category: Proportions and Probability

Difficulty: Medium

Strategic advice: Probability is $\frac{\# \text{ of desired outcomes}}{\# \text{ of possible outcomes}}$.

Getting to the answer: Jamal wants the probability of selecting a white sock to be $\frac{1}{5}$. Since there are already 10 white socks, the ratio of desired outcomes (white socks) to possible outcomes (all socks) must be $\frac{1}{5}$ $= \frac{10}{50}$. To get to 50 total socks, Jamal will need to add 40 black socks, or (**H**). (K) is a trap. The question asks for the number of black socks Jamal needs to add, not the total number of socks that should be in the suitcase.

7. C

Category: Patterns, Logic & Data

Difficulty: Medium

Strategic advice: Not every question about geometric sequences requires the formula.

Getting to the answer: A geometric sequence is simply a sequence in which each term except the first is equal to the previous term times some constant. Since the ratio between the second and first term is $\frac{12}{3} = 4$, each term is the previous term times 4, and $r = 12 \div 4 = 48$. You can check your answer by seeing whether it gives the correct fourth term: $48 \times 4 = 192$. Yes, this works.

8. G

Category: Trigonometry

Difficulty: Medium

Strategic advice: Remembering SOHCAHTOA alone can get you through a lot of Trigonometry questions.

Getting to the answer: The problem is essentially asking for the length of $\overline{BC}$. The only length you

are given is that of the hypotenuse of the triangle, so eliminate (J) and (K) as tan does not use it. $\overline{BC}$ is opposite $\angle D$, the 37° angle, and adjacent to $\angle B$, the $90 - 37 = 53°$ angle, so you're looking for either sin 37° or cos 53° in the choices. The former is (**G**).

9. A

Category: Trigonometry

Difficulty: Medium

Strategic advice: The Pythagorean theorem is often helpful in trigonometry questions.

Getting to the answer: Since sine $= \frac{\text{opposite}}{\text{hypotenuse}}$, cosecant $= \frac{\text{hypotenuse}}{\text{opposite}}$. Sketch a right triangle and fill in the sides provided by $\sin\theta = \frac{\sqrt{11}}{2\sqrt{3}}$:

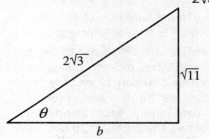

The length side of side b can be found by the Pythagorean theorem:

$(\sqrt{11})^2 + b^2 = (2\sqrt{3})^2$

$11 + b^2 = (4 \times 3)$

$b^2 = 12 - 11 = 1$

$b = 1$

So if $b = 1$, $\cos\theta = \frac{1}{2\sqrt{3}}$, (**A**)

10. K

Category: Trigonometry

Difficulty: Medium

Strategic advice: Don't try to do problems like this in your head. Set up an equation that relates the thing you're looking for to the things you know and then solve for the thing you're looking for.

Getting to the answer: You know the angle of elevation and the distance from the base of the flagpole, and you're looking for the height of the flagpole. That means you know one angle, the side adjacent to it, and the side opposite it. Which trig function describes the relationship between an angle and the opposite and adjacent sides? Tangent does.

Tan 40° $= \frac{f}{100}$, where f is the height of the flagpole. Therefore, $100 \tan 40° = f$. The question tells you that tan 40° is approximately 0.839, so f is approximately 100(0.839) = 83.9. The best approximation of this is (**K**).

11. E

Category: Operations
Difficulty: Medium
Strategic advice: A square outside of parentheses means to square every term inside the parentheses.
Getting to the answer: $(5\sqrt{3})^2 = 5^2(\sqrt{3})^2 = 25 \cdot 3 = 75$

12. G

Category: Patterns, Logic & Data
Difficulty: High
Strategic advice: If you're not sure how to find the missing terms, Backsolving is a great alternative.
Getting to the answer: The total difference between 12 and 32 is 32 − 12 = 20. This difference is spread over 4 parts: the difference between 12 and the first blank, the difference between the first and second blanks, the difference between the second and third blanks, and the difference between the third blank and 32. Therefore, each part has a difference of $\frac{20}{4} = 5$. So 12 + 5 = 17, 17 + 5 = 22, 22 + 5 = 27, and 27 + 5 = 32, and the missing numbers are 17, 22, and 27.

13. C

Category: Patterns, Logic & Data
Difficulty: Medium
Strategic advice: Consider the situation carefully; just because all cats in Cooperville are gray does not mean all gray cats are in Cooperville.
Getting to the answer: Since all cats in Cooperville are gray, Cat B must be gray (since it is in Cooperville). (D) and (E) are definitely false. Neither (A) nor (B) has to be true—a gray cat could be in Cooperville, or it could be somewhere else.

14. J

Category: Trigonometry
Difficulty: High
Strategic advice: All you need to remember for the ACT is SOHCAHTOA. Other necessary formulas will be given in the question.

Getting to the answer: The question tells you that sin $(a + b)$ = sin a cos b + sin b cos a for all values of a and b, and the question asks for sin $(x + y)$. All you need to do is plug the appropriate values into the equation sin x cos y + sin y cos x, and simplify. Remember, sin $= \dfrac{\text{opposite}}{\text{hypotenuse}}$ and cos $= \dfrac{\text{adjacent}}{\text{hypotenuse}}$. Work carefully; it's easy to get the wrong side of a triangle.

sin x cos y + sin y cos x

$= \dfrac{4}{5} \cdot \dfrac{5}{13} + \dfrac{12}{13} \cdot \dfrac{3}{5}$

$= \dfrac{20}{65} + \dfrac{36}{65}$

$= \dfrac{56}{65}$

15. E

Category: Trigonometry
Difficulty: Medium
Strategic advice: Cosecant is $\dfrac{20}{4} = 5$.

Getting to the answer: Since sine $= \dfrac{\text{opposite}}{\text{hypotenuse}}$, cosecant $= \dfrac{\text{hypotenuse}}{\text{opposite}}$. The hypotenuse of this triangle is r, and the side opposite $\angle Q$ is q. Therefore, the cosecant of Q is $\dfrac{r}{q}$.

Quarter 4

Answer Key

1. **B**
2. **J**
3. **B**
4. **F**
5. **C**
6. **G**
7. **D**
8. **H**
9. **D**
10. **G**
11. **D**
12. **G**
13. **A**
14. **J**
15. **A**
16. **J**
17. **D**

18. **G**
19. **B**
20. **H**
21. **D**
22. **H**
23. **A**
24. **G**
25. **B**
26. **H**
27. **A**

PASSAGE I

1. **B**

Category: Figure Interpretation
Difficulty: Medium
Strategic advice: When dealing with Roman numeral questions, start by examining the statements that appear most frequently in the answer choices.

Getting to the answer: Statement II is clearly true; there are arrows labeled respiration going from the green plants and carbohydrates, the animals, and the other animals or animal parasites stages back to the carbon dioxide stage. Eliminate (A). Statement I is false because the diagram shows that the carbon in animals can move to other animals through the process of "animal digestion." An animal that only eats other animals is participating in the carbon cycle when it digests its prey, so eliminate (C). Statement III is not true because some carbon dioxide is released into the air by fermentation and putrefaction. Since only Statement II is true, (**B**) is correct.

2. **J**

Category: Figure Interpretation
Difficulty: Medium
Strategic advice: When there are multiple possible correct answers to a question, it's best to go straight to the answer choices.

Getting to the answer: According to the diagram, there are four direct sources of atmospheric carbon dioxide: fermentation by decay bacteria, respiration by green plants, respiration by animals, and respiration by other animals or animal parasites. (**J**) correctly cites the respiration of animal parasites.

(F) is incorrect because green-plant carbohydrates do not undergo fermentation directly.

(G) is incorrect because, according to the diagram, plant photosynthesis *removes* CO_2 from the atmosphere. (H) is incorrect because, as in (F), the digestion of plant matter by animals is an indirect source of carbon dioxide in the atmosphere. It fuels animal respiration, which in turn returns carbon dioxide to the atmosphere.

3. **B**

Category: Figure Interpretation
Difficulty: Medium
Strategic advice: Remember that the answer to a Figure Interpretation question is in the diagram.

Getting to the answer: The arrow signifying animal respiration and the arrow signifying photosynthesis are linked in the diagram by the "CO_2 in air or dissolved in water" box. Animal respiration is one of the sources of carbon for carbon dioxide, and the carbon dioxide in turn provides carbon for the process of photosynthesis. Therefore, (**B**), "Animal respiration provides vital gases for green plants," best describes this relationship.

(A) is incorrect because respiration functions to put carbon dioxide into the air, and photosynthesis removes it from the air.

(C) is incorrect because animal respiration contributes carbon dioxide for photosynthesis and therefore helps, rather than inhibits, photosynthesis.

(D) is contradicted by the diagram; animal respiration and photosynthesis are linked by the carbon dioxide in the air.

4. **F**

Category: Figure Interpretation
Difficulty: Medium
Strategic advice: Make sure you understand all of the ways that the different elements in a diagram relate to each other before you predict what will happen when one is reduced or eliminated.

Getting to the answer: According to the diagram, the only way that carbon dioxide can enter the carbon cycle is through photosynthesis, in which it is taken up by green plants. Therefore, if green plants were eliminated, the carbon cycle would probably come to a complete stop (**F**) is correct.

(G) is incorrect because animals are not the only source of carbon dioxide. Green plants emit it through respiration, decay bacteria through fermentation and putrefaction, and animal parasites though respiration. (H) is incorrect because animal digestion is one of many sources of carbon dioxide in the air. Without animal digestion, the carbon cycle would still continue because other processes add carbon dioxide to the air.

(J) is incorrect for the same reasons. Decay bacteria are one of many sources for atmospheric carbon dioxide.

5. C

Category: Scientific Reasoning

Difficulty: Medium

Strategic advice: Use only what the figures and supporting paragraphs tell you to answer Scientific Reasoning questions.

Getting to the answer: Decay bacteria, according to the diagram, get carbon from the carbon compounds of dead plants and animals and add to the supply of carbon dioxide in air and water through fermentation and putrefaction. Since there is no other way to get carbon from dead plants and animals back to carbon dioxide, you know that a drop in decay bacteria will reduce the amount of carbon available for forming carbon dioxide. The carbon dioxide level will not be greatly affected, though, because there are other sources of carbon for carbon dioxide.

(A) is incorrect because decay bacteria are not the sole source of carbon dioxide.

(B) is incorrect because the bacteria emit carbon dioxide; they don't consume it.

(D) is incorrect because decay bacteria emit carbon dioxide. If they were eliminated from the cycle, it is unlikely that the amount of carbon dioxide would increase. Additionally, there is no evidence that the cycle would become unbalanced.

PASSAGE II

6. G

Category: Figure Interpretation

Difficulty: Low

Strategic advice: Don't get confused when you're bouncing back and forth between two figures.

Getting to the answer: To find the answer to this question, you have to look at Tables 1 and 2. Table 1 shows the conductivity when 10.0 g of each solute is dissolved in 100 mL of water, and Table 2 shows the conductivity when the amount of solute is tripled. Check each answer choice individually, and remember

that you're looking for the solute that *doesn't* increase in conductivity as its concentration increases.

(F) NaCl conducts 5.4 volts at 10.0 g and 10.6 volts at 30.0 g. That's an increase, so it's not the answer you're looking for.

(**G**) $C_{12}H_{22}O_{11}$ conducts 0.0 volts at both 10.0 g and 30.0 g. It shows no increase in conductivity as its concentration increases, so this is the exception you're looking for.

(H) $HC_2H_3O_2$ conducts 1.9 volts at 10.0 g and 3.0 volts at 30.0 g, so this choice is incorrect.

(J) The conductivity of $MgCl_2$ also increases, from 1.6 to 2.6 volts, as its concentration increases, so this choice is also incorrect.

7. D

Category: Figure Interpretation

Difficulty: Medium

Strategic advice: Remember to research your answers in the passage.

Getting to the answer: You know that the conductivity of $MgCl_2$ solutions goes up as temperature and $MgCl_2$ concentration go up, so you should look for the answer choice with the highest temperature and the greatest amount of $MgCl_2$.

(A) You know from Table 1 that 10 g of $MgCl_2$ in 100 mL of 35°C water will conduct 1.6 volts.

(B) 20 g is halfway between 10 and 30 g, so you can estimate that 20 g of $MgCl_2$ in 100 mL of 35°C water will conduct about 2.1 volts.

(C) Putting 20 g of $MgCl_2$ in 200 mL of 35°C water gives the same concentration as putting 10 g in 100 mL. This will give you 1.6 volts again.

(**D**) You know from Table 3 that 30 g of $MgCl_2$ in 100 mL of 70°C water will conduct 4.0 volts. This, then, is the largest amount of electricity and the correct answer.

8. H

Category: Figure Interpretation

Difficulty: Medium

Strategic advice: Never assume anything on the ACT Science Test. All of the answers can be found in the passage.

Getting to the answer: The 70°C in the question stem should tell you that you need to look at Table 3. The conductivity of 30 g of $C_{12}H_{22}O_{11}$ at 70°C was 0.0 volts, so you know that will contribute nothing to the new solution's conductivity. The conductivity of

30 g of $HC_2H_3O_2$ at 70°C was 4.9 volts. The conductivity of a mix of the two will simply be the conductivity of $HC_2H_3O_2$, or (**H**).

(F) lists the conductivity of $C_{12}H_{22}O_{11}$, so that's incorrect.

(G) would be tempting if you tried to average the conductivity of $C_{12}H_{22}O_{11}$ and $HC_2H_3O_2$, but you're given no instruction to do that, so it is incorrect.

(J) is incorrect because it is much larger than what could be expected.

9. D

Category: Figure Interpretation

Difficulty: High

Strategic advice: Some Figure Interpretation questions will ask you to "read between the lines" of a figure.

Getting to the answer: You're not given any data for conductivity at 50°C, but you *are* given the conductivity of each of the solutes at 35°C in Table 2 and at 70°C in Table 3. 50°C is just about halfway between these two temperatures, so you can make a good estimate of conductivity at this temperature. Go back to Tables 2 and 3. You can see that for every solute except NaCl, conductivity increases as temperature increases. (**D**) matches this.

(A) is the exact opposite of what happens, so it is incorrect.

(B) is incorrect for all of the electrolyte solutions, but it could be tempting if you confused electrolytes with nonelectrolytes.

(C) is incorrect because it doesn't take into account that NaCl doesn't behave like the other electrolytes in this situation.

10. G

Category: Scientific Reasoning

Difficulty: High

Strategic advice: Try to predict an answer to Scientific Method questions. If you can't, however, don't waste time. Move directly to the answer choices.

Getting to the answer: What do you know about the role of water in this passage? Check the passage text to find out. Water was the solvent in each experiment. Measuring the conductivity of water by itself shows how much of the conductivity can be attributed to water, so (**G**) is correct.

(F) is incorrect because the passage states that water is the solvent in each experiment.

(H) is incorrect because the ability of water to dissolve the salts was never mentioned in the passage.

(J) is incorrect because water does not conduct electricity at all.

11. D

Category: Scientific Reasoning

Difficulty: Medium

Strategic advice: Identifying the scientific method when you finish reading a passage will help on Scientific Method questions.

Getting to the answer: It's difficult to predict an answer to this question, so go straight to the answer choices.

(A) Experiment 3 already tested the effect of temperature change on conductivity.

(B) To change solute color, you'd have to chemically change the solutes. Then you'd be studying a new solute, not its color.

(C) The effect of water on conductivity was already tested in all three experiments.

(**D**) Replacing water with different solvents would tell you more about conductivity. This is the correct answer.

PASSAGE III

12. G

Category: Scientific Reasoning

Difficulty: Low

Strategic advice: When you're asked to contrast two studies, focus on one at a time to avoid confusion.

Getting to the answer: Study 1 compared the physical characteristics of monarch milkweed plants with non-monarch milkweed plants, so eliminate answer choices that don't accurately describe the study.

(F) In Study 1, physical characteristics of monarch plants were studied, not monarch caterpillars. Cross this off.

(**G**) Milkweed plants were examined, so keep this for now.

(H) You weren't told whether or not monarch caterpillars were removed from the plants in Study 1, so cross off this answer choice.

(J) Cross this off too—monarch milkweeds, not monarch caterpillars, were examined in Study 1. The correct answer, then, must be (G). Of course, if you had more than one answer choice remaining, you'd have to go back and check Study 3.

13. A

Category: Figure Interpretation
Difficulty: High

Strategic advice: Many times, you'll be able to find the answer to a difficult Science question by eliminating answer choices that contradict the passage.

Getting to the answer: This question could be very confusing if you overthink it and very simple if you don't. You're not given any information that relates the properties of the non-monarch milkweed plants to predators, but the ACT won't give you a question you can't answer. As always, when you're stumped, go straight to the answer choices.

(A) According to Table 1, non-monarch plants have a high pH. So this is a possibility.

(B) Table 1 says non-monarch plants have a low concentration of plant proteins, so (B) cannot be the correct answer.

(C) Table 1 says non-monarch plants don't have blossoms, so they can't possibly protect the plants from being eaten.

(D) Nothing in Table 1, or the entire passage for that matter, mentions thorns. This can't be the correct answer. The correct answer, then, must be (**A**).

14. J

Category: Figure Interpretation
Difficulty: Medium

Strategic advice: When a question requires you to jump back and forth between figures, work carefully and make notes to keep the information organized.

Getting to the answer: First make sure you know which kinds of plants were in Group 2. The first paragraph in Study 3 says that monarch milkweeds were in Groups 1 and 2 and that the caterpillars on the plants in Group 2 remained untouched. Table 1 tells you that 20–30 monarch caterpillars live on each monarch milkweed plant. so the correct answer must be (**J**). (F) states the number of caterpillars typically found on non-monarch milkweeds and is a tempting wrong answer for those who move too quickly.

15. A

Category: Figure Interpretation
Difficulty: Medium

Strategic advice: Zero in on where you'll find your answers. Don't get distracted by all of the extraneous information in the passage!

Getting to the answer: Characteristics of non-monarch milkweed plants are represented in Table 1, so you should start there. Since any number of combinations of characteristics is possible, you'll have to go straight to the answer choices on this one.

(A) Thin leaves, no blossoms, and growing in direct sunlight are all characteristics of non-monarch milkweeds. Keep this choice.

(B) Low pH is a characteristic of monarch milkweeds, so this cannot be the correct choice.

(C) Fragrant blossoms, partial sun, and low pH are characteristic of monarch milkweeds, so this also cannot be correct.

(D) Thick leaves are characteristic of monarch milkweeds, so this must also be incorrect. Only (**A**) remains and is the correct answer.

16. J

Category: Figure Interpretation
Difficulty: High

Strategic advice: When a Figure Interpretation question doesn't tell you exactly where to go to find the answer, find the places where key words from the question stem appear in the figures.

Getting to the answer: Where can you find information about plant proteins and nectar? They're mentioned in Tables 1 and 2. Table 1 tells you that monarch plants produce high levels of plant proteins and that their blossoms produce nectar. Table 2 tells you that monarch caterpillars feed on plant-based proteins and nectar. Therefore, you can predict that the correct answer will contain this information. (**J**) does just that.

(F) is incorrect because you're not given any information that relates plant proteins to grazing animals.

(G) is incorrect because you're not given any information that relates nectar to grazing animals.

(H) is incorrect for the same reasons that (F) and (G) are incorrect.

PASSAGE IV

17. D

Category: Patterns
Difficulty: Medium

Strategic advice: A common type of Patterns question will ask you to extend trends in the data beyond what is shown.

Getting to the answer: Start with Figure 3. What are the patterns in that data? Regardless of the surface, oscillation time increases as m increases. Or, read the other way, oscillation time decreases as m decreases. So when you decrease m to less than 100 on Earth, you'll get an oscillation time of less than 1 sec. Only (**D**) offers this.

(A) might be the oscillation time for a spring on Jupiter, and (B) and (C) are too high to be correct.

18. G

Category: Patterns

Difficulty: Medium

Strategic advice: Use your pencil to continue the lines off the plots when required.

Getting to the answer: This question directs you to Figure 4. What are the patterns in that data? For each planetary surface, oscillation time increases as L increases. When you increase L beyond what is shown on the table, keep the rate of increase the same as what's shown. Extend the line for Earth until you hit 3 sec. That will make an L greater than 250. (H) and (J) are less than 250, so cross them off. L on Earth at 1 sec. is 125 cm, and L at 2 sec. is almost 250 cm. You can approximate that L at 3 sec. will be about 375 cm. Only (**G**) comes close.

19. B

Category: Patterns

Difficulty: Medium

Strategic advice: Just like Figure Interpretation questions, some Patterns questions will require you to combine information from multiple figures.

Getting to the answer: The only thing that makes this question tricky is identifying gravitational acceleration in the figures. To find it, you have to combine the planet information from the graphs with the table that lists the actual gravitational acceleration from each planet.

For any given m in Figure 3 or L in Figure 4, oscillation time is highest for Jupiter, in the middle for Earth, and lowest for Titan. According to Table 1, Jupiter has the highest gravitational acceleration at 24.9 m/sec^2, followed by Earth at 9.8 m/sec^2, followed by Titan, at 1.1 m/sec^2. As gravitational acceleration increases, oscillation time increases, (**B**).

If oscillation time stayed the same as gravitation acceleration increased, as (C) says, then the lines for Jupiter, Earth, and Titan would lie on top of each other, which is obviously not the case.

(A) can't be right, because then oscillation time for Titan would be the highest, followed by Earth, with Jupiter at the bottom.

20. H

Category: Patterns

Difficulty: Medium

Strategic advice: Approach Patterns questions methodically and you'll eliminate careless mistakes.

Getting to the answer: According to Figure 3, a spring will have an oscillation time of 2.25 sec on Jupiter's surface when an m of 100 g is attached. What m would give the same spring on Earth an oscillation time of 2.25 sec? Figure 3 only shows oscillation times up to just under 2.0 sec on Earth, so you'll have to continue the line on your own. Extend the line that corresponds to 2.25 sec to the right and then sketch the Earth line until it intersects 2.25 sec. It looks like the intersection would happen close to an m of 1,500 g. That's approximately 15 times the m for Jupiter, or (**H**).

50 times greater than the m for Jupiter, (F), and 50 times less, (G), are far too high and too low to be correct. You might accidentally pick (J), 15 times less than the m for Jupiter, if you were hurrying.

21. D

Category: Patterns

Difficulty: Low

Strategic advice: When questions introduce a totally new element, like this one does, make sure you understand how and where it fits into the existing data before you attempt to answer the question.

Getting to the answer: If the gravitational acceleration on Mercury is 3.7 m/sec^2, then it is greater than Titan's and less than Earth's. Therefore, all of Mercury's oscillation times would be more than Titan's but less than Earth's. This matches (**D**), so stop there.

PASSAGE V

22. H

Category: Scientific Reasoning

Difficulty: Low

Strategic advice: If you can predict more than one right answer, go straight to the answer choices.

Getting to the answer:

(F) is incorrect because samples were taken daily in both experiments.

(G) is incorrect because both phosphates and nitrates were measured in both experiments.

(**H**) is correct. Experiment 1 sampled groundwater, while Experiment 2 sampled stream water.

(J) is incorrect since neither experiment measured algae or bacteria concentrations.

23. A

Category: Patterns

Difficulty: Low

Strategic advice: Use Step 2 of the Kaplan Method to focus only on the relevant data.

Getting to the answer: You're looking only at phosphate and suspended sediment concentrations in Stream 1. On June 1, phosphate concentration is 7.1 and sediment is 33.5. For June 2, phosphates are higher and so are sediments. Both peak on June 4 and go back down on June 5. Every day that shows an increase in phosphate concentration also shows an increase in sediment concentration, so (**A**) is correct.

24. G

Category: Figure Interpretation

Difficulty: Low

Strategic advice: Take advantage of easy points like these!

Getting to the answer: Make sure you're looking at the column labeled "Nitrate concentration," then just read down for the highest concentration in Dormitory 2. That happened on June 2, when the concentration was 26.4 mg/L, or (**G**).

25. B

Category: Scientific Reasoning

Difficulty: Low

Strategic advice: Some questions will just require you to go back to the introductory material.

Getting to the answer: In Experiment 2, the scientists "suspected that runoff water carrying fertilizers was another source of the nutrients." Which answer choice restates this hypothesis? Only (**B**) does.

26. H

Category: Patterns

Difficulty: Medium

Strategic advice: Double-check the direction of desired changes. Here, you're looking for something that will *decrease* the amount of nitrogen and phosphorous in the pond.

Getting to the answer: Since phosphates and nitrates are getting into the pond via wastewater from the dormitories and runoff from the farms, reducing either of these sources would work. (**H**) should reduce the amount of nitrates and phosphorous.

(F) and (G) would probably *increase* the amount of nutrients flowing into the pond.

(J) is not supported by the passage. Neither experiment involved removing plants from the pond, so whether this would have any effect on the amount of nitrogen or phosphorous is unknown.

27. A

Category: Patterns

Difficulty: Medium

Strategic advice: Take note of patterns described in the question stem.

Getting to the answer: You're told that phosphates are more likely to be removed from the water as they get farther from their source. Therefore, there will most likely be fewer phosphates in a sample from farther away than there were in the original sample. The original Dormitory 1, June 2 phosphate concentration was 6.6 mg/L. Which of the answer choices is less than this? Only (**A**) is.

ANSWERS AND EXPLANATIONS

Preview Quiz

Answer Key

1. **B**
2. **H**
3. **A**
4. **G**
5. **D**

1. B

Category: Verb Tenses

Difficulty: Low

Strategic Advice: Use dates as context clues to determine what verb tense to use.

Getting to the Answer: The passage begins in the past—in 1940—so the appropriate verb will be in the past tense. (**B**) corrects the error.

2. H

Category: Connections

Difficulty: Medium

Strategic Advice: When looking at a connection between two sentences, first determine how the sentences are related.

Getting to the Answer: The sentence preceding the connection states that the bridge "enjoyed a relatively short life." The sentence that starts with "Also" says that the bridge "taught important lessons." These are contrasting ideas, so you need a contrast word to join them. "But" in (**H**) accomplishes this.

3. A

Category: Word Choice

Difficulty: High

Strategic Advice: When a preposition is underlined, determine if it's the correct preposition to use.

Getting to the Answer: The sentence is correct as written because the state officials are physically in Washington.

"From" in (B) implies that while the state officials originated in Washington, they are now somewhere else. (C) "Between" implies that two items or places are being compared. (D) "Among" implies that more than two locations or items are involved.

4. G

Category: Wordiness

Difficulty: Medium

Strategic Advice: Don't use more words than are necessary to get a point across.

Getting to the Answer: Because the sentence earlier states that state officials "saw a need for a bridge across Puget Sound," you don't need to include "of the Sound" after "on the other side." We already know that the "other side" is of the Sound. (**G**) correctly omits "of the Sound."

5. D

Category: Organization

Difficulty: Low

Strategic Advice: Start with the most appropriate choice for the topic sentence and work your way through the paragraph.

Getting to the Answer: Sentence [3] is the most general and is therefore the topic sentence. Knowing Sentence [3] comes first is sufficient to mark (**D**) as the correct answer. Sentence [1] describes at which point across Puget Sound the bridge was built and is therefore second. Sentence [2] must then come after Sentence [4], because the latter describes the construction and the former describes the result of that construction.

Quarter 2

Answer Key

1. **B**
2. **H**
3. **D**
4. **G**
5. **A**
6. **H**
7. **C**
8. **J**
9. **B**
10. **J**
11. **D**
12. **J**
13. **B**
14. **H**

PASSAGE I

1. B

Category: Inference
Difficulty: Medium
Strategic Advice: When you don't receive a line reference, rely on your notes to avoid too much rereading of the passage.
Getting to the Answer: The author refers only briefly to Emil, but the key statements are Alexandra's—that Emil "is so different from the rest of us" (lines 26–27) and that she "would rather have Emil grow up" in the city "than like his brothers." Predict something like *have a life different from hers.*
(A) Opposite; the passage suggests that she wants something different for him.
(**B**) Correct. This matches the thrust of the prediction.
(C) Distortion; Alexandra says she would rather he be like Carl.
(D) Out of Scope; she wants Emil to be like Carl, not to live with him.

2. H

Category: Inference
Difficulty: Medium
Strategic Advice: Remember that the correct inference will be a small step removed from what is said in the passage.
Getting to the Answer: In the first paragraph, Alexandra ponders the lack of change in Carl—that he had not become "self-satisfied." "Self-satisfied" is not a desirable characteristic, so she must be relatively happy about that. Look for a match to that sentiment.
(F) Distortion; nothing in the paragraph suggests that she is "charmed."
(G) Out of Scope; Alexandra does not appear "perplexed," and the author makes no allusion to Carl's reason for returning.
(**H**) This matches the tone and content of the prediction.
(J) Out of Scope; if anything, her mental picture of him suggests a certain sympathy.

3. D

Category: Inference
Difficulty: Medium
Strategic Advice: A prediction of even a single word can capture the tone (positive, negative) of the correct choice.

Getting to the Answer: Based on the cited lines, you can make a prediction even as simple as *a failure* or *depressed* and still be on the right track.
(A) Distortion; "lucky" is too positive.
(B) Distortion; "fortunate" is too positive.
(C) Distortion; the tone is right, but Carl is dissatisfied with his life in New York, not with life in Nebraska.
(**D**) Correct. This matches Carl's tone in the passage; it also captures the gist of what he says.

4. G

Category: Writer's View
Difficulty: High
Strategic Advice: When the question encompasses a large section of the passage, your notes are even more critical; turn there first.
Getting to the Answer: The cited conversation takes up most of the passage, so you're better off working from your notes. Note that Alexandra's thoughts are the first things the author mentions and that Alexandra speaks last (and more) in this excerpt. These facts, and the content of those closing comments, should lead you to the correct answer.
(F) Distortion; Carl is certainly unhappy, but the author never indicates that he longs for "the simple life" as a solution.
(**G**) Correct. This matches well with the gist of the closing paragraph.
(H) Out of Scope; the author makes only brief allusion to Lou's and Oscar's opinions of Alexandra, and nothing in the passage indicates that the author sympathizes with that assessment.
(J) Distortion; the second sentence suggests that Alexandra feels some "disdain for the 'city man,'" but the author doesn't emphasize this point.

5. A

Category: Writer's View
Difficulty: High
Strategic Advice: With unusual questions, a quick review of your notes will prepare you well, even if a prediction is difficult to make.
Getting to the Answer: Focus first on "the author's characterization" of Alexandra—that she's *determined, hard-working,* and *wants the best for Emil.* Then skim the quotes to see which one best embodies those sentiments.

(A) Correct; this appropriately captures her determination and her concern for her brother's welfare.

(B) Misused Detail; for this to be right, the author would have had to have painted Alexandra as more critical of Carl.

(C) Extreme; while this might represent her determination, it also suggests that Alexandra is stubborn, and does not address her concern for Emil.

(D) Misused Detail; this suggests that Alexandra is more focused on the negative aspects of her life than on a hopeful view of the future (at least for Emil).

PASSAGE II

6. **H**

Category: Function
Difficulty: Medium
Strategic Advice: Language like "in order to" clearly signals that you're dealing with a Function question.
Getting to the Answer: Move to the end of paragraph 1 and read for context. The author states, "So deeply embedded in the country's consciousness is the ideal of a freestanding dwelling that even young children" will depict a generic house in that fashion. The author seems to talk about children's sketches *to emphasize how completely the ideal of the American house has permeated the American mindset.*

(F) Out of Scope; the author doesn't reference "simplicity of design."

(G) Misused Detail; the author mentions "the traditional family" in paragraph 5, but it has nothing to do with the cited example.

(H) Correct; this matches the tone and content of the prediction.

(J) Distortion; this picture of the American house may have seeped into the general consciousness, but this is not the same thing as the "desire for" such a house.

7. **C**

Category: Function
Difficulty: Medium
Strategic Advice: To understand the function of a paragraph—how it fits in—you must have a grasp of the passage's main idea and how the author advances it.

Getting to the Answer: Good notes are critical in a situation like this. Check your notes on the fourth paragraph; it is the last one to deal with the traditional American house. The next paragraph looks at how the American house is changing. Predict that the paragraph serves to *transition from a discussion of the "traditional" American house to a discussion of how it is changing.*

(A) Out of Scope; the author presents no example in this paragraph.

(B) Distortion; the paragraph does begin by acknowledging that the American house was not "perfect or universal," but the paragraph does not focus on any negative aspect of the model.

(C) Correct; this matches the prediction.

(D) Out of Scope; the paragraph does not contain any "counterargument."

8. **J**

Category: Function
Difficulty: Medium
Strategic Advice: Even with Function questions, you should be able to move quickly when given a line reference.

Getting to the Answer: Read around the reference to understand why the author refers to these rooms. The sentence including the reference is enough; the author describes two aspects of the 1920s house: a style of architecture and "a concern for cleanliness." He then offers an example of each aspect; "shiny white-surfaced" after "yet" certainly evokes cleanliness. Predict *give an example of "cleanliness"* as your answer.

(F) Distortion; the author never indicates that these specific rooms are common to all "American houses."

(G) Distortion; discussion of the "family room" follows this detail, but the author describes no such cause-and-effect relationship.

(H) Distortion; the author never implies that homes of the 1850s were "unsanitary."

(J) Correct; this matches nicely.

PASSAGE III

9. **B**

Category: Inference
Difficulty: High

Strategic Advice: Don't read too much into your inference. Huge logical leaps will not be rewarded.

Getting to the Answer: Your notes should lead you to the end of the first paragraph, where Rosemary considers her advanced age. She "could not take anything for granted" but "was glad she could still write at all." A good prediction would be *acceptance*.

(A) Misused Detail; Rosemary is certainly sad over her inability to pursue her schooling, but this doesn't describe her view of her advanced age.

(**B**) This matches the prediction perfectly.

(C) Out of Scope; nothing in the paragraph supports this choice.

(D) Distortion; although she is thankful for the little she can do, you cannot characterize this as "optimism."

10. **J**

Category: Inference
Difficulty: Low

Strategic Advice: Many inferences will be only slightly removed from the passage; don't make it harder than it has to be.

Getting to the Answer: Consult your notes; Victor plays a role in very few paragraphs. In the fourth one, you see that Rosemary is disturbed by her grandson's decision to take an easy course in college. This works fine as a prediction.

(F) Out of Scope; the author never mentions this.

(G) Out of Scope; the author never depicts this.

(H) Distortion; Rosemary is surprised at how late Victor sleeps, but she doesn't express the feeling that he has stayed with her too long.

(**J**) This matches nicely.

11. **D**

Category: Writer's View
Difficulty: High

Strategic Advice: Prediction should always be your first instinct. With some difficult questions, however, a quick skim of the choices can help you understand what you're looking for.

Getting to the Answer: Here you are looking for the structure the author chooses in telling his story. In this case, he relates events in the present between Rosemary and Victor, events that then prompt Rosemary to remember how her father prevented her from pursuing her schooling.

(A) Distortion; Rosemary's old age and restriction from going to school are certainly "hardships," but the passage revolves around more than just a series of such events.

(B) Opposite; the story actually unfolds from present to past, not chronologically.

(C) Extreme; "the greatest disappointment in her life" is too extreme an expression of Rosemary's feelings. The memory only came back to her after hearing Victor talk about the "gut" class.

(**D**) This matches the structure of the passage and is correct.

12. **J**

Category: Inference
Difficulty: Low

Strategic Advice: Most question stems will give you clues as to where in your notes or the passage to find support for the answer.

Getting to the Answer: Your notes should remind you that the author discusses "Rosemary's father" near the end of the passage. The question is fairly open-ended, but you can at least predict something to do with her father's strictness and the way he denied her dreams to go to school.

(F) Extreme; nothing in the passage indicates that Rosemary's father didn't love her.

(G) Opposite; the passage suggests that he didn't see much benefit in getting an education.

(H) Opposite; the passage indicates that he's very stubborn.

(**J**) Correct. In the last paragraph, Rosemary comments, "There was no arguing with Papa when he spoke that way"; she also wonders what would have happened "if somehow she had found the strength to defy him."

13. **B**

Category: Function
Difficulty: Low

Strategic Advice: Function questions focus on the *why*, not the what.

Getting to the Answer: Go back and read around the cited lines to figure out why the author includes Rosemary's memory of her father. The lines preceding the memory are "If she had been allowed to continue her studies, she would never have taken a 'gut.'" Predict that the memory has something to do with Rosemary's disapproval of how Victor is treating his education.

(A) Misused Detail; while the memory offers glimpses of how Rosemary grew up, this is not the author's purpose in mentioning the memory.

(**B**) Correct; this matches your prediction nicely.

(C) Out of Scope; this answer's too general—just because Rosemary's life was like this doesn't mean everyone's life was like hers.

(D) Out of Scope; Rosemary cries in the memory, but this detail has nothing to do with the passage as a whole.

14. **H**

Category: Function

Difficulty: Medium

Strategic Advice: Use your Passage Map as a guide for Function questions.

Getting to the Answer: Think about what the quotation marks around the word "gut" mean in relation to the characters in the story. Your Passage Map should help you predict that Rosemary is disgusted by the term.

(F) Out of Scope; this is Victor's term, so it's not the author's way of describing the course—Victor uses "gut" to describe his course.

(G) Out of Scope; this may be true, but the passage does not said anything about Victor's slang.

(**H**) Correct; this matches the gist of your prediction.

(J) Out of Scope; this might be true also, but it's not the reason the author puts the term in quotation marks.

Quarter 3

Answer Key

1. **C**
2. **F**
3. **B**
4. **J**
5. **B**
6. **H**
7. **D**
8. **G**
9. **D**
10. **H**
11. **B**
12. **H**
13. **C**
14. **H**
15. **C**

16. **H**
17. **D**
18. **G**
19. **C**
20. **J**
21. **D**
22. **H**

1. **C**

Category: Connections

Difficulty: Medium

Strategic Advice: When the choices are connecting words, first determine the relationship between the ideas expressed.

Getting to the Answer: The original sentence incorrectly uses the contrasting transition "on the other hand." However, the description in this sentence is an example of the idea presented in the preceding sentence. This makes (**C**) correct. (B) and (D) do not indicate the correct relationship between the sentences.

2. **F**

Category: Connections

Difficulty: Medium

Strategic Advice: Be careful not to introduce a new error with your answer choice.

Getting to the Answer: There is a contrast relationship between these two complete sentences, making "However," the appropriate connecting word. The sentence is correct as written.

(G) and (H) incorrectly indicate a similarity between the sentences, while (J) creates a run-on.

3. **B**

Category: Connections

Difficulty: Medium

Strategic Advice: Take the context of the paragraph into consideration. A grammatically correct sentence may have a style error.

Getting to the Answer: The connecting word "Indeed" adds emphasis, mistakenly indicating that this sentence is an amplification of what has come before. A connecting word showing contrast, such as "Nevertheless," is needed to show the relationship between the sentences.

(C) incorrectly suggests similarity between the ideas in the two sentences, while (D) suggests a cause-and-effect relationship that does not exist.

4. J

Category: Verb Tenses

Difficulty: Low

Strategic Advice: Always check to make sure an underlined verb conveys the most logical sequence of events, based on context.

Getting to the Answer: "For forty years" indicates that there should be a verb indicating action starting in the past and continuing up to the present.
(**J**) provides the correct meaning.
(G) and (H) do not indicate the correct time period.

5. B

Category: Verb Tenses

Difficulty: Medium

Strategic Advice: Context clues will let you know what tense is most appropriate and logical.

Getting to the Answer: The passage sets up this verb by noting that "In the past," the narrator responded in a certain way every time her friend wanted to do dangerous things.
(**B**) correctly indicates that the narrator's reactions occurred entirely in the past.
(C) and (D) do not fit the sequence of events.

6. H

Category: Verb Tenses

Difficulty: Low

Strategic Advice: Other verbs will provide context for determining whether an underlined verb is in the correct and logical tense.

Getting to the Answer: The narrator is describing something that is about to happen, so the past tense does not make sense. The present tense verb in (**H**) is the most logical in context.
(G) is illogical in context.
(J) is unnecessarily wordy and awkward in context.

7. D

Category: Wordiness

Difficulty: Low

Strategic Advice: Eliminating redundancies in the sentence will yield clearer, more concise writing.

Getting to the Answer: Extra words make the sentence awkward and redundant. "During the last five decades of the 20th century" sufficiently indicates the length of time that Gregory Hines was a performer, thus making the underlined phrase unnecessary.
(**D**) is the correct answer.

8. G

Category: Wordiness

Difficulty: Medium

Strategic Advice: For Wordiness questions, always look for the most concise and grammatically correct answer choice.

Getting to the Answer:
(H) and (J) are redundant.
(**G**) is correct; it is the most concise answer choice that doesn't contain a redundancy.

9. D

Category: Wordiness

Difficulty: Low

Strategic Advice: Don't say it twice! Eliminate redundancies in your answer choices.

Getting to the Answer: "Various" and "different" mean the same thing.
(A), (B), and (C) are used correctly.
(**D**) is the only choice that contains a redundancy.

10. H

Category: Verb Tenses

Difficulty: Low

Strategic Advice: Don't change the verb tense unless you're sure it makes sense in the context of the passage.

Getting to the Answer: The underlined verb is in the singular form, which doesn't match its plural subject, "advertisements."
(**H**) corrects the agreement error without introducing another error.
(G) incorrectly uses "which" and the past tense, which does not make sense in context.
(J) incorrectly uses "who," which refers only to people.

11. B

Category: Word Choice

Difficulty: Low

Strategic Advice: Trust your ear. If something sounds wrong, there's probably an error.

Getting to the Answer: Check the meaning of the sentence. As it is written, it is awkward and doesn't make much sense. The underlined portion should contain an adverb. (**B**) corrects the error and uses the correct preposition. (C) and (D) use incorrect prepositions for the context.

12. H

Category: Word Choice
Difficulty: Medium
Strategic Advice: Use "which" to refer to things, not to people.
Getting to the Answer: The original sentence incorrectly uses "which" to refer to people, in this case, "customers."
(**H**) is correct.
(G) incorrectly uses "whom," which refers to an object but not a subject.
(J) omits a necessary comma.

13. C

Category: Verb Tenses
Difficulty: Medium
Strategic Advice: Use the simplest tense that conveys the correct sequence of events and has the correct meaning.
Getting to the Answer: The addition of "were" to "used to" gives it the meaning of being accustomed to something, whereas the correct tense is just the simple past.
(**C**) corrects this error.
(B) misuses the idiom "used to" as well as maintains the incorrect helping verb.
(D) also incorrectly structures the idiom.

14. H

Category: Verb Tenses
Difficulty: Low
Strategic Advice: The verb must correctly convey the time when the event happened
Getting to the Answer: Since the entire passage concerns events of the past, the future perfect is incorrect here.
(**H**) fixes the error by using the correct verb tense for an action that occurred before another past action.
(G) uses the simple future, and (J) inserts the present.

15. C

Category: Word Choice
Difficulty: Medium
Strategic Advice: Use the sentence to determine which synonym is not correct in context.
Getting to the Answer: Ella's father was famous for his medical practice, so the synonym for "known" that does not have the right connotation is in (**C**)—it is too negative. The choices in (A), (B), and (D) are all positive and would all make sense in context.

16. H

Category: Word Choice
Difficulty: Medium
Strategic Advice: Use context to determine which preposition is idiomatically correct.
Getting to the Answer: Idiomatically, "coupled" in this context requires the preposition "with," so (**H**) is correct. The linking is not being done "by" anything, so (G) does not work. Deleting the preposition entirely, as in (J), does not make sense.

17. D

Category: Verb Tenses
Difficulty: Medium
Strategic Advice: A sentence must have a predicate verb to be complete.
Getting to the Answer: The predicate verb of this sentence currently follows a relative pronoun, which turns the sentence into a fragment.
(**D**) corrects the error with the verb in the appropriate past tense.
(B) removes the pronoun but mistakenly uses the present tense.
(C) removes the pronoun but uses the gerund form, which cannot be a predicate verb in a sentence.

18. G

Category: Wordiness
Difficulty: High
Strategic Advice: Eliminate unnecessary words to avoid redundancy and create clear, concise writing.
Getting to the Answer: The art is mentioned in the previous sentence, so referring to it with a pronoun is the best option.
(**G**) does so correctly.

(H) uses a relative pronoun, which does not make sense in context.

(J) is also unnecessarily wordy.

19. C

Category: Word Choice

Difficulty: High

Strategic Advice: Use the sentence to determine meaning and context and then eliminate all choices that do not fit.

Getting to the Answer: The sentence indicates that taking pictures of children yielded artwork that conveyed the subjects' joy, so the connotation of yielding must be the correct replacements. Only "owned" in (C) has the wrong connotation.

(A), (B), and (D) all work as synonyms for "produced" in context of the sentence.

20. J

Category: Word Choice

Difficulty: Medium

Strategic Advice: A pronoun must be in the appropriate case for its role in the sentence.

Getting to the Answer: The pronoun here needs to be in the subjective case, as it is the subject of the modifying clause.

(J) puts the pronoun into the correct case.

(G) inserts a preposition that does not make sense in context.

(H) uses the possessive case of the pronoun, which does not work in this sentence.

21. D

Category: Verb Tenses

Difficulty: Medium

Strategic Advice: Use the simplest tense that conveys the correct sequence of events.

Getting to the Answer: Since the entire passage is in the past, the best verb tense here is the simple past.

(D) makes the correction.

(B) not only introduces a conditional situation, but it also makes the idiom incorrect.

(C) eliminates the meaning of time passing and does not make sense in context.

22. H

Category: Word Choice

Difficulty: High

Strategic Advice: Check an underlined pronoun to make sure it is in the correct case.

Getting to the Answer: The relative pronoun here is the subject of the relative clause, so it should be in the subjective case.

(H) correctly uses "who" in the sentence.

(G) does not correct the error and incorrectly changes the meaning. Since the pronoun refers to persons, the change to "that" in (J) is incorrect.

Quarter 4

Answer Key

1. C
2. G
3. A
4. G
5. B
6. H
7. D
8. H
9. D
10. J
11. B
12. G
13. B
14. G
15. D
16. J

1. C

Category: Writing Strategy

Difficulty: Low

Strategic Advice: Though the shortest choice is often the correct answer on the ACT, it is not always the correct answer.

Getting to the Answer: The proposed revision adds detail to the original, providing information about the freshness of the produce in the boxes. This is relevant to the paragraph, so (C) is the answer.

This particular detail does not clearly emphasize the benefits of the CSA, so (D) is incorrect.

2. G

Category: Writing Strategy
Difficulty: Medium

Strategic Advice: Think of this as a matching question. Match the phrase to the answer choice that best describes it.

Getting to the Answer: The phrase in question explains how farmers benefit from the CSA. (**G**) is the only choice that matches this content. The phrase does not refer to the narrator's family, so (F) is incorrect.

Farmers who do not sell to the CSA are not mentioned in the essay, so (H) is out.

(J) is incorrect because the first paragraph provides a brief explanation of a CSA, making the information relevant.

3. A

Category: Writing Strategy
Difficulty: Medium

Strategic Advice: If you're not sure whether to remove a phrase, try reading the sentence without it. Does the sentence still make sense? Does it lead naturally into the following sentence?

Getting to the Answer: Removing the description of when the bunch arrived makes the sentence less clear and informative, so the answer must be (A) or (B). (A) identifies that pointing out when the bunch came and what effect it had on the writer helps emphasize the importance of freshly-delivered vegetables. (B) clarifies when the bunch came, but the point of the description is that deliveries came regularly and were fresh, not that broccoli came in June in particular. (**B**) effectively explains why the author should not delete the phrase. (A) is incorrect because the paragraph is not focused on June vegetables.

4. G

Category: Writing Strategy
Difficulty: Medium

Strategic Advice: The correct answer choice will be clearly connected to the other details in the paragraph or effectively summarize the ideas in the paragraph. On the ACT, a strong concluding sentence won't introduce a new topic.

Getting to the Answer: The paragraph describes how the narrator's family has positively reacted to the CSA. Only (**G**) is connected to this idea, and the sentence is

a natural follow-up to the information about what the narrator's brother has eaten because of the family's CSA membership. The other choices are not connected to the topic of the family's positive experience with the CSA.

5. B

Category: Writing Strategy
Difficulty: Low

Strategic Advice: Use your elimination skills. Once you've determined whether or not to add the proposed sentence, you can immediately eliminate two wrong answer choices.

Getting to the Answer: This paragraph describes how the family cooked and baked with the overwhelming amount of zucchini they received. This detail is relevant to that idea, so it should be included. Therefore, (C) and (D) are incorrect. (**B**) is correct. The family's cooking skills are not a main point in the paragraph, so (A) is incorrect.

6. H

Category: Writing Strategy
Difficulty: Medium

Strategic Advice: The correct answer to this type of Writing Strategy question will be connected to the main idea of the passage, so start with pinpointing the main idea.

Getting to the Answer: The main idea of this passage is that one family has enjoyed their experience with a community-supported agriculture association but has also discovered some drawbacks. This does not match the much more general, informative purpose given in the question, making (F) and (G) incorrect. (**H**) correctly identifies the focus of the essay. (J) contradicts the essay, which does provide some information on membership.

7. D

Category: Organization
Difficulty: Medium

Strategic Advice: When asked to order sentences in a paragraph properly, save time by identifying an appropriate topic sentence and eliminating those choices that don't start with that sentence.

Getting to the Answer: (**D**) is the best order for the sentences here. There's nothing for "for example" in the first sentence to refer to, so NO CHANGE won't be correct. Where sentence 2 is placed in (B), there is no antecedent for "this camouflage." Sentence 3 sounds more like an introduction than a conclusion, making (C) incorrect.

8. H

Category: Organization
Difficulty: High
Strategic Advice: Remember to take into consideration any corrections you've made in earlier questions when tackling those relating to the passage as a whole.
Getting to the Answer: First, determine which paragraph makes the most logical introduction to the passage; it's paragraph 4 here. After you eliminate the choices that do not begin with paragraph 4, only (H) remains.

9. D

Category: Writing Strategy
Difficulty: Medium
Strategic Advice: If a Writing Strategy question appears early in the passage, flag it and return after you've read the passage through.
Getting to the Answer: (D) is the best choice with which to open this passage.
(A) and (C) repeat information that is already in the passage.
(B) would be more appropriate in paragraph 3.

10. J

Category: Wordiness
Difficulty: Low
Strategic Advice: Plug answer choices back into the sentence to see whether more concise versions of the selection are logical in context.
Getting to the Answer: The phrase "a people" is not necessary to the meaning of this sentence; (J) omits it.
(G) does not properly relate the two clauses.
(H) uses "that," rather than "who," to refer to people.

11. B

Category: Sentence Sense
Difficulty: Low
Strategic Advice: Make sure all sentences have subjects and predicate verbs and that they express complete thoughts.

Getting to the Answer: The second sentence here is a fragment; (B) creates one grammatically correct sentence.
(C) inserts an unnecessary comma.
(D) misuses the colon.

12. G

Category: Writing Strategy
Difficulty: High
Strategic Advice: Read question stems carefully. The purpose of a sentence or phrase may be different from the purpose of the passage as a whole.
Getting to the Answer: The phrase "those people wealthy enough to afford it" is meant to convey the idea that chocolate at that time was very expensive. Nothing in this paragraph indicates that chocolate didn't appeal to the people who couldn't afford it, so (F) is incorrect. Cortez would have had no way of knowing how expensive chocolate would be when he brought back the cacao beans, which eliminates (H). The author indicates that the beverage was considered "unusual" before it caught on with the wealthy people of Europe, so the latter could not explain the former, eliminating (J).

13. B

Category: Writing Strategy
Difficulty: High
Strategic Advice: If a question stem does not ask you to determine the relevance of a potential addition, you must find a logical purpose for it.
Getting to the Answer: This description would provide some color to the passage. It would not "weaken" or "not fit with the topic," so eliminate (A) and (C). It would not say anything about the author's opinion of chocolate either, so (D) is incorrect as well.

14. G

Category: Organization
Difficulty: High
Strategic Advice: Finding the best topic sentence will help you answer paragraph organization questions quickly.
Getting to the Answer: Sentence 4 is the most logical topic sentence here, eliminating (F) and (H). "In fact," in sentence 3, doesn't logically follow from sentence 4, eliminating (J).

15. D

Category: Writing Strategy

Difficulty: Low

Strategic Advice: You may be asked to determine *whether* additional information is relevant, *where* it is relevant, or both.

Getting to the Answer: Information concerning tea is Out of Scope for this passage; (**D**) is correct.

16. J

Category: Writing Strategy

Difficulty: Medium

Strategic Advice: You are likely to see this question format at least once or twice on the ACT; read the question stem carefully.

Getting to the Answer: This passage concerns only chocolate; it would not fulfill the requirements of an assignment to write about culinary trends in history.

Homework Answers and Explanations

Quarter 2

Answer Key

1. **C**
2. **G**
3. **D**
4. **F**
5. **C**
6. **H**
7. **D**
8. **G**
9. **A**
10. **H**
11. **B**
12. **F**
13. **D**
14. **H**
15. **B**
16. **F**
17. **A**
18. **G**
19. **D**
20. **F**

PASSAGE I

In the first two paragraphs, the author shows Miss Brill preparing to go to the park, putting on her fur; she seems to think of it as a living thing. Once there, she sits on a bench, where she likes to eavesdrop (paragraph 3). In paragraphs 4–6, she observes those around her, seeing them as actors in a play. A band plays music; she envisions everyone in the park singing (paragraph 7). In the next paragraph, two young lovers sit down beside her; she eavesdrops again. They make fun of her (paragraphs 9–11). In the last two paragraphs, Miss Brill leaves the park. She skips her normal stop at the bakery, returns home, and puts her fur away. As she does, she hears crying.

1. C

Category: Inference

Difficulty: Medium

Strategic Advice: With generally worded questions, skim your notes and look for the choice that matches the general thrust of the passage.

Getting to the Answer: Look through your notes for the point where Miss Brill first enters the park (paragraph 3). She "always looked forward to the conversation"—the conversation of others. Use this as a prediction.

(A) Distortion; paragraph 1 indicates that she hasn't worn the fur in a while, but she seems to go to the park every week regardless.

(B) Distortion; she doesn't even speak to anyone.

(**C**) Correct; the paragraph supports this.

(D) Misused Detail; she seems to enjoy the band, but this is not the reason she goes to the park.

2. G

Category: Detail

Difficulty: Medium

Strategic Advice: When you receive limited help from the stem, count on your notes to help you confirm or rule out choices based on the passage.

Getting to the Answer: Miss Brill observes many things, so work through the choices if need be. You should see the reference to the girls meeting the soldiers in paragraph 5, confirming (G) as correct.

(F) Distortion; Miss Brill sees a woman throw away a bunch of violets "as if they'd been poisoned" (line 37). The flowers are not actually poisoned.

(**G**) Correct; this matches what the author writes in paragraph 5.

(H) Distortion; the old man in paragraph 4 is selling flowers, not planting them.

(J) Distortion; she envisions, but doesn't actually see, the lovers arriving on (not "boarding") a yacht.

3. **D**

Category: Detail

Difficulty: Medium

Strategic Advice: Most questions will not give line references. Taking good notes is the key to finding answers in the passage.

Getting to the Answer: Every part of her routine seems intact until lines 77–78, where the author tells you that Miss Brill "usually bought a slice of honey-cake at the baker's." Line 84 states, however, "But today she passed the baker's by." Look for this among the choices.

(A) Distortion; she doesn't speak to the couple.

(B) Out of Scope; this is only a metaphor in the passage.

(C) Opposite; this is the major part of her routine.

(**D**) Correct; this is confirmed in the last two paragraphs.

4. **F**

Category: Writer's View

Difficulty: Medium

Strategic Advice: When asked for the author's view of the main character, you can support your initial perception of this with your notes.

Getting to the Answer: The author shows Miss Brill going to the park alone to watch and listen to others; she does not interact with them, also returning home alone. Her major interaction is with her fur. You can predict that the author paints Miss Brill as *lonely*.

(**F**) Correct; this matches the prediction nicely.

(G) Opposite; Miss Brill is certainly not "an outgoing woman." She doesn't speak to a single person during the course of the story.

(H) Extreme; although the young boy and girl make fun of Miss Brill, it is not clear that she is "frequently ridiculed."

(J) Misused Detail; though she imagines the people in the park as actors on the stage, she does not actually dream of "pursuing an acting career."

5. **C**

Category: Inference

Difficulty: Medium

Strategic Advice: Even on Inference questions, line references in the stem are a great help; take advantage and move quickly to leave time for more difficult questions.

Getting to the Answer: The entrance of the boy and girl immediately follows Miss Brill's idea that the "whole company" of people in the park would begin singing along with the band. She has made up a background story for the young couple whom she pictures as the hero and heroine of the "play."

(A) Opposite; the passage makes clear that they don't really know each other.

(B) Out of Scope; while Miss Brill is an eavesdropper, the author never indicates that she has overheard this information.

(**C**) Correct; this matches the thrust of the passage.

(D) Distortion; nothing suggests that she is "overly concerned about their relationship."

6. **H**

Category: Vocab-in-Context

Difficulty: Low

Strategic Advice: You can deduce the meaning of virtually any term in a passage, familiar or unfamiliar, by interpreting the surrounding context.

Getting to the Answer: Miss Brill has been imagining that everyone in the park is taking part in a play. Predict something like *group* or *cast* (as in cast of characters).

(F) Out of Scope; this is a common meaning of the word that doesn't make sense in context.

(G) Opposite; these people are really strangers to Miss Brill.

(**H**) Correct; this matches the prediction nicely.

(J) Out of Scope; this is a common meaning of the word that doesn't make sense in context.

7. **D**

Category: Inference

Difficulty: Medium

Strategic Advice: The correct answer will not stray far from the passage; don't make too big a logical leap.

Getting to the Answer: Directly after hearing the couple's unkind remarks, Miss Brill goes home, eschews her normal stop at the bakery, and hears crying in her room—her own, though she might attribute it to her fur. Predict something like *people were making fun of her*.

(A) Distortion; the author never suggests that Miss Brill truly dreams of acting on stage.

(B) Extreme; the author never suggests this. Miss Brill may have forgotten it by next week.

(C) Out of Scope; the author never indicates that anyone other than Miss Brill envisions such a play.

(**D**) Correct; this matches the thrust of the prediction.

8. **G**

Category: Detail

Difficulty: Medium

Strategic Advice: Most questions will not give line references. Taking good notes is critical to finding the answer in the passage quickly.

Getting to the Answer: Consult your notes, looking for the first reference to the park activities as a play. Paragraph 6 indicates that Miss Brill makes this connection after seeing "a little brown dog."

(F) Misused Detail; this comes from earlier in the passage.

(**G**) Correct; this matches the research above.

(H) Distortion; neither Miss Brill nor the other people actually sing.

(J) Misused Detail; this comes from earlier in the passage.

9. **A**

Category: Inference

Difficulty: Medium

Strategic Advice: Try to work from your notes as much as possible, only referring to the passage for confirmation as needed.

Getting to the Answer: Miss Brill imagines that the fur's "sad little eyes" talk to her. She thinks, "Oh, how sweet it was to see them snap at her again" (lines 6–7). As the notes above summarize, she sees the fur as a *living thing*.

(**A**) Correct; this matches the thrust of the prediction.

(B) Opposite; the first paragraph clearly indicates that the fur is more than just "a fashion accessory."

(C) Distortion; Miss Brill has not yet had her realization that the park is like a stage.

(D) Out of Scope; Miss Brill never seems to consider that others might find the fur humorous.

10. **H**

Category: Generalization

Difficulty: Medium

Strategic Advice: Rely on your notes and, if unsure, stick with the overall tone you perceive in the paragraph.

Getting to the Answer: Miss Brill imagines that "she heard something crying" (line 90) when she puts the fur back in its box. It may be her crying, or she may imagine that the fur cries. Either way, the paragraph conveys sadness or hurt feelings. Look for a choice that matches that sentiment.

(F) Extreme; the passage does not support such a strong word as "never."

(G) Out of Scope; the author does not suggest this.

(**H**) Correct; this matches the tone and content of the paragraph.

(J) Out of Scope; nothing supports this conclusion.

PASSAGE II

In this passage, the author describes the career of a successful female photographer. In the first paragraph, he explains how women photographers have had a major impact on the field. In the second paragraph, he reviews the life of Julia Margaret Cameron, a nineteenth-century intellectual who developed a voracious interest in photography. The third paragraph details her record of success. The final paragraph contrasts her allegorical pictures and her portrait photographs; modern critics much prefer the latter.

11. **B**

Category: Generalization

Difficulty: Medium

Strategic Advice: With generally worded questions, look for the choice that best matches the author's purpose and tone.

Getting to the Answer: The author's purpose is to discuss the impressive photographic work of Julia Margaret Cameron. In the second paragraph, the author describes her as "the first woman to have achieved eminence in photography." Look for a choice that matches this focus.

(A) Distortion; she was far from "a traditional homemaker," and this part of her life was hardly the focus of the passage.

(**B**) Correct; the author says as much, and the last paragraph indicates that he is not alone.

(C) Opposite; paragraph 3 contradicts this.

(D) Distortion; any "eccentricity" was not so significant as to prevent her from being appreciated.

12. F

Category: Detail

Difficulty: Low

Strategic Advice: When you don't receive a line reference, count on your notes to help you find support for the answer in the passage.

Getting to the Answer: Look to your notes to find where the author discusses "modern critics"—the last paragraph. In lines 66–67, the author writes, "Contemporary taste much prefers her portraits."

(F) Correct; this matches what you find in the text.

(G) Opposite; modern critics don't like these works.

(H) Misused Detail; this comes from paragraph 3.

(J) Out of Scope; the author never suggests this.

13. D

Category: Generalization

Difficulty: High

Strategic Advice: When faced with a question on a paragraph, first consult your notes on the paragraph.

Getting to the Answer: Your notes should indicate that the author uses this paragraph to give background on Cameron's life and on her interest in photography. The dates used in the passage tell you that he does this chronologically. Use this as your prediction.

(A) Out of Scope; the author recounts events, not "anecdotes."

(B) Distortion; the paragraph also discusses her personal life, and her importance to the field comes after this.

(C) Out of Scope; the author never mentions this.

(D) Correct; this matches the prediction well.

14. H

Category: Function

Difficulty: Medium

Strategic Advice: For Function questions, remember to read around the reference (sometimes as much as the entire paragraph) to understand what the author is doing.

Getting to the Answer: Near the end of the paragraph, the author indicates that Cameron

"worked ceaselessly" and overcame the technological limitations of the time. All of this shows how she "devoted herself wholly to this art" (line 45). Use this as the basis for your prediction.

(F) Out of Scope; the first part of the second paragraph indicates that she was relatively well off.

(G) Distortion; modern critics do value her portraits.

(H) Correct; this matches the prediction.

(J) Out of Scope; the passage focuses on only one such photographer.

15. B

Category: Vocab-in-Context

Difficulty: Medium

Strategic Advice: Some Vocab-in-Context questions will ask you to "translate" a phrase.

Getting to the Answer: Read around the reference for context. Cameron considered photography a "divine art" to which she was wholly devoted. You can predict something like *was her purpose in life.*

(A) Distortion; the second paragraph suggests that Cameron's social life was anything but conventional.

(B) Correct; this matches the prediction nicely.

(C) Out of Scope; this draws from a different meaning of "vocation."

(D) Out of Scope; don't be misled by "divine" and "devoted." The author is not speaking about Cameron's religious beliefs.

16. F

Category: Generalization

Difficulty: Medium

Strategic Advice: A question on the main point of a passage or paragraph can be easily answered if you've taken good notes.

Getting to the Answer: Return to your notes on the third paragraph; they should reflect that it details Cameron's record of success. Look for a match to that.

(F) Correct; this matches the gist of the prediction.

(G) Extreme; to say that she is "the greatest photographer that ever lived" goes beyond anything stated or implied in the passage.

(H) Misused Detail; the third paragraph does not mention modern appraisals of Cameron.

(J) Out of Scope; the author does not make such a statement.

17. A

Category: Function

Difficulty: High

Strategic Advice: The function of a part of the passage will be closely tied to the text immediately surrounding it. You shouldn't have to look far.

Getting to the Answer: The author introduces these two assessments directly after lauding Cameron's achievements as "notable." He follows their comments by saying that no other woman photographer can match her level of success. The two opinions emphasize how impressive her accomplishments were.

(A) Correct; this matches the purpose of the reference.

(B) Misused Detail; this comes from the next paragraph.

(C) Out of Scope; don't misconstrue Watts's inscription (lines 55–56). Nothing in the paragraph suggests any "envy."

(D) Misused Detail; this pulls from the next paragraph.

18. G

Category: Detail

Difficulty: Low

Strategic Advice: You should be able to find distinctive details (such as proper names or italicized words) easily, even without line references.

Getting to the Answer: You shouldn't have taken any detailed names down in your notes, but a quick skim of the passage should help you find this title quickly. Read a few lines before, and you should see that this is an example of the "allegorical…native scenes" that Victorian critics loved and modern critics devalue.

(F) Out of Scope; this work is contrasted with the portraits.

(G) Correct; this matches what the author writes in the paragraph.

(H) Distortion; this refers to an aspect of Cameron's photographic portraits, not her allegorical work.

(J) Opposite; Cameron's contemporaries liked works such as this.

19. D

Category: Detail

Difficulty: Medium

Strategic Advice: Don't get confused on NOT questions; make sure you're answering the question that was asked.

Getting to the Answer: Check your notes to determine where the two sets of critics are discussed: the last paragraph. Based on your notes, you could predict that modern critics would not agree with the high esteem that Victorians felt for Cameron's allegorical pictures.

(A) Distortion; while Cameron did base some of her photographs on poems, neither set of critics takes a stand on the practice.

(B) Distortion; the author never states that Victorian critics felt this way about any of her work.

(C) Opposite; based on the paragraph, modern critics would agree with this.

(D) Correct; the author makes clear that the two camps disagree on this matter.

20. F

Category: Writer's View

Difficulty: Medium

Strategic Advice: Many Writer's View questions can be answered with a quick review of the author's purpose and tone.

Getting to the Answer: The author says that Cameron "achieved eminence" (line 11) in her field, that she "devoted herself wholly to this art" (line 45), and that "No other female artist of the nineteenth century achieved such acclaim" (lines 58–60). You can predict *appreciative,* or even something as simple as *positive.*

(F) Correct; this matches the author's tone.

(G) Opposite; this is too negative.

(H) Distortion; the author uses too many words of praise for this to work.

(J) Out of Scope; the passage doesn't support this characterization.

Quarter 3

Answer Key

1. **B**
2. **J**
3. **D**
4. **J**
5. **A**
6. **J**
7. **D**
8. **H**
9. **B**

10. **G**
11. **C**
12. **G**
13. **D**
14. **F**
15. **C**
16. **J**
17. **A**
18. **J**
19. **D**
20. **H**
21. **D**
22. **G**
23. **D**
24. **H**
25. **C**
26. **H**
27. **A**
28. **G**
29. **C**
30. **F**

SHERLOCK HOLMES

1. B

Category: Wordiness
Difficulty: Medium

Strategic Advice: When you see a compound phrase underlined, ask yourself if the two words mean essentially the same thing. If so, the correct answer choice will be one or the other.

Getting to the Answer: The description of Sherlock Holmes as "ingenious" and "extremely clever" is redundant because these two adjectives mean the same thing. You only need to use one of the two to get the point across.

2. J

Category: Connections
Difficulty: Medium

Strategic Advice: Make sure any connecting words or phrases are appropriate in context.

Getting to the Answer: "Therefore" is a signal that what follows is a logical conclusion based on the given information. "Therefore" doesn't make sense here

because you can't conclude that everyone knows the phrase "Elementary, my dear Watson" just because everyone knows of Holmes's detective abilities.

3. D

Category: Wordiness
Difficulty: Medium

Strategic Advice: When "OMIT the underlined portion" is a given option, ask yourself if the underlined information is relevant.

Getting to the Answer: The underlined sentence has nothing to do with the topic of the paragraph. It should be omitted.

4. J

Category: Wordiness
Difficulty: Medium

Strategic Advice: The shortest answer choice will not always be correct, but it's a good place to start.

Getting to the Answer: The ACT looks for simplicity in style. "To be remembered" is the most concise way to phrase the underlined idea.

5. A

Category: Connections
Difficulty: Medium

Strategic Advice: When faced with a Connections question, examine the ideas being combined; how are they related?

Getting to the Answer: "In fact" is the appropriate signal phrase here; the selection is correct as written. "Despite this," "Regardless," and "Yet" all indicate a contrast between ideas. There is no contrast, however; Conan Doyle did not want to be remembered as the author of Sherlock Holmes stories, so he ended the character's life.

6. J

Category: Sentence Sense
Difficulty: High

Strategic Advice: Make sure any modifying phrases are properly placed for what they are intended to modify.

Getting to the Answer: As written, this sentence tells us that Sherlock Holmes himself, not his creator, "had enough of his famous character." (**J**) rewords the selection so that the modifying phrase refers to Conan Doyle.

7. D

Category: Wordiness
Difficulty: Low

Strategic Advice: Just because a sentence refers to the subject of a passage does not mean it is necessarily relevant in context.

Getting to the Answer: The fact that Conan Doyle was knighted has nothing to do with the rest of the paragraph. This sentence should be omitted.

8. H

Category: Wordiness
Difficulty: Medium

Strategic Advice: You can always omit wording that doesn't add anything useful to a sentence, but first verify that it isn't needed for grammar or logic.

Getting to the Answer: The phrasing of this sentence is two examples (automatic writing and spiritual medium) and explanations for each. The question asks whether you want to get rid of the explanation for one of them. Doing so would make the sentence no longer parallel, and would remove useful information (what "automatic writing" is), so it should not be done, eliminating (J). The right answer will be the shortest answer that retains the useful information, which is (**H**).

9. B

Category: Sentence Sense
Difficulty: Low

Strategic Advice: To be complete, a sentence must have a subject and predicate (main) verb in an independent clause.

Getting to the Answer: As written, this is a sentence fragment, since neither of the clauses is independent. By omitting "that," you make the second clause independent; (**B**) is correct.
(C) is incorrect grammatical structure.
(D) leaves the first clause as a sentence fragment.

10. G

Category: Verb Tenses
Difficulty: High

Strategic Advice: Make sure verb tenses accurately reflect the time period(s) referenced.

Getting to the Answer: Sherlock Holmes is a fictional character, so a verb phrase that implies he may be speaking sometime in the future ("will...have to say") is incorrect. The same is true of "going to say" in (H). "Had...said" in (J) indicates that Sherlock Holmes actually had some comment on Conan Doyle's interest in spiritualism.
"Would...have said," in (G), is the appropriate verb phrase in this context.

MY RAFTING ADVENTURE

11. C

Category: Verb Tenses
Difficulty: Medium

Strategic Advice: The –ing verb form can never be the main verb in a sentence.

Getting to the Answer: This sentence discusses something that started several years ago and is still continuing. "Has been" in (C) is the proper tense to express this.
(B) does not agree with the singular subject "white-water rafting."
The past tense in (D) is inappropriate in context.

12. G

Category: Word Choice
Difficulty: Medium

Strategic Advice: Pronouns like "nothing" are grammatically singular.

Getting to the Answer: Since the sentence starts out using "have drifted," "has ever matched" in (**G**) is the only choice that uses a consistent tense.
(F) does not agree with its singular subject.
(H) leaves the meaning of the second clause incomplete.
(J) uses an inconsistent verb tense.

13. D

Category: Word Choice
Difficulty: Low

Strategic Advice: In the subject of a sentence, the subjective pronoun case is correct.

Getting to the Answer: (A) and (B) use the incorrect case, whereas (C) is unnecessarily wordy.

14. F

Category: Verb Tenses

Difficulty: Low

Strategic Advice: Unless multiple time frames are referenced, verb tenses should remain consistent.

Getting to the Answer: This sentence is correct as written.
(G) and (H) introduce inconsistent verb tenses.
(J) is unnecessarily wordy.

15. C

Category: Word Choice

Difficulty: Medium

Strategic Advice: Most tested idioms will hinge on preposition usage.

Getting to the Answer: In this context, "by" is the idiomatically correct preposition with "replaced." None of the other prepositions forms a correct idiom.

16. J

Category: Wordiness

Difficulty: Medium

Strategic Advice: When a compound phrase is underlined, check to see if the words have similar meanings.

Getting to the Answer: "Halt" and "stop" mean essentially the same thing; the selection should be omitted.

17. A

Category: Word Choice

Difficulty: High

Strategic Advice: On many questions, all of the answer choices will be grammatically correct. You must determine which one is correct in context.

Getting to the Answer: This sentence is correct as written. Although all of the other choices are correctly constructed idioms, none is appropriate in context.

18. J

Category: Verb Tenses

Difficulty: Medium

Strategic Advice: Use context clues to determine the correct verb tense.

Getting to the Answer: Since this passage is written primarily in the past tense, (J) provides the consistent choice.
The conditional in (G) and the present in (H) are inappropriate tenses in context.

19. D

Category: Wordiness

Difficulty: Medium

Strategic Advice: When OMIT is among the answer choices, read the sentence without the underlined selection; OMIT is frequently the correct choice when it is offered.

Getting to the Answer: The selection and both (B) and (C) contain redundant information; the correct choice is to OMIT the underlined material.

20. H

Category: Verb Tenses

Difficulty: Medium

Strategic Advice: Be consistent in verb tense choices unless there is a clear reason to introduce a new tense.

Getting to the Answer: "Went" in the first part of the sentence is your clue; "received" is the best choice here.
(F), (G), and (J) use inconsistent tenses.

THE HISTORY OF MARBLES

21. D

Category: Word Choice

Difficulty: Medium

Strategic Advice: Pronouns must agree in number with their antecedent nouns.

Getting to the Answer: The antecedent noun here is the plural "names," so the pronoun should be plural as well.
(A) and (B) use a singular pronoun.
(C) uses "there," a homophone of the plural possessive pronoun "their" and incorrect in this context.

22. G

Category: Word Choice

Difficulty: Medium

Strategic Advice: A verb must agree in number with its subject noun, which may not be the noun closest to it in the sentence.

Getting to the Answer: Here, the plural "marbles" is the object of "regarding"; the subject of the verb is the singular "word."

(F) and (J) use plural verb forms.

(H) creates a sentence fragment.

The singular verb form in (**G**) is correct.

23. D

Category: Word Choice

Difficulty: High

Strategic Advice: Many answer choices will be correctly structured idioms; choose the one that makes sense in context.

Getting to the Answer: All of the answer choices here are proper idioms but, in this context, "manipulated in a variety of ways" is correct.

24. H

Category: Verb Tenses

Difficulty: Medium

Strategic Advice: Verbs in a compound must be in parallel form.

Getting to the Answer: (G), (H), and (J) all make the verbs parallel, so you must determine which uses the appropriate tense.

The tenses used in (G) and (J) change the meaning of the original sentence; (**H**) is correct here.

25. C

Category: Verb Tenses

Difficulty: Medium

Strategic Advice: Determine the main verb tense of the passage; most sentences will use this tense.

Getting to the Answer: This passage is written primarily in the present tense; (**C**) is the consistent choice here.

(A) and (D) use the past tense; additionally, the singular verb in (D) is incorrect with the plural "varieties."

(B) is incorrect grammatical structure.

26. H

Category: Word Choice

Difficulty: Low

Strategic Advice: Pronouns must agree in person and number with their antecedents.

Getting to the Answer: The antecedent here is the plural "players," so the singular "his or her" in (F) is incorrect.

(G) and (J) use second- and first-person pronouns, respectively, which are also inappropriate with this antecedent.

"Their marbles," in (**H**), is correct here.

27. A

Category: Word Choice

Difficulty: Medium

Strategic Advice: The noun closest to a verb in the sentence may not be its subject.

Getting to the Answer: Here, the plural "marbles" is the object of the preposition "of," not the subject of the verb "spans"; the subject is the singular "popularity," so this sentence is correct as written.

(B) does not agree with the singular subject.

The verb form in (C) creates a grammatically incorrect sentence.

(D) is unnecessarily wordy.

28. G

Category: Word Choice

Difficulty: Medium

Strategic Advice: The antecedent of a pronoun may appear in an earlier sentence.

Getting to the Answer: The antecedent of "It" is the plural "games" in the sentence before, so the pronoun should be plural.

(F) and (J) use singular pronouns.

(H) changes the meaning of the sentence.

29. C

Category: Word Choice

Difficulty: Medium

Strategic Advice: On the ACT, the longest answer choice is rarely correct.

Getting to the Answer: (A), (B), and (D) are all idiomatically incorrect constructions; only the idiom in (**C**) is correct.

30. F

Category: Wordiness
Difficulty: High
Strategic Advice: Some sentences will be correct as written.
Getting to the Answer: This sentence contains no error.
(G) improperly uses an adjective ("actual") to modify a verb ("has").
(H) and (J) make the sentence unnecessarily wordy.

Quarter 4

Answer Key

1. **B**
2. **H**
3. **A**
4. **H**
5. **C**
6. **H**
7. **A**
8. **F**
9. **C**
10. **G**
11. **A**
12. **F**
13. **C**

URBAN LEGENDS

1. B

Category: Organization
Difficulty: High
Strategic Advice: To order sentences within a paragraph quickly, find a logical topic sentence and eliminate those choices that don't place that sentence first.
Getting to the Answer: Here, the most logical topic sentence is 3, which eliminates (A) and (C).
(D) puts sentence 7 next, but that sentence doesn't logically follow from sentence 3's introduction of "some characteristic features."

2. H

Category: Writing Strategy
Difficulty: Medium
Strategic Advice: Read question stems carefully. The purpose of a detail or paragraph may be different from the purpose of the passage as a whole.
Getting to the Answer: The cookie recipe legend is mentioned here as an example of urban legends that have proliferated over the Internet. The writer uses the word "supposedly" to refer to the woman's actions, so the detail can't be used for proof that some urban legends are true, as (F) suggests. Although the example says that the woman spread the recipe via e-mail, there's no reason to think the Internet was necessary for the legend to spread, which eliminates (G). The example does not rebut the paragraph's assertion that many urban legends flourish over the Internet, eliminating (J).

3. A

Category: Writing Strategy
Difficulty: Medium
Strategic Advice: Use the clues in the question stem to help you eliminate inappropriate answer choices.
Getting to the Answer: The question stem gives an important clue to the best answer—the purpose of the inserted sentence is "to describe the different kinds" of stories. (**A**) is the only choice that does this.
(B) explains how the stories were told.
(C) explains why more is not known about the stories.
(D) describes the length of some stories.

4. H

Category: Writing Strategy
Difficulty: Medium
Strategic Advice: When asked to add information, use context to help you determine the best place for it.
Getting to the Answer: Paragraph 5 describes a rather frightening legend—alligators living underneath the city in the sewer system. The sentence "Other urban legends seem to be designed to instill fear" is an appropriate topic sentence for this paragraph.
(F) and (J) place the sentence at the end of the passage and the end of paragraph 5 respectively, which is illogical for a sentence that introduces a new topic. Placing the new sentence where (G) suggests interrupts the flow of information in paragraph 3.

5. C

Category: Writing Strategy

Difficulty: Medium

Strategic Advice: This question format is very common on the ACT. Read the question stem carefully to determine exactly what you're being asked.

Getting to the Answer: Although paragraph 6 provides some general information about the purpose and topics of the myths and legends of primitive societies, no specifics are given. This makes (**C**) the best answer. (D) incorrectly states that the essay provides no information on the topic.

6. H

Category: Organization

Difficulty: High

Strategic Advice: Finding a logical introduction and conclusion will help you quickly determine the appropriate order for the paragraphs.

Getting to the Answer: Paragraph 6 is the most logical introductory paragraph for this passage, since it introduces and defines the concept of the urban legend. Since only (**H**) puts paragraph 6 first, there's no need to look further.

THE SPACE SHUTTLE

7. A

Category: Writing Strategy

Difficulty: Medium

Strategic Advice: When asked whether or not to add new information, take tone and point of view into consideration.

Getting to the Answer: This paragraph is best as written.
(C) and (D) are too positive for the rest of the paragraph, and they contradict the remainder of the essay.
(B) uses "you," which is not consistent with the rest of the essay.

8. F

Category: Writing Strategy

Difficulty: Medium

Strategic Advice: Read context carefully for "purpose" questions.

Getting to the Answer: This paragraph lists some of the accomplishments of the shuttle program. (G) is incorrect because the history was outlined in the first two paragraphs. Even though this paragraph does discuss things that happened in the past, the emphasis is on "significant firsts." The paragraph neither predicts "the future of the shuttle program," (H), nor provides "an alternative reason" for its cost, (J).

9. C

Category: Writing Strategy

Difficulty: Medium

Strategic Advice: Consider the tone and point of view of any new information you're asked to add.

Getting to the Answer: (A) is too negative, and (B) is too positive in the context of the passage. Also, (B)'s "is abound with" is grammatically incorrect.
There is no evidence for (D).
(**C**) is the best choice here.

10. G

Category: Writing Strategy

Difficulty: Low

Strategic Advice: The purpose of a paragraph or detail may be different from the purpose of the entire passage; read the question stems carefully.

Getting to the Answer: The author knows her audience and therefore uses the age of the readers as a way of providing a contextual framework; (**G**) is correct here. The age of the students has nothing to do with the shuttle program's "successes and failures," (F); the "general history of NASA's greatest accomplishments," (H); or "the topic of the essay," (J).

MARIA MERIAN

11. A

Category: Writing Strategy

Difficulty: Medium

Strategic Advice: Many wrong answer choices will be consistent with the passage but fail to answer the question asked.

Getting to the Answer: This section of the passage is about Merian's accomplishments, so more examples of this would be the most appropriate way to strengthen the essay; (**A**) is the best choice here.
(B) and (D) are Out of Scope for this passage.

(C) is redundant and doesn't merit a separate paragraph.

12. F

Category: Organization
Difficulty: High
Strategic Advice: Learn to identify appropriate topic sentences; this will help you answer Organization questions concerning sentence order.
Getting to the Answer: These sentences are already in the most logical order.

13. C

Category: Writing Strategy
Difficulty: Medium
Strategic Advice: Don't let the wording of this question stem throw you; the testmaker is asking you about the purpose of the passage as a whole.
Getting to the Answer: This passage is a brief biographical sketch of Maria Merian, an artist/scientist who lived in the late seventeenth and early eighteenth centuries. Since Medieval Europe is not mentioned in the passage, you can rule out (A) as being Out of Scope. Professional art historians, mentioned in (B), would most likely not be satisfied with this essay, since it concentrates on Merian's personal history and does not give a critical evaluation of Merian's art and its place in art history. There is nothing in the essay to help the prospective visitor to Amsterdam, so (D) is incorrect. The essay seems to be aimed at the general reader who has an interest in art history, which is consistent with (**C**).

ANSWERS AND EXPLANATIONS

Quarter 2 Lesson

1. **C**
2. **J**
3. **B**
4. **F**
5. **B**
6. **G**
7. **D**
8. **F**
9. **D**
10. **F**
11. **C**
12. **H**

Passage I

1. C

Category: Scientific Reasoning
Difficulty: Low

Strategic Advice: Even if you're certain you know the answer, it only takes a few seconds to glance back at the passage to double-check.

Getting to the Answer: This question asks you to identify something specific about the design of the researchers' experiment: What did they vary? If you didn't identify the parts of the scientific reasoning when you read the passage, you'll have to go back to research your answer. The paragraph before Table 1 explains that the researchers intentionally changed the temperature in the habitats, (**C**).

(A) is incorrect because the passage states that 50 frogs were studied in both experiments.

(B) is incorrect because the passage does not mention humidity.

(D) is incorrect and a very predictable wrong answer. The amount of oxygen that the frogs absorbed varied according to temperature, but this factor was not varied intentionally by the researchers.

2. J

Category: Scientific Reasoning
Difficulty: Low

Strategic Advice: Experiments usually differ in either their method or what they're measuring.

Getting to the Answer: The same method was used in both experiments, so check to see if they measured different things. Experiment 1 measured oxygen absorption, and Experiment 2 measured carbon dioxide elimination. That matches (**J**).

(F) could be immediately eliminated because only one species of tree frog is discussed.

(G) can be eliminated by a quick glance at Tables 1 and 2.

(H) can be eliminated by a quick glance at Table 2.

3. B

Category: Scientific Reasoning
Difficulty: Medium

Strategic Advice: When you're asked "Why?" about one step of the method, your task is to identify the purpose of that step.

Getting to the Answer: Researchers adjusted the temperature in the habitats and then allowed time for the temperature to reach equilibrium. You know that the purpose of the experiment was to test how temperature affected the frog's oxygen absorption, so find the connection between these two ideas. The researchers wouldn't get accurate readings of the oxygen absorption at each temperature until the frogs adjusted their oxygen intake to the newest temperature change. Only (**B**) comes close to this.

(A) is incorrect because nowhere in the passage does it state that additional oxygen was removed from the habitats between temperature changes.

(C) is incorrect for the same reason. Researchers never adjusted carbon dioxide levels in the habitats.

(D) can be crossed off immediately because humidity isn't mentioned in the passage.

4. F

Category: Scientific Reasoning
Difficulty: Low

Strategic Advice: Questions that ask "Why?" require reasoning, not science, skills.

Getting to the Answer: Remember the purpose of this experiment—to investigate how temperature affects the tree frog's rate of exchange of gas through its skin and lungs. If the researchers are testing how one variable affects something, they need to be able to isolate it and change it at their will. (**F**) encompasses this idea.

(G) can be eliminated because nothing in the passage mentions predators.

(H) is incorrect because food supply is also never mentioned.

(J) is misleading, but incorrect, because the researchers wish to measure, not control, the frogs' oxygen intake.

Passage II

5. B

Category: Scientific Reasoning
Difficulty: Medium

Strategic Advice: Don't ever go back and reread the entire passage to answer one question.

Getting to the Answer: This passage explains the method in great detail, so if you can't recall what was kept constant, start with the answer choices.

(A) wasn't kept constant. Experiment 2 talks about heating the solutions.

(B) is possible. The amount of rhodium complex present isn't explicitly stated, but Experiment 1 does tell you that "the two solutions were identical in all other ways." Keep this.

(C) is incorrect. Sodium acetate was only added in Experiment 3.

(D) is also incorrect, again because sodium acetate was only used in Experiment 3. The answer, then, must be (**B**).

6. G

Category: Scientific Reasoning
Difficulty: High

Strategic Advice: Questions that ask you to identify a useful next step require that you combine an understanding of the purpose with an understanding of the methods in the different experiments.

Getting to the Answer: The purpose of the experiment was to figure out which conditions favored Substance 1 and which favored Substance 2. Varying the pH of the rhodium complex solutions, as in Experiment 1, produced two different substances. You know that a pH of 5.0 (acidic) produces Substance 2 and a pH of 8.2 (basic) produces Substance 1. Finding out what a pH of 7 would produce would certainly tell you more about which conditions favor each substance, so (**G**) is correct.

(F) is incorrect because you're given no evidence that concentration affects substance development.

(H) is incorrect because Experiment 2 already tried heating the solutions, and it only affected Substance 1.

(J) is incorrect because, again, there's no evidence that temperature affects the development of

Substance 2. Also, freezing the solutions would likely make a reaction impossible.

7. D

Category: Scientific Reasoning
Difficulty: High

Strategic Advice: The question stem mentions acetates, so start by looking at Experiment 3.

Getting to the Answer: Substance 2 is formed in Solution A when heated, but it is not formed when sodium acetate is added before heating. This supports the statement that Substance 2 may react to form other, more readily dissolved compounds in the presence of certain acetates. Also, the final product in Experiment 3 is a liquid, which indicates that the substance formed might have dissolved into the rhodium complex, which is further support for (**D**). None of the other choices involves the presence of any type of acetate.

Passage III

8. F

Category: Conflicting Viewpoints
Difficulty: Low

Strategic Advice: Just as in the Reading Test, some questions will ask you for the purpose of a statement.

Getting to the Answer: In the middle of his argument, Scientist 2 states, "Mitochondrial DNA and ribosomal proteins differ from those of bacteria. Therefore,..." The word "Therefore" indicates that a conclusion will follow—mitochondria could not have evolved from prokaryotes, leading to answer choice (**F**).

(G) is incorrect but tempting because it uses the word "aerobic," which appears earlier in the passage.

(H) is incorrect because it's never an issue in the passage.

(J) is incorrect because it's the exact opposite of Scientist 2's argument.

9. D

Category: Conflicting Viewpoints
Difficulty: High

Strategic Advice: Because this question asks about both Scientists, only answer it after reading both and answering all questions that only have to do with one or the other.

Getting to the Answer: This question asks whether the shape of mitochondrial DNA being similar to the structure of prokaryotic DNA weakens either scientist's argument. Neither scientist deals directly with DNA shape, and both suggest that prokaryotes led to the existence of mitochondria (though they disagree on how). Without more information, there's no reason to think the shape resembling prokaryotic DNA is an issue. The answer is (**D**).

Passage IV

10. F

Category: Conflicting Viewpoints
Difficulty: Low
Strategic Advice: Points of agreement can often be found by process of elimination.

Getting to the Answer: Because the researchers disagree about what causes schizophrenia, rule out (H) and (J), which discuss the causes of the illness. Researcher 2 does not mention Parkinson's disease, so (G) cannot be correct either. Both researchers do mention that drugs have been effective in the treatment of schizophrenia's symptoms, so (**F**) is correct.

11. C

Category: Conflicting Viewpoints
Difficulty: Medium
Strategic Advice: First, identify what Researcher 2 believes causes schizophrenia. Then look for an answer choice that addresses that.

Getting to the Answer: Researcher 2's hypothesis is that schizophrenia is caused by early childhood exposure to double-blind communications. Only (**C**) addresses this cause. (A) and (B) relate to Researcher 1's hypothesis, so they can't be correct. (D) is not addressed by either researcher.

12. H

Category: Conflicting Viewpoints
Difficulty: Low
Strategic Advice: Start by asking yourself what each researcher believes causes schizophrenia.

Getting to the Answer: Researcher 1 believes schizophrenia is "related to hyperactivity of the dopaminergic system." One possibility is the over-release of dopamine, a neurotransmitter. A virus that targets neurotransmitters, then, could

cause schizophrenia. Researcher 2 says that schizophrenia is an emotional disorder caused by dysfunction within the family. Since these findings would support the hypothesis of Researcher 1 only, (**H**) is the correct answer.

Quarter 2 Quiz

1. **A**
2. **G**
3. **B**
4. **F**
5. **D**
6. **H**
7. **C**
8. **F**
9. **A**
10. **G**
11. **D**
12. **J**
13. **B**

Passage V

1. A

Category: Scientific Reasoning
Difficulty: Low
Strategic Advice: The question refers to Experiment 2 only, so the correct answer will involve sunlight, which was tested in that experiment.

Getting to the Answer: Table 2 shows that the average length of the leaves increased from 5.3 cm to 12.4 cm as the amount of sunlight increased from 0 to 3 hours per day. But as the amount of sunlight increased further, leaf size decreased. (**A**) summarizes this best.

(B) and (C) are irrelevant, as humidity and water weren't tested in Experiment 2.

(D) misstates the relationship shown in Experiment 2.

2. G

Category: Figure Interpretation
Difficulty: Low
Strategic Advice: Remember, some Figure Interpretation questions will ask you to read between two data points.

Getting to the Answer: Table 1 gives leaf widths at 35% and 55% humidity as 1.8 and 2.0 cm, respectively. The leaf width at 40% humidity would most likely be between those two figures. Only (**G**) fits in this range.

3. **B**

Category: Scientific Reasoning
Difficulty: Medium
Strategic Advice: Go back and check the passage to find where the variables in this question were tested.

Getting to the Answer: All of the answer choices involve humidity and sunlight, which were investigated in Experiments 1 and 2, respectively. In Table 1, leaf length and width were greatest at 75% humidity. In Table 2, they were greatest at 3 hours per day of sunlight. Combining these two conditions, as in (**B**), would probably produce the largest leaves.

4. **F**

Category: Scientific Reasoning
Difficulty: Low
Strategic Advice: Check the opening text for variables that were kept constant through the experiments.

Getting to the Answer: Each experiment begins with a statement that five groups of seedlings were used. Therefore, (**F**) is correct. (G), (H), and (J) all list variables that were manipulated in Experiments 1 and 3.

5. **D**

Category: Scientific Reasoning
Difficulty: Medium
Strategic Advice: Design questions hinge on your understanding of why the experiments were set up the way they were.

Getting to the Answer: The three experiments tested how different factors affected the growth of 3 separate batches of 5 groups of 25 seedlings. If the seedlings were not equally capable of further growth, then changes in leaf size and density could not be reliably attributed to researcher-controlled changes in humidity, sunlight, and temperature. (**D**), then, is the correct answer.

(A) is incorrect because all of the seedlings were 2–3 cm tall.

(B) is incorrect because the seedlings must already have germinated, or sprouted, to have reached 2–3 cm.

(C) is incorrect because the seedlings' ability to produce flowers was never studied.

6. **H**

Category: Scientific Reasoning
Difficulty: High
Strategic Advice: Remember, you're looking for the answer choice that best probes further the question of what factors relate to *Cycas* leaf size and density—the purpose of the experiments.

Getting to the Answer: Each of the three experiments investigated a different factor. To produce the most useful new data, researchers would probably want to vary a fourth condition. Soil mineral content, as in (**H**), would be an appropriate factor to examine.

(F) is incorrect because counting the number of leaves more than 6 cm long wasn't the purpose of these experiments.

(G) and (J) are irrelevant to *Cycas* leaf size and density, so they cannot be correct.

Passage VI

7. **C**

Category: Conflicting Viewpoints
Difficulty: Medium
Strategic Advice: Ask yourself how the new information in the question stem relates to each scientist's viewpoint.

Getting to the Answer: Scientist 2 argues that the amount of oxygen in the air does not affect the number of times a person yawns. Scientist 1 argues that it does. Therefore, you can eliminate (A) and (B), because these statements contradict Scientist 1's viewpoint. You can also eliminate (D), because Scientist 2 argues that stretching is a function of yawning. The correct answer, then, is (**C**).

8. **F**

Category: Conflicting Viewpoints
Difficulty: Medium
Strategic Advice: Go back to the passage to find what evidence Scientist 2 uses to support his viewpoint.

Getting to the Answer: Scientist 2 states, "Particularly striking support for this theory is found in the behavior of people who are paralyzed on one side of their bodies from a stroke. It has been observed that such people can stretch limbs on the otherwise paralyzed sides of their bodies when they yawn." This matches (**F**).

(G) might be tempting because it starts off right, so be sure you're reading carefully.

(H) would support Scientist 1's viewpoint.

(J) is incorrect because Scientist 2 does not cite this as "the best evidence."

9. A

Category: Conflicting Viewpoints
Difficulty: Medium
Strategic Advice: To counter a statement, ask yourself which answer choice would make it untrue.

Getting to the Answer: If a person's oxygen levels don't change after a yawn, then yawns can't function to increase the amount of oxygen in the blood. (**A**) is correct.

(B) is incorrect because it supports, rather than counters, the statement.

(C) is incorrect because you're told that an increase in oxygen flushes out excess carbon dioxide. (D) is incorrect because a decrease in carbon dioxide, then, would support the statement. (D) is irrelevant to the statement.

10. G

Category: Conflicting Viewpoints
Difficulty: Medium
Strategic Advice: Start with the answer choices for "both scientists" questions.

Getting to the Answer: You can immediately eliminate (J), because this is the viewpoint of Scientist 2. You can eliminate (F) because, while both scientists agree that yawns occur primarily during periods of tiredness or boredom, neither states this as *a cause* of yawns.

That leaves (G) and (H), which both reference details found in the introductory material. Since (H) misstates what is said in that introduction, where we are told that yawns are *associated* with acute myocardial infarction and aortic dissection but we are *not* told about a causal relationship. (**G**) must be the correct answer.

11. D

Category: Conflicting Viewpoints
Difficulty: Low
Strategic Advice: You should answer this question before you read the viewpoint of Scientist 2.

Getting to the Answer: Scientist 1's main argument is that a lack of oxygen in the bloodstream leads to an increase in the number of yawns. That leads you to (**D**).

(A) distorts what Scientist 1 says about carbon dioxide excess.

(B) is related to Scientist 2, not Scientist 1.

(C) distorts the passage.

12. J

Category: Conflicting Viewpoints
Difficulty: Medium
Strategic Advice: Look for clues about what sort of answer you need in the answer choices.

Getting to the Answer: All of the answer choices reference details from the opening paragraph. All you need to do is identify which one is correct. The passage states, "Yawning has been associated with drowsiness or weariness, as well as acute myocardial infarction and aortic dissection (vasovagal reactions)." This matches (**J**). It doesn't matter that you don't know what either term means!

(F), (G), and (H) all distort details that appear in the passage.

13. B

Category: Conflicting Viewpoints
Difficulty: High
Strategic Advice: You can save time on this question by reading each answer choice only until you reach a false statement.

Getting to the Answer: To predict what conclusion each scientist will draw from that information, think about how it relates to her viewpoint.

(A) reverses the scientists' viewpoints. Scientist 2 would conclude that a lack of sleep caused an increased need to stretch, and Scientist 1 would conclude that a lack of sleep caused an increased need for oxygen.

(**B**) gets the relationship right. Scientist 1 would likely conclude that a lack of sleep caused an increased need for oxygen, and Scientist 2 would likely conclude that a lack of sleep caused an increased need to stretch.

(C) is wrong about Scientist 2. Only Scientist 1 would say that a lack of sleep caused an increased need for oxygen.

(D) is wrong about Scientist 1. Only Scientist 2 would say that a lack of sleep caused an increased need to stretch.

Quarter 3 Lesson

1. **C**
2. **J**
3. **A**
4. **H**
5. **E**
6. **H**
7. **E**
8. **G**

1. C

Category: Coordinate Geometry

Difficulty: Medium

Strategic Advice: Be sure to memorize the formulas you'll need before Test Day.

Getting to the Answer: The distance formula is

$$\sqrt{(x_1 - x_2)^2 + (y_1 - y_2)^2}$$

Plug in the x-and y-values of points A and B to find AB:

$$\sqrt{(7 - 1)^2 + (1 - 5)^2} = \sqrt{6^2 + (-4)^2}$$
$$= \sqrt{36 + 16}$$
$$= \sqrt{52}$$
$$= 2\sqrt{13}$$

2. J

Category: Coordinate Geometry

Difficulty: Medium

Strategic Advice: Remember to use the slope intercept formula: $y = mx + b$

Getting to the Answer: You know two points on the line: (1, 21) and (4, 42). Find the values of each variable. Identify the slope: $\frac{(42 - 21)}{(4 - 1)} = \frac{21}{3} = 7$. Plug in the values of either point; choose (1, 21) and get $21 = 7(1) + b$. Simplify the equation to get $b = 14$. (**J**) is correct.

3. A

Category: Coordinate Geometry

Difficulty: Medium

Strategic Advice: Parallel lines have the same slope.

Getting to the Answer: Isolate y to find the slope:

$4x + 3y = 15$

$3y = -4x + 15$

$y = -\frac{4}{3}x + 5$

The slope of the original line is $-\frac{4}{3}$. The only choice with the same slope is (**A**).

4. H

Category: Coordinate Geometry

Difficulty: Medium

Strategic Advice: When a line segment is divided in half, it creates two line segments of equal length.

Getting to the Answer: Use the information given in the question stem to determine the lengths of all the line segments. Since (G) is the midpoint of FH, $GH = FG = 13$. HK is 18 and $HJ = JK$, so each is half of HK and $HJ = JK = 9$. Line segment GJ, then, is made up of $GH + HJ = 13 + 9 = 22$. The answer is (**H**).

5. E

Category: Coordinate Geometry

Difficulty: Medium

Strategic Advice: Knowing the graphs of equations is key to solving certain Coordinate Geometry questions.

Getting to the Answer: Use variable manipulation to add 36 to both sides of the equation: $x^2 + y^2 = 36$. This matches the equation of a circle, so you can eliminate (B), (C), and (D). The equation of a circle is $x^2 + y^2 = r^2$, where r is the radius of that circle. The radius is 6, so the diameter is $6 \times 2 = 12$ and (**E**) is correct.

6. H

Category: Coordinate Geometry

Difficulty: Medium

Strategic Advice: When in doubt, sketch it out!

Getting to the Answer: Since both ends of a parabola stretch out to infinity, the only way to avoid intersecting with a downward-facing parabola is to stay above it. Therefore, if an equation contains points inside the parabola, we can eliminate it. This allows us to immediately discard (F) and (G). The equation in (J) can be rewritten as $y = -2x + 8$, which will intersect the parabola, so (J) is wrong as well. (K) can also go, as it is an upward-facing parabola with its vertex at the origin. As the only choice left, (**H**) must be correct and it is: the equation can be rewritten as $y = 2x + 8$. This is the equation of a line with a y-intercept of 8 and an x-intercept of -4.

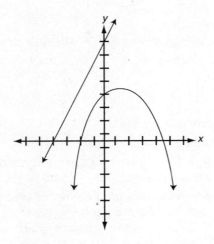

7. E

Category: Coordinate Geometry

Difficulty: Medium

Strategic Advice: Remember FOIL (First, Outer, Inner, Last) to factor a quadratic equation.

Getting to the Answer: The question asks for possible values of x. You know that $x^2 - 4x - 6 = 6$. Set the equation equal to zero: $x^2 - 4x - 12 = 0$. FOIL this equation to get $(x - 6)(x + 2) = 0$. X could equal either 6 or –2; therefore, (**E**) is correct.

8. G

Category: Coordinate Geometry

Difficulty: Medium

Strategic Advice: Most questions about linear equations rely on the slope, rise over run.

Getting to the Answer: Find two points on the graph. Any points will do, so pick ones that are easy to work with. Here, (0,2) and (1,–1) will work well. The slope of this line is as follows:

$$\frac{y_2 - y_1}{x_2 - x_1} = \frac{-1 - 2}{1 - 0} = \frac{-3}{1} = -3$$

Only one answer choice has this slope—(**G**). If more than one answer choice had the correct slope, you'd just need to see which one had the correct y-intercept, $b = 2$.

Quarter 3 Quiz

Answer Key

1. **D**
2. **G**

3. **B**
4. **K**
5. **A**
6. **G**
7. **D**
8. **K**

1. D

Category: Coordinate Geometry

Difficulty: Low

Strategic Advice: The distance formula, $\sqrt{(x_1 - x_2)^2 + (y_1 - y_2)^2}$, provides the length of the line segment between two points. You'll want to memorize this by Test Day, since it won't be provided for you.

Getting to the Answer:

$$\sqrt{[3 - (-2)]^2 + (-6 - 6)^2}$$
$$= \sqrt{5^2 + (-12)^2}$$
$$= \sqrt{169}$$
$$= 13$$

2. G

Category: Coordinate Geometry

Difficulty: Medium

Strategic Advice: Some questions are simpler than they sound at first. Make sure you read the whole question before you decide whether to skip it or not.

Getting to the Answer: The "perpendicular bisector" is just the line that divides $\overline{AB}$ into two equal parts and crosses it at a 90° angle. Since you're looking for the point of intersection of this line with $\overline{AB}$, all you need to find is the point that divides $\overline{AB}$ into two equal parts. This is just the midpoint of $\overline{AB}$. To find the midpoint, find the average of the x-coordinates of A and B and the average of the y-coordinates of A and B.

$$\frac{1 + 7}{2} = \frac{8}{2} = 4$$
$$\frac{5 + 1}{2} = \frac{6}{2} = 3$$

The midpoint of $\overline{AB}$ is (4,3).

3. B

Category: Coordinate Geometry

Difficulty: Low

Strategic Advice: This problem calls for the midpoint formula: $\frac{(x_1 + x_2)}{2}, \frac{(y_1 + y_2)}{2}$

Getting to the Answer: Using V and W, let $(x_1 + x_2) =$ $(-2 + 4)$ and $(y_1 + y_2) = (-7 + 5)$. The average x value is given as 1: $\frac{(-2 + 4)}{2} = \frac{2}{2} = 1$, which checks out. The average y value is $\frac{(-7 + 5)}{2} = \frac{-2}{2} = -1$. The midpoint of line VW is therefore $(-1, 1)$; $p = -1$ and (**B**) is correct.

4. K

Category: Coordinate Geometry
Difficulty: Medium
Strategic Advice: Remember that parallel lines have slopes that are negative reciprocals of one another.
Getting to the Answer: Since line m is perpendicular to a line with a slope of $-\frac{4}{5}$, the slope of line m must be $\frac{5}{4}$. Eliminate (G), (H), and **J**. Next, you know that the line passes through point $(4, 3)$, so plug them into both remaining choices. If $x = 4$, then $(F) = \left(\frac{5}{4}\right)(4) + 2$ $= 5 + 2 = 7$. $(K) = \left(\frac{5}{4}\right)(4) - 2 = 5 - 2 = 3$. Therefore, (**K**) is correct.

5. A

Category: Coordinate Geometry
Difficulty: High
Strategic Advice: This problem may look a little intimidating. Think about what it's asking for before you start making any calculations.
Getting to the Answer: Both of the given points on line m have the same y-coordinate, so m is the horizontal line $y = 5$. The shortest way to get from point C to line m is to move vertically. If you start at point C $(3,3)$ and move up 2 units, you reach $(3,5)$, which is on line m. The shortest distance between point C and line m is 2.

6. H

Category: Coordinate Geometry
Difficulty: Medium
Strategic Advice: Perpendicular lines have negative reciprocal slopes. Parallel lines have equal slopes.
Getting to the Answer: Slope is rise over run, or $\frac{(y^2 - y^1)}{(x^2 - x^1)}$.
The slope of the line containing the points $(5,6)$ and $(6,10)$ is $\frac{10 - 6}{6 - 5} = \frac{4}{1} = 4$. The slope of line l is the negative reciprocal of that, or $-\frac{1}{4}$.

7. D

Category: Coordinate Geometry
Difficulty: Medium
Strategic Advice: Factoring quadratics requires FOIL.
Getting to the Answer: $x^2 - 6x + 1 = -4$
$x^2 - 6x + 5 = 0$
$(x - 1)(x - 5) = 0$
$x = 1$ or 5
(**D**) is correct

8. K

Category: Coordinate Geometry
Difficulty: Medium
Strategic Advice: Remember the order of operations, or PEMDAS.
Getting to the Answer: The radical around the first term in this equation cancels out the square, leaving $x^2 + 4$ as the first term. The next set of terms is a different of squares: $(x + 2)(x - 2) = x^2 - 4$. Their difference equals $x^2 + 4 - (x^2 - 4) = 4 - (-4) = 8$. (**K**) is correct.

Quarter 4 Lesson

Answer Key

1. **A**
2. **H**
3. **D**
4. **H**
5. **D**
6. **G**
7. **A**
8. **G**
9. **E**
10. **H**
11. **E**
12. **K**

1. A

Category: Plane Geometry
Difficulty: Low
Strategic Advice: When the question does not provide a figure, draw one yourself.

Getting to the Answer: Since lines $\overline{PQ}$ and $\overline{RS}$ are perpendicular, ∠*PQR* must form a 90°angle. If point *L* cannot be in the interior of ∠*PQR*, it must be in the interior of ∠*PQS* and the measure of ∠*LQR* must be greater than 90°. Only *A* is greater than 90°.

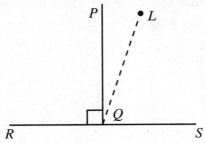

2. H

Category: Plane Geometry

Difficulty: Low

Strategic Advice: To answer questions about lines and angles, figure out which angles are equal and which are supplementary.

Getting to the Answer: ∠*CRP* = ∠*ATR* since *CD* and *AB* are parallel. ∠*ATR* and ∠*ATQ* are supplementary, so the measure of ∠*ATQ* = 180° − 110° = 70°.

3. D

Category: Plane Geometry

Difficulty: Medium

Strategic Advice: The interior angles of every triangle add up to 180°. This figure contains three triangles: *ABC, ABD,* and *BCD*.

Getting to the Answer: Begin by adding any information to the diagram that isn't already in it. Here, you know that ∠*BD* and ∠*CBD* are both 50° (since $\overline{BD}$ bisects ∠*ABC*). The question stem also tells you that ∠*BAD* is 60°. Since ∠*BAC* is a triangle, ∠*BCA* is 180° − 100° − 60° = 20°. Since ∠*BDC* is a triangle, ∠*BDC* is 180° − 50° − 20° = 110°.

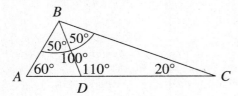

4. H

Category: Plane Geometry

Difficulty: High

Strategic Advice: Whenever a question doesn't seem to have enough information, look for subtle relationships.

Getting to the Answer: V *ABC* and V *EBD* are similar since they share the same angles. (Remember, the acute angles formed when a transversal crosses two parallel lines are all equal.) Since the sides of similar triangles are proportional, *BC:BD* will be equal to *BA:BE*. Since *ABC* is a multiple of a 3:4:5 triangle, *AB* = 8. (If you didn't spot the Pythagorean triplet, you could use the Pythagorean theorem to find the missing leg instead.)

$$\frac{8}{BE} = \frac{6}{6+9}$$

$$8(15) = 6BE$$

$$20 = BE$$

$$AE = 20 - 8 = 12$$

5. D

Category: Plane Geometry

Difficulty: Low

Strategic Advice: If a geometry question doesn't provide a figure, draw your own.

Getting to the Answer: The space between the wall and the point where the ladder touches the ground forms the base of a right triangle. The ladder is its hypotenuse, and the distance from the ground to the top of the ladder is the height. You might notice that this is a multiple of a 3:4:5 Pythagorean triplet, so *w* must equal 16.

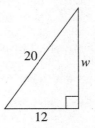

If you didn't spot the triplet, you could use the Pythagorean theorem to find the height.

$$12^2 + w^2 = 20^2$$

$$144 + w^2 = 400$$

$$w^2 = 256$$

$$w = 16$$

6. G

Category: Plane Geometry

Difficulty: Low

Strategic Advice: Every time you see a circle, find the radius first.

Getting to the Answer: The circumference of a circle is $2\pi r$. This circle's *circumference* is 2π, so $r = 1$. Area equals $\pi r2$, so this circle's area is $\pi(1)^2 = \pi$.

7. A

Category: Plane Geometry

Difficulty: Medium

Strategic Advice: Every part of a sector is proportional to the whole circle.

Getting to the Answer: Since the question asks for the length of the arc, you need to find the circumference of the circle.

$d = 2r = 6$

$C = 2\pi r = 6$

The ratio between the central angle of a sector and 360° is the same as the ratio between the arc length and the circumference.

$$\frac{60}{360} = \frac{x}{6\pi}$$

$60(6\pi) = 360x$

$\pi = x$

8. G

Category: Plane Geometry

Difficulty: Medium

Strategic Advice: Once you have identified the given information in an ACT problem, ask yourself: "What can I do with what I know?"

Getting to the Answer: Start with the pentagon. Since the perimeter of a polygon is the sum of all its sides, multiply the length of AB by 5 to determine perimeter of the pentagon: $24 \times 5 = 120$. Both the pentagon and the octagon have the same perimeter, so the perimeter of the octagon must also equal 120. Divide this sum by the number of sides: $120 \div 8 = 15$. (**G**) is the correct answer.

9. E

Category: Plane Geometry

Difficulty: Medium

Strategic Advice: Since you need to transfer information from the square to the circle, find a side they share.

Getting to the Answer: Since the area of the square is 16, each side is 4 units long. A side of the square

is the radius of the circle. Therefore, the area of the circle is $\pi(4)^2 = 16\pi$.

10. H

Category: Plane Geometry

Difficulty: Medium

Strategic Advice: Since you need to move information from one part of the figure to another, look for things they have in common.

Getting to the Answer: Notice that a side of the square is the same length as the diameter of the circle. The perimeter of the square is 16 inches, so each side is 4 inches long and the area of the square is 16 square inches. Since the diameter of the circle is 4 inches, its radius is 2 inches and the area of the circle is $\pi(2)2 = 4$ square inches. The area of the shaded region is the area of the square minus the area of the circle, or $16 - 4\pi$ square inches.

11. E

Category: Plane Geometry

Difficulty: Medium

Strategic Advice: When an ACT problem asks you for the sum of every surface of a solid, find the total surface area.

Getting to the Answer: To get the total surface area of the plank, find the area of each individual surface and then find the sum. The plank's dimensions are 3, 5, and 30, so there are two surfaces of $3 \times 5 = 15$, two surfaces of $3 \times 30 = 90$, and two surfaces of $5 \times 30 = 150$. Therefore, the total surface area is $15 + 15 + 90 + 90 + 150 + 150 = 510$.

12. K

Category: Plane Geometry

Difficulty: Medium

Strategic Advice: The key to solving problems with multiple figures is to transfer information from one figure to another.

Getting to the Answer: The base of the triangle passes through the center of the circle, which means that the base is the circle's diameter and the height is the circle's radius. The circumference of the circle is 36π, so the radius is $\frac{1}{2} \times 36 = 18$ and the diameter is 18 $18 \times 2 = 36$. Therefore, the area of the triangle is $\frac{1}{2} \times 36 \times 18 = 324$.

Quarter 4 Quiz

Answer Key

1. **D**
2. **H**
3. **D**
4. **G**
5. **A**
6. **G**
7. **D**

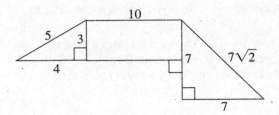

1. D

Category: Plane Geometry

Difficulty: Medium

Strategic Advice: All the acute angles formed when a transversal crosses two parallel lines are equal, as are all the obtuse angles.

Getting to the Answer: The combination of the angle marked 46° and the right angle corresponds to the angle marked y: $46° + 90° = 136° = y$.

2. H

Category: Plane Geometry

Difficulty: Low

Strategic Advice: Anytime you see intersecting lines on the ACT, look for vertical angles and supplementary angles.

Getting to the Answer: $\angle b$ and $\angle c$ are supplementary and add up to 180°. a and b are congruent, and $\angle c$ and $\angle d$ are vertical and congruent. Therefore, angles a and d are supplementary and equal 180°. $\angle a + \angle b + \angle c + \angle d = 360°$.

3. D

Category: Plane Geometry

Difficulty: Medium

Strategic Advice: Complex and composite figures should be divided into simpler shapes. Then you can easily find the area of each simple figure and add these areas together to find the total area.

Getting to the Answer: Break the complex figure into easy-to-work-with rectangles and triangles:

The base of the triangle on the left can be found by subtracting the length of the rectangle from the length of the rectangle plus triangle. The height of the triangle on the right can be found by noticing that the triangle is a 45–45–90 triangle, since its base and hypotenuse are in the ratio $x:x\sqrt{2}$. Therefore, the base and height are the same.

Area of triangle on left: $\frac{1}{2}(4)(3) = 6$.

Area of rectangle: $10(3) = 30$.

Area of triangle on right: $\frac{1}{2}(7)(7) = 24.5$.

Total area: $6 + 30 + 24.5 = 60.5$.

4. G

Category: Plane Geometry

Difficulty: Medium

Strategic Advice: Always be on the lookout for special right triangles. Spotting them will save you valuable time on Test Day.

Getting to the Answer: Since ABC is equilateral, its altitude $\overline{BD}$ bisects its base $\overline{AC}$. Therefore, $AD = 2\sqrt{2}$. You may recognize these two sides of triangle ABD as part of a 30–60–90 triangle (with a side ratio of $x:x\sqrt{3}:2x$). Either this ratio or the Pythagorean theorem will let you find the length of $\overline{BD}$: $2\sqrt{6}$.

5. A

Category: Plane Geometry

Difficulty: Medium

Strategic Advice: Once you have identified the given information in the question stem, ask yourself: "What can I do with what I know?"

Getting to the Answer: Determine what kind of right triangle is presented by finding the remaining angle. If the angles given are 30° and 90°, then the remaining angle must be 60°. The ratio of sides in a 30:60:90 right triangle are $x:x\sqrt{3}:2x$. Since the side opposite the 30° angle is the shortest side, x, the side opposite the 60° angle is equal to $x\sqrt{3}$. Set $4 = x\sqrt{3}$ and solve for x. x equals 2.3 or (**A**).

6. **G**

Category: Plane Geometry

Difficulty: Low

Strategic Advice: Be sure you answer the right question. It's easy to get off track and solve for the wrong thing.

Getting to the Answer: The perimeter is the distance around the parallelogram. Since $WX = ZY = 8$ and $WZ = XY$, the total perimeter is $8 + 8 + XY + XY$.

$16 + 2XY = 30$

$2XY = 14$

$XY = 7$

7. **D**

Category: Plane Geometry

Difficulty: Medium

Strategic Advice: No formulas are provided on the ACT, so you'll need to memorize them.

Getting to the Answer: The volume of a cylinder is $\pi r^2 h$. This cylinder's height is 5 inches and its radius is 4 inches, so the volume is $\pi(4)^2(5) = 80\pi$.

Quarter 2 Homework

Answer Key

1. **B**
2. **J**
3. **A**
4. **H**
5. **B**
6. **F**
7. **D**
8. **F**
9. **C**
10. **G**
11. **D**
12. **H**
13. **A**
14. **H**
15. **D**
16. **H**
17. **B**
18. **F**
19. **B**
20. **H**
21. **D**
22. **F**
23. **B**
24. **F**
25. **C**
26. **F**
27. **D**
28. **G**
29. **A**
30. **H**

PASSAGE I

1. **B**

Category: Scientific Reasoning

Difficulty: Low

Strategic Advice: This Scientific Reasoning question can easily be answered by reading information off Table 1.

Getting to the Answer: Bus 3 (built in 1996) is much newer than Bus 1 (1984) or Bus 2 (1982). Do the data in the table support the hypothesis that newer buses emit a smaller percentage of hydrocarbons than older buses? Yes. For any sample time, Bus 3 emits a lower percentage of hydrocarbons than either Bus 1 and Bus 2, and on average Bus 1 is lower than Bus 2. Answer (**B**) is a match.

Be careful of (C). It's true that the highest percentage of hydrocarbons was emitted by the 1982 bus, but you should have immediately crossed this choice off, as well as (D), as they both incorrectly answered the question "No."

2. **J**

Category: Scientific Reasoning

Difficulty: High

Strategic Advice: Questions that ask how to test a new variable should control everything except the new variable.

Getting to the Answer: If the student wants to investigate whether carbon monoxide gas is affecting the hydrocarbons reading, he would have to run some kind of test that determines whether the gas chromatograph correctly measures hydrocarbons when carbon monoxide is also present. Testing a control sample with known percentages of carbon monoxide and hydrocarbons, (**J**), would certainly tell the student whether the gas chromatograph was giving correct readings.

(**F**) won't work. Adding hydrocarbons to the collection bag would increase the percentage of hydrocarbons in the exhaust, but it wouldn't address the carbon monoxide issue.

(**G**) won't work either. The teacher's car won't tell the student anything new about measuring hydrocarbons when carbon monoxide is present.

(**H**) is incorrect. Nothing in the passage suggests that testing oxygen will tell the student anything about carbon monoxide and hydrocarbons.

3. A

Category: Scientific Reasoning

Difficulty: Medium

Strategic Advice: When a question asks why a particular piece of equipment was used, make sure you understand the experimental setup before answering.

Getting to the Answer: The students were collecting exhaust samples to determine what percentage of the exhaust was composed of hydrocarbons, so they'd want to keep each exhaust sample as pure as possible. A bag attached to the tailpipe would collect the exhaust before it mixed with, and was diluted by, the outside air, (**A**).

(**B**) violates the students' purpose. They wanted to compare the percentages of hydrocarbons in the exhaust. Adding air and other gases would make their results unreliable.

(**C**) is incorrect because you know that the collection bag captures all of the exhaust, not only hydrocarbons.

(**D**) is incorrect because you're given no reason to assume the bag filters anything from the exhaust.

4. H

Category: Scientific Reasoning

Difficulty: Low

Strategic Advice: If you've learned to read critically and identify the parts of the scientific method as you go, you should be able to answer this question easily.

Getting to the Answer: In Experiment 1, students took exhaust samples at varying times from buses of the same model that were built in different years. Only (**H**) states either of these elements, so it is correct.

(**F**) is tempting because it mentions time, but it does so incorrectly. The exhaust samples were collected

at 30-second intervals, but the time of day they were collected wasn't mentioned.

(**G**) is incorrect. The same method of collection was used for each sample with each bus.

(**J**) is incorrect because you're told that 5 mL of each exhaust sample were injected into the gas chromatograph.

5. B

Category: Figure Interpretation

Difficulty: Low

Strategic Advice: Remember to ask yourself, "Where is the information I need?"

Getting to the Answer: The goal is to test emissionswhen they're at their peak. Check Table 1 and Table 2 and note at which time each bus emits the highest percentage of hydrocarbons. Bus 1 emits peak hydrocarbons (12%) at 90 seconds, Bus 2 at 120 seconds (22.9%), and Bus 3 at 90 seconds (6%). This matches (**B**).

6. F

Category: Scientific Reasoning

Difficulty: Medium

Strategic Advice: If you were able to note the purpose of Experiment 2 as you read, you won't have to go back to the text to answer this question. If you couldn't, then look for the purpose in the short paragraph that follows the *Experiment* 2 subhead.

Getting to the Answer: The purpose of Experiment 2 was to find the percentage of hydrocarbons in the exhaust of the same three buses used in Experiment 1 after they had idled for 15 minutes and their engines were warm. This matches (**F**).

(**G**) is incorrect. No mention is made in the passage of calibrating the gas chromatograph.

(**H**) is incorrect because the experiment tests only hydrocarbons. (Nitrogen oxides are mentioned as one cause of ozone in the opening paragraph, but don't let this confuse you.)

(**J**) is incorrect because the effectiveness of the exhaust collection bag is never mentioned or tested.

PASSAGE II

7. D

Category: Scientific Reasoning

Difficulty: High

Strategic Advice: Finding statements both scientists agree on can be time-consuming, so start with the answer choices on this one.

Getting to the Answer: To find the answer quickly, remember that only one scientist needs to disagree for the choice to be incorrect.

(A) is incorrect, because Scientist 2 states, "Between 400 and 680 km, activity once again increases."

(B) is incorrect because Scientist 2 says that the quakes "result from the slippage that occurs when rock in a descending tectonic plate undergoes a phase change." This has nothing to do with fluids.

(C) is incorrect because Scientist 2 says that "mantle rock below 300 km is probably totally dehydrated."

(**D**) is the only point of agreement. Scientist 1 says that "below 50 km, rock is under too much pressure to fracture normally." Scientist 2 says, "Deep-focus earthquakes cannot result from normal fractures...at depths greater than 50 km."

8. F

Category: Scientific Reasoning
Difficulty: Medium

Strategic Advice: You should answer this question first, after you finish reading Scientist 1's viewpoint.

Getting to the Answer: Scientist 1 says that water trapped in rock causes deep-focus earthquakes. The correct answer should build on this theory.

(**F**) is exactly what you're looking for. Evidence that water can exist at the depths of deep-focus earthquakes would support the idea that water could cause the earthquakes.

(G) is incorrect because proof that these earthquakes happen doesn't necessarily lend support to *why* Scientist 1 thinks they happen.

(H) is incorrect because phase changes aren't mentioned by Scientist 1. (They are mentioned by Scientist 2. This answer choice could be tempting if you read both viewpoints before attempting this question.)

(J) is incorrect because Scientist 1 argues that water causes deep-focus earthquakes, not quakes shallow enough to have been caused by sewer lines.

9. C

Category: Scientific Reasoning
Difficulty: Medium

Strategic Advice: When a question asks about assumptions shared by both scientists, check the

introductory material for common ground. If the answer isn't there, go straight to the answer choices and eliminate those with which just one scientist would agree.

Getting to the Answer: Both scientists believe that Earth's crust (surface layer) is composed of mobile tectonic plates, (**C**). In describing the plates as being "forced down into the mantle," Scientist 1 implies that they are normally in the crust. Scientist 2 makes reference to "a descending tectonic plate."

(A) is incorrect because the introductory paragraph says that most earthquakes originate less than 20 km below Earth's surface.

(B) is incorrect because neither scientist assumes that surface quakes are caused by trapped fluids.

(D) is incorrect because neither scientist discusses how deep-focus earthquakes are detected.

10. G

Category: Scientific Reasoning
Difficulty: Medium

Strategic Advice: A hypothesis is refuted when evidence that contradicts the claim is introduced.

Getting to the Answer: Scientist 2 believes that deep-focus earthquakes are the result of slippage caused by phase changes. Scientist 2, therefore would, not expect deep quakes to occur below 680 km where, according to the last sentence of the passage, "No phase changes are predicted." Recording a quake with an origin below that depth, (**G**), would send Scientist 2 back to the drawing board, or at least in search of deeper phase changes.

(F) is incorrect because Scientist 2 doesn't believe deep-focus quakes are caused by water.

(H) is incorrect because only the phase changes undergone by rock in Earth's crust are relevant.

(J) is incorrect because this would support Scientist 2's hypothesis.

11. D

Category: Scientific Reasoning
Difficulty: Low

Strategic Advice: Just as in the Reading Test, some Scientific Reasoning questions will ask about a detail in the passage.

Getting to the Answer: The final sentence of Scientist 1's paragraph mentions that, when fluids were injected into the ground at the Rocky Mountain Arsenal, the unintended result was "a series of shallow-focus earthquakes." The opening words "In fact" signal that this final sentence is meant to illustrate the previous sentence, which refers to experiments in which trapped fluids caused rock to fail at lower than normal shear stress. The implication is that the quakes at the arsenal occurred because the fluid wastes lowered the shear stress failure point of the rock, (**D**).

(A) and (B) are incorrect because dehydration and the slab of calcium magnesium silicate belong in Scientist 2's paragraph.

(C) is incorrect because it confuses the Rocky Mountain Arsenal incident with the deep-sea trenches that are mentioned in the previous two sentences.

12. H

Category: Scientific Reasoning
Difficulty: Medium
Strategic Advice: Evidence that supports a hypothesis will offer support to one or more elements of the hypothesis.

Getting to the Answer: Scientist 2 claims that the slippage involved in deep-focus earthquakes results from phase changes. To support this contention, she cites laboratory work that produced similar phase changes and slippage in a slab of calcium magnesium silicate. But neither scientist says that mantle rock is composed of calcium magnesium silicate. If the slippery slab is to serve as evidence for Scientist 2's theory, it must at least be similar to mantle rock, (**H**).

(F) might help refute Scientist 1's hypothesis, but it would not strengthen Scientist 2's.

(G) and (J) would both weaken Scientist 2's hypothesis.

13. A

Category: Scientific Reasoning
Difficulty: Medium
Strategic Advice: Since the question stem doesn't give you any indication of where to start, go straight to the answer choices.

Getting to the Answer: The first sentence of the opening paragraph says that "the *focus* (point of origin) of most earthquakes lies less than 20 km below Earth's surface." This matches (**A**).

(B) is the exact opposite of the correct answer.

(C) and (D) can be easily eliminated, as volcanic activity and destructive power are not mentioned in the passage.

PASSAGE III

14. H

Category: Scientific Reasoning
Difficulty: Low
Strategic Advice: To determine what was investigated, look at what was varied and what was measured.

Getting to the Answer: In Experiment 1, the scientists varied the concentration and the temperature of sucrose solutions, and they measured the osmotic pressure. Therefore, they were investigating the effect of concentration and temperature on osmotic pressure, (**H**).

(F) is predictably incorrect. Solvent and concentration were investigated in Experiment 2.

(G) can be ruled out easily because volume isn't mentioned anywhere in the passage.

(J) is incorrect. Experiment 1 tested the effect of temperature on osmotic, not atmospheric, pressure.

15. D

Category: Scientific Reasoning
Difficulty: Low
Strategic Advice: To answer questions about an experiment's design, start with what the scientists are trying to measure.

Getting to the Answer: You're told in the opening paragraph that osmotic pressure is the pressure required to prevent osmosis. To measure the osmotic pressure of a solution, scientists need to be able to tell when osmosis is and isn't happening. If both solutions were clear, this would be very difficult! Adding a dye to the pure water means that the sucrose solution will start to turn blue when the water (the solvent) moves across the membrane. (**D**) matches this.

(A) is tempting because it's so close. The dye showed when osmosis began, not when it was completed.

(B) could be crossed off immediately because ions were never mentioned in the passage.

(C) is irrelevant.

16. H

Category: Patterns
Difficulty: Low
Strategic Advice: Go through the variables in the answer choices one by one to determine whether osmotic pressure depends on each.

Getting to the Answer: The answer choices all involve temperature, concentration, and solvent in different combinations. Start with temperature—does osmotic pressure vary with temperature? Check Table 1. For a 1.00 mol/L solution at 298 K, the osmotic pressure is 24.47 atm. For the same solution at 348 K, the osmotic pressure is 28.57 atm. Apparently, temperature influences osmotic pressure. Cross off (G), because it doesn't include temperature.

Next, try solvent. A 0.50 mol/L solution of ethanol at 298 K has the same osmotic pressure as 0.05 mol/L solutions of acetone, diethyl ether, and methanol, according to Table 2, and the same as water, according to Table 1. Therefore, osmotic pressure is not dependent on solvent. Cross off (F) and **J**, leaving just (**H**)—the correct answer.

(For practice, double-check that osmotic pressure is indeed dependent on concentration. Look at any solvent from Table 1 or Table 2 to see that when concentration goes up, so does osmotic pressure.)

17. **B**

Category: Patterns
Difficulty: Medium

Strategic Advice: To figure out what will happen under these conditions, you have to understand what osmotic pressure means.

Getting to the Answer: Go back to the definition of osmotic pressure given in the introduction. Osmotic pressure is the external pressure required to prevent osmosis. So, for osmosis to occur, the external pressure must be less than the osmotic pressure of the solution.

The solution in this question is a 0.1 mol/L aqueous sucrose solution at 298 K. Because it's aqueous, you should know to look at Table 1. There, you can read that the osmotic pressure for this solution is 2.45 atm. Since the external pressure in this question is less than that, it won't prevent osmosis, and water will move across the membrane.

The passage also tells you about the direction of movement during osmosis. The solvent (here, water) moves from the side with a lower concentration of dissolved solids to the side with a higher concentration of dissolved solids. So the pure water will move from the pure-water side to the sucrose-solution side, (**B**).

Be careful of (A), which reverses the proper relationship!

18. **F**

Category: Scientific Reasoning
Difficulty: Medium

Strategic Advice: With Roman numeral questions, start by investigating the statement that appears most often in the answer choices.

Getting to the Answer: Statement I appears three times, so start there. The results in Table 2 show that osmotic pressure does not depend on the solvent (you also determined this in question 16), so Statement I is valid. Cross off (G) because it doesn't contain Statement I.

Next, evaluate Statement II. Is osmotic pressure dependent on anything besides temperature? In question 16, you determined that it was dependent on temperature and concentration. The data in Table 2 verify this, so cross off (H) because it contains II.

Finally, consider Statement III. Check the definition of osmotic pressure—it's the amount of pressure required to *prevent* osmosis. So when osmotic pressure is exceeded, osmosis won't happen, and Statement III is false. (**F**) is correct.

19. **B**

Category: Figure Interpretation
Difficulty: Low

Strategic Advice: You should do this question first and grab the easy points.

Getting to the Answer: Find methanol at 0.5 mol/L, which is in Table 2. The text above the table says that all the trials were conducted at the same temperature (298 K). Therefore, all you have to do is read across the row. The osmotic pressure listed is 12.23 atm, (**B**).

PASSAGE IV

20. **H**

Category: Patterns
Difficulty: Medium
Strategic Advice: What are the patterns in the data?

Getting to the Answer: The patterns are remarkablysimilar throughout the graphs, except for the hollow squares in Figure 3. Instead of orienting themselves in either direction of migration, the birds that were raised in a windowless room displayed a more or less random orientation. The fact that these were the only birds raised without ever seeing any stars, whether real or projected, suggests that indigo buntings need repeated exposure to the stars to orient themselves properly for migration. (**H**) is the correct answer.

(F), (G), and (J) are incorrect because Experiments 1 and 2 do not include birds that were not exposed to stars.

21. D

Category: Scientific Reasoning
Difficulty: High

Strategic Advice: To answer this kind of question, first identify which factors researchers identified as having an effect on the experiment in question. Then look for an answer that investigates this factor further.

Getting to the Answer: Only raising newborn indigo buntings in a windowless room with diffuse light affected their ability to orient themselves for migration. The correct answer choice should further investigate this situation.

A is incorrect because it doesn't probe the situation you identified as having an effect on migration orientation.

(B) is incorrect because nothing in the passage suggests that there might be a link between migration orientation and diet.

(C) is incorrect because nothing in the passage suggests that raising indigo buntings with full night-sky exposure will affect their ability to orient themselves for migration. There's also no reason to suspect that viewing the ground affects orientation ability.

(**D**) is correct. This experiment could tell you whether exposure to the stars must occur by any particular stage in an indigo bunting's life.

22. F

Category: Scientific Reasoning
Difficulty: Medium

Strategic Advice: Remember that purpose can often be found in the paragraph following the experiment heading.

Getting to the Answer: Experiment 3 isolated newborn indigo buntings from adults and raised one set in a planetarium with a projected view of the normal night sky and the other in a windowless room with diffuse light. This matches (**F**).

(G) is incorrect because seasonal temperature variations aren't mentioned in Experiment 3 (or in the passage at all).

(H) is incorrect because it fails to mention the windowless room or the isolation of newborns from adults. This is the purpose of Experiment 2.

(J) is incorrect because other species of migratory birds are not discussed in Experiment 3.

23. B

Category: Scientific Reasoning
Difficulty: High

Strategic Advice: To identify which statement would weaken the hypothesis, ask yourself whether each would be impossible if the hypothesis were true.

Getting to the Answer: Start with Statement I. Under these conditions, the newborn indigo buntings would never have seen the stars before having been placed in outdoor cages. It's still possible, however, that they could learn how to orient themselves on the spot from the adult indigo buntings. Cross off (A) and (D), as they contain Statement I.

Statement II would weaken the hypothesis. It would demonstrate that the birds are able to orient themselves when the stars are not visible. (**B**), then, must be the correct answer, as it is the only remaining choice that contains Statement II.

(Statement III also does not weaken the hypothesis, as the opening paragraph describes indigo buntings as "night-flying." The behavior of birds that migrate by day is irrelevant to indigo buntings.)

24. F

Category: Patterns
Difficulty: Medium

Strategic Advice: Identify the pattern shown in Experiment 3; then look for a match among the answer choices.

Getting to the Answer: Figure 3 shows the birds raised in a windowless room (the hollow squares) orienting themselves pretty much in all directions. Their inability to choose any particular direction almost certainly stems from their lack of exposure either to the stars or to adult birds that were familiar with the stars, rather than from the month (September) and projected constellations (fall). Changing the month and the projected constellations, then, is unlikely to enable them to display any particular orientation. (**F**) restates this pattern.

25. C

Category: Patterns
Difficulty: Medium

Strategic Advice: Remember, many questions will require you to combine information from multiple experiments.

Getting to the Answer: Newborn indigo buntings raised in a planetarium in isolation from adult birds oriented themselves fairly well under (projected) September constellations (see the black squares in Figure 3). Experiment 1 showed that adult indigo buntings in outdoor cages were able to orient themselves to the night sky. Most likely then, newborns raised in isolation in outdoor cages would also orient themselves appropriately, (**C**). There is no reason to suppose that the birds would orient themselves correctly in one migratory season and not the other, so (A) and (B) are incorrect. (D) is the opposite of what you're looking for.

PASSAGE V

26. F

Category: Scientific Reasoning

Difficulty: High

Strategic Advice: To answer this question, you must understand Scientist 2's point about the Pauli exclusion principle.

Getting to the Answer: Scientist 2 says that the quark model is wrong because it violates the Pauli exclusion principle, which states that no two particles of half-integer spin can occupy the same state. He says that in the $\Delta++$ baryon, for example, the presence of two up quarks in the same state would violate the principle, so the model must be incorrect. If Scientist 1 were able to show, however, that quarks do not have half-integer spin, (**F**), she could argue that the Pauli exclusion principle does not apply to quarks and thus counter Scientist 2's objections.

Evidence that the $\Delta++$ baryon exists, (G), or that quarks have fractional charge, (H), isn't going to help Scientist 1 because neither has anything to do with the Pauli exclusion principle.

Evidence that quarks have the same spin as electrons, (J), would only support Scientist 2's position.

27. D

Category: Scientific Reasoning

Difficulty: Medium

Strategic Advice: What does Scientist 1 state about the $\Delta++$ baryon?

Getting to the Answer: Scientist 1 doesn't say anything about the $\Delta++$ baryon specifically, but she does say that all baryons "are composed of three quarks." Scientist 2 tells you that the $\Delta++$ baryon "supposedly consists solely of three up quarks."

Scientist 1 believes in the quark model and that

each up quark has a charge of $+2/3$. So the three up quarks that together make up the $\Delta++$ baryon would have a total charge of $+2$, (**D**).

28. G

Category: Scientific Reasoning

Difficulty: Low

Strategic Advice: When a scientist offers several reasons for his opinions, any one or combination of these reasons could be a correct answer.

Getting to the Answer: Scientist 2 thinks that the quark model is flawed for two reasons: quarks would have been detected experimentally if they existed, and the quark model violates the Pauli exclusion principle. The first reason is paraphrased in (**G**), the correct answer.

(F) is incorrect because the existence of individual baryons, including protons, has been verified experimentally. Scientist 2 never says that he thinks particles cannot have fractional charge, (H), nor does he complain that the quark model doesn't include electrons as elementary particles, (J).

29. A

Category: Scientific Reasoning

Difficulty: Low

Strategic Advice: Questions like this are really just testing your ability to locate a detail in the passage.

Getting to the Answer: The deep inelastic scattering experiments, according to Scientist 1, showed that the proton has a substructure. The three distinct lumps that were found to bounce high-energy electrons back and scatter them through large angles were the three quarks that make up the proton (at least in Scientist 1's view), so (**A**) is correct.

30. H

Category: Scientific Reasoning

Difficulty: High

Strategic Advice: Reread the lines concerning deep inelastic scattering.

Getting to the Answer: Scientist 1 says that, in deep inelastic scattering, "high-energy electron beams were fired into protons. While most of the electrons incident on the proton passed right through, a few bounced back. The number of electrons scattered through large angles indicated that there are three distinct lumps within the proton."

Earlier, Scientist 1 stated that "all baryons, one of which is the proton, are composed of three quarks." If the three lumps were indeed quarks, then this supports the quark model because, in the quark model, the proton consists of three quarks. (**H**) matches this. (F) and (G) are incorrect because protons are baryons and not mesons.

Baryons, such as the proton, are all supposed to consist of three quarks, so this rules out (J).

Quarter 3 Homework

Answer Key

1. **D**
2. **H**
3. **E**
4. **H**
5. **D**
6. **K**
7. **B**
8. **K**
9. **A**
10. **G**
11. **C**
12. **K**
13. **E**
14. **K**

1. D

Category: Coordinate Geometry
Difficulty: Medium
Strategic Advice: Use the FOIL technique to expand polynomials.

Getting to the Answer: First, set the equation equal to zero: $2x^2 - 2x - 12 = 0$. The common factor in this equation is 2. Divide by 2 to get $x^2 - x - 6 = 0$. The constant term is negative, so one factor must be positive and the other must be negative. The numbers 2 and -3 sum to -1 and multiply to -6. $(x + 2)(x - 3) = 0$, so x can be -2 or 3. Adding these values results in 1, so (**D**) is correct.

2. H

Category: Coordinate Geometry
Difficulty: Medium

Strategic Advice: Begin by solving each equation for y to find out each line's slope.

Getting to the Answer: Solve for y in the first equation: $7y = -5x + 49$, which reduces to $y = -\frac{5}{7}x + 7$. Then solve for y in the second equation: $7y = 6x + 21$, which reduces to $y = \frac{6}{7}x + 3$. $7 - 3 = 4$, so (**H**) is correct.

3. E

Category: Coordinate Geometry
Difficulty: Medium

Strategic Advice: With variables in the answer choices, this question is a great candidate for Picking Numbers; Pick Numbers to check your work.

Getting to the Answer: Midpoint formula $= \frac{(x_1 + x_2)}{2}, \frac{(y_1 + y_2)}{2}$. Let $(x_1, y_1) = (x + 4, x + 5)$, and $(x_2, y_2) = (x + 2, x - 1)$.

$$\frac{(x + 4) + (x + 2)}{2} = \frac{2x + 6}{2} = x + 3$$

$$\frac{(x + 5) + (x - 1)}{2} = \frac{2x + 4}{2} = x + 2$$

(**E**) is correct.

4. H

Category: Coordinate Geometry
Difficulty: Medium

Strategic Advice: Most questions about linear equations rely on the slope. Make sure you know that the slope of a line is $\frac{y_2 - y_1}{x_2 - x_1}$

Getting to the Answer: Since the two lines are parallel, their slopes are equal. The slope of the first line is $\frac{16 - 1}{2 - 1} = \frac{15}{1} = 15$ and the slope of the second line is $\frac{25 - (-5)}{a - (-10)} = \frac{30}{a + 10}$. Set these equal to each other and solve for a:

$$\frac{30}{a + 10} = 15$$

$$30 = 15a + 150$$

$$-120 = 15a$$

$$-8 = a$$

5. D

Category: Coordinate Geometry
Difficulty: Low

Strategic Advice: When a line intersects the y-axis, x = 0. When a line intersects the x-axis, y = 0.

Getting to the Answer: Set y equal to 0 and solve for x to find the value of x at which the line intersects the x-axis:

$3x + 0 = 9$

$3x = 9$

$x = 3$

6. K

Category: Coordinate Geometry

Difficulty: Low

Strategic Advice: Draw a quick sketch. Notice that the answers are fairly different, so you only need a general idea of the solution in order to get the correct answer.

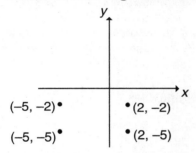

Getting to the Answer: As you can see in the diagram above, the fourth coordinate must be (–5, –5).

7. B

Category: Coordinate Geometry

Difficulty: Medium

Strategic Advice: The easiest way to find the slope of a line is to put the equation in slope-intercept form, $y = mx + b$.

Getting to the Answer:

$4x + 3y = 9$

$3y = -4x + 9$

$y = -\frac{4}{3}x + 3$

The slope, m, is the coefficient of x, or $-\frac{4}{3}$.

8. K

Category: Variable Manipulation

Difficulty: Medium

Strategic Advice: If you're not sure which answer is correct, try plugging in points from the number line.

Getting to the Answer: The shaded region includes all the values between –1.5 and –2.5, exclusive. Since –1.5 is larger than –2.5, the inequality should be –1.5 >x > –2.5. Plugging in x = –2 eliminates (F), (G), and (J).

(H) includes numbers that aren't in the shaded region, such as –2.9.

9. A

Category: Coordinate Geometry

Difficulty: Medium

Strategic Advice: Don't jump right into using your graphing calculator; often some simple algebra is the best way to the right answer.

Getting to the Answer: The easiest way to find the y-intercept (the value of y when the graph crosses the y-axis) is to plug in x = 0:

$12(0) - 3y = 12$

$-3y = 12$

$y = -4$

10. G

Category: Operations

Difficulty: Medium

Strategic Advice: If the labels are missing on a number line, you can find the length of each interval by finding the difference in the endpoints (how much the total interval is) and dividing by the number of subintervals.

Getting to the Answer: The unmarked interval goes from 2.7 to 2.8, so it must be 0.1 units long. It's divided into 10 equally spaced subintervals, each which must be $\frac{0.1}{10}$ = 0.01 units long.

A B   C   D E

2.7 2.72 2.74 2.762.78 2.8

E is approximately 2.78, so (**G**) is the closest.

11. C

Category: Coordinate Geometry

Difficulty: Medium

Strategic Advice: Be sure to read the question carefully. This one gives you an equation that's x in terms of y, not y in terms of x.

Getting to the Answer: First, translate the description into an equation: $x = 9 + 3y$. Then put it into slope-intercept form:

$x = 9 + 3y$

$\frac{1}{3}x - 3 = y$

As you can see from the equation, the slope is $\frac{1}{3}$.

12. K

Category: Coordinate Geometry

Difficulty: Low

Strategic Advice: Most coordinate geometry questions rely on the slope. Make sure you remember that slope is $\frac{rise}{run}$.

Getting to the Answer:

$$\frac{y_2 - y_1}{x_2 - x_1} = \frac{\frac{3}{4} - 0}{\frac{1}{3} - 0}$$

$$= \frac{\frac{3}{4}}{\frac{1}{3}}$$

$$= \frac{3}{4} \times \frac{3}{1}$$

$$= \frac{9}{4}$$

13. E

Category: Coordinate Geometry

Difficulty: High

Strategic Advice: Backsolving is a great option here if you're not sure how to set this problem up algebraically or if you're not confident about your variable manipulation skills. Most students will also find Backsolving to be the faster way to solve this problem.

Getting to the Answer: Plug the given coordinates into the distance formula ($\sqrt{(x_1 - x_2)^2 + (y_1 - y_2)^2}$), set the distance equal to 4, and solve for r:

$$\sqrt{(r - 10)^2 + (6 - r)^2} = 4$$
$$(r - 10)^2 + (6 - r)^2 = 16$$
$$(r^2 - 20r + 100) + (36 - 12r + r^2) = 16$$
$$2r^2 - 32r + 136 = 16$$
$$2r^2 - 32r + 120 = 0$$
$$r^2 - 16r + 60 = 0$$
$$(r - 10)(r - 6) = 0$$
$$r = 10 \text{ or } r = 6$$

Only 10 is an answer choice, so (**E**) is correct. To Backsolve, you still need to know the distance formula to figure out whether (A), (B), and (D) are correct, but notice that E gives the points (10,6) and (10,10). Since the x-coordinate is the same, you can see that the distance between the points is $10 - 6 = 4$ without using the formula.

14. K

Category: Percents

Difficulty: Medium

Strategic Advice: Always make sure you're solving for the right thing.

Getting to the Answer: At first glance, this question may look like an Average or Weighted Average question, making answers (F) and (G) tempting. The question asks for the combined increase, though, which means we need to know the actual numbers. (J) is tempting as well, because since the time periods are the same, we may want to just add the two percentages. However, Picking Numbers will show us the answer. With Percent questions, we should always start with 100. If there were 100 people in City Q in 1970, and it increased by 20%, in 1980 there were 120. If there were 120 in 1980, and it increased by another 30% of that, there were 156 people in 1990. 156 is a 56% increase over 100, so the answer is (**K**).

Quarter 4 Homework

Answer Key

1. **C**
2. **G**
3. **E**
4. **H**
5. **A**
6. **G**
7. **B**
8. **G**
9. **D**
10. **H**
11. **D**
12. **H**
13. **D**
14. **H**
15. **E**
16. **J**
17. **D**
18. **G**
19. **B**

1. C

Category: Plane Geometry

Difficulty: Medium

Strategic Advice: Always make sure you're solving for the right thing.

Getting to the Answer: Say the rectangle is l centimeters long. Then it is $2l$ centimeters wide and $x = 2l(l) = 2l^2$. If both the length and width are doubled, the new area is $4l(2l) = 8l^2$. This is 4 times x. If you have trouble keeping the variables straight, try Picking Numbers. If the rectangle is 1 centimeter by 2 centimeters, its area is 2. When both dimensions are doubled, the new area is $2(4) = 8$, or 4 times the original area.

2. G

Category: Plane Geometry

Difficulty: Medium

Strategic Advice: Since area formulas you need forgeometry aren't printed in the test, you'll need tomemorize them ahead of time.

Getting to the Answer: If the base of the triangle is b, then its height is $3b$. Since the area of a triangle ishalf the base times the height, $\frac{1}{2}(b)(3b) = 216$.

$$3b^2 = 432$$
$$b^2 = 144$$
$$b = 12$$

3. E

Category: Plane Geometry

Difficulty: Low

Strategic Advice: Evaluate Roman numeral statements one at a time, starting with the one that appears in the most answer choices.

Getting to the Answer: The figure is a polygon, since all its sides are straight. Eliminate (B) and (C). The figure is a quadrilateral, since it has four sides. Eliminate (A). The figure is not a rectangle, since not all its angles are 90°. Eliminate (D), leaving (**E**) as the only possible answer.

4. H

Category: Plane Geometry

Difficulty: Medium

Strategic Advice: Remember the triangle inequality theorem: every side of a triangle must be less than the sum of and greater than the difference between the other two sides.

Getting to the Answer: If one side of the triangle is 7, the other two sides must add up to more than 7. Since all three sides are integers, the smallest number the other two sides can add up to is 8. Therefore, the smallest possible perimeter is $7 + 8 = 15$.

5. A

Category: Plane Geometry

Difficulty: Medium

Strategic Advice: Many questions combine several ideas. This question combines plane geometry with variable manipulation.

Getting to the Answer: The areas of the two rectangles are equal, so $(a + 2)b = a(b + 3)$.

$$ab + 2b = ab + 3a$$
$$2b = 3a$$
$$\frac{2b}{3} = a$$

6. G

Category: Plane Geometry

Difficulty: Medium

Strategic Advice: Triangles appear in many problems that do not at first glance seem to involve them.

Getting to the Answer: The area of a parallelogram is its base times its height. Remember that the height of a parallelogram is only the same as its side length if the parallelogram is a rectangle. Since the base is 6 and the area is 24, the height of this parallelogram (QT) is 4. Since T is the midpoint of $\overline{PS}$, $PT = 3$. Now that you know two sides of the right triangle PQT, you can easily find the third, either by noticing that it is a Pythagorean triplet or by using the Pythagorean theorem. $PQ = 5$, so $RS = 5$. The perimeter is the distance all the way around the figure, or $6 + 5 + 6 + 5 = 22$.

7. B

Category: Plane Geometry

Difficulty: Medium

Strategic Advice: Whenever a figure is made of more than one simple figure, look for a part ofthe figure that is part of two simple figures to move information from one to the other.

Getting to the Answer: The diameter of circle R is the radius of circle S. First, find the diameter of circle R from its area:

$$\pi r^2 = 6$$
$$r^2 = \frac{6}{\pi}$$
$$r = \sqrt{\frac{6}{\pi}}$$
$$d = 2\sqrt{\frac{6}{\pi}}$$

Now use the diameter of R as the radius of S to find the area of S:

$$A = \pi r^2$$
$$A = \pi\left(2\sqrt{\frac{6}{\pi}}\right)^2 = \pi\left(4 \times \frac{6}{\pi}\right) = \frac{24\pi}{\pi} = 24$$

8. G

Category: Plane Geometry

Difficulty: Medium

Strategic Advice: In any ACT question that involves a circle, identify the radius first.

Getting to the Answer: Since the radii of a circle must all be the same length, $OP = OR$. Therefore, the angles opposite those two sides of triangle POR are also equal. $\angle ROQ$ is supplemental to $\angle POR$, so $\angle POR$ measures $180° - 50° = 130°$. The interior angles of a triangle always add up to $180°$, so if the two equal angles each measure $x°$, then $2x + 130 = 180$, $2x = 50$, and $x = 25$. $\angle RPQ$ is one of these equal angles, so it measures $25°$.

9. D

Category: Plane Geometry

Difficulty: Low

Strategic Advice: Be sure to solve for the right thing. It can be easy to get sidetracked on geometry problems.

Getting to the Answer: Since $\overline{EC}$ is a straight line, the three angles $\angle ABC$, $\angle ABF$, and $\angle FBE$ add up to $180°$. Therefore, $\angle ABC + 30° + 30° = 180°$, so $ABC = 120°$.

10. H

Category: Plane Geometry

Difficulty: Medium

Strategic Advice: Always be on the lookout for special triangles.

Getting to the Answer: You should recognize a triangle with side lengths of 6, 8, and 10 as a Pythagorean triplet. It is a right triangle with legs of length 6 and 8, so its area is $\frac{1}{2}(6)(8) = 24$. Since the perimeter of the square is 28, each of its sides is $\frac{28}{4} = 7$ units long,

and its area is $7^2 = 49$. The difference between the areas of the two shapes is $49 - 24 = 25$.

11. D

Category: Plane Geometry

Difficulty: High

Strategic Advice: If there doesn't seem to be enough information to solve a Plane Geometry question, look for subtle relationships such as similar triangles.

Getting to the Answer: Since ABC is a right triangle with legs of 15 and 20, it is a multiple of a 3:4:5 Pythagorean triplet, and its hypotenuse is 25. (You could also use the Pythagorean theorem to find the hypotenuse.) The right triangles ABC and ADB are similar because they both have a right angle and $\angle BAD$. Therefore, the third angle in each triangle is also the same, and the triangles are similar. The ratio between the longer leg of each triangle is the same as the ratio between the hypotenuses. Therefore,

$$\frac{20}{AD} = \frac{25}{20}$$
$$20 \times 20 = 25 \times AD$$
$$16 = AD$$

12. H

Category: Plane Geometry

Difficulty: Medium

Strategic Advice: Look at diagrams carefully. It can be easy to get confused.

Getting to the Answer: The ribbon that goes over the top and down the front of the present crosses the top and bottom in the short (10-inch) direction and the front and back in the medium (14-inch) direction. The ribbon that goes around the sides crosses the sides in the short (10-inch) direction and the front and back in the long (22-inch) direction. Therefore, the total length of both pieces of ribbon is $2(10) + 2(14) + 2(10) + 2(22) = 112$ inches.

13. D

Category: Plane Geometry

Difficulty: Low

Strategic Advice: Remember the geometry formulas; they won't be given to you on the test.

Getting to the Answer: The circumference of a circle is π times the diameter. Therefore, since the circumference of this circle is 36π, the diameter must be 36.

14. H

Category: Plane Geometry

Difficulty: Medium

Strategic Advice: Any complex figure on the ACT can be broken up into simple figures you know how to work with.

Getting to the Answer: Add a line to this trapezoid to create a rectangle and a right triangle:

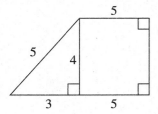

Since the base of the right triangle is 3 and its hypotenuse is 5, you know that it's a 3:4:5 triangle and the height is 4. If you didn't spot that, you could have used the Pythagorean theorem.

Area of triangle: $\frac{1}{2}(3)(4) = 6$.

Area of rectangle: $(4)(5) = 20$.

Total area of trapezoid: $20 + 6 = 26$.

You could also solve this problem using the formula for the area of a trapezoid: $\frac{b_1 + b_2}{2} \times h$.

15. E

Category: Plane Geometry

Difficulty: Medium

Strategic Advice: More difficult Plane Geometry questions may require you to add a line to the figure. More often than not, you'll create a useful triangle.

Getting to the Answer: Add line segment $\overline{OD}$ to create the triangles OCD and OED. Since this line segment is a radius of the circle, as are $\overline{OC}$ and $\overline{OE}$, each triangle is isosceles, and the angles across from the equal sides are also equal. Therefore, $\angle CDO$ measures 70° and $\angle ODE$ measures 45°. Together, they form $\angle CDE$, which measures 70° + 45° = 115°.

16. J

Category: Plane Geometry

Difficulty: Medium

Strategic Advice: If a Plane Geometry question doesn't provide a diagram, sketch your own.

Getting to the Answer: Since $\overline{AB}$ and $\overline{BC}$ arecongruent, the angles opposite those sides of the triangle will be

equal. A sketch will make this much clearer:

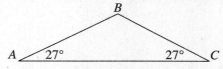

Since the interior angles of a triangle always add up to 180°, $\angle ABC = 180° - 27° - 27° = 126°$.

17. D

Category: Plane Geometry

Difficulty: Medium

Strategic Advice: Right triangles appear even in questions that don't seem at firstglance to have them.

Getting to the Answer: The diagonal of a square divides it into two 45–45–90 triangles. Since the sides of a 45–45–90 triangle are in the ratio $x:x:x \sqrt{2}$, each side of the square is $4\sqrt{2}$ inches long. The area of the square is $\left(4\sqrt{2}\right)^2 = 32$ square inches.

18. G

Category: Plane Geometry

Difficulty: High

Strategic Advice: Be sure not to stop too soon. Here, it's easy to find the difference between the outside and inside dimensions of the picture frame and forget that w is half that difference.

Getting to the Answer: Sincethe diagonal of a square divides it into two 45–45–90 triangles and the sides of a 45–45–90 triangle are in the ratio $x:x:x \sqrt{2}$, each side of the interior square is 4 inches long. The outside length of the frame is the interior length plus the width of the frame on each side, or $4 + 2w$. Since this equals 6, $4 + 2w = 6$, $2w = 2$, and $w = 1$ inch.

19. B

Category: Plane Geometry

Difficulty: Medium

Strategic Advice: You'll need to remember the formulas for area, perimeter, and volume since they will not appear on the test.

Getting to the Answer: The area of a triangle is half the base times the height.

$\frac{1}{2}(3 + 12)YS = 45$

$15 \times YS = 90$

$YS = 6$

ANSWERS AND EXPLANATIONS

Preview Quiz

Answer Key

1. **B**
2. **F**

1. B

Category: Figure Interpretation
Difficulty: Low

Strategic Advice: Remember to ask yourself the third Figure Interpretation question—Where is the information I need?

Getting to the Answer: To answer this question, you have to examine the third column of the table, transmittance range. For a material to transmit light at a wavelength of 25 μm, its transmittance range—the range of wavelengths over which the material is transparent—must include 25 μm. Only potassium bromide (0.3–29 μm) and cesium iodide (0.3–70 μm) have transmittance ranges that include 25 μm, so (**B**) is correct.

2. F

Category: Figure Interpretation
Difficulty: Medium

Strategic Advice: A hypothesis is contradicted when information proves part or all of it to be untrue.

Getting to the Answer: The material that contradicts this hypothesis is going to have poor chemical resistance, but a transmittance range less than 10 μm. Lithium fluoride, (**F**), fits the bill: its chemical resistance is poor, and its transmittance range is less than 6 μm wide.

(G) and (J) are incorrect because both flint glass and quartz have excellent chemical resistance.

(H) is out because cesium iodide has a transmittance range nearly 70 μm wide.

Quarter 2

Answer Key

1. **B**
2. **F**
3. **B**
4. **H**
5. **D**

1. B

Category: Writer's View
Difficulty: High

Strategic Advice: When the question encompasses a large section of the passage, your notes are even more critical; turn there first.

Getting to the Answer: The cited conversation takes up most of the passage, so you're better off working from your notes. Note that Alexandra's thoughts are the first things the author mentions and that Alexandra speaks last (and more) in this excerpt. These facts, and the content of those closing comments, should lead you to the correct answer.

(A) Distortion; Carl is certainly unhappy, but the author never indicates that he longs for "the simple life" as a solution.

(**B**) Correct. This matches well with the gist of the closing paragraph.

(C) Out of Scope; the author makes only brief allusion to Lou's and Oscar's opinions of Alexandra, and nothing in the passage indicates that the author sympathizes with that assessment.

(D) Distortion; the second sentence suggests that Alexandra feels some "disdain for the 'city man,'" but the author doesn't emphasize this point.

2. F

Category: Writer's View
Difficulty: High

Strategic Advice: With unusual questions, a quick review of your notes will prepare you well, even if a prediction is difficult to make.

Getting to the Answer: Focus first on "the author's characterization" of Alexandra—that she's *determined, hard-working,* and *wants the best for Emil.* Then skim the quotes to see which one best embodies those sentiments.

(**F**) Correct; this appropriately captures her determination and her concern for her brother's welfare.

(G) Misused Detail; for this to be right, the author would have had to have painted Alexandra as more critical of Carl.

(H) Extreme; while this might represent her determination, it also suggests that Alexandra is stubborn.

(J) Misused Detail; this suggests that Alexandra is more focused on the negative aspects of her life than on a hopeful view of the future (at least for Emil).

3. B

Category: Inference

Difficulty: Medium

Strategic Advice: When you don't receive a line reference, rely on your notes to avoid too much rereading of the passage.

Getting to the Answer: The author refers only briefly to Emil, but the key statements are Alexandra's—that Emil "is so different from the rest of us" (lines 26–27) and that she "would rather have Emil grow up" in the city "than like his brothers." Predict something like *have a life different from hers.*

(A) Opposite; the passage suggests that she wants something different for him.

(B) Correct. This matches the thrust of the prediction.

(C) Distortion; Alexandra says she would rather he be like Carl.

(D) Out of Scope; she wants Emil to be like Carl, not to live with him.

4. H

Category: Inference

Difficulty: Medium

Strategic Advice: Remember that the correct inference will be a small step removed from what is said in the passage.

Getting to the Answer: In the first paragraph, Alexandra ponders the lack of change in Carl—that he had not become "self-satisfied." "Self-satisfied" is not a desirable characteristic, so she must be relatively happy about that. Look for a match to that sentiment.

(F) Distortion; nothing in the paragraph suggests that she is "charmed."

(G) Out of Scope; Alexandra does not appear "perplexed," and the author makes no allusion to Carl's reason for returning.

(H) This matches the tone and content of the prediction.

(J) Out of Scope; if anything, her mental picture of him suggests a certain sympathy.

5. D

Category: Inference

Difficulty: Medium

Strategic Advice: A prediction of even a single word can capture the tone (positive, negative) of the correct choice.

Getting to the Answer: Based on the cited lines, you can make a prediction even as simple as *a failure* or *depressed* and still be on the right track.

(A) Distortion; "lucky" is too positive.

(B) Distortion; "fortunate" is too positive.

(C) Distortion; the tone is right, but Carl is dissatisfied with his life in New York, not with life in Nebraska.

(D) Correct. This matches Carl's tone in the passage; it also captures the gist of what he says.

Quiz

Answer Key

1. **A**
2. **G**
3. **C**

1. A

Category: Function

Difficulty: Medium

Strategic Advice: Sometimes you can determine function from your notes, without having to return to the passage.

Getting to the Answer: These references fall in the third and fourth paragraphs, which discuss the relationship between arms and art as shown in Greek and Roman mythology. If you do return to the passage, note the sentence before the first example: "In classical antiquity, too, there was a close relationship between art and arms." These examples look at additional aspects of the connection between art and arms.

(A) Correct; this matches the thrust of the passage.

(B) Out of Scope; the author doesn't discuss "divine arts."

(C) Misused Detail; though Hephaestos's work certainly sounds both beautiful and well crafted, the author doesn't use the two paragraphs primarily to make these points.

(D) Distortion; the gods themselves seem to have been the artists here. The passage offers no support for this choice.

2. G

Category: Generalization

Difficulty: Low

Strategic Advice: When you take notes, you should always identify the author's purpose. Questions like this will be much easier if you do.

Getting to the Answer: Your notes should reflect that the author describes the long interrelation between arms and art. Look for that among the choices.

(F) Distortion; the author never implies that one element was more important than the other.

(**G**) Correct; this is slightly different from the prediction but still captures the main idea of the passage.

(H) Misused Detail; this is too narrow. The author makes only a brief reference to the influence of Christianity.

(J) Misused Detail; the author only mentions the Renaissance in the final paragraph.

3. C

Category: Detail

Difficulty: Medium

Strategic Advice: With NOT questions, a quick scan of the choices can cut down on your research.

Getting to the Answer: This question encompasses the whole passage, making your research more time-consuming. Scan the choices first; at worst, you'll know the four specific spots you need to look for, and one or two may jump out at you as more likely choices. Wayland the Smith and Achilles might ring a bell, but Heinrich Schliemann should not do so as much—start there. Scanning for proper names, you can see that the author discusses him in lines 41–46; Schliemann seems to be an archaeologist. Therefore, he did not create such works; he only discovered the remains of some of them.

(A) Opposite; the author mentions this in the first paragraph.

(B) Opposite; the author mentions this in the fifth paragraph.

(**C**) Correct; Schliemann's "work" does not exemplify this "interplay."

(D) Opposite; the author mentions this in the sixth paragraph.

Quarter 3

Answer Key

1. **C**
2. **F**
3. **B**
4. **H**
5. **D**
6. **J**
7. **C**
8. **G**
9. **C**
10. **J**
11. **B**
12. **H**
13. **A**

1. C

Category: Connections

Difficulty: Medium

Strategic Advice: When the choices are connecting words, first determine the relationship between the ideas expressed.

Getting to the Answer: The original sentence incorrectly uses the contrasting transition "on the other hand." However, the description in this sentence is an example of the idea presented in the preceding sentence. This makes (**C**) correct.

(B) and (D) do not indicate the correct relationship between the sentences.

2. F

Category: Connections

Difficulty: Medium

Strategic Advice: Be careful not to introduce a new error with your answer choice.

Getting to the Answer: There is a contrast relationship between these two complete sentences, making "However," the appropriate connecting word. The sentence is correct as written.

(G) and (H) incorrectly indicate a similarity between the sentences, while (J) creates a run-on.

3. B

Category: Connections

Difficulty: Medium

Strategic Advice: Take the context of the paragraph into consideration. A grammatically correct sentence may have a style error.

Getting to the Answer: The connecting word "Indeed" adds emphasis, mistakenly indicating that this sentence is an amplification of what has come before. A connecting word showing contrast, such as "Nevertheless," is needed to show the relationship between the sentences. (C) incorrectly suggests similarity between the ideas in the two sentences, while (D) suggests a cause-and-effect relationship that does not exist.

4. **H**

Category: Connections

Difficulty: Low

Strategic Advice: Connection words must reflect a logical transition between ideas.

Getting to the Answer: The sentence as written suggests cause and effect, but it needs a contrast. (**H**) provides the correct transition. (G) does not correct the error. (J) provides the wrong transition and also creates a run-on.

5. **D**

Category: Wordiness

Difficulty: Low

Strategic Advice: Don't say it twice! Eliminate redundancies in your answer choices.

Getting to the Answer: "Discontent" and "unhappiness" mean the same thing; (**D**) eliminates the redundancy. (A), (B), and (C) all retain redundancies.

6. **J**

Category: Connections

Difficulty: Medium

Strategic Advice: Eliminate illogical or unnecessary transitions.

Getting to the Answer: No transition is necessary. (**J**) provides the best correction. (G) is unnecessarily wordy. (H) would also introduce an error in logic.

7. **C**

Category: Connections

Difficulty: Low

Strategic Advice: Use context to make sure that a connecting word conveys a logical link between ideas.

Getting to the Answer: The correct transition needs to indicate that an explanation is coming. (**C**) does so. (B) indicates contrast instead. (D) suggests cause-and-effect rather than explanation.

8. **G**

Category: Wordiness

Difficulty: Medium

Strategic Advice: Eliminating unnecessary words will yield clearer, more concise writing.

Getting to the Answer: Extra words make the sentence awkward and redundant. (**G**) preserves the meaning while getting rid of unnecessary words. (H) and (J) are still redundant.

9. **C**

Category: Wordiness

Difficulty: Medium

Strategic Advice: Eliminating unnecessary words will yield clearer, more concise writing.

Getting to the Answer: Extra words make the sentence awkward; (**C**) preserves the meaning while getting rid of unnecessary words. (B) and (D) are still overly wordy.

10. **J**

Category: Wordiness

Difficulty: Medium

Strategic Advice: Always consider "OMIT the underlined portion" when it is an option.

Getting to the Answer: Information about King Arthur is not relevant to this passage; the sentence should be omitted.

11. **B**

Category: Connections

Difficulty: Medium

Strategic Advice: Choose specific language to express ideas clearly.

Getting to the Answer: The best transition here will specify the time being discussed. (**B**) does so. (C) remains somewhat vague. (D) is concise but not specific about when the events took place.

12. **H**

Category: Wordiness

Difficulty: Low

Strategic Advice: If there's a simpler way to say something, choose the answer that does so.

Getting to the Answer: The adverb "eagerly" is all that's necessary here. (F) is unnecessarily wordy; both (G) and (J) are grammatically incorrect.

13. A

Category: Connections

Difficulty: High

Strategic Advice: A connecting word or phrase must convey the logical sequence of events.

Getting to the Answer: The context indicates that the first part of the sentence happened before the second part, so any alternative must also do so. (A) does not relate to time. (B), (C), and (D) all preserve the meaning.

Quarter 4

Answer Key

1. **B**
2. **F**
3. **B**
4. **F**
5. **B**
6. **G**
7. **C**

1. B

Category: Operations

Difficulty: Low

Strategic Advice: The square root of a number is the factor of the number that when multiplied by itself gives you the original number.

Getting to the Answer: Find the two perfect squares that $\sqrt{42}$ is between: $\sqrt{36}$ and $\sqrt{49}$, or 6 and 7. So, 6 is the largest integer less than $\sqrt{42}$.

2. F

Category: Trigonometry

Difficulty: Medium

Strategic Advice: The mnemonic SOHCAHTOA is an excellent way to remember the most commonly tested trigonometric functions on the ACT.

Getting to the Answer: The word SOHCAHTOA helps you remember that

$\sin = \dfrac{\text{opposite}}{\text{hypotenuse}}$, $\cos = \dfrac{\text{adjacent}}{\text{hypotenuse}}$, and

$\tan = \dfrac{\text{opposite}}{\text{adjacent}}$. $\overline{VX}$ is opposite the given angle and you are given the value of the hypotenuse, so the correct answer will involve the sin function:

$\sin 55° = \dfrac{\text{opposite}}{\text{hypotenuse}}$

$\sin 55° = \dfrac{\text{opposite}}{14}$

14 sin 55° = opposite That's (**F**).

3. B

Category: Plane Geometry

Difficulty: High

Strategic Advice: Did you notice how four of the fiveanswer choices resemble the Pythagorean theorem? This should prompt you to try thinking about this word problem as a geometry problem involving triangles. Remember: The answer choices give us great clues about how to tackle a problem!

Getting to the Answer: First, figure out where each person has gone. Bob drove at 60 mph and went north for half an hour and then east for an hour, so he has gone 30 miles north and 60 miles east. Linda drove at 50 mph for one hour east and half an hour north, so she went 50 miles east and 25 miles north. Drawing a diagram will be very helpful in making sense of this problem:

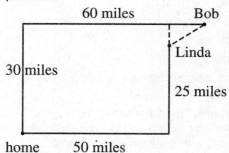

From the diagram, you can see that the distance between Bob and Linda when they both arrive at work is the hypotenuse of a right triangle. One side of the triangle is (30 − 25), and the other side is (60 − 50). Use the Pythagorean theorem: $a^2 + b^2 = c^2$; $(30 − 25)^2 + (60 − 50)^2 = c^2$. Now evaluate which of the answer choices gives you an equivalent expression. Since the answer choices haven't been simplified, there's no need to simplify your answer.

(**B**), or $c\sqrt{(60-50)^2 + (25-30)^2}$, is the only equivalent expression. (Since any number squared is positive, $(30-25)^2$ is equivalent to $(25-30)^2$.)

4. F

Category: Patterns, Logic & Data

Difficulty: High

Strategic Advice: A graphing calculator can be a big help when you're comparing functions.

Getting to the Answer: $f(g(x)) = 3^{g}(x)$. This question wants to know which of the functions $g(x)$ in the answer choices will make $f(g(x))$ the biggest when x is greater than 2. In all cases, a is some constant greater than or equal to 3. The easiest way to think about an abstract question like this one is to Pick Numbers. Try looking at $x = 3$ and $a = 10$ (which will make the logarithm in (K) easy to compute).

(F) $g(x) = ax = 3(10) = 30$

(G) $g(x) = \dfrac{a}{x} = \dfrac{10}{3} = 3\dfrac{1}{3}$

(H) $g(x) = \dfrac{a}{x} = \dfrac{3}{10}$

(J) $g(x) = a + x = 10 + 3 = 13$

(K) $g(x) = \log_a x = \log_{10} 3 \approx 0.477$

Since $f(g(x)) = 3^{g(x)}$ will be largest when $g(x)$ is largest, (**F**) produces the largest value of $f(g(x))$. You also could have plugged in $a = 10$ (or some other constant) and then graphed the five functions.

(F) $f(g(x)) = 3^{10x}$

(G) $f(g(x)) = 3^{\frac{10}{x}}$

(H) $f(g(x)) = 3^{\frac{x}{10}}$

(J) $f(g(x)) = 3^{10 + x}$

(K) $f(g(x)) = \log_{10} x$

(F) will be larger than the other graphs for every value of x greater than 2.

5. B

Category: Proportions and Probability

Difficulty: Medium

Strategic Advice: Make sure you understand the situation before you start calculating. What's really going on here?

Getting to the Answer: Town A's population starts out at 9,400 and decreases by 100 people every year. Town B's population starts out at 7,600 and increases by 100 people each year. You could set up a chart that

shows the population of each town every year, or you could set up an equation: $9,400 - 100x = 7,600 + 100x$ (here, x is the number of years since 2000).

$9,400 = 7,600 + 200x$.

$1,800 = 200x$

$9 = x$

So the towns' populations will be equal in 2009.

6. G

Category: Variable Manipulation

Difficulty: Medium

Strategic Advice: There are many possible ways to approach this question. Two are shown below, but others are certainly possible. Choose whichever method is fastest and easiest for you.

Getting to the Answer: Most people find questions like this easiest to Backsolve. Since it will be difficult to tell whether you need a smaller or a larger number, you should start with the answer choices that are easiest to evaluate:

(F) $\sqrt[3]{45} = 3\sqrt[3]{5}$

$45 = 3(5)$

$45 = 15$

That's not true, so try another value of ...

(G) $\sqrt[2]{45} = 3\sqrt[2]{5}$

$6.708... = 6.708...$

These are equal, so (**G**) is correct. Alternatively, you could take the original equation, raise both sides to the nth power, and solve for n:

$\sqrt[n]{45} = 3\sqrt[n]{5}$

$(\sqrt[n]{45}) = (3\sqrt[n]{5})^n$

$45 = 3^n \cdot 5$

$9 = 3^n$

$3^2 = 3^n$

$2 = n$

7. C

Category: Plane Geometry

Difficulty: Medium

Strategic Advice: Since you are not given values for the length and width of the flowerbed, you can Pick Numbers.

Getting to the Answer: Say the width of the flowerbed is 2 and the length is 4. That means the area of the flowerbed will be 8. Double the width and the length to get the dimensions of the vegetable garden: 4 and 8.

This gives the vegetable garden an area of 32, which is 4 times 8, the area of the flowerbed. So the answer is (C).

Algebraically: If the width of the flowerbed is w, its length is $2w$ and its area is $2w^2$. The vegetable garden's width is then $2w$ and its length is $4w$, so the area would be $8w^2$, which is 4 times the area of the flower bed.

Quiz (Math)

Answer Key

1. **E**
2. **J**
3. **A**
4. **K**
5. **C**
6. **F**
7. **B**
8. **H**
9. **B**

1. E

Category: Proportions and Probability
Difficulty: Low
Strategic Advice: This is a great one to Backsolve because you know 20% of the answer should turn out to be 10. Alternatively, you could use your knowledge that percent $= \frac{\text{part}}{\text{whole}} \times 100\%$ to set up an equation.
Getting to the Answer: Let x be the number of students in the class. Then 20% of x is 10:

$0.2x = 10$
$x = 50$

2. J

Category: Plane Geometry
Difficulty: Low
Strategic Advice: Questions like this are simply testing if you remember how many degrees are in a line. Remember that the arc between two points on a line is a half circle, or 180°.
Getting to the Answer: $20° + 40° + x° = 180°$
$x° = 120°$

3. A

Category: Patterns, Logic, & Data
Difficulty: Low
Strategic Advice: Even if you forget what "arithmetic" means, you should still be able to recognize the pattern.
Getting to the Answer: Each term is 3 less than the previous term.
Fourth term $= 1 - 3 = -2$.
Fifth term $= (-2) - 3 = -5$.
Be sure not to stop too soon—the fourth term is a tempting, but wrong, answer choice.

4. K

Category: Proportions and Probability
Difficulty: Low
Strategic Advice: Whenever you see a proportion (two fractions set equal to each other), you can cross-multiply to solve.
Getting to the Answer:

$\frac{20}{8} = \frac{c}{10}$
$20(10) = 8c$
$c = 25$

5. C

Category: Coordinate Geometry
Difficulty: Low
Strategic Advice: On problems without a diagram, drawing one is an excellent idea.
Getting to the Answer: $\overline{GH} \cong \overline{HK}$ means that the line segments $\overline{GH}$ and $\overline{HK}$ are congruent, or equal in length. For these two segments to have equal lengths, the points must be arranged like this:

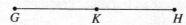

As you can see, K is the midpoint.

6. F

Category: Operations
Difficulty: Low
Strategic Advice: On problems early in the Math Test, you can sometimes let your calculator do most of the work for you.
Getting to the Answer: Yarn cut off $= 4(1.2) = 4.8$ yards. Yarn remaining $= 50 - 4.8 = 45.2$ yards.

7. B

Category: Variable Manipulation

Difficulty: Low

Strategic Advice: Be careful with positives and negatives and remember to follow the order of operations. You can count on some of the wrong answer choices coming from careless mistakes.

Getting to the Answer:

$14 - 3[(-2) + 3]$

$= 14 - 3(1)$

$= 11$

8. H

Category: Proportions and Probability

Difficulty: Low

Strategic Advice: Remembering how to convert among percents, fractions, and decimals will be a key skill on the ACT.

Getting to the Answer:

15% of 3,200 = 0.15(3,200) = 480

3,200 + 480 = 3,680

9. B

Category: Operations

Difficulty: Low

Strategic Advice: You can use your calculator to quickly find the fourth root of 90, or you can compare the fourth power of the integers in the answer choices.

Getting to the Answer:

$2^4 = 16$

$3^4 = 81$

$4^4 = 256$

If $x^4 = 90$, then x must be between 3 and 4, since 90 is between 3^4 and 4^4.

Quiz (Science)

Answer Key

1. **B**
2. **G**
3. **C**
4. **J**
5. **D**
6. **G**
7. **D**
8. **F**
9. **C**
10. **G**
11. **D**

PASSAGE I

1. B

Category: Figure Interpretation

Difficulty: Low

Strategic Advice: This question represents a case in which it's faster to go to the answer choices first.

Getting to the Answer: Searching for the lowest value of the 20 in Table 2 is time-consuming. Instead, start with the lowest value among the answer choices. (D), like (C), is far lower than the values in Table 2—in fact, both are values from Table 1. (B) is the lowest value in Table 2. It was recorded in room 4 on day 1. (A) is the highest value in Table 2.

2. G

Category: Figure Interpretation

Difficulty: Low

Strategic Advice: Don't answer low-difficulty questions like this one from memory. It's worth taking an extra ten seconds to look back at the table to be sure you get the right answer.

Getting to the Answer: All of the values in Table 2 are recorded to the nearest 0.1 mm Hg.

(F) is a trap for those who mistakenly refer to Table 1, in which values are recorded to the nearest 0.01°C.

3. C

Category: Patterns

Difficulty: Medium

Strategic Advice: Pick one data point at a time and check it against the answer choices. Eliminate any that don't contain that data point.

Getting to the Answer: Start by checking the answer choices for the point from Day 1 (745.2 mm Hg, 18.03°C).
Eliminate (A), (B), and (D), as they don't contain this point. Only (C) correctly represents this data point, so this must be the correct answer.

4. J

Category: Patterns

Difficulty: Low

Strategic Advice: For questions that ask you to describe a data trend in words, be sure to make a prediction before checking the answer choices.

Getting to the Answer: Circle the Room 3 column in Table 2 so your eye doesn't accidentally wander. Reading down the column, you can see that the average daily air pressure decreases every day. (J) matches this perfectly.

(F) describes the pressure changes for Room 1. (G) describes the temperature changes (Table 1) for Room 3.

(H) is the opposite of the correct answer.

5. D

Category: Scientific Reasoning

Difficulty: Medium

Strategic Advice: Pay close attention to the definitions of new terms introduced in the question stem. Make sure to account for all referenced quantities.

Getting to the Answer: (D) is correct because you are given only the temperatures of each room. You know nothing about the exact quantities of heat provided to the room or the amount absorbed by the room's contents.

(A), (B), and (C) all suggest knowledge of these quantities.

PASSAGE II

6. G

Category: Scientific Reasoning

Difficulty: Low

Strategic Advice: Before looking at the choices, determine for yourself what factors would support the given hypothesis or cause it to be rejected. In this case, the hypothesis would be supported only if the results showed higher Hg concentrations in swordfish and shark than in catfish and crabs.

Getting to the Answer: The results do indeed show higher Hg concentrations for swordfish and sharks, so the hypothesis is confirmed as in (G).

The "Yes" part of (F) is correct, but the reason given contradicts the data in Table 2, so it is incorrect.

(H) is also incorrect; the lowest Hg concentration was indeed in catfish, but this does not cause the hypothesis to be rejected.

(J) contradicts the data in Table 2.

7. D

Category: Scientific Reasoning

Difficulty: High

Strategic Advice: Refer to the passage to understand the process in question on Scientific Method questions. In this case, refer to the description of CVAFS.

Getting to the Answer: The passage mentions that CVAFS "indicates the relative concentrations of various elements and compounds." A properly working CVAFS, then, should be able to correctly measure the relative concentrations of Hg and Pb. Using a sample of known concentrations of Hg and Pb, as in (D), would support or reject the accuracy of the CVAFS in detecting the presence of Pb.

Nothing in the passage supports either (A) or (C).

(B) is similarly unrelated to the passage.

8. F

Category: Patterns

Difficulty: Medium

Strategic Advice: Try to find a correlation between any new information given in the question stem and the information in the passage.

Getting to the Answer: Since new data on water temperature are introduced, try to find a correlation between water temperature and Hg concentration. Compare the average Hg concentrations in Tables 1 and 2 to see that, for all three common species (crab, swordfish, and sharks), the cold-water specimens have higher Hg concentrations than do the warm-water specimens. (F) is correct, since the northern Atlantic Ocean is the coldest location.

9. C

Category: Scientific Reasoning

Difficulty: Low

Strategic Advice: The factors intentionally varied are the ones researchers purposefully changed in the course of the experiment.

Getting to the Answer: Look back at Table 2. It shows that researchers intentionally tested four different kinds of fish, which matches (C).

(A) is incorrect, since the volume of tissue was never discussed.

(B) is incorrect because all four species in Experiment 2 were extracted from water of the same temperature.

(D) is incorrect, since CVAFS is the only method of analysis mentioned.

10. G

Category: Patterns
Difficulty: Medium
Strategic Advice: Questions like this use a lot of words to hide a very simple concept. In this case, all you're really asked to do is identify which fish would be most likely to have the greatest Hg concentration.

Getting to the Answer: Tables 1 and 2 tell you that swordfish have the highest Hg concentrations and that cold-water fish have higher Hg concentrations than the same species from warm water. A swordfish caught in cold water would likely have the greatest Hg concentration of all the listed specimens, then, making (**G**) correct.

11. D

Category: Scientific Reasoning
Difficulty: Medium
Strategic Advice: Think about the experimental method used, and try to predict an answer before looking at the choices.

Getting to the Answer: Increasing the volume of tested material while maintaining the same volume of Hg in the sample would lead to a smaller fraction of Hg content, regardless of water temperature. (**D**) is perfect.

(C) is incorrect because nothing in the passage indicates that the contamination would affect warm- and cold-water fish differently.

Homework
Quarter 2

Answer Key

1. **C**
2. **G**
3. **D**
4. **H**

---

5. **D**
6. **G**
7. **D**
8. **F**
9. **A**
10. **G**

1. C

Category: Detail
Difficulty: Medium
Strategic Advice: You will usually find answers to basic questions on the subject of the passage in the first paragraph.

Getting to the Answer: This question basically asks for a definition of the topic of the passage. Turn to the first paragraph; in the first sentence, the authors write, "Enlightenment ideas were put forth by a variety of intellectuals...known as the *philosophes*." Use this as your prediction.

(A) Misused Detail; the *philosophes* were influenced by Locke, but they were also influenced by other thinkers and institutions.

(B) Opposite; the first paragraph contradicts this, stating that the *philosophes* were "not formally trained or associated with a university."

(**C**) Correct; this restates the idea in the first sentence of the passage.

(D) Distortion; it seems unlikely that they would be scientists if they were "more literary than scientific" (lines 11–12).

2. G

Category: Generalization
Difficulty: Medium
Strategic Advice: Good notes will help you to limit your rereading of the passage.

Getting to the Answer: Your notes should point you to the last paragraph. Skim it again to get a feel for Voltaire's usual forms of writing and then work through the choices.

(F) Distortion; the authors describe Voltaire as "representative" of the views of the *philosophes*. In paragraph 2, the authors state that the sources of the *philosophes*'s philosophy were found in the Scientific Revolution. Voltaire would thus be unlikely to have criticized that movement.

(G) Correct; this fits. The last paragraph discusses Voltaire's wit and the facts that he "wrote...drama" and "indirectly criticized French society."

(H) Distortion; the last paragraph states that Voltaire "came to admire" English government.

(J) Out of Scope; while the final paragraph says that Voltaire "wrote poetry," the authors make no allusion to this type of poetry.

3. D

Category: Detail
Difficulty: Medium
Strategic Advice: Detail questions with line references aren't usually that challenging; move quickly through them.

Getting to the Answer: The sentence including the quote also includes a "therefore." Look to the preceding sentence to see that this statement flows from Locke's belief that "What human beings become depends on their experiences." Use this as your prediction.

(A) Opposite; the authors indicate that Locke "pictured the human brain at birth as a blank sheet of paper" (lines 41–42).

(B) Distortion; the authors do refer to humans as "more malleable than had been assumed," but they make no connection between this and age.

(C) Out of Scope; the authors don't state this.

(D) Correct; this matches the text.

4. H

Category: Detail
Difficulty: Low
Strategic Advice: With Roman numeral questions, start with the statement that appears most frequently.

Getting to the Answer: Your notes should remind you that Newton is discussed in the third paragraph. Start with Statement I, since it appears in three choices. In lines 27–28, you read that Newton saw the universe as "ordered, mechanical, material, and only originally set in motion by God." So the first statement is part of Newton's view; eliminate (J). The quote also confirms Statement III; eliminate (F) and (G) since they don't include that statement. You don't need to check Statement II; **(H)** is the correct answer.

5. D

Category: Detail
Difficulty: Medium
Strategic Advice: Skim if you're unsure; italics are easy to spot in the passage.

Getting to the Answer: Skimming the passage shows you that these works appear in the fourth and sixth paragraphs. Common sense should help, too; a discussion of revelation as truth would probably not be found in a treatise on government, for example. In lines 50–53, you find the statement that Locke's psychology "rejected the notion that...revelation was a reliable source of truth." This is the last point made about Locke's *Essay Concerning Human Understanding*.

(A) Misused Detail; Voltaire wrote this.

(B) Misused Detail; this work by Locke focused on political ideas.

(C) Misused Detail; Voltaire wrote this.

(D) Correct; this matches the research above.

6. G

Category: Inference
Difficulty: Medium
Strategic Advice: This question basically asks for the relationship between two paragraphs; focus on the transitions between them.

Getting to the Answer: The paragraph discussing Locke begins, "Locke...agreed with Newton but went further. This English thinker would not exempt even the mind from the mechanical laws of the material universe" (lines 37–40). Use this as your prediction.

(F) Out of Scope; the authors never mention that any of Locke's work contradicted beliefs of Newton's.

(G) Correct; this matches the research above.

(H) Out of Scope; the authors never state this.

(J) Out of Scope; the authors never discuss "Newton's political ideas."

7. D

Category: Generalization
Difficulty: High
Strategic Advice: Some generally worded questions won't allow you to pinpoint a part of the passage to research. Work through the choices if you're stumped.

Getting to the Answer: The question stem doesn't give you much of a clue where to look in the passage for support. Based on the tone and thrust of the passage, if you work through the choices, (D) seems like it doesn't fit. If time allows, you could confirm this by skimming the passage, knowing that three of these phrases will turn up in some form. Lines 60–66 show that the *philosophes* admired England, which seemed to "allow greater individual freedom, tolerate religious differences," and have freed itself "from traditional institutions." The *philosophes* wanted to see these things take root in their countries as well. Only (D) isn't mentioned.

(A) Opposite; the *philosophes* were in favor of this.

(B) Opposite; the *philosophes* were in favor of this.

(C) Opposite; the *philosophes* were in favor of this.

(D) Correct; the passage doesn't support this. The *philosophes* actually accepted this science.

8. F

Category: Inference

Difficulty: Medium

Strategic Advice: Find the appropriate paragraph and focus on both content and tone.

Getting to the Answer: Look at your notes for the "England" paragraph or at the paragraph itself. Notice that the authors take an approving tone toward England: "England's approach seemed to work." Look for something in line with this view.

(F) Correct; the authors do list "political reform" as a part of England's approach that "seemed to work."

(G) Distortion; the authors actually say that the *philosophes* did tend "to idealize" England.

(H) Misused Detail; the authors do not connect Voltaire's exile to this stability.

(J) Distortion; the authors mention the Scientific Revolution in a different context.

9. A

Category: Generalization

Difficulty: Medium

Strategic Advice: Even the tone, or "charge," of a relationship can work as a prediction.

Getting to the Answer: Your notes should lead you to the last paragraph. The authors say that Voltaire's status as an "outspoken critic" caused him to run afoul of (get in trouble with) these authorities. Predict something like *were repressive or hard to deal with*.

(A) Correct; this matches the tone and gist of the prediction and the text.

(B) Out of Scope; the author never directly states that Voltaire wrote any satires, making this choice too much of a logical leap.

(C) Distortion; they certainly weren't indifferent to Voltaire, whom the authors describe as "representative" of *philosophes*. The passage doesn't support this inference.

(D) Out of Scope; the passage doesn't support this.

10. G

Category: Vocab-in-Context

Difficulty: Medium

Strategic Advice: Read for context before moving to the choices.

Getting to the Answer: The surrounding text gives the context: "He wrote poetry, drama, history, essays, letters, and scientific treatises...Few people in history have dominated their age intellectually as did Voltaire." Predict something like *studies*.

(F) Distortion; this draws from the similar word "treaty" but doesn't fit in context.

(G) Correct; this matches the prediction.

(H) Distortion; this draws from the similar word "treaty" but doesn't fit in context.

(J) Out of Scope; it doesn't make sense that a scientific document would focus on "moral lessons."

Quarter 3: Writing

Example Essays

PROMPT 1

SCORE OF 6

With the explosion in information technology, many companies are developing applications to enhance students' learning. Some of these companies are profit-based and some are non-profit, entering this endeavor to benefit students and society, not themselves. Because the personal data of technology users is marketable, three perspectives have arisen about the usage of the students' personal information. Some believe this data should never be shared, because it is collected from persons below the legal age of consent. Others believe that the data can be shared, but only among not-for-profit developers who will use the data for further non-profit projects. Finally, some believe that use of this technology, with real-time feedback, implies that the user understands and agrees that the information they provide will be freely available to anyone, for any purpose. Because disclosure of personal information can have serious consequences, and because the students using this software cannot legally consent to a contract, personal information obtained from educational technology should never be shared without consent from the students' parents or guardians.

One doesn't have to look very far to find examples of harm caused by personal information obtained improperly from the internet. My uncle's identify was stolen from his PayPal account, and, while the money that was stolen was replaced, he had to close all his bank accounts and change all his credit cards. Recently, Sony, a major company was hacked and their company emails were posted on the internet. Educational technology companies should keep the welfare of their student users foremost and not share information obtained through the use of their software. Perhaps I might want to try to take a difficult course online, and then fail it because either the course was too hard, or because I wasn't able to learn it well from the technology. If that information was shared and published on the internet, it might negatively affect my college applications, even though I was just taking an extra class to try to improve myself. Because of the potential harm caused by abuse of personal information, educational technology companies should not share their students' information.

Others would argue that the information generated by students' activity on the educational software provides valuable information to improve the technology and should be shared with non-profit entities working to improve educational outcomes. While this may seem to be an acceptable compromise, this view assumes that the sensitive personal data obtained from students will never be stolen or misused. Again, from current events, we know that employees can steal data, as did Edward Snowden, and that even sophisticated systems such as PayPal and Sony can be hacked. If non-profit educational technology companies want to share data, they could strip off all personal identifiers and share information such as number of users, average scores, average time spent, etc. as long as there were no way to trace any information back to the individual student. This could further the goal of developing educational technology while preserving the privacy of students. Without protecting the identities of individual students, this data should not be shared, even with not-for-profit entities.

The third view is that students using educational technology understand and agree that, because they're using a real-time application with continuous data sharing, their information can be shared indiscriminately with any organization, for any purpose. This perspective is severely flawed in two ways: it assumes that students would think about and agree to this sharing, and it is getting permission for this sharing from students below the legal age of consent. Because most websites offer some privacy protection, for example, any shopping, credit card or banking site is protected, technology users tend to assume their data is protected. Even Facebook and Google, which rely on users sharing information, encourage their subscribers to limit those who can observe or contribute to their accounts. Students are far more likely to assume their data on educational websites is similarly protected, rather than to think that they are agreeing to limitless distribution of their information. Even if students agreed to this sharing, if they are under the age of 18, they're not able to legally consent to this activity. Educational technology companies should not distribute student information.

If educational technology companies want to use the personal information of their subscribers to further improve their products, they have two options. First, they could disclose their proposed usages and obtain permission from the parents or legal guardians of their users. Second, they could strip off any information that could personally identify the students and use that information in any way they choose. The tremendous success of Khan Academy, a free non-profit educational website that only collects an email address from its users, indicates that these technologies can be developed and improved rapidly without risking the harm to students that could be generated from data sharing.

Through the examples of my uncle's identity theft, Sony's hacking and Edward Snowden, it is clear that there are many potential problems facing students if their personal information is shared. These risks exist whether the is used to generate profits or for altruistic purposes. Student information obtained from educational websites should not be distributed to other entities without the permission of the student's parents or guardians.

SCORE OF 5

Educational technology companies are generating extensive data through the use of their programs. Non-profit companies want to use this information to improve their offerings more quickly, and for-profit companies want to defray some of the costs of developing these products through the sale of their users' information. Some people believe that any data collected from students under the age of 18 should be completely protected, others believe that that data may be shared among non-profit companies, and others believe that the data may be shared with anyone, because the students are using a real-time system and thus, have no expectation of privacy. Because of all the problems that may arise if information is used inappropriately, student data obtained from educational technology should not be shared.

Those who say student data should be completely protected are correct, because of the many problems that can arise if data is misused. Email bullying has caused many students to suffer – some have even committed suicide when their personal secrets have been revealed. If students scores were ever stolen from an educational website, and published, it could lead to similar trauma. Student data should be completely protected.

Many non-profit educational technology companies want to share student data among themselves to share ideas and more quickly improve their products. While this is a lofty and admirable goal, it is outweighed by the dangers inherent in sharing data. After all, Khan Academy is a very successful educational technology program that has risen up very quickly on its own. From one man producing YouTube videos for his niece, Khan Academy is rapidly growing to fulfill its goal of providing a free education to anyone in the world. Their success indicates that data sharing is not necessary to produce excellent educational technology.

Finally, those who would distribute student information for any purpose, including advertising, are reckless in the extreme. Students use educational technology to learn; they don't expect to be targeted by advertisers as a result of their search for knowledge or self-improvement. To assume that students know that their information will be shared, just because they're using a real-time application, really doesn't make any sense. When we buy something from the internet, our important identity and financial data are protected. Yes, we may later see an advertisement or a recommendation for another product, but even though the sale was made in real-time, our personal information is protected. Users of educational technology sites would expect no less.

Because so many serious problems can arise from the misuse of personal information, data from students under the age of 18 on educational websites should be completely protected. To allow non-profit companies to use it, still exposes innocent students to harmful consequences. To allow for-profit companies to use it is not only wrong, but possibly illegal, because the information is obtained from children.

SCORE OF 4

Educational technology companies are considering sharing the data they collect. Some think any data-sharing is wrong, because most of the students who generate that data are under the age of 18. Some think that it's acceptable to share data among non-profit companies to improve their products, while some believe that the data can be shared with anyone for any reason. Data shouldn't be shared because of the dangers that may arise when students' data is shared.

The safest route is for educational technology companies to never share their student data. Any time data is shared, there's a risk that it will be stolen and misused. I had to get a new Target credit card last year after one of their employees stole a lot of credit card numbers. Perhaps an employee of an educational technology company might do the same thing, and my test scores or home address could be posted on the internet. It's not worth taking that chance. When I'm using an educational website, I expect my information will remain private.

Non-profit educational technology companies are trying to help people learn and improve. Some of them would like to share student data to modify and improve their products more quickly, but again, any data sharing brings risks. The more people have access to data, the more likely it is that there may be someone who would steal or misuse it. The risks of the harm that may come about from sharing the information are greater than the benefits that may arise.

To use the information students provide on educational websites to make money is wrong. Students are using these sites to improve themselves and to learn. To take that opportunity to use their personal information just to make more money is taking advantage of them. Educational websites should never sell or make money from their students.

Student data is personal and private, and it's important for companies to recognize that. Even non-profit companies should protect students' information and privacy. The risk of damage that may occur if personal information is misused is greater than any advantage that might come from sharing that data.

SCORE OF 3

Three perspectives have been offered in regards to ed tech companies sharing the data they collect from elementary and high school students. Some people believe students data should be wholly protected, some people believe it can be shared as long as it's just being used to make the programs better, and some think that everyone should be able to use the data however they like. I agree that students data should be wholly protected because a lot of times, when your information is on the internet, it can cause problems.

My mom is always checking my computer to make sure I don't use the internet wrong. She doesn't let me put our address in my Facebook, even if I just want my friends to be able to come over. She says that somehow crooks could find out where we live. If my school was giving my address out, she'd be upset.

I bet the companies would want to share students information to be able to make their programs better, but it's not worth the risk. Why should I have to worry about bad stuff happeneing to me just because I use some companies website?

And of course companies want to make more money, but I don't want them to make money by making my life more dangerous. That's not fair. Why should they make money off my information? I'm just doing what I have to for my classes.

So the only right thing is for companies to protect student information. This way, students can learn more, and still be safe.

Score of 2

There's three perspectives on sharing student information. First, it should be wholly protected. Second, it should be exclusively available to not-for-profit tech developers. Third, it can be used by anyone. I think it should be protected.

I use the Khan Academy website a lot, and really like it. It enables me to review tough subjects that were covered in my classes and to get in some extra math practice. All I needed to do to use Khan Academy was provide an email account. I used my "trash" email account because I didn't want a lot of extra spam coming to my regular email. But to my surprise, I didn't get any spam from them. I'm more likely to use their site now that I know my information is safe, and that they are not using my email to send me a lot of unwanted advertisements. If I thought they might give my information to other companies, I wouldn't sign up.

Score of 1

I don't want anyone, from any company to have my personal information. I don't want people to know where I live or what I'm doing. I certainly don't want anyone to know my grades if I don't tell them. Privacy is important, and just because I'm trying to learn on the internet, and not in a classroom, I shouldn't have to give up my privacy.

Prompt 2

Score of 6

The costs of a college education are rising rapidly, and have made a college degree prohibitively expensive for many students. To alleviate this problem, three approaches have been suggested. The first would provide low-interest loans to students, and remove any responsibility from the states to provide reduced tuition; the second would provide funding for employment programs to enable graduates to find work so they could repay their tuition loans; and the last would offer reduced tuition to in-state students as part of the state's responsibility to improve the welfare of society as a whole. Because state colleges and universities receive substantial funding from state taxes, and because these state taxes are paid by residents of the state, state colleges and universities should offer substantial tuition discounts to in-state students.

Some would argue that a college education will pay for itself through the increased earnings of graduates, and that since this increased earning-power enables graduates to pay off student loans, the state has no responsibility to provide discounted tuition to residents. These people would think that making low-interest loans available to students would be sufficient. However, this view overlooks the fact that the very source of funding for state colleges and universities is the citizens of the state itself. Because state residents (or their parents) have paid state taxes for years to support their local colleges, they should be eligible for reduced tuition.

Others would argue that the funds dedicated to state colleges should be used for employment programs so graduates are able to find work and pay off their loans, thus learning financial responsibility and fiscal planning. This view would create an entire new tier of administrators between graduates and their potential employers. The money that could be used for lower tuition would instead be dedicated to paying the salaries of the advisors and administrators who would be assisting the graduates. It would be a much more efficient use of the state's resources to simply provide lower tuition to in-state students. In addition, the value of this plan in generating financial responsibility and fiscal planning skills is overstated. Tuition, while substantial, is only one part of the costs of a college education. Students will still learn financial responsibility and fiscal planning as they pay for books, equipment, housing, transportation, food and other living expenses. Providing an employment-assistance service to college graduates is not a wise use of taxpayers' funds dedicated to education.

Stats should provide reduced tuition to their residents as an extension of the social contract. The founding fathers of our country insisted on the provision of education to every citizen and demanded that states offer free public education. In today's world, a high-school diploma is no longer sufficient for many jobs. The increasing complexity of technology, and our dependence on it, demands more highly-trained workers in engineering, computer science, management sciences, economics and social systems. As demands on our nation's workers increase, the level of education supported by the state must also increase. Providing a lower-cost tuition to in-state students is not only fair because of the support residents have provided these schools through their taxes, but also because a well-educated population will improve the welfare of the citizens of the state as a whole. Businesses will be more willing to open factories and operations in states where well-educated employees are available. Technology companies are known to "cluster" in areas like Northern California, Austin, Texas and the North Carolina Triangle where major state-sponsored colleges generate qualified graduates. More businesses mean more taxes to generate funds for the state, as well as more support services such as restaurants, retail operations and personal services that provide even more employment opportunities for the state's residents. Because residents of the state have provided the funds that have supported local colleges and universities, and because a better-educated population will lead to improvements in the general welfare of the entire state, local residents should be offered reduced tuition to state schools.

As states and students struggle with the rising costs of education, states must recognize the value of a well-educated population, invest in their residents and use the money raised by state taxes to provide reduced tuition to in-state students. Other schemes, such as low-cost loans or employment-assistance services, divert the money residents have paid to fund education to banks, administrators and program managers. These funds are more efficiently and appropriately used to directly support residents through low-cost tuition to state colleges and universities.

SCORE OF 5
College costs are rising quickly, even much faster than the overall cost of living. Because the high costs are making it impossible for many qualified students to attend college, some have proposed that states offer

support to students to enable accepted students to attend state colleges and universities. Three forms of this support have been proposed: low-cost student loans, employment assistance for graduates and lower-cost tuition to state residents. Because an educated population benefits the state as a whole, and because funds to support state colleges and universities are generated by taxes paid by state residents, states should assist qualified students with low-cost student loans.

While it may seem that low-cost student loans could relieve the state of the need to provide further assistance, this is not the case. For most non-technical degrees, the tuition costs alone for college can come to more than $50,000. For scientific and technical degrees, like engineering and medicine, the costs are much higher because these degree programs take longer to complete. My sister graduated 5 years ago with a degree in elementary education, and college loans of $70,000. Her starting salary was under $30,000. Even with a lower interest rate than she's paying, it would take her many years to pay off her loans. During this time, she won't be able to buy a house, a new car or have much discretionary spending. My sister teaches fourth grade in a public school. She's an example of a hard-working person whose education is contributing to the welfare of society as a whole. If she could buy a home or hire a housekeeper once a month, these types of modest expenditures would contribute to strengthening the local economy. Low-cost student loans as a solution to the problem of higher tuition are short-sighted. They may seem to relieve the burden on the students, but they actually prevent dedicated graduates from contributing to local economies for extended periods of time.

Offering employment services to students assumes that graduates are not able to find work to pay off their loans. But for the students who are contributing the most to the welfare of society, like my sister, this is not the case. Almost every municipality is looking for more excellent teachers, nurses, doctors, police officers, computer programmers and other well-educated professionals. Locating suitable employment is not the problem – the problem is the large amount of debt graduates accumulate through their college careers. Even if jobs were hard to find, this plan doesn't guarantee graduates a position. What if the state located a position far away from a graduate's family? Or found a position that paid substantially below the average market rate for that job? Would the student have to accept whatever position the state identified? The faulty assumptions behind this plan make it a poor choice.

The best of these three proposals is the one where states offer qualified resident students tuition discounts. This would enable students to graduate with much more manageable tuition loans. While it may seem to be the most expensive option, that is a short-term view. In the long run, it may even generate enough money to pay for itself through the improved business climate. If major companies relocated to the state because of the excellent, qualified workforce created by the reduced tuition program, the tax revenues generated by that company could not only defray many tuition subsidies, but also contribute to the state's general revenue.

To improve their business environment, and thus, improve the overall welfare of the community, states should enable their qualified students to attend local colleges and universities. The best way to defray the ever-rising costs of tuition is for the states to offer tuition discounts to these students that are funded by taxes. Low-cost loans and job-placement programs are insufficient to provide qualified students the assistance they need and deserve.

SCORE OF 4

The cost of going to college is so high, it's keeping many good students from attending so it's been suggested that states should come up with some ways to assist student in funding their high education To address the question of whether states should assist students or not, three views have been presented. Some say the states have no obligation to help because students will be able to repay their student loans once they start working. Others say that the states should start and support job placement services that enable graduates to find work quickly; while others believe the states should assist students with tuition discounts. I think the best approach is for states to offer their students reduced tuition to state colleges and universities because the money used to support state schools is raised from taxes paid by the residents, and this will enable state residents to become better educated, improving the society as a whole.

Some would say that states have no obligation to assist their students because a college education will enable them to work and pay off their student loans. However, this overlooks the fact that even though employed, many graduates do not earn enough to pay off their loans, and the longer you have a loan, the more you end up paying. My sister graduated from college 5 years ago and has been teaching fourth grade ever since. But she says that after paying for her rent, car, food and insurance she only has enough left

over to make the minimum payment on her student loans. She says it's going to take her another 12 years to finish paying her student loans. Because her job helps her students and so makes our state a better place to live, the state should've helped her graduate without the burden of a large debt from student loans.

Others believe that states should use some of the money they raise for schools for setting up job placement services that will enable their college graduates to find work quickly, but in my opinion, this will not be very helpful. My sister was able to find a job quickly, but still struggles to pay off her loans, so this idea wouldn't help her at all. For many people, the problem isn't finding a job, but in the large amount of money they've had to borrow to finish college.

I think the best solution is for the states to use taxes to provide lower-cost tuition for graduates. My parents have paid property taxes here my whole life, and we pay sales tax on everything we buy. Part of those taxes should be used to support the state colleges and universities. My sister is helping the state by working in a public school educating children. It is the responsibility of the state to assist its residents, especially those like my sister, who are making the state a better place to live. States should use the money raised by our taxes to help our best and brightest improve our communities.

College tuition goes up every year. It's important for states to assist their residents because more educated people make the state a better place to live. Those who say the state has no responsibility to help ignore the benefits that come to the society as a whole from a more educated population. Those who say the state should assist college students by providing an employment service after graduation are assuming that the graduates can't find work, and this is not always the case. States should assist their residents with lower tuitions funded by state taxes.

SCORE OF 3

Going to college is very, very expensive. Because the cost of tuition can prevent some students from going college, three views have been presented to assist them. These are: first, for states to offer low-cost loans, second, for states to provide services that will assist graduates to secure employment so they can repay their loans, and finally, for states to offer tuition discounts to residents. I think that states should give us lower tuition.

Because our parents have paid taxes, and the out-of-state students haven't, I think that it's only fair that we get lower tuitions. That way, any student who is accepted will be able to attend college. I live in Florida and the television ads are always saying that the state lottery contributes a lot of money to education, so some of that money can be used for lower tuition.

If you get a student loan, you have to pay it back and it's easy to end up with huge student loans, so I don't think low-cost student loans are a good idea. The state should do more to help us because we are going to live and work here and make the state a better place. If we're improving the community by getting a good education, the state should help us to do this. Just as the state builds roads to help us get around, and hospitals to take of us when we're sick, and pays police and firemen to keep us safe, the state should help us get a good education. These are all things that make our communities better places to live.

Having a job service for college graduates shouldn't be needed. If you can't get a job, why would you go to college? For the state to find you a job after college seems unnecessary. And that doesn't do anything about the high cost of college. States should be doing something to help make college less expensive so more of us can go.

Because educating it's citizens makes the state a better place to live, just like having good roads, good hospitals and good public services, the states should provide free or reduced tuition for all students who receive acceptance letters. Low-cost student loans and job-placement services are not enough help.

SCORE OF 2

I'm hoping to go to college, but I don't know...it's very expensive and my family is already paying for my brother's college. My parents say that I'll have to come up with some way to help them. Just like my brother, he works in the dorm and over the summer he works with a landscape company. There are 3 ideas to help students like me go to college, their can be low-cost loans from the state or the state can help people find jobs or the state can give students free tuition. My parents say some states give the students that live there a discount on tuitions, and I think that's a very good idea. After all, we live here and will work here, and so it's good for the state if we have college degrees. People with college degrees can become engineers or computer programmers, and if you don't have a degree, you can't. We need more engineers and programmers because so many things run on computers.

If there are a lot of people with college degrees in our state, then that's good for the state. More people will want to come here to live, and that means more

people will be buying houses, cars and food etc here. That will create more jobs for other people like saleman and store clerks, and that will help the state. I don't think low-cost loans or job programs will be that helpful.

SCORE OF 1

I don't think I'm going to be able to go to college, because it's too expensive. I think it would be a good thing for the state to provide lower tuition because if I go to college, I'll be able to get a good job, get married and raise a family. I won't be able to take care of my family without a college degree. If I do go to college, I'll be able to make sure my kids have a good life. If I have to get a loan to finish college, I don't think I will because I don't want to owe a lot of money. It's too hard to pay back.

Quarter 3

Answer Key

1. **D**
2. **H**
3. **A**
4. **J**
5. **B**
6. **J**
7. **D**
8. **J**
9. **D**
10. **G**
11. **D**
12. **G**
13. **D**
14. **H**
15. **C**
16. **H**
17. **A**
18. **G**
19. **C**
20. **F**

1. D

Category: Wordiness

Difficulty: Medium

Strategic Advice: Sometimes a redundancy will be included in the underlined selection; the underlined material may also be redundant because the idea is present somewhere else in the sentence.

Getting to the Answer: Because the word "live" is used later in the sentence, all choices but (D) contain unnecessary information.

2. H

Category: Word Choice

Difficulty: High

Strategic Advice: Learn the differences between "its" and "it's"—the former is the possessive form of "it"; the latter is the contraction of "it is" or "it has."

Getting to the Answer: "Its'" is not a word, so that rules out (F). Because the "unique anatomy" belongs to the sloth, the possessive "its" is correct here. (G) uses the contraction for "it is or it has," and (J) incorrectly uses an adverb ("uniquely") to modify a noun ("anatomy").

3. A

Category: Punctuation

Difficulty: Medium

Strategic Advice: Use commas to separate nonessential descriptive phrases from the rest of the sentence.

Getting to the Answer: This sentence is correct as written. (B) misuses the semicolon, which is correct when used to combine two independent clauses. The first sentence created by (C) is a fragment. (D) uses a transition word that is inappropriate in context.

4. J

Category: Word Choice

Difficulty: Low

Strategic Advice: Adjectives can only modify nouns and pronouns; all other parts of speech are modified by adverbs.

Getting to the Answer: The verb phrase "are... adapted" needs to be modified by an adverb, so (J) is the correct choice. None of the other choices makes sense in context.

5. B

Category: Connections/Word Choice

Difficulty: Medium

Strategic Advice: Pronouns must agree in number with their antecedent nouns.

Getting to the Answer: "Instead" properly relates the ideas in the two sentences, so that shouldn't be changed. However, the paragraph is discussing "a sloth," so "it," not "they," is the proper pronoun.

6. J

Category: Connections

Difficulty: Medium

Strategic Advice: When answering a Connections question, first determine how the ideas are related.

Getting to the Answer: The sloth's skill as a swimmer contrasts with its inability to move swiftly on land, so you're looking for a word that expresses contrast. "Because," in the original section, indicates cause-and-effect, and "Similarly," in (H), indicates similarity, so those are clearly incorrect. Of the two remaining options, (G) is not grammatically correct when plugged back in to the sentence. (J) is the correct choice.

7. D

Category: Verb Tenses

Difficulty: Medium

Strategic Advice: Make sure verb tenses logically sequence the events discussed.

Getting to the Answer: Most passages will use more than one verb tense; context will help you determine which one is correct. Since the sentence already states that a sloth "can hang," "can look," (D) is the correct choice here. The past perfect "had been looking" in (B) is inconsistent, and (C) is unnecessarily wordy.

8. J

Category: Wordiness

Difficulty: Low

Strategic Advice: Check underlined compounds for redundancy. If the words have similar meanings, look for an answer that eliminates one of them.

Getting to the Answer: "Protect" and "defend" mean essentially the same thing; (J) eliminates "defend." Both (G) and (H) use "protects" with "to," which is incorrect; the infinitive is "to protect."

9. **D**

Category: Wordiness
Difficulty: Medium
Strategic Advice: When OMIT is offered as an answer choice, examine the relevance of the underlined information.
Getting to the Answer: This passage concerns the sloth; discussion of the howler monkey is irrelevant.

10. **G**

Category: Sentence Sense
Difficulty: Medium
Strategic Advice: A dependent clause cannot stand alone as a sentence.
Getting to the Answer: The sentence beginning with "Which" is actually a fragment. (**G**) correctly makes the dependent clause a part of the first sentence. (H) uses a connecting phrase that is inappropriate in context. (J) creates a grammatically incorrect sentence.

11. **D**

Category: Word Choice
Difficulty: Medium
Strategic Advice: Pronouns must agree in number with their antecedent nouns.
Getting to the Answer: The antecedent noun here is the plural "names," so the pronoun should be plural as well. (A) and (B) use a singular pronoun. (C) uses "there," a homophone of the plural possessive pronoun "their," and is incorrect in this context.

12. **G**

Category: Word Choice
Difficulty: Medium
Strategic Advice: A verb must agree in number with its subject noun, which may not be the noun closest to it in the sentence.
Getting to the Answer: Here, the plural "marbles" is the object of "regarding"; the subject of the verb is the singular "word." (F) and (J) use plural verb forms; (H) creates a sentence fragment. The singular verb form in (**G**) is correct.

13. **D**

Category: Word Choice
Difficulty: High
Strategic Advice: Many answer choices will be correctly structured idioms; choose the one that makes sense in context.
Getting to the Answer: All of the answer choices here are proper idioms but, in this context, "manipulated in a variety of ways" is correct.

14. **H**

Category: Verb Tenses
Difficulty: Medium
Strategic Advice: Verbs in a compound must be in parallel form.
Getting to the Answer: (G), (H), and (J) all make the verbs parallel, so you must determine which uses the appropriate tense. The tenses used in (G) and (J) change the meaning of the original sentence; (**H**) is correct here.

15. **C**

Category: Verb Tenses
Difficulty: Medium
Strategic Advice: Determine the main verb tense of the passage; most sentences will use this tense.
Getting to the Answer: This passage is written primarily in the present tense; (**C**) is the consistent choice here. (A) and (D) use the past tense; additionally, the singular verb in (D) is incorrect with the plural "varieties." (B) is incorrect grammatical structure.

16. **H**

Category: Word Choice
Difficulty: Low
Strategic Advice: Pronouns must agree in person and number with their antecedents.
Getting to the Answer: The antecedent here is the plural "players," so the singular "his or her" in (F) is incorrect. (G) and (J) use second- and first-person pronouns, respectively, which are also inappropriate with this antecedent. "Their marbles," in (**H**), is correct here.

17. **A**

Category: Word Choice

Difficulty: Medium

Strategic Advice: The noun closest to a verb in the sentence may not be its subject.

Getting to the Answer: Here, the plural "marbles" is the object of the preposition "of," not the subject of the verb "spans"; the subject is the singular "popularity," so this sentence is correct as written. (B) does not agree with the singular subject. The verb form in (C) creates a grammatically incorrect sentence. (D) is unnecessarily wordy.

18. **G**

Category: Word Choice

Difficulty: Medium

Strategic Advice: The antecedent of a pronoun may appear in an earlier sentence.

Getting to the Answer: The antecedent of "It" is the plural "games" in the sentence before, so the pronoun should be plural. (F) and (J) use singular pronouns. (H) changes the meaning of the sentence.

19. **C**

Category: Word Choice

Difficulty: Medium

Strategic Advice: On the ACT, the longest answer choice is rarely correct.

Getting to the Answer: (A), (B), and (D) are all idiomatically incorrect constructions; only the idiom in (**C**) is correct.

20. **F**

Category: Wordiness

Difficulty: High

Strategic Advice: Some sentences will be correct as written.

Getting to the Answer: This sentence contains no error. (G) improperly uses an adjective ("actual") to modify a verb ("has"). (H) and (J) make the sentence unnecessarily wordy.

Quarter 4

Answer Key

1. B
2. K
3. A
4. F
5. C
6. H
7. E
8. J
9. C
10. F
11. C
12. J
13. C
14. F

1. **B**

Category: Plane Geometry

Difficulty: High

Strategic Advice: Whenever two triangles have two equal angles, they are similar triangles. When you notice a triangle within a triangle, like the one in this figure, pay special attention to the angles that are shared by both triangles.

Getting to the Answer: The triangle with hypotenuse b that is formed by the dotted line is similar to $\triangle PQR$. The sides of this triangle, therefore, will be in proportion to the sides of $\triangle PQR$. Your job, then, is to evaluate the answer choices to find which ratio describes the ratio of the smaller triangle to $\triangle PQR$. Side d is the shortest side of the smaller triangle, and a is the shortest side of $\triangle PQR$. Side c is the longer leg of the smaller triangle, and b is the longer leg of $\triangle PQR$. Therefore, the ratio between the two pairs of sides is the same, and $\frac{d}{a} = \frac{b}{c}$, (**B**).

2. **K**

Category: Variable Manipulation

Difficulty: High

Strategic Advice: Each problem is worth the same amount, so don't spend too much time on any one problem. Problems that ask how many different values of something there are tend to be particularly lengthy, so it's a good idea to save them for the end of the test.

Getting to the Answer: One way to solve this is to make all of the numerators 3: $\frac{3}{33} < \frac{3}{n} < \frac{3}{27}$.
This inequality is true for all values of n between 27 and 33: 28, 29, 30, 31, and 32. That's 5 integer values of n. You can also solve this algebraically. The fastest way is to first take the reciprocals, which will reverse the inequalities (since $\frac{1}{3} < \frac{1}{2}$ but 3 < 2): $11 > \frac{n}{3} > 9$. Now multiply each term by 3: $33 > n > 27$. Once again, you get five solutions: n = 28, 29, 30, 31, or 32.

3. **A**

Category: Trigonometry

Difficulty: Medium

Strategic Advice: The key to many trigonometry problems is the basic definitions: $\sin = \frac{opposite}{hypotenuse}$; $\cos = \frac{adjacent}{hypotenuse}$; $\tan = \frac{opposite}{adjacent}$. Use the mnemonic SOHCAHTOA to help you remember which trig function goes with which sides of the right triangle.

Getting to the Answer:

$$\tan 37° = \frac{4.3}{x}$$
$$x(\tan 37°) = 4.3$$
$$x = \frac{4.3}{\tan 37°}$$

4. **F**

Category: Coordinate Geometry

Difficulty: High

Strategic Advice: The points that two or more graphs have in common are the points where each graph has the same values of x and y.

Getting to the Answer: Since each of the first two equations is equal to $-2y$, set the right sides equal to each other:

$$-x + 4 = -2y = x + 4$$
$$-x + 4 = x + 4$$
$$-x = x$$
$$-2x = 0$$
$$x = 0$$

Now plug back in to solve for y:

$$-2y = x + 4$$
$$-2y = 0 + 4$$
$$-2y = 4$$
$$y = -2$$

The only solution to the first two equations is (0,–2). Does this point work in the third equation?

$$5y = -6x + 8$$
$$5(-2) = -6(0) + 8$$
$$-10 \neq -2$$

It doesn't, which means no point will work in all three equations. The graphs have no points in common, (**F**).

5. **C**

Category: Plane Geometry

Difficulty: High

Strategic Advice: When calculating the area of an irregular shape, see if you can divide it into simpler shapes for which you know the area formulas.

Getting to the Answer: The volume of the shovel will be the area of this cross section multiplied by the width of the shovel. Since you know the area formula for rectangles (base × height) and for triangles ($\frac{1}{2}$ × base × height), imagine that this figure is a rectangle with a right triangle cut out.

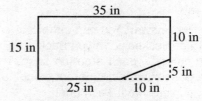

The area of the rectangle is (15)(35) = 525 square inches. The area of the triangle is $\frac{1}{2}$ (10)(5) = 25 square inches. So the area of the cross section is 525 – 25 = 500 square inches. Multiply this area by the third dimension, the width of the shovel: (500)(40) = 20,000 cubic inches.

6. **H**

Category: Trigonometry

Difficulty: High

Strategic Advice: Since the sides of the box are perpendicular to the top and bottom, angles like ZYX will be right angles. Imagine that you rotate this angle, and you'll see that ZYW is also a right angle.

Getting to the Answer: Since $WX = 12$ and $XY = 5$, you can use the Pythagorean triplet 5:12:13 to find that $WY = 13$. Then triangle ZWY, if you put it down flat on the page, looks like this:

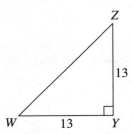

You can save yourself some work by recognizing that this is a 45–45–90 triangle (since the legs are the same length), which means that $\sin ZWY = \sin 45°$ $= \frac{\sqrt{2}}{2}$. (If you don't have the sine of 45° memorized, this is still pretty simple: $\sin = \frac{\text{opposite}}{\text{hypotenuse}}$, and the hypotenuse of a 45–45–90 triangle is the length of a leg times $\sqrt{2}$, so $\sin 45° = \frac{13}{13\sqrt{2}} = \frac{\sqrt{2}}{2}$.)

7. E

Category: Variable Manipulation
Difficulty: High
Strategic Advice: Sometimes questions will look harder than they actually are because they're written to intimidate you.
Getting to the Answer: You can either solve this algebraically or Backsolve. If you Backsolve, remember that "if and only if"—don't stop too soon. There are really three possibilities in different combinations in the answer choices. Test each one.

If $a = 0$, then:
$(a - b)^2 = (0 - b)^2 = (-b)^2 = b^2$
$a^2 - b^2 = 0^2 - b^2 = -b^2$
$b^2 \neq -b^2$ unless $b = 0$, so you can eliminate (A) and (D).

If $b = 0$, then:
$(a - b)^2 = (a - 0)^2 = a^2$
$a^2 - b^2 = a^2 - 0^2 = a^2$
$a^2 = a^2$, so you can eliminate (C) ($b = 0$ alone is enough to make them equal; you don't need $a = 0$ as well).

If $a = b$, then:
$(a - b)^2 = (0)^2 = 0$
$a^2 - b^2 = a^2 - a^2 = 0$

$0 = 0$, so either $a = b$ or $b = 0$ will make the statement $(a - b)^2 = a^2 - b^2$ true. (**E**) is correct.

To set it up algebraically, set $(a - b)^2$ equal to $a^2 - b^2$ and see what you can solve for.
$(a - b)^2 = a^2 - b^2$
$a^2 - 2ab + b^2 = a^2 - b^2$
$-2ab + b^2 = -b^2$
$-2ab = -2b^2$
$ab = b^2$
This is true if $a = b$ or if $b = 0$.

8. J

Category: Variable Manipulation
Difficulty: High
Strategic Advice: If you have trouble keeping track of the variables, you can Pick Numbers, but many people will find it slightly faster to work with the variables.
Getting to the Answer: The rectangle has area $(x + 3)(x + 7) = x^2 + 10x + 21$, and the square has area x^2. The area after removing the square is $x^2 + 10x + 21 - x^2 = 10x + 21$.

9. C

Category: Proportions and Probability
Difficulty: High
Strategic Advice: Little words like "at least" make a big difference.
Getting to the Answer: You can get exactly 2 heads three ways: THH, HTH or HHT. You can get exactly 3 heads one way: HHH. So you can get at least 2 heads in 4 ways. Each flip has 2 possible outcomes, so the probability of getting tails (or heads) on any one flip is $\frac{1}{2}$.

Probability of THH $= \frac{1}{2} \cdot \frac{1}{2} \cdot \frac{1}{2} = \frac{1}{8}$.

Probability of HTH $= \frac{1}{2} \cdot \frac{1}{2} \cdot \frac{1}{2} = \frac{1}{8}$.

Probability of HHT $= \frac{1}{2} \cdot \frac{1}{2} \cdot \frac{1}{2} = \frac{1}{8}$.

Probability of HHH $= \frac{1}{2} \cdot \frac{1}{2} \cdot \frac{1}{2} = \frac{1}{8}$.

Probability of any of the four is $\frac{1}{8} + \frac{1}{8} + \frac{1}{8} + \frac{1}{8} = \frac{4}{8} = \frac{1}{2}$.

10. F

Category: Coordinate Geometry

Difficulty: High

Strategic Advice: Don't get thrown off by the variables. If the question stem talks about distance, plug into the distance formula.

Getting to the Answer: The distance between $(a,2)$ and $(16,a)$ is $\sqrt{(a-2)^2 + (16-a)^2} = 10$.

Square both sides:

$(a-2)^2 + (16-a)^2 = 100$

FOIL out the parentheses:

$(a^2 - 4a + 4) + (256 - 32a + a^2) = 100$

$2a^2 - 36a + 260 = 100$

To solve for a, first get one side of the equation equal to 0:

$2a^2 - 36a + 160 = 0$

Then factor. Dividing by 2 will make factoring easier:

$a^2 - 18a + 80 = 0$

$(a-8)(a-10) = 0$

$a - 8 = 0$ or $a - 10 = 0$

$a = 8$ or $a = 10$

Backsolving would also be a good way to solve this problem.

11. C

Category: Variable Manipulation

Difficulty: High

Strategic Advice: Picking Numbers can turn one of the hardest problems on the test into one of the most manageable.

Getting to the Answer: Choose $t = 6$ so that you can easily find when you compute x.

$x = \frac{1}{3}t + 2 = \frac{1}{3}(6) + 2 = 2 + 2 = 4$

$y = 4 - t = 4 - 6 = -2$

Now plug $x = 4$ into the equations in the answer choices and see if you get -2 for y:

(A) $y = 2 - \frac{1}{3}x = 2 - \frac{1}{3}(4) = \frac{6}{3} - \frac{4}{3} = \frac{2}{3}$. This isn't -2, so eliminate.

(B) $y = 4 - x = 4 - 4 = 0$. This isn't -2, so eliminate.

(C) $y = 10 - 3x = 10 - 3(4) = 10 - 12 = -2$. This is a match.

(D) $y = -2 - 3x = -2 - 3(4) = -2 - 12 = -14$. This isn't -2, so eliminate.

(E) $y = 6 - 3x = 6 - 3(4) = 6 - 12 = -6$. This isn't -2, so eliminate.

Algebraically, you could solve the first equation for t and plug this into the equation for y to eliminate t:

$x = \frac{1}{3}t + 2$

$x - 2 = \frac{1}{3}t$

$t = 3(x - 2) = 3x - 6$

$y = 4 - t = 4 - (3x - 6) = 4 - 3x + 6 = 10 - 3x$

12. J

Category: Number Properties

Difficulty: High

Strategic Advice: Many problems will tell you everything you need to know (even if you've never seen a complex number!).

Getting to the Answer:

$(i-1)^2(i+1) = (i-1)(i-1)(i+1)$

You can save some work by multiplying the last two parentheses first:

$(i-1)^2(i+1) = (i-1)(i^2 - 1)$

i is the square root of -1, so we can substitute. $i^2 = -1$:

$(i-1)(-1-1)$

$= 1(i-1)(-2)$

$= -2i + 2$.

Since there is -1 outside of the parentheses, make sure to multiply the entire thing by -1, which is (J).

If you FOILed $(i-1)(i-1)$ first, you should have arrived at the same answer, just with more work.

13. C

Category: Coordinate Geometry

Difficulty: High

Strategic Advice: If you can tell at a glance that a problem is going to take several minutes, save it until you've done all the easier problems.

Getting to the Answer: In the equation of an ellipse, $\frac{(x-h)^2}{a^2} + \frac{(y-k)^2}{b^2}$, the center is at (h,k), the length of the horizontal axis is $2a$, and the length of the vertical axis is $2b$. Putting this together, this ellipse looks something like this:

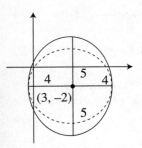

The largest circle possible is dotted on the diagram. Notice that it has the same center as the ellipse and has radius 4. In the equation of a circle, $(x - h)^2 + (y - k)^2 = r^2$, (h,k) is the center, and r is the radius. Plugging into the formula, this circle's equation is $(x - 3)^2 + (y + 2)^2 = 4^2 = 16$, which is (**C**).

14. F

Category: Plane Geometry

Difficulty: High

Strategic Advice: Picking Numbers can make a theoretical problem much more concrete.

Getting to the Answer: If you're not sure which answer choice makes the most sense, assume each side starts with length 1 and try each answer out. The area starts as $1 \times 1 = 1$, so triple the area is 3.

(H) area $= (1 \times 9)(1 \times 9) = 81$. This is too big.

(G) area $= (1 \times 3)(1 \times 3) = 9$. Still too big.

(F) area $= (1 \times \sqrt{3})(1 \times \sqrt{3}) = \sqrt{3} \times \sqrt{3} = 3$. This is perfect.

Quarter 4: Science

Answer Key

1. **D**
2. **J**
3. **B**
4. **H**
5. **C**
6. **G**
7. **B**
8. **H**
9. **A**
10. **G**

1. D

Category: Scientific Reasoning

Difficulty: High

Strategic Advice: Don't be put off by new terms that appear in the question stem. They'll always be defined for you.

Getting to the Answer: Total internal reflection occurs when the first medium has a higher refractive index than the second. So the correct answer is a pair of materials in which the refractive index of the first material is greater than that of the second. All you have to do is read the refractive indexes in Table 1 for each answer choice.

(A), (B), and (C) all have lower refractive indices for the first material than the second, so they are incorrect. Only (**D**) has the correct relationship; the refractive index for flint glass (1.66) is greater than that of calcium fluoride (1.43).

2. J

Category: Patterns

Difficulty: Medium

Strategic Advice: If an answer choice is untrue for any one material, then it's not a valid general statement.

Getting to the Answer: The easiest way to answer this question is to use the first couple of materials and test each hypothesis on them.

(F) and (G) are incorrect because the transmittance range of lithium fluoride is wider than its useful prism range.

Comparing the data on lithium fluoride and calcium fluoride rules out (H) because transmittance range does NOT increase as useful prism range decreases. In fact, looking down the rest of the table, you see that transmittance range seems to decrease as useful prism range decreases.

(**J**) is the only choice left, and the data on lithium fluoride and calcium fluoride, as well as all the other materials, confirm that the transmittance range is always wider than, and includes within it, the useful prism range.

3. B

Category: Patterns

Difficulty: Medium

Strategic Advice: Start by asking yourself where you saw information about lead oxide.

Getting to the Answer: According to the footnote to Table 1, quartz infused with lead oxide is flint glass. A comparison of the properties of pure quartz and flint glass shows that the transmittance range of flint glass is narrower than that of quartz but that its refractive index is greater. This supports (**B**).

PASSAGE II

4. H

Category: Scientific Reasoning
Difficulty: Medium

Strategic Advice: When you're reading Conflicting Viewpoints passages, it's important to note both what scientists agree *and* disagree on.

Getting to the Answer: In his argument, Scientist 1 states that the surface of Triton is covered with a thick layer of methane and nitrogen. Scientist 2 mentions methane-nitrogen polar ice caps, so (**H**) is correct.

(F) and (G) are incorrect because only Scientist 1 proposes volcanic activity and internal heating by radioactive decay.

(J) is incorrect because only Scientist 2 proposes nitrogen-methane "snowfall."

5. C

Category: Scientific Reasoning
Difficulty: High

Strategic Advice: To answer this question, first go back to the passage and reread the part where Scientist 2 discusses high-resolution images. Remember, the answer is in the passage.

Getting to the Answer: Scientist 2 proposes that small craters—which constitute some of Triton's surface features—arose from the impact of small meteorites over a long period of time, so (**C**) is correct.

You can eliminate (A) immediately because Scientist 2 doesn't discuss planetoids.

(B) is incorrect because the impact of meteorites has nothing to do with volcanic activity.

(D) is incorrect because nowhere in Scientist 1's argument does he say that low-resolution images were used.

6. G

Category: Scientific Reasoning
Difficulty: Medium

Strategic Advice: Always begin Roman numeral questions by examining the statement that appears most frequently in the answer choices.

Getting to the Answer: First consider Statement I. There is no need to chemically analyze Triton's surface because both scientists agree that there is a layer of nitrogen and methane on the surface. Therefore, Statement I is incorrect. (G) is the only choice that does not include Statement I, so (**G**) is correct.

Statements II and III are both correct because both subsurface temperature and core radioactivity readings would settle the question of whether Triton could sustain volcanic activity.

7. B

Category: Scientific Reasoning
Difficulty: Medium

Strategic Advice: If you can't recall the points of disagreement, research the answer choices one by one.

Getting to the Answer: The scientists most clearly disagree about the physical process responsible for the features found on Triton, (**B**). Scientist 1 claims that a number of geological features are caused by volcanic activity, whereas Scientist 2 believes the same features are caused by glacier-like movement of ice caps and "snowfall."

The scientists do agree on what features are observed and the chemical composition of the surface of Triton, so (A) and (C) are incorrect.

(D) is incorrect because the origin of Triton is discussed only by Scientist 2.

8. H

Category: Scientific Reasoning
Difficulty: Medium

Strategic Advice: You should have answered this question first, before reading Scientist 2's viewpoint.

Getting to the Answer: To answer this question, you must know Scientist 1's viewpoint: a number of features on Triton arise from volcanic activity. Therefore, if evidence of an active volcano were found in the images, this hypothesis would be supported, so (**H**) is correct.

(F) would not support this hypothesis; the fact that the surfaces of the three moons are composed of the same elements doesn't prove that they all must exhibit volcanic activity. It is clear from Scientist 1's viewpoint that volcanic activity requires an *internal* heat source. The external properties are not relevant to this argument.

(G) is incorrect because Scientist 1 doesn't discuss small craters.

(J) is incorrect because it pertains to Scientist 2's viewpoint.

9. A

Category: Scientific Reasoning
Difficulty: High
Strategic Advice: Consider how this new information fits into both Scientist 1 and Scientist 2's viewpoints.

Getting to the Answer: Scientist 1 believes that radioactive decay may provide the energy for volcanic eruptions in Triton, but Scientist 2 says that Triton has been cooling in a stable orbit and is too small to still support radioactive decay. If new research suggested that slow radioactive decay could, in fact, continue in small bodies for up to 10 billion years, this information would support the view of Scientist 1 only, (**A**).

10. G

Category: Scientific Reasoning
Difficulty: Medium
Strategic Advice: Any generalizations must be consistent with what Scientist 2 stated in the passage.

Getting to the Answer: Go back and reread what Scientist 2 said about Triton's orbit. His third sentence states that Triton's "unusual orbit—it revolves in the direction opposite to the planet's rotation—indicates that it was captured by Neptune." If Triton's orbit is unusual in that it revolves in the direction opposite Neptune's rotation, then most moons must revolve in the same direction as their planet's rotation, (**G**).

(F) might be tempting because Scientist 2 does state that Triton's original orbit must have been highly elliptical. However, there is no indication that this elliptical orbit is typical of other moons.

(H) and (J) are irrelevant to the information in the passage

KAPLAN

TEST PREP AND
ADMISSIONS

ACT®*

Practice Test E
Test with Explanations

For Courses Starting on or After 6/2/2015

ENGLISH TEST

45 Minutes—75 Questions

Directions: In the following five passages, certain words and phrases are underlined and numbered. In the right-hand column are alternatives for each underlined portion. Select the one that best conveys the idea, creates the most grammatically correct sentence, or is most consistent with the style and tone of the passage. If you decide that the original version is best, select NO CHANGE. You may also find questions that ask about the entire passage or a section of the passage. These questions will correspond to small, numbered boxes in the test. For these questions, decide which choice best accomplishes the purpose set out in the question stem. After you've selected the best choice, fill in the corresponding oval on your Answer Grid. For some questions, you'll need to read the context in order to answer correctly. Be sure to read until you have enough information to determine the correct answer choice.

Passage I

American Jazz

<u>One of the earliest</u> music forms to originate in the United
₁
States was Jazz. Known as truly Mid-American because of

<u>it's</u> having origins in several locations in middle America,
₂
this music developed almost simultaneously in New Orleans,

Saint Louis, Kansas City, and Chicago.

   At the start of the twentieth century, musicians all along

the Mississippi River familiar with West African folk music

[3] blended it with European classical music from the early

   nineteenth century. This combination was adopted by art-

ists in the region who began to use minor chords and

1. **A.** NO CHANGE
   B. One of the most earliest
   C. The most early
   D. The earliest

2. **F.** NO CHANGE
   G. its
   H. its's
   J. its'

3. At this point, the writer is considering adding the following phrase:
       —rich with syncopation—
   Given that it is true, would this be a relevant addition to make here?
   A. Yes, because it can help the reader have a better understanding of the music being discussed.
   B. Yes, because it helps explain to the reader why this music became popular.
   C. No, because it fails to explain the connection between this music and the button accordion.
   D. No, because it is inconsistent with the style of this essay to mention specific musical forms.

GO ON TO THE NEXT PAGE

syncopation, in their own music, ragtime and blues. At the
4
same time, brass bands and gospel choirs adopted Jazz music,
and it became a true blend of cultures. Eventually, a unique
music style developed; based on a blend of the many different
5
cultures in America at the time. It was American Jazz and
6
became the first indigenous American style to affect music in
the rest of the world.

[1] One of the true greats of American Jazz was Cabell
"Cab" Calloway III. [2] He was born in New York in 1907,
but his family moved to Chicago during his teen years.
[3] Growing up, Cab made his living working as a shoe
7

shiner and he was a waiter. [4] During these years, he also
8
spent time at the racetrack, where he walked horses to keep

them in good shape. [9] [5] After graduating from high

---

4. **F.** NO CHANGE
   G. syncopation in their own music,
   H. syncopation, in their own music
   J. syncopation in their own music

5. **A.** NO CHANGE
   B. style developed based on
   C. style developed based on,
   D. style, developed based on

6. **F.** NO CHANGE
   G. This style, known as American Jazz,
   H. Being known as American Jazz, it
   J. It being American Jazz first

7. Which of the following alternatives to the underlined
   portion would NOT be acceptable?
   A. earned his living by
   B. made his living from
   C. made his living on
   D. earned his living

8. **F.** NO CHANGE
   G. as well
   H. being
   J. OMIT the underlined portion

9. The writer is considering deleting the following clause
   from the preceding sentence (placing a period after the
   word *racetrack*):

   where he walked horses to keep them in good shape.

   Should the writer make this deletion?
   A. Yes, because the information is unrelated to the topic
   addressed in this paragraph.
   B. Yes, because the information diminishes the musical
   accomplishments and successes of Cab Calloway.
   C. No, because the information explains the reference to
   the racetrack, which might otherwise puzzle readers.
   D. No, because the information shows how far Cab
   Calloway came in his life.

GO ON TO THE NEXT PAGE

school in Chicago, <u>where</u> Cab got his first performance job in
                         10
a revue called "Plantation Days." [6] His strong and impressive

voice soon gained him <u>popularity in the top Jazz circles</u> of the
                              11

United States. [12]

Many others have followed Cab's lead <u>and have moved</u>
                                            13
<u>from the east coast to middle America.</u> Like other folk
         13
music forms, American Jazz has a rich history and unique

sound that <u>means it'll stick around for a while</u>.
                  14

10. F. NO CHANGE
    G. it was there that
    H. was where
    J. OMIT the underlined portion

11. A. NO CHANGE
    B. popularity: in the top Jazz circles
    C. popularity, in the top Jazz circles,
    D. popularity in the top Jazz circles,

12. Upon reviewing this paragraph and finding that some information has been left out, the writer composes the following sentence incorporating that information:

    > He became widely known as "The man in the zoot suit with the reet pleats."

    This sentence would most logically be placed after sentence:
    F. 3.
    G. 4.
    H. 5.
    J. 6.

13. Given that all the choices are true, which one would most effectively tie together the two main subjects of this essay?
    A. NO CHANGE
    B. and have added to the rich tradition of American Jazz.
    C. such as George Duke and Earl Klugh.
    D. and have signed large recording contracts.

14. F. NO CHANGE
    G. causes it to be an enduring institution with a timeless appeal.
    H. makes many people enjoy it.
    J. ensures its continued vitality.

> Question 15 asks about the essay as a whole.

15. Suppose the writer's goal was to write a brief essay focusing on the history and development of American Jazz music. Would this essay successfully fulfill this goal?
    A. Yes, because the essay describes the origins of American Jazz music and one of its important figures.
    B. Yes, because the essay mentions the contributions American Jazz music has made to other folk music traditions.
    C. No, because the essay refers to other musical forms besides American Jazz music.
    D. No, because the essay focuses on only one American Jazz musician, Cab Calloway.

GO ON TO THE NEXT PAGE

Passage II

My Grandfather's Internet

My grandfather is possibly the least technologically capable writer in the world. He refused to use anything but his pen and paper to write until last year. (He said, he didn't need any keys or mouse pads between his words and himself.) Consequently, when he has went to buy a computer—because of the knowledge that his editor refused to read another hand-written novel—he resisted connecting it to the Internet for several months. He said he had no need to find information on a World Wide Web. [20]

Grandpa's editor, however, was clever and, knowing exactly how my grandfather could use it, described how the Internet would improve his life. However, Grandpa could get instant feedback, and praise from the publishing company, read online reviews, and do research for his characters much faster. Finally, Grandpa connected to the Internet, and he hasn't logged off yet.

Grandpa is fascinated by all the things he can do on the World Wide Web. He has found that chat rooms are wonderful places to have long conversations with people interesting enough to be characters in his books.

16. F. NO CHANGE
    G. world he refused
    H. world refusing,
    J. world, and has been refusing

17. A. NO CHANGE
    B. said
    C. said, that
    D. said, that,

18. F. NO CHANGE
    G. had went
    H. went
    J. goes

19. A. NO CHANGE
    B. due to the fact that
    C. because
    D. so

20. Given that all are true, which of the following additions to the preceding sentence (after *World Wide Web*) would be most relevant?
    F. that was on his computer.
    G. when he had a set of encyclopedias right there in his office.
    H. with other people on it.
    J. where he might get a computer virus.

21. A. NO CHANGE
    B. Additionally, Grandpa
    C. Conversely, Grandpa
    D. Grandpa

22. F. NO CHANGE
    G. feedback and, praise
    H. feedback and praise
    J. feedback and praise,

For example, he says, by clicking the "close" button he can
23

just ignore them who aren't interesting. Grandpa's favorite
24

website is Google.com. Google.com is a search engine that

searches millions of sites for whatever word he types in,

which is very convenient when he needs to know
25

how the native people of Africa developed the game

Mancala. For him, Grandpa says that, in merely a few
26

seconds, to be able to find anything he wants is a source of
26

pure joy.
26

[1] As for his writings, Grandpa uses the Internet not only for

research but also for making them more creative and checking

his word choice. [2] Explaining his new vocabulary to his edi-

tor, Grandpa points to his new computer and admits that
27

an Internet connection was a good idea after all. [3] I am sure

Grandpa hasn't explored the entire Internet yet, but I am sure
28

he will continue to find new and better ways of using it. 29
28

23. A. NO CHANGE
    B. To illustrate,
    C. On the one hand,
    D. On the other hand,

24. F. NO CHANGE
    G. the people
    H. it
    J. their talking

25. A. NO CHANGE
    B. convenient, when
    C. convenient. When
    D. convenient; when

26. F. NO CHANGE
    G. For him, Grandpa says that to be able to find anything he wants, is a source of pure joy for him, in merely a few seconds.
    H. Grandpa says a source of pure joy for him is that he is able to find anything he wants, in merely a few seconds.
    J. Grandpa says that being able to find anything he wants in merely a few seconds is source of pure joy for him.

27. A. NO CHANGE
    B. pointing
    C. having pointed
    D. Grandpa has pointed

28. F. NO CHANGE
    G. and he probably won't explore the rest of it either.
    H. and so his editor will have to teach him to find things faster.
    J. and his editor knows just that.

29. Upon reviewing Paragraph 5 and realizing that some information has been left out, the writer composes the following sentence:

    He uses the dictionary and thesaurus websites religiously.

    The most logical placement for this sentence would be:

    A. before sentence 1.
    B. after sentence 1.
    C. after sentence 2.
    D. after sentence 3.

GO ON TO THE NEXT PAGE

Question 30 asks about the essay as a whole.

30. The writer is considering deleting the first sentence of Paragraph 1. If the writer removed this sentence, the essay would primarily lose:
   F. information about aspects of technology that his grandfather does not use.
   G. humor that sets the mood for the piece.
   H. important details about the Internet that his grandfather might enjoy.
   J. a justification for his grandfather's reluctance to use the Internet.

Passage III

Chickasaw Wandering

<u>In</u> the twilight of a cool autumn evening, I walked with a
31

gathering of people to the center of a field in Oklahoma.

Although I didn't know <u>more of the people who</u> walked with
32

me, <u>a few of them I did know quite well.</u> We were Chickasaw
33

Indians, and some of us had waited for years to make this

journey <u>across</u> the Chickasaw territory to the ornately
34

31. A. NO CHANGE
    B. On
    C. With
    D. From

32. F. NO CHANGE
    G. more of the people whom
    H. most of the people who
    J. most of the people whom

33. The writer wants to balance the statement made in the earlier part of this sentence with a related detail that suggests the unity of the people. Given that all of the following choices are true, which one best accomplishes this goal?
    A. NO CHANGE
    B. we each had our own reasons for being there.
    C. I hoped I would get to know some of them.
    D. I felt a kinship with them.

34. Which of the following alternatives to the underlined portion would NOT be acceptable?
    F. among
    G. over
    H. on
    J. through

GO ON TO THE NEXT PAGE

6

decorated capital of Tishomingo. [35]

For my whole life I had been shown <u>other Chickasaw's</u>
₃₆
<u>pictures</u>— many of them the ancestors of the
₃₆

<u>people, who walked along with me,</u> to the Festival that evening.
₃₇

<u>My father and grandmother helped preserve tribal history</u>
₃₈
<u>by collecting books and newspaper clippings.</u> Books about
₃₈
the history and traditions of our tribe were stacked on the
bookshelves, and framed portraits of members of our tribe
decorated the walls of these rooms. When I was growing up,
I would often find my father or grandmother in one of the
rooms, my father reading a book and my grandmother listening to ancient tribal music

    <u>That room</u> held everything I knew about being a
₃₉

<u>Chickasaw, and unlike</u> many Chickasaw, my family had
₄₀
moved away from Oklahoma all the way to Seattle. Once a

year, the tribe held a Festival and Annual Meeting <u>that was</u>
₄₁
<u>always well attended.</u>
₄₁

35. The writer is considering revising the preceding sentence by deleting the phrase "to the ornately decorated capital of Tishomingo" (placing a period after the word *territory*). If the writer did this, the paragraph would primarily lose:

  A. information comparing the narrator's own journey to similar ones made by members of other tribes.
  B. details describing the destination of the people the narrator is traveling with.
  C. details that establish the time and place of the events of the essay.
  D. interesting but irrelevant information about the Chickasaw.

36. F. NO CHANGE
  G. pictures in which other Chickasaw were present
  H. pictures of other Chickasaw
  J. other Chickasaw whose pictures had been taken

37. A. NO CHANGE
  B. people who, walked along with me
  C. people, who walked along, with me
  D. people who walked along with me

38. F. NO CHANGE
  G. Some of those pictures had been reprinted in books my father and grandmother collected.
  H. My grandmother and father proudly displayed these pictures in their homes.
  J. Like other Chickasaw, my father and grandmother had each set aside a room in their own home to the tribe.

39. A. NO CHANGE
  B. Her rooms
  C. Those rooms
  D. This room

40. F. NO CHANGE
  G. Chickasaw unlike
  H. Chickasaw, unlike
  J. Chickasaw. Unlike

41. Given that all of the choices are true, which one provides information most relevant to the main focus of this paragraph?

  A. NO CHANGE
  B. notable for its exquisite dancing.
  C. in south central Oklahoma.
  D. that lasted several days.

GO ON TO THE NEXT PAGE

Before they moved to Seattle, my grandmother and father had always attended this event. However, the tribe owned no land in Seattle on which a ceremonial house could be built and <u>Chickasaw ceremonies conducted.</u> Since I had never been
to Oklahoma, I had never been to a Chickasaw event or

walked in our territory. <u>Still,</u> I had never even known any other Chickasaw children. Finally, my father, grandmother, and I all took a trip to participate in the Festival. As we walked together through the open plain, hundreds of <u>crickets chirping</u> softly from the grass. The insects accompanied our

march <u>like</u> the spirits of our ancestors singing to us on our way home.

42. F. NO CHANGE
G. Chickasaw ceremonies were conducted there.
H. there were Chickasaw ceremonies conducted there.
J. the conducting of Chickasaw ceremonies.

43. A. NO CHANGE
B. Meanwhile
C. In fact,
D. On the other hand,

44. F. NO CHANGE
G. crickets, which chirped
H. crickets that chirped
J. crickets chirped

45. A. NO CHANGE
B. just as
C. as like
D. such as

Passage IV

Topping the Washington Monument

During the midday hours of December 6, <u>1884, engineers</u>

and workers braced themselves for the <u>days</u> dangerous mission. Winds that rushed past the workers at speeds of

nearly sixty miles per hour <u>threatened</u> to postpone

<u>and delay</u> the capstone ceremony marking the placement of

46. F. NO CHANGE
G. 1884, and engineers
H. 1884. Engineers
J. 1884; engineers

47. A. NO CHANGE
B. days'
C. day's
D. days's

48. F. NO CHANGE
G. had been threatened
H. will have threatened
J. threatens

49. A. NO CHANGE
B. to a later time
C. by delaying
D. OMIT the underlined portion

8

the capstone atop the Washington Monument. 50

Eighty-five years of fundraising and planning had brought

about this moment. In 1799, attorney and Congressman John
51
Marshall proposed a monument to honor the young nation's

Revolutionary War hero and first president. 52 Architect

Robert Mills, who planned the monument that would
53

memorialize Washington. Meanwhile, the monument would
54
be in the form of a 500-foot obelisk made of marble and

topped with a 100-pound capstone of aluminum.

In 1861, construction on the monument was halted because

supplies and men were needed to fight the Civil War. During

the war, the monument stood only 176 feet tall, and the

ground around it served as grazing land for livestock used

to feed the Union army. Fifteen years passed before work

resumed on the monument. The workers had the entire
55

monument's history in their minds during they're attempt to
56
place its capstone.
56

50. The writer is considering deleting the following from the preceding sentence:

> marking the placement of the capstone atop the Washington Monument.

If the writer were to delete this phrase, the essay would primarily lose:

F. a minor detail in the essay's opening paragraph.
G. an explanation of the term *capstone ceremony*.
H. the writer's opinion about the significance of the capstone ceremony
J. an indication of the capstone ceremony's significance to the American people.

51. A. NO CHANGE
B. attorney, and Congressman
C. attorney and Congressman,
D. attorney, and Congressman,

52. If the writer were to delete the preceding sentence, the paragraph would primarily lose:

F. an explanation of Washington's heroic acts of war.
G. details about what John Marshall thought the monument he envisioned should look like.
H. background information about why Washington was being honored with a monument.
J. biographical information about John Marshall.

53. A. NO CHANGE
B. Mills, planner of
C. Mills planned
D. Mills creating

54. F. NO CHANGE
G. Therefore, the
H. However, the
J. The

55. A. NO CHANGE
B. started
C. began
D. restarted again

56. F. NO CHANGE
G. they're attempt to place it's
H. their attempt to place its
J. their attempt to place it's

GO ON TO THE NEXT PAGE

9

The crowd cheered as, attached to the top of the
57

monument, the capstone was hoisted up. More than
57

eight decades and more than eighty years of planning and
58

building had come to a conclusion, and the Washington
59

Monument was finally complete.

57. A. NO CHANGE
   B. As the crowd cheered, the capstone was hoisted up and attached to the top of the monument.
   C. As the crowd cheered, attached to the top of the monument, the capstone was hoisted up.
   D. The capstone was hoisted up as the crowd cheered and attached to the top of the monument.

58. F. NO CHANGE
   G. decades amounting to more than eighty years
   H. decades–over eighty years–
   J. decades

59. Which of the following alternatives would be LEAST acceptable in terms of the context of this sentence?
   A. reached completion,
   B. come to a halt,
   C. come to an end,
   D. ended,

Question 60 asks about the essay as a whole.

60. Suppose the writer had intended to write a brief essay that describes the entire process of designing and building the Washington Monument. Would this essay successfully fulfill the writer's goal?

   F. Yes, because it offers such details as the materials used to make the capstone and shaft of the monument.
   G. Yes, because it explains in detail each step in the design and construction of the monument.
   H. No, because it focuses primarily on one point in the development of the monument rather than on the entire process.
   J. No, because it is primarily a historical essay about the early stages in the development of the monument.

Passage V

Why Lions Roar

   Research by biologists and environmental scientists has found several reasons that lions roar. Lions, which live in groups called prides, are very social creatures that communicate with one another in many ways. Roaring, the sound most often
61

61. A. NO CHANGE
   B. Roaring
   C. Roaring:
   D. Roaring is

GO ON TO THE NEXT PAGE

associated with lions, <u>perform</u> several key functions within
the pride.

62. F. NO CHANGE
    G. perform,
    H. performs,
    J. performs

<u>One of these defense</u> involves protecting the pride's land.
When prides take large pieces of land and claim them as their

63. A. NO CHANGE
    B. One of these, defense,
    C. One of these being defense,
    D. One of these is defense and it

own, they will roar to keep away intruders, <u>those are usually</u>
other lions. This "No Trespassing" warning serves to keep the

64. F. NO CHANGE
    G. most often these are
    H. and are typically
    J. usually

peace <u>because</u> it helps prevent competing prides from fighting
over food or for mates.

65. Which of the following alternatives to the underlined
portion would be the LEAST acceptable?
    A. although
    B. in that
    C. since
    D. as

<u>Lions also roar</u> to stay in contact with one another when
members of a pride are separated by long distances. Like all

66. F. NO CHANGE
    G. It's also the case that roaring is employed
    H. In addition, roaring is a way
    J. Roaring is also used

large cats, lions have <u>intense</u> hearing, which makes it possible
for them to hear other members of their pride from great

67. A. NO CHANGE
    B. cunning
    C. acute
    D. vivid

distances. <u>Frequently, everyday</u> activities like hunting

68. F. NO CHANGE
    G. Quite regularly, everyday
    H. Many times, everyday
    J. Everyday

<u>call upon animals' sharp instincts</u>; in order to reunite, the
pride members roar to find one another.

69. Given that all of the choices are true, which is the best
replacement for the underlined selection to provide a
logical reason for the action described in the second clause
of the sentence?
    A. NO CHANGE
    B. disperse a pride over large areas of land
    C. require the pride to travel some distance
    D. involve the entire pride.

<u>Finally,</u> lions use roars to attract potential mates. During
mating season, males will try to attract females from the pride

70. F. NO CHANGE
    G. Nevertheless,
    H. Second,
    J. Thus,

by roaring, displaying their manes, <u>they rub</u> against females
and fighting one another. Often a male that does not belong
to a pride will try to enter the pride and mate with females
inside the pride. When this occurs,

71. A. NO CHANGE
    B. rubbing
    C. rubbed
    D. rub

GO ON TO THE NEXT PAGE

the <u>alpha or, dominant, male</u> instructs all the other males in
                72

the pride to roar toward the outsider. <u>The outsider is scared</u>
                                                    73
<u>during his preparation for the fight partly by the roaring.</u> The
            73

combined roaring of the males <u>make</u> the pride sound much
                                    74
larger than it actually is.

    Future research on lions will help us understand more
about the reasons they roar. What is already <u>clear, is that</u>
                                                        75
often the lion's roar is meant to be heard. Whether
communicating with one another or threatening intruders,
lions roar to get attention.

72. **F.** NO CHANGE
    G. alpha, or dominant, male
    H. alpha or dominant male,
    J. alpha or, dominant male

73. **A.** NO CHANGE
    B. The purpose of the roaring is to help scare the outsider during his preparation for the fight.
    C. Fear in the outsider is raised, during preparation for the fight, by the roaring.
    D. The roaring helps scare the outsider during his preparation for the fight.

74. **F.** NO CHANGE
    G. have the effect of making
    H. are intended to make
    J. makes

75. **A.** NO CHANGE
    B. clear is that,
    C. clear is, that
    D. clear is that

STOP! DO NOT TURN THE PAGE UNTIL TOLD TO DO SO.

NO TEST MATERIAL ON THIS PAGE

MATHEMATICS TEST

60 Minutes—60 Questions

Directions: Solve each of the following problems, select the correct answer, and then fill in the corresponding space on your answer sheet.

Don't linger over problems that are too time-consuming. Do as many as you can, then come back to the others in the time you have remaining.

The use of a calculator is permitted on this test. Though you are allowed to use your calculator to solve any questions you choose, some of the questions may be most easily answered without the use of a calculator.

Note: Unless otherwise noted, all of the following should be assumed.

1. Illustrative figures are *not* necessarily drawn to scale.
2. All geometric figures lie in a plane.
3. The term *line* indicates a straight line.
4. The term *average* indicates arithmetic mean.

---

1. In a class, 10 students are receiving honors credit. This number is exactly 20% of the total number of students in the class. How many students are in the class?

   A. 12
   B. 15
   C. 18
   D. 20
   E. 50

2. In the figure below, points *A*, *B*, and *C* are on a straight line. What is the measure of angle *DBE* ?

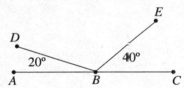

   F. 60°
   G. 80°
   H. 100°
   J. 120°
   K. 140°

3. What is the fifth term of the arithmetic sequence 7, 4, 1, … ?

   A. −5
   B. −2
   C. 1
   D. 4
   E. 14

DO YOUR FIGURING HERE.

GO ON TO THE NEXT PAGE

4. What value of c solves the following proportion?

$$\frac{20}{8} = \frac{c}{10}$$

DO YOUR FIGURING HERE.

  F.   4
  G. 16
  H. 18
  J. 22
  K. 25

5. If G, H, and K are distinct points on the same line, and $\overline{GK} \cong \overline{HK}$, then which of the following must be true?

  A. G is the midpoint of $\overline{HK}$
  B. H is the midpoint of $\overline{GK}$
  C. K is the midpoint of $\overline{GH}$
  D. G is the midpoint of $\overline{KH}$
  E. K is the midpoint of $\overline{KG}$

6. Four pieces of yarn, each 1.2 meters long, are cut from the end of a ball of yarn that is 50 meters long. How many meters of yarn are left ?

  F. 45.2
  G. 45.8
  H. 46.8
  J. 47.2
  K. 47.8

7. If $x = -2$, then $14 - 3(x + 3)$?

  A. −1
  B. 11
  C. 14
  D. 17
  E. 29

8. $-|-6| - (-6) = ?$

  F. −36
  G. −12
  H.   0
  J. 12
  K. 36

9. A car dealership expects an increase of 15% in its current annual sales of 3,200 cars. What will its new annual sales be?

  A. 3,215
  B. 3,248
  C. 3,680
  D. 4,700
  E. 4,800

GO ON TO THE NEXT PAGE

15

10. If $x^4 = 90$ (and x is a real number), then x lies between which two consecutive integers?

F. 2 and 3
G. 3 and 4
H. 4 and 5
J. 5 and 6
K. 6 and 7

11. If $47 - x = 188$, then $x = $?

A. −235
B. −141
C. 4
D. 141
E. 235

12. To complete a certain task, Group A requires 8 more hours than Group B, and Group B requires twice as long as Group C. If h is the number of hours required by Group C, how long does the task take Group A, in terms of h ?

F. $10h$
G. $16h$
H. $10 + h$
J. $2(8 + h)$
K. $8 + 2h$

13. In the standard (x,y) coordinate plane, three corners of a rectangle are $(2,-2)$, $(-5,-2)$, and $(2,-5)$. Where is the rectangle's fourth corner?

A. $(2,5)$
B. $(-2,5)$
C. $(-2,2)$
D. $(-2,-5)$
E. $(-5,-5)$

14. Which of the following is a simplified form of $5a - 5b + 3a$?

F. $5(a - b + 3)$
G. $(a - b)(5 + 3a)$
H. $a(8 - 5b)$
J. $8a - 5b$
K. $2a - 5b$

DO YOUR FIGURING HERE.

GO ON TO THE NEXT PAGE

15. In the parallelogram below, what is the measure of angle *FEG* ?

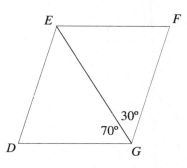

DO YOUR FIGURING HERE.

A. 30°
B. 40°
C. 50°
D. 60°
E. 70°

16. What is the slope of any line parallel to the line $4x + 3y = 9$?

F. -4

G. $-\dfrac{4}{3}$

H. $\dfrac{4}{9}$

J. 4

K. 9

17. If $x > 0$ and $3x^2 - 7x - 20 = 0$, then $x =$?

A. $\dfrac{5}{3}$

B. 3
C. 4
D. 7
E. 20

18. The lengths of the sides of a triangle are 2, 5, and 8 centimeters. How many centimeters long is the shortest side of a similar triangle that has a perimeter of 30 centimeters?

F. 4
G. 7
H. 10
J. 15
K. 16

GO ON TO THE NEXT PAGE

19. A shirt that normally sells for $24.60 is on sale for 15% off. How much does it cost during the sale, to the nearest dollar?

    A. $ 4
    B. $10
    C. $20
    D. $21
    E. $29

20. Which of the following is a factored form of $3xy^4 + 3x^4y$?

    F. $3x^4y^4(y + x)$
    G. $3xy(y^3 + x^3)$
    H. $6xy(y^3 + x^3)$
    J. $3x^4y^4$
    K. $6x^5y^5$

21. If $x - 2y = 0$ and $3x + y = 7$, what is the value of x ?

    A. −1
    B. 0
    C. 1
    D. 2
    E. 3

22. There are three feet in a yard. If 2.5 yards of fabric cost $4.50, what is the cost per foot?

    F. $ 0.60
    G. $ 0.90
    H. $ 1.50
    J. $ 1.80
    K. $11.25

23. The figure below shows a square overlapping with a rectangle. One vertex of the rectangle is at the center of the square. What is the area of the shaded region, in square inches?

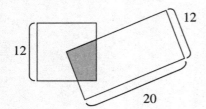

    A. 9
    B. 18
    C. 36
    D. 72
    E. 144

DO YOUR FIGURING HERE.

GO ON TO THE NEXT PAGE

DO YOUR FIGURING HERE.

24. A salesperson earns $7h + 0.04s$ dollars, where h is the number of hours worked, and s is the total amount of her sales. What does she earn for working 15 hours with $120.50 in sales?

   F. $109.82
   G. $153.20
   H. $226.10
   J. $231.50
   K. $848.32

25. A floor has the dimensions shown below. How many square feet of tiles are needed to cover the entire floor? (Note: All angles are right angles)

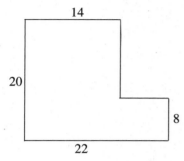

   A.   64
   B.   96
   C. 160
   D. 344
   E. 484

26. Which of the following is the graph of the solution set of $x - 2 < -4$?

   F.

   G.

   H.

   J.

   K.

GO ON TO THE NEXT PAGE

DO YOUR FIGURING HERE.

27. Which of the following is less than $\frac{3}{5}$?

   A. $\frac{4}{6}$

   B. $\frac{8}{13}$

   C. $\frac{6}{10}$

   D. $\frac{7}{11}$

   E. $\frac{4}{7}$

28. What is the area, in square feet, of a right triangle with sides of length 7 feet, 24 feet, and 25 feet?

   F. 56
   G. 84
   H. $87\frac{1}{2}$
   J. 168
   K. 300

29. When the graduating class is arranged in rows of 6 people each, the last row is one person short. When it is arranged in rows of 7, the last row is still one person short. When arranged in rows of 8, the last row is *still* one person short. What is the least possible number of people in the graduating class?

   A. 23
   B. 41
   C. 71
   D. 167
   E. 335

30. A triangle has sides of length 3.5 inches and 6 inches. Which of the following CANNOT be the length of the third side, in inches?

   F. 2
   G. 3
   H. 4
   J. 5
   K. 6

GO ON TO THE NEXT PAGE

31. For all $b > 0$, $\dfrac{4}{5} + \dfrac{1}{b} = ?$

  A. $\dfrac{4}{5b}$

  B. $\dfrac{5}{5b}$

  C. $\dfrac{4b + 5}{5b}$

  D. $\dfrac{5}{5 + b}$

  E. $\dfrac{4b + 5}{5 + b}$

DO YOUR FIGURING HERE.

32. In the right triangle below, how long is side $\overline{EF}$?

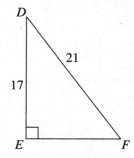

  F. $\sqrt{21^2 - 17^2}$

  G. $\sqrt{21^2 + 17^2}$

  H. $21^2 - 17^2$

  J. $21^2 + 17^2$

  K. $21 - 17$

33. If the length of a square is increased by 2 inches and the width is increased by 3 inches, a rectangle is formed. If each side of the original square is b inches long, what is the area of the new rectangle, in square inches?

  A. $2b + 5$
  B. $4b + 10$
  C. $b^2 + 6$
  D. $b^2 + 5b + 5$
  E. $b^2 + 5b + 6$

34. If $\sin \beta = \dfrac{8}{17}$ and $\cos \beta = \dfrac{15}{17}$, then $\tan \beta = ?$

  F. $\dfrac{7}{17}$

  G. $\dfrac{8}{15}$

  H. $\dfrac{23}{17}$

  J. $\dfrac{15}{8}$

  K. $\dfrac{120}{17}$

GO ON TO THE NEXT PAGE

35. Which of the following best describes the graph on the number line below?

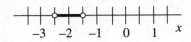

A. $-|x| = -2$
B. $-|x| < 0.5$
C. $-3 < x < -1$
D. $-1.5 < x < -2.5$
E. $-1.5 > x > -2.5$

36. A basketball team made 1-point, 2-point, and 3-point baskets. 20% of their baskets were worth 1 point, 70% of their baskets were worth 2 points, and 10% of their baskets were worth 3 points. To the nearest tenth, what was the average point value of their baskets?

F. 1.4
G. 1.7
H. 1.8
J. 1.9
K. 2.0

37. In the triangle below, if $\overline{CD}$ is 3 centimeters long, how many centimeters long is CE?

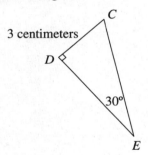

A. 3
B. $3\sqrt{2}$
C. $3\sqrt{3}$
D. 6
E. 9

38. What is the largest possible product for two odd integers whose sum is 42 ?

F. 117
G. 185
H. 259
J. 377
K. 441

GO ON TO THE NEXT PAGE

39. In the figure below, lines *l* and *m* are parallel, lines *n* and *p* are parallel, and the measures of two angles are as shown. What is the value of *x* ?

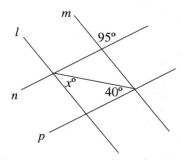

A. 40
B. 45
C. 50
D. 70
E. 85

40. In the (*x, y*) coordinate plane, what is the *y*-intercept of the line $12x - 3y = 12$?

F. −4
G. −3
H. 0
J. 4
K. 12

41. Among the points graphed on the number line below, which is closest to *e* ?
(Note: $e \approx 2.718281828$)

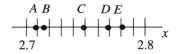

A. *A*
B. *B*
C. *C*
D. *D*
E. *E*

42. For what value of *a* would the following system of equations have no solution?
$$-x + 6y = 7$$
$$-5x + 10ay = 32$$

F. $\dfrac{5}{3}$
G. 3
H. 6
J. 30
K. 60

GO ON TO THE NEXT PAGE

43. The expression $(360 - x)°$ is the degree measure of a nonzero obtuse angle if and only if:

   A. $0 < x < 90$
   B. $0 < x < 180$
   C. $180 < x < 270$
   D. $180 < x < 360$
   E. $270 < x < 360$

44. If $p - q = -4$ and $p + q = -3$, then $p^2 - q^2 = ?$

   F. 25
   G. 12
   H. 7
   J. –7
   K. –12

45. The sides of a triangle are 6, 8, and 10 meters long. What is the angle between the two shortest sides?

   A. $30°$
   B. $45°$
   C. $60°$
   D. $90°$
   E. $135°$

46. In the standard (x, y) coordinate plane, if the x-coordinate of each point on a line is 9 more than three times the y-coordinate, the slope of the line is:

   F. –9
   G. –3
   H. $\dfrac{1}{3}$
   J. 3
   K. 9

DO YOUR FIGURING HERE.

GO ON TO THE NEXT PAGE

24

47. A tree is growing at the edge of a cliff, as shown below. From the tree, the angle between the base of the cliff and the base of the house near it is 62°. If the distance between the base of the cliff and the base of the house is 500 feet, how many feet tall is the cliff?

DO YOUR FIGURING HERE.

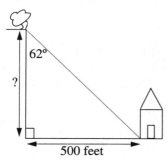

500 feet

A. $500 \cos 62°$

B. $500 \tan 62°$

C. $\dfrac{500}{\sin 62°}$

D. $\dfrac{500}{\cos 62°}$

E. $\dfrac{500}{\tan 62°}$

48. Two numbers have a greatest common factor of 9 and a least common multiple of 54. Which of the following could be the pair of numbers ?

F. 9 and 18
G. 9 and 27
H. 18 and 27
J. 18 and 54
K. 27 and 54

49. Five functions, each denoted $b(x)$ and each involving a real number constant $k > 1$, are listed below. If $a(x) = 5^x$, which of these 5 functions yields the greatest value of $a(b(x))$, for all $x > 2$?

A. $b(x) = \dfrac{k}{x}$

B. $b(x) = \dfrac{x}{k}$

C. $b(x) = kx$

D. $b(x) = x^k$

E. $b(x) = \sqrt[k]{x}$

GO ON TO THE NEXT PAGE

50. Line segments $\overline{WX}$, $\overline{XY}$, and $\overline{YZ}$ which represent the 3 dimensions of the rectangular box shown below, have lengths of 12 centimeters, 5 centimeters, and 13 centimeters, respectively. What is the cosine of $\angle ZWY$?

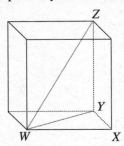

DO YOUR FIGURING HERE.

F. $\dfrac{13\sqrt{2}}{12}$

G. 1

H. $\dfrac{12}{13}$

J. $\dfrac{\sqrt{2}}{2}$

K. $\dfrac{5}{13}$

51. A certain circle has an area of 4π square centimeters. How many centimeters long is its radius?

A. $\dfrac{1}{4}$

B. 2

C. 4

D. 2π

E. 4π

GO ON TO THE NEXT PAGE

52. The equation of line *l* below is $y = mx + b$. Which of the following could be an equation for line *q* ?

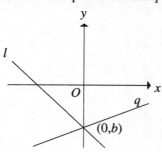

DO YOUR FIGURING HERE.

F. $y = \dfrac{1}{2}mx$

G. $y = \dfrac{1}{2}mx - b$

H. $y = \dfrac{1}{2}mx + b$

J. $y = -\dfrac{1}{2}mx - b$

K. $y = -\dfrac{1}{2}mx + b$

53. The equation $x^2 - 6x + k = 0$ has exactly one solution for *x*. What is the value of *k* ?

A. 0
B. 3
C. 6
D. 9
E. 12

54. In the standard (x, y) coordinate plane, what is the slope of the line through the origin and $\left(\dfrac{1}{3}, \dfrac{3}{4}\right)$?

F. $\dfrac{1}{4}$

G. $\dfrac{1}{3}$

H. $\dfrac{5}{12}$

J. $\dfrac{3}{4}$

K. $\dfrac{9}{4}$

GO ON TO THE NEXT PAGE

DO YOUR FIGURING HERE.

55. If R, S, and T are real numbers and $RST = 2$, which of the following *must* be true?

A. $RT = \dfrac{2}{S}$

B. R, S, and T are all positive
C. Either $R = 2$, $S = 2$ or $T = 2$
D. Either $R = 0$, $S = 0$ or $T = 0$
E. Either $R > 2$, $S > 2$ or $T > 2$

56. A square has sides of length $(w + 5)$ units. Which of the following is the remaining area of the square, in square units, if a rectangle with sides of length $(w + 2)$ and $(w - 3)$ is removed from the interior of the square?

F. 31
G. $9w + 19$
H. $11w + 31$
J. $w^2 + 10w + 25$
K. $2w^2 + 9w + 19$

57. What is the smallest positive value for θ where $\sin 2\theta$ reaches its minimum value?

A. $\dfrac{\pi}{4}$

B. $\dfrac{\pi}{2}$

C. $\dfrac{3\pi}{4}$

D. π

E. $\dfrac{3\pi}{2}$

58. In the standard (x, y) coordinate plane, if the distance between the points $(r, 6)$ and $(10, r)$ is 4 coordinate units, which of the following could be the value of r ?

F. 3
G. 4
H. 7
J. 8
K. 10

59. Calleigh puts 5 nickels into an empty hat. She wants to add enough pennies so that the probability of drawing a nickel at random from the hat is $\dfrac{1}{6}$. How many pennies should she put in?

A. 1
B. 5
C. 10
D. 25
E. 30

GO ON TO THE NEXT PAGE

60. How many different integer values of x satisfy the inequality $\frac{1}{5} < \frac{3}{x} < \frac{1}{3}$?

F. 1
G. 2
H. 3
J. 4
K. 5

DO YOUR FIGURING HERE.

STOP! DO NOT TURN THE PAGE UNTIL TOLD TO DO SO. DO NOT RETURN TO THE PREVIOUS TEST.

READING TEST

35 Minutes—40 Questions

Directions: This test contains four passages, each followed by several questions. After reading each passage, select the best answer to each question and fill in the corresponding oval on your Answer Grid. You may refer to the passages while answering the questions.

Passage I

PROSE FICTION: This passage is adapted from Nathaniel Hawthorne's short story "Rappaccini's Daughter."

Giovanni still found no better occupation than to look down into the garden beneath his window. From its appearance, he judged it one of those botanic gardens that were of earlier date in Padua than elsewhere in Italy
5 or in the world. Or, not improbably, it might once have been the pleasure-place of an opulent family; for there was the ruin of a marble fountain in the center, sculptured with rare art, but so woefully shattered that it was impossible to trace the original design from the chaos
10 of remaining fragments. The water, however, continued to gush and sparkle into the sunbeams as cheerfully as ever. A little gurgling sound ascended to the young man's window, and made him feel as if the fountain were an immortal spirit that sung its song unceasingly
15 and without heeding the vicissitudes around it, while one century embodied it in marble and another scattered the perishable embellishments on the soil. All about the pool into which the water subsided grew various plants that seemed to require a plentiful supply of moisture for the
20 nourishment of gigantic leaves, and, in some instances, flowers gorgeously magnificent. There was one shrub in particular, set in a marble vase in the midst of the pool, that bore a profusion of purple blossoms, each of which had the luster and richness of a gem; and the whole
25 together made a show so resplendent that it seemed enough to illuminate the garden, even had there been no sunshine. Every portion of the soil was peopled with plants and herbs, which, if less beautiful, still bore tokens of assiduous care, as if all had their individual virtues,
30 known to the scientific mind that fostered them. Some were placed in urns, rich with old carving, and others in common garden pots; some crept serpent-like along the ground or climbed on high, using whatever means of ascent was offered them. One plant had wreathed itself
35 round a statue of Vertumnus, which was thus quite veiled and shrouded in a drapery of hanging foliage, so happily arranged that it might have served a sculptor for a study.

While Giovanni stood at the window he heard a rustling behind a screen of leaves, and became aware
40 that a person was at work in the garden. His figure soon emerged into view, and showed itself to be that of no common laborer, but a tall, emaciated, sallow, and sickly-looking man, dressed in a scholar's garb of black. He was beyond the middle term of life, with gray hair, a thin,
45 gray beard, and a face singularly marked with intellect and cultivation, but which could never, even in his more youthful days, have expressed much warmth of heart.

Nothing could exceed the intentness with which this scientific gardener examined every shrub that grew
50 in his path: it seemed as if he were looking into their inmost nature, making observations in regard to their creative essence, and discovering why one leaf grew in this shape and another in that, and why such and such flowers differed among themselves in hue and perfume.
55 Nevertheless, in spite of this deep intelligence on his part, there was no approach to intimacy between himself and these vegetable existences. On the contrary, he avoided their actual touch or the direct inhaling of their odors with a caution that impressed Giovanni most
60 disagreeably; for the man's demeanor was that of one walking among malignant influences, such as savage beasts, or deadly snakes, or evil spirits, which, should he allow them one moment of license, would wreak upon him some terrible fatality. It was strangely frightful to the
65 young man's imagination to see this air of insecurity in a person cultivating a garden, that most simple and innocent of human toils, and which had been alike the joy and labor of the unfallen parents of the race. Was this garden, then, the Eden of the present world? And this man, with
70 such a perception of harm in what his own hands caused to grow—was he the Adam?

The distrustful gardener, while plucking away the dead leaves or pruning the too luxuriant growth of the shrubs, defended his hands with a pair of thick gloves.

GO ON TO THE NEXT PAGE

75 Nor were these his only armor. When, in his walk through
    the garden, he came to the magnificent plant that hung its
    purple gems beside the marble fountain, he placed a kind
    of mask over his mouth and nostrils, as if all this beauty
    did but conceal a deadlier malice; but, finding his task
80 still too dangerous, he drew back, removed the mask, and
    called loudly, but in the infirm voice of a person affected
    with inward disease.

1. Of the plants mentioned in the passage, which of the
following did Giovanni find to be the most exceptional?

  A. The plant wreathed around the statue
  B. The plant that crept along the ground
  C. The plant with the gigantic leaves
  D. The plant with the purple blossoms

2. In order to ensure that he is safe from the plants, the
gardener:

  I.   handles them only indirectly.
  II. avoids looking directly at them.
  III. avoids breathing their odors.

  F. I and II only
  G. I and III only
  H. II and III only
  J. I, II, and III

3. It can reasonably be inferred from the passage that the
gardener, as compared with Giovanni, is a:

  A. more religious man.
  B. less cautious man.
  C. more cautious man.
  D. less religious man.

4. Which of the following actions performed by the gardener
disturbs Giovanni?

  I.   Indicating disregard or disapproval of the
       plants
  II. Avoiding directly inhaling the odors of the
       plants
  III. Looking at the inmost nature of the plants

  F. I only
  G. II only
  H. III only
  J. I and II only

5. As described in the third paragraph, the gardener's actions
suggest that he is a man who:

  A. is very alert.
  B. knows all there is to know about plants.
  C. loves nature.
  D. resembles Adam.

6. The narrator suggests that the plant with "a profusion of
purple blossoms" (line 23) could:

  F. sprout gems.
  G. produce light.
  H. overrun the garden.
  J. grow very quickly.

7. The narrator takes the point of view of:

  A. a gardener.
  B. Giovanni.
  C. a scientist.
  D. an unknown third party.

8. When Giovanni questions whether the garden is "the Eden
of the present world" and whether the gardener is Adam
(lines 68–71), he is expressing his belief that the gardener:

  F. goes about his work with great care.
  G. has every reason to be distressed by the plants.
  H. should treat the plants with reverence.
  J. should not appear so afraid of the plants.

9. According to the passage, Giovanni characterizes the area
beneath his window as a:

  A. botanic garden.
  B. center for rare art.
  C. place for people with plants.
  D. pleasure-place for the community.

10. In the third paragraph (lines 48–71), the author suggests
that the gardener's relationship with the plants was partly
characterized by:

  F. the gardener's impatience with the plants.
  G. the gardener's interest in understanding the plants.
  H. the gardener's desire to harm the plants.
  J. the gardener's anger toward the plants.

GO ON TO THE NEXT PAGE

Passage II

SOCIAL SCIENCE: This passage is adapted from "Look First to Failure" by Henry Petroski, which appeared in the October 2004 issue of *Harvard Business Review*. It discusses a paradox in the field of engineering.

Engineering is all about improvement, and so it is a science of comparatives. "New, improved" products are ubiquitous, advertised as making teeth whiter, wash fluffier, and meals faster. Larger engineered systems
5 are also promoted for their comparative edge: the taller building with more affordable office space, the longer bridge with a lighter-weight roadway, the slimmer laptop with greater battery life. If everything is a new, improved version of older technology, why do so many products
10 fail, proposals languish, and systems crash?

To reengineer anything—be it a straight pin, a procurement system, or a Las Vegas resort—we first must understand failure. Successes give us confidence that we are doing something right, but they do not necessarily
15 tell us what or why. Failures, on the other hand, provide incontrovertible proof that we have done something wrong. That is invaluable information.

Reengineering anything is fraught with risk. Take paper clips. Hundreds of styles were introduced in the
20 past century, each claiming to be an improvement over the classic Gem. Yet none displaced it. The Gem maintains its privileged position because, though far from perfect, it strikes an agreeable balance between form and function. Each challenger may improve on one aspect of
25 the Gem but at the expense of another. Thus, a clip that is easier to attach to a pile of papers is also more likely to fall off. Designers often focus so thoroughly on the advantages that they fail to appreciate (or else ignore) the disadvantages of their new design.

30 Imagine how much more complex is the challenge of reengineering a jumbo jet. The overall external form is more or less dictated by aerodynamics. That form, in turn, constrains the configuration of the interior space, which must accommodate articulated human passengers
35 as well as boxy luggage and freight. As much as shipping clerks might like fuselages with square corners, they must live with whale bellies. It is no wonder that Boeing invited stakeholders, including willing frequent flyers, to participate in designing its Dreamliner—so the
40 users would buy into the inevitable compromises. The resulting jetliner will succeed or fail depending on how convincingly those compromises are rationalized.

Logically speaking, basing a reengineering project—whether of a product or a business process—on
45 successful models should give designers an advantage:
They can pick and choose the best features of effective existing designs. Unfortunately, what makes things work is often hard to express and harder to extract from the design as a whole. Things work because they work in
50 a particular configuration, at a particular scale, and in a particular culture. Trying to reverse-engineer and cannibalize a successful system sacrifices the synergy of success. Thus John Roebling, master of the suspension bridge form, looked for inspiration not to successful
55 examples of the state of the art but to historical failures. From those he distilled the features and forces that are the enemies of bridges and designed his own to avoid those features and resist those forces. Such failure-based thinking gave us the Brooklyn Bridge, with its signature
60 diagonal cables, which Roebling included to steady the structure in winds he knew from past example could be its undoing.

But when some bridge builders in the 1930s followed effective models, including Roebling's, they ended
65 up with the Tacoma Narrows Bridge, the third-longest suspension bridge in the world and the largest ever to collapse in the wind. In the process of "improving" on Roebling's design, the very cables that he included to obviate failure were left out in the interests of economy
70 and aesthetics.

When a complex system succeeds, that success masks its proximity to failure. Imagine that the Titanic had not struck the iceberg on her maiden voyage. The example of that "unsinkable" ship would have embold-
75 ened success-based shipbuilders to model larger and larger ocean liners after her. Eventually the Titanic or one of those derivative vessels would probably have encountered an iceberg with obvious consequences. Thus, the failure of the Titanic contributed much more
80 to the design of safe ocean liners than would have her success. That is the paradox of engineering—and of reengineering.

11. All of the following are mentioned as constraints on the design of a jumbo jet EXCEPT:
   A. the shape of the human body.
   B. fuel consumption.
   C. aerodynamics.
   D. freight handling.

GO ON TO THE NEXT PAGE

12. When the author says Boeing wants stakeholders to "buy into" the Dreamliner's inevitable compromises (lines 37–40), he means the company hopes that:

    F. passengers will be willing to invest in the company to support Dreamliner development.
    G. engineers will be able to satisfy all the needs of passengers, freight handlers, and pilots.
    H. users will be willing to pay extra to have their specific needs met.
    J. users will understand and accept that the jet will not meet all their needs perfectly.

13. The author believes the sinking of the Titanic contributed more to the safety of ocean travel than its success would have because:

    A. engineers realized they could not be so careless.
    B. later ships carried more lifeboats.
    C. shipbuilders were able to learn from mistakes in the Titanic's design before they built more ships with the same weakness.
    D. passengers were more likely to take out insurance before a voyage.

14. The purpose of the passage is to convey the idea that:

    F. failed systems often have more to teach us than do successful ones.
    G. sophisticated engineering projects are more difficult than they seem.
    H. the best way to design a system is to reverse-engineer successful models.
    J. today's engineering is so technically advanced that there is little to learn from the past.

15. Based on the passage, which of the following contributed to the failure of the Tacoma Narrows Bridge?

    A. The engineers copied the design for the Brooklyn Bridge too closely.
    B. The wind at Tacoma Narrows was stronger than in Brooklyn.
    C. The engineers ignored the aesthetic aspect of the design.
    D. The final design omitted diagonal cables.

16. The author inserts the final paragraph (lines 71–82) in order to:

    F. emphasize that the designers of the Titanic should have studied earlier ships more thoroughly.
    G. make the point that all ocean liners will eventually encounter icebergs and sink.
    H. illustrate how the failure of a complex design may contribute more to long-term technical development than its success would have.
    J. point out that the designs of ocean liners and bridges both involve significant risks.

17. The main purpose of the Gem paper clip example is to show that:

    A. paper clips are indispensable to modern business.
    B. attempting to redesign a paper clip is a waste of time.
    C. engineers should study the effectiveness of the paper clip before beginning a design project.
    D. redesigning a successful product risks damaging its effectiveness.

18. According to the passage, the Gem paper clip continues to be the most popular because:

    F. it features an excellent compromise between ease of attachment and security.
    G. it was invented long before alternative designs.
    H. people are familiar with the name and don't want to risk trying new products.
    J. it is unlikely to fall off in use.

19. In the context of this passage, "failure-based thinking" (lines 58–59) refers to:

    A. a counterproductive habit that engineers adopt that inhibits their creativity.
    B. the process of taking inspiration from analyzing the causes of past failures.
    C. an example of how cannibalizing a successful system can create synergy.
    D. an approach to design that was discredited with the collapse of the Tacoma Narrows Bridge.

20. When the author says engineering is a "science of comparatives" (line 2), he means that:

    F. engineers are always compared to other scientists.
    G. engineered products are only better if they are bigger or faster than other products.
    H. engineers' designs are generally evaluated based on whether they offer improvements over previous designs of the same product.
    J. engineering tools are used to compare the discoveries of scientists.

GO ON TO THE NEXT PAGE

Passage III

HUMANITIES: This passage is an excerpt from the concluding chapter of Emily Post's *Etiquette*, a 1922 guide to proper manners and behavior.

Whether we Americans are drifting toward or from finer perceptions, both mental and spiritual, is too profound a subject to be taken up except on a broader scope than that of the present volume. Yet it is a commonplace
5 remark that older people invariably feel that the younger generation is speeding swiftly on the road to perdition. But whether the present younger generation is really any nearer to that frightful end than any previous one, is a question that we, of the present older generation, are
10 scarcely qualified to answer. To be sure, manners seem to have grown lax, and many of the amenities apparently have vanished. But do these things merely seem so to us because young men of fashion do not pay party calls nowadays and the young woman of fashion is informal?
15 It is difficult to maintain that youth today is so very different from what it has been in other periods of the country's history, especially as "the capriciousness of beauty," the "heartlessness" and "carelessness" of youth, are charges of a too suspiciously bromidic flavor to carry
20 conviction.

The present generation is at least ahead of some of its "very proper" predecessors in that weddings do not have to be set for noon because a bridegroom's sobriety is not to be counted on later in the day! That young
25 people of today prefer games to conversation scarcely proves degeneration. That they wear very few clothes is not a symptom of decline. There have always been recurring cycles of undress, followed by muffling from shoe-soles to chin. We have not yet reached the undress
30 of Pauline Bonaparte, so the muffling period may not be due!

However, leaving out the mooted question whether etiquette may not soon be a subject for an obituary rather than a guide-book, one thing is certain: we have
35 advanced prodigiously in aesthetic taste.

Never in the recollection of any one now living has it been so easy to surround oneself with lovely belongings. Each year's achievement seems to stride away from that of the year before in producing woodwork, ironwork,
40 glass, stone, print, paint, and textile that is lovelier and lovelier. One cannot go into the shops or pass their windows on the streets without being impressed with the ever-growing taste of their display. Nor can one look into the magazines devoted to gardens and houses and house-
45 furnishings and fail to appreciate the increasing wealth of the beautiful in environment.

That such exquisite "best" as America possessed in her Colonial houses and gardens and furnishings should ever have been discarded for the atrocities of the
50 period after the Civil War is comparable to nothing but Titania's *Midsummer Night's Dream* madness that made her believe a donkey's features more beautiful than those of Apollo!

Happily, however, since we never do things by
55 halves, we are studying and cultivating and buying and making, and trying to forget and overcome that terrible marriage of our beautiful Colonial ancestress with the dark-wooded, plush-draped, jig-sawed upstart of vulgarity and ignorance. In another country her type would be
60 lost in his, forever! But in a country that sent a million soldiers across three thousand miles of ocean, in spite of every obstacle and in the twinkling of an eye, why even comment that good taste is pouring over our land as fast as periodicals, books, and manufacturers can take
65 it? Three thousand miles east and west, two thousand miles north and south, white tiled bathrooms have sprung like mushrooms seemingly in a single night, charming houses, enchanting gardens, beautiful cities, cultivated people, created in thousands upon thousands of instances
70 in the short span of one generation. Certain great houses abroad have consummate quality, it is true, but for every one of these, there are a thousand that are mediocre, even offensive. In our own country, beautiful houses and appointments flourish like field flowers in summer; not
75 merely in the occasional gardens of the very rich, but everywhere.

And all this means? Merely one more incident added to the many great facts that prove us a wonderful nation. (But this is an aside merely, and not to be talked about
80 to anyone except just ourselves!) At the same time it is no idle boast that the world is at present looking toward America; and whatever we become is bound to lower or raise the standards of life. The other countries are old; we are youth personified! We have all youth's glorious
85 beauty and strength and vitality and courage. If we can keep these attributes and add finish and understanding and perfect taste in living and thinking, we need not dwell on the Golden Age that is past, but believe in the Golden Age that is sure to be.

GO ON TO THE NEXT PAGE

21. The main purpose of the passage can most closely be described as an effort to:

    A. encourage optimism about America's future.
    B. describe various trends in American fashion.
    C. compare the younger generation to earlier ones.
    D. deplore the decline of America's youth.

22. The author's attitude toward the subject of the passage can best be characterized as:

    F. cautious ambivalence.
    G. strong disapproval.
    H. hopeful positivism.
    J. rational objectivism.

23. It can be reasonably inferred that the author believes that the Golden Age:

    A. occurred in Europe.
    B. occurred during the Colonial period.
    C. occurred during the post-Civil War period.
    D. lies in the future.

24. According to the first and second paragraphs, the author describes the younger generation, as compared to earlier generations, as:

    F. opposed to earlier standards.
    G. opposed to strong moral foundations.
    H. in favor of more rigid rules of etiquette.
    J. exhibiting the same basic level of decorum.

25. As described in the passage, the effect of post-Civil War aesthetics on earlier styles is best summarized by which of the following?

    A. Post-Civil War aesthetics had a powerful impact on initial post-war generations but no impact on more recent ones.
    B. Post-Civil War aesthetics impacted popular style temporarily but subsequently waned in influence.
    C. Post-Civil War aesthetics impacted American style by challenging its definition of beauty.
    D. Post-Civil War aesthetics' impact was limited by the traditions of craftsmen and America's preference for conventional styles.

26. When the author states, "the muffling period may not be due!" (lines 30–31), she most likely is implying that:

    F. youthful tastes have not reached extremes.
    G. trends are inevitably cyclical.
    H. Americans are more modest than Europeans.
    J. fashion is subject to whim.

27. The passage indicates that the primary purpose for setting a wedding at noon was to:

    A. follow the rules of previous generations.
    B. prevent the groom from doubting his commitment to get married.
    C. work around the typical behavior of bridegrooms.
    D. allow for conversation only after the wedding.

28. According to the author, the basis of the older generation's complaints about the younger is grounded in:

    F. the disappearance of familiar manners and styles.
    G. the decline of empathy in interpersonal relationships.
    H. the growing informality of social ritual.
    J. the rapidity of change.

29. The author describes the quality of certain great houses as "consummate" (line 71) because their quality:

    A. challenges community standards.
    B. reveals expert and artful construction.
    C. overpowers the designs of neighboring houses.
    D. typifies architectural trends.

30. The comparison in the fifth paragraph (lines 47–53) between America's change in style and "Titania's *Midsummer Night's Dream* madness" most directly refers to the similar confusion between:

    F. past and present.
    G. dream and reality.
    H. ugliness and beauty.
    J. inaccuracy and accuracy.

GO ON TO THE NEXT PAGE

Passage IV

NATURAL SCIENCE: This passage is adapted from a Wikipedia. com entry on particle accelerators. It describes two different devices used to accelerate subatomic particles.

In linear accelerators, particles are accelerated in a straight line, with the target at the end of the line. Low energy accelerators such as cathode ray tubes and X-ray generators use a single pair of electrodes with a DC volt-
5 age of a few thousand volts between them. In an X-ray generator, the target is one of the electrodes.

Higher energy accelerators use a linear array of plates to which an alternating high energy field is applied. As the particles approach a plate, they are accelerated
10 toward it by an opposite polarity charge applied to the plate. As they pass through a hole in the plate, the polarity is switched so that the plate now repels the particles, which are now accelerated by it toward the next plate. Normally, a stream bunches particles that are acceler-
15 ated, so a carefully controlled AC voltage is applied to each plate to repeat this for each bunch continuously.

As the particles approach the speed of light, the switching rate of the electric fields becomes so high as to operate at microwave frequencies, and so microwave
20 cavities are used in higher energy machines instead of simple plates. High energy linear accelerators are often called linacs.

Linear accelerators are very widely used. Every cathode ray tube contains one, and they are also used to
25 provide an initial low-energy kick to particles before they are injected into circular accelerators. They can also produce proton beams, which can produce "proton-heavy" medical or research isotopes, as opposed to the "neutron-heavy" ones made in reactors.
30

In circular accelerators, the accelerated particles move in a circle until they reach sufficient levels of energy. The particle track is bent into a circle using dipole magnets. The advantage of circular accelerators over linacs is that components can be reused to accelerate
35 the particles further, as the particle passes a given point many times. However, they suffer a disadvantage in that the particles emit synchrotron radiation.

When any charged particle is accelerated, it emits electromagnetic radiation. As a particle travelling in a
40 circle is always accelerating towards the center of the circle, it continuously radiates. This has to be compensated for by some of the energy used to power the accelerating electric fields, which makes circular accelerators less efficient than linear ones. Some circular accelerators
45 have been deliberately built to generate this radiation
50 (called synchrotron light) as X-rays—for example, the Diamond Light Source being built at the Rutherford Appleton Laboratory in England. High energy X-rays are useful for X-ray spectroscopy of proteins, for example.

Synchrotron radiation is more powerfully emitted by lighter particles, so these accelerators are invariably electron accelerators. Consequently, particle physicists are increasingly using heavier particles, such as protons, in their accelerators to achieve higher levels of energy.
55 The downside is that these particles are composites of quarks and gluons, which makes analyzing the results of their interactions much more complicated.

The earliest circular accelerators were cyclotrons, invented in 1929 by Ernest O. Lawrence. Cyclotrons have a single pair of hollow "D"-shaped plates to accel-
60 erate the particles and a single dipole magnet to curve the track of the particles. The particles are injected in the center of the circular machine and spiral outwards toward the circumference.

65 Cyclotrons reach an energy limit because of relativistic effects at high energies, whereby particles gain mass rather than speed. As the Special Theory of Relativity means that nothing can travel faster than the speed of light in a vacuum, the particles in an accelerator normally travel very close to the speed of light. In
70 high energy accelerators, there is a diminishing return in speed as the particle approaches the speed of light. The effect of the energy injected using the electric fields is therefore to increase their mass markedly, rather than their speed. Doubling the energy might increase the
75 speed a fraction of a percent closer to that of light, but the main effect is to increase the relativistic mass of the particle.

Cyclotrons no longer accelerate electrons when they have reached an energy for about 10 million electron
80 volts. There are ways of compensating for this to some extent—namely, the synchrocyclotron and the isochronous cyclotron. They are nevertheless useful for lower energy applications.

85 To push the energies even higher—into billions of electron volts—it is necessary to use a synchrotron. This is an accelerator in which the particles are contained in a doughnut-shaped tube, called a storage ring. The tube has many magnets distributed around it to focus the particles and curve their track around the tube, and
90 microwave cavities similarly distributed to accelerate them. The size of Lawrence's first cyclotron was a mere four inches in diameter. Fermilab now has a ring with a beam path of four miles.
95

GO ON TO THE NEXT PAGE

31. The main idea of the passage is that:
- **A.** linear accelerators are more efficient than circular accelerators.
- **B.** particles in accelerators cannot travel at the speed of light.
- **C.** linear and circular accelerators have important, but different, uses.
- **D.** the cyclotron is a useful type of circular accelerator.

32. The passage states that magnets affect particles by:
- **F.** influencing the direction particles travel.
- **G.** creating curved particles.
- **H.** increasing the acceleration of particles.
- **J.** causing an increase in the particles' energy levels.

33. The passage states that which of the following causes an increase in particle mass?
- **A.** A particle reaching the speed of light
- **B.** Acceleration of a particle in a vacuum
- **C.** Using heavier particles
- **D.** Injecting energy using electric fields

34. As it is used in line 56, the word *quarks* most nearly refers to:
- **F.** objects made up of electrons.
- **G.** objects made up of radiation.
- **H.** components of protons.
- **J.** components of gluons.

35. According to the passage, which of the following CANNOT be a result of using a circular accelerator?
- **A.** Particles that emit electromagnetic radiation
- **B.** Reuse of components to accelerate particles
- **C.** Particles that emit synchrotron radiation
- **D.** An initial low kick of energy in particles

36. Which of the following statements would the author most likely agree with?
- **F.** Linear accelerators are of limited use.
- **G.** Using particles such as protons in such experiments is not possible, since they are composites of quarks and gluons.
- **H.** Circular accelerators have improved little since Lawrence's first cyclotron.
- **J.** Depending on the desired result, both linear and circular accelerators are valuable tools.

37. According to the passage, what is one effect of particles passing through the hole in the plate of higher energy accelerators?
- **A.** The mass of the particles increases.
- **B.** The charge of the particles changes.
- **C.** The particles lose energy.
- **D.** The particles are repelled and accelerated toward the next plate.

38. The passage suggests that the greatest difference between a cyclotron and a synchrotron is that:
- **F.** cyclotrons are not useful.
- **G.** synchrotrons accelerate particles in a circle.
- **H.** synchrotrons can overcome limitations that cyclotrons cannot.
- **J.** synchrotrons are capable of causing particles to curve more closely to the edge of the tube.

39. How does the information about the size of Lawrence's first cyclotron and the size of Fermilab's ring function in the passage?
- **A.** It suggests that, over time, there has been progress in improving the size and capabilities of particle accelerators.
- **B.** It proves that cyclotrons are important for particle acceleration because they were invented by Lawrence.
- **C.** It indicates that the inventors at Fermilab were more capable than Lawrence was.
- **D.** It emphasizes the difference between cyclotrons and synchrotrons.

40. What is the main idea of the ninth paragraph (lines 66–79)?
- **F.** Cyclotrons can accelerate particles to nearly the speed of light.
- **G.** As the speed of particles in an accelerator approaches the speed of light, they gain more mass than speed.
- **H.** The speed of particles diminishes when particles get close to the speed of light.
- **J.** Energy limits are reached in cyclotrons because the mass of the particles becomes too high.

STOP! DO NOT TURN THE PAGE UNTIL TOLD TO DO SO. DO NOT RETURN TO THE PREVIOUS TEST.

SCIENCE TEST

35 Minutes—40 Questions

Directions: This test contains seven passages, each followed by several questions. After reading each passage, select the best answer to each question and fill in the corresponding oval on your Answer Grid. You may refer to the passages while answering the questions. You may NOT use a calculator on this test.

Passage I

A panel of engineers designed and built a pressurized structure to be used for shelter by geologists during extended research missions near the South Pole. The design consisted of 4 rooms, each with its own separate heating and air pressure control systems. During testing, the engineers found the daily average air temperature, in degrees Celsius (°C), and daily average air pressure, in millimeters of mercury (mm Hg), in each room. The data for the first 5 days of their study are given in Table 1 and Table 2.

Table 1

Day	Daily average air temperature (°C)			
	Room 1	Room 2	Room 3	Room 4
1	19.64	19.08	18.67	18.03
2	20.15	19.20	18.46	18.11
3	20.81	19.19	18.62	18.32
4	21.06	19.51	19.08	18.91
5	21.14	19.48	18.60	18.58

Table 2

Day	Daily average air pressure (mm Hg)			
	Room 1	Room 2	Room 3	Room 4
1	748.2	759.6	760.0	745.2
2	752.6	762.0	758.7	750.3
3	753.3	760.2	756.5	760.4
4	760.1	750.8	755.4	756.8
5	758.7	757.9	754.0	759.5

1. The lowest daily average air pressure recorded during the first 5 days of the study was:
   A. 762.0 mm Hg.
   B. 745.2 mm Hg.
   C. 21.14 mm Hg.
   D. 18.03 mm Hg.

2. According to Table 2, daily average air pressures were recorded to the nearest:
   F. 0.01 mm Hg.
   G. 0.1 mm Hg.
   H. 1.0 mm Hg.
   J. 10 mm Hg.

GO ON TO THE NEXT PAGE

3. Which of the following graphs best represents a plot of the daily average air temperature versus the daily average air pressure for Room 4?

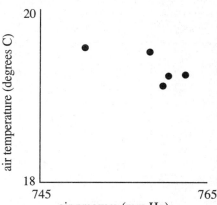

A.

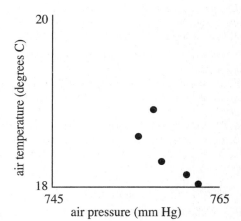

B.

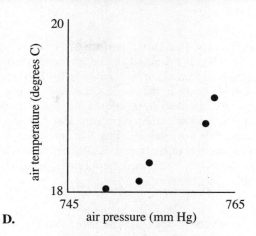

D.

4. Which of the following most accurately describes the changes in the daily average air pressure in Room 3 during days 1–5?

F. The daily average air pressure increased from days 1 to 4 and decreased from days 4 to 5.

G. The daily average air pressure decreased from days 1 to 2, increased from days 2 to 4, and decreased again from days 4 to 5.

H. The daily average air pressure increased only.

J. The daily average air pressure decreased only.

5. Suppose the *heat absorption modulus* of a room is defined as the quantity of heat absorbed by the contents of the room divided by the quantity of heat provided to the entire room. Based on the data, would one be justified in concluding that the heat absorption modulus of Room 1 was higher than the heat absorption modulus of any of the other rooms?

A. Yes, because the quantity of heat provided to Room 1 was greater than the quantity of heat provided to any of the other rooms.

B. Yes, because the quantity of heat not absorbed by the contents of Room 1 was greater than the quantity of heat not absorbed by the contents of any of the other rooms.

C. No, because the quantity of heat absorbed by the contents of Room 1 was less than the quantity of heat absorbed by the contents of any of the other room.

D. No, because the information provided is insufficient to determine heat absorption modulus.

C.

GO ON TO THE NEXT PAGE

Passage II

Humans can experience toxic symptoms when concentrations of mercury (Hg) in the blood exceed 200 parts per billion (ppb). Frequent consumption of foods high in Hg content contributes to high Hg levels in the blood. On average, higher Hg concentrations are observed in people whose diets consist of more extreme amounts of certain types of seafood. A research group proposed that sea creatures that live in colder waters acquire greater amounts of Hg than those that reside in warmer waters. The researchers performed the following experiments to examine this hypothesis.

Experiment 1

Samples of several species of consumable sea life caught in the cold waters of the northern Atlantic Ocean were chemically prepared and analyzed using a cold vapor atomic fluorescence spectrometer (CVAFS), a device that indicates the relative concentrations of various elements and compounds found within a biological sample. Comparisons of the spectra taken from the seafood samples with those taken from samples of known Hg levels were made to determine the exact concentrations in ppb. Identical volumes of tissue from eight different specimens for each of four different species were tested, and the results are shown in Table 1, including the average concentrations found for each species.

Table 1				
Specimen	Hg concentration in cold-water species (ppb):			
	Cod	Crab	Swordfish	Shark
1	160	138	871	859
2	123	143	905	820
3	139	152	902	839
4	116	177	881	851
5	130	133	875	818
6	134	148	880	836
7	151	147	910	847
8	109	168	894	825
Average	133	151	890	837

Experiment 2

Four species caught in the warmer waters of the Gulf of Mexico were examined using the procedure from Experiment 1. The results are shown in Table 2.

Table 2				
Specimen	Hg concentration in warm-water species (ppb):			
	Catfish	Crab	Swordfish	Shark
1	98	113	851	812
2	110	122	856	795
3	102	143	845	821
4	105	128	861	803
5	94	115	849	798
6	112	136	852	809
7	100	129	863	815
8	117	116	837	776
Average	105	125	852	804

6. Given that shark and swordfish are both large predatory animals, and catfish and crab are smaller non-predatory animals, do the results of Experiment 2 support the hypothesis that the tissue of larger predatory fish exhibits higher levels of Hg than does the tissue of smaller species?

   F. Yes; the lowest concentration of Hg was found in swordfish.
   G. Yes; both swordfish and shark had Hg concentrations that were higher than those found in either catfish or crab.
   H. No; the lowest concentration of Hg was in catfish.
   J. No; both catfish and crab had concentrations of Hg that were higher than those found in either swordfish or shark.

7. A researcher, when using the CVAFS, was concerned that lead (Pb) in the tissue samples might be interfering with the detection of Hg. Which of the following procedures would best help the researcher explore this trouble?

   A. Flooding the sample with a large concentration of Pb before using the CVAFS
   B. Using the CVAFS to examine a non-biological sample
   C. Collecting tissue from additional species
   D. Testing a sample with known concentrations of Hg and Pb

GO ON TO THE NEXT PAGE

8. Based on the results of the experiments and the data in the table below, sharks caught in which of the following locations would most likely possess the largest concentrations of Hg in February?

Location	Average water temperature (°F) for February
Northern Atlantic Ocean	33
Gulf of Mexico	70
Northern Pacific Ocean	46
Tampa Bay	72

F. Northern Atlantic Ocean
G. Northern Pacific Ocean
H. Gulf of Mexico
J. Tampa Bay

9. Which of the following factors was intentionally varied in Experiment 2?

A. The volume of tissue tested
B. The method by which the marine organisms were caught
C. The species of marine organism tested
D. The method of sample analysis

10. The governments of many nations require frequent testing of seafood to determine Hg concentration levels. According to the experiments, in order to determine the maximum concentration of Hg found in a collection of seafood specimens, from which of the following specimens would it be best to take sample tissue?

F. A crab caught in cold water
G. A swordfish caught in cold water
H. A catfish caught in warm water
J. A swordfish caught in warm water

11. How might the results of the experiments be affected if the chemical preparation described in Experiment 1 introduced Hg-free contaminants into the sample, resulting in a larger volume of tested material? The measured concentrations of Hg would be:

A. the same as the actual concentrations for both cold-water and warm-water specimens.
B. higher than the actual concentrations for both cold-water and warm-water specimens.
C. lower than the actual concentrations for cold-water specimens, but higher than the actual concentrations for warm-water specimens.
D. lower than the actual concentrations for both cold-water and warm-water specimens.

GO ON TO THE NEXT PAGE

Passage III

A student performed three exercises with a battery and four different light bulbs.

Exercise 1

The student connected the battery to a fixed outlet designed to accept any of the four bulbs. She then placed four identical light sensors at different distances from the outlet. Each sensor was designed so that a green indicator illuminated upon the sensor's detection of incident light, while a red indicator remained illuminated when no light was detected. The student darkened the room and recorded the state of each sensor while each bulb was lit. The results are shown in Table 1.

Table 1				
Sensor distance (cm)	Sensor indicator color			
	Bulb 1	Bulb 2	Bulb 3	Bulb 4
50	green	green	green	green
100	red	green	green	green
150	red	red	green	green
200	red	red	red	green

Exercise 2

The battery produced an *electromotive force* of 12 Volts. The student was given a device called an ammeter, which is used to measure the *current* passing through an electric circuit. She completed the circuit by connecting the battery, the ammeter, and each of the four light bulbs, one at a time. She measured the associated current in Amperes (A) for each bulb and calculated the *impedance* (Z) in Ohms (Ω) for each from the following formula:

$$Z = \text{electromotive force} \div \text{current}.$$

The results are shown in Table 2.

Table 2		
Light bulb	Current (A)	Z (Ω)
1	0.2	60
2	0.3	40
3	0.4	30
4	0.6	20

Exercise 3

The *power rating* (P) of each light bulb was printed near its base. P gives the time rate of energy consumption of the bulb and is related to the *brightness* (B) of light at a given distance from the bulb. B is calculated in Watts per meter squared (W/m^2) from the following formula:

$$B = \frac{P}{4x\pi^2}$$

where r is the distance in meters (m) from the bulb, and P is measured in Watts (W).

The student calculated B for each bulb at a distance of 1 m. The results are shown in Table 3.

Table 3		
Light bulb	P (W)	B (W/m^2)
1	2.4	0.19
2	3.6	0.29
3	4.8	0.38
4	7.2	0.57

12. If the student had tested a fifth light bulb during Exercise 2 and measured the current passing through it to be 1.2 A, the Z associated with this bulb would have been:

    F. 1 Ω.
    G. 10 Ω.
    H. 14.4 Ω.
    J. 100 Ω.

13. Based on the results of Exercise 2, a circuit including the combination of which of the following batteries and light bulbs would result in the highest current in the circuit? (Assume Z is a constant for a given light bulb.)

    A. A 10 V battery and Bulb 1
    B. An 8 V battery and Bulb 2
    C. A 6 V battery and Bulb 3
    D. A 5 V battery and Bulb 4

14. With Bulb 3 in place in the circuit in Exercise 1, how many of the sensors were unable to detect any incident light?

    F. 1
    G. 2
    H. 3
    J. 4

15. Which of the following equations correctly calculates B (in W/m^2) at a distance of 2 m from Bulb 2?

    A. $B = \dfrac{2}{4\pi(3.6)^2}$

    B. $B = \dfrac{2}{4\pi(2.4)^2}$

    C. $B = \dfrac{3.6}{4\pi(2)^2}$

    D. $B = \dfrac{2.4}{4\pi(2)^2}$

GO ON TO THE NEXT PAGE

16. Another student used the approach given in Exercise 3 to calculate B at a distance of 1 m from a fifth light bulb. He determined that, for this fifth bulb, B = 0.95 W/m². Accordingly, P for this bulb was most likely closest to which of the following values?

   F.   0.1 W
   G.   6 W
   H.   12 W
   J.   18 W

17. Exercise 1 and Exercise 2 differed in that in Exercise 1:

   A.   4 light sensors were used.
   B.   4 different light bulbs were used.
   C.   the electromotive force of the battery was varied.
   D.   the current was highest for Bulb 1.

GO ON TO THE NEXT PAGE

Passage IV

The electrons in a solid occupy *energy states* determined by the type and spatial distribution of the atoms in the solid. The probability that a given energy state will be occupied by an electron is given by the *Fermi-Dirac distribution function*, which depends on the material and the temperature of the solid. Fermi-Dirac distribution functions for the same solid at 3 different temperatures are shown in the figure below.

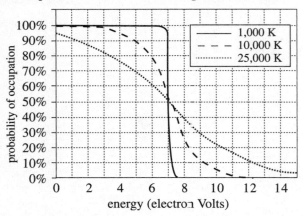

(Note: 1 electron Volt (eV) = 1.66×10^{-19} Joules (J); eV and J are both units of energy. At energies above 15 eV, the probability of occupation at each temperature continues to decrease.)

18. The steepness of the slope of each distribution function at the point where its value equals 50% is inversely proportional to the average *kinetic energy* of the atoms in the solid. Which of the following correctly ranks the 3 functions, from *least* to *greatest*, according to the average kinetic energy of the atoms in the solid?

F. 25,000 K; 10,000 K; 1,000 K
G. 25,000 K; 1,000 K; 10,000 K
H. 10,000 K; 1,000 K; 25,000 K
J. 1,000 K; 10,000 K; 25,000 K

19. Based on the figure, at a temperature of 1,000 K, the probability of a state at an energy of 20 eV being occupied by an electron will most likely be:

A. less than 5%.
B. between 5% and 50%.
C. between 50% and 90%.
D. greater than 90%.

20. Based on the figure, which of the following sets of Fermi-Dirac distribution functions best represents an unknown solid at temperatures of 2,000 K, 20,000 K, and 50,000 K?

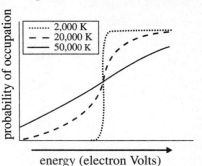

F.

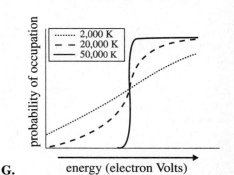

G.

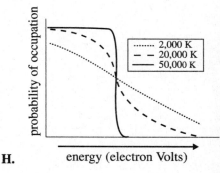

H.

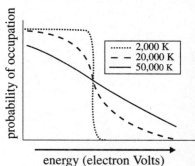

J.

GO ON TO THE NEXT PAGE

21. Based on the figure, the probability of a 5 eV energy state being occupied by an electron will equal 80% when the temperature of the solid is closest to:

   A. 500 K.
   B. 5,000 K.
   C. 20,000 K.
   D. 30,000 K.

22. The *de Broglie wavelength* of an electron energy state decreases as the energy of the state increases. Based on this information, over all energies in the figure, as the de Broglie wavelength of an electron energy state decreases, the probability of that state being occupied by an electron:

   F. increases only.
   G. decreases only.
   H. increases, then decreases.
   J. decreases, then increases.

GO ON TO THE NEXT PAGE

Passage V

A soda beverage is typically a solution of water, various liquid colorings and flavorings, and CO_2 gas. *Solubility* is defined as the ability of a substance to dissolve, and the solubility of CO_2 in a soda depends on the temperature and pressure of the system. As the temperature of a sealed container of soda changes, so does the solubility of the CO_2. This results in changes in the concentration of CO_2 in both the soda and the air in the container. The following experiments were performed to study the solubility of CO_2 in sodas.

Experiment 1

The apparatus shown in Figure 1 was assembled with an H_2O bath at room temperature (25°C). After 10 minutes, the air pressure above the soda was measured in kilo-Pascals (kPa) by reading the value directly from the pressure gauge. Additional trials were performed at different temperatures and with other sodas in the container. The results are shown in Table 1.

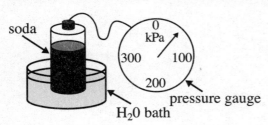

Figure 1

Table 1			
Soda	Pressure (kPa) at:		
	0°C	25°C	50°C
A	230	237	256
B	214	234	253
C	249	272	294
D	223	243	282
E	209	228	247

Experiment 2

An apparatus similar to those used by companies that produce soda was constructed so that measured amounts of compressed CO_2 gas could be injected into each soda until the solution reached its maximum concentration of CO_2. The apparatus consisted of an air-sealed flask containing only soda and no air. Starting with sodas from which all of the CO_2 had been carefully removed, CO_2 was injected and the maximum CO_2 concentration for each soda was recorded. From the maximum concentrations, the solubility of CO_2 in each soda was calculated for three different temperatures at equal pressures. Solubility was recorded in centi-Molars per atmosphere (cM/atm), and the results are shown in Table 2.

Table 2			
Soda	CO_2 solubility (cM/atm) at:		
	0°C	25°C	50°C
A	3.59	3.51	3.45
B	3.58	3.50	3.37
C	3.67	3.57	3.48
D	3.62	3.53	3.41
E	3.54	3.46	3.29

23. Which of the following bar graphs best expresses the pressures of the container contents from Experiment 1 at 25°C?

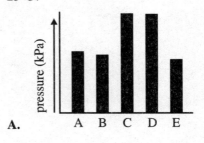

A.

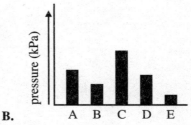

B.

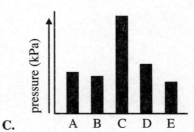

C.

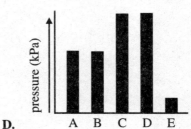

D.

GO ON TO THE NEXT PAGE

24. Which of the following figures best depicts the change in position of the needle on the pressure gauge while attached to the container holding Soda C in Experiment 1?

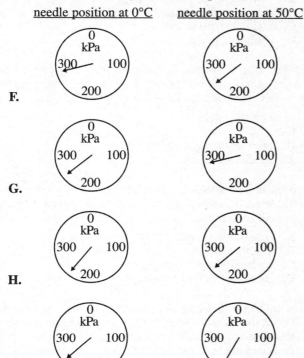

25. A student hypothesized that, at a given pressure and temperature, the higher the sugar content of a soda, the higher the solubility of CO_2 in that soda. Do the results of Experiment 2 and all of the information in the table below support this hypothesis?

Soda	Sugar content (grams per 12 ounces)
A	23
B	32
C	38
D	40
E	34

A. Yes; Soda A has the lowest sugar content and the lowest CO_2 solubility.
B. Yes; Soda D has a higher sugar content and CO_2 solubility than Soda C.
C. No; the higher a soda's sugar content, the lower the soda's CO_2 solubility.
D. No; there is no clear relationship in these data between sugar content and CO_2 solubility.

26. According to the results of Experiment 2, as the temperature of the soda increases, the CO_2 solubility of the soda:

F. increases only.
G. decreases only.
H. increases, then decreases.
J. decreases, then increases.

27. Which of the following figures best illustrates the apparatus used in Experiment 2?

A.

B.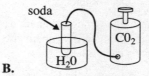

C.

D.

28. Which of the following statements best explains why, in Experiment 1, the experimenter waited 10 minutes before recording the pressure of the air above the soda? The experimenter waited to allow:

F. all of the CO_2 to be removed from the container.
G. time for the soda in the container to evaporate.
H. the contents of the container to adjust to the temperature of the H_2O bath.
J. time for the pressure gauge to stabilize.

GO ON TO THE NEXT PAGE

Passage VI

Straight-chain conformational isomers are carbon compounds that differ only by rotation about one or more single carbon bonds. Essentially, these isomers represent the same compound in a slightly different position. One example of such an isomer is butane (C_4H_{10}), in which two methyl (CH_3) groups are each bonded to the main carbon chain. The straight-chain conformational isomers of butane are classified into 4 categories.

1. In the *anti* conformation, the bonds connecting the methyl groups to the main carbon chain are rotated 180° with respect to each other.

2. In the *gauche* conformation, the bonds connecting the methyl groups to the main carbon chain are rotated 60° with respect to each other.

3. In the *eclipsed* conformation, the bonds connecting the methyl groups to the main carbon chain are rotated 120° with respect to each other.

4. In the *totally eclipsed* conformation, the bonds connecting the methyl groups to the main carbon chain are parallel to each other.

The anti conformation is the lowest energy and most stable state of the butane molecule, since it allows for the methyl groups to maintain maximum separation from each other. The methyl groups are much closer to each other in the gauche conformation, but this still represents a relative minimum or *metastable* state, due to the relative orientations of the other hydrogen atoms in the molecule. Molecules in the anti or gauche conformations tend to maintain their shape. The eclipsed conformation represents a relative maximum energy state, while the totally eclipsed conformation is the highest energy state of all of butane's straight-chain conformational isomers.

Two organic chemistry students discuss straight-chain conformational isomers.

Student 1

The *active shape* (the chemically functional shape) of a butane molecule is always identical to the molecule's lowest-energy shape. Any other shape would be unstable. Because the lowest-energy shape of a straight-chain conformational isomer of butane is the anti conformation, its active shape is always the anti conformation.

Student 2

The active shape of a butane molecule is dependent upon the energy state of the shape. However, a butane molecule's shape may also depend on temperature and its initial isomeric state. Specifically, in order to convert from the gauche conformation to the anti conformation, the molecule must pass through either the eclipsed or totally eclipsed conformation. If the molecule is not given enough energy to reach either of these states, its active shape will be the gauche conformation.

29. According to the passage, molecules in conformation states with relatively low energy tend to:
    A. convert to the totally eclipsed conformation.
    B. convert to the eclipsed conformation.
    C. maintain their shape.
    D. chemically react.

30. The information in the passage indicates that when a compound changes from one straight-chain conformational isomer to another, it still retains its original:
    F. energy state.
    G. shape.
    H. number of single carbon bonds.
    J. temperature.

31. Student 2's views differ from Student 1's views in that only Student 2 believes that a butane molecule's active shape is partially determined by its:
    A. initial isomeric state.
    B. energy state.
    C. hydrogen bonding angles.
    D. proximity of methyl groups.

32. A student rolls a ball along the curved path shown below. Given that points closer to the ground represent states of lower energy, the ball coming to rest at the position shown corresponds to a butane molecule settling into which conformational isomer state?

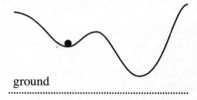

    F. Anti
    G. Gauche
    H. Eclipsed
    J. Totally eclipsed

33. Suppose butane molecules are cooled so that each molecule is allowed to reach its active shape. Which of the following statements is most consistent with the information presented in the passage?
    A. If Student 1 is correct, all of the molecules will be in the anti conformation.
    B. If Student 1 is correct, all of the molecules will have shapes different from their lowest-energy shapes.
    C. If Student 2 is correct, all of the molecules will be in the anti conformation.
    D. If Student 2 is correct, all of the molecules will have shapes different than their lowest-energy shapes.

GO ON TO THE NEXT PAGE

34. Which of the following diagrams showing the relationship between a given butane molecule's shape and its relative energy is consistent with Student 2's assertions about the energy of butane molecules, but is NOT consistent with Student 1's assertions about the energy of butane molecules?

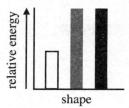

F.

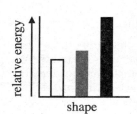

G.

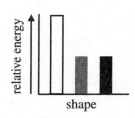

H.

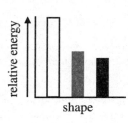

J.

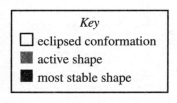

Key
☐ eclipsed conformation
▨ active shape
■ most stable shape

35. Student 2 says that a butane molecule may settle into a moderately high-energy conformation. Which of the following findings, if true, could be used to *counter* this argument?

A. Once a molecule has settled into a given conformation, all of its single carbon bonds are stable.

B. Enough energy is available in the environment to overcome local energy barriers, driving the molecule into its lowest-energy conformation.

C. During molecule formation, the hydrogen bonds are formed before the carbon bonds.

D. Molecules that change their isomeric conformation tend to lose their chemical functions.

GO ON TO THE NEXT PAGE

Passage VII

The survival of plant life depends heavily on the availability of nitrogen in the environment. Although about 72% of Earth's atmosphere consists of N_2 gas, this form of nitrogen is inaccessible to plants, since a plant cell is incapable of breaking the triple bond between the two nitrogen atoms. Certain bacteria in soil, however, are capable of processing N_2 into ammonia (NH_4), a form of nitrogen that plants can utilize. This process is called *nitrogen fixation*. Plant roots extract nitrogen in the form of ammonia from the soil and release back into the soil various forms of nitrogen as metabolic byproducts. After a plant dies, it also releases various forms of nitrogen as it decays. Figure 1 shows how the concentration of ammonia in the soil affects the growth rate of a certain bean plant. Figure 2 shows the typical ammonia concentrations found in soil at various depths beneath the surface. Figure 3 shows the concentrations of two different forms of nitrogen found at equal depths beneath the soil surface in 3 different environments. The concentrations in all 3 figures are given in units of parts per million (ppm).

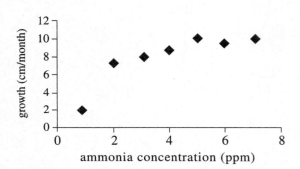

Figure 1

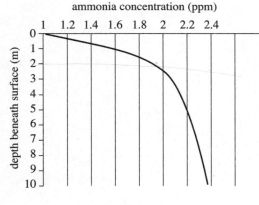

Figure 2

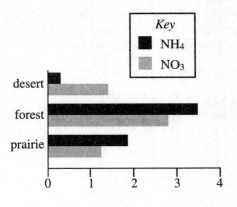

Figure 3

36. Assume that the soil samples in Figure 3 were extracted from a depth of 2 m beneath the soil surface. According to figures 2 and 3, the soil samples analyzed in Figure 2 were most likely taken from which environment?

F. Desert
G. Forest
H. Prairie
J. The environment from which the samples were taken cannot be determined from the information given in figures 2 and 3 alone.

37. The data in Figure 3 support which of the following statements about nitrogen fixation?

A. Forest bacteria are incapable of nitrogen fixation.

B. Desert bacteria are incapable of nitrogen fixation.

C. Bacteria capable of nitrogen fixation are much more prevalent in a forest environment than in a desert environment.

D. Bacteria capable of nitrogen fixation are much less prevalent in a forest environment than in a desert environment.

38. Bean plants at higher altitudes tend to grow faster than those at lower altitudes. According to Figure 1, this most likely occurs because the soil at higher altitudes:

F. supports fewer bacteria capable of nitrogen fixation.
G. has a higher concentration of forms of nitrogen other than ammonia.
H. has a lower ammonia concentration.
J. has a higher ammonia concentration.

GO ON TO THE NEXT PAGE

39. According to Figure 1, the minimum ammonia concentration that allows for maximum bean plant growth rate is approximately:

   A. 2 ppm.
   B. 3 ppm.
   C. 5 ppm.
   D. 7 ppm.

40. Figure 1 shows that the bean plant's growth rate increases the most between which of the following ammonia concentrations?

   F. Between 1 ppm and 2 ppm
   G. Between 2 ppm and 3 ppm
   H. Between 3 ppm and 4 ppm
   J. Between 4 ppm and 5 ppm

STOP! DO NOT TURN THE PAGE UNTIL TOLD TO DO SO. DO NOT RETURN TO THE PREVIOUS TEST.

30 *Minutes*

Directions: This is a test of your writing skills. You will have thirty (30) minutes to write an essay in English. Before you begin planning and writing your essay, read the writing prompt carefully to understand exactly what you are being asked to do. Your essay will be evaluated on the evidence it provides of your ability to do the following:

- Express judgments by evaluating the three perspectives given in the prompt, taking a position on an issue, and explaining the relationship among all four ideas
- Develop a position by using logical reasoning and by supporting your ideas
- Maintain a focus on the topic throughout the essay
- Organize ideas in a logical way
- Use language clearly and effectively according to the conventions of standard written English

You may use the unlined pages in this test booklet to plan your essay. These pages will not be scored. *You must write your essay in pencil on the lined pages in the answer folder.* Your writing on those lined pages will be scored. You may not need all the lined pages, but to ensure you have enough room to finish, do NOT skip lines. You may write corrections or additions neatly between the lines of your essay, but do NOT write in the margins of the lined pages. *Illegible essays cannot be scored, so you must write (or print) clearly.*

If you finish before time is called you may review your work. Lay your pencil down immediately when time is called.

Collegiate Fields of Study

Students pursuing higher education with the intent to commit to a particular field of study often determine that a different concentration is a better fit and subsequently make a change. Many students base their initial field of study on their interests, strengths, and experiences in high school. Some students complete the program they originally selected, but many others find that college unearths new passions and prospects. Additionally, collegiate study often exposes students to job markets, which help students evaluate the availability of jobs in their desired field; this is often a driving factor in changing their concentration since students seek financial security upon graduation. Should high schools incorporate career-oriented programs to help students make better decisions regarding their majors? Making better-informed choices before entering college will help students wisely allocate their time and money during their college careers, and will prevent graduates from entering a career field without background knowledge regarding job availability.

Read and carefully consider these perspectives. Each discusses the importance of providing high school students with the necessary knowledge to choose appropriate fields of study in college.

Perspective One	Perspective Two	Perspective Three
High schools should hold career-oriented seminars at least once a semester during the regular school day to help students make more directed decisions when choosing collegiate fields of study. These seminars will help students explore career options, post-graduate position availability, and job requirements. Armed with this knowledge, students can make better-informed choices that will help them to avoid spending unnecessary time and money in both college and job markets.	High schools should retain their current primary focus, but should offer optional after-school career-focused seminars conducted by professionals so students can learn about options before attending college. Students who take advantage of this resource will be able to make better decisions, and these seminars will allow teachers to continue to focus on the core curriculum and assist students academically.	High schools should partner with colleges and professionals to embed career-oriented options into current courses. The job market information will be relevant to the class in which it is presented. Although students will only receive career-based information centered on the courses in which they are enrolled, this approach guarantees that each student is offered course-specific advice.

Planning Your Essay

Use the space below and on the following blank pages to generate ideas and plan your essay. You may wish to consider the following as you think critically about the task:

Strengths and weaknesses of the three given perspectives
- What insights do they offer, and what do they fail to consider?
- Why might they be persuasive to others, or why might they fail to persuade?

Your own knowledge, experience, and values
- What is your perspective on this issue, and what are its strengths and weaknesses?
- How will you support your perspective in your essay?

Use this page to *plan* your essay.
Your work on this page will *not* be scored.

**Use this page to *plan* your essay.
Your work on this page will *not* be scored.**

KAPLAN

TEST PREP AND ADMISSIONS

1-800-KAP-TEST | kaptest.com

KAPLAN

TEST PREP AND ADMISSIONS

ACT®*

Practice Test E
Answers & Explanations

For Courses Starting On or After 6/2/2015

English

American Jazz

1. **A** **Category:** Word Choice
   Difficulty: Low
   Strategic Advice: The superlative adjective form will use *–est* or *most*—not both.
   Getting to the Answer: This sentence needs NO CHANGE. "Earliest" is the correct superlative adjective to refer to all "music forms."
   B uses "most" with "earliest," which is grammatically incorrect.
   C uses "most early," which is also incorrect; "most" is only used with words that do not have an *–est* superlative form.
   D uses the right adjective, but creates a subject–verb agreement error; "The earliest… forms" does not agree with the singular verb form "was."

2. **G** **Category:** Punctuation
   Difficulty: High
   Strategic Advice: "It's" is a contraction of *it is* or *it has*. If neither of these makes sense when substituted for the contraction, the contraction is incorrect.
   Getting to the Answer: It doesn't make sense to say "because of it is (or has) having," so we know **F** is incorrect. **G** substitutes the correct singular possessive adjective, "its," meaning that the "origins" belong to American Jazz.
   H and **J** use spellings that are never correct.

3. **A** **Category:** Writing Strategy
   Difficulty: High
   Strategic Advice: Just determining whether or not the suggested information is relevant gives you a 50–50 chance of getting the question right.
   Getting to the Answer: First, determine if the new information is relevant or not. Here, it is, since the paragraph discusses the way that different musical forms came together to form American Jazz; eliminate **C** and **D**. **B** is Out of Scope for the paragraph, which concerns the development, not the popularity, of American Jazz. **A** is correct.

4. **G** **Category:** Punctuation
   Difficulty: Medium
   Strategic Advice: If a phrase is set off by a comma or commas, the sentence must make sense without it.
   Getting to the Answer: The phrase "ragtime and blues" should be set of from the rest of the sentence with a comma because it is not essential to the meaning of the sentence; **G** is correct.
   Removing the phrase set off by commas in **F** does not result in a logical sentence.
   H incorrectly separates a prepositional phrase from the rest of the sentence.
   J eliminates the commas, making the sentence difficult to understand.

English

5. B **Category:** Punctuation
Difficulty: Medium
Strategic Advice: If a semicolon is used to combine clauses, the clauses must be independent.
Getting to the Answer: This sentence incorrectly places a semicolon between an independent and a dependent clause. **B** eliminates the incorrect semicolon.
C incorrectly inserts a comma between a preposition and its object.
D separates a subject from its verb with a comma, which is also incorrect.

6. G **Category:** Word Choice
Difficulty: Medium
Strategic Advice: When an underlined selection includes a pronoun, make sure its antecedent is clear and unambiguous.
Getting to the Answer: There are several singular nouns in the sentence previous to this one ("style," "blend," "America," "the time") that could be antecedents for the pronoun "It." **G** replaces the pronoun with the appropriate noun. **H** and **J** do not address the ambiguity issue.

7. C **Category:** Word Choice
Difficulty: Medium
Strategic Advice: When an English Test question has a stem, read it carefully. This one asks you to determine the unacceptable choice, which means three of the choices will be correct in context.
Getting to the Answer: Although "made his living on" is a properly constructed idiom, it is inappropriate in this context, since it refers to the location where the living was made, rather than the occupation itself. **C** is the correct choice here. **A**, **B**, and **D** are all acceptable in the sentence.

8. J **Category:** Connections
Difficulty: Medium
Strategic Advice: When OMIT is an option, check to see if the underlined selection is necessary to the meaning of the sentence.
Getting to the Answer: "He was" isn't necessary here; "working as a shoe shiner and a waiter" properly provides a compound object for the preposition.
G uses incorrect grammatical structure
J leaves the meaning of the second clause incomplete.

9. C **Category:** Writing Strategy
Difficulty: High
Strategic Advice: When facing a question about deleting information, read the sentence without the suggested deletion.
Getting to the Answer: The information that Cab Calloway "spent time at the racetrack" doesn't make sense coming directly after a sentence that discusses the jobs he held, unless we also know that Calloway worked at the track. **C** is correct; without this explanation, readers might be confused.
A is incorrect; the information does relate to the topic at hand.
B is also wrong; the information has nothing to do with Calloway's accomplishments or successes.
Other information in the sentence tells us how far Cab Calloway came in his life; it's not necessary to keep this clause for the reason that **D** suggests.

10. **J** **Category:** Sentence Sense
     Difficulty: Medium
     Strategic Advice: Although OMIT will not always be the correct answer when it's offered, always consider the possibility that the selection is either redundant or used incorrectly.
     Getting to the Answer: As written, this sentence is a fragment, with no independent clause. Eliminating "where," as **J** suggests, corrects this error.
     G is unnecessarily wordy.
     H does not address the fragment error.

11. **A** **Category:** Punctuation
     Difficulty: Medium
     Strategic Advice: The ACT tests only a few very specific punctuation rules; make sure your answer choice follows these rules.
     Getting to the Answer: **A** is correct; no punctuation is needed here.
     B inserts a colon which, on the ACT, will only be correct when used to introduce a brief explanation, definition, or list.
     C treats the phrase "in the top Jazz circles" as nonessential information, but the sentence does not make sense when read without it.
     D inserts an unneeded comma before a prepositional phrase.

12. **J** **Category:** Organization
     Difficulty: Medium
     Strategic Advice: Since NO CHANGE is not an answer choice, the sentence must be relevant; you'll need to determine its most logical placement.
     Getting to the Answer: "Widely known" is a good context clue. It doesn't make sense that he was well-known when he was a shoe shiner and waiter (**F**), when he was walking racehorses (**G**), or when he first began performing (**H**); **J** places the sentence most logically.

13. **B** **Category:** Writing Strategy
     Difficulty: Low
     Strategic Advice: Your Reading skills will be helpful in answering questions like this one.
     Getting to the Answer: The two topics of this essay are Cab Calloway and American Jazz. **B** is the only choice that mentions both of these topics and relates them to one another.
     A, **C**, and **D** all fail to mention American Jazz, the second main subject of the passage.

14. **J** **Category:** Writing Strategy
     Difficulty: Medium
     Strategic Advice: In addition to following the rules of grammar, style, and usage, the correct answer choice must also be consistent with the tone of the passage.
     Getting to the Answer: The phrase "it'll stick around for a while" is too informal and slangy for the rest of this passage. **J** matches the tone of the essay and provides a logical conclusion.
     G is unnecessarily wordy.
     H doesn't provide a logical conclusion to the passage; it concerns Jazz's popularity rather than its endurance.

English

15. **A** **Category:** Writing Strategy
Difficulty: Medium
Strategic Advice: Once you determine whether or not the passage satisfies the conditions in the question stem, you can immediately eliminate two of the four choices.
Getting to the Answer: First, you'll need to determine whether or not this essay focuses on "the history and development of American Jazz music." Since it does, you can eliminate both "no" choices, **C** and **D**. Now focus on the reasoning. **B** misstates the information in the passage, which tells us that Jazz developed from folk music, not the other way around. **A** is the correct choice here.

My Grandfather's Internet

16. **F** **Category:** Sentence Sense
Difficulty: Medium
Strategic Advice: Approximately 25% of ACT English Test questions will require NO CHANGE.
Getting to the Answer: This sentence contains no error; **F** is correct.
G creates a run-on sentence.
H would be acceptable if the comma were placed after "world," but is incorrect punctuated this way.
J introduces a verb tense that is inappropriate in context.

17. **B** **Category:** Punctuation
Difficulty: Medium
Strategic Advice: When commas are the issue, remember your tested rules.
Getting to the Answer: This sentence does not meet any of the tested conditions for proper comma usage; **B** is correct.
A separates the verb from its object.
C and **D** do not address the error; "said that" would be acceptable without the commas but, as written, these choices are incorrect.

18. **H** **Category:** Verb Tenses
Difficulty: Medium
Strategic Advice: Unless context tells you that more than one time frame is referred to, verb tenses should remain consistent.
Getting to the Answer: This sentence discusses something that happened in the past; **H** is correct.
F and **G** incorrectly use "went" with "has" and "had," respectively; the correct past participle for the verb *to go* is "gone."
J uses the present tense, which is incorrect in context.

19. **C** **Category:** Wordiness
Difficulty: Low
Strategic Advice: Many ACT Style questions will have four answer choices that are grammatically correct; your goal is to find the best one.

Getting to the Answer: "Because" is all that is needed here; **C** is the best choice. **A** and **B** are unnecessarily wordy.

D creates an illogical relationship between the clauses; the editor's refusal to read hand-written manuscripts was the cause, not the result, of the grandfather's decision to buy a computer.

20. **G** **Category:** Writing Strategy
    Difficulty: High
    Strategic Advice: An added sentence or clause must be relevant to the topic of the passage and consistent with its tone.
    Getting to the Answer: The theme of this passage up to this point is the grandfather's preference for the old-fashioned way of doing things. **G** provides a low-tech alternative to the Internet: "a set of encyclopedias."
    F and **H** are redundant; we already know the World Wide Web is on the computer and that other people use it.
    J is Out of Scope; nothing in the passage indicates that the writer's grandfather is concerned about computer viruses.

21. **D** **Category:** Connections
    Difficulty: Medium
    Strategic Advice: Make sure Connections words are both logical and necessary.
    Getting to the Answer: This sentence needs nothing to link it to the sentence that precedes it. **D** eliminates the unnecessary words.
    A incorrectly uses "however" to link the two sentences. This would indicate that the second sentence contradicts the first, which it does not.
    B uses "additionally," which means the second sentence is building upon the first sentence. This is not the case here either.
    "Conversely," in **C**, indicates a contradiction to what came before, which is inappropriate here.

22. **H** **Category:** Punctuation
    Difficulty: Medium
    Strategic Advice: Use commas only between items in a series of three or more items; a compound does not require a comma.
    Getting to the Answer: This sentence treats the compound "feedback and praise" as two separate items in this series of clauses. The conjunction "and," however, is not correct between the first two items in a longer series. **H** eliminates the incorrect comma.
    G places a comma after the conjunction "and," which is not correct in a series.
    J treats "from the publishing company" as an item in the series, which does not make sense in a list of uses for a computer.

23. **D** **Category:** Connections
    Difficulty: Medium
    Strategic Advice: Make sure Connections words properly relate the words or clauses they connect.
    Getting to the Answer: The second sentence here provides a different point than the first; Grandpa is saying that he can talk to interesting people for a long time or he can ignore uninteresting people. **D** uses the appropriate Connection.

English

A and **B** indicate that the second sentence will provide a specific example of the first, but this is not the case.

D suggests that the writer will introduce a contrasting perspective after discussing Grandpa's use of the "close" button, but she does not do so.

24. **G** **Category:** Word Choice
Difficulty: Low
Strategic Advice: When the underlined word is a pronoun, make sure its antecedent is clear and that it is in the proper case.
Getting to the Answer: Since you wouldn't say "them people," **F** is incorrect; *those* would be the proper pronoun here. However, since *those* is not among the answer choices, you'll need to find a logical replacement for the pronoun. **G** correctly indicates who isn't interesting.
H incorrectly uses "it" to refer to people.
J creates a sentence that is grammatically incorrect.

25. **A** **Category:** Punctuation
Difficulty: Medium
Strategic Advice: If you read the sentence and don't find a problem with it, don't be afraid to choose NO CHANGE. It will be the correct choice about 25% of the time.
Getting to the Answer: This sentence contains no error; **F** is correct here.
B treats the phrase "which is very convenient" as nonessential information, but the sentence does not make sense without it.
The second sentence created by **H** is a fragment.
J misuses the semicolon splice, which is only correct when combining two independent clauses.

26. **J** **Category:** Sentence Sense
Difficulty: High
Strategic Advice: When an entire sentence is underlined, choose the clearest revision.
Getting to the Answer: As written, this sentence is wordy and convoluted. While not much briefer, **J** is easier to understand; "in merely a few seconds" is placed directly after the phrase it modifies, "being able to find anything he wants," and "for him" follows the phrase it modifies, "a source of pure joy."
F, **G**, and **H** are all less concise and more awkward than **J**; additionally, **G** incorrectly places a comma between the sentence's subject and predicate verb.

27. **A** **Category:** Verb Tenses
Difficulty: Medium
Strategic Advice: Unless context makes it clear that more than one time frame is being referenced, verb tenses should remain consistent.
Getting to the Answer: This sentence needs NO CHANGE; the present tense is correct in context.
B and **C** create sentence fragments.
D introduces a verb tense that is inappropriate in context.

English

28. **F** **Category:** Sentence Sense
Difficulty: Low
Strategic Advice: Don't just read for errors in grammar and usage; read for logic as well.
Getting to the Answer: Here, **F** is the only choice that is both consistent with the passage and uses the proper contrast transition "but."
Nothing in the passage indicates that Grandpa won't continue to explore the Internet, as **G** suggests, or that his editor believes this to be the case, as in **J**.
H doesn't follow logically from the first clause of the sentence.

29. **B** **Category:** Organization
Difficulty: Medium
Strategic Advice: When asked to add information, read the new sentence into the passage at the suggested points to determine its best placement.
Getting to the Answer: This sentence adds information about how Grandpa uses the websites he accesses, so placing it before sentence 1, as **A** suggests, is illogical. **C** and **D** both place the new information too far from the discussion of Grandpa's use of the Internet. **B** is the most logical place for this new sentence.

30. **J** **Category:** Writing Strategy
Difficulty: Medium
Strategic Advice: Whenever you are asked to consider deleting something, think about why the author included that information—what purpose does it serve?
Getting to the Answer: The first sentence of this passage tells us that Grandpa does not know how to use technology. This explains why Grandpa did not want to use the Internet; **J** is correct.
F misstates a detail from the passage; the sentence in question tells us only that Grandpa does not like to use technology, not the specific technologies he avoids.
The first sentence is not particularly humorous, which eliminates **G**.
H can be eliminated as well, since no justification for Grandpa's technophobia is provided.

Chickasaw Wandering

31. **A** **Category:** Word Choice
Difficulty: Low
Strategic Advice: Most Idioms question will hinge on preposition usage.
Getting to the Answer: This sentence needs NO CHANGE; "In the twilight" is the appropriate idiom in this context.
B is idiomatically incorrect usage.
C and **D** would require more information to be correct; neither "With the twilight" nor "From the twilight" is an acceptable idiom by itself.

32. **H** **Category:** Word Choice
Difficulty: High
Strategic Advice: Some constructions might be grammatically correct but inappropriate in context.

English

Getting to the Answer: Although "more of the people who" is a grammatically correct construction, it is used incorrectly here. It was "most of the people" the writer did not know; **H** makes the correction without introducing a new error.

G does not address the error; additionally, it uses the objective pronoun form "whom" where "who" is correct.

J corrects the incorrect use of "more", but adds a new error by changing "who" to "whom."

33. **D** **Category:** Writing Strategy
Difficulty: Medium
Strategic Advice: Read question stems carefully and use Keywords to determine the correct answer choice.
Getting to the Answer: The Keyword in this question stem is "unity." **D** mentions "kinship," which suggests a family-like relationship between the writer and the other walkers.
A indicates that the writer knew some of the people, but you can know people without feeling unity with them.
B's mention of each walker having his or her own reasons for being there suggests the opposite of unity.
Being interested in knowing people, as **C** suggests, does not convey unity.

34. **F** **Category:** Word Choice
Difficulty: Low
Strategic Advice: Read question stems carefully to determine what the question is asking. Here, you are looking for the one unacceptable answer, which means that three of the choices will be appropriate in context.
Getting to the Answer: You can "journey over," (**G**) "journey on," (**H**) and "journey through" (**J**) a territory; you cannot "journey among" it. **F** is the correct choice here.

35. **B** **Category:** Writing Strategy
Difficulty: Medium
Strategic Advice: Questions like this one require you to use the "purpose of a detail" skills from your Reading lessons.
Getting to the Answer: When a question stem asks you to determine what a paragraph would lose with information deleted, it's asking the purpose of that information. Here, what's being deleted is the information about the writer's destination; **B** is the correct choice.
The phrase in question does not compare "the narrator's...journey" to any others (**A**) or "establish the time and place of the events of the essay" (**C**), nor is it "about the Chickasaw," as **D** suggests.

36. **H** **Category:** Sentence Sense
Difficulty: High
Strategic Advice: When all of the answer choices are wordier than the original selection, ask yourself if there is a grammatical or logical need for a longer phrase.
Getting to the Answer: As written, the sentence does not make clear whether the writer is talking about pictures *of* other Chickasaw or pictures *belonging to* other Chickasaw. **H** makes this clear.
G is unnecessarily wordy.
J changes the meaning of the phrase, indicating that it was "Chickasaw," and not "pictures," that the writer had been shown.

37. **D** **Category:** Punctuation
Difficulty: Medium
Strategic Advice: Only very specific comma uses are tested on the ACT. If commas are used in any other way, they will be incorrect.
Getting to the Answer: The underlined selection does not meet any of the tested requirements for comma usage; **D** is correct.
A treats the phrase "who walked along with me" as nonessential information, but the sentence does not make sense without it.
B inserts a comma within a phrase modifying "people."
C treats another necessary phrase, "who walked along," as nonessential.

38. **J** **Category:** Connections
Difficulty: High
Strategic Advice: Each sentence in the passage must lead logically into the next.
Getting to the Answer: Look at the sentence preceding the selection and the one that follows. You need to find a choice that transitions from the idea of the pictures the writer had been shown and somewhere that "Books...were stacked on the bookshelves." **J** does this best.
F, **G**, and **H** all explain where the pictures came from but do not lead logically into the sentence that follows.

39. **C** **Category:** Word Choice
Difficulty: Low
Strategic Advice: Remember to read for logic as well as grammar and usage.
Getting to the Answer: We know there are two rooms: the father's and the grandmother's; **C** correctly conveys this.
A and **D** refer to a single room, but the writer has been talking about two rooms.
B seems to indicate that both rooms belong to the writer's grandmother, but this contradicts the passage.

40. **J** **Category:** Connections
Difficulty: Medium
Strategic Advice: Connection words, such as conjunctions, must logically join the ideas they are used to combine.
Getting to the Answer: The two clauses here do not relate to one another in a way that makes it logical for them to be joined into a single sentence; one clause concerns the rooms displaying pictures of Chickasaw and the other the writer's family's move to Seattle. **J** makes each clause a separate sentence.
G and **H** create run-on sentences.

41. **C** **Category:** Writing Strategy
Difficulty: High
Strategic Advice: When NO CHANGE is offered as an option, you'll need to determine the logic and relevance of any potential new material.
Getting to the Answer: The information in the underlined sentence, while related to the topic being discussed, does not logically lead from the idea that the writer and his family had moved to Seattle to the reason they were then unable to attend the Annual Meetings. This means you can eliminate **A**. By pointing out the location of these meetings, **C** connects the two ideas: the meetings were too far away from the family's new home.

English

B is Out of Scope—dancing at the Festivals is never mentioned in the passage—and still fails to logically connect the ideas.

D also fails to provide a logical reason for the writer's family not attending the meetings.

42. **F** **Category:** Wordiness
Difficulty: Medium
Strategic Advice: Be wary of answer choices that are significantly longer than the original selection. Barring errors of grammar or logic, these will be incorrect.
Getting to the Answer: There is no need to make this sentence any longer; **F** is correct.
G, **H**, and **J** are all wordier than the original and violate the parallel structure required for the compound "built and…conducted."

43. **C** **Category:** Connections
Difficulty: Low
Strategic Advice: Connections words and phrases must logically combine the ideas they connect.
Getting to the Answer: This sentence builds on the preceding one by giving more evidence to make the point of the first sentence. **C** correctly reflects this relationship.
A and **D** use inappropriate contrast Connections.
B indicates two events occurring simultaneously, which is illogical in context.

44. **J** **Category:** Sentence Sense
Difficulty: Medium
Strategic Advice: A sentence can have multiple verbs and still be a fragment. Remember, the –*ing* verb form by itself can never be the predicate (main) verb in a sentence.
Getting to the Answer: As written, this sentence is a fragment; neither clause is independent. **J** gives the sentence a correct predicate verb, "chirped."
G and **H** do not address the error.

45. **A** **Category:** Word Choice
Difficulty: Medium
Strategic Advice: Some idiomatic phrases are only correct as part of a longer construction.
Getting to the Answer: **A** is correct here; "like" can stand alone as a comparison in this context.
B does not properly complete the idiomatic construction "just as…so."
C uses the grammatically incorrect "as like."
D uses an idiom that means "for example," which is inappropriate in context.

46. F   Category: Punctuation
Difficulty: Medium
Strategic Advice: An introductory clause should be set off with a comma.
Getting to the Answer: This sentence is punctuated appropriately; **F** is correct.
G incorrectly places a comma and a coordinating conjunction between an independent clause and a prepositional phrase.
The first sentence created by **H** is a fragment.
J improperly places a semicolon between an independent clause and a prepositional phrase.

47. C   Category: Punctuation
Difficulty: Medium
Strategic Advice: When apostrophe use is the issue, use context to determine whether a plural or a possessive is required; eliminate answer choices that use the apostrophe in ways that are never correct.
Getting to the Answer: As written, this sentence uses the plural "days," which doesn't make sense in context, so you can eliminate **A**. Although there are circumstances in which a noun ending in *s* will be made possessive by adding *'s*, the rules for this usage are quite complicated and are not tested on the ACT; eliminate **D**. Since the sentence is discussing one specific day (December 6, 1884), the plural possessive in **B** can also be eliminated. "Day's," the singular possessive, is what is called for here; **C** is correct.

48. F   Category: Verb Tenses
Difficulty: Low
Strategic Advice: Use context to determine the appropriate tense of underlined verbs.
Getting to the Answer: There is no contextual reason to change verb tenses in this sentence; since "rushed" is in the past tense, "threatened" is correct.
G changes the meaning of the sentence, making the wind the object of the threat, rather than its cause.
H uses a tense that indicates actions that will happen in the future, but these actions have already occurred.
J uses the singular verb form "threatens" with the plural noun "winds."

49. D   Category: Wordiness
Difficulty: Low
Strategic Advice: Whenever OMIT is presented as an option, check the underlined selection for relevance and redundancy.
Getting to the Answer: Here, "postpone" and "delay" mean essentially the same thing; OMIT is the correct choice here.
B still contains redundant wording; "to a later time" is understood in "postpone."
C is also redundant; there is no other way to "postpone" something than "by delaying" it.

50. G   Category: Writing Strategy
Difficulty: Medium
Strategic Advice: Remember your "purpose of a detail" skills from ACT Reading; that's what question stems like this one are asking for.
Getting to the Answer: Here, the phrase marked for deletion is the definition of "capstone ceremony"; **G** correctly explains what the essay would lose if the clause were deleted.

English

Since the term "capstone ceremony" is not something most people are familiar with, this "detail" is not "minor," as **F** suggests.

Nothing in the phrase reflects the writer's opinion or the ceremony's significance to the American people, which eliminates **H** and **J**.

51. **A** **Category:** Punctuation
Difficulty: Medium
Strategic Advice: Remember your tested comma rules; if a comma is used in any other way in the underlined selection, it will be incorrect.
Getting to the Answer: None of the conditions for comma usage are met by this sentence, so A is correct.
B and **D** insert commas between the two parts of a compound; this is never correct comma usage.
C treats "attorney and Congressman" as nonessential information, but leaving it out makes it unclear who John Marshall was.

52. **H** **Category:** Writing Strategy
Difficulty: High
Strategic Advice: When a question stem suggests deleting a sentence, first determine the sentence's purpose in the passage.
Getting to the Answer: The sentence in question says that the monument was proposed to honor a war hero and president; **H**'s "background information about why Washington was being honored" is the purpose of this detail in the passage.
F is Out of Scope; the sentence merely tells us that Washington was a Revolutionary War hero, not what he did to become one.
G is also Out of Scope; nowhere in the passage is this discussed.
J is Out of Scope as well; the passage contains no biographical information about John Marshall.

53. **C** **Category:** Sentence Sense
Difficulty: Medium
Strategic Advice: A sentence may be a fragment even if it contains multiple nouns and verb forms.
Getting to the Answer: As written, this sentence consists of a single dependent clause. Only **C** creates a complete sentence by adding an appropriate predicate verb, "planned."
B and **D** do not address the fragment error.

54. **J** **Category:** Connections
Difficulty: Low
Strategic Advice: When evaluating Connections words, consider the possibility that no Connection is needed.
Getting to the Answer: This sentence needs nothing to link it to the sentence that precedes it; **J** is the best choice here.
F indicates that the actions in the two sentences occurred concurrently, which is illogical.
G indicates that the second sentence is the result of the first, which also doesn't make sense in context.
H links the two sentences with a contrast Connection, which is inappropriate here as well.

55. A **Category:** Word Choice
Difficulty: Medium
Strategic Advice: If two answer choices mean the same thing and work in grammatically similar ways, you can eliminate them both, since only one answer choice can be correct.
Getting to the Answer: Since work was done on the monument, stopped, and then started again, "resumed," choice **A**, is the most appropriate.
B and **C** do not convey the idea that this work was a continuation of work that was done in the past.
D is redundant; "again" is indicated by the prefix *re–* in "restarted."

56. H **Category:** Word Choice
Difficulty: Medium
Strategic Advice: Replacing contractions with the full phrase can help you determine correct usage.
Getting to the Answer: "They're" is a contraction of *they are*, so first determine if the contraction is appropriate here. Since "during they are attempt" doesn't make sense, you can quickly eliminate **F** and **G**. Now turn to the difference between the remaining choices: the possessive "its" versus the contraction "it's." Try replacing the contraction with *it is* or *it has*; neither makes sense, so you can eliminate **J** as well. **H** is correct here.

57. B **Category:** Sentence Sense
Difficulty: Medium
Strategic Advice: In most cases, a descriptive phrase will modify the first noun that follows it.
Getting to the Answer: As written, this sentence refers to the capstone as "attached to the top of the monument." However, this doesn't make sense, since the sentence concerns placing the capstone there. **B** creates the most logical sentence: The crowd cheers while the capstone is hoisted up, then the capstone is attached.
C and **D** make it sound as if the crowd, not the capstone, was "attached to the top of the monument."

58. J **Category:** Wordiness
Difficulty: Low
Strategic Advice: Look for words and phrases that mean the same thing; using them together will not be correct on the ACT.
Getting to the Answer: "Eight decades" and "eighty years" are the same amount of time. **J** eliminates the redundancy.
F, **G**, and **H** all include redundant information.

59. B **Category:** Writing Strategy
Difficulty: High
Strategic Advice: Read question stems carefully. This one asks for the LEAST acceptable alternative, which means that three choices will work in context.
Getting to the Answer: "Conclusion," "completion," "end," and "halt" all have similar meanings but, in this context, "come to a halt" implies that the project was not completed. Since context tells us the project was completed, **B** is the least acceptable choice.
A, **C**, and **D** would all be acceptable in context.

English

60. H **Category:** Writing Strategy
Difficulty: Medium
Strategic Advice: Question stems like this one appear frequently on the ACT. Answer the "yes" or "no" part of the question first, then tackle the reasoning behind your choice.
Getting to the Answer: The question stem asks if this essay would satisfy an assignment to write about "the entire process of designing and building the Washington Monument." Since the passage focuses primarily on the capstone ceremony, you can immediately eliminate the "yes" choices, **F** and **G**. **J**'s reasoning is that the essay focuses on "the early stages" of the monument's construction, but the opposite is true. **H** is correct here.

Why Lions Roar

61. A **Category:** Punctuation
Difficulty: Medium
Strategic Advice: Keep tested punctuation rules in mind; uses other than these will be incorrect on the ACT.
Getting to the Answer: This sentence is punctuated correctly; the phrase separated out by the commas is not essential to the meaning of the sentence.
By eliminating the first comma, **B** incorrectly leaves the subject and verb of the sentence separated by a comma.
C misuses the colon which, on the ACT, will only be correct when used to introduce or emphasize a brief explanation, description, or list.
D creates a sentence that is grammatically incorrect.

62. J **Category:** Word Choice
Difficulty: Medium
Strategic Advice: The test maker frequently places a plural object near a verb with a singular subject. Always determine the proper subject of an underlined noun; it will generally not be the noun closest to it in the sentence.
Getting to the Answer: The singular "Roaring," not the plural "lions," is the subject of the verb "perform." **J** puts the verb in the proper singular form without introducing any additional errors.
G does not address the error and also incorrectly places a comma between the verb and its object.
H corrects the agreement error, but also inserts the incorrect comma.

63. B **Category:** Punctuation
Difficulty: High
Strategic Advice: Always read for logic as well as usage and style.
Getting to the Answer: As written, this sentence uses the plural "these" to modify the singular "defense." By putting commas around "defense," **B** makes "One of these" refer to "functions," and identifies "defense" as a function of roaring.
C creates a sentence that is grammatically incorrect.
D is unnecessarily wordy.

64. J   Category: Sentence Sense
Difficulty: Medium
Strategic Advice: There are several ways to correct a run-on sentence, but only one answer choice will do so without introducing any new errors.
Getting to the Answer: This sentence is a run-on; the underlined selection begins a new independent clause. **J** corrects the error by making the final clause dependent. **G** does not address the error.
H eliminates the run-on error, but it is unnecessarily wordy.

65. A   Category: Connections
Difficulty: Low
Strategic Advice: Read question stems carefully. You can determine the least acceptable Connections word simply by finding the one that is inconsistent with the other three.
Getting to the Answer: Since NO CHANGE is not given as an option, you're looking for the Connection that cannot be substituted for "because." "In that" (**B**), "since" (**C**), and "as" (**D**) can all mean "because"; "although" (**A**) indicates contrast, not cause-and-effect.

66. F   Category: Wordiness
Difficulty: Low
Strategic Advice: Be suspicious of answer choices that are significantly longer than the original selection. They won't always be incorrect, but make sure the longer phrase is necessary for logic or grammatical correctness.
Getting to the Answer: There is no reason for a longer sentence; **F** is correct.
G, **H**, and **J** are all unnecessarily wordy.

67. C   Category: Word Choice
Difficulty: High
Strategic Advice: Some Word Choice questions will require you to use skills you've learned in your Reading sessions.
Getting to the Answer: "Intense" means *extreme* or *forceful*, "cunning" means *clever*, "acute" means *extremely sharp or intense*, and "vivid" means *having the clarity and freshness of immediate experience*. Of these, the one most logical to modify "hearing" in this context is **C**, "acute."

68. J   Category: Wordiness
Difficulty: Medium
Strategic Advice: Use context clues to determine when words are used redundantly.
Getting to the Answer: Something that is described as "everyday" can be assumed to be done "frequently"; **J** eliminates the redundancy.
F, **G**, and **H** all use words or phrases that are redundant with "everyday."

69. B   Category: Writing Strategy
Difficulty: High
Strategic Advice: Remember the first rule in the Kaplan Method: Read until you have enough information to answer the question.
Getting to the Answer: The second clause here tells us the pride members have to "reunite," so the logical answer choice will concern their being separated. **B** is the choice most consistent with the question stem.

Neither **A** nor **D** involve the pride becoming separated.
Although **C** mentions the pride traveling, it does not indicate that they become separated when they do so.

70. **F** **Category:** Connections
Difficulty: Medium
Strategic Advice: Connections words and phrases must logically transition between the ideas they combine.
Getting to the Answer: Each paragraph in this essay describes a way in which roaring helps lions survive. This paragraph discusses the final use lions have for their roars; "Finally" is the best Connection here.
G uses "nevertheless," which indicates a contrast that is not present here.
H uses "second," but this is the essay's third point.
J signifies a conclusion, which is inappropriate in this context.

71. **B** **Category:** Sentence Sense
Difficulty: Low
Strategic Advice: Run-on sentences can be corrected in a number of ways, but only one answer choice will do so without introducing additional errors.
Getting to the Answer: As written, this sentence is a run-on, so you can eliminate **A** right away. **B**, **C**, and **D** all make the second clause dependent, but only **B** follows the rules of parallel structure required in the series "roaring…displaying…and fighting."

72. **G** **Category:** Punctuation
Difficulty: High
Strategic Advice: Commas are never correct when used to separate a subject and verb.
Getting to the Answer: As written, the sentence treats the word "dominant" as nonessential information, but the sentence does not make sense without it. **G** correctly sets off the phrase "or dominant" from the rest of the sentence; the sentence is still both logical and grammatically correct with this information removed.
H incorrectly places a comma between a subject and its predicate verb.
J places a comma after a non-coordinating conjunction, which is also incorrect.

73. **D** **Category:** Sentence Sense
Difficulty: Medium
Strategic Advice: In most cases, the passive voice will make a sentence unnecessarily wordy and may cause modifier errors as well.
Getting to the Answer: This sentence is written in the passive voice, making it unclear what the phrase "by the roaring" is intended to modify. **D** creates the clearest sentence. The passive voice in **B** and **C** makes them unnecessarily wordy.

74. **J** **Category:** Word Choice
Difficulty: Medium
Strategic Advice: Don't mistake the object of a preposition for the subject of a verb.
Getting to the Answer: Here, the plural "males" is the object of the preposition "of"; the subject of the verb here in the singular "roaring." **G**, **H**, and **J** all correct the agreement error, but **G** and **H** are unnecessarily wordy.

75. D Category: Punctuation
Difficulty: Medium
Strategic Advice: Remember your tested comma rules. If a sentence doesn't satisfy one or more of those requirements, commas will be incorrect.
Getting to the Answer: This sentence does not meet any of the tested requirements for comma usage; **D** is correct.
A puts a comma between the sentence's subject and its predicate verb.
B incorrectly places a comma between "that" and the clause it introduces.
The comma in **C** separates the verb "is" from its object.

Math

1. **E**   **Category:** Proportions and Probability
   Difficulty: Low
   Strategic Advice: This is a great one for Backsolving, because you know 20% of the answer should turn out to be 10. Alternatively, you could use your knowledge that

   $percent = \dfrac{part}{whole} \cdot 100\%$ to set up an equation.

   Getting to the Answer: Let x be the number of students in the class. Then 20% of x is 10:

   $0.2x = 10$

   $x = 50$

2. **J**   **Category:** Plane Geometry
   Difficulty: Low
   Strategic Advice: Questions like this are simply testing if you remember how many degrees are in a line. Remember that the arc between two points on a line is a half circle, or 180°.
   Getting to the Answer:
   $20° + 40° + x° = 180°$
   $x° = 120°$

3. **A**   **Category:** Patterns, Logic, & Data
   Difficulty: Low
   Strategic Advice: Even if you forget what "arithmetic" means, you should still be able to recognize the pattern.
   Getting to the Answer: Each term is 3 less than the previous term.

   Fourth term = $1 - 3 = -2$

   Fifth term = $(-2) - 3 = -5$

   Be sure not to stop too soon—the fourth term is a tempting, but wrong, answer choice.

4. **K**   **Category:** Proportions and Probability
   Difficulty: Low
   Strategic Advice: Whenever you see a proportion (two fractions set equal to each other), you can cross-multiply to solve.
   Getting to the Answer:
   $\dfrac{20}{8} = \dfrac{c}{10}$

   $20(10) = 8c$

   $c = 25$

5. **C**   **Category:** Coordinate Geometry
   Difficulty: Low
   Strategic Advice: On problems like this without a diagram, drawing one is an excellent idea.
   Getting to the Answer: $\overline{GK} \cong \overline{HK}$ means that the line segments $\overline{GK}$ and $\overline{HK}$ are congruent, or equal in length. For these two segments to have equal lengths, the

points must be arranged like this:

G ————— K ————— H

As you can see, *K* is the midpoint.

6. **F** **Category:** Operations
Difficulty: Low
Strategic Advice: On early problems, you can sometimes let your calculator do most of the work for you.
Getting to the Answer:
Yarn cut off = 4(1.2) = 4.8 yards
Yarn remaining = 50 − 4.8 = 45.2 yards

7. **B** **Category:** Variable Manipulation
Difficulty: Low
Strategic Advice: Be careful with positives and negatives, and remember to follow the order of operations. You can count on some of the wrong answer choices coming from careless mistakes.
Getting to the Answer:
$14 - 3[(-2) + 3]$
$= 14 - 3(1)$
$= 11$

8. **H** **Category:** Operations
Difficulty: Low
Strategic Advice: Remember the order of operations. In PEMDAS, absolute value counts as parentheses, so you must evaluate it first.
Getting to the Answer:
$-|-6| - (-6)$
$= -(6) - (-6)$
$= -6 + 6$
$= 0$

9. **C** **Category:** Proportions and Probability
Difficulty: Low
Strategic Advice: Remembering how to convert between percents, fractions, and decimals will be a key skill on the ACT.
Getting to the Answer:
15% of 3200 = 0.15(3200) = 480
3200 + 480 = 3680

10. **G** **Category:** Operations
Difficulty: Low
Strategic Advice: You can use your calculator to quickly find the fourth root of 90, or you can compare the fourth power of the integers in the answer choices.
Getting to the Answer:
$2^4 = 16$
$3^4 = 81$
$4^4 = 256$
If $x^4 = 90$, then x must be between 3 and 4, since 90 is between 3^4 and 4^4.

Math

11. **B** **Category:** Variable Manipulation
Difficulty: Low
Strategic Advice: You can use your calculator for the arithmetic here. It will take only a few seconds and will help you avoid mistakes.
Getting to the Answer:
$$47 - x = 188$$
$$47 = 188 + x$$
$$-141 = x$$

12. **K** **Category:** Variable Manipulation
Difficulty: Low
Strategic Advice: Don't jump at the first answer that seems right; on the other hand, don't think that the most complicated answer has to be right, either!
Getting to the Answer:
Time for Group C = h
Time for Group B = $2h$
Time for Group A = $8 + 2h$

13. **E** **Category:** Coordinate Geometry
Difficulty: Low
Strategic Advice: Draw a quick sketch. Notice that the answers are fairly different, so you just need a general idea in order to get the correct answer.
Getting to the Answer:

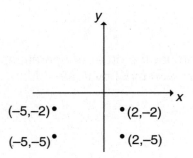

As you can see in the diagram above, the fourth coordinate must be (–5,–5).

14. **J** **Category:** Variable Manipulation
Difficulty: Low
Strategic Advice: Before you try anything too fancy, check for like terms.
Getting to the Answer: Combine the like variables $5a$ and $3a$ to find that $5a - 5b + 3a = 8a - 5b$.

15. **E** **Category:** Plane Geometry
Difficulty: Medium
Strategic Advice: Even if you forget all the properties of a parallelogram, you can figure out problems like this by using the fact that opposite sides are parallel.

Math

Getting to the Answer: Redraw the diagram, and it's clear that *FEG* and *EGD* are alternate interior angles. Therefore, the measure of *FEG* is also 70°.

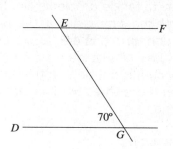

16. G **Category:** Coordinate Geometry
Difficulty: Medium
Strategic Advice: The easiest way to find the slope of a line is to put the equation in slope-intercept form, $y = mx + b$.
Getting to the Answer:
$$4x + 3y = 9$$
$$3y = -4x + 9$$
$$y = -\frac{4}{3}x + 3$$

The slope, m, is the coefficient of x, or $-\frac{4}{3}$.

17. C **Category:** Variable Manipulation
Difficulty: Medium
Strategic Advice: When you need to factor a quadratic equation, make sure one side is equal to zero before you begin. Then you know that one factor or the other must be equal to zero.
Getting to the Answer: Since 3 is a prime number, the factorization must be $(3x \pm \_\_)(x \pm \_\_)$. You know one of the last two numbers must be positive and the other negative, since they multiply to a negative number (-20). At this point you can use trial and error with the factors of -20 to find $(3x + 5)(x - 4) = 0$. If the product is equal to zero, then one of the factors must be equal to zero, so $3x + 5 = 0$ or $x - 4 = 0$. The left equation gives you a negative value for x, which contradicts the question stem, while the right equation gives you $x = 4$.

18. F **Category:** Plane Geometry
Difficulty: Medium
Strategic Advice: In similar shapes, each side is scaled up or down by the same factor, and the perimeter is scaled up or down by that same factor.
Getting to the Answer: The perimeter of the original triangle is $2 + 5 + 8 = 15$. Since the similar triangle has a perimeter twice as long, each side must also be twice as long. The smallest side is $2(2) = 4$.

19. D **Category:** Proportions and Probability
Difficulty: Low
Strategic Advice: You can often save a step in percentage problems if you figure out what percentage is *left*.
Getting to the Answer: If the shirt is 15% off, then the sale price is 100% − 15% = 85% of the original price.
$24.60(0.85) = 20.91 \approx 21$

Math

20. **G** **Category:** Variable Manipulation
    Difficulty: Medium
    Strategic Advice: One way to tackle problems like this is to multiply out the factored answers to see if they match the expression in the problem.
    Getting to the Answer: Each term has a 3, an x, and a y, so you can take out a greatest common factor of $3xy$. What's left from each factor when you divide this out? The first term has no more coefficient or x, and it has 3 ys left, so the term turns into y^3. Similarly, the second term becomes x^3. The factored form is $3xy(y^3 + x^3)$, which you can check by distributing.

21. **D** **Category:** Variable Manipulation
    Difficulty: Medium
    Strategic Advice: If the question asks you for x, that means you don't care about y—get rid of it!
    Getting to the Answer: You can eliminate y using one of two methods.
    Substitution:
    $$3x + y = 7$$
    $$y = 7 - 3x$$
    $$x - 2y = x - 2(7 - 3x) = 0$$
    $$x - 14 + 6x = 0$$
    $$7x = 14$$
    $$x = 2$$
    Combination:
    Multiply the second equation by 2: $2(3x + y) = 2(7)$
    $$6x + 2y = 14$$

    Add to the first equation: $\quad\quad 6x + 2y = 14$
    $$\underline{+\ x - 2y = 0\quad}$$
    $$7x = 14$$
    $$x = 2$$

22. **F** **Category:** Operations
    Difficulty: Low
    Strategic Advice: Writing out the units on conversion problems will help you avoid mistakes.
    Getting to the Answer: First find the cost per yard: $\dfrac{4.50 \text{ dollars}}{2.5 \text{ yards}} = 1.80 \dfrac{\text{dollars}}{\text{yards}}$.

    Then find the cost per foot (notice that yards cancel):

    $$1.80 \frac{\text{dollars}}{\text{yards}} \bullet \frac{1 \text{ yard}}{3 \text{ feet}} = 0.60 \frac{\text{dollars}}{\text{foot}}$$

23. **C** **Category:** Plane Geometry
    Difficulty: High
    Strategic Advice: Sometimes the answer choices give you a hint on how to solve the problem. Here, they are simple enough that you know you don't have to do any fancy calculations. In fact, they're different enough that you might even be able to just eyeball the answer.
    Getting to the Answer: Draw in lines that go from the center of the square to the edge at right angles.

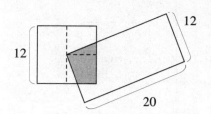

As you can see, the gray triangle is the same size as the white triangle. (The portion of the upper 90° angle formed by the gray triangle is the same as the portion of the rectangle's 90° angle formed by the gray triangle. Therefore, the portion of the lower 90° angle formed by the white triangle is also the same.)

If you move the gray triangle to where the white triangle is, you'll see that the shaded area is exactly $\frac{1}{4}$ of the square.

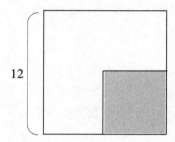

Since the area of the square is 12 • 12 = 144, the area of the shaded region is $\frac{1}{4}(144) = 36$.

24. **F** **Category:** Operations
Difficulty: Low
Strategic Advice: Questions like this may seem complicated at first, but all you need to do is plug the given numbers into the formula.
Getting to the Answer:
  $h = 15$ and $s = 120.50$
  $7h + 0.04s$
= 7(15) + 0.04(120.50)
= 105 + 4.82
= 109.82

25. **D** **Category:** Plane Geometry
Difficulty: Low
Strategic Advice: Whenever you're faced with an odd shape, try to divide it into two or more shapes that are familiar.
Getting to the Answer: This shape can be divided into two rectangles. The width of the smaller one is the difference between the width of the entire shape and the width of the larger rectangle, or 22 – 14 = 8. The area of any rectangle is length times width.

Math

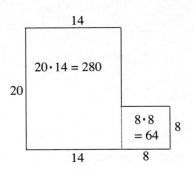

As you can see in the diagram, the total area of this shape is 280 + 64 = 344.

26. **G** **Category:** Variable Manipulation
Difficulty: Low
Strategic Advice: Don't forget that inequalities work exactly the same as equalities, except that the direction of the sign changes when you multiply or divide by a negative number.
Getting to the Answer:
$x - 2 < -4$
Add 2 to both sides:
$x < -2$
Everything less than −2 is everything to the left of −2, exactly what **G** shows.

27. **E** **Category:** Operations
Difficulty: Low
Strategic Advice: On the ACT Math test, you have an average of one minute per question. If a problem can be solved quickly using your calculator, take advantage of it. For example, you can use your calculator to compare fractions by finding the decimal equivalents.
Getting to the Answer:

$\dfrac{3}{5} = 0.6$

A $\dfrac{4}{6} = 0.\overline{66}$

B $\dfrac{8}{13} = 0.61538\ldots$

C $\dfrac{6}{10} = 0.6$

D $\dfrac{7}{11} = 0.\overline{63}$

E $\dfrac{4}{7} = 0.57142\ldots$

Only **E** is smaller than 0.6.

28. **G** **Category:** Plane Geometry
Difficulty: Medium
Strategic Advice: In a right triangle, the hypotenuse is always the longest side, and the other two sides are the legs.

Getting to the Answer: The legs are 7 and 24. Area $= \frac{1}{2}bh$

$$= \left(\frac{1}{2}\right)(7)(24)$$

$$= 84$$

29. D Category: Number Properties
Difficulty: Medium
Strategic Advice: You need to figure out how to turn this word problem into math. If the last row is one person short of 6, how does the number of students relate to multiples of 6?
Getting to the Answer: This is just another way of saying that the number of students is one less than a multiple of 6, one less than a multiple of 7, and one less than a multiple of 8. The least common multiple of 6, 7, and 8 is 168. One less is 167, **D**. You can find the least common multiple by finding the prime factors of each number:
$6 = 2 \cdot 3$
$7 = 7$
$8 = 2 \cdot 2 \cdot 2$
To get all these factors in one number, you need one 3, one 7, and three 2s, or $3 \cdot 7 \cdot 2 \cdot 2 \cdot 2 = 168$.
E produces the right arrangement, but it is not the smallest possible number. **A** is 2 *more* then a multiple of 7, which means the last row will have 2 people (or be 5 people short). **B** is 1 *more* than a multiple of 8, which means the last row will be 7 people short. **C** is 1 *more* than a multiple of 7, which means the last row will be 6 people short.

30. F Category: Plane Geometry
Difficulty: Low
Strategic Advice: There will usually be one question that tests your knowledge of the Triangle Inequality Theorem. If you're not sure how to proceed, try drawing a sketch.
Getting to the Answer: The Triangle Inequality Theorem states that any side of a triangle is less than the sum of and more than the difference between the other two, so the third side must be at least $6 - 3.5 = 2.5$ inches. **F** is too small.

31. C Category: Variable Manipulation
Difficulty: Medium
Strategic Advice: Fractions are always added in the same way, whether they include variables or not. You must get both fractions in terms of a common denominator, then add the numerators.
Getting to the Answer:

$$\frac{4}{5} = \frac{4b}{5b}$$

$$\frac{1}{b} = \frac{5}{5b}$$

$$\frac{4b}{5b} + \frac{5}{5b} = \frac{4b + 5}{5b}$$

Math

32. F **Category:** Plane Geometry
Difficulty: Medium
Strategic Advice: In the Pythagorean Theorem, $a^2 + b^2 = c^2$, c represents the hypotenuse (the longest side).
Getting to the Answer:

$$a^2 + b^2 = c^2$$
$$17^2 + b^2 = 21^2$$
$$b^2 = 21^2 - 17^2$$
$$b = \sqrt{21^2 - 17^2}$$

33. E **Category:** Variable Manipulation
Difficulty: Medium
Strategic Advice: When you multiply binomials, don't forget to use FOIL. If you just multiply the first terms together and the last terms together, you're missing two terms.
Getting to the Answer: The new length is $b + 2$, and the new width is $b + 3$.

$$\text{Area} = l \cdot w$$
$$= (b + 2)(b + 3)$$
$$= b^2 + 3b + 2b + 6$$
$$= b^2 + 5b + 6$$

34. G **Category:** Trigonometry
Difficulty: Low
Strategic Advice: If you have sine and cosine, find tangent with the formula $\tan x = \dfrac{\sin x}{\cos x}$.

Getting to the Answer:

$$\tan x = \frac{\sin x}{\cos x}$$
$$= \frac{\dfrac{8}{17}}{\dfrac{15}{17}}$$
$$= \frac{8}{17} \cdot \frac{17}{15}$$
$$= \frac{8}{15}$$

35. E **Category:** Variable Manipulation
Difficulty: Medium
Strategic Advice: If you're not sure which answer is correct, try plugging in points from the number line.
Getting to the Answer: The shaded region includes all the values between −1.5 and −2.5. Since −1.5 is larger than −2.5, the inequality should be $-1.5 > x > -2.5$. Plugging in $x = -2 \bullet 2.5$ eliminates **A**, **B**, and **D**. **C** includes numbers that aren't in the shaded region, such as −2.9.

36. J **Category:** Operations
Difficulty: Medium
Strategic Advice: To make the question a little easier to follow, Pick Numbers for the total number of baskets. Imagine that they made a total of 100 baskets.
Getting to the Answer: If the team made 100 baskets, then they made 20 1-point baskets, 70 2-point baskets, and 10 3-point baskets. The average point value of all the baskets is the total number of points divided by the total number of baskets:

$$\frac{20(1) + 70(2) + 10(3)}{100}$$

$$= \frac{20 + 140 + 30}{100}$$

$$= \frac{190}{100}$$

$$= 1.9$$

37. D **Category:** Plane Geometry
Difficulty: Medium
Strategic Advice: If you can use 45–45–90 triangles or 30–60–90 triangles instead of trigonometry, do it. (Similarly, look for the Pythagorean Triplets before you use the Pythagorean Theorem.)
Getting to the Answer: The sides in a 30–60–90 triangle are in the ratio $x{:}x\sqrt{3}{:}2x$. You have been given the side opposite the 30 degree angle, which is x. You want the side opposite the 90 degree angle, which is $2x$. Since $x = 3$, $CE = 2x = 6$.

38. K **Category:** Number Properties
Difficulty: Medium
Strategic Advice: On this type of problem, you want the numbers to be either as close together or as far apart as possible. Try out a few possibilities; you should see a pattern.
Getting to the Answer:
$3 \bullet 39 = 117$
$5 \bullet 37 = 185$
$7 \bullet 35 = 245$
As you can see, the products are increasing, so it looks like you want the two numbers to be as close together as possible. Since half of 42 is 21, try $21 \bullet 21 = 441$. Since this is the largest possible answer choice, you can be sure it's correct.

39. B **Category:** Plane Geometry
Difficulty: Medium
Strategic Advice: Parallel lines provide lots of information—look for congruent and supplementary angles.

Math

Getting to the Answer:

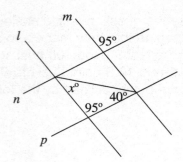

Since both sets of lines are parallel, you can tell that the missing angle in the triangle corresponds to the angle marked 95°. The three interior angles of the triangle sum to 180°:

$$40° + 95° + x° = 180°$$
$$x° = 45°$$

40. **F** **Category:** Coordinate Geometry
Difficulty: Medium
Strategic Advice: Don't jump right in to using your graphing calculator; often some simple algebra is the best way to the right answer.
Getting to the Answer: The easiest way to find the y-intercept (the value of y when the graph crosses the y-axis) is to plug in $x = 0$:
$$12(0) - 3y = 12$$
$$-3y = 12$$
$$y = -4$$

41. **B** **Category:** Operations
Difficulty: Medium
Strategic Advice: If the labels are missing on a number line, you can find the length of each interval by finding the difference in the endpoints (how much the total interval is) and dividing by the number of subintervals.
Getting to the Answer: The unmarked interval goes from 2.7 to 2.8, so it must be 0.1 units long. It's divided into 10 equally spaced subintervals, each which must be $\frac{0.1}{10} = 0.01$ units long.

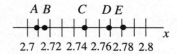

E is approximately 2.718, so you want a point between 2.71 and 2.72. **B** is the closest.

42. **G** **Category:** Coordinate Geometry
Difficulty: High
Strategic Advice: If the system has no solution, there are no values of x and y that make both equations true. If the system has infinitely many solutions, then every set of x and y that works in one equation will also work in the other.
Getting to the Answer: These two linear equations will have no solutions (points of intersection) if they are parallel. Write both equations in slope-intercept form, then set the slopes equal and solve for a.

$$-x + 6y = 7$$
$$6y = x + 7$$
$$y = \frac{1}{6}x + \frac{7}{6}$$

$$-5x + 10ay = 32$$
$$10ay = 5x + 32$$
$$y = \frac{5}{10a}x + \frac{32}{10a}$$

$$\frac{1}{6} = \frac{5}{10a}$$

$$10a = 30$$
$$a = 3$$

43. C Category: Plane Geometry
Difficulty: Medium
Strategic Advice: "If and only if" means the answer always gives you an obtuse angle, and it gives you all obtuse angles.
Getting to the Answer: An angle is obtuse if its measure is between 90° and 180°, non-inclusive. That's everything wider than a right angle and smaller than a straight line.
Try plugging in the end values of each range:
A $0 < x < 90$: $360 - 0 = 360$, $360 - 90 = 270$. This answer gives angles from 270° to 360°.
B $0 < x < 180$: $360 - 0 = 360$, $360 - 180 = 180$. This answer gives angles from 180° to 360°.
C $180 < x < 270$: $360 - 180 = 180$, $360 - 270 = 90$. This answer gives angles from 90° to 180°—exactly what you're looking for.
D $180 < x < 360$: $360 - 180 = 180$, $360 - 360 = 0$. This answer gives angles from 0° to 180°.
E $270 < x < 360$: $360 - 270 = 90$, $360 - 360 = 0$. This answer gives angles from 0° to 90°.
Only **C** gives the entire set of obtuse angles and nothing more.

44. G Category: Variable Manipulation
Difficulty: Medium
Strategic Advice: Always be on the lookout for the three classic quadratics—they'll save you a lot of time.
Getting to the Answer:
$$p^2 - q^2 = (p + q)(p - q)$$
$$= (-3)(-4)$$
$$= 12$$

45. D Category: Plane Geometry
Difficulty: Low
Strategic Advice: Remember, time is short on the ACT. Do they really expect you to apply something like the law of cosines here?
Getting to the Answer: If you recognized the Pythagorean Triplet (3:4:5) scaled up by 2, then you realized that this is a right triangle. The right angle is always between the two shortest sides (and opposite the longest side, the hypotenuse).

Math

46. H Category: Coordinate Geometry
Difficulty: Medium
Strategic Advice: Be sure to read the question carefully. This one gives you an equation that's x in terms of y, not y in terms of x.
Getting to the Answer: First, translate the description into an equation: $x = 9 + 3y$. Then put it into slope-intercept form:

$$x = 9 + 3y$$

$$\frac{1}{3}x - 3 = y$$

As you can see from the equation, the slope is $\frac{1}{3}$.

47. E Category: Trigonometry
Difficulty: High
Strategic Advice: Remember SOHCAHTOA. When you're presented with a trigonometry problem, your first step should be to identify the sides you're given and the side you're trying to find. Then figure out which trig function gives you a relationship between the side you know and the side you want to know.
Getting to the Answer: The distance between the cliff and the house is opposite the given angle. The height of the cliff is adjacent. The trig function that gives a relationship between the opposite and the adjacent sides is tangent.

$$\tan 62° = \frac{500}{\text{height}}$$

$$\text{height} \cdot \tan 62° = 500$$

$$\text{height} = \frac{500}{\tan 62°}$$

48. H Category: Number Properties
Difficulty: Medium
Strategic Advice: Prime factorizations can help you find the greatest common factor and least common multiple.
Getting to the Answer:
$9 = 3 \bullet 3$
$18 = 2 \bullet 3 \bullet 3$
$27 = 3 \bullet 3 \bullet 3$
$54 = 2 \bullet 3 \bullet 3 \bullet 3$

	GCF	LCM
9 and 18	$3 \bullet 3 = 9$	$2 \bullet 3 \bullet 3 = 18$
9 and 27	$3 \bullet 3 = 9$	$3 \bullet 3 \bullet 3 = 27$
18 and 27	$3 \bullet 3 = 9$	$2 \bullet 3 \bullet 3 \bullet 3 = 54$
18 and 54	$2 \bullet 3 \bullet 3 = 18$	$2 \bullet 3 \bullet 3 \bullet 3 = 54$
27 and 54	$3 \bullet 3 \bullet 3 = 27$	$2 \bullet 3 \bullet 3 \bullet 3 = 54$

Only **H** fits the description. All the other pairs have either a lower common multiple or a greater common factor.

49. D Category: Patterns, Logic, & Data
Difficulty: High

Strategic Advice: You can make abstract questions like this one easier to handle by Picking Numbers. Be sure the numbers you pick obey any restrictions in the question stem. **Getting to the Answer:** Try $k = 2$ and $x = 4$. (These numbers will make the radical in **E** easy to calculate.)

A $b(4) = \dfrac{2}{4} = \dfrac{1}{2}$

B $b(4) = \dfrac{4}{2} = 2$

C $b(4) = 2(4) = 8$

D $b(4) = 4^2 = 16$

E $b(4) = \sqrt[2]{4} = 2$

The largest $b(x)$ is **D**. When this is plugged into $a(b(x)) = 5^{b(x)}$, the largest value of $b(x)$ will produce the largest value of $a(b(x))$. For the values of k and x allowed in this question, **D** is always the largest, so it is correct.

Another way to approach this problem is to use a graphing calculator. Pick a value for k, then graph each answer choice on your calculator at the same time to see which one has the largest value when x is greater than 2.

50. J **Category:** Trigonometry
Difficulty: High
Strategic Advice: If you're not sure where to get started, try working backwards. What are you looking for? The cosine of $\angle ZWY$. What do you need to find that? The lengths of the hypotenuse and the adjacent leg, WZ and WY. How can you find those lengths? By using the given side lengths and your knowledge of right triangles. Now that you've figured out how to get from what you have to what you need, you can go ahead and get there.
Getting to the Answer: WXY is a right triangle. You know that WX is 12 and XY is 5, so WY must be 13. If you didn't spot the 5:12:13 triplet, you could have used the Pythagorean Theorem.) WYZ is also a right triangle. You know that WY and YZ are both 13, so WZ must be $13\sqrt{2}$. (Again, you could have used the Pythagorean Theorem if you didn't spot the 45–45–90 triangle.) The cosine of an angle is the adjacent leg over the hypotenuse, so the cosine of $\angle ZWY$ is WY over WZ, or $\dfrac{13}{13\sqrt{2}} = \dfrac{1}{\sqrt{2}} = \dfrac{\sqrt{2}}{2}$.

51. B **Category:** Plane Geometry
Difficulty: Low
Strategic Advice: On circle questions, it's important to distinguish between radius and diameter.
Getting to the Answer:
$$\text{Area} = \pi r^2 = 4\pi$$
$$r^2 = 4$$
$$r = 2$$

52. K **Category:** Coordinate Geometry
Difficulty: Medium
Strategic Advice: Remember that lines with positive slope rise to the right, and lines with negative slope rise to the left.
Getting to the Answer: The lines have the same y-intercept, so line q must also have "$+ b$" at the end of its equation. You may have been fooled by the fact that b is

negative, but imagine that the y-intercept was at –2: the equation would be $y = mx + (-2)$. This eliminates **F**, **G**, and **J**.

Line l has a negative slope, so $m < 0$, and line q has a positive slope. Since $\frac{1}{2}m < 0$, this cannot be the slope of line q, so its equation must be $y = -\frac{1}{2}mx + b$.

53. D Category: Variable Manipulation
Difficulty: Medium
Strategic Advice: Always solve quadratics by factoring. Each factor will give you a solution.
Getting to the Answer: If the equation has only one solution, that means the factors are the same. To get a middle term of $-6x$, you must have factors of $(x - 3)(x - 3)$. Multiply it out to get $(x - 3)(x - 3) = x^2 - 3x - 3x + 9 = x^2 - 6x + 9$. This means that $k = 9$.

54. K Category: Coordinate Geometry
Difficulty: Low
Strategic Advice: Most coordinate geometry questions rely on the slope. Make sure you remember that slope is $\frac{\text{rise}}{\text{run}}$.
Getting to the Answer:

$$\frac{y_2 - y_1}{x_2 - x_1} = \frac{\frac{3}{4} - 0}{\frac{1}{3} - 0}$$

$$= \frac{\frac{3}{4}}{\frac{1}{3}}$$

$$= \frac{3}{4} \cdot \frac{3}{1}$$

$$= \frac{9}{4}$$

55. A Category: Number Properties
Difficulty: Medium
Strategic Advice: Don't accidentally add your own assumptions. For example, the question never says that the variables are integers.
Getting to the Answer:
A is true. It follows immediately from dividing both sides by S.

B, **C**, and **E** are disproved by $R = -3$, $S = -2$, and $T = \frac{1}{3}$.

D can never be true, because then the product would be 0.

56.   H   Category: Plane Geometry
Difficulty: High
Strategic Advice: Although this is a geometry question, the part that's most likely to trip you up is the variable manipulation. Work carefully, and remember that you can Pick Numbers if you run into trouble with w.
Getting to the Answer: The area of the square is $(w + 5)^2 = w^2 + 10w + 25$. The area of the rectangle is $(w + 2)(w - 3) = w^2 - w - 6$. The area of the square after the rectangle is removed is $w^2 + 10w + 25 - (w^2 - w - 6) = 11w + 31$, **H**.
If you had any trouble with the math, Picking Numbers can simplify things. Say $w = 5$. Then the square has sides of length 10 and an area of 100. The rectangle's sides are length 7 and length 2, so its area is 14. The area of the square after the rectangle is removed is $100 - 14 = 86$. Plug $w = 5$ into each answer choice to find that only **H** equals 86.

57.   C   Category: Trigonometry
Difficulty: Medium
Strategic Advice: First figure out where sine reaches a minimum, then worry about where the 2θ comes in.
Getting to the Answer: The sine function first reaches its minimum of -1 at $\frac{3\pi}{2}$, so

$$2\theta = \frac{3\pi}{2}$$
$$\theta = \frac{3\pi}{4}$$

58.   K   Category: Coordinate Geometry
Difficulty: High
Strategic Advice: Backsolving is a great option here if you're not sure how to set this problem up algebraically or if you're not confident about your variable manipulation skills.
Getting to the Answer: Plug the given coordinates into the distance formula $(\sqrt{(x_1 - x_2)^2 + (y_1 - y_2)^2})$, set the distance equal to 4, and solve for r.

$$\sqrt{(r - 10)^2 + (6 - r)^2} = 4$$
$$(r - 10)^2 + (6 - r)^2 = 16$$
$$(r^2 - 20r + 100) + (36 - 12r + r^2) = 16$$
$$2r^2 - 32r + 136 = 16$$
$$2r^2 - 32r + 120 = 0$$
$$r^2 - 16r + 60 = 0$$
$$(r - 10)(r - 6) = 0$$
$$r = 10 \text{ or } r = 6$$

Only 10 is an answer choice, so **K** is correct.
To Backsolve, you still need to know the distance formula to figure out whether **F**, **G**, **H**, and **J** are correct, but notice that **K** gives the points (10,6) and (10,10). Since the x-coordinate is the same, you can see that the distance between the points is $10 - 6 = 4$ without using the formula.

Math

59. **D** **Category:** Proportions and Probability
Difficulty: Medium
Strategic Advice: This is a great candidate for Backsolving. For each answer, add that number to 5 to find the total. Is the probability of getting a nickel $\frac{1}{6}$?
Getting to the Answer: You know that $\frac{1}{6}$ of the total should be 5 nickels. Let x be the total:

$$\frac{1}{6}x = 5$$
$$x = 30$$

If the total is 30, the number of pennies is $30 - 5 = 25$.

60. **K** **Category:** Variable Manipulation
Difficulty: High
Strategic Advice: Each question is worth the same amount, so don't spend too much time on any one. Problems that ask how many different values of something there are tend to be particularly lengthy, so it's a good idea to save them for the end of the test.
Getting to the Answer: One way to solve this is to make all of the numerators 3:

$$\frac{3}{15} < \frac{3}{x} < \frac{3}{9}$$

This inequality is true for all values of x between 9 and 15. That's 10, 11, 12, 13, and 14: 5 integer values of x.
You can also solve this algebraically. The fastest way is to first take the reciprocals, which will reverse the inequalities (since $\frac{1}{3} < \frac{1}{2}$ but 3 > 2):

$$5 > \frac{x}{3} > 3$$

Multiply everything by 3 to find $15 > x > 9$. Again, the five integer values of x are 10, 11, 12, 13, and 14.

Reading

Passage I

1. **D** **Category:** Detail
   Difficulty: Medium
   Strategic Advice: Good notes will help lead you quickly to the section of the passage you need to research.
   Getting to the Answer: In lines 21–27, Giovanni notices "one shrub in particular" that seems to "illuminate the garden." The plant he is speaking about is the one with "a profusion of purple blossoms." In the next sentence, he considers other plants that are "less beautiful" than the one with purple blossoms. This should lead you to **D.**
   A Misused Detail; the plant that is wreathed around the statue (lines 34–37) is shown in a positive light, but these lines do not indicate that Giovanni finds the plant to be exceptional.
   B Misused Detail; in lines 32–33, there is information about plants that "crept serpent-like along the ground," yet no specific plant is mentioned, nor are any viewed as being special.
   C Misused Detail; in line 20, "gigantic leaves" are mentioned, but not a specific plant's leaves.
   D Correct; this matches the research above.

2. **G** **Category:** Detail
   Difficulty: Medium
   Strategic Advice: If you are able to determine that a certain statement is correct (or incorrect), you can include (or eliminate) all answer choices that include that statement.
   Getting to the Answer: Normally, you would start with the statement that appears most frequently, but all statements here appear an equal number of times. Your notes should indicate that the narrator discusses the gardener's interaction with the plants principally in paragraphs 3 and 4. Skim those paragraphs for the information in the three statements. In lines 57–59, you see that the gardener avoids the "actual touch or the direct inhaling of [the plants'] odors." Based on this, you know that Statements I and III are valid; eliminate all choices that don't include both of them (**F** and **H**). Paragraph 4 offers alternate confirmation of these two statements. A quick skim of the paragraphs offers no support for Statement II; eliminate **J.**
   F Distortion; this lacks Statement III.
   G Correct; the passage supports both statements.
   H Distortion; this lacks Statement I.
   J Out of Scope; the passage doesn't support the second statement.

3. **C** **Category:** Generalization
   Difficulty: Medium
   Strategic Advice: Generalization questions can be challenging because the answers will not be directly stated in the passage. Remember, though, that the answers will be supported by information within the passage, usually in more than one spot.
   Getting to the Answer: Your notes should help you to see that the gardener is shown as being very cautious when he gardens. For instance, in line 74, it is stated that the gardener wears gloves to protect himself. He also wears other "armor," the mask that he puts over his mouth and nostrils, in line 78. In lines 64–68, Giovanni is disturbed

by the fact that the gardener takes so much caution with the plants, indicating that Giovanni himself would not take these types of precautions. A good prediction is *cautious man*.

A Distortion; Giovanni alludes to Adam and the Garden of Eden, but this does not indicate that the gardener is more religious.

B Opposite; the narrator depicts the gardener as being very cautious, behavior that disturbs Giovanni.

C Correct; this matches the research above.

D Distortion; Giovanni alludes to Adam and the Garden of Eden, but this does not indicate that the gardener is less religious.

4. **J** **Category:** Detail

Difficulty: Medium

Strategic Advice: In Roman numeral questions, start with the statements that appear more frequently.

Getting to the Answer: Statements I and II appear more frequently than the third one does, so start there. In lines 59–60, the gardener "impressed Giovanni most disagreeably" by avoiding the inhalation of the plants' odors; Statement II is valid then. Eliminate **F** and **H**. (Note that this means you don't have to investigate Statement III.) In the following lines, Giovanni becomes upset that "the man's demeanor was that of one walking among malignant influences," which supports Statement I. **J** is the choice.

F Distortion; this does not include Statement II.

G Distortion; this does not include Statement I.

H Misused Detail; the narrator describes the gardener as doing this, but not that it disturbs Giovanni.

J Correct; the passage supports both statements.

5. **A** **Category:** Generalization

Difficulty: Medium

Strategic Advice: Some questions will ask you to read between the lines. Although this can sometimes be difficult, remember that the answer will always be supported by information in the passage.

Getting to the Answer: The gardener, in lines 57–59, avoids directly touching the plants or "inhaling...their odors." He is also described as a "scientific gardener," who seems to be "looking into" the nature of the plants. You can infer that he is observant and seems to understand the essence of the plants. Predict that he is *focused* or *attentive*.

A Correct; this matches the research above.

B Extreme; lines 48–54 indicate that the gardener knows a lot about plants. The narrator suggests, however, that he discovers this information as he works, not that he already knows all there is to know about plants.

C Opposite; the fact that he refuses to touch or smell the plants goes against the idea that he loves nature.

D Misused Detail; Giovanni mentions Adam in lines 69–71, but there is no indication that the gardener actually resembles him.

6. **G** **Category:** Inference

Difficulty: Medium

Strategic Advice: Don't "over-infer." The correct choice will be closely related to something stated in the passage.

Getting to the Answer: In lines 24–27, the plant is described as seemingly able to

"illuminate the garden, even had there been no sunshine." From this, you can infer that the plant seemed capable of producing light, which matches **G**.
F Distortion; in line 24, the narrator states that each blossom "had the luster and richness of a gem." To say that the plant could sprout gems stretches the metaphor too far.
G Correct; this matches the prediction nicely.
H Distortion; the narrator suggests that the plant could shed light on the garden, not overrun it like a weed.
J Out of Scope; nowhere in the passage is there any indication that the plant grows very quickly.

7. **D** **Category:** Writer's View
Difficulty: Low
Strategic Advice: Take the time to predict an answer before looking at the answer choices; this will help you avoid being tempted by incorrect answer choices.
Getting to the Answer: The passage is not told directly from Giovanni's point of view; the reader understands what Giovanni is thinking, yet this information comes from an unidentified narrator. Look for this among the choices.
A Misused Detail; the narrator refers to the gardener in the third person.
B Misused Detail; the narrator refers to Giovanni in the third person.
C Misused Detail; the gardener is described as being scientific, yet that does not indicate that the narrator is a scientist.
D Correct; this matches the prediction.

8. **J** **Category:** Function
Difficulty: Medium
Strategic Advice: Read the referenced lines carefully to determine the author's intent.
Getting to the Answer: These statements are made after the narrator describes Giovanni as being disturbed by the insecurities the gardener shows while cultivating the garden. The narrator mentions Eden and Adam to show how far the gardener's behavior is from these ideals—he should display more positive feelings for the plants he tends.
F Misused Detail; Giovanni seems to recognize this in the gardener earlier in the paragraph, but this has no relation to the references to Adam and Eden.
G Opposite; Giovanni finds the gardener's behavior inexplicable.
H Distortion; while these are Biblical references, Giovanni never implies that the gardener should show the plants respect, religious or otherwise.
J Correct; this matches the prediction.

9. **A** **Category:** Detail
Difficulty: Low
Strategic Advice: When you don't receive line references, good notes will help you know where to research.
Getting to the Answer: Your notes should indicate that every paragraph but the first focuses on Giovanni's observation of the gardener, so look to the first paragraph. Scan the choices first, then look for the match.
A Correct; in line 3, Giovanni refers to the garden as "one of those botanic gardens," different from most in the world.
B Distortion; rare art is mentioned in line 8, but this refers specifically to the marble fountain, not to the garden as a whole.
C Distortion; this answer is a misreading of lines 27–28, where the narrator states that "the soil was peopled with plants and herbs." He is not referring to actual people.

D Distortion; in lines 5–6, the narrator states that the garden "might once have been the pleasure-place of an opulent family." He never states that it was such a locale for "the community."

10. **G** **Category:** Generalization
Difficulty: High
Strategic Advice: When given line references in the question stem, go back to those lines in the text and, if necessary, read the sentences before and after those lines.
Getting to the Answer: The paragraph begins by describing the gardener as examining the plants intently and "looking into [the plants'] inmost nature," "discovering why one leaf grew in this shape and another in that" (lines 50–53). He seems interested in understanding what the plants are made up of. The remainder of the paragraph discusses his apparent fear of the plants. Look for one of these ideas in the correct choice.
F Opposite; the paragraph indicates that he is quite patient, intently seeking to understand the plants' inmost qualities.
G Correct; this matches the first part of the paragraph.
H Distortion; the gardener seems to fear the plants may harm him, but he does not seem to want to harm the plants.
J Out of Scope; there is no indication that the gardener is angry with the plants.

Passage II

11. **B** **Category:** Detail
Difficulty: Low
Strategic Advice: You are looking for three things that ARE mentioned and one that IS NOT. Don't get the two confused.
Getting to the Answer: First check your notes to see that the author mentions jumbo jet design in paragraph 4. Research the passage and cross off each choice that is referenced in the paragraph.
A Opposite; the author mentions this in line 34.
B Correct; the author does not reference this in the passage.
C Opposite; the author mentions this in line 32.
D Opposite; the author mentions this in line 35.

12. **J** **Category:** Vocab-in-Context
Difficulty: Medium
Strategic Advice: The test maker frequently gives you uncommon usages of common words. You need to read carefully to understand the intended meaning of the phrase.
Getting to the Answer: The Boeing example starts by pointing out that the plane's design will be limited in ways that will make it impossible to satisfy everyone. You can assume that the company wants to come close enough to satisfying all the plane's users that those users will be happy with the final design.
F Out of Scope; the author doesn't discuss such investments.
G Extreme; the passage tells you that there will be compromises.
H Out of Scope; the cost to users is not mentioned.
J Correct; this matches the thrust of the text.

13. C **Category:** Detail
Difficulty: Medium
Strategic Advice: You need to find the details used as evidence for this belief.
Therefore, your answer will come straight from the passage.
Getting to the Answer: Your passage notes should send you to the last paragraph.
The author asks you to "imagine" that the Titanic hadn't sunk on her first trip. In the
author's opinion, there would have been many ships designed just like the Titanic and
potentially many more disasters. Look for an answer choice that reflects this idea.
A Out of Scope; there is no evidence that ship designers were careless before the
Titanic sank.
B Out of Scope; the number of lifeboats is not mentioned.
C Correct; this matches the idea in the text.
D Out of Scope; the passage never discusses insurance.

14. F **Category:** Generalization
Difficulty: Medium
Strategic Advice: The answer should come from your overall understanding of the
passage, not from specific details.
Getting to the Answer: Your active reading told you that this passage is about the
importance of learning from failure. The passage title—"Look First to Failure"—is an
excellent clue. Therefore, look for an answer choice that mentions the positive aspects
of studying failures.
F Correct; this matches the prediction.
G Out of Scope; the author does not address whether or not projects "seem" difficult.
H Opposite; in lines 52–53, the author tells you that reverse engineering "sacrifices the
synergy of success."
J Opposite; the author says that studying past failures is an excellent way to learn.

15. D **Category:** Detail
Difficulty: Medium
Strategic Advice: Use your notes to find the correct paragraph and predict the answer
before looking at the choices; you will reach your answer more quickly and be less
likely to fall into traps set by the test maker.
Getting to the Answer: Based on your notes, you should go directly to paragraph
6. It tells you that the engineers for the Tacoma Narrows Bridge tried to improve on
Roebling's design for the Brooklyn Bridge and left out "the very cables that he included
to obviate failure." The prior paragraph identifies those cables.
A Opposite; deviations from the design of the Brooklyn Bridge were the cause of the
failure of the Tacoma Narrows Bridge.
B Out of Scope; the author doesn't discuss any difference in the wind strength between
the two bridges.
C Opposite; the engineers' concern for "economy and aesthetics" were what caused
them to leave out the critical cables.
D Correct; this matches your research.

16. H **Category:** Function
Difficulty: High
Strategic Advice: Use your notes to help you understand the writer's purpose in
selecting this specific example.
Getting to the Answer: Because this is the final paragraph, it is likely that its meaning
will be closely related to the overall purpose of the passage. Lines 79–81 state that
Titanic's failure contributed more to ocean liner safety than its success would have.

Reading

Note that the correct choice may not be stated so specifically.
F Distortion; the author's point is about design in general, not just the Titanic.
G Distortion; the article is not about the fate of ocean liners.
H Correct; this matches the prediction well.
J Out of Scope; this is true, but it's not the function of the paragraph.

17. D Category: Function
Difficulty: Medium
Strategic Advice: Focus on how an example fits into the overall point the author is making.
Getting to the Answer: Use your notes to locate the paper clip example—paragraph 3. The author points out that challengers to the Gem may be able to improve on one aspect of its design but not another. This reiterates the topic sentence, "Reengineering anything is fraught with risk." The example is probably meant to emphasize this point.
A Out of Scope; the paragraph is not about the importance of paper clips.
B Extreme; the example points out the risks of reengineering in general.
C Distortion; the author does not suggest any redesign of the paper clip.
D Correct; this captures the idea in the prediction above.

18. F Category: Detail
Difficulty: Low
Strategic Advice: Use your notes to research paragraph 3. To avoid traps, predict your answer before reading the choices.
Getting to the Answer: The paragraph tells you that the Gem clip is easy to use and doesn't fall off. Challengers have improved on one aspect of the Gem clip but have sacrificed the other.
F Correct; this choice addresses the compromise predicted.
G Out of Scope; function, not timing, determines success.
H Out of Scope; brand awareness and familiarity are not mentioned.
J Distortion; this mentions only one of the benefits the author lists.

19. B Category: Detail
Difficulty: Medium
Strategic Advice: When dealing with unfamiliar or passage-specific terms, read around the reference carefully.
Getting to the Answer: "Failure-based thinking" in this reference is related to Roebling's *successful* design of the Brooklyn Bridge. A careful reading shows you that Roebling was able to succeed because he understood where others had failed. You need to look for a positive use of "failure" in your answer choice.
A Out of Scope; the author doesn't discuss such a habit.
B Correct; this matches the prediction and the thrust of the text.
C Distortion; this choice can be tempting because it uses several key words from the paragraph, but the passage says cannibalizing can *sacrifice* synergy, not *create* it.
D Opposite; the Tacoma Bridge collapse supports the author's theory because the designers of that bridge failed to use "failure-based thinking."

20. H Category: Vocab-in-Context
Difficulty: Medium
Strategic Advice: To answer this question, you need to understand the author's use of the term *in context*. First, read the entire sentence and, if necessary, the sentences before and after.

Getting to the Answer: "So" in the middle of the sentence tells you that the first and second halves of the sentence are closely linked. From this, you conclude that "comparatives" relates to improvements. You need to look for an answer choice that tells you that engineering is measured by its ability to make improvements.

F Out of Scope; the comparison is between products, not individuals.
G Distortion; "bigger" and "faster" are only two possible measures of improvement.
H Correct; this matches the prediction.
J Out of Scope; the author doesn't deal with such comparisons.

Passage III

21.   **A**   **Category:** Generalization
Difficulty: Medium
Strategic Advice: When considering a passage's main purpose, look for clues about the author's attitude as well as passage content.
Getting to the Answer: This passage is overflowing with positive language. The author declares that Americans have "advanced prodigiously in aesthetic taste," that they have "all youth's glorious beauty and strength and vitality and courage," and ends with her conviction that the Golden Age is "sure to be."
A Correct; this best captures the overall tone and purpose.
B Misused Detail; the author alludes to this, but it isn't her primary emphasis.
C Misused Detail; the author alludes to this, but it isn't her primary emphasis.
D Opposite; this contradicts the author, who states, "It is difficult to maintain that youth today is so very different from what it has been" in the past.

22.   **H**   **Category:** Writer's View
Difficulty: Low
Strategic Advice: Most authors will present opposing points of view in the course of making their argument. Make sure to distinguish the author's attitude towards her own point of view from her attitude regarding opposing points of view.
Getting to the Answer: The author recognizes the "commonplace remark" that "the younger generation is speeding swiftly on the road to perdition," but then counters it with her own argument that the younger generation is not so unlike previous generations. She later points out that America is returning to its earlier and more beautiful sense of style. Look for a choice that captures this generally positive attitude.
F Distortion; this suggests that the author is uninvolved emotionally, which is clearly not the case.
G Opposite; the author only disapproves of a few select topics.
H Correct; this matches the research above.
J Distortion; this implies a balanced overview of the subject, while the author is instead quite opinionated.

23.   **D**   **Category:** Inference
Difficulty: Low
Strategic Advice: Remember to make inferences carefully, making sure they are based on information the passage provides.
Getting to the Answer: Throughout the passage, the author focuses on America's future and provides evidence that it is bright. In the concluding paragraph, she writes,

Reading

"the world is at present looking toward America" and encourages a focus not on any prior perceived Golden Age, but on "the Golden Age that is sure to be."
A Distortion; the author references Europe but makes no clear connection between it and a "Golden Age."
B Distortion; though the author praises this era, she does not specifically link the Colonial period to any "Golden Age that is past."
C Opposite; this cannot be the Golden Age because the author criticizes the post-Civil War period.
D Correct; this matches the text.

24. **J** **Category:** Detail
Difficulty: Medium
Strategic Advice: Comparisons are often made to emphasize certain points. Look for which traits of the objects being compared the author is focusing on.
Getting to the Answer: The author describes the ways in which the younger generation has changed the rules of etiquette, but concludes by saying that many of the charges against the younger generation lack "conviction." She goes on to state that characteristics of the younger generation are not symptoms of "degeneration" or "decline."
F Distortion; "earlier standards" are never directly discussed.
G Distortion; while the author notes that others believe the younger generation to be "on the road to perdition," she contradicts this perspective in the following sentence.
H Opposite; the author notes in lines 10–11 that "manners seem to have grown lax.
J Correct; this best summarizes the author's opinions.

25. **B** **Category:** Detail
Difficulty: Medium
Strategic Advice: When you don't get line references, use your notes to help you find the reference.
Getting to the Answer: In the fifth paragraph, the author states that traditional styles were "discarded" for post-Civil War "atrocities," but the next paragraph goes on to say that Americans are "trying to forget" post-Civil War "vulgarity." Look for a choice that captures the negative view of the era's aesthetic and its lessening impact.
A Extreme; the author notes that we are "trying to forget" post-Civil war aethetics, not that they have had "no impact" at all.
B Correct; this captures the thrust of the text.
C Out of Scope; the author does not say this.
D Out of Scope; the passage doesn't support this.

26. **F** **Category:** Inference
Difficulty: High
Strategic Advice: Some citations make little sense on their own. For these, understanding context is especially important.
Getting to the Answer: The citation is preceded by the author's assertion, "There have always been recurring cycles of undress," and it concludes a sentence beginning, "We have not yet reached the undress of Pauline Bonaparte." This comparison suggests that the current state of affairs is not as bad as some previous to it.
F Correct; this captures the idea in the text.
G Misused Detail; the author does say that there are "recurring cycles of undress," but this is not the function of the citation.

H Out of Scope; the author does not compare European and American styles of dress.
J Out of Scope; the author emphasizes cycles of fashion, not its unpredictability.

27. **C** **Category:** Detail
Difficulty: Low
Strategic Advice: This question focuses on a specific detail in the passage. Locating and understanding that detail in the context of the passage will lead you straight to the correct answer.
Getting to the Answer: Your notes should help you find this in the second paragraph. The passage states that weddings were held at noon "because a bridegroom's sobriety is not to be counted on" after that point.
A Out of Scope; the passage doesn't indicate this.
B Out of Scope; the passage doesn't indicate this.
C Correct; this matches up well with the text.
D Out of Scope; the passage doesn't indicate this.

28. **F** **Category:** Generalization
Difficulty: Medium
Strategic Advice: This question is asking you to make a distinction between cause and effect. Make sure not to confuse the two.
Getting to the Answer: The second paragraph offers examples of how customs have changed and follows them with denials of common critical interpretations of these changes—the criticism seems to be based simply on the fact that things have changed.
F Correct; this captures the thrust of the reference.
G Misused Detail; the author makes reference to "heartlessness," but this doesn't describe the basis for those accusations.
H Misused Detail; the author makes reference to this, but informality alone is not the cause of older generations' complaints.
J Out of Scope; the rate of change is not addressed.

29. **B** **Category:** Inference
Difficulty: High
Strategic Advice: Even if you do not know the meaning of the word cited, the relationship between the subject of the citation and its context will give you clues about the comment's function in the sentence.
Getting to the Answer: These "great houses" are compared to others that are "mediocre" or "even offensive." This allows you to infer that these houses of "consummate quality" are of a very high quality; look for a match to this among the choices.
A Out of Scope; the author doesn't indicate that these homes "challenge" a community's expectations.
B Correct; this matches the thrust of the author.
C Out of Scope; the context doesn't support this.
D Misused Detail; architectural trends are not discussed in this part of the passage.

30. **H** **Category:** Inference
Difficulty: Low
Strategic Advice: The question stem hints at what is being compared. Draw on the context to make a more specific comparison.
Getting to the Answer: In Titania's madness, she believed that a donkey was more beautiful than a god, which indicates that she mistook something ugly for something beautiful. The author compares this to America's embrace of unattractive post-Civil War

style instead of the more "exquisite" Colonial style.
F Out of Scope; time was not an issue in Titania's experience.
G Distortion; this may seem to apply to Titania's experience, but there was no "dream" element to America's changing patterns of style.
H Correct; this matches the prediction.
J Out of Scope; this doesn't make sense from the standpoint of American style.

Passage IV

31. **C** **Category:** Generalization
      Difficulty: Low
      Strategic Advice: Be sure to predict an answer before looking at the answer choices; predicting will help you avoid trap answers.
      Getting to the Answer: Your notes should help you to predict an answer for this on every passage. Throughout this passage, the author discusses how linear and circular accelerators work and how they differ in their uses.
      A Misused Detail; although this does appear, it is not the main idea of the entire passage.
      B Misused Detail; this appears in the passage, but it is not the main idea.
      C Correct; this matches the prediction well.
      D Misused Detail; based on the passage, cyclotrons do seem to be a useful type of circular accelerator, but this is not the main idea of the entire passage.

32. **F** **Category:** Detail
      Difficulty: Medium
      Strategic Advice: Think of Detail questions as matching questions. The answer choice will always match a detail stated directly in the passage.
      Getting to the Answer: In lines 89–91, the author writes, "The tube has many magnets distributed around it to focus the particles and curve their track around the tube." The magnets, by focusing the particles and their curve, influence the direction in which the particles travel; use this as your prediction.
      F Correct; this matches the prediction well.
      G Distortion; this misconstrues the statement that the magnets curve the particles' track "around the tube" (line 91). The particles' track is curving, not the particles themselves.
      H Distortion; the microwave cavities accelerate the particles (line 92), not the magnets.
      J Out of Scope; there is no indication that the magnets impact the energy levels of the particles.

33. **D** **Category:** Detail
      Difficulty: Medium
      Strategic Advice: On Detail questions, avoid incorrect choices that contain details from the passage not relevant to the question being asked.
      Getting to the Answer: According to lines 73–75, "The effect of the energy injected using the electric fields is therefore to increase their mass."
      A Distortion; the passage states that particles do not reach the speed of light.
      B Distortion; this misconstrues the reference to a vacuum in line 70.
      C Out of Scope; there is no indication in the passage that using heavier particles will cause particle mass to increase.
      D Correct; this matches what is stated in the text.

34. H **Category:** Vocab-in-Context
Difficulty: Medium
Strategic Advice: When answering Vocab-in-Context questions, read the entire sentence that contains the vocabulary word to decipher its meaning; then look at the choices.
Getting to the Answer: In lines 53–55, the author states that heavier particles, such as protons, are being used in accelerators. In the following sentence, you see that "these particles are composites of quarks and gluons." It follows that quarks help make up protons.
F Misused Detail; electron accelerators are mentioned in lines 51–53, but there is no indication that electrons are what make up a quark.
G Out of Scope; there is no mention of radiation in this paragraph, nor is there any indication that a quark is made up of radiation.
H Correct; this matches the prediction.
J Distortion; gluons and quarks seem to be roughly equivalent. Neither is a component of the other.

35. D **Category:** Detail
Difficulty: Medium
Strategic Advice: Some questions will ask you what CANNOT be possible. Make sure you take the time to read the question carefully, so that you don't select what is possible.
Getting to the Answer: In lines 25–27, the passage states that linear accelerators "are also used to provide an initial low-energy kick to particles before they are injected into circular accelerators." These lines show that linear accelerators provide this kick, not the circular accelerator, as **D** suggests.
A Opposite; in lines 39–40, the author states that "When any charged particle is accelerated, it emits electromagnetic radiation," which means that the circular accelerator can cause this.
B Opposite; in lines 35–36, the author states that parts of circular accelerators "can be reused to accelerate the particles further."
C Opposite; in lines 37–38, the author states that circular accelerators suffer a disadvantage in that the particles emit synchrotron radiation.
D Correct; this misconstrues a detail from the paragraph.

36. J **Category:** Generalization
Difficulty: Medium
Strategic Advice: Some questions will ask you to read between the lines. Although this can sometimes be difficult, remember that the answer will always be supported by information in the passage.
Getting to the Answer: The passage discusses how linear and circular accelerators work. Some information is also given on how they differ, how they can be used, and some different types of accelerators. Based on this information, it would seem that they have different uses, yet both linear and circular accelerators are valuable in their own ways,
F Extreme; the author states, for example, that linear accelerators can be used to "provide an initial low energy kick."
G Extreme; the author states in lines 53–55 that physicists are using particles like protons in accelerators.
H Distortion; besides the first circular accelerator invented by Lawrence in 1929, the passage mentions other types of circular accelerators, such as the synchrotron, which

is able to push energies into the billions of electron volts versus the 10 million electron volts that a cyclotron can push energies to.

J Correct; this statement fits in with the thrust of the passage.

37. D   Category: Detail
Difficulty: Medium
Strategic Advice: To get more points on Test Day, predict answers; this will keep you from being tempted to pick incorrect choices that distort or misuse information from the passage.
Getting to the Answer: Your notes can help direct you to the second paragraph. Lines 11–14 include the information needed to answer this question. Once the particles have passed through the hole in the plate, the plate repels the particles, which are accelerated towards the next plate.
A Out of Scope; the author does not state this.
B Out of Scope; the author does not state this.
C Out of Scope; the author does not state this.
D Correct; this matches the research above.

38. H   Category: Inference
Difficulty: High
Strategic Advice: Remember that even though the answers for Inference questions will not be directly stated in the passage, they will be supported by information in the passage.
Getting to the Answer: Use your notes to find where the author discusses these items. The author writes that synchrotrons can push energy levels higher than cyclotrons can. Look for this distinction among the choices.
F Extreme; as stated in lines 84–85, cyclotrons are still useful for lower energy applications.
G Distortion; circular accelerators accelerate particles in a circle, and cyclotrons and synchrotrons are both types of circular accelerators.
H Correct; this matches the research above.
J Out of Scope; the author never indicates that synchrotrons cause particles to move closer to the edge of the tube.

39. A   Category: Function
Difficulty: Medium
Strategic Advice: When you come across Function questions, remember that context is crucial to understanding the purpose of a particular passage element.
Getting to the Answer: After discussing the "storage ring," the author recalls the earliest cyclotron, from 1929, and shows the size difference between it and a modern counterpart. You can predict that the author means to *show the progress made in the technology.*
A Correct; this matches the prediction.
B Misused Detail; the passage indicates that cyclotrons are important, but not because Lawrence invented them.
C Distortion; simply due to the passage in time and the natural pace of progress, this is likely true. This is not, however, the author's purpose in making this statement.
D Distortion; this is not the purpose of this reference.

40. G Category: Generalization
Difficulty: Medium
Strategic Advice: Go back and read the lines mentioned in the question. Taking the time to research the passage will help ensure that the answer you choose is supported by the passage, which means more points on Test Day.
Getting to the Answer: Throughout this paragraph, the main focus is on how particles in high energy accelerators approach the speed of light, and that when they do so, the main effect is an increase in the relativistic mass of the particle.
F Misused Detail; the author references this in line 71, but it is not the main idea of the paragraph.
G Correct; this matches the research above.
H Distortion; this choice is a misinterpretation of the information in lines 71–73.
J Distortion; energy limits are not reached because the mass increases. The mass increases in particles as they come closer to traveling at the speed of light.

Science

Passage I

1. **B** **Category:** Figure Interpretation
   Difficulty: Low
   Passage Type: Data Representation
   Strategic Advice: This question represents a case where it's faster to go to the answer choices first.
   Getting to the Answer: Searching for the lowest value of the 20 in Table 2 is time consuming. Instead, start with the lowest value among the answer choices.
   D, like **C**, is far lower than the values in Table 2—in fact, both are values from Table 1.
   B is the lowest value in Table 2. It was recorded in Room 4 on Day 1.
   A is the highest value in Table 2.

2. **G** **Category:** Figure Interpretation
   Difficulty: Low
   Passage Type: Data Representation
   Strategic Advice: Don't answer low-difficulty questions like this one from memory. It's worth taking an extra ten seconds to look back at the table to be sure you get the right answer.
   Getting to the Answer: All of the values in Table 2 are recorded to the nearest 0.1 mm Hg.
   F is a trap for those who mistakenly refer to Table 1, in which values are recorded to the nearest 0.01°C.

3. **C** **Category:** Patterns
   Difficulty: Medium
   Passage Type: Data Representation
   Strategic Advice: Pick one data point at a time and check it against the answer choices. Eliminate any that don't contain that data point.
   Getting to the Answer: Start by checking the answer choices for the point from Day 1 (745.2 mm Hg, 18.03°C). Eliminate **A**, **B**, and **D**, as they don't contain this point. Only **C** correctly represents this data point, so this must be the correct answer.

4. **J** **Category:** Patterns
   Difficulty: Low
   Passage Type: Data Representation
   Strategic Advice: For questions that ask you to describe a data trend in words, be sure to make a prediction before checking the answer choices.
   Getting to the Answer: Circle the Room 3 column in Table 2, so your eye doesn't accidentally wander. Reading down the column, you can see that the average daily air pressure decreases every day. **J** matches this perfectly.
   F describes the pressure changes for Room 1.
   G describes the temperature changes (Table 1) for Room 3.
   H is the opposite of the correct answer.

5. **D** **Category:** Scientific Reasoning
   Difficulty: Medium

Passage Type: Data Representation
Strategic Advice: Pay close attention to the definitions of new terms introduced in the question stem. Make sure to account for all referenced quantities.
Getting to the Answer: D is correct because you are given only the temperatures of each room. You know nothing about the exact quantities of heat provided to the room or the amount absorbed by the room's contents. **A**, **B**, and **C** all suggest knowledge of these quantities.

Passage II

6. **G Category:** Scientific Reasoning
    Difficulty: Low
    Passage Type: Research Summary
    Strategic Advice: Before looking at the choices, determine for yourself what factors would support the given hypothesis or cause it to be rejected. In this case, the hypothesis would be supported only if the results showed higher Hg concentrations in swordfish and shark than in catfish and crab.
    Getting to the Answer: The results do indeed show higher Hg concentrations for swordfish and shark, so the hypothesis is confirmed as in **G**.
    The "Yes" part of **F** is correct, but the reason given contradicts the data in Table 2, so it is incorrect.
    H is also incorrect; the lowest Hg concentration was indeed in catfish, but this does not cause the hypothesisto be rejected.
    J contradicts the data in Table 2.

7. **D Category:** Scientific Reasoning
    Difficulty: High
    Passage Type: Research Summary
    Strategic Advice: Refer to the passage to understand the process in question on Scientific Method questions. In this case, refer to the description of CVAFS.
    Getting to the Answer: The passage mentions that CVAFS "indicates the relative concentrations of various elements and compounds." A properly working CVAFS, then, should be able to correctly measure the relative concentrations of Hg and Pb. Using a sample of known concentrations of Hg and Pb, as in **D**, would support or reject the accuracy of the CVAFS in detecting the presence of Pb.
    Nothing in the passage supports either **A** or **C**.
    B is similarly unrelated to the passage.

8. **F Category:** Patterns
    Difficulty: Medium
    Passage Type: Research Summary
    Strategic Advice: Try to find a correlation between any new information given in the question stem and the information in the passage.
    Getting to the Answer: Since new data on water temperature is introduced, try to find a correlation between water temperature and Hg concentration. Compare the average Hg concentrations in Tables 1 and 2 to see that, for all three common species (crab, swordfish, and shark), the cold-water specimens have higher Hg concentrations than do the warm-water specimens. **F** is correct, since the Northern Atlantic Ocean is the coldest location.

Science

9. **C** **Category:** Scientific Reasoning
    Difficulty: Low
    Passage Type: Research Summary
    Strategic Advice: The factors intentionally varied are the ones researchers purposefully changed in the course of the experiment.
    Getting to the Answer: Look back at Table 2. It shows that researchers intentionally tested four different kinds of fish, which matches **C**.
    A is incorrect, since the volume of tissue was never discussed.
    B is incorrect because all four species in Experiment 2 were extracted from water of the same temperature.
    D is incorrect, since CVAFS is the only method of analysis mentioned.

10. **G** **Category:** Patterns
    Difficulty: Medium
    Passage Type: Research Summary
    Strategic Advice: Questions like this use a lot of words to hide a very simple concept. In this case, all you're really asked to do is identify which fish would be most likely to have the greatest Hg concentration.
    Getting to the Answer: Tables 1 and 2 tell you that swordfish have the highest Hg concentrations and that cold water fish have higher Hg concentrations than the same species in warm water. A swordfish caught in cold water would likely have the greatest Hg concentration of all the listed specimens, then, making **G** correct.

11. **D** **Category:** Scientific Reasoning
    Difficulty: Medium
    Passage Type: Research Summary
    Strategic Advice: Think about the experimental method used, and try to predict an answer before looking at the choices.
    Getting to the Answer: Increasing the volume of tested material while maintaining the same volume of Hg in the sample would lead to a smaller fraction of Hg content, regardless of water temperature. **D** is perfect.
    C is incorrect, because nothing in the passage indicates that the contamination would affect warm- and cold-water fish differently.

Passage III

12. **G** **Category:** Patterns
    Difficulty: Medium
    Passage Type: Research Summary
    Strategic Advice: When a question introduces new data, try to relate it to patterns in the data given. Occasionally, some basic math may be required.
    Getting to the Answer: The equation in Exercise 2 tells you how to calculate the answer. Z = electromotive force ÷ current = $(12\text{ V}) ÷ (1.2\text{ A}) = 10\ \Omega$. Even if you missed the equation, you can note from Table 2 that Z decreases as current increases and at least eliminate **J**.
    Also, if you noticed that Z and current are inversely proportional (either by looking at the equation or Table 2), you could see that *double* the current of Bulb 4 results in *half* the Z of Bulb 4.

13. **D** **Category:** Patterns
Difficulty: High
Passage Type: Research Summary
Strategic Advice: Challenging Pattern Analysis questions may require you to do some basic math. Here, noticing the pattern of decreasing Z with increasing current is not enough. You must actually apply the given equation.
Getting to the Answer: Since Z = electromotive force ÷ current, current = electromotive force ÷ Z. You have to apply this equation to each answer choice and calculate which gives the highest current. You must use the Z values for each light bulb from Table 2.

For **A**, current = (10 V) ÷ (60 Ω) = $\frac{1}{6}$ A.

For **B**, current = (8 V) ÷ (40 Ω) = $\frac{1}{5}$ A.

For **C**, current = (6 V) ÷ (30 Ω) = $\frac{1}{5}$ A.

For **D**, current = (5 V) ÷ (20 Ω) = $\frac{1}{4}$ A. **D**, then, gives the largest current.

14. **F** **Category:** Figure Interpretation
Difficulty: Medium
Passage Type: Research Summary
Strategic Advice: Sometimes, a question may require you to combine a detail from the passage with data in a figure. Read the question carefully for clues regarding which part of the passage and which table you'll need.
Getting to the Answer: According to Table 1, Bulb 3 produced one red indicator light and three green indicator lights. The text above Table 1 explains that green indicators illuminate when light is detected and red indicators illuminate when no light is detected. For Bulb 3, then, only one sensor did not detect any light, **F**.
Beware of the trap in **H** for those who confuse the meaning of red and green indicators.

15. **C** **Category:** Figure Interpretation
Difficulty: Medium
Passage Type: Research Summary
Strategic Advice: This question certainly looks more intimidating than it is. Work methodically and you'll get the answer in no time.
Getting to the Answer: First, find the equation for B in the passage. It's listed in Exercise 3 as B = $\frac{P}{4\pi r^2}$. The text explains that P is the power rating in Watts and r is the distance in meters from the bulb. You're given r in the question stem (2 meters), but you'll need to find P. P is listed in Table 3 as 3.6 watts for Bulb 2. Plugging in P = 3.6 and r = 2 gives you **C**.
A is the result if you accidentally swap the values of P and r.
B and **D** are the results if you mistakenly use the P for Bulb 1.

16. **H** **Category:** Scientific Reasoning
Difficulty: High
Passage Type: Research Summary
Strategic Advice: Since you are not permitted to use your calculator during the Science Test, there must be a way to estimate seemingly involved calculations. Look for ways to make the math easier than it appears.

Science

Getting to the Answer: Since $B = \dfrac{P}{4\pi^2}$, $P = 4\pi^2 B$. You're given in the question stem that the bulb is 1 m away, so you can plug r = 1 into the equation. You're also given that B = 0.95 W/m². Plugging r and B into the equation for P gives:
$P = 4\pi(1 \text{ m})^2(0.95 \text{ W/m}^2)$.
Since π is slightly larger than 3, and 0.95 is slightly smaller than 1,
$P \approx 4(3)(1 \text{ m}^2)(1 \text{ W/m}^2) = 12$ W, **B**.
Even without calculating, you can eliminate **F** and **G** by comparing B for the fifth bulb with all of the B values from Table 3. 0.95 is just less than double the B value for Bulb 4, which had a P value of 7.2 Watts. Since B increases with P, you know your answer must be greater than 7.2.

17. **A** **Category:** Scientific Reasoning
Difficulty: Low
Passage Type: Research Summary
Strategic Advice: Look first at the tables for the similarities and differences between the two exercises. It's often easier to read information from those than from the text.
Getting to the Answer: No light sensors were used in Exercise 2, so **A** is correct.
B is incorrect because 4 different light bulbs were used in both exercises.
C is incorrect because a 12 V battery was used for both exercises.
D is incorrect because Table 2 shows that the current was lowest for Bulb 1.

Passage IV

18. **J** **Category:** Scientific Reasoning
Difficulty: High
Passage Type: Data Representation
Strategic Advice: Don't be intimidated by presentation of unfamiliar science. The answers to the questions must come from the passage and the data given, NOT from outside information.
Getting to the Answer: All three curves happen to intersect at 50%, so look at their slopes at this point of intersection. "Inversely proportional" means that the average kinetic energy is lower for steeper slopes. The 1,000 K curve has the steepest slope and therefore the lowest average kinetic energy. The 10,000 K curve has the next steepest slope and therefore the next lowest kinetic energy, and the 25,000 K curve has the least steep slope and the highest kinetic energy. **J** is correct.

19. **A** **Category:** Patterns
Difficulty: Low
Passage Type: Data Representation
Strategic Advice: Locate the correct data set and extrapolate beyond the given data by using your pencil to continue the curve.
Getting to the Answer: The 1,000 K curve appears to reach 0% at energies above approximately 8 eV. The note under the graph says that the curves all continue to decrease beyond 15 eV, so the value of the 1,000 K curve should still be 0% at an energy of 20 eV. Only **A** agrees with this.

20. **J** **Category:** Patterns
Difficulty: Medium

Passage Type: Data Representation
Strategic Advice: The correct answer will depict the same trends as the figure in the passage. Identify those trends before you check the answer choices
Getting to the Answer: There are two trends in the figure that accompanies Passage IV: probability of occupation decreases as energy increases, and the curves get shallower as temperature increases. Look for both of these patterns to be represented in the correct answer.
You can immediately eliminate **F** and **G**, since the curves in these choices increase in value with an increase in energy, behavior opposite to that of the curves in the figure. **J** is perfect because these curves decrease with increasing energy and because the lowest temperature (2,000 K) curve has the steepest slope, just as the figure shows.

21. **C** **Category:** Figure Interpretation
Difficulty: High
Passage Type: Data Representation
Strategic Advice: Sometimes a question will ask you to predict the placement of data points that are in between those actually shown on a graph. The answer choices for these questions will be spaced far enough apart so that a rough estimate will be enough.
Getting to the Answer: Locate the point corresponding to an 80% probability of occupation of a 5 eV energy state. It lies between the 10,000 K and 25,000 K curves. The temperature of the solid, then, must be between 10,000 K and 25,000 K. **C** must be correct, since it is the only choice in this range.

22. **G** **Category:** Patterns
Difficulty: High
Passage Type: Data Representation
Strategic Advice: Questions that introduce technical terms can be very confusing. Remember, though, that you don't need to understand what they mean, just how they fit into the question.
Getting to the Answer: It doesn't matter whether you've ever heard of the de Broglie wavelength before (or whether you can pronounce it!). Everything you need to know is in the question stem. As the de Broglie wavelength decreases, the energy increases. What happens to probability as energy increases? The figure clearly shows that the values on all three curves decrease with increasing energy. **G**, then, is the correct answer.
You can eliminate **H** and **J** because the figure doesn't show any curve changing from an increase to a decrease, or vice versa, so these can't be correct.

Passage V

23. **C** **Category:** Patterns
Difficulty: Medium
Passage Type: Research Summary
Strategic Advice: On questions that ask you to generate a graph from a data set, identify a few points and check for the answer choice in which they all appear.
Getting to the Answer: The bars on the graph need to represent the values in the 25°C column of Table 1. Soda C gives the largest value, and Soda D gives the second largest value. Eliminate **A** and **D** because neither shows this trend.

C shows Sodas A, B, and E all very close to each other, and **B** shows Soda A higher than Sodas B and E. Checking back with Table 1, you'll see that the pressures in Sodas A, B, and E are fairly equally spaced at 25°C, so **C** is correct.

24. **G** **Category:** Patterns
Difficulty: Low
Passage Type: Research Summary
Strategic Advice: Make sure you understand the meaning of new and unusual diagrams.
Getting to the Answer: Start by looking back at Table 1 and jotting down the pressures of Soda C at 0°C (249 kPa) and 50°C (294 kPa). **G** shows the gauge at 249 kPa at 0°C and 294 kPa at 50°C, so this is the correct answer.
F shows the opposite relationship between 0°C and 50°C.
Beware of **H**, which shows the values for Soda B.

25. **D** **Category:** Scientific Reasoning
Difficulty: Medium
Passage Type: Research Summary
Strategic Advice: Pick a few data points that stand out and look for correlations between the two relevant sets of data (in this case, sugar content and solubility).
Getting to the Answer: Soda D has the highest sugar content (40 grams per 12 ounces), but, according to Table 2, it has lower solubility than Soda C. This means higher sugar content doesn't always give higher solubility. The theory is not true, so eliminate **A** and **B**.
C is incorrect because, while Soda D has the highest sugar content, it doesn't have the lowest solubility (Soda E does).
Only **D**, then, is true.

26. **G** **Category:** Patterns
Difficulty: Low
Passage Type: Research Summary
Strategic Advice: Read across each row to identify the trend in the data.
Getting to the Answer: If you read across each row in Table 2, you'll see that the solubility values for each soda decrease with increasing temperature, with no exceptions. **G**, then, is the correct answer.

27. **A** **Category:** Scientific Reasoning
Difficulty: Medium
Passage Type: Research Summary
Strategic Advice: Refer to the passage for a description of the experiment in question, paying close attention to detail.
Getting to the Answer: Experiment 2 says, "The apparatus consisted of an air-sealed flask containing only soda and no air," and "CO_2 was injected." So you're looking for an apparatus built to allow CO_2 to be injected into a sealed container of soda. Only **A** shows this setup.
B is incorrect because it shows the soda immersed in an H_2O bath, which was only the case in Experiment 1.
C is incorrect because it shows an apparatus that injects H_2O into soda.
D is incorrect because it shows an apparatus that injects CO_2 into H_2O.

28. H **Category:** Scientific Reasoning
Difficulty: Medium
Passage Type: Research Summary
Strategic Advice: Sometimes a question requires you to infer things not directly stated in the passage. Draw only conclusions that MUST follow from the passage.
Getting to the Answer: The passage states that the H_2O bath is at room temperature, but soda temperatures are what matter. You can predict that 10 minutes allows the soda to reach the same temperature as the H_2O.
H correctly explains how the H_2O and soda reach the same temperature.
F and **G** are incorrect because CO_2 and soda evaporation aren't mentioned in Experiment 1.
In **J** the chronology is backwards—you need the pressure gauge to stabilize during the reading of the pressure, not beforehand.

Passage VI

29. C **Category:** Scientific Reasoning
Difficulty: Medium
Passage Type: Conflicting Viewpoints
Strategic Advice: Reread where the passage discusses "low energy," paying close attention to the details.
Getting to the Answer: The passage states, "The anti conformation is the lowest energy and most stable state of the butane molecule," and "Molecules in the anti or gauche conformations tend to maintain their shape." **C**, then is a perfect match.
A and **B** are the opposite of what you're looking for—the low energy molecules *don't* change their shape.
D is incorrect because the passage never mentions chemical reactions.

30. H **Category:** Scientific Reasoning
Difficulty: Medium
Passage Type: Conflicting Viewpoints
Strategic Advice: Refer to the passage, paying close attention to detail. Eliminate choices that contradict the passage or ones that don't logically follow from statements made in the passage.
Getting to the Answer: The passage states that "*Straight-chain conformational isomers* are carbon compounds that differ only by rotation about one or more single carbon bonds," and "isomers represent the same compound in a slightly different position." The number of carbon bonds, then, must not vary between different isomers of the same compound. **H** matches perfectly.
F and **G** contradict the statements in the passage.
J is not mentioned in the passage.

31. A **Category:** Scientific Reasoning
Difficulty: Medium
Passage Type: Conflicting Viewpoints
Strategic Advice: When the question stem says "only Student 2 believes," you know you're looking for an answer choice with which Student 1 would disagree.
Getting to the Answer: Student 1 believes that a molecule's active shape is *always* identical to its lowest-energy shape. Student 2 believes that "The active shape of a butane molecule is dependent upon the energy state of the shape," but also that there

Science

are two other factors, namely temperature and initial isomeric state, that affect active shape. Temperature does not appear in the choices, so **A** is the only possibility.

32. **G** **Category:** Scientific Reasoning
Difficulty: High
Passage Type: Conflicting Viewpoints
Strategic Advice: Don't be intimidated by questions that ask you to apply the logic of the passage to a totally different situation. Try to find structural similarities between the passage and the new situation.
Getting to the Answer: The question stem tells you that the two dips in the path represent states of lower energy. The lowest dip is closer to the ground and represents the lowest energy state, and the smaller, higher dip is a higher energy state. The ball is in the dip that is higher off the ground, so check the passage to find the name of the second-lowest energy state. According to the information at the beginning of the passage, the anti conformation is the lowest energy state, and the gauche conformation is the next lowest ("The methyl groups are much closer to each other in the gauche conformation, but this still represents a relative minimum or *meta-stable* state"). **G**, then, is the correct answer.

33. **A** **Category:** Scientific Reasoning
Difficulty: Medium
Passage Type: Conflicting Viewpoints
Strategic Advice: Make sure you understand the fundamentals of both arguments presented in the passage before you tackle this question.
Getting to the Answer: Student 1 believes that a molecule's active shape and its lowest-energy shape are the same thing. Therefore, Student 1 believes that all molecules in their active shape are in the anti conformation. This matches **A**. Student 2 believes that some of the molecules will settle into the gauche conformation, so you can eliminate **C**.
B is incorrect and the opposite of what Student 1 believes.
D is incorrect because Student 2 only believes that some of the molecules will have shapes different from that of their lowest-energy shapes.

34. **J** **Category:** Scientific Reasoning
Difficulty: High
Passage Type: Conflicting Viewpoints
Strategic Advice: Look for agreements between the graphs and the viewpoint of each student.
Getting to the Answer: Student 2 believes that the energy of a molecule's active shape may be slightly higher than that of its most stable shape, while Student 1 believes that a molecule's most stable shape and its active shape are always the same. **J**, then, depicts a situation in which the active shape has a higher energy than the most stable shape, so it is the correct answer.
H is incorrect because Student 1 believes that the active shape and most stable shape are always the same, and you're looking for a choice Student 1 would disagree with. Both students agree that the energy of the eclipsed conformation is higher than that of either the active or most stable shape, so you could immediately eliminate **F** and **G**.

35. **B** **Category:** Scientific Reasoning
Difficulty: High
Passage Type: Conflicting Viewpoints

Strategic Advice: Be sure to understand an argument thoroughly before attempting to counter it.

Getting to the Answer: Student 2 says that a butane molecule may settle into a moderately high-energy conformation. This, he says, is because "in order to convert from the gauche conformation to the anti conformation, the molecule must pass through either the eclipsed or totally eclipsed conformation. If the molecule is not given enough energy to reach either of these states, its active shape will be the gauche conformation." According to Student 2, then, without being given enough energy, the butane molecule can't always settle from the gauche (second-lowest energy) to the anti (lowest energy) state. If **B** was true, and the molecule could get enough energy from the environment to get into the lowest state, then this would counter his argument.

C and **D** are incorrect because hydrogen bonds, carbon bonds, and chemical functions aren't related to Student 2's argument.

A is not clearly relevant, and, if anything, supports the argument of Scientist 2.

Passage VII

36. **H** **Category:** Figure Interpretation
    Difficulty: High
    Passage Type: Data Representation
    Strategic Advice: Some questions ask you to apply information from one figure to information from another figure. Attack these questions step by step on Test Day.
    Getting to the Answer: Use your pencil to draw a horizontal line from 2 m on Figure 2 to the curve. You'll see that it intersects the curve at about 1.9 ppm. The ammonia concentration at a depth of 2 m in Figure 2, then, is about 1.9 ppm.
    Now move to figure 3. The ammonia (NH_4) concentration, represented by the black bar, is about 1.9 ppm for samples taken from a prairie. **H** is correct.

37. **C** **Category:** Patterns
    Difficulty: High
    Passage Type: Data Representation
    Strategic Advice: Look back at Figure 3 and try to determine the relationship between environment and NO_3. Then examine the answer choices.
    Getting to the Answer: Figure 3 shows that forests have the highest NO_3 concentration, followed by deserts and prairies. The passage explains that bacteria capable of nitrogen fixation lead to an increase in soil nitrogen levels. Therefore, high nitrogen levels may be a direct result of a high prevalence of nitrogen-fixing bacteria. **C** states just this and is the correct answer.
    A and **B** are incorrect because Figure 3 indicates that both forest and desert bacteria are capable of nitrogen fixation.
    D presents the opposite and incorrect conclusion.

38. **J** **Category:** Patterns
    Difficulty: Low
    Passage Type: Data Representation
    Strategic Advice: Compare any new information with the given figure. Don't try to answer the question from memory!
    Getting to the Answer: In Figure 1, plants grow faster in soil of higher ammonia concentration. Since no other explanations for changes in growth rate are given, you

can only refer to the effects of ammonia concentration. **J** is correct.

H is the exact opposite of what you're looking for.

F is incorrect because Figure 1 doesn't show any information relating to nitrogen-fixing bacteria.

G is incorrect because Figure 1 doesn't compare nitrogen and ammonia.

39. **C** **Category:** Figure Interpretation
    Difficulty: Medium
    Passage Type: Data Representation
    Strategic Advice: Mark up the graph to find the exact value of the data point you're looking for.
    Getting to the Answer: Figure 1 shows that the growth rate reaches a peak for an ammonia concentration of 5 ppm and appears to level off for higher concentrations. This matches **C**.

    The concentration in **D** gives a similar growth rate to **C**, but it is not the *minimum* concentration that does this, so it is incorrect.

40. **F** **Category:** Figure Interpretation
    Difficulty: Low
    Passage Type: Data Representation
    Strategic Advice: On a curve, large rates of increase are represented by steep slopes.
    Getting to the Answer: The greatest positive change in growth rate occurs between concentrations of 1 ppm and 2 ppm, **F**. The other choices give less drastic changes in growth rate.

Writing Test
Level 6 Essay

It is the rare high school student who knows exactly what his career will be and pursues it single-mindedly. High school is a time to master a solid educational base and explore future opportunities, therefore high schools need to expose students to career opportunities. The question is how this is best done. Some argue that required attendance at career-oriented seminars will allow students to explore careers and job requirements. Others emend this to optional after-school career-focused seminars, while still others feel that schools, colleges and professionals should partner to embed career-oriented options into existing courses. Because exploring options is so important to deciding on a career, I agree that students should be required to attend career seminars at least once a semester, and that they should be given by college representatives and career professionals.

The second option, that of providing optional seminars after-school, would be helpful to students already interested in exploring options, but unfortunately many students don't think that far ahead. Some do not have a family background that encourages college or professional careers, and those students would likely not attend seminars that they feel is of no interest to them. This does not serve the purpose of exposing all students to career options. Although after-school seminars do not interrupt the core curriculum, some students are not able to stay after school and would miss the seminars. In any case, a seminar of an hour or two per semester would not interfere with core instruction. There is no need to make students stay after school, or to exclude the very students who need college and career information the most. This option does not consider any but the already-interested student, the exact opposite of what is intended.

Those who go much further and would have career-oriented options embedded into current courses miss the fact that not all students take the same courses, so those who do not take courses with career-options embedded in them will not be exposed to these opportunities. Also, if the options are taught in a class relevant to it, who would choose which classes and options to incorporate? Some might be ok but others might not interest anyone. Furthermore, this option would take up class time and teachers may not be able to teach everything they need to. The argument says that all students would be given course-specific advice, but to guarantee that every student gets that advice means that there will have to be a lot of options offered in every class, from art to history, and a lot of classes interrupted. This approach takes up school time. The same professionals and college representatives can give seminars and not have to develop whole programs that would go into high school classes. This may be overkill. We don't need to have entire embedded programs to be exposed to career possibilities.

The first perspective of required seminars is the best one. The seminars would only take up a few hours each semester, so would not interrupt classes, and could be held during assembly times. In my school weekly assemblies are required and have various programs. Career-oriented seminars could be one of those programs once a semester. When this is required, all students will be exposed to career options and have some background knowledge before they go to college. I don't agree that not going to college already knowing what you want to do is a waste of time and money, since you learn a great deal before you decide on a career. But I do agree that if you have some information about a lot of different careers, you have a good basis to keep exploring, and that basis should be provided in high school to give students a jump start on their thinking about careers.

Grader's Comments:

This essay stays squarely focused on the prompt, explores the implications of all three perspectives, and presents the author's opinion in both the opening and closing paragraphs. Specific examples are provided, including school assemblies, reference to art and history classes, students who will and will not take advantage of seminars, and those who cannot attend after-school seminars.

Writing

The writer displays good use of the conventions of writing, including high-level vocabulary with phrases such as "core curriculum" and "solid educational base." Though the writer also uses lower-level words ("overkill," "ok"), they do not reduce the impact of the writing. There is a clear introduction covering all perspectives and introducing the writer's point of view, and though there is no concluding paragraph, the last sentence of the final paragraph serves the purpose. Grammar and punctuation are correct, with only one misused word ("emend"). Transition words and phrases are well-placed ("Some," "Others," "Furthermore") and though not every paragraph opens with a transition, each paragraph is clearly separate and discusses one of the three options.

The author's position is well-reasoned and supported, and critical thinking is clearly displayed. Though her point of view could be developed somewhat further, it is evident that this writer has understood the argument and different points of view, considered the pros and cons of each, and taken a solid stand of her own.

Level 4 Essay

I think it's really important to tell students about jobs and careers and high school is a good place to do this but we already spend enough time in school without having to go to lectures after school. Seminars should be scheduled during the school day when we are already there. Also, we have so much work to do in all of our classes that there shouldn't be more added even though it might be helpful. Also, I like airplane mechanics and I'll bet there wouldn't be anything about that in any of my current classes.

My school has assemblys that are mostly a waste of time since nobody pays attention. Now, if they did something interesting like having people talk about what they do, we'd be more likely to actually listen, especially if the people talking to us had really impressive jobs. I doubt we'd listen to a lab technician, but someone who builds airplanes would have a lot of good info to share.

Asking students to stay after school to learn about careers is a great way to have really terrible attendance at the seminars. Plus, it's really unfair to students who have after-school activities. There is no way that the star of the football team is going to miss practice just to attend an assembly.

My friends and I are always thinking about what we should do after high school, and I know my mom and dad are super worried about it, so learning about jobs in school would really help. Maybe someone who comes to talk to us will tell us about a job I didn't even know existed. I once met a flebologist, which was really neat because I had no idea what that even meant. When he told me that he studies vains, I was really interested. Who knew that you could spend your whole career helping people with disorders in their vains? I don't think I want to be a flebologist, but I might miss out on knowing what that is if my school only talks about medical careers in bio or chem class. Since I am taking physics, maybe an engineer would come to talk to my class, but I know for sure that I don't want to be an engineer. Plus physics is hard enough without trying to fit in extra time to talk about careers, we barely get through everything we need to discuss in one class period as it is.

In-school assemblies are the best way to get information about careers to students since we'll actually pay attention, we won't have to stay after school, and we won't take up important class time.

Grader's Comments:

The writer stays on topic throughout the essay, but doesn't explore each perspective with the same depth of analysis. While the writer adequately expresses her views, she needs to offer a full discussion of each perspective rather than concentrating on her own opinion.

The writing style is adequate, but the essay includes grammatical errors that should be avoided, such as run-on sentences ("I think it's really important to tell students about jobs and careers and high school is a good place to do this but we already spend enough time in school without having to go to lectures after school") and comma splices ("Plus physics is hard enough without trying to fit in extra time to talk about careers, we barely get through everything we need to discuss in one class period as it is"). The writer has a few spelling mistakes, writing "assemblys" for "assemblies," "vains" for "veins," and "flebologist" for "phlebologist." Though the writer has organized the essay into five paragraphs, there are no transitions at the beginning of each paragraph, and the last paragraph includes only one sentence.

Word choice could be improved by avoiding simpler words and phrases ("I'll bet", "super worried, and "for sure"). In addition, the writer should write "biology" instead of "bio" and "chemistry" instead of "chem." In all, the writer needs to offer a more comprehensive analysis of the issue and express her ideas with more complex vocabulary and sentence structure.

Level 2 Essay

I dont need anyone to tell me what to do when I get out of school I already know I will work in my uncles garage and hes going to teach me everything I need to no about it. I only go to school because I have to and noone can tell me that I need to learn more than I need.

Maybe other kids want to go to colege and they dont know what they will work at so they can listen to poeple tell them what to do but not me. I like cars and my uncle says I good at them so thats what I will do. Besides people talk a lot but that dosnt mean there right so maybe you wont find out what you want even if you listen to them.

Grader's Comments:

The essay is off-topic, misses the point of the prompt and task, is very poorly written and shows little, if any, logical reasoning. The author has a definite point of view but it is not relevant to any of the perspectives, thus does not fulfill the requirements of the essay. He has not considered any point of view other than his own and a fleeting, derogatory reference to other students and those who may present job information. His only support is that he already knows what he will do and needs no other information about careers.

Conventions of English are flaunted in every category. There are numerous misspellings, including "no" for "know," "noone" for "no one," "poeple" for "people," and "colege" for "college." Contractions lack apostrophes, sentences are confusing ("noone can tell me that I need to learn more than I need"), necessary words are missing ("uncle says I good at them"), and the first sentence is a run-on one.

Though there are two paragraphs, there is no introduction or conclusion, and neither paragraph attempts to reference any perspective. The author seems to have taken this task as an opportunity to vent his own annoyance at school and those students who are not sure of their career paths, but does so without logical reasons, support, or clarity.

Writing

KAPLAN

TEST PREP AND ADMISSIONS

1-800-KAP-TEST | kaptest.com/act

MATH

NUMBER LINES

A **number line** is a straight line that extends infinitely in either direction, on which real numbers are represented as points.

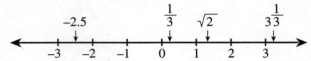

As you move to the right on a number line, the values increase.

Conversely, as you move to the left, the values decrease.

Zero is neither positive nor negative but is considered an even number

Primes

Prime number: A **prime** number is an integer greater than 1 that has no factors other than 1 and itself. The number 1 is not prime. The number 2 is the first prime number and the only even prime.

Prime factorization: The **prime factorization** of a number is the expression of the number as the product of its prime factors. To determine a number's prime factorization, keep factoring until you only have prime factors left.

Example: Find the prime factorization of 1,050.

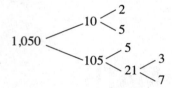

The prime factorization of 1,050 is $2 \times 3 \times 5^2 \times 7$.

NUMBER PROPERTIES

Number Types

Real numbers: All numbers on the number line.

Rational numbers: All numbers that can be expressed as the ratio of two integers (all integers and fractions). In decimal form, rational numbers are defined as numbers that have no decimal or have a terminating or repeating decimal, for example, 11.25, $3.\overline{33}$, etc.

Irrational numbers: All real numbers that are not rational, both positive and negative: for example, π or the square root of 2.

Integers: All numbers with no fractional or decimal parts: multiples of 1.

Imaginary Numbers: Imaginary numbers are numbers that when squared give a negative result. The imaginary number I cycles through 4 different values every time it is multiplied. These values are as follows:

i = Sq root of -1

$i^2 = -1$

$i^3 = -i$

$i^4 = 1$

this cycle will repeat itself over and over again.

Properties of –1, 0, 1, and Numbers in Between

Properties of zero: Adding or subtracting zero from a number does not change the number.

Any number multiplied by zero equals zero.

Division by zero is **undefined**. When given an algebraic expression, be sure that the denominator is not zero.

Properties of 1 and –1: Multiplying or dividing a number by 1 does not change the number.

Multiplying or dividing a number by –1 changes the sign.

Example: $y \times (-1) = -y$; $6 \times (-1) = -6$; $-2 \div (-1) = -(-2) = 2$; $(x - y) \times (-1) = -x + y$

Note: The sum of a number and –1 times that number is equal to zero.

Example: $a + (-a) = 0$; $8 + (-8) = 0$; $0 \times (-1) = 0$

The **reciprocal** of a number is 1 divided by the number. For a fraction, the reciprocal can be found by just interchanging the denominator and the numerator. The product of a number and its reciprocal is 1. Zero has no reciprocal, since $\frac{1}{0}$ is undefined.

Properties of numbers between –1 and 1: The reciprocal of a number between 0 and 1 is greater than the number.

Example: The reciprocal of $\frac{2}{3} = \frac{1}{\frac{2}{3}} = \frac{3}{2} = 1\frac{1}{2}$, which is greater than $\frac{2}{3}$.

The reciprocal of a number between –1 and 0 is less than the number.

Example: The reciprocal of $-\frac{2}{3} = \frac{1}{-\left(\frac{2}{3}\right)} = -\frac{3}{2} = -1\frac{1}{2}$, which is less than $-\frac{2}{3}$.

The square of a number between 0 and 1 is less than the number.

Example: $\left(\frac{1}{2}\right)^2 = \frac{1}{2} \times \frac{1}{2} = \frac{1}{4}$, which is less than $\frac{1}{2}$.

Multiplying any positive number by a fraction between 0 and 1 gives a product smaller than the original number.

Example: $6 \times \frac{1}{4} = \frac{6}{4} = 1\frac{1}{2}$, which is less than 6.

Multiplying any negative number by a fraction between 0 and 1 gives a product greater than the original number.

Example: $(-3) \times \frac{1}{6} = -\frac{1}{2}$, which is greater than –3.

Odds and Evens

Even numbers are integers that are divisible by 2, and odd numbers are integers that are not divisible by 2. Odd and even numbers may be negative; 0 is even.

Operations with Signed Numbers

Addition: Like signs: Add the absolute values and keep the same sign.

Example: $(-6) + (-3) = -9$

Unlike signs: Take the difference of the absolute values and keep the sign of the number with the larger absolute value.

Example: $(-7) + (+3) = -4$

Subtraction: Subtraction is the opposite of addition. Pay careful attention to the signs, particularly when subtracting a negative number; subtracting a negative number is the same as adding it.

Example: $(-5) - (-10) = (-5) + (+10) = +5$

Multiplication and division: The product or the quotient of two numbers with the same sign is positive.

Example: $(-2) \times (-5) = +10; \frac{-50}{-5} = +10$

The product or the quotient of two numbers with opposite signs is negative.

Example: $(-2) \times (+3) = -6; \frac{-6}{+2} = -3$

Consecutive Numbers

A list of numbers is **consecutive** if the numbers either occur at a fixed interval or exhibit a fixed pattern. Consecutive numbers could be in ascending or descending order.

NUMBER PROPERTIES EXERCISE

Solve the following problems. (Answers follow.)

1. $(-3) \times (4) \left(-\frac{1}{6}\right) \times \left(-\frac{1}{12}\right) \times 16 =$

2. $|6 + (-3)| - |-3 + 6| =$

3. $\left(-\frac{1}{4}\right)^2 =$

4. Which of the following numbers is divisible by 3: 241, 1,662, 4,915, or 3,131?

5. Which of the following numbers is divisible by 4: 126, 324, 442, or 598?

6. Which of the following numbers is divisible by 6: 124, 252, 412, or 633?

7. What are the first five prime numbers greater than 50?

Find the prime factorization of each of the following.

8. 12

9. 48

10. 162

11. 208

Decide whether each of the following is odd or even. (Don't calculate! Use logic.)

12. $42 \times 21 \times 69$

13. $24 + 32 + 49 + 151$

14. $\left(\frac{90}{45} + \frac{25}{5}\right) \times 4$

15. $(2,610 + 4,987)(6,321 - 4,106)$

16. $\frac{1}{2} + \frac{1}{3} + \frac{1}{4} =$

17. $\frac{12}{25} + \frac{13}{5} =$

18. $\frac{6}{21} + \frac{7}{3} =$

19. $\frac{1}{16} - \frac{3}{4} + 1\frac{7}{8} =$

20. $4\left(\frac{1}{3} + \frac{1}{12}\right) =$

21. $\frac{1}{2}\left(\frac{1}{3} + \frac{1}{4}\right) =$

22. $\frac{1}{24}(36 + 60) =$

23. $0.021 + 0.946 + 1.324 =$

24. $\left(\frac{12}{16} - \frac{3}{6}\right)^3 =$

25. $1.69 \times 0.002 =$

26. $30.17 \times 1.01 =$

27. $7 + 5 \times \left(\frac{1}{4}\right)^2 - 6 \div (2 - 3) =$

28. $4(1.24 - (0.8)^2) + 6 \times \frac{1}{3} =$

29. $\dfrac{\frac{5}{6} + \frac{3}{2} + 2}{\frac{1}{3} + \frac{4}{9} + 4} =$

30. $\dfrac{0.25 \times (0.1)^2}{0.5 \times 40} =$

ANSWER KEY—NUMBER PROPERTIES EXERCISE

1. $-\dfrac{8}{3}$

2. 0

3. $\dfrac{1}{16}$

4. 1,662

5. 324

6. 252

7. 53, 59, 61, 67, 71

8. $2 \times 2 \times 3$

9. $2 \times 2 \times 2 \times 2 \times 3$

10. $2 \times 3 \times 3 \times 3 \times 3$

11. $2 \times 2 \times 2 \times 2 \times 13$

12. Even

13. Even

14. Even

15. Odd

16. $\dfrac{13}{12}$ or $1\dfrac{1}{12}$

17. $\dfrac{77}{25}$ or $3\dfrac{2}{25}$

18. $\dfrac{55}{21}$ or $2\dfrac{13}{21}$

19. $\dfrac{19}{16}$ or $1\dfrac{3}{16}$

20. $\dfrac{5}{3}$ or $1\dfrac{2}{3}$

21. $\dfrac{7}{24}$

22. 4

23. 2.291

24. $\frac{1}{64}$

25. 0.00338

26. 30.4717

27. $13\frac{5}{16}$

28. 4.4

29. $\frac{39}{43}$

30. 0.000125

RATIOS

A ratio is a comparison of two quantities by division.

Ratios may be written either with a fraction bar $\left(\frac{x}{y}\right)$, with a colon ($x{:}y$) or with English terms (ratio of x to y).

Ratios should, when possiblebe reduced to lowest terms

Example: Joe is 16 years old, and Mary is 12.

The ratio of Joe's age to Mary's age is $\frac{16}{12}$ (Read "16 to 12.")
$\frac{16}{12} = \frac{4}{3}$, or 4:3

In a ratio of two numbers, the numerator is often associated with the word *of*; the denominator is often associated with the word *to*.

Example: In a box of doughnuts, 12 are sugar and 18 are chocolate. What is the ratio of sugar doughnuts to chocolate doughnuts?

$$\text{Ratio} = \frac{\text{of sugar}}{\text{to chocolate}} = \frac{12}{18} = \frac{2}{3}$$

Ratios are often expressed as a **proportion**., which is simply an equation in which two ratios are set equal to one another.

Ratios typically deal with "parts" and "wholes." The whole is the entire set: The part is a certain section of the whole.

The ratio of a part to a whole is usually called a fraction. "What fraction of the workers are female?" means the same thing as "What is the ratio of the number of female workers to the total number of workers?"

A fraction can represent the ratio of a part to a whole:

Example: There are 15 men and 20 women in a class. What fraction of the students are female?

$$\text{Fraction} = \frac{\text{Part}}{\text{Whole}}$$
$$= \frac{\text{\# of female students}}{\text{Total \# of students}}$$
$$= \frac{20}{15 + 20}$$
$$= \frac{20}{35}$$
$$= \frac{4}{7}$$

This means that $\frac{4}{7}$ of the students are female, or 4 out of every 7 students are female, or the ratio of female students to total students is 4:7.

Part: Part Ratios and Part : Whole Ratios

A ratio can compare either a part to another part or a part to a whole. One type of ratio can readily be converted to the other *if* all the parts together equal the whole and there is no overlap among the parts.

Ratios with more than two terms: Ratios involving more than two terms are governed by the same principles. These ratios contain more relationships, so they convey more information than two-term ratios. Ratios involving more than two terms are usually ratios of various parts, and the sum of these parts does equal the whole, which makes it possible to find *part : whole* ratios as well.

Example: Given that the ratio of men to women to children in a room is 4:3:2, what other ratios can be determined?

Quite a few. The *whole* here is the number of people in the room, and since every person is either a man, a woman, or a child, you can determine *part:whole* ratios for each of these parts. Of every 9 (4 + 3 + 2) people in the room, 4 are men, 3 are women, and 2 are children. This gives you three *part:whole* ratios:

The ratio of men:total people = 4 : 9 or $\frac{4}{9}$

The ratio of women:total people = 3 : 9 = 1 : 3 or $\frac{1}{3}$

The ratio of children:total people = 2 : 9 or $\frac{2}{9}$

In addition, from any ratio of more than two terms, you can determine various two-term ratios among the parts.

The ratio of women:men = 3 : 4

The ratio of men:children = 4 : 2 = 2 : 1

And finally if you were asked to establish a relationship between the number of adults in the room and the number of children, you would find that this would be possible as well. For every 2 children, there are 4 men and 3 women, which is 4 + 3 or 7 adults. So:

The ratio of children : adults = 2 : 7, or

The ratio of adults : children = 7 : 2

Ratio versus Actual Number

Ratios are always reduced to simplest form. If a team's ratio of wins to losses is 5 : 3, this does not necessarily mean that the team has won 5 games and lost 3. For instance, if a team has won 30 games and lost 18, the ratio is still 5 : 3. Unless you know the **actual number** of games played (or the actual number won or lost), you don't know the actual values of the parts in the ratio.

Example: In a classroom of 30 students, the ratio of the boys in the class to students in the class is 2 : 5. How many are boys?

This is a part to whole ratio (boys:students); write it as a fraction. Multiplying this fraction by the actual whole gives the value of the corresponding part. There are 30 students; $\frac{2}{5}$ of them are boys, so the number of boys must be $\frac{2}{5} \times 30 = 12$.

Ratio problems that do not contain any actual values, just ratios, are best solved by Picking Numbers. Just make sure that the numbers you pick are divisible by both the numerator and denominator of the ratio.

Example: A building has $\frac{2}{5}$ of its floors below ground. What is the ratio of the number of floors above ground to the number of floors below ground?

(A) 5 : 2

(B) 3 : 2

(C) 4 : 3

(D) 3 : 5

(E) 2 : 5

Pick a value for the total number of floors, one that is divisible by both the numerator and denominator of $\frac{2}{5}$ Let's say 10. Since $\frac{2}{5}$ of the floors are below ground, $\frac{2}{5} \times 10$, or 4 floors are below ground. This leaves 6 floors above ground. Therefore, the ratio of the number of floors above ground to the number of floors below ground is 6 : 4, or 3 : 2, (B).

Rates

A **rate** is a ratio that relates two different kinds of quantities. Speed, which is the ratio of distance traveled to time elapsed, is an example of a rate.

Average Rate (Average *A* per *B*)

Note: You will frequently see the term "average rate". Don't simply take the two rates add them together and divide by 2 - this is a trap answer. Instead be sure to use the formula:

Average miles per hour = $\frac{\text{Total miles}}{\text{Total hours}}$

Example: John travels 30 miles in two hours and then 60 miles in three hours. What is his average speed in miles per hour?

$\frac{(30 + 60) \text{ miles}}{(2 + 3) \text{ hours}} = \frac{90 \text{ miles}}{5 \text{ hours}} = 18$ miles/hour

Variation

Direct variation: When two quantities x and y vary directly, their relationship can be expressed by the equation $y = kx$, where k is a constant. In direct variation, one variable increases when the other increases and decreases when the other decreases. Direct variation problems can be solved by using proportions.

Example: A certain recipe makes six servings for every 8 eggs used in it. If Bob uses 12 eggs in this recipe, how many servings does he make?

Set up the situation as a proportion:

$\frac{6 \text{ servings}}{8 \text{ eggs}} = \frac{x \text{ servings}}{12 \text{ eggs}}$

$72 = 8x$

$9 = x$

So Bob makes 9 servings. Or use the direct variation equation:

$6 = 8k$

$\frac{6}{8} = \frac{3}{4} = k$

$y = \frac{3}{4}(12) = 9$

Inverse variation: When two quantities x and y vary inversely, their relationship can be expressed by the equation $xy = k$. In inverse variation, one variable decreases when the other increases and increases when the other decreases

Example: If Mary can walk from home to school in 30 minutes at a rate of 3 miles per hour, how fast would she have to run to travel the same distance in 15 minutes?

Set up an equation:

(0.5 hour)(3 miles per hour) = 1.5 miles

(0.25 hour)(x miles per hour) = 1.5 miles

x miles per hour = 6 miles per hour

Proportions

A proportion is simply an equation in which two ratios are set equal to one another. When working with proportions, be sure to notice any changes in units.

Example: Every inch on a particular map represents 70 miles. Approximately how many inches on the map will a 260-mile-long river be?

Set up a proportion: $\dfrac{1 \text{ inch}}{70 \text{ miles}} = \dfrac{x \text{ inches}}{70 \text{ miles}}$

Cross-multiply and solve: $260 = 70x$

$$\dfrac{260}{70} \cong 3.7$$

The river will be about 3.7 inches long on the map.

EQUATIONS

Order of Operations

PEMDAS = **P**lease **E**xcuse **M**y **D**ear **A**unt **S**ally. This mnemonic will help you remember the order of operations.

P = Parentheses

E = Exponents

M = Multiplication

D = Division in order from left to right

A = Addition

S = Subtraction in order from left to right

Example:

First perform any operations within *Parentheses.* $30 - 5 \times 4 + (7 - 3)^2 \div 8$

(If the expression has parentheses within parentheses, $30 - 5 \times 4 + 4^2 \div 8$

work from the innermost out.)

Next, raise to any powers indicated by *Exponents.* $30 - 5 \times 4 + 16 \div 8$

Then do all *Multiplication* and *Division* in order from left to right. $30 - 20 + 2$

Last, do all *Addition* and *Subtraction* in order from left to right. 12 $10 + 2$

12

Laws of Operations

Commutative law: Addition and multiplication are both **commutative**; it doesn't matter in what order the operation is performed.

Division and subtraction are *not* commutative.

Example: $3 - 2 \neq 2 - 3$; $6 \div 2 \neq 2 \div 6$

Associative law: Addition and multiplication are also **associative**; the terms can be regrouped without changing the result.

Example: $(a + b) + c = a + (b + c)$ $(a \times b) \times c = a (b \times c)$

$(3 + 5) + 8 = 3 + (5 + 8)$ $(4 \times 5) \times 6 = 4 \times (5 \times 6)$

$8 + 8 = 3 + 13$ $20 \times 6 = 4 \times 30$

$16 = 16$ $120 = 120$

Distributive law: The **distributive law** of multiplication allows us to "distribute" a factor among the terms being added or subtracted. In general, $a(b + c) = ab + ac$.

Example: $4(3 + 7) = 4 \times 3 + 4 \times 7$

$4 \times 10 = 12 + 28$

$40 = 40$

Division can be distributed in a similar way.

Example: $\frac{3+5}{2} = \frac{3}{2} + \frac{5}{2}$

$\frac{8}{2} = 1\frac{1}{2} + 2\frac{1}{2}$

$4 = 4$

Terminology

A **term** is a numerical constant or the product (or quotient) of a numerical constant and one or more variables. Examples of terms are $3x$, $4x^2yz$, and $\frac{2a}{c}$.

An **algebraic expression** is a combination of one or more terms. Terms in an expression are separated by either + or − signs. Examples of expressions are $3xy$, $4ab + 5cd$, and $x^2 - 1$.

In the term $3xy$, the numerical constant 3 is called a **coefficient**. In a simple term such as z, 1 is the coefficient. A number without any variables is called a **constant term**. An expression with one term, such as $3xy$, is called a **monomial**; one with two terms, such as $4a + 2d$, is a **binomial**; one with three terms, such as $xy + z - a$, is a **trinomial**. The general name for expressions with more than one term is **polynomial**.

Substitution

Substitution is a method used to evaluate an algebraic expression or to express an algebraic expression in terms of other variables.

Example: Evaluate $3x^2 - 4x$ when $x = 2$.

Replace every x in the expression with 2 and then carry out the designated operations. Remember order of operations (PEMDAS).

$3x^2 - 4x = 3(2)^2 - 4(2) = 3 \times 4 - 4 \times 2 = 12 - 8 = 4$

Example: Express $\frac{a}{b-a}$ in terms of x and y if $a = 2x$ and $b = 3y$.

Replace every "a" with $2x$ and every "b" with $3y$:

$\frac{a}{b-a} = \frac{2x}{3y - 2x}$

Operations with Polynomials

All of the laws of arithmetic operations, are also applicable to polynomials.

The process of simplifying an expression by subtracting or adding together terms with the same variable component is called **combining like terms.**

Distributive law: $3a(2b - 5c) = (3a \times 2b) - (3a \times 5c) = 6ab - 15ac$

Note: The product of two binomials can be calculated by applying the distributive law twice.

Example: $(x + 5)(x - 2) = x \times (x - 2) + 5 \times (x - 2)$

$= x \times x - x \times x + 5 \times x - 5 \times 2$

$= x^2 - 2x + 5x - 10$

$= x^2 + 3x - 10$

A simple mnemonic for this is **FOIL**, which means that the products immediately after all the parentheses have been removed appear in the order **F**irst, **O**uter, **I**nner, **L**ast. The FOIL method for the above multiplication would look like this:

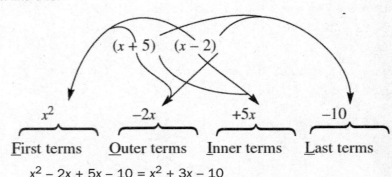

Products of the ⠀⠀⠀⠀ First terms ⠀⠀ Outer terms ⠀⠀ Inner terms ⠀⠀ Last terms

$x^2 - 2x + 5x - 10 = x^2 + 3x - 10$

Factoring Algebraic Expressions

Factoring a polynomial means expressing it as a product of two or more simpler expressions.

Common monomial factor: When there is a monomial factor common to every term in the polynomial, it can be factored out by using the distributive law.

Example: $2a + 6ac = 2a(1 + 3c)$ (Here, $2a$ is the greatest common factor of $2a$ and $6ac$.)

Difference of two squares: The difference of two squares can be factored into a product:
$a^2 - b^2 = (a - b)(a + b)$

Example: $9x^2 - 1 = (3x)^2 - (1)^2 = (3x + 1)(3x - 1)$

Polynomials of the form $a^2 + 2ab + b^2$: Any polynomial of this form is equivalent to the square of a binomial. Notice that $(a + b)^2 = a^2 + 2ab + b^2$ (try FOIL).

Factoring such a polynomial is just reversing this procedure.

Example: $x^2 + 6x + 9 = (x)^2 + 2(x)(3) + (3)^2 = (x + 3)^2$

Polynomials of the form $a^2 - 2ab + b^2$: this form is equivalent to the square of a, the binomial is the difference of two terms: $(a - b)^2 = a^2 - 2ab + b^2$.

Polynomials of the form $x^2 + bx + c$: The polynomials of this form can sometimes be factored into a product of two binomials. The product of the first terms in each binomial must equal the first term of the polynomial. The product of the last terms of the binomials must equal the third term of the polynomial. The sum of the remaining products must equal the second term of the polynomial. Factoring can be thought of as the FOIL method backwards.

Example: $x^2 - 3x + 2$

You can factor this into two binomials, each containing an x term. Start by writing down what you know.
$x^2 - 3x + 2 = (x \quad)(x \quad)$

In each binomial on the right, you need to fill in the missing term. The product of the two missing terms will be the last term in the polynomial: 2. The sum of the two missing terms will be the coefficient of the second term of the polynomial: −3. Try the possible factors of 2 until you get a pair that adds up to −3. There are two possibilities: 1 and 2, or −1 and −2. Since $(-1) + (-2) = -3$, you can fill −1 and −2 into the empty spaces.

Thus, $x^2 - 3x + 2 = (x - 1)(x - 2)$.

Note: Whenever you factor a polynomial, you can check your answer by using FOIL to obtain the original polynomial.

EQUATIONS EXERCISE—WORD PROBLEMS

Translate the following directly into algebraic form. Do not reduce the expressions. (Answers follow.)

1. z is x less than y.

2. The sum of 5, 6, and a

3. If n is greater than m, the positive difference between twice n and m

4. The ratio of $4q$ to $7p$ is 5 to 2.

5. The product of a decreased by b and twice the sum of a and b

6. A quarter of the sum of a and b is 4 less than a.

7. Double the ratio of z to a plus the sum of z and a equals z minus a.

8. If $500 is taken from F's salary, then the combined salaries of F and G will be double what F's salary would be if it were increased by one-half of itself.

9. The sum of a, b, and c is twice the sum of a minus b and a minus c.

10. The sum of y and 9 decreased by the sum of x and 7 is the same as dividing x decreased by z by 7 decreased by x.

ANSWER KEY—EQUATIONS EXERCISE—WORD PROBLEMS

1. $z = y - x$

2. $5 + 6 + a$

3. $2n - m$

4. $\dfrac{4a}{7p} = \dfrac{5}{2}$

5. $(a - b) - 2(a + b)$

6. $\dfrac{a+b}{4} = a - 4$

7. $\dfrac{2z}{a} + z + a = z - a$

8. $F - 500 + G = 2\left(F + \dfrac{F}{2}\right)$

9. $a + b + c = 2\left[(a - b) + (a - c)\right]$

10. $(y + 9) - (x + 7) = \dfrac{x - z}{7 - x}$

EQUATIONS EXERCISE

Solve the following problems. (Answers follow.)

Simplify expressions 1–10; factor expressions 11–20.

1. $2x + 4y + 7x - 6y =$

2. $2x(4y + 3x) =$

3. $x(x^2 + x + 1) - x^2 =$

4. $(y^2 + 1)(x^2 + 1) =$

5. $(2a - b)(2a + b) =$

6. $(4x + y)(x + 4y) - 17xy =$

7. $(x^2 - 1)(x^2 + 1) =$

8. $xyz\left(\dfrac{1}{xy} + \dfrac{x}{zy} + \dfrac{1}{x}\right) =$

9. $\left(\dfrac{zxy}{z}\right)\left(\dfrac{z^2y}{x}\right)\left(\dfrac{z}{y^2}\right) =$

10. $\left(\dfrac{x^4}{y^3}\right)\left(\dfrac{y^2}{x^3}\right)\left(\dfrac{x}{y}\right) =$

11. $x^2 + xy + x =$

12. $y^3 + 2y^2 + y =$

13. $5x^2 - 5 =$

14. $x^4 - x^2 =$

15. $x^2 - 6x + 9 =$

16. $x^2 + 10x + 25 =$

17. $x^2 + x + \dfrac{1}{4} =$

18. $x^2 - 4x + 4 =$

19. $x^2 + 7x + 10 =$

20. $x^2 + 10x + 9 =$

KAPLAN

ANSWER KEY—EQUATIONS EXERCISE

1. $9x - 2y$

2. $8xy + 6x^2$

3. $x^3 + x$

4. $x^2y^2 + x^2 + y^2 + 1$

5. $4a^2 - b^2$

6. $4x^2 + 4y^2$

7. $x^4 - 1$

8. $z + x^2 + yz$

9. z^3

10. $\dfrac{x^2}{y^2}$

11. $x(x + y + 1)$

12. $y(y + 1)^2$

13. $5(x - 1)(x + 1)$

14. $x^2(x - 1)(x + 1)$

15. $(x - 3)^2$

16. $(x + 5)^2$

17. $\left(x + \dfrac{1}{2}\right)^2$ or $\dfrac{(2x + 1)^2}{4}$

18. $(x - 2)^2$

19. $(x + 2)(x + 5)$

20. $(x + 9)(x + 1)$

Equations and Unknowns

If a problem has one equation and involves more than one variable, you can only solve for one variable in terms of the others. To do this, try to get the desired variable alone on one side and all the other variables on the other side.

Example: In the formula $V = \dfrac{PN}{R + NT}$, solve for N in terms of P, R, T, and V.

1. Clear denominators by cross-multiplying.

   $\dfrac{V}{1} = \dfrac{PN}{R + NT}$

   $V(R + NT) = PN$

2. Remove parentheses by distributing.

   $VR + VNT = PN$

3. Put all terms containing N on one side and all other terms on the other side.

   $VNT - PN = -VR$

4. Factor out the common factor N.

   $N(VT - P) = -VR$

5. Divide by the coefficient of N to get N alone.

   $N = \dfrac{-VR}{VT - P}$

Note: You can reduce the number of negative signs in the answer by multiplying both the numerator and the denominator of the fraction on the right side by -1.

$N = \dfrac{VR}{P - VT}$

Simultaneous Equations

In general, if you want to find numerical values for all your variables, you will need as many different equations as you have variables. If you are given two different equations with two variables, one way to solve them is combine the equations to obtain a unique solution set. Isolate the variable in one equation, then plug that expression into the other equation. Substitution, as noted above, is alternate method.

Example: Find the values of m and n if $m = 4n + 2$ and $3m + 2n = 16$.

1. $m = 4n + 2$. Substitute $4n + 2$ for m in the second equation.

   $3(4n + 2) + 2n = 16$

   $12n + 6 + 2n = 16$

2. Solve for n.

   $14n = 10$

   $n = \dfrac{10}{14} = \dfrac{5}{7}$

3. To find the value of m, substitute $\dfrac{5}{7}$ for n in the first equation and solve.

   $m = 4\left(\dfrac{5}{7}\right) + 2$

   $m = \dfrac{20}{7} + \dfrac{14}{7} = \dfrac{34}{7}$

Quadratic Equations

The polynomial $ax^2 + bx + c$ set equal to 0, i– is called a quadratic equation. Since it is an equation, you can find the value(s) for x which make the equation work.

Example: $x^2 - 3x + 2 = 0$

To find the solutions, or roots, start by factoring $x^2 - 3x + 2$ into $(x - 2)(x - 1)$, making your quadratic equation $(x - 2)(x - 1) = 0$.

Now there are two binomials whose product is equal to 0 The only time that a product of two terms will equal 0 is when at least one of the terms is 0. If the product of $(x - 2)$ and $(x - 1)$ is equal to 0, either the first factor equals 0 or the second factor equals 0. To find the roots, set the two binomials equal to 0. That gives you $x - 2 = 0$ or $x - 1 = 0$.

Solving for x, you get $x = 2$ or $x = 1$. As a check, plug in 1 and 2 into the equation $x^2 - 3x + 2 = 0$, and you'll see that either value makes the equation work.

INEQUALITIES

Inequality symbols:

> greater than

Example: $x > 4$ means x can be all numbers greater than 4.

< less than

Example: $x < 0$ means x can be all numbers less than zero (the negative numbers).

$\geq$ greater than or equal to

Example: $x \geq 2$ means x can be -2 or any number greater than -2.

$\leq$ less than or equal to

Example: $x \leq \frac{1}{2}$ means x can be $\frac{1}{2}$ or any number less than $\frac{1}{2}$.

A range of values is often expressed on a number line. Two ranges are shown below.

(a)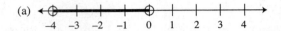

(b)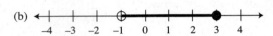

(a) represents the set of all numbers between -4 and 0, excluding the endpoints -4 and 0, or $-4 < x < 0$.

(b) represents the set of all numbers greater than -1, and up to and including 3, or $-1 < x \leq 3$.

Solving Inequalities: Use the same methods used in solving equations with two exceptions:

Multiplying or dividing by a negative number reverses the direction of the inequality.

If the inequality $-3x < 2$ is multiplied by -1, the resulting inequality is $3x > -2$.

Note: The solution set to an inequality is not a single value but a range of possible values. Omit this number line since problem is omitted.

FUNCTIONS

Some ACT questions focus on evaluating **functions**; function problems are just substitution problems with a little window dressing Remember the order of operations (Parentheses, Exponents, Multiplication and Division, Addition and Subtraction) and work carefully.

Example: If $r(x) = (x + 6)^2$, $r(-4) = (-4 + 6)^2 = (2)^2 = 4$.

You may also see more complex questions involving composition of functions.

Example: If $w(a) = a + 6$, $v(b) = b^2$, and $u(c) = c - 5$, what is the value of $u(v(w(1)))$?

Just follow the order of operations—start with the innermost parentheses.

$w(1) = 1 + 6 = 7$

$v(w(1)) = v(7) = 7^2 = 49$

$u(v(w(1))) = u(49) = 49 - 5 = 44$

Domain and Range

The **domain** of a function is the set of values of x for which the function is defined. The **range** of a function is the set of values of the function that exist. In other words, domain is input and range is output.

Example: If $f(x) = x^2 + \sqrt{2}$, the domain of $f(x)$ includes all numbers greater than or equal to 0, since you cannot take the square root of a negative number. The range is also all numbers greater than or equal to 0, since both x^2 and $\sqrt{2}$ must be at least 0.

Symbols

You may see strange symbols on the ACT. The question stem in these problems will always define the action for the symbol.

Example: Let $x*$ be defined by the equation $x* = \dfrac{x^2}{1 - x^2}$. Evaluate $\left(\dfrac{1}{2}\right)^*$.

$$\left(\frac{1}{2}\right)^* = \frac{\left(\frac{1}{2}\right)^2}{1 - \left(\frac{1}{2}\right)^2} = \frac{\frac{1}{4}}{1 - \frac{1}{4}} = \frac{\frac{1}{4}}{\frac{3}{4}} = \frac{1}{3}$$

Linear Functions

A linear function is a function whose graph is a straight line. The standard form of the equation of a line is $y = mx + b$, where m is the slope of the line and b is the y-intercept. To find the slope of a line that passes through the points (x_1, y_1) and (x_2, y_2), use the formula $m = \dfrac{y_2 - y_1}{x_2 - x_1}$. You can find the y-intercept by plugging m and a point on the line into the equation of the line $y = mx + b$ and solving for b. Many questions can also be solved by sketching the line and estimating the slope and y-intercept.

Example: What is the equation of the line that passes through the points $(1, 2)$ and $(3, 4)$?

First, find the slope.

$$m = \frac{4 - 2}{3 - 1} = \frac{2}{2} = 1$$

Then plug in one of the given points to find the y-intercept.

$2 = 1(1) + b$

$2 = 1 + b$

$1 = b$

So the equation of the line is $y = x + 1$.

Parallel lines: Parallel lines have the same slope.

Perpendicular lines: Perpendicular lines have negative reciprocal slopes.

Quadratic Functions

A quadratic function is a function in the form $f(x) = ax^2 + bx + c$. The graph of a quadratic function is a parabola.

Example: If $w(x) = x^2 - 16$, at what values of x does the graph of $w(x)$ cross the x-axis?

A curve crosses the x-axis when its y-value equals 0. Set $w(x)$ equal to 0 and solve for x to find the values of x at which the graph crosses the x-axis.

$x^2 - 16 = 0$

$x^2 = 16$

$x = -4$ or $x = 4$

You could also sketch the function by picking several values of x and calculating the corresponding values of y, then observe the locations at which the function crosses the x-axis.

Functions as Models

Some ACT questions may ask you to relate a function to a real-life situation. One common type of question will provide a chart or graph and ask which of several answer choices best describes the information in it. It's usually easiest to solve these questions by picking a few data points from the chart or graph and plugging them into the equations in the answer choices to see which equation works for all the points in the chart or graph.

Example:

Week	Number of Customers
1	5
2	11
3	21
4	35 make this graph shorter

Mr. Lee's Snack Shop has been open for eight weeks. The table above shows how many customers have visited the shop each week. If c = the number of customers and t = the week, which of the following equations best fits the information in the table above?

(A) $c = t + 4$

(B) $c = 2t + 5$

(C) $c = t^2 + 7$

(D) $c = t^2 + 4$

(E) $c = 2t^2 + 3$

The only equation that fits all the weeks in the table is (E).

EXPONENTS

Rules of Operation with Powers

In the term $3x^2$, 3 is the **coefficient**, x is the **base**, and 2 is the **exponent**. An exponent tells you how many times to multiply the number by itself. For instance $4^3 = 4 \times 4 \times 4$.

To multiply two terms with the same base, keep the base and add the exponents.

Example: $2^2 \times 2^3 = (2 \times 2)(2 \times 2 \times 2)$ or $= (2 \times 2 \times 2 \times 2 \times 2)$

$$= 2^5$$

To divide two terms with the same base, keep the base and subtract the exponent of the denominator from the exponent of the numerator.

Example: $4^4 \div 4^2 = \dfrac{4 \times 4 \times 4 \times 4}{4 \times 4}$ or $4^4 \div 4^2 = 4^{4-2}$

$$= \dfrac{4 \times 4}{1} \qquad\qquad\qquad\qquad 4^2$$

$$= 4^2$$

To raise a power to an exponent, multiply the exponents.

Example: $(3^2)^4 = (3 \times 3)^4$ or $(3^2)^4 = 3^{2 \times 4}$

$= (3 \times 3)(3 \times 3)(3 \times 3)(3 \times 3)$ $= 3^8$

$= 3^8$

Any nonzero number raised to the zero power is equal to 1. For example $a^0 = 1$.

A negative exponent convert. is the inverse of the same number with the exponent.

$$a^{-n} = \frac{1}{a^n} \text{ or } \left(\frac{1}{a}\right)^n$$

Example: $2^{-3} = \left(\dfrac{1}{2}\right)^3 = \dfrac{1}{2^3} = \dfrac{1}{8}$

A fractional exponent indicates a **root**.

$a^{\frac{1}{n}} = \sqrt[n]{a}$ ("the nth root of a." If no "n" is present, the radical sign means the positive square root.)

Example: $8^{\frac{1}{3}} = \sqrt[3]{8} = 2$

Logarithms

Logarithms are another way of expressing exponents. Log28 =3 is just a different way of saying 23 =8. When an expression is written as a log, the base will become a subscrip, the result is written right next to it and the equal sign tells you what the base is raised to in order to get the result, which is the logarithm. Try to think of the result and the exponent as just switching places.

Powers of 10

The exponent of a power of 10 tells us how many zeros the number would contain if written out.

Example: $10^6 = 1{,}000{,}000$ (six zeros) since 10 multiplied by itself six times is equal to 1,000,000.

When multiplying a number by a power of 10, move the decimal point to the right the same number of places as the number of zeros in that power of 10.

When dividing by a power of 10, move the decimal point the corresponding number of places to the left. (Note that dividing by 10^4 is the same as multiplying by 10^{-4}.)

Large numbers or small decimal fractions can be expressed more conveniently using scientific notation. Scientific notation means expressing a number as the product of a decimal between 1 and 10 and a power of 10.

Example: $5,600,000 = 5.6 \times 10^6$
Example: $0.00000079 = 7.9 \times 10^{-7}$

Radicals

Rules of operations with roots: Every positive number has two square roots, one positive and one negative. Zero has only one square root, 0. Negative numbers do not have any real square roots. The positive square root of 25 is 5, since $5^2 = 25$; the negative square root of 25 is –5.

By convention, the symbol $\sqrt{}$ (radical) means the **positive** square root only.

Example: $\sqrt{9} = -3$

Even though there are two different numbers whose square is 9 (both 3 and –3), $\sqrt{9}$ is positive number 3 only.

Addition and subtraction: Only like radicals can be added to or subtracted from one another.

Example: $2\sqrt{3} + 4\sqrt{2} - \sqrt{2} - 3\sqrt{3} = (4\sqrt{2} - \sqrt{2}) + (2\sqrt{3} - 3\sqrt{3})$ [Note: $\sqrt{2} = 1\sqrt{2}$]
$= 3\sqrt{2} + (-\sqrt{3})$
$= 3\sqrt{2} - \sqrt{3}$

Multiplication and division: To multiply or divide one radical by another, multiply or divide the numbers outside the radical signs, then the numbers inside the radical signs.

Example: $(6\sqrt{3}) \times (2\sqrt{5}) = (6 \times 2) \times (\sqrt{3} \times \sqrt{5}) = 12\sqrt{3 \times 15} = 12\sqrt{15}$

Example: $\dfrac{4\sqrt{18}}{2\sqrt{6}} = \left(\dfrac{4}{2}\right)\left(\dfrac{\sqrt{18}}{\sqrt{6}}\right) = 2\left(\sqrt{\dfrac{18}{6}}\right) = 2\sqrt{3}$

If the number inside the radical is a multiple of a perfect square, the expression can be simplified by factoring out the perfect square.

Example: $\sqrt{72} = \sqrt{36 \times 2} = \sqrt{36} \times \sqrt{2} = 6\sqrt{2}$

Radical Equations

A **radical equation** is an equation that includes a square root. Isolate the radical on one side of the equation, then square both sides to remove the radical.

Example: If $m - \sqrt{m + 6} = 0$, what is the value of m?

$m - \sqrt{m + 6} = 0$
$m = \sqrt{m + 6}$
$m^2 = (\sqrt{m + 6})^2$
$m^2 = m + 6$
$m^2 - m - 6 = 0$
$(m - 3)(m + 2) = 0$
$m = 3$ or $m = -2$

Rational Equations

A **rational equation** is an equation that contains a fraction in which the numerator and denominator are both polynomials, and work just like simpler equations. Picking Numbers and Backsolving are excellent techniques to use on rational equations.

If you choose to solve this type of problem algebraically, start by cross multiplying, then simplify and solve.

Example: If $\dfrac{x-2}{x+4} = \dfrac{1}{x-2}$, and x does not equal 2 or –4, what is the value of x?

Cross-multiply: $(x-2)(x-2) = x+4$

$x^2 - 4x + 4 = x + 4$

$x^2 - 5x = 0$

$x(x-5) = 0$

$x = 0$ or $x = 5$

TRIANGLES

General Triangles

A **triangle** is a closed figure with three angles and three straight sides.

The sum of the interior angles of any triangle is 180 degrees.

Each interior angle is supplementary to an adjacent exterior angle. The degree measure of an exterior angle is equal to the sum of the measures of the two nonadjacent (remote) interior angles, or 180° minus the measure of the adjacent interior angle.

In the figure, a, b, and c are interior angles. Therefore, $a + b + c = 180$. The exterior angle d is equal to the sum of the two remote interior angles: a and b.

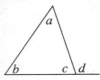

The **altitude** (or height) of a triangle is the perpendicular distance from a vertex to the side opposite the vertex. The altitude can fall inside the triangle, outside the triangle, or on one of the sides.

Altitude = AD

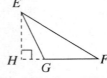
Altitude = EH

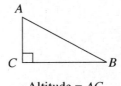
Altitude = AC

Sides and angles: The length of any side of a triangle is less than the sum of the lengths of the other two sides and greater than the positive difference between the lengths of the other two sides.

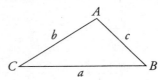

$b + c > a > b - c$

$a + b > c > a - b$

$a + c > b > a - c$

If the lengths of two sides of a triangle are unequal, the greater angle lies opposite the longer side, and vice versa. In the figure, if $A > B > C$, then $a > b > c$.

Area of a triangle: The area of a triangle is $\frac{1}{2}$ base × height

Example: In the following diagram, the base has length 4 and the altitude length 3, so you write:

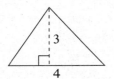

KAPLAN

$A = \frac{1}{2}bh$

$= \frac{1}{2} \times 4 \times 3 = 6$

When two sides of a triangle are perpendicular to each other, the area is easy to find. In a right triangle, the two sides that form the 90° angle are called the **legs.** Then the area is one-half the product of the legs, or

$A = \frac{1}{2}bh$

$= \frac{1}{2}(\text{Leg}_1)(\text{Leg}_2)$

Perimeter of a triangle: The **perimeter** of a triangle is equal to the sum of the lengths of the sides.

Example: In the triangle below, the sides are of lengths 5, 6, and 8. Therefore, the perimeter is 5 + 6 + 8, or 19.

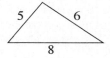

Isosceles triangles: An **isosceles triangle** is a triangle that has two sides of equal length. The two equal sides are called **legs** and the third side is called the **base**.

Since the two legs have the same length, the two angles opposite the legs must have the same measure. In the figure below, $PQ = PR$ and $\angle R = \angle Q$.

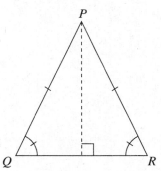

Equilateral triangles: An **equilateral triangle** has three sides of equal length and three 60° angles.

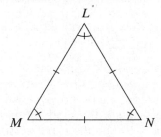

Similar triangles: Triangles are **similar** if they have the same shape—if corresponding angles have the same measure. For instance, any two triangles whose angles measure 30°, 60°, and 90° are similar. In similar triangles, corresponding sides are in the same ratio. Triangles are **congruent** if corresponding angles have the same measure and corresponding sides have the same length.

Example: What is the perimeter of △*DEF* below.

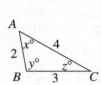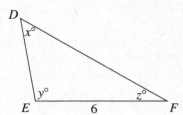

Each triangle has an *x*° angle, a *y*° angle, and a *z*° angle; therefore, they are similar, and corresponding sides are in the same ratio. *BC* and *EF* are corresponding sides; each is opposite the *x*° angle. Since *EF* is twice the length of *BC*, *each* side of △*DEF* will be twice the length of the corresponding side of △*ABC*. Therefore, *DE* = 2(*AB*), or 4, and *DF* = 2(*AC*), or 8. The perimeter of △*DEF* is 4 + 6 + 8 = 18.

The ratio of the areas of two similar triangles is the square of the ratio of corresponding lengths. For instance, in the example above, because each side of △*DEF* is 2 times the length of the corresponding side of △*ABC*, △*DEF* must have 2^2 or 4 times the area of △*ABC*:

$$\frac{\text{Area }(\triangle DEF)}{\text{Area }(\triangle ABC)} = \left(\frac{DE}{AB}\right)^2 = \left(\frac{2}{1}\right)^2 = 4$$

Right Triangles

A right triangle has one interior angle of 90°. The longest side (which lies opposite the right angle, the largest angle of a right triangle) is called the **hypotenuse**. The other two sides are called the **legs**.

Pythagorean theorem: $(\text{Leg}_1)^2 + (\text{Leg}_2)^2 = (\text{Hypotenuse})^2$ or $a^2 + b^2 = c^2$

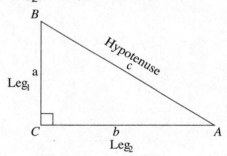

Some sets of integers happen to satisfy the Pythagorean theorem. These sets of integers are commonly referred to as Pythagorean Triplets. One very common set to remember is 3, 4, and 5. This is the most common kind of right triangle on the SAT. In addition, any multiple of these lengths makes another Pythagorean Triplet: for instance, $6^2 + 8^2 = 10^2$, so 6, 8, and 10 also make a right triangle. One other triplet that appears occasionally is 5, 12, and 13.

Example: What is the length of the hypotenuse of an isosceles right triangle with legs of length 4? Since you're told the triangle is isosceles, you know two of the sides have the same length. You know the hypotenuse can't be the same length as one of the legs (the hypotenuse must be the longest side), so it must be the two legs that are equal. Therefore, in this example, the two legs have length 4, and you can use the Pythagorean theorem to find the hypotenuse.

$$\text{Hypotenuse}^2 = 4^2 + 4^2$$
$$= 16 + 16$$
$$= 32$$
$$\text{Hypotenuse} = \sqrt{32} + 4\sqrt{2}$$

There are two special kinds of right triangles, that always have the same ratios. They are:

$1:1:\sqrt{2}$

(for isosceles right triangles)

$1:\sqrt{3}:2$

(for 30–60–90 triangles)

You could use the Pythagorean theorem to find the sides in these triangles as well.

RIGHT TRIANGLES AND TRIGONOMETRY

The ACT will have 3-4 questions testing trigonometry concepts of sine, cosine, and tangent. The acronym SOHCAHTOA explains the relationship of these terms.

The Sine of an angle is the measure of the side **Opposite** the angle divided by **the hypotenuse**;

(Sine = $\dfrac{\text{opposite}}{\text{hypotenuse}}$ or SOH)

The Cosine of an angle is the measure of the side **adjacent** to the angle divided by the **hypotenuse**;

(Cosine = $\dfrac{\text{adjacent}}{\text{hypotenuse}}$ or CAH)

The tangent of an angle is the measure of the side **opposite** the angle divided by the **hypotenuse**;

(Tangent = $\dfrac{\text{opposite}}{\text{adjacent}}$ or TOA)

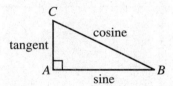

The reciprocals of these functions are less frequently tested but good to know.

Cotangent = $\dfrac{1}{\text{tangent}}$ or $\dfrac{\text{adjacent}}{\text{opposite}}$

Secant   = $\dfrac{1}{\text{cosine}}$ or $\dfrac{\text{hypotenuse}}{\text{adjacent}}$

Cosecant = $\dfrac{1}{\text{sine}}$ or $\dfrac{\text{hypotenuse}}{\text{opposite}}$

TRIANGLES EXERCISE

Solve the following problems. (Answers follow.)

> The sum of the measures of the angles in a triangle is 180°.

In 1–4, find the missing angles.

1.

x =

2.
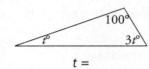

t =

3.
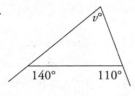

v =

4.
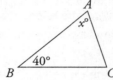

AB = BC

x =

> In a right triangle, $\text{Leg}_1^2 + \text{Leg}_2^2 = \text{Hypotenuse}^2$.

In 5–12, find the missing sides.

5.
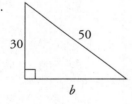

b =

6.
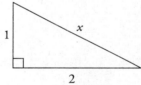

x =

7.
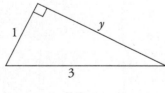

v =

8.
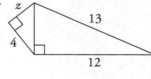

z =

> The ratio of the sides in an isosceles right triangle is $1:1:\sqrt{2}$

9.

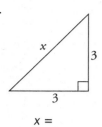

x =

10.

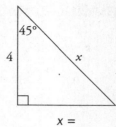

x =

The ratio of the sides in a 30–60–90 triangle is 1:√3:2.

11.

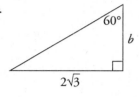

b =

12.

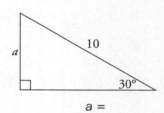

a =

The area of a triangle is $\frac{1}{2}$ (base × height).

In 13–16, find the area of the triangles.

13.

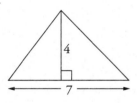

Area =

14.

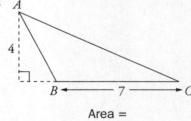

Area =

15.

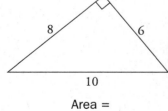

Area =

16.

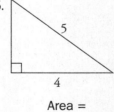

Area =

ANSWER KEY—TRIANGLES EXERCISE

1. 60

2. 20

3. 70

4. 70

5. 40

6. $\sqrt{5}$

7. $\sqrt{8}$ or $2\sqrt{2}$

8. 3

9. $\sqrt{18}$ or $3\sqrt{2}$

10. $4\sqrt{2}$

11. 2

12. 5

13. 14

14. 14

15. 24

16. 6

DATA ANALYSIS

To answer questions about graphs and charts pull the correct information from the graph or chart. Identify the title, the *x*-axis, the *y*-axis, and any labels in the chart or graph before you begin. Be sure you know exactly what information is being presented. Pay careful attention to units of measurement.

Example:

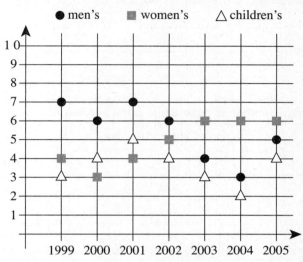

Jackets Sold at Mike's Sporting Goods, in thousands

● men's   ■ women's   △ children's

In this graph, the *x*-axis represents years and the *y*-axis represents jackets sold (in thousands). The graph includes three different types of jackets, which you would need to distinguish to answer questions about the graph.

Questions about pie charts often rely on your knowing the total amount represented by the chart. Be sure to spot that crucial piece of information.

Example:

**Pets Seen at
Veterinary Clinic Last Week**

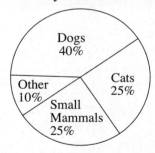

Total number of pets = 260

How many cats were seen at the veterinary clinic last week? 25% of 260, or 260 × 0.25 = 65.

Matrices

Matrix problems involve combining information from more than one chart.

Example:

Plants in Tom's Garden		
	# of plants	# of vegetables per plant
tomato	3	18
pepper	5	10
zucchini	1	24

Number of Vegetables Used in Recipes		
	1 pan of vegetable lasagna	1 jar of pasta sauce
tomato	5	20
pepper	4	5
zucchini	4	2

If Tom makes two jars of pasta sauce and one pan of vegetable lasagna from the vegetables in his garden, how many tomatoes will he have left over?

Tom has a total of 3 × 18 = 54 tomatoes. He uses a total of (2 × 20) + 5 = 45 tomatoes in the recipes. Therefore, he has 54 − 45 = 9 tomatoes left over.

WRITING

VERB TENSES

English has six tenses, each of which has a simple form and a progressive form.

	Simple	Progressive
Present	I work	I am working
Past	I worked	I was working
Future	I will work	I will be working
Present Perfect	I have worked	I have been working
Past Perfect	I had worked	I had been working
Future Perfect	I will have worked	I will have been working

Verb tenses should accurately reflect the time frame(s) discussed in a sentence.

1. **Use the present tense for:**

   Actions or states occurring in the present time:

   *I **am** a student.*

   *They **are studying** the Holy Roman Empire.*

   Habitual actions:

   *They **eat** in the cafeteria every day.*

   *My father never **drinks** coffee.*

   Things that are always true:

   *Grass **is** green.*

   *Students **take** geometry during their junior year.*

2. **Use the past tense for actions or states that took place at a specific time in the past and are now completed.**

   *Norman **broke** his toe when he **tripped** over his son's tricycle.*

3. **Use the future tense for actions expected in the future.**

   *I **will call** you on Wednesday.*

4. **Use the present perfect tense for:**

   Actions and states that started in the past and continue into the present:

   *I **have been living** here for two years.*

   Actions and states that occurred a number of times in the past and may occur again in the future:

   *I **have heard** that song several times on the radio.*

   Actions and states that occurred at an unspecified time in the past:

   *Anna **has seen** that movie already.*

5. **Use the past perfect tense for past actions or states that were completed prior to other past actions or states.**

   The more recent past event is expressed in the simple past, and the earlier past event is expressed in the past perfect.

When I **turned on** my computer this morning, I realized that I **had exited** the program without saving my work.

6. **Use the future perfect tense for a future actions or states that will take place before other future actions or states.**

   By the end of this week, I **will have worked** four hours of overtime.

Irregular verbsmay have different forms for the simple past tense and for the past participle used with the perfect tenses.

Here are some common irregular verbs:

Present	Past	Past Participle
Am	Was	Been
Begin	Began	Begun
Bring	Brought	Brought
Come	Came	Come
Do	Did	Done
Drive	Drove	Driven
Eat	Ate	Eaten
Fall	Fell	Fallen
Get	Got	Got/gotten
Grow	Grew	Grown
Know	Knew	Known
Leave	Left	Left
Read	Read	Read
Ride	Rode	Ridden
Run	Ran	Run
Speak	Spoke	Spoken
Take	Took	Taken
Wear	Wore	Worn
Write	Wrote	Written

VERB TENSES EXERCISE

Choose the appropriate verb tense in the following examples.

1. They *had been/have been* calling Susan when she arrived at their house.

2. There *are/were* so many reports of psychic activity that one cannot easily dismiss the phenomenon.

3. I was just about to *sit/sat* down and take a nap when the doorbell rang.

4. Tony thanked Tina for the present that she *had given/gived* him.

5. When I *was/am* older, I will move out of my parents' house and get my own apartment.

6. All last summer, I *swam/swum* in our pool; as a result, my hair turned green.

7. Jeff walked right into a beehive and was badly *stang/stung*.

8. By the end of next week, I *have finished/will have finished* my term paper.

9. As soon as the sun set, the vampire *rised/rose* out of his coffin.

10. Sabrina's mom *had laid/laid* the baby boy down after he fell asleep.

ANSWER KEY—VERB TENSES EXERCISE

1. had been

2. are

3. sit

4. had given

5. am

6. swam

7. stung

8. will have finished

9. rose

10. laid

PRONOUNS

Personal pronouns are identified by person, gender, number, and case.

Person	Number	Subjective	Objective	Possessive
First Person	Singular	I	Me	My, mine
Second Person	Singular	You	You	Your, yours
Third Person: Masculine	Singular	He	Him	His
Feminine	Singular	She	Her	Her
Neutral	Singular	It	It	Its
Third Person	Plural	They	Them	Their, theirs

1. **A pronoun's antecedent is the noun to which it refers.**

   Pronouns must agree in both gender and number with their antecedent nouns. A singular pronoun should stand in for a singular antecedent; a plural pronoun should stand in for a plural antecedent.

   Mary was late for work because *she* forgot to set the alarm.

   Seniors will get *their* report cards next Friday.

   A pronoun's antecedent may appear after it in a sentence.

   Because *she* forgot to set the alarm, *Mary* was late for work.

   After *their* report cards are issued, the *seniors* will practice for graduation.

2. **Use the subjective case:**

   When a pronoun is the subject of a verb:

   She works for an insurance company.

   My brother is thrilled that ***he got*** *a part in the school play.*

   After ***they return*** *from vacation, the Madigans will be moving to Boston.*

   As the subject of a verb that is not stated but understood:

   Gary is taller than ***she*** *(is).*

   They arrived earlier than ***we*** *(did).*

3. **Use the objective case:**

   When a pronoun is the object of a verb, verb form, or preposition:

   Give that to ***me.***

   I called ***him*** *on the phone.*

   Asking ***them*** *to go was a big mistake.*

   In comparisons between objects of verbs that are not stated but understood:

   She calls you more than (she calls) ***me.***

   They'll have to pay professionals more than (they'll have to pay) ***us.***

4. **Use the relative pronouns *who* and *whom* when referring to people.**

   Who is the subjective case pronoun used to refer to people.

   The woman ***who*** *is standing at the piano is my sister.*

Whom is the objective case pronoun used to refer to people.

*The woman with **whom** I am staying is my sister.*

If you're not sure whether *who* or *whom* is correct in a sentence, try this:

*Sylvester, (**who** or **whom**?) is afraid of the dark, sleeps with the lights on.*

Look at the relative pronoun and turn its clause into a question.

***Who** or **whom** is afraid of the dark?*

Then answer the question with a personal pronoun.

***He** is.*

If you answer the question with a subjective case pronoun the subjective case *who* is correct.

*Sylvester, **who** is afraid of the dark, sleeps with the lights on.*

If you answer the question with an objective case, the objective case *whom* is correct.

*To (**who** or **whom**?) should I address the letter?*

Adress it to him, so the form should be To whom should I address the letter?

5. **Use the relative pronouns *which* and *that* to refer to inanimate objects.**

    Generally, *which* is used to introduce a phrase or clause set off by commas, and *that* is used within the body of a sentence.

    *The hotel **that** we stayed in had an indoor swimming pool.*

    *The hotel, **which** has an indoor swimming pool, is one of our favorites.*

6. **Pronouns must have clear, unambiguous antecedents.**

    A pronoun is *ambiguous* if it is used with no antecedent.

    *WRONG: Joe doesn't like the music **they** play on this radio station.*

    Who are *they*? We can't tell, because there is no antecedent for the pronoun.

    A pronoun is also ambiguous when it could logically refer to more than one antecedent.

    *WRONG: Linda and Amy went to the concert in **her** car.*

    Whose car did they use? We don't know, since *her* could refer to either Linda or Amy.

    Ambiguity errors can be corrected by replacing the pronoun with the appropriate noun.

    *Joe doesn't like what **the disc jockeys** play on this radio station.*

    *Linda and Amy went to the concert in **Amy's** car.*

PRONOUN AGREEMENT EXERCISE

Choose the appropriate pronoun in the following examples.

1. The *Declaration of Independence* argues that people have a right to fight for *one's/their* rights.

2. The employees respected their manager's energy, even if they didn't always understand *her/their* ideas.

3. Nobody who visits the Grand Canyon can help but feel that *he/they* saw something impressive.

4. The audience gave a standing ovation, enthusiastically showing *its/their* approval.

5. The children were annoyed because *it was/they were* only allowed to watch an hour of television a day.

6. When the whale breached the water, the group ran over to the side of the boat as though *it was/they were* one body.

7. People are bound to get angry when *she realizes/they realize* that this "once in a lifetime opportunity" is really just a scam.

8. One should always be aware of *their/one's* surroundings when sitting in a public place.

9. The number of people required to change a lightbulb *is/are* a common premise for a joke.

10. Mr. Matray was famous for giving his students partial credit on *his/their* experiment reports.

ANSWER KEY—PRONOUN AGREEMENT EXERCISE

1. their

2. her

3. he

4. its

5. they were

6. it

7. they realize

8. one's

9. is

10. their

PRONOUN CASE EXERCISE

Choose the appropriate pronoun in the following examples.

1. To *who/whom* shall I address this letter?

2. The writer, about *who/whom* I had read, was disappointing in person.

3. Dominic hates it when anyone does better than *he/him* in class.

4. Years later, my mom still talks about her tenth-grade teacher and wonders what happened to *she/her*.

5. Benjamin Franklin was a proponent of the American philosophical movement *which/who* tried to reconcile material gain and spirituality.

6. Betsy and *I/me* were friends for a long time before she moved away.

7. I really appreciated it when you gave that birthday card to *I/me*.

8. Leslie and *she/her* can be annoying when they drink too much caffeine.

9. Even though people thought it couldn't happen, you and *we/us* have managed to become good friends.

10. Although Carol plays tennis very infrequently, *she/her* is a better player than Sharon.

ANSWER KEY—PRONOUN CASE EXERCISE

1. whom

2. whom

3. he

4. her

5. which

6. I

7. me

8. she

9. we

10. she

WHO, WHICH, AND *THAT* EXERCISE

Choose *who*, *which*, or *that* for each of the following sentences.

1. Our knowledge of UN intervention in foreign affairs is based on a report _____ the governor received.

2. The truck, _____ was full of logs, could not proceed up the hill.

3. The Constitution essentially endorsed the concept _____ all people are created equal.

4. The incumbents _____ will be nominated for reelection are on the stage.

5. Expectations for growth in the coming year, _____ economists inside and outside the administration approved, will be reported next month.

6. Give these ballet shoes to the dancer _____ is sitting backstage.

ANSWER KEY—*WHO, WHICH,* AND *THAT* EXERCISE

1. that

2. which

3. that

4. who

5. which

6. who

PRONOUN SHIFT EXERCISE

Choose the appropriate pronoun in the following examples.

1. Conventional wisdom has it that one should not be too uptight; otherwise, *one/you* will miss out on the fun in life.

2. The puppy in the window looked so plaintive that one felt sorry for it, and *one/you* wanted to buy it immediately.

3. When a camper visits Glacier Park, *she/they* is given advice on how to avoid grizzly bears.

4. By being alert, you can reduce the odds that *one/you* will be a crime victim.

5. One cannot help but be amazed by the scientific advances in the past century, especially if *one/you* studies the history of science.

6. You shouldn't care what other people say about you, but sometimes *one/you* can't help feeling hurt by critical remarks.

7. It is really hard for one to understand the immensity of a giant redwood tree until *one/you* is standing under it.

8. You may not be fond of classical music, but this new compilation of Chopin's greatest hits will still greatly impress *one/you*.

9. One should not go camping unless *one has/you have* a good pair of hiking boots.

10. When in Rome, one should do as the Romans do, but in English-speaking countries, *one/you* should call the Italian city of Livorno "Leghorn."

ANSWER KEY—PRONOUN SHIFT EXERCISE

1. one

2. one

3. she

4. you

5. one

6. you

7. one

8. you

9. one has

10. one

PRONOUN AMBIGUITY EXERCISE

Circle the ambiguous pronouns in the following examples, and rewrite the part of each sentence that is unclear.

1. The number of people who call tech support to ask questions about computers shows that they are confusing.

    Rewrite:

    _____

    _____

2. Some people prefer women's pro basketball because they do not talk as much trash as men's.

    Rewrite:

    _____

    _____

3. Don't believe everything you read in print because you do not know if they are telling the truth.

    Rewrite:

    _____

    _____

4. Many people went to the PTA-sponsored prom party because they weren't chaperoned.

    Rewrite:

    _____

    _____

5. Susan told Mary that she needed to eat more protein.

    Rewrite:

    _____

    _____

6. People placed bets on the Superbowl teams, confident that they would win.

    Rewrite:

    _____

    _____

7. Todd searched the Internet to see what kinds of cheap airfare they had.

    Rewrite:

    _____

    _____

8. The miniseries was well acted, but they failed to get all the historical details right.

   Rewrite:

   _____

   _____

9. Before going to college, Sam gave Alex a copy of her favorite CD.

   Rewrite:

   _____

   _____

10. They've really done a great job with the latest handbook.

    Rewrite:

    _____

    _____

ANSWER KEY—PRONOUN AMBIGUITY EXERCISE

1. Ambiguous pronoun: *they*

   Rewrite: The number of people who call tech support to ask questions about computers shows that *computers* are confusing.

2. Ambiguous pronoun: *they*

   Rewrite: Some people prefer women's pro basketball because *the female players* do not talk as much trash as the men.

3. Ambiguous pronoun: *they*

   Rewrite: Don't believe everything you read in print because you do not know if *the writers* are telling the truth.

4. Ambiguous pronoun: *they*

   Rewrite: Many people went to the PTA-sponsored prom party because *there weren't any chaperones*.

5. Ambiguous pronoun: *she*

   Rewrite: Susan told Mary *to eat more protein*.

6. Ambiguous pronoun: *they*

   Rewrite: *People were confident that they would win when they placed bets on the Superbowl teams.*

7. Ambiguous pronoun: *they*

   Rewrite: Todd searched the Internet to see what kinds of cheap airfare *the airlines* had.

8. Ambiguous pronoun: *they*

   Rewrite: The miniseries was well acted, but *the producers* failed to get all the historical details right.

9. Ambiguous pronoun: *her*

   Rewrite: Before going to college, Sam gave *a copy of her favorite CD to Alex*.

10. Ambiguous pronoun: *they*

    Rewrite: *The authors* have really done a great job with the latest handbook.

USAGE REVIEW

1. A **phrase** is a group of words that does not contain both a subject and a verb.

   looking out the window

   behind the scenes

2. A **clause** is a group of words that contains both a subject and a verb. Clauses can be independent, meaning they can stand alone as sentences:

   I was looking out the window.

   Fresh corn is now on sale at the farmer's market.

   or subordinate, meaning they cannot:

   because I was looking out the window

   which is now on sale at the farmer's market

3. A **sentence** is a group of words that contains at least one independent clause and expresses a complete thought. To do so, a sentence must contain a subject, about which something is said, and a predicate verb, which says something about the subject.

   I was looking out the window when the car passed by.

   We went behind the scenes to learn how a television news show is produced.

   Fresh corn is one of the vegetables now on sale at the farmer's market.

RUN-ONS AND FRAGMENTS

1. **A sentence that does not contain at least one independent clause is a fragment.**

   A sentence fragment may be grammatically incomplete because it lacks a subject or a predicate verb:

   WRONG: Fresh corn on sale at the farmer's market.

   WRONG: Going behind the scenes to learn how a news show is produced.

   Or logically incomplete because other elements necessary for it to express a complete thought are missing:

   WRONG: I was looking out the window when.

   WRONG: Because fresh corn is on sale.

   A sentence fragment can be corrected by adding the missing element(s) to the sentence:

   *Fresh corn **is** on sale at the farmer's market.*

   Or by combining it with an independent clause:

   *Going behind the scenes to learn how a news show is produced, **our media class learned a great deal in a very short time.***

2. **A sentence containing multiple independent clauses that are not properly combined is a run-on.**

   WRONG: The children had been playing in the park they were covered with mud.

   WRONG: The children had been playing in the park, they were covered with mud.

   A run-on sentence can be corrected by making each clause a separate sentence:

   The children had been playing in the park. They were covered with mud

   By combining the independent clauses with a semicolon:

*The children had been playing in the **park; they** were covered with mud.*

By making one of the clauses subordinate:

Because the children had been playing in the park, *they were covered with mud.*

The children who had been playing in the park *were covered with mud.*

The children had been playing in the park, ***which was why they were covered with mud.***

Or by joining the clauses with a comma and a coordinating conjunction:

The children had been playing in the park, ***and*** *they were covered with mud.*

The children had been playing in the park, ***so*** *they were covered with mud.*

(Coordinating conjunctions include *for, and, nor, but, or, yet,* and *so.* Use the mnemonic FANBOYS to help you remember them.)

SENTENCE STRUCTURE EXERCISE

Circle the subject and the predicate verb in the following examples.

1. The weather forecast promised sunshine for the upcoming weekend.

2. The number of people requesting a refund is too large for the store to accommodate.

3. By accident, I opened my book to exactly the page that I wanted.

4. Low-fat ice cream does not taste as good as regular ice cream.

5. After visiting New Orleans, Susan understood why it was called "The Big Easy."

6. Only when the heels on his boots gave out did Seppy buy a new pair.

7. Grant celebrated getting into college by going out for pizza.

8. Exhausted from the arduous course, the cyclists took a well-deserved break at the top of the hill.

9. Most people believe that if something sounds too good to be true, it probably is.

10. The color blue has been proven to have a calming effect on human beings.

ANSWER KEY—SENTENCE STRUCTURE EXERCISE

In each example, the subject is underlined and the verb is in italics.

1. The <u>weather forecast</u> *promised* sunshine for the upcoming weekend.

2. The <u>number of people</u> requesting a refund *is* too large for the store to accommodate.

3. By accident, <u>I</u> *opened* my book at exactly the page that I wanted.

4. <u>Low-fat ice cream</u> *does not taste* as good as regular ice cream.

5. After visiting New Orleans, <u>Susan</u> *understood* why it was called "The Big Easy."

6. Only when the heels on his boots gave out *did* <u>Seppy</u> *buy* a new pair.

7. <u>Grant</u> *celebrated* getting into college by going out for pizza.

8. Exhausted from the arduous course, <u>the cyclists</u> *took* a well-deserved break at the top of the hill.

9. <u>Most people</u> *believe* that if something sounds too good to be true, it probably *is*.

10. <u>The color blue</u> *has been proven* to have a calming effect on human beings.

SENTENCE FRAGMENTS EXERCISE

Make the following sentence fragments into complete sentences. You may need to modify the sentence structure, cross out superfluous words, or replace the verb.

1. After great deliberation, the CEO of the corporation, deciding to end his bid to acquire the software company.

   Rewrite:

   _____

   _____

2. Upon discovering the theft in the office, the employees, suspecting one another.

   Rewrite:

   _____

   _____

3. The toy store employees, overwhelmed by children and adults, trying to keep the shelves fully stocked with action figures.

   Rewrite:

   _____

   _____

4. The point of going to school is not only to get an education, also socializing.

   Rewrite:

   _____

   _____

5. The fashion industry, by going to local high schools and seeing what styles teenagers were favoring, designing a new line.

   Rewrite:

   _____

   _____

6. Weddings being popular occasions because they tend to be joyous, with great dancing, cheering, and feasting.

   Rewrite:

   _____

   _____

7. The scholar, observing the tendency of TV ads to be cynical, offbeat, and humorous, calling them postmodern.

   Rewrite:

   _____

   _____

8. The knight, determined to save his castle, fighting mightily to the end.
   Rewrite:

   _____

   _____

9. Designed by Japanese immigrants, the tea gardens reflecting the aesthetics of the East.
   Rewrite:

   _____

   _____

10. Because Erin likes word games, she frequently doing the crossword puzzle.
    Rewrite:

    _____

    _____

ANSWER KEY—SENTENCE FRAGMENTS EXERCISE

(Your answers may differ.)

1. After great deliberation, the CEO of the corporation decided to end his bid to acquire the software company.

2. Upon discovering the theft in the office, the employees began to suspect one another.

3. The toy store employees, overwhelmed by children and adults, tried to keep the shelves fully stocked with action figures.

4. The point of going to school is not only to get an education, but also to socialize.

5. By going to local high schools and seeing what styles teenagers were favoring, the fashion industry was able to design a new line.

6. Weddings are popular occasions because they tend to be joyous, with great dancing, cheering, and feasting.

7. Observing the tendency of TV ads to be cynical, offbeat, and humorous, the scholar called them postmodern.

8. The knight, determined to save his castle, fought mightily to the end.

9. Designed by Japanese immigrants, the tea gardens reflect the aesthetics of the East.

10. Because Erin likes word games, she frequently does the crossword puzzle.

RUN-ON SENTENCES EXERCISE

Correct the following examples, using conjunctions or semicolons.

1. The historic center of town was restored, with its new look it once again bustled with activity.

   Rewrite:

   _____

   _____

2. Matt is a fencing pro, he hopes to go to the Olympics someday.

   Rewrite:

   _____

   _____

3. The European countries had a bad harvest last year, the price of wheat has risen dramatically.

   Rewrite:

   _____

   _____

4. Tea has less caffeine per cup than coffee, therefore, it is favored as a more healthy "pick-me-up."

   Rewrite:

   _____

   _____

5. The fossil was in near-perfect condition, every bone was in place, and you could even see traces of feathers.

   Rewrite:

   _____

   _____

6. U-shaped valleys were made by glaciers, V-shaped valleys were made by rivers.

   Rewrite:

   _____

   _____

7. Aaron couldn't wait until summer, there would be a wide variety of fresh fruit available.

   Rewrite:

   _____

   _____

8. Michael discovered that there is no such thing as a quick fix when it comes to dieting, the secret to maintaining a healthy weight is eating nutritious food and exercising.

   Rewrite:

   _____

   _____

9. The company wasted a lot of resources on perks for management, the employees became disgruntled.

   Rewrite:

   _____

   _____

10. Logical thinking is essential to scientific research, the irony is that scientists who make important discoveries often do so on a hunch.

    Rewrite:

    _____

    _____

ANSWER KEY—RUN-ON SENTENCES EXERCISE

(These are not the only ways to correct the run-ons; your answers may differ.)

1. The historic center of town was restored; with its new look, it once again bustled with activity.

2. Matt is a fencing pro, and he hopes to go to the Olympics someday.

3. The European countries had a bad harvest last year, so the price of wheat has risen dramatically.

4. Tea has less caffeine per cup than coffee; therefore, it is favored as a more healthy "pick-me-up."

5. The fossil was in near-perfect condition; every bone was in place, and you could even see traces of feathers.

6. U-shaped valleys were made by glaciers, and V-shaped valleys were made by rivers.

7. Aaron couldn't wait until summer, as there would be a wide variety of fresh fruit available.

8. Michael discovered that there is no such thing as a quick fix when it comes to dieting; the secret to maintaining a healthy weight is eating nutritious food and exercising.

9. The company wasted a lot of resources on perks for management, so the employees became disgruntled.

10. Logical thinking is essential to scientific research, but the irony is that scientists who make important discoveries often do so on a hunch.

CONJUNCTIONS EXERCISE

Choose the appropriate conjunction in each sentence.

1. The house was not only built out of flimsy material, *but/and* also greatly overpriced.

2. Neither Luke *nor/or* Leia knew that they were siblings.

3. Yoshi's driver's license was revoked, *and/but* he continues to drive anyway.

4. Professor Smith was late for class *and/because* he had a flat tire.

5. Josh got into the semifinals at the tennis tournament *because/but* he worked hard for it.

6. *Because/Although* she claimed not to be a feminist, she understood feminist issues thoroughly.

7. Some people believe that human beings should strive to function out of sheer rationality *but/and* suppress their emotions.

8. Since Brian dislikes math *but/and* chemistry, he does poorly in both subjects.

9. I'm not sure if I'll be able to attend the reception, *although/because* I'll be extremely busy that day.

10. The car skidded and threatened to go off a cliff, *but/and* Andrew managed to get control of it again.

ANSWER KEY—CONJUNCTIONS EXERCISE

1. but

2. nor

3. but

4. because

5. because

6. although

7. and

8. and

9. because

10. but

SUBJECT–VERB

1. A verb must agree with its subject in person.

A first-person subject means someone is making a statement about himself. First-person subjects are the pronouns *I* and *we*.

I am going to Paris.

We are going to Paris.

A second-person subject means someone is speaking directly to someone else. The second-person subject is the pronoun *you*.

You are going to Paris.

A third-person subject makes a statement about some other person, place, or thing. The third-person subjects are the pronouns *he*, *she*, *it*, and *they*, as well as all nouns.

He is going to Paris.

Annalise is going with him.

The flight will take eight hours.

2. A verb must agree with its subject in number.

A singular subject requires the singular form of a verb.

Michelle takes the bus to school every morning.

A plural subject requires the plural form of the verb.

Many students take the bus to school every morning.

Michelle and Abby take the bus to school every morning.

A verb's subject is often not the noun closest to it in the sentence.

Wild animals in jungles all over the world are endangered.

Be sure to "match" all verbs to their appropriate subject nouns.

3. Collective nouns are grammatically singular.

Collective nouns are nouns that name entities with more than one member, such as *group*, *team*, and *family*. Even though these nouns represent more than one person, they are grammatically singular and require singular verb forms.

The collection of paintings entitled "Matisse in Morocco" is one of the most widely viewed art exhibits in recent years.

A committee to study the feasibility of the renovations was appointed by the mayor.

4. Only when collective nouns are in plural form do they require plural verbs.

My collections of rare coins and canceled stamps are worth more than I thought.

Several committees were involved in choosing the final design.

SUBJECT-VERB EXERCISE

Choose the appropriate verb in the following examples.

1. Vico believes that coffee grown in Latin American countries *taste/tastes* better than coffee grown anywhere else.

2. Ice skating, with its emphasis on technique, artistry, and discipline, *is/are* one of the most demanding sports.

3. Although she worked hard in school, the alternative music scene and its interesting personalities *were/was* what truly interested Julie.

4. There *is/are* a great deal of proof that Shakespeare is the sole author of the plays attributed to him.

5. Of the many movements in art today, the emergence of modern Chinese painters *is/are* the most exciting.

6. Despite the attempt to block the publication of the book, there *is/are* many people who want to read it.

7. The movie wasn't good, but the soundtrack, with its fanfare and stirring themes, *was/were* exciting.

8. Of all the injuries Dan got while mountain climbing, the bruising of his ribs *was/were* the most painful.

9. Basketball, with its unusual athletes and gravity-defying plays, *has/have* become America's favorite sport.

10. Dmitri wants to run his own business someday, so selling magazines *is/are* something that he does not mind doing.

ANSWER KEY—SUBJECT-VERB EXERCISE

1. tastes

2. is

3. were

4. is

5. is

6. are

7. was

8. was

9. has

10. is

COMPOUND SUBJECT-VERB EXERCISE

Choose the appropriate verb in the following examples.

1. During the interview, Marian pointed out that her drive, experience, and professionalism *make/ makes* her an excellent candidate for the job.

2. Neither the critics nor the producers *understand/understands* the reason for the movie's cult-like status.

3. Pancakes, eggs, and sausage *is/are* Genevieve's favorite breakfast.

4. Greed, along with gullibility, *is the reason/are the reason* that so many people bought junk bonds.

5. Both my mom and my dad *is/are* supportive of my decision to put off college for a year.

6. Julie, as well as the rest of the class, *is/are* glad to volunteer for a worthy cause.

7. Polls show that the number of people who do not care about the latest government scandal *has/have* increased.

8. Unfamiliarity with the exam, combined with nerves, *is/are* a big reason why so many people don't do their best.

9. Neither the approaching storm nor the warning on all radio frequencies *is/are* convincing Justin to give up the search for survivors.

10. Location, location, and location *is/are* supposed to be the most important factor in real estate decisions.

ANSWER KEY—COMPOUND SUBJECT-VERB EXERCISE

1. make

2. understand

3. is

4. is the reason

5. are

6. is

7. has

8. is

9. is

10. is

PARALLELISM

1. Parallel Structure in a Series

Matching constructions must be expressed in parallel form. When a sentence contains a series or list, the items must exhibit parallel structure.

*WRONG: I love **skipping**, **jumping**, and **to play** tiddlywinks.*

*WRONG: I love **to skip**, **jump**, and **to play** tiddlywinks.*

*I love to **skip**, **jump**, and **play** tiddlywinks.*

*I love **to skip**, **to jump**, and **to play** tiddlywinks.*

*I love **skipping**, **jumping**, and **playing** tiddlywinks.*

COMPARISONS

1. Comparisons and Parallelism

Grammatically correct comparisons must compare logicalally similar things.

*WRONG: **To visualize** success is not the same as **achieving** it.*

***To visualize** success is not the same as **to achieve** it.*

***Visualizing** success is not the same as **achieving** it.*

*WRONG: **The rules of chess** are more complex than **checkers**.*

***The rules of chess** are more complex than **those of checkers**.*

***Chess** is more complex than **checkers**.*

PARALLELISM EXERCISE

Make all appropriate items in the following sentences parallel.

1. Mozart's contributions to Western music include the introduction of new instruments such as the oboe, the refinement of the symphonic form, and emphasizing melody.

   Rewrite:

   _____

   _____

2. Letting children make their own decisions is to be a good parent.

   Rewrite:

   _____

   _____

3. After training at an obedience school, my dog is able to sit, to heel, and plays dead.

   Rewrite:

   _____

   _____

4. The talk show host promised to stop exploiting his guests, cease covering sensational stories, and that substantial issues would become his top priority.

   Rewrite:

   _____

   _____

5. The success of any television show depends on the actors, the sponsors, and it must have good scripts.

   Rewrite:

   _____

   _____

6. Before we leave, we must turn out the lights, lock the door, and leaving a note for Cindy.

   Rewrite:

   _____

   _____

ANSWER KEY—PARALLELISM EXERCISE

(Your answers may differ.)

1. Mozart's contributions to western music include the introduction of new instruments such as the oboe, the refinement of the symphonic form, and an emphasis on melody.

2. Letting children make their own decisions is being a good parent.

3. After training at an obedience school, my dog is able to sit, to heel, and to play dead.

4. The talk show host promised to stop exploiting his guests, cease covering sensational stories, and make substantial issues his top priority.

5. The success of any television show depends on the actors, the sponsors, and the scripts.

6. Before we leave, we must turn out the lights, lock the door, and leave a note for Cindy.

COMPARISONS EXERCISE

Circle the items that are being compared, then rewrite each sentence so that the compared items are parallel.

1. Jane Austen's books are still famous today as much for her acute observation of human behavior as they are because people just love to read her witty dialogue.
   Rewrite:
   _____
   _____

2. In order to pass the proficiency exam, you must be both a fluent speaker of French and able to read it.
   Rewrite:
   _____
   _____

3. Cathy prefers to sleep late than going out for breakfast.
   Rewrite:
   _____
   _____

4. The quality of sound on a compact disc is much better than a cassette tape.
   Rewrite:
   _____
   _____

ANSWER KEY—COMPARISONS EXERCISE

1. Compared items: observation of human behavior and witty dialogue

    Rewrite: Jane Austen's books are still famous today as much for her acute observation of human behavior as for her witty dialogue.

2. Compared items: fluent speaker and able to read it

    Rewrite: In order to pass the proficiency exam, you must be both a fluent speaker and reader of French.

3. Compared items: sleep late and going out for breakfast

    Rewrite: Cathy prefers sleeping late to going out for breakfast.

4. Compared items: quality of sound on a compact disc and a cassette tape

    Rewrite: The quality of sound on a compact disc is much better than that on a cassette tape.

IDIOMS

1. Some idioms must be constructed in a certain way to be correct.

Between . . . and:

RIGHT: **Between** *hot hogs* **and** *hamburgers, I prefer hamburgers.*

Not only . . . but also:

RIGHT: This semester, Matt is taking **not only** *chemistry* **but also** *biology.*

As . . . as:

RIGHT: That suit is **as** *expensive* **as** *this one.*

Either . . . or/Neither . . . nor:

Either *Debby* **or** *Alec will meet the plane*

2. Common Idioms

There is no complete list of all possible idioms. Notice how they are used as you read, especially in your ACT practice.

3. Infinitives, Gerunds, and Participles

Infinitives are verb forms that are preceded by the word *to*, such as *to eat, to grow, to run*.

Gerunds are verb forms that end with *-ing* and act as nouns. (*Swimming* is my hobby; *skating* is fun.)

Participles are verb forms that end with *-ing* that act as adjectives (*swimming* pool, *skating* rink).

In Writing section questions, if you see an infinitive or a gerund underlined, check for idioms errors.

Try to establish a list of words followed by infinitives, or followed by gerunds.

PREPOSITIONS EXERCISE

Choose the appropriate preposition in the following examples.

1. cannot put up *with/by* his reckless behavior.

2. The amulet supposedly protects one *from/of* evil spirits.

3. I get really tired of waiting *with/on* customers in my new job.

4. The suspect repeatedly told the police that he should not be charged *for/with* the crime.

5. Compared *to/by* French, English has many more words.

6. Since he was a small boy, Joe dreamed *about/to* traveling to distant lands.

7. Rick and Steve were total opposites; there were no two things that they could agree *upon/with*.

8. Cybil politely told the hostess that she did not care *for/about* spinach.

9. Because he is colorblind, Jake has a hard time distinguishing red *from/between* blue.

10. After I became familiar *with/to* the format of the test, I got a much higher score.

ANSWER KEY—PREPOSITIONS EXERCISE

1. with

2. from

3. on

4. with

5. to

6. about

7. upon

8. for

9. from

10. with

INFINITIVES AND GERUNDS EXERCISE

In each sentence, identify and correct the idiomatic error, if there is one.

1. Through this new ad campaign, we hope for tripling our gross income by the end of the year.

    Rewrite:

    _____

    _____

2. Despite the Preservation Society's efforts to save the old mill, the overwhelming majority of city council members voted to raze it.

    Rewrite:

    _____

    _____

3. Questioning a store owner's right of carrying a gun is not the purpose of this City Council meeting.

    Rewrite:

    _____

    _____

4. Arthur Rubinstein was long ranked among the world's finest pianists, although he was sometimes known as playing several wrong notes in a single performance.

    Rewrite:

    _____

    _____

5. Grading research papers over the years, the professor became expert at recognizing submissions that had been plagiarized or inadequately documented.

    Rewrite:

    _____

    _____

ANSWER KEY—INFINITIVES AND GERUNDS EXERCISE

1. Replace *for tripling* with *to triple*.

2. This sentence has no idiomatic error; the use of infinitives (*to save* and *to raze*) is correct.

3. Replace *of carrying* with *to carry*.

4. Replace *as playing* with *to play*.

5. This sentence has no idiomatic error; the use of the gerunds (*grading* and *recognizing*) is correct.

MODIFIERS

1. **Often modifying phrases can sound correct but are not, due to misplaced modifiers. When a sentence begins with a phrase, followed by a coma, read carefully and ask what is being described; you will then be able to spot the error.**

   WRONG: ***Flying*** *for the first time, the* **roar** *of the jet engines frightened the child.*

   As this sentence is written, the phrase *Flying for the first time* describes *the roar of the jet engines.* What should this phrase logically be modifying?

   Flying for the first time, *the* **child** *was frightened by the roar of the jet engines.*

2. **Use adjectives to modify nouns and pronouns.**

   A woman in a **white** *dress stood next to the* **old** *tree.*

   The **leaky** *boat hadn't been used in* **many** *years.*

3. **Use adverbs to modify verbs, adjectives, and other adverbs.**

   Many, but not all, adverbs end in -ly.

   The interviewer looked **approvingly** *at the* **neatly** *dressed applicant.*

   That movie was **very** *long.*

   Don't eat **too quickly**.

MODIFIERS EXERCISE

Rewrite each example so that the modifier is positioned to modify the proper word or phrase.

1. Staring blankly, the computer screen flickered while Joanna sat at her desk.

   Rewrite:

   _____

   _____

2. Carrying a basket on her hip, the water jug was supported by the woman.

   Rewrite:

   _____

   _____

3. Reflecting the sunlight, the sun shone down on the ocean.

   Rewrite:

   _____

   _____

4. Dripping with grease, Grandmother placed the casserole on the table.

   Rewrite:

   _____

   _____

5. Running on only one cylinder, Sarah slowly drove the car into the garage.

   Rewrite:

   _____

   _____

6. Raised by the aquarium staff, Michael fed the baby sea otters.

   Rewrite:

   _____

   _____

7. Painted in brilliant hues of green, the artist sold his painting of the forest for more than he had anticipated.

   Rewrite:

   _____

   _____

8. Breaking into a canter, Leanne rode the horse around the ring.

   Rewrite:

   _____

   _____

9. Pushing the baby bird out of the nest, George watched as the mother bird encouraged her young to fly.

   Rewrite:

   _____

   _____

10. Developed in secrecy, the scientist patented the vaccine.

    Rewrite:

    _____

    _____

ANSWER KEY—MODIFIERS EXERCISE

1. Staring blankly, Joanna sat at her desk while the computer screen flickered.

2. Carrying a basket on her hip, the woman supported the water jug.

3. The sun shone down on the ocean, which reflected the sunlight.

4. Grandmother placed the casserole, dripping with grease, on the table.

5. Sarah slowly drove the car, running on only one cylinder, into the garage.

6. Michael fed the baby sea otters that were raised by the aquarium staff.

7. The artist sold his painting of the forest, painted in brilliant hues of green, for more than he had anticipated.

8. The horse broke into a canter as Leanne rode around the ring.

9. As George watched, the mother bird pushed the baby bird out of the nest, encouraging her young to fly.

10. The scientist patented the vaccine she had developed in secrecy.

AMBIGUOUS MODIFIERS EXERCISE

Rewrite the sentences below to correct the ambiguous modifiers.

1. Ted and Patricia stood talking about the play in the hallway.

   (The play was in a theater.)

   Rewrite:

   _____

   _____

2. The dentist instructed him regularly to brush his teeth.

   (The dentist only spoke to him once a year.)

   Rewrite:

   _____

   _____

3. Laurel said in her house she had all the nice photos.

   (Laurel said this in school.)

   Rewrite:

   _____

   _____

ANSWER KEY—AMBIGUOUS MODIFIERS EXERCISE

1. Ted and Patricia stood in the hallway, talking about the play.

2. The dentist instructed him to brush his teeth regularly.

3. Laurel said she had all the nice photos in her house.

Does there need to be a narrative on comparatives/superlatives?

COMPARATIVES/SUPERLATIVES EXERCISE

Choose the right form for the adjectives and adverbs in the following examples.

1. Among cherries, strawberries, and plums, I like cherries *better/the best*.

2. Steve is the *nicer/nicest* twin in the Johnson family.

3. Of all the Harry Potter books, I like the first one *more/the most*.

4. Tim gets to stay up late because he is the *older/oldest* of the three of us.

5. When the five of us sing, Crystal attracts *more/the most* attention from the audience.

6. Between thé English landscape painters Turner and Constable, I like Turner *better/the best*.

7. Of all my responsibilities, ordering office supplies is the *less/least* important.

8. After reading *Anna Karenina* and *War and Peace*, I found *War and Peace* to be the *more/most* interesting.

ANSWER KEY—COMPARATIVES/SUPERLATIVES EXERCISE

1. the best

2. nicer

3. the most

4. oldest

5. the most

6. better

7. least

8. more

ADJECTIVES AND ADVERBS EXERCISE

Choose the appropriate adjective or adverb in the following examples.

1. Gordon works much more *quick/quickly* since he got his new computer.

2. Though he had been nervous beforehand, Miles played his violin *beautiful/beautifully* for the audition.

3. Pete got a scholarship to a school that will be really *good/well* for him.

4. Keesha's science project showed how *easy/easily* technology can be used.

5. Fed up, Kevin's brother told him to stop behaving in such a *childish/childishly* manner.

6. The inner city will be the first area to suffer if we have another economic slump, according to a *new/newly* printed report.

7. Dil steered the car *smooth/smoothly* into the narrow parking space.

8. Jim was appreciative when his younger sister *thoughtful/thoughtfully* remembered his birthday.

9. It is sad to see that this office building, which was once full of *busy/busily* people, has become deserted and run-down.

10. Most people had great difficulty with the test, but because Juan had studied, he found it very *easy/easily*.

ANSWER KEY—ADJECTIVES AND ADVERBS EXERCISE

1. *quickly* (modifies the verb *works*)

2. *beautifully* (modifies the verb *played*)

3. *good* (modifies the noun *school*)

4. *easily* (modifies the verb phrase *can be used*)

5. *childish* (modifies the noun *manner*)

6. *newly* (modifies the verb form *printed*)

7. *smoothly* (modifies the verb *steered*)

8. *thoughtfully* (modifies the verb *remembered*)

9. *busy* (modifies the noun *people*)

10. *easy* (modifies the pronoun *it*)

WORDINESS

1. **Having unnecessary words in a sentence can result in a style problem; be concise in your writing.**

   *WORDY: The supply of **musical instruments that are antique** is limited.*

   *CONCISE: The supply of **antique musical instruments** is limited.*

   *WORDY: We **were in agreement with each other** that Max should be captain.*

   *CONCISE: We **agreed** that Max should be captain.*

2. **Words or phrases are redundant when they have basically the same meaning in the context in which they are used.**

   *WRONG: The school was **founded and established** in 1906.*

   Don't use two words when one will do.

   *The school was **founded** in 1906.*

   *The school was **established** in 1906.*

3. **A word is used redundantly when its meaning is implicit in the meaning of another word.**

   *WRONG: I felt a sense of **nervous anxiety** before the curtain rose.*

   The idea of being nervous is part of the meaning of the word *anxiety*. Using them together is redundant.

   *I felt **nervous** before the curtain rose.*

   *I felt a sense of **anxiety** before the curtain rose.*

WORDINESS EXERCISE

Cross out the unnecessary words in each of the sentences below.

1. Duke Ellington eventually came to New York because of the opportunities that awaited and were there for young musicians.

2. Albert Schweitzer was not only an accomplished doctor but also a talented musician as well.

3. As it had been developed by a scientific team at the university, the new formula facilitates the diagnosis of certain congenital diseases.

4. Developing a suitable environment for house plants is in many ways like when you are managing soil fertilization in city parks.

ANSWER KEY—WORDINESS EXERCISE

1. Cross out *awaited and* or *and were there*.

2. Cross out *as well*.

3. Cross out *As it had been*.

4. Cross out *when you are*.

PUNCTUATION

A. Commas - The ACT test 4 comma rules; use a comma to:

- Separate items in a series or list. On the ACT, whenever, there is a list of 3 or more things, there must be a comma before the word *and.*

Example: I went to the store to buy milk, eggs, and bread.

- Set off nonessential information within the sentence;
- Set off introductory phrases
- Separate two independent clauses that are set off by a FANBOYS word.

B. Semicolons and colons - while not as heavily tested on the ACT as comma usage is, it is useful to know the following rules:

i. Semicolons: Use a semicolon to:

- Join two independent clauses if there is no FANBOYS word between them;
- Separate items in a series or list, if those Items already have commas.

ii. Use a colon to

- Introduce or emphasize a short phrase, question, explanation, example or list.

C. Dashes and apostrophes.

i. Dashes: Use dashes to:

- Set off explanatory elements within a sentence
- Indicate a hesitation or break in thought.

ii. Apostrophes: Use an apostrophe to:

- Indicate the possessive form of a noun
- indicate a contraction

Know the difference between these words:

It's and it's

Theirs and there's

Who's and whose

Science

There will be a few very actual science questions on the ACT science test - 4 at the most. The ACT science test is actually a test of reading comprehension. Reading through the science passages requires time management - you have roughly 5 minutes per passage for reading the passage, noting the information in graphs and charts and answering the questions.

To maximize the limited time, it is crucial to read for key information. Make notes and keep track of several important points:

- Purpose of an experiment - what are the researchers trying to find out? Why are they conducting the experiment?
- The Method(s) used - what are the researchers doing? Take note of what is kept constant and what is changed.
- The Result (s) - what did the researchers find out?

There will be graphs and charts in most, if not all, passages. Take a few seconds to make note of units of measurement, variables and trends in the data. Ask:

- what does the figure show?
- what are the units of measurement?

When there are two or more scientists mentioned in a passage, keep track of what theories and experiments they disagree about and the topics on which they agree.